Duke Ellington's America

DUKE ELLINGTON'S AMERICA

Harvey G. Cohen

The University of Chicago Press

CHICAGO AND LONDON

Harvey G. Cohen teaches cultural history at the Centre for Cultural, Media and Creative Industries Research, King's College London.

The University of Chicago Press, Chicago 60637
The University of Chicago Press, Ltd., London
© 2010 by The University of Chicago
All rights reserved. Published 2010
Printed in the United States of America

19 18 17 16 15 14 13 12 11 10   2 3 4 5

ISBN-13: 978-0-226-11263-3 (cloth)
ISBN-10: 0-226-11263-2 (cloth)

Library of Congress Cataloging-in-Publication Data

Cohen, Harvey G.
    Duke Ellington's America / Harvey G. Cohen.
        p. cm.
    Includes bibliographical references and index.
    ISBN-13: 978-0-226-11263-3 (cloth : alk. paper)
    ISBN-10: 0-226-11263-2 (cloth : alk. paper) 1. Ellington,
Duke, 1899–1974. 2. African American jazz musicians—
Biography. I. Title.
    ML410 .E44C56 2010
    781.65092—dc22
    [B]
                                                2009033288

♾ The paper used in this publication meets the minimum
requirements of the American National Standard for
Information Sciences—Permanence of Paper for Printed
Library Materials, ANSI Z39.48-1992.

FOR MY GRANDPARENTS GUEST,
AND MY PARENTS, WHO STARTED
ME ON THIS ROAD OF CULTURE

CONTENTS

ACKNOWLEDGMENTS

This book has been brewing for over a decade, and it would not have been possible without the support of dozens of people, whom I am very happy to thank here.

First on the list is the Smithsonian Institution. About twenty years ago, John Hasse, the Smithsonian's curator of American music, led the effort to purchase Duke Ellington's personal and business records, along with the clippings scrapbooks that Duke Ellington, Inc., maintained. These hundreds of thousands of pages of documents, along with the forty Smithsonian oral interviews with former Ellington associates, formed the backbone of my work. Hasse also generously put me in contact with surviving Ellington associates, offered insight into my manuscript, and became a valued friend.

The staff of the Archives Center at the Smithsonian's National Museum of American History, where the Ellington papers reside, were not only professional, but versed in the questions and issues surrounding Ellington, freely sharing their expertise and opinions and showing me areas to explore further. Reuben Jackson, Annie Kuebler, and Scott Schwartz were particularly generous in making the mysteries of Ellingtonia clearer to me. Chief archivist John Fleckner and his staff, David Haberstich, Catherine Keen, Mimi Minnick, Craig Orr, Deborra Richardson, Wendy Shay, Vanessa Simmons, and Susan Strange made my days at the Smithsonian some of the most pleasant ones I've ever experienced in a research context. Volunteers Ted Hudson and Ben Pubols, from the Washington, D.C., branch of the Duke Ellington Society, were also instrumental. James Rhoan and Stephanie Thomas in the museum's library facilitated my months of exploration through the microfilmed Ellington clippings scrapbooks. Cutbacks in funding and personnel have placed a noticeable strain on the Archives Center staff since the turn of the century, allowing them significantly less time for the scholarly interaction that proved so important to me in my work on this book. The Smithsonian's collections represent an essential and diverse academic resource compiled over many decades, and the recent deemphasizing and underfunding of the institution's academic mission is an unfortunate, shortsighted, and just plain stupid circumstance that will hopefully be corrected in upcoming years.

A yearlong fellowship from the John W. Kluge Center at the Library of Congress enabled me to conduct final research and finish the first draft of this book. Thanks to the center's directors while I was in residence, Prosser

Gifford and Carolyn Brown, as well as staff members Regina Thielke and Mary Lou Reker, for all their support. The staff in the library's Recorded Sound Division generously and repeatedly provided their expertise on American music and helped me find the hidden nuggets in their audio and document collections: Larry Applebaum, Jeremy Bartczak, Sam Brylawski, Bryan Cornell, Gene DeAnna, Karen Fishman, Jan McKee, and David Sager. The people in the Motion Picture Division provided similar advice and support while I viewed their unparalleled collection of rare Ellington films and TV appearances: Jennifer Ormson, Christel Schmidt, and Zoran Sinobad.

Other archives also proved indispensable. Robert Heger, Walter Hill, and Martin McGann guided me through the maze of paper at the National Archives II in College Park, Maryland. Martin Manning, at the U.S. State Department's library in Washington, D.C., unearthed a lot of material for me concerning Ellington's State Department tours. Betty Austin and Michael Dabrishus of the Special Collections Division at the University of Arkansas in Fayetteville took me through their collection of Senator William Fulbright's papers, the most complete, least censored, and easily accessible set of papers dealing with 1960s and 1970s State Department tours that I encountered during my research. Dan Morganstern, David Berger, Tad Hershorn, and Annie Kuebler helped me find rare recordings, articles, and promotional materials at the Institute for Jazz Studies at Rutgers University in Newark. In London, Peter Symes's photo research skills and contacts helped me assemble the pictures in this book, most of which have not been published in decades, if ever.

I was lucky to be able to spend time with numerous Ellington family members and associates, who besides providing me with valuable information also bestowed upon me an invaluable sense of the age they lived in and the man they knew. Sharing time with these people, sometimes on several occasions, provided the most enjoyable hours of work on this book: George Avakian, Wilma Cockerell, Yvonne Lanauze Duke, Ruth Ellington, Ruth Fegley, Claire Gordon, Irving Gordon, Phoebe Jacobs, Michael James, Herb Jeffries, Harold Jovien, Brooks Kerr, Maurice Lawrence, Henrietta Livingston, Gerald Marks, Paul Mills, Albert Murray, Wally Orlinsky, H. Robert Udkoff, and Patricia Willard. I thank them all profusely.

Professors at the University of Maryland gave me an excellent grounding in American history and culture and the tools to write and document it: James Gilbert and David Sicilia, as mentors, colleagues, and friends, have given me tough and accurate advice on my work and career for years, as have Ira Berlin, Daphne Duval Harrison, Alfred Moss, Robyn Muncy, Stephan Palmie, Barry Lee Pearson, and Howard Smead. David Sicilia also guided me in the intricacies of marketing, accounting, and business history and helped me decode the sometimes confusing business documents in the Smithsonian's Ellington collection. George Chauncey, Robin Kelley, Lawrence Levine, and Mark Tucker generously shared their expertise with me and helped me explore ideas when I called on them intermittently, despite the fact that I did not attend their universities. Going above and beyond the call of duty was David Grimsted from the University of Maryland, whose careful editing and always insightful comments taught me more than anyone else ever has about writing, editing, and framing an argument. He has greatly influenced and improved this work, and I thank him for his friendship and the extensive amount of time he spent on this project.

I was also privileged to have several readers of various sections of my manuscript, who shaped this final product: Jeff Coster, Sjef Hoefsmit, Cheryl Hurwitz, Robert Morrow, Janine C. Stines, and Edmund F. Wehrle. Some close and patient friends read through large parts or all of this book before publication, and offered incisive suggestions: Avram Goldstein, Ted Hudson, Kevin Lafferty, and Dennis Mulqueeney. My two anonymous readers for the University of Chicago Press did an excellent job of pointing out various shortcomings and merits; hopefully I will discover their secret identities sometime and thank them in person. Naturally, all the faults in the manuscript are mine, not those named above. Tom Vincent and Scott Weston, my lawyers in residence, helped me navigate through the various legal documents in the Smithsonian's Ellington collections. I've also received copious amounts of support and camaraderie from my colleagues at the Centre for Cultural, Media and Creative Industries Research at King's College London: Ruth Adams, Christopher Hamnett, Richard Howells, Hye-Kyung Lee, and Ralph Parfect.

A special and enduring thanks goes to Doug Mitchell, my editor at the University of Chicago Press, who understood and believed in this book before almost anyone else, and not just because he's an accomplished jazz drummer. Our numerous breakfasts at various history conferences across the United States over the years were inspirational, informative, and hilarious gabfests that helped shape this book, and completely dissipated the boredom that usually attends such scholarly weekends. I felt privileged as an author to have my manuscript combed over so closely by Chicago's excellent copy editor Katherine Frentzel; let's just say she caught quite a few errors and taught me a lot about grammar and punctuation through the efficient marking of my manuscript. Thanks also to Tim McGovern, Levi Stahl, and everyone else who worked on my book at the Press.

My grandparents Milo and Pearl Guest introduced me to the power and beauty of culture, music, history, and a good story; my mother first gave me a sense of politics and the world; and my father sparked my fascination with music. They all float around this book in their subtle ways.

INTRODUCTION

The struggle over how the story of Duke Ellington's life would be told began long before his passing in 1974. In the fall of 1964, Duke Ellington mostly listened as longtime collaborator and friend Billy Strayhorn and journalist Carter Harman debated the theme of a projected film about Ellington's life. Harman wanted the film to focus on Ellington's surmounting of racial discrimination, particularly how he and the band traveled through the South in the 1930s in a hired Pullman car to avoid dealing with segregated establishments and the occasional violence black entertainers faced on the road:

HARMAN: I can see, in the story of Duke Ellington, a lot of good opportunities for a dramatic presentation of the [race] problems, you know. That Pullman car thing, that's a great scene, a marvelous—

STRAYHORN: Listen. Do you know the way this should be done? It should be done the same way as they did Louis Pasteur.

HARMAN: Accomplishment.

STRAYHORN: Yeah, the drama of the accomplishment, and the incidents that accompanied all the accomplishments . . . it was a helluva picture and it was only about what he did, the battles he was up against to do it, the people he had to beat down, the drama . . . this should be done the same way.

HARMAN: The thing is music.

STRAYHORN: There is more material to the business . . . The drama . . . is in his maintaining a position which he happened to establish very early. And the drama is in his maintaining it . . . staying up there is the thing. Well, he established a certain position, which wasn't easy to get to either. But he had to struggle to get to this position, but then it was much harder, it's still harder, it's still a struggle to keep people from making you bow down, to playing what they want you to do . . .

HARMAN: I think the story probably is a racial theme, I mean, that's the theme, the accomplishment.

STRAYHORN: Well, no, I don't think it should be racial because I don't think he's racial. He's not racial. He is an individual and he has set himself up.

HARMAN: OK, I'm not talking about race. I'm talking about the struggle against the scene.

STRAYHORN: Well, I think it shouldn't be put in that context . . . you don't have to say the darn thing.

HARMAN: But that's what it is though.[1]

*

Ellington's contribution to the conversation was to wonder if Hollywood could be convinced "that this is sufficiently interesting from the point of view of the audience." Hollywood still shows no interest, yet both Strayhorn and Harman were right: Ellington's story is one of remarkable creative and popular staying power, and one richly integrated with American history during the transformative years of the twentieth century.

This book seeks to understand Ellington's achievements and contributions over a half century in the context of the pragmatic realities he faced and skillfully manipulated while sustaining a long, varied, and rare career in the fickle world of popular music. It documents Ellington's status as a "culture hero," a world-famous public figure who "mediates public tensions," serving as a totem for important and controversial changes occurring in the larger society.[2] Thousands of documents demonstrate how Ellington mediated the tensions between popular and serious American art, intellectual and popular culture, creativity and conformity, democracy and communism, and especially between blacks and whites. Through his actions and his work over a half century, he changed American culture, transforming the nation's cultural and racial landscape.

This book includes the voice of Ellington as much as possible, probably more than any previous work. Within five decades of clippings stored in the Ellington Scrapbooks at the Smithsonian, many eloquent Ellington quotations are hidden in the obscure columns of newspapers gathered from around the world. When faced with unimaginative questions, Ellington gave pat answers, but, when inspired, he revealed insight, a stunning wit, and knowledge of history. His words make clear that when he produced images and music that went against the usual dictates of how blacks and American music were viewed, he knew full well what he was doing.

Ellington's beliefs concerning racial equality were molded during his youth in turn-of-the-century Washington, D.C., where an emphasis on black identity, pride, and history was imparted to black children. They were taught to command, rather than demand, respect for the race. Ellington carried himself in a manner consistent with this attitude, in the way he walked, the way he spoke. Music proved an optimal venue for Ellington to change and challenge American racial life. It was less controversial than the speeches and writings of black spokespeople because it did not demand acceptance for a particular position. As a musician, Ellington subverted stereotypes about how blacks dressed, acted, and created. More importantly, music served as a form of activism that reflected Ellington's long-term priorities of infiltration and circumvention, rather than confrontation.

Strayhorn's insistence that Ellington was "not racial" was true in the sense that the composer never put race ahead of music. Yet the black media of the 1930s dubbed him a leading "race man," and a large portion of the pragmatic realities Ellington confronted dealt with Harman's racial "scene." No black American before Ellington had ever enjoyed such a lengthy career, or been so widely hailed as a major serious artistic figure. Such a career was rare for any American when Ellington entered the popular-music profession in the late 1910s, an era of harsh Jim Crow denigration on the streets and in the media.

Ellington did not fight for civil rights in the manner of political activists, but he contributed much to the cause, much of it unrecognized because it lay outside the annals of overt racial protest. His devotion to his race and his determination to document its achievements and character infused much of his best work, and surfaced repeatedly in his comments to the press. Ellington's history as a "race leader" will be closely followed throughout this book, from the jungle trappings of the all-black Cotton Club shows of the 1920s to Ellington's unique participation in the civil rights movement in the 1960s.

In many ways, Ellington shared an aesthetic problem with other major black artists of his time. How do black artists write about the history, character, and problems connected with race and create great art and understanding without it devolving into polemic? And how do such minority artists develop a large enough audience to support their art, while staying true to their ideals? Ellington, along with black writers Langston Hughes, Zora Neale Hurston, and Claude McKay, wanted to be recognized as a great artist, not just as a black artist. In a later era, Albert Murray argued that being viewed primarily as a "black writer" made one's work easier to dismiss, but that it was "no slight feat" for an African American artist "to fuse white and black America into one interested and approving audience." Ellington accomplished this feat over his long career by creatively celebrating the black American experience without standing on a soapbox. For him, the most effective protest in the American scene was to live and create in a way that undermined racial barriers and stereotypes. His career shows how much the racial changes in the United States owed to infiltrators like Ellington, who softened the enemy so that protest could develop effectively.[3]

The marketing of Ellington forms another major theme of this book. The deliberate marketing campaign designed by Ellington and manager Irving Mills between 1926 and 1939 sought to establish Ellington as a serious composer and a "genius." It was an unusual and effective way to promote American music, and aside from limited campaigns for Scott Joplin at the turn of the century, unprecedented for a black artist. Because of this campaign, the public came to expect that entering an Ellington show or purchasing an Ellington recording involved serious art as well as entertainment. At the time, the segregated market for "race records" by and exclusively for blacks would have been the most likely outlet for Ellington, but Ellington aimed at the multiracial mainstream from the start; that was where he viewed his music as belonging, and the white market formed the most lucrative part of the business. To tap this, the marketing campaign compared Ellington to leading white artists in the popular and classical worlds. This created a brand endowed with qualities that reverberated in the American imagination: artistry, respectability, genius, black pride, black history, freedom, and America itself. Such notions brought large rewards even during the height of the Great Depression. In the decades that followed the creation of Ellington's mass-media image, Ellington himself as well as record companies, the media, and the United States government took these references and used them to their own advantage.

But the branding of Ellington yielded more than financial reward. Ellington was a leading figure in establishing a serious, international respect for American music during a time when American art was seen as coarse and derivative. American universities offered almost no courses on American art of any kind, and European precedents were held up as the sole standard by American critics and educators when Ellington began his career, yet he was hailed as a serious composer on both sides of the Atlantic by 1933. In *The Story of Louis Pasteur,* the 1936 film that Strayhorn and Harman referenced in their conversation, Pasteur passionately opposes scientific "bigotry" and "ignorance" during the mid-nineteenth century in his efforts to impel doctors to adopt sterilization of surgical instruments. Perhaps Strayhorn's reticence to have a film about Ellington concentrate too closely on race grew from his recognition that Ellington dealt with bigotry on more levels than just that one.

Economic exploitation of artists was pervasive. With Ellington's knowledge and tacit approval, Mills made millions of dollars during ensuing decades by putting his name to dozens of Ellington's compositions of the 1920s and 1930s that he almost certainly did not help write. Mills's heirs still receive royalties from this material. This situation will be analyzed closely, along with other disputes over songwriting credit within the Ellington orchestra. However, after the Ellington/Mills relationship unraveled in 1939, the strong foundation provided by Mills's marketing enabled Ellington to enjoy success and wide artistic freedom well into the 1970s. The story of the second half of Ellington's career, too long ignored and belittled, will be treated more thoroughly in this work than in any previous book.

Ellington's attention to marketing also surfaced in the variety of his musical releases over the years. Part of the reason for his decades of popularity rested in his ability to constantly develop and institute changes in his music, qualities essential for long-term success in the novelty-driven, star-making machinery of the entertainment world. This approach worked well with his free-ranging approach to composing and creativity. For example, in 1956–57, Ellington released a live Newport Jazz festival concert featuring a new extended suite; an album connected with a TV special that fancifully and humorously portrayed the history of jazz; a programmatic celebration of the works of Shakespeare; and *Ellington Indigos,* an easy-listening selection of well-known standards, some by Ellington. Such unpredictability kept audiences, especially core Ellington fans, interested over long periods of time, and the conceptual projects Ellington often pursued gave marketers something concrete and new to sell.

He was both an entertainer and a serious artist, relishing both identities and seeing no contradiction between them. At the moment of his greatest exposure on the pop charts during World War II, one could simultaneously hear Ellington's compositions on jukeboxes across the country and at Carnegie Hall. In the 1950s and afterward, dates with symphony orchestras became common. Like much of the lasting and most significant American musical art of the twentieth century (by Louis Armstrong, the Carter Family, Aaron Copland, Bob Dylan, and others), Ellington's music proved over decades that great popularity and great art could coexist.

Ellington's business strategies represent another essential facet of the pragmatic realities that shaped his career. This book marks the first time that the Ellington business records housed at the Smithsonian Institution have been used extensively. Ellington's commitment to composing was expensive—especially his insistence on carrying an eighteen-piece orchestra fifty-two weeks a year filled with some of the finest jazz musicians ever, so he could hear new compositions hours after they were rendered. This, in turn, mandated that the band draw large audiences and fees. No big band besides the Ellington orchestra survived the demise of the Swing Era without interruption. As Strayhorn pointed out, staying on top proved even more of a struggle than the band's initial rise to stardom. Ellington's efforts to keep his music before the public in that difficult period when musical trends were moving away from big bands and toward pop vocalists, R&B, and rock and roll demonstrates much about his artistic process and personal resolve. From the 1920s to the 1970s, audiences shifted and generation gaps surfaced, yet Ellington, aided by his steady stream of songwriting royalties, always found enough profit amid the ever-changing popular-music marketplace to keep his band and entourage on the road, and his artistry in record stores. Ellington's business strategies also demonstrate how his activities strongly resembled those of other black American entrepreneurs of his time, especially his priority of building community and supporting friends and family rather than operating purely for profit.

The enormous cache of personal, business, musical, and media documents stored at the Smithsonian make clear that Ellington's significance went far beyond the musical realm. His music and his actions put him at the center of several contested areas of American society, history, and culture during his time, and especially the racial one—Ellington took strong positions in each area that contradicted stereotypes that needed revamping. I hope that this book adequately demonstrates that, as rich as Ellington's music is, a closer examination of his life and career makes clear his status as a rich figure in American history as well as in American music.

1
WASHINGTON/ NEW YORK

Prelude

Ellington's parents, James and Daisy, strictly maintained that all people were equal, and no race better than another. This marked a characteristic attitude of the black middle-class of turn-of-the-century Washington, D.C. Social and political progress, according to the mindset of this community, would not occur through political agitation and protest, but by high achievement and radiating a sense of respectability. Washington's black children were made aware of the violence and discrimination of the Jim Crow era, yet also were taught that skilled achievers would be recognized no matter their color. Ellington's younger sister Ruth explained how the Ellington family's social life reflected this sentiment:

> In our house . . . while I was growing up, people of all colors were there. More whites than coloreds. My father was like that. [Duke] didn't talk about color. In our house, you didn't talk about color. I remember when I was about five years old in Washington I was standing down in the front garden with my cousin and the people passing our house were various colors. And she pointed out to me that these people had different colors. I had never heard anybody talk about color. So I ran upstairs to my father with whom I had all my, quote, intellectual conversations, and I thought that I ought to impart this information to him and he was reading the newspaper and when I told him what my cousin Elizabeth said he put the paper down and said two words: "Nonsense, Ruthie!" And he put his newspaper back up. So I went downstairs and I never mentioned color again [giggles]. That's probably why I am the way I am now about color.[1]

This attitude of recognizing the best in each category, rather than categorizing people and accomplishments by color, represented the Ellington ethos. After flirtations with sports and art, the teenaged Ellington gravitated toward the field of music, which, at the time he was born, represented one of the few areas in the country in which blacks earned money and respect at the highest level, competing and collaborating with whites at the top of a profession. Ellington's background, and the black cultural figures who preceded him, proved essential in his ability to create the most distinguished oeuvre in American music.

✱

The Washington, D.C., into which Edward Kennedy "Duke" Ellington was born on 29 April 1899 proved a perfect springboard for his genius and ambitions. It was a center of black musical and intellectual resistance to racism, and probably the best place to be an African American at the turn of the century, though certainly not without racial problems. The city was a bastion of the black middle class, to which Ellington's family tenuously belonged. The community's black leaders did not so much fight against the racist system in America as quietly and determinedly circumvent it. The dignity and pride they sought to instill in the Washington black community, especially its young people, avoided challenging and confronting the social and political realities of the time, but instead sought to rise above them. From his upbringing, from the mentors and cultural figures who came before him, Ellington adopted a method of assertive yet nonconfrontational activism in dealing with matters of race, prejudice, and black achievement.

Even before the Civil War, Washington represented a better place than usual for blacks to live. Laws against blacks were rarely enforced, the majority of blacks were free by the 1830s, and the first black public school opened in 1807, followed by many more in ensuing decades, probably more in relation to population than anywhere else in the United States. After the Civil War, Washington gained a reputation as a center of "respectable Negro society," serving as a haven from exploitive sharecropping in the South designed to resemble slavery, most of the worst Jim Crow discrimination, and increased incidence of lynchings and racial violence. It boasted the largest black urban community in the nation—31 percent of its inhabitants. Until the Woodrow Wilson administration ushered in an era of increased segregation in 1913, the federal government treated and hired local blacks with relative equality.[2]

Booker T. Washington noted in the late 1870s that African Americans could "live a life of ease" in the nation's capital, and the argument gained more credence by the time of Ellington's birth. A few blacks were born to limited wealth, but most were in small businesses or professions as teachers, barbers, lawyers, dentists, college-trained clergy, and, thanks to the strong federal-government presence, civil servants and social workers. For whites, such occupations represented middle-class status, but in the black community these were viewed as elite occupations. Three national African American papers ran society columns reporting on the activities of the elite black Washingtonians, and some black observers criticized them for being overly obsessed with status and material objects, a view Langston Hughes endorsed when he stayed in Washington for a period in the mid-1920s.[3]

Washington's elite black community adopted many of the trappings and beliefs of the white American middle class of the nineteenth century: "respectability, church membership, family stability, home ownership, hard work, good education, and refinement." The same values were cherished in the Ellington household. Jacqueline Moore traced the development of the black middle class in Washington, D.C., and documented a distinct difference between the philosophies of this group in the 1880s and in the first two decades of the twentieth century. While the group in both periods placed emphasis on manners, etiquette, and dress, the middle-class blacks of the earlier period stressed assimilation into white society by cultivating an image of respectability grounded in highbrow culture. A black opera company was founded in the city in the 1870s, and the intellectual American Negro Academy developed in 1897, amid other cultural activities such as literary organizations, (often classical) music programs, plays, poetry readings, and lecture series for blacks.

By the turn of the century, however, whites had still not accepted such attempts at bridging the racial divide and generally viewed all blacks as inferior, no matter their level of refinement or the fact that some of them lived in better circumstances than many whites. Black elites increasingly stressed racial solidarity, with "an emphasis on black culture and a closer identity with the black masses," according to Willard B. Gatewood. Assimilation no longer represented their top priority. They steered their children toward "careers that would help the black community achieve independence from white society [and] . . . worked more openly for racial justice" and uplift. Moore found that the black children of Ellington's generation and their middle-class parents in Washington, D.C., believed that "if they worked quietly behind the scenes to contradict negative images of African Americans, they could bring whites to accept them as equals without open conflict."[4] Such a strategy, with its emphasis on subtle challenge instead of head-on attack and on the unity of black culture, encapsulated Ellington's views on race relations almost perfectly.

Washington's black churches played a major role in building community, as black churches had for more than a century in American history. Church leadership emphasized racial uplift and solidarity, and supported the teaching of the "social gospel," a popular religious trend among white Protestant churches that encouraged congregants to use their churches as centers for aiding and enlightening the urban poor, and reforming society. Black churches expanded the notion to include speaking out against discrimination and racial violence. Black businessmen also played a role in promoting black pride in Washington, goaded in part by their realization that, because of Jim Crow discrimination, they needed to rely on their black clientele almost exclusively. The Shaw neighborhood, where Ellington principally grew up, was the main black business district.

Most importantly, race pride was emphasized in Washington's black schools, and emerged as a major influence in the generation of black youngsters that came of age in the early twentieth century. Moore reported that administrators assembled a curriculum that purposely "counteracted negative stereotypes" of blacks. In the 1960s, when arguments between integration and segregation roiled American politics, Ellington felt that the separated schools for blacks in his youth constituted "a very good thing for the Negro." "What used to happen was that they were concerned with you being representative of a great and proud race," he recalled. "They used to pound it into you, you go to the English class, that [race pride] was more important than the English." Students wrote papers concerning morality and the value of community. They studied great African civilizations, and one school assigned African folk tales. Washington's black youth also received a strong grounding in black history, using an African American history book cowritten by the local black scholar Carter G. Woodson. At Armstrong High School, where Ellington attended in the mid-1910s, the principal "had his students render black folk songs." No other students in the country were given such detailed training and instruction in black history and identity. Moore found that this strategy of instilling race pride and opportunity paid dividends: "The children of this social elite who came to prominence in the early twentieth-century were more secure in their position, expected a certain measure of success and believed it was the responsibility of the elite to lead the race to better things."[5]

Ellington reported in his autobiography that his teachers (and his father) taught him that African Americans needed to cultivate especially good manners and speech and that blacks in his neighborhood were careful not to mix with any below-average people—black or white. "At that time there was some kind of movement to desegregate the schools in Washington, D.C.," Ellington explained. "Who do you think were the first to object? Nobody but the proud Negroes of Washington, who felt that the kind of white kids we would be thrown in with were not good enough." His eighth-grade instructor, Miss Boston, told her classes flatly that "your responsibility is to command respect for the race." This atmosphere, combined with the occasional sight in Washington of African American judges, lawyers, and other professionals led young black men for generations to believe that, as Washington musician and educator Billy Taylor recalled, "any field that I wanted to go into, I had the possibility of success." A generation after Ellington left his hometown, this kind of education continued and was still rare for its time: his son Mercer recalled that he received instruction in black history in Washington, but not when he moved to New York City to be with his father in the early 1930s. While sometimes snobbish, the culture and environment of black Washington forwarded the impression of the personal worth and innate equality of blacks without taking a dangerously assertive stance.[6]

Racial pride and support flourished first in the Ellington home.[7] This was not uncommon; D.C.'s black families provided protection for their children against Jim Crow, and gave them a strong sense of security and identity. The families were usually very close, which helped them take advantage of opportunities. Parents taught their children to stand up for themselves without showing disrespect. Such descriptions fit the Ellingtons snugly. They were a close and "almost unbelievably loving" family, by all accounts. At an early age, his mother Daisy repeatedly told Ellington: "Edward, you are blessed. You don't have anything to worry about. Edward, you are blessed!" In his autobiography, written when he was past the age of seventy, Ellington intimated that he still believed her words to be true. Ruth Ellington, his sister, reported that the family acted as if the sentiment were true, noting without malice that "everything was [done] for Edward." Ellington corroborated this in a 1958 interview:

> I never had it so good as when I was a kid. I didn't have to move a muscle. My mother brought me up in the palm of her hand, she really spoiled me. And it wasn't just my mother. It was my mother's 14 sisters and brothers and my father and his 18 sisters and brothers. When they got through spoiling me, I was really spoiled.

Six years later, he reminisced about frequent trips with his mother to his grandmother's house to visit his aunts. They used to all play in "a great big backyard with four pear trees surrounded by a grape orchard . . . We used to eat the pears in the summertime, and in the fall they would always be preserving and canning, you know, this big thing," Ellington recalled. "They were cooking constantly . . . I don't know too much about the neighbors because this was such a tight-knit family circle that neighbors never even entered into it . . . I was so busy wrapped up in family."

Ellington's family history confirmed the notion that an African American could accomplish anything, as long as hard work accompanied the desire. Ellington's son Mercer recalled that Daisy's side of the family (the Kennedys) included "principals, doctors, lawyers, and so forth." According to Ruth Ellington, their maternal grandfather "was born a slave, and was a son of [an] Irish slave master, who freed him before Lincoln freed the slaves and put him in business contracting and building. He ended up a millionaire . . . and there's still about a quarter of a million dollars of his estate that's left."

Apparently, the grandfather's estate was bequeathed to other branches of the Kennedy family tree, and not to the Ellingtons. Ellington's first cousin Bernice Wiggins (her mother was Daisy's sister) claimed that their mothers' family had white and Native American antecedents as well as African American, and were related to Frederick Douglass and Charles Drew, the pioneer of blood transfusions.

Ellington's family certainly did not live the lifestyle of the wealthy before Duke's commercial success in the early 1930s. But they did lead a secure existence as a black middle-class family, though their income would not have qualified them for such status in the white community. In the 1960s, Ellington recalled that his family knew "no poverty," and that "my mother fed me with a silver spoon all my life." Ellington's parents lived and acted like they were among the black upper crust, but were not. Their grandson Mercer Ellington classified them as "menials." Their middle-class aspirations reflected the desire to assert dignity and pride more than the family's actual economic and social position. Part of this pride communicated itself in what Mercer and Wiggins viewed as the tradition of art and music on both sides of Ellington's family tree. Mercer recalled that, within the family, it was stressed to "do something different. Do something that identifies you as an individual."

Ruth Ellington characterized her father, James E. Ellington, often called "J. E.," as "a Chesterfieldian gentleman, very charming." J. E. passed onto his son his eloquent way with words, particularly with the ladies. He entertained people at home with his barbershop quartet, and played whist (a card game) prodigiously. His many sisters were warm and outgoing; Ruth claimed that her brother's penchant for kisses and telling people "love you madly" came from the Ellington side of the family. As his son recalled, J. E. also played a little piano: "In spite of the fact that he only played by ear, he only played operatic music [laughs] and he would sing along with it," especially the arias. He worked in various capacities in some of the finer white homes as waiter, coachman, driver, and butler. Since his family could not afford to provide him with a formal education, his main education came from a long-term assignment as a butler and a houseman with Dr. Cuthbert, a white man who allowed him to partake of a large personal library that J. E. "read omnivorously." Because of these experiences, J. E. knew fine wines, and insisted that the Ellington dinner table be laid out in a formal manner, and that the family's clothing match that ambience.

Ellington's mother Daisy made sure the Ellington home radiated a Victorian sensibility. She was the oldest girl in a large family of Kennedys, a very musical family in which most of her siblings played some sort of instrument. Daisy was "very responsible, very puritanical . . . in other words, diametrically opposed to my father," according to Ruth. She wore "pinched nose glasses, and was a real Victorian lady." Daisy played piano, particularly hymns, ragtime, and "waltzes with a kind of beat," but disapproved of the blues. She "taught [her son] how to play" the piano, since he "did not respond to formal piano lessons as a small boy." He also played some harmonica as "a young kid." Edward also learned many piano chords from Florence Hargrove, one of Daisy's sisters. "And that's when he got really interested in [music, at the age of fifteen] . . . she began to show him how [Irving Berlin's 1911 hit] 'Alexander's Ragtime Band' [was played]," according to Hargrove's daughter, Bernice Wiggins. Ruth Ellington recalled the prim nature of her childhood home, even years after Ellington had left Washington:

> I'll never forget the first time I heard Edward's music. Of course we'd heard it at home [years before], playing ragtime, but here he was playing his music with his own band on the radio from New York, coming out of this old-fashioned horn-speaker. I think radio had just been invented . . . or at least just launched commercially. It was quite a shock. Here we were, my mother and I, sitting in this very respectable Victorian living room, my mother so puritanical she didn't even wear lipstick, and the announcer from New York tells us we are listening to "Duke Ellington and his Jungle Music!"

Yet Daisy felt very proud of her son's accomplishments, and Ruth remembered being at shows by her brother where her mother tapped her feet to the rhythm, and often was still clapping after everyone else had stopped.

Ellington initially resisted being a musician as a young man. He rejected formal piano lessons as a kid, and concentrated on athletics—"football, baseball, track, everything." But an experience the morning after his first professional music gig at the age of fifteen changed his mind: "three of the prettiest girls you've ever seen looking up at [my] window, saying 'Mrs. Ellington, is Edward ready?' She said, 'Yes, darling, he's coming right down.' And I ain't been no athlete since. That was the end of my athletic career," Ellington recalled, laughing heartily. Even after this signal event, a painting career also competed for Ellington's attention, and he proved talented enough to win a scholarship to the Pratt Institute in New York. He ended up refusing it, but his talents in this area enlarged his bankroll during his early days as a musician in Washington. "After I started playing the piano professionally . . . I got a sign shop and you know, you came to get a sign painted, I said 'Who's playing your music?' and if you came to get your music played, I'd say 'Who's painting your signs?'" Ellington said in 1969, laughing at the memory. "Oh, I was a pretty smart kid when I was young. I'm not too smart now."[8]

Various stories exist explaining how Edward Ellington became "the Duke." Some claimed that Daisy's proclivity to dress her son up in dandified clothes inspired schoolmates to refer to him as "the Duke," a name pinned on Ellington as a young teen. Ellington said the accolade came from a

> schoolmate of mine, Edgar McEntry. He was a boyhood pal of mine, we used to travel around a lot together. And through high school. And he was a pretty elegant cat, you know, he was a swinger of his day, actually. He was very well dressed, you know. I'm naturally the sloppy type, you know. But then I had to keep up with him, so I began to tag on little things of, you know, dressing and so on. So, I think he felt that in order for me to be eligible for his constant companionship that I should have a title. And so with that, he called me Duke. And it sort of stayed there.

In any case, family members in later years recalled that Ellington, as a high school student, predicted his massive success and later ducal status. Wiggins remembers her cousin saying that "one of these days, everybody in the world is going to call me Duke Ellington, ze grand, ze great, and ze glorious Duke Ellington." An Ellington cousin named Katherine said that a great aunt of his challenged his prediction, and Ellington replied that "crowds will be running to see the grand noble Duke, and bells will be ringing." He "used to practice" for this eventuality as a boy on the front steps of his house in Washington, D.C., making his cousins bow and curtsy to him. Wiggins recalled another afternoon at the Ellington family home:

> I never will forget . . . he came in one evening and he said, "Mother, dear," and she turned around and looked at him and he always would come in and kiss her on both side of the cheeks and she says, "What have you been up today?" as a mother would. He said, "Mother, your son is going to be one of the great musicians in the world." He says, "Someday . . . I'm gonna be bowin' before the kings and queens." And Aunt Daisy used to say, "The boy's talking foolish." But that came true. As the day he lived and died . . . He foresaw his destiny in many, many years.[9]

The race pride among Washington blacks also involved a sense of class stratification. "I could play the dances but I couldn't mingle with all the highfalutin doctors and lawyers and all the fancy chicks from the university," complained longtime Ellington drummer and friend Sonny Greer in 1979. "They looked at me like I was nothin'." Ellington portrayed the policies concerning different classes within the black community as something taught in black families. "I don't know how many castes of Negroes there were in the City at the time, but I do know that if you decided to mix carelessly with another you would be told that one just did not do that sort of thing," wrote Ellington. "It might be wonderful for somebody, but not for me and my cousins."

Yet, Ellington also spent significant time as a teenager in a less rarified area of black Washington, at Frank Holliday's poolroom in the Shaw neighborhood, next door to the Howard Theater, where major black touring acts regularly played. The poolroom attracted a mix of people who Ellington claimed educated him as much as his schoolteachers did: "pool sharks," lawyers, well-traveled "Pullman car porters," "professional and amateur gamblers," a slew of piano players, and Dr. Charles Drew.[10]

Alternating impressions of aloofness and snobbery as well as warmth and inclusiveness were seen by fans and by those close to Ellington, probably influenced by the contrasting worlds he inhabited in Washington, D.C. Phoebe Jacobs, a club manager, professional associate, and personal friend of Ellington and his family recalled that "Ellington was a snob," and cited examples of his taste in home furnishings or his proclivity to break dates with people at the last minute if something or someone more interesting came up. But for Jacobs, this pride and bearing had mostly positive manifestations:

> "Regal" and "elegant" [are] the two words you have to use for Ellington . . .
> His whole demeanor, the way he held his head, the way he held his shoulders, the way he placed his feet on the ground. He knew who he was. He had great self-esteem . . . And you could put him with a President, or you could put him with a porter, and he would have the same warmth and ability to communicate.[11]

Ellington's many Washington mentors provided him with a varied education, and stressed a vision of black history expressed through music. One of his first musical employers, Russell Wooding, wrote an operetta called *Halcyon Days in Dixie* (1921), which represented an "attempt at music drama based on themes of Negro life and music." Earlier, Ellington studied fundamentals and harmony with Henry Grant, one of the most active musicians and producers on the local black musical scene. In 1911, Grant directed the choir in a Howard University–sponsored production entitled *The Evolution of the Negro in Picture, Song and Story,* which celebrated black history. In 1915, the opening of a historic dramatic pageant entitled *The Star of Ethio-*

pia constituted a "major community event" in Washington, D.C. Originally produced in 1913 by the groundbreaking black scholar and spokesperson W. E. B. DuBois, and featuring J. Rosamond Johnson as musical director, the show depicted ten thousand years of black history. The structure and content of both the Grant and DuBois productions foreshadowed Ellington's extended work of 1943, *Black, Brown and Beige: A Tone Parallel of the American Negro*. Perhaps most importantly for Ellington's future ambitions, Grant "believed that standards of excellence could apply to popular music" and that "popular music could be taken seriously."[12]

Writers Amiri Baraka and Robert Palmer pointed out that blacks in Africa and America used music to teach behavior and impart messages to prepare young men for manhood. This tradition emanated from the long-standing practice of African griots, whose main function consisted of passing on to the young generation meticulously memorized songs and poetry that chronicled the history of African peoples, instead of the history books used by Western civilizations. Ellington honored and expanded this tendency of his musical forebears, penning many programmatic tributes to black cultural figures and historical settings throughout his career. In his autobiography, he reflected upon how the early African American Broadway and jazz composers "sent a message" through their music and made historical facts and personal emotions known through their writing: "The audience didn't know . . . but the cats in the band did."[13]

Ellington followed a nontraditional path of musical education, refusing to enter the conservatory, despite urgings from peers and family members. "People were trying to get me to go study music from [age] 16 to 26," he noted in 1964. "I had no formal education . . . as far as music was concerned, except for piano lessons when I was a kid. But all the time I was asking questions. So, I mean, I was getting the education I wanted, I wasn't getting me a lot of education I wasn't going to have any use for." Ellington knew that conservatories taught none of the African American music tradition he grew up with and wished to carry forward. So, he informally studied with various black mentors, such as Doc Perry and Henry Grant, in their homes as well as in Holliday's poolroom, asking them to show him certain skills, and then practicing at home until he had perfected them:

> Then I'd go to someone else and ask some questions. I'd go to the harmony teacher [Grant], and took, I don't know how many lessons, half a dozen maybe . . . I got to the point where . . . I discovered that F-sharp is not a G-flat. That was the end of my lessons there because I found out what I wanted to know [laughs]. And this adjusted my perspective as to how I

should pursue the next phase of my learning. It was a matter of learning what I wanted to learn, rather than learning what was in the order of the book that is normally taught in the normal music curriculum.

Ellington's wife, Edna, whom he began to court while they were in high school, also taught him sight reading and music theory.

While Ellington learned fundamentals of music theory and composition, he also steeped himself in the techniques of nonschooled jazz and blues musicians, whose rawness and passion he admired and sought to duplicate. This dichotomy, a trademark of the Ellington sound, represented a hallmark of the Washington musical environment: "Everybody seemed to get something out of the other's playing—the ear cats [those who learned music by ear instead of formal training] loved what the schooled cats did, and the schooled guys, with fascination, would try what the ear cats were doing." In 1972, Ellington further described this atmosphere: "the guys who were schooled musicians were captive of the guys who were not schooled, and vice versa. And it was this great exchange, and there I was right in the middle, and my embryo, sort of, was nurtured in this." As Helen Oakley Dance, close to Ellington and the band from the 1930s to the 1970s, recalled, "Duke, as much as he prized all the accomplishment, he equally prized the bottom of the ladder, the gutter, as he loved to refer to it." Such musicians were "close to the real roots and they were the ones that could produce it, whereas . . . the well-educated people who were smooth sophisticated musicians, they did not relate to that, it wasn't there." Ellington wished to be proficient in both areas. Many times during recording sessions, Dance heard Ellington exhorting his band to "get it in the gutter!" especially when recording bluesy compositions.[14]

White musical culture also played an important role during Ellington's early years. In Washington's black community, concert music thrived alongside African American popular song. Ellington's first piano teacher, Marietta Clinkscales, taught him concert pieces and classical technique. In church, Ellington learned white as well as black hymns and songs. Daisy Ellington continued that tradition at home, frequently playing nostalgic Victorian parlor songs and religious hymns such as "Meditation" (1896) and "The Rosary" (1900) on the family piano. Ellington was very close to his mother, and, as Mark Tucker pointed out, the songs she played were recalled and referenced by him throughout his life, especially in his more wistful and elegiac compositional moods. "The Single Petal of a Rose" (1959) and the bridge to "In a Sentimental Mood" (1935), two of Ellington's most nostalgic compositions, both featured the same key (D-flat), and similar melodies and structure to both "Meditation" and "The Rosary." As a result of this cross-racial musical background, Ellington tended to judge music and people not by style, category, or by race, but by how skilled and affecting they were. Throughout his life, he reiterated his view that there existed only two kinds of music, "the good kind and the other kind." Ellington's background in this regard also helped explain the close friendships he had with both blacks and whites, something of a rarity for the time.[15]

When Ellington first began forming bands in the late 1910s, his repertoire included songs associated with both black and white culture, and he played for both black and white audiences, almost always segregated. Ellington's father's work as a caterer for society functions, including some at the White House during the Harding administration in the early 1920s, provided connections for Ellington's bands to score coveted "society jobs." These were lucrative performances for a usually all-white audience at official functions at embassies, political gatherings, and private mansions. Bands at these dates usually featured ragtime-style pianists (as Ellington was at the time) who performed dance music of Tin Pan Alley popular songs, along with the newly popular black jazz sounds. On the other side of the social spectrum, Ellington's early bands also played for alcohol-soaked college-aged black and white audiences in Georgetown. Like other so-called East Coast commercial bands, they played the range of popular music from cotillion dance tunes, country tunes, music hall hits, popular novelties, tangos, and waltzes to ragtime and blues. Ellington pointed out in his autobiography that this multigenre training proved profitable when his band the Washingtonians had their first long engagement in New York City during the mid-1920s. After the band's regular sets, Ellington and Greer worked the late-night crowd "answering requests, we sang anything and everything—pop songs, jazz songs, dirty songs, torch songs, Jewish songs" and receiving twenty-dollar bills for their trouble.[16]

The mixing of black music and white, especially evident in Washington, D.C., and New York City, became more commonplace in America in the decades after the turn of the century, wielding a huge influence on twentieth-century popular song. Before the rise of the mass media and popular music sales charts in the 1920s and 1930s, blues and country artists and recordings could sometimes not be accurately classified by race. Nor could many other American genres. Ragtime existed as a danceable amalgam of European and African musical traditions. New Orleans black brass bands combined European brass with African rhythmic patterns. European composers Antonin Dvorak and Maurice Ravel, among others, utilized African and

African American rhythms and folk melodies in their work. A great deal of musical and cultural cross-pollination surfaced in the songs churned out by Tin Pan Alley. The nature of American music took hold during this period, bringing together various cultural elements and communities in the United States. Eventually, by the mid-twentieth century, the influences were traded back and forth so frequently that the appellation of "American music" would be more correct than denoting it by color. Ellington received the training to communicate in this new form as a young man, and spoke about it long before scholars acknowledged it. "There's really no distinction anymore between white music and colored music," Ellington told a journalist in 1948. "It's sort of a hybrid thing. They have each borrowed so much from the other."[17]

In the area of religion, this melding of black and white influences proved particularly common and significant. The Great Awakenings of the eighteenth and nineteenth centuries led to the establishment of the first independent black churches in the country, many of them featuring black interpretations of the emotionally rich Isaac Watts and Charles Wesley hymns from England, as well as original and African-influenced compositions in their services. These institutions, such as the African Methodist churches, served as environments where blacks defined their own identities in public, defying preconceived white notions of their history and destiny. Many whites were comforted by black acceptance of Christianity in the nineteenth century, but not all of them realized that blacks used Biblical stories in their own subtle and subversive ways.[18] Music and religion have long acted as uniting forces for some blacks and whites in American history. In his Sacred Concerts in the 1960s and 1970s, Ellington continued this tradition, even when it became politically unpopular among some groups of black and white Americans. But he also was a resolute supporter and creator of what he called "Negro music," a style of music that consciously documented and communicated a more exclusively African American experience.

Ellington learned how to run a band musically and professionally during the late 1910s, a skill probably as important as his musical lessons. After a booking agent took an egregious 90 percent commission for an Ellington performance, Ellington became his own manager and booker. Starting in 1918, he chose the songs, booked the gigs, collected the fees, and paid his musicians personally. His genial personality and skill at networking and advertising made him an effective businessman. He placed ads in Washington-area newspapers and telephone directories for his band, promising "Colored Syncopators" playing "irresistible jass" for "select patrons." Ellington became so successful at these activities that he regularly booked several bands in one night, under the name of the Duke's Serenaders:

> I was a pretty rich kid before I was 20. I had a society band; in fact, I had five or six of them going at one time . . . It got so we would go for days from one party to another. They really gave parties then, especially the Virginia aristocrats and horse show people just across the line from Washington. They were the sort of people they name counties for in Virginia, Madison and names like that.[19]

Playing at high-society functions also meant that Ellington and his band had to have formal clothes for their shows. Dress and image, important for Ellington personally since boyhood, became an imperative for the band, a trademark of his groups until at least the 1950s. He also became involved in African American–organized Washington music unions to improve business and musical skills and standards.

By 1920, however, Washington started to lose its reputation as a haven for American blacks. President Wilson's 1913 purge of blacks from federal government work eliminated many prestigious jobs for them. The violence against blacks following World War I included a race riot that raged for five days, provoked by false reports of black men attacking white women. The attacks by whites inspired blacks to take up arms against them. "Blacks were proud of their solidarity" by the end of the riot, David Levering Lewis reported. "And whites were sobered by it." But the lowest moment of the era in D.C. race relations occurred at the dedication of the Lincoln Memorial in 1922, when blacks were segregated from the main audience by a rope and a dirt road, and a black speaker at the event honoring the president who freed the slaves could not even sit on the dais. Ellington and band members Sonny Greer and Otto Hardwicke left Washington for New York shortly after this last event.[20]

Before 1922, Ellington earned a very good living, making by his own account $10,000 per year (about $116,000 in today's dollars), though this figure may not be reliable. Still, by 1919, he had bought a house for his new family (wife Edna and son Mercer), as well as a new car worth $2,000. He could easily have remained in Washington and thrived. Hardwicke recalled that Ellington felt "reluctant" to leave his well-established career, and that he and Greer had to convince him to go. But, as Ellington stated in his autobiography, "it is always more important to know what's happening than it is to make a living." Being at the vortex of the music and artists that Ellington and his bandmates loved seemed to be the major pull of Manhattan. New York City formed the center of the radio, recording, and publishing industries. It boasted the best theaters and show-business personalities galore. "It was New York that filled our imagination," Ellington recalled, listing as proof the dozens of artists that he, Greer, and Hardwicke admired when they were in their early twenties. "We were awed by the never-ending roll of great talents there . . . Harlem, to our minds, did indeed have the world's most glamorous atmosphere. We had to go there."[21]

One of the reasons Ellington gained international prominence and respect in New York, as well as hundreds of thousands of dollars during the 1920s and 1930s while the Harlem Renaissance writers struggled to survive during the same period, is that a century-long tradition of successful black music productions and performers preceded him there. According to James Weldon Johnson, the influential songwriter, pianist, historian, and political activist (and Ellington mentor) of the early twentieth century, the lengthy and rich history of black music and theater in New York City began in the 1820s. Blacks and whites performed together in house bands, and multiracial audiences attended. While minstrel shows formed the mainstay of black theatrical expression in this period and throughout the nineteenth century, original dramas and Shakespeare plays were also staged, sometimes at expensive prices. Eileen Southern's research indicated that blacks composed a "considerable amount of art music" before the Civil War, most of it lost.[22]

Following the Civil War, black performers increasingly entered the show business profession, especially in the field of "black minstrelsy," one of the few areas in which white audiences accepted black performers during the last third of the nineteenth century. Black minstrels were forced by tradition and economic pressure to uphold some white minstrel traditions, utilizing "coon songs" and blackface make-up on already black faces. But black minstrelsy did not connote an entirely negative proposition for black Americans. It provided blacks with a foot in the American stage door in the 1870s and 1880s, allowing them to get training in all aspects of theater production, which led to more satisfying and less degrading black stage productions in the 1890s. In addition, black minstrels changed the content of minstrel presentations to include more humanistic portrayals of black life and to excise and ameliorate the most stinging racist caricatures of the genre.[23]

In the immediate post–Civil War years, blacks worked on other fronts besides minstrel shows to establish their own cultural identities and gain a presence in the professional entertainment world. The Fisk Jubilee Singers represented the most famous example of this trend, with their formal dress standard and serious artistic purpose providing a strikingly different vision of black Americans for whites raised on an entertainment diet of the minstrel show. A new respect for black artistic achievement was also reflected in the publishing of the first two books dedicated to African American music, an 1861 collection of spirituals, and *Slave Songs of the United States* (1867).[24]

America rushed forward in the so-called Progressive Era during the decades near the turn of the century, innovation constantly surfacing in the realms of both industry and culture. The country was gaining "velocity," as Ellington put it, and the music that best represented this zeitgeist, that became most identified with an American aesthetic, was African American music. The quick pace and alternating rhythms of ragtime reflected the fast pace of the urban city. The blues allowed room for an individualistic working-class perspective and narrative rare in European-based music. It expressed black feelings concerning racism, the modern alienation of working in physically bruising dead-end jobs, as well as universal sorrows of lost love. Furthermore, African American musical devices such as syncopation, call-and-response, blue notes, and ninth chords provided the underpinnings for the major American popular musical trends that swept the country and the world during the twentieth century—jazz, swing, rock and roll, soul, and the golden age of American songwriting, as epitomized by the work of Irving Berlin, George Gershwin, and Jerome Kern, among others. As DuBois passionately claimed in the last chapter of *The Souls of Black Folk,* black music provided an important, though imperfect, meeting point for blacks and whites throughout the 1800s, and its role in this matter increased exponentially during the twentieth century through the present day.

Early black successes on Broadway in the 1890s by songwriters and performers such as Bob Cole and the brothers J. Rosamond and James Weldon Johnson established blacks as artistic and economic forces on a national level, providing early precedents for Ellington's achievements. More than any other figure in the black Broadway constellation, Will Marion Cook proved a huge personal and musical influence on the young Ellington. Thanks to financial help organized by the famous black activist and author Frederick Douglass, Cook received a formal European conservatory education and played piano and violin as well as composed and conducted. Discrimination in the classical music world kept him from employment, and inspired comments about how he seemed to have an inordinate amount of talent for a black person. Such treatment infuriated Cook and led him to try his hand at the new market for black musical productions on Broadway, where he enjoyed more success. With his learned and superior manner, conservatory background, and European interests (which Ellington adopted, to a degree), Cook was a leader among the black artistic community. One of his main goals was to prod black productions to present "real pictures of Negro life" and "black exploration of realistic drama as opposed to farce comedy" of the minstrel tradition. In an interview published on his seventieth birthday, Ellington warmly recalled the many occasions he and Cook rode in an open taxicab through Central Park in the mid-1920s, discussing questions of music and race "while [Cook's] beautiful white hair was flowing in the breeze." Ellington felt so moved by Cook that he named his son Mercer after Cook's son.[25]

At the turn of the century, Bert Williams represented the preeminent figure in efforts by blacks to establish themselves as serious and nationally successful entertainment figures in New York City. Though mostly known as a comedian, his "regal quality" and melancholy tinged stage presence marked Williams as someone beyond the slapstick clowning of the minstrel performer. Critics and audiences recognized him as an artist who brought comedy to a higher and more insightful plane, much as Charlie Chaplin would in the 1910s. Though he felt discouraged because stage conventions forced him to don blackface (which he resented), and because audiences only accepted him in humorous roles, his list of show business achievements are second to none among blacks of his era, and even among most of his white peers. Williams was the first black entertainer to win widespread national appeal among both white and black audiences. He achieved international success in black Broadway musicals as well as in his long stints in the lavishly budgeted Ziegfeld revues, writing a good deal of his own material. He was the first African American to enjoy a major career in the record business, and one of the only black performers to be cross-promoted with classical singers such as Enrico Caruso. Williams was the most famous African American of his day aside from political spokesperson Booker T. Washington, and Washington felt that Williams achieved more than he had on behalf of the black race. "He has smiled his way into people's hearts," Washington mused. "I have been obliged to fight my way."[26] In his ability to attain the pinnacles of show business, reach black and white audiences, and have a strong, if nonpolitical effect on issues and impressions of race in America, Williams provided a significant precedent for Ellington in the conduct of his career. They both asserted dignity and position on an international level while rocking no racist's boat.

Progress on behalf of African Americans was evident in the field of popular music as well as on Broadway during the opening decades of the twentieth century, as seen in the examples of Scott Joplin and James Reese Europe. With "Maple Leaf Rag" (1898), Joplin became the first black American composer to enjoy a million-seller, ushering in an international passion for ragtime music. The marketing strategies of John Stark, the white publisher of "Maple," also were rare and significant. In advertisements, Stark insisted that ragtime, especially Joplin's, represented "the equal of classical music" in quality.[27] Such claims were unprecedented for a black composer, and clashed with the views of white and black moral authorities who argued that the syncopated strains of ragtime signified a dangerous influence on young people. Stark and Joplin's efforts to market a sense of artistry and respectability in black music, and to attract a highbrow multiracial audience, would be duplicated and amplified by Ellington and his manager three decades later.

Of all the black musical figures preceding Ellington, James Reese Europe came closest to achieving the kind of career Ellington enjoyed and Joplin dreamed of: multiracial international success in highbrow and popular circles. If not for his tragic death at the age of thirty-nine at the end of World War I, Europe may well have brought jazz to a wider audience a decade before Ellington and Louis Armstrong did, and changed the entire direction and definition of black music. Europe's talents centered in the areas of bandleading, arranging, and promotion more than in composing. His leadership in the Clef Club during the 1910s in New York City brought about improved working opportunities and reduced discrimination for black musicians. The club's signature moment occurred on 2 May 1912, when Europe's Clef Club orchestra, performing a "serious and dignified program of African American music," became the first black orchestra to play Carnegie Hall. The audience for the show probably represented the first integrated audience for a concert in America. The enthusiastic reaction ensured numerous future bookings at "nearly all the best functions," including gigs for upper-class clientele on yachts and in mansions, in both America and Europe. The orchestra returned to Carnegie Hall the next year, anticipating Ellington's annual Carnegie visits from 1943 to 1948. Shortly after the first Carnegie show, Europe became the first black bandleader to receive a major recording contract. Yet acclaim remained constricted, especially among the large segment of the critical community that only deemed music as being worthy of respect if it adopted European forms. A critic reviewing the 1912 Carnegie concert for *Musical America* offered advice:

> If the Negro Symphony Orchestra will give its attention in the coming year to a movement or two of a Haydn symphony and play it at its next concert, and if the composers, who this year took such obvious pleasure in conducting their marches, tangos, and waltzes, will write short movements for orchestra, basing them on classic models, next year's concert will inaugurate a

new era for the Negro musician in New York and will aid him in being appraised at his full value and taken seriously.

Europe replied to this kind of sentiment much as Ellington would thirty years later: "We have developed a kind of symphony music that, no matter what else you think, is different and distinctive, and that lends itself to the playing of the peculiar compositions of our race." As if that were not enough, Europe spent the end of his career serving overseas in World War I in combat and as a regiment leader, and as the leader of an orchestra that drew exuberant crowds and praise across France, where Europe is credited with introducing jazz to the European continent. Ellington had a direct connection to Europe, since his sister Mary taught Ellington in school, and he regularly asked his Washington friends about her welfare throughout his life.[28]

In the years following World War I, African Americans began to lay claim to a presence in the mass media beyond their previous incursions in Broadway productions and popular song. A black literary movement called the Harlem Renaissance arose in New York City in the 1920s. It shared many goals with the black musical artists of previous decades. Both groups promoted artistic expression as a way of breaking down prejudice, achieving racial uplift, displaying the humanity and achievement of blacks, and documenting their history and identity. Both groups also wished to make money by creating best-selling products. While Renaissance authors rarely mingled or collaborated with jazz musicians such as Ellington and Armstrong, the proximity and excitement emanating from both groups created a synergy that inspired media coverage and black artistic achievement, and further established New York City as an international center of black artistic and intellectual activity. Before it was safe to politically confront the forces of American racism through public protest, the arts represented an area where, despite the paltry sales of Renaissance authors, blacks could safely challenge the false suppositions of black inferiority behind Jim Crow discriminations and bring alternate messages concerning blacks to a national audience.

Though the Harlem Renaissance participants engineered important precedents and released some excellent work, the black musicians and composers of the 1895–1940 period succeeded in developing a broad cross-racial appeal far more effectively. Multiple reasons accounted for this. For one, no professional literary tradition or national market existed for black authors before the 1920s, particularly in the realm of fiction.[29] American blacks formed a minority of 10–12 percent during this period, and purchased few books. National publishers hesitated committing promotional resources for such books until they felt certain a large enough audience existed. Moreover, Southern bookstores tended to refuse to stock books by or sympathetic to blacks, and many publishers were intimidated by the potential of a Southern boycott of their catalog if they attempted to distribute books by black authors.

Black musicians and composers of the period, on the other hand, enjoyed a readymade audience and long-term historic acceptance in various distribution systems and venues, while African American authors still felt they had to prove themselves as artists. This situation enabled many black musicians to earn a living—something with which all Harlem Renaissance writers experienced difficulty.[30]

Perhaps most importantly, the work of the best Renaissance writers confirmed an important hypothesis made by one of the American theorists that Renaissance intellectuals took most to heart. In his 1917 essay "Trans-National America," Randolph Bourne argued that the diversity of American society formed the source of its strength and renewal. He warned against allowing the Anglo-Saxon vision of assimilation through mass conformity to come to fruition because new people, voices, and culture kept America from the stagnation that, in his opinion, afflicted the less diverse nations of Europe. To Bourne, writing as American industry and technology proved predominant during World War I, America's "trans-national" identity represented the essence of the democratic vision and the key to its greatness, even if it made some less enlightened, more prejudiced people uncomfortable at times.[31] Numerous black and immigrant artists had proved by the 1920s that American diversity shaped the most vital strands in American music; by the end of the 1920s, the more distinctive works by Langston Hughes, Zora Neale Hurston, Nella Larsen, Claude McKay, Wallace Thurman, and Jean Toomer, among others, proved that new black voices bestowed a unique vibrancy onto American literature as well.

The world of black music in the 1920s provided an illustrative counter to the Harlem Renaissance. Where black authors felt a need to prove themselves to publishers and academics, jazz and blues artists knew from the start that, as blacks playing music of their own composition and arrangement, they were situated outside the environs of high culture. They were not attempting to measure up to European standards. They employed no standards but their own, and those of their largely black audience.[32] While many Renaissance writers labored to present an image of African American culture as being equal to European culture, black musicians of the 1920s showcased black culture as American, but also as something vibrant and apart. The more successful musicians did not have to wait for reviews of their work or for sales accountings from publishers. They witnessed the money and respect their work garnered in clubs every night, as well as the fact that companies clamored to release their recordings to a national (if mostly segregated) audience. While many Renaissance authors wrote of their fears concerning what skin color meant, artists like Ellington, Armstrong, and Bessie Smith celebrated their heritage, and did not draw color lines around blacks. Even amidst the white elite audiences, minstrel-like trappings, and semi-nude dancers of the Cotton Club, Ellington played compositions that celebrated black culture in all its hues: "Black and Tan Fantasie," "Black Beauty," "Creole Rhapsody." Early nattily dressed jazz pioneers like Armstrong, Sidney Bechet, Coleman Hawkins, Earl Hines, King Oliver, and many more, especially Ellington, radiated black pride. While many in the Renaissance were asking for acceptance and permission from cultural and academic vanguards, Ellington, by the early 1930s, earned the acceptance they were striving for as an artist creating at the highest levels of culture.

But Ellington and his jazz and blues brethren did not receive contemporary recognition for achieving the goals of the Harlem Renaissance more effectively than the writers and intellectuals. While some modern-day accounts include jazz and blues artists as part of the Renaissance, this represents a revisionist view.[33] The often elite and effete sensibilities of the movement's leaders kept the purveyors of popular music at a distance and downgraded their cultural contributions and significance. The Renaissance intellectuals applied the same standards to music as they did to literature: they tended to only recognize music that emulated European standards. As Samuel A. Floyd documented, they hoped for great African American achievement in classical music, and encouraged composers to take the themes of supposedly primitive jazz, blues, and plantation melodies, and transform them into orchestrated, conventionally Western works of art. Howard University professor Alain Locke urged Renaissance composers to create "jazz classics," not the "trashy type" of jazz usually purveyed in clubs, and declared that popular black jazz, blues, and ballads would never be viewed as "great Negro music."[34]

The musical prescriptions of the Harlem Renaissance intellectuals like Locke erected an unnecessary wall between the intellectuals and jazz musicians during the 1920s. "Those of us in the music and entertainment business were vaguely aware that something exciting was happening, but we weren't directly involved," wrote bandleader Cab Calloway in the 1970s. Benny Carter, the multitalented composer, player, and arranger, noted the divide between the two groups. "We in music knew there was much going on in literature, but our worlds were far apart," he recalled. "We sensed that the black cultural as well as moral leaders looked upon us as undignified."[35] The educated backgrounds, dapper appearances, and eloquent speaking styles of artists such as Ellington, Carter, and bandleader Fletcher Henderson could have served as a bridge between the two groups, but, sadly, neither side took up the challenge.

During the Harlem Renaissance, just as jazz and blues began to achieve mass commercial exposure and success, numerous critics in the white media, especially those who usually covered classical and opera, disparaged the music and the people who wrote and performed it. For some, jazz contributed to the social disintegration endemic in American cities. They felt that traditional music (i.e., classical or Victorian) inculcated traditional values, while jazz, as practiced by whites as well as blacks, somehow "had the Devil in it." They complained that its "sensual" and "carnal" rhythms "ruined youth" and threatened to turn back the clock of progress for Western civilization. Jazz improvisation was even decried as "bolshevistic" by one 1920s account.

In their enthusiasm to belong to the highbrow world of art and criticism, Harlem Renaissance intellectuals adopted some of the tone and prejudiced standards of these white critics. But the irony of this situation was that the most threatening possibility to many of these white critics was the notion that African Americans were capable of creating great and lasting art, a goal Renaissance leaders held dear. Neil Leonard reported that many cultural observers of the era wanted to make sure jazz stayed "in its place" and out of the confines of the concert hall. "Keep your dirty paws off your betters," thundered English critic Ernest Newman in a prominent 1926 editorial in the *New York Times*. He further called jazz musicians "musical illiterates," insisted that "there are no [real] composers" in jazz, and crowed that the collected brains of those who write jazz "would not fit in Johann Strauss' hat." In addition, because the jazz style was identified in the 1920s with black Southern history and immoral practices such as brothels (something largely disproven by later historians), some in the black media in the North, most notably the *Chicago Defender,* also criticized jazz music and musicians. One *Defender* article advised that "if you are now in a jazz band, do not give up proper study on your instrument. You may be called upon to render real service and play good music."[36] Up-and-coming black musicians and composers in the 1920s, like the young Ellington, faced artistic resistance from both the black and white critical establishments.

During the 1920s, blacks also gained a significant presence in another facet of the mass media besides the publishing industry, one with more relevance to Ellington's ambitions: the recording industry. Technological innovations during that decade made phonographs and discs more affordable, which increased sales and allowed black artists an unprecedented opportunity to reach a national audience.

Before 1920, African American musicians rarely appeared on commercial recordings, and when they did, one did not usually find authentic black music embedded into the grooves. Bert Williams released over eighty sides, many of them excellent, but grounded in orchestrated Broadway-styled arrangements. More often, blacks appeared performing "coon songs" from minstrel shows, novelty pieces, or, on recordings by such artists as the Fisk Jubilee Singers, rearranged plantation melodies and spirituals in a European concert style, which tended to excise some of the African American qualities of the songs. These recordings of black artists were generally produced and arranged by whites for a white audience.

Usually, blacks did not appear on records featuring African American music before the 1920s, because the major labels believed that white artists "covering" black music represented a more marketable proposition to middle- and upper-class white audiences. The Original Dixieland Jazz Band, an all-white ensemble from New Orleans, represented the most famous example of this tendency. Black jazz musicians inspired them (although they sometimes denied this), yet they were marketed as the "creators of jazz." While the ODJB's releases of the late 1910s were watered-down versions of jazz with a novelty feel (the horns often imitated animal noises), they also broke sales records previously held by Caruso and John Philip Sousa discs. The huge commercial potential for jazz and black music was first realized with these releases.

Finally, events of the World War I era, especially the Great Migration, led to changes in the recording industry. Black entrepreneurs such as W. C. Handy and Perry Bradford initiated efforts to inform the major record companies of the potential for a profitable, largely urban black market for recordings by blacks, especially female blues singers. According to legendary record executive John Hammond, Mamie Smith's "Crazy Blues" (1920) represented an "overwhelming success" that sold "exclusively to blacks" in the range of one hundred thousand. The "race market" had arrived, and the recordings that catered to it multiplied exponentially in the months and years to come.[37]

Jim Crow pervaded the early African American record market. Records by blacks were known as "race records," and were generally not available at the same stores where white artists' records were sold. In the rare cases when they were, they were sold "under the counter." African American recordings were advertised in black newspapers, not the white press. The discs were not listed in the monthly record company bulletins sent to white-patronized stores. Separate bulletins were issued until at least the mid-1930s. Ads for "race records" frequently featured stereotypical and offensive portraits of blacks and never featured cross-promotion with white artists. But numerous historians have subsequently argued that "race record" did not automatically represent a derogatory term denoting segregation, but was probably adopted from the *Chicago Defender*, which viewed the term "race" as signifying "black pride and solidarity" in the 1920s. As Albert Murray noted, the term "race man" or "race woman" suggested an ideal black or a black leader.

Segregation ruled on the radio just as it did in the record stores of the 1920s. Blacks were almost never heard on the radio, especially on the national level, until Ellington's late-night broadcasts from the Cotton Club in the late 1920s. Thanks to an edict by the Hays office, such music was also forbidden in motion pictures.[38]

With the new "race records," black musicians, publishers, talent scouts, and songwriters enjoyed increasing autonomy over the material recorded and released. Early blues and jazz artists received a great deal of latitude in the recording studio since production costs were low, royalties existed only for the most popular artists, and airplay was nonexistent.[39] Despite the promising arrival of an African American record market in the 1920s, opportunities were limited for black recording artists—their records did not enjoy anywhere near the influence or sales of white artists, a situation that Ellington and his management had a leading role in changing.

Black musicals returned to Broadway in the early 1920s, following a hiatus largely initiated by World War I, led by Eubie Blake and Noble Sissle's hugely successful *Shuffle Along* (1921). It broke a longstanding taboo concerning African American Broadway musicals: the portrayal of serious romantic love between black characters. It contributed to the renewal of New York City's reputation as an environment of opportunity and acceptance for black performers, one that fueled the explosion of jazz talent in the city during the 1920s. As scholar Ted Gioia pointed out, New York City whites possessed a more accurate picture of black culture, thanks to shows like *Shuffle Along* and the previous turn-of-the-century black Broadway productions, and thus were more inclined to support black music there than anywhere else in the world. Despite the hit status of *Shuffle Along*, prejudice surfaced during its run. While blacks were allowed to sit in what had previously been considered the seats of white people in the auditorium, segregation was still observed, with the balcony reserved for blacks only. In addition, band members were made to memorize the score since, according to Blake, "people didn't believe that black people could read music—they wanted to think that our ability was just natural talent."[40] No further black Broadway hits of the caliber of *Shuffle* surfaced in the 1920s. Progress for blacks in the entertainment world was not only slow—sometimes it was reversible.

When Ellington became involved with the New York music scene in March 1923, his business and musical education needed to rise to new levels.[41] A tougher competition existed for musical jobs than he had faced in Washington. According to Ellington, it felt "a little terrifying" being in New York City with the "millions" of skilled pianists there in the mid-1920s. The first time Ellington, Greer, and Hardwick ventured to New York, they were back in D.C. within three months because of their inability to secure a regular income (though there was no paucity of smaller jobs, alcohol-fueled Prohibition-era partying, pool hustling, and hanging out with famous musicians). They were back to stay in New York by the summer, and eventually, Ellington recalled, legendary New York pianists like Fats Waller, James P. Johnson, and Willie "The Lion" Smith used to listen to Ellington play during that period and "they thought I was pretty good." The competition made Ellington better, and Smith became an important Ellington mentor.

Ellington had to learn how to maneuver in the recording and publishing worlds in New York. In 1923, at Ellington's first recording session (playing piano with Elmer Snowden's Novelty Band), the band, which included Greer and Hardwick, turned in a subdued performance much like the "under-conversation" music for which Ellington and his compatriots were famous in the Washington society scene. The record company rejected the session because, as Snowden said later, "it wasn't the kind of *Negro* music they wanted." The polite sound that made Washington's high-society audiences happy would not fly in New York City. Besides, white bandleaders Paul Whiteman and Vincent Lopez had already established a market for sweeter sounds. At that time, record companies generally assumed that black jazz bands, in order to sell records, needed to create their own distinctive segregated market with "hot" music rather than the sweeter style of jazz. In 1924, Snowden left the band, partly for the aforementioned reasons, but mostly, according to longtime Ellington associate Tom Whaley, because Greer found out that the band had received pay raises that Snowden failed to pass on to the band.

With Snowden's departure, Ellington reluctantly became the leader of a band called the Washingtonians, which featured the remaining members of the Snowden band, even though he would have rather concentrated his time on writing songs and selling them to publishers. Songwriting and arranging represented relatively new endeavors for Ellington. During the 1914–23 period of performing in Washington, only three original Ellington compositions can be accounted for, none of them copyrighted or published. By 1924, he was actively peddling his songs on Tin Pan Alley, but garnered no notable commercial successes until 1925, and it was probably not until 1925 that the Washingtonians regularly played Ellington compositions during gigs. The Washingtonians were surprised at how quickly Ellington mastered songwriting and arranging and developed his own musical voice. According to Washingtonian band member Louis Metcalf:

> One thing which surprised all of us—when Duke started arranging for the band . . . he started bringing in some music there that we'd never heard before and we were sort of wondering what it would sound like.
>
> I never forget he brought in an arrangement on "St. Louis Blues" and he had every horn playing the melody in a different key, and it sound awful, you know. But I come to found out it wasn't the sound of harmony he was after, it was effects. And after we played and rehearsed the thing for about 2 hours, it began to soak in what this man was doing, you know? Actually, it sounded like a train coming through the woods or forest, you know, and he had the whole works in there, you know. And we just couldn't believe it, because we know the man didn't do any studying for arrangement. But it was just a natural gift, just naturally a born arranger, and from then, far as I can see, he never looked back since.

The Washingtonians did good business and established a reputation as a live act at their extended engagements at the Hollywood Club (after 1925, the Kentucky Club) in a basement on West 49th Street. Greer recalled that "the bandstand was so small, it could hardly hold a fight." The band regularly played until 9:00 AM, and the club became a place where celebrities gathered after their own gigs in Manhattan, attracting such black and white luminaries as Armstrong, Berlin, Gershwin, Fanny Brice, Fletcher Henderson, and Al Jolson. The club was also a place where Ellington experimented with and furthered his writing and arranging skills. "We were the first group [of our kind] to have what you would call arrangements. It was unheard of," according to Greer. In 1972, Ellington talked about his writing process and some of his influences during his band's run at the Kentucky Club:

> I always wanted to sound like Fletcher Henderson's band, not that I had much success . . . practically every afternoon we'd go to one of the [several] movie houses where they had a symphony orchestra in the pit, many of them on Broadway . . . they'd have a regular symphonic work as the overture, then they would do a sort of presentation with a small group or a large group

of people, depending on which day it was. And you'd sit there to the symphony for two or three shows and then you'd go to the Kentucky Club and [try to] make your six-piece band sound like a symphony. And of course you didn't have any success but it was a lot of fun. The same thing with Fletcher's band, you say "I want to try to make it sound like that." No success, but what came out of it had some sort of little unique thing about it and it attracted attention.

But their recording-studio experiences during 1925–26 were disappointing. According to Mark Tucker, the Washingtonians recorded less than comparable New York bands of the time and probably suffered from record-company interference. The discs' sound balance was poor, and the band mostly recorded non-Ellington compositions pushed on them by black publishers and record companies. Nine of the first ten Washingtonian recordings were popular songs that Ellington and the band did not compose or, presumably, play as part of their repertoire. Tucker summed up the situation:

> If the Washingtonians had been better readers, like Fletcher Henderson's musicians, the results might have been more impressive. But Ellington did not have this kind of ensemble [yet]. His was a group accustomed to regular rehearsals, during which arrangements were worked out collectively and, for the most part, orally. Given a choice, Ellington probably would have recorded pieces his group played more often and cared more about.

Ellington faced a common Catch-22 of the music business: he was not allowed to perform his own work without a proven track record or powerful manager behind him. The mid-1920s represented a learning period—the problems with sound quality, record-company interference, lack of support for original material, and the economic and artistic limits of aiming only for a segregated black market were eventually tackled and turned around by Ellington and his powerful manager, Irving Mills.

During the mid-1920s, Ellington also initiated his first efforts to fit the lessons of the post-1895 African American music tradition into his own writing. At this early juncture, he did not yet extend the parameters of what his forebears accomplished, but he brought some of the concepts of Blake, Cook, and others into the jazz-oriented field before most other black songwriters. Like Blake and Sissle's work in 1921, Jo Trent's lyrics for the 1925 Ellington song "With You" treated African American love seriously. "Jig Walk," an Ellington and Trent composition from the same year, made a proud if simple statement about the influence of black music and dance.

"Show these kind folk New York's dancing craze," goes the lyric. "It has got that big Broadway ablaze." Through the use of novel chromatic changes, different harmonic colorings, and chords with flatted "blue notes," Ellington's early works consistently brought a fresh, more authentic African American musical flavor to compositions aimed toward Tin Pan Alley. The belief that black popular music could be infused with excellence is evident during Ellington's forays in the music business during the pre–Cotton Club 1920s.

Yet, an ad for a Gennett record by Duke Ellington and the Washingtonians (and other records by other artists) from 1926 in the *Chicago Defender* features a minstrel caricature of a Sambo-like character in a suit. In the not too distant future, Ellington, with help from Mills, would correct this anomaly between the subtext of his music and the way it was marketed.[42]

Long before and more eloquently than any of his peers, Langston Hughes saw and reported the contradictions between the Harlem Renaissance artistic dictates and the problems of creating an African American artistic tradition. As a young man, Hughes lived both in black and white neighborhoods, went to both black and white schools, and followed working-class black culture, especially the blues. Like Ellington, he had interacted with poor as well as middle-class people, and knew more than most blacks about black history, especially the activities of his own lineage (Hughes's abolitionist maternal grandfather participated in John Brown's raid in 1859). But Hughes also evinced an interest in Jewish culture and white American poets such as Walt Whitman and Carl Sandburg. He was more versed in the various strata of class and race than most Renaissance intellectuals.

Hughes's 1926 essay "The Negro Artist and the Racial Mountain" presented a cogent summary of the problems facing black art and its acceptance in America. He argued that art that dealt with explicitly black themes, styles, and syntax had never been accepted or encouraged by critics of any color. He warned that "the mountain standing in the way of any true Negro art in America" was the urge "toward whiteness, the desire to pour racial individuality into the mold of American standardization, and to be as little Negro and as much American as possible." In what must have been a purposeful dig at Renaissance hoi polloi, Hughes praised "the low-down folks, the so-called common element" who took joy in being black, and enthusiastically supported musical forms like jazz and blues. "They still hold their individuality in the face of American standardizations," he enthused. "And they accept what beauty is their own without question." Hughes called for art that celebrated the black experience and assumed that the black world "was as interesting as any other world" and needed to be documented and celebrated. By publishing his essay in the *Nation,* he purposely directed his remarks to a national audience of left-leaning elite intellectuals, the same audience that supported the Harlem Renaissance and the views of its spokespeople. Hughes summed up with sentiments that resembled common intellectual currencies of the 1960s:

> We younger Negro artists who create now intend to express our individual dark-skinned selves without fear or shame. If white people are pleased we are glad. If they are not, it doesn't matter. We know we are beautiful. And ugly too.[43]

The Ellington orchestra recorded their first sides in December 1926, six months after Hughes's stirring call to black artists. Those initial recordings included "Black and Tan Fantasie" and "East St. Louis Toddle-O," two compositions that celebrated black culture in ways analogous to Hughes's works. The first was lightly based on a church song well known among black parishioners that co-composer Bubber Miley's mother used to play for him, and the second attempted to musically document the tired yet determined lope of a certain older black resident of Harlem.[44] No evidence exists that Ellington read Hughes's words (although they did become friends in the 1930s), but the "Racial Mountain" essay resembled Ellington's own views and concerns on racial art, which he would expound upon for the rest of his career.

Ellington and Hughes fulfilled the goals of the Harlem Renaissance more than any other figures, even if both were largely dismissed by the Renaissance leadership of the 1920s and 1930s. Both of their careers sustained decades of notoriety and artistic development that few black artists enjoyed before them. But Ellington succeeded financially in a way that Hughes did not, despite intense efforts by Hughes to create revenue-generating books and shows. While Renaissance leaders decried the fact that blacks were denied access to the rights and institutions that brought economic and artistic success (property owning, higher education, loans and financing, better job opportunities), Ellington lived out an unprecedented vision of success for blacks starting in the late 1920s. He became the embodiment of the key tenets of black pride, quality, and achievement stressed in the background and training he received in Washington, D.C. The large group of educated middle-class blacks Ellington grew up among won the opportunity to shape their own culture and institutions. They used this power to try to create a generation of youthful black achievers less hindered by the manacles of race in America, and Ellington became the most famous product of their culture.

By 1926, Ellington was aware of what he had to do to make a living and to make creative strides. Late that year, he signed a contract with manager and publisher Irving Mills, who shared enough of Ellington's vision to facilitate the slow development of a music that expanded the definition and acceptance of African American and American popular music. Ellington, with a truly American musical style that drew from black as well as white inspirations, could not reach his full commercial potential in a segregated music-business world. He needed the biggest audience possible, like any commercial artist. Despite the dictates of the white-run music business and the prejudice that surrounded what could and could not be considered great art, Ellington and Mills realized that his music could potentially appeal to a broad cross-section of all races, and sell widely.

With these developments, the stage was set for a truly distinctive American music to be presented on a national scale and for the recognition and celebration of the African American contribution to American culture. Various prejudices would be toppled in the American twentieth century—not just racial and political ones, but cultural ones as well. Ellington's personal background and the artists who came before him set the groundwork for the contribution he made during the rest of his career, on and off the bandstand.

2

THE MARKETING PLAN

[During and after 1926] the additions to the band really started coming fast, but not till the most important change in Duke's life took place. Whether you judge it as good or bad, hate him or admire him, the advent of Irving Mills is pivotal in the life of Edward Kennedy Ellington and all those associated with him. When Mills stepped in, accident and chance stepped out; big business took over and the rise of the Ellington orchestra was made inevitable. That with this rise should also come serious disillusionment for the men in the band, a deepening sense of personal and collective tragedy which has never left these brilliant musicians, that, too, was inevitable.   BARRY ULANOV, Ellington's first biographer, 1946

Any new consumer product that does not disappear quickly as just a fad or fashion is probably related to deep social currents.
     MICHAEL SCHUDSON, historian of marketing, 1984[1]

In the fall of 1926, music publisher Irving Mills became Duke Ellington's manager, publisher, and business partner.[2] They had known each other informally for years: Ellington spent time in the mid-1920s on the "professional floor" at Mills Music, where "composers, lyricists, bandleaders, singers and vaudevillians gathered" to write, audition, buy, and sell songs. He also played solo piano on a 1925 recording, backing up Mills's vocal on a blues song. Some accounts indicate that the Ellington band's rendition of the Ellington–Bubber Miley composition "Black and Tan Fantasie" at the Kentucky Club in midtown Manhattan is what initially impressed Mills.

FIGURE I. A rare shot of Duke Ellington and his band, probably taken during the Christmas season of 1928. An elegantly attired African American orchestra would appear less threatening to white audiences of the period, who, told of "genius" and assured of "class" in the advertisements and marketing of the band, would be more likely to purchase Ellington's sheet music, show tickets, and recordings. Standing (*left to right*): Joe Nanton, Arthur Whetsol, Harry Carney, Freddie Guy, Wellman Braud, Freddie Jenkins. Seated: Johnny Hodges, Sonny Greer, Cootie Williams. On floor: Duke Ellington. Kendall/Bolden Collections/Symil.

In 1958, Ellington told the story a different way. "We were playing [W. C. Handy's] 'St. Louis Blues,'" he recalled, one of the most recognizable and covered songs of the twentieth century. "And he asked what it was. When I told him, he said it sure sounded nothing like it. So maybe that gave him ideas." In any case, Mills felt so strongly about Ellington's potential as a bandleader as well as a composer that he entered an area of the music business that he had previously not been involved with: band managing. "If I hadn't raved about him when I heard him the first night, he might have just been . . . another one of the bandleaders working in the café," Mills mused, several decades later. "I was very fortunate, Duke was very fortunate."

From 1926 to 1939, Mills and Ellington designed and carried out an influential marketing plan that made Ellington an international figure, allowed him to surmount the segregation of the mass media, and cemented his reputation as an important composer. With the rise of a national music market in the 1920s and the popularity of "canned" music emanating from radio and records, recording artists more than ever before required powerful management. Success at the local level would not be as profitable or dependable as in decades past. To compete in this new mass media at the highest level, recording artists needed more than a solitary manager. They needed an agency armed with personnel supervising the various aspects of the music business for an artist: recordings, sheet music, touring, film, merchandising, promotion, and newspaper publicity. This is the role Mills played in launching both Ellington's career and in establishing a new standard and philosophy for managing artists in the music business. The precedents established by Mills provided the blueprint for the powerful agencies that emerged a decade later to supervise the unprecedentedly lucrative business dealings of the big bands of the Swing Era in the 1930s and 1940s.[3]

The Ellington/Mills partnership occurred during an auspicious period for American music and its business.[4] Changes were brewing in the 1920s that transformed the American cultural landscape. In looking back on his career, Ellington often remarked that success entailed "doing the right thing for the right people at the right time." The year 1926 represented the ideal moment to unleash Ellington's array of talents to a national audience.

Radio arrived in 1920, but not until 1926 did it represent a national phenomenon. Prices for equipment dropped yearly, enabling more people to afford it. Sixteen million Americans listened to radio by 1925, and sixty million—roughly 40 percent of American households—were tuned in by 1930.

The record industry reached new commercial and artistic heights as well.

A significant drop in the price of phonographs in the early 1920s generated increased record sales, thus enabling record companies to expand the scope of their offerings. While the larger companies spent much of the 1910s attempting to appeal to a high-class white audience paying premium prices for the finest classical recordings, the 1920s found these companies and a host of new independent companies releasing more popular music, including music for the sometimes controversial dancing crazes that began in the 1910s. Starting in 1920, formerly benighted record companies finally discovered the profit potential of the African American music market, which increased exponentially as the decade wore on.

Conditions for Ellington, Mills, and many others in the music business were further improved by the introduction of electronic recording in 1925, which, with the use of a condenser microphone instead of a recording horn, increased the range of recorded sound by two and a half octaves. A more natural, less muddy sound resulted. Drum sets had overpowered the older technology and tended to be left aside before, but thanks to electronic recording, the great American love affair with rhythm, be it in jazz, blues, country, or Broadway, could be captured fully. Sales increased with the introduction of this new technology, and many believe that a commercial and artistic golden age of recording resulted in the late 1920s.

These developments were key components in the creation of a mass media. In the United States before the 1920s, entertainment was locally based. Plentiful live music existed for public enjoyment in large and small cities, in public and private venues. Player pianos were affordable and widespread among upper- and middle-class families. Live home sing-alongs were common sources of recreation and a leading reason why the sheet-music market predominated in the music business before the mid-1930s.

But the rise of a national mass media in the 1920s changed the ways in which American music was disseminated. As radio and recordings became more affordable and widespread, broadcasts and recordings were distributed throughout the country. More than ever before, audiences in Louisiana and California heard and bought the same music as did people in New York. Over time, this nationalizing of popular music precipitated a decline in artists performing in strictly regional styles.[5] Charts that listed the best-selling records in the country began appearing in *Variety* in the 1920s. The notion of what popular music encompassed was increasingly being decided on a national basis, with local influences holding less sway. Radio and record companies began pushing for grouping musical artists into easily classified genres (such as pop, jazz, country, black, white, etc.) that helped sell records and radio commercial time, and build more predictable audience behavior.

This kind of intensive national promotion and marketing proved even more important for black artists than for white. To promote Ellington successfully as a popular attraction and serious composer, Mills needed to accomplish more than just selling his music and the band that performed it; he had to create an image that circumvented the ingrained negative or limited images associated with black Americans. In order to gain access to the most lucrative and widest possible national market, Mills positioned Ellington to appeal to all races, something unprecedented on a national scale in mid-1920s Jim Crow America.

For the most part, the entertainment and music business worlds were highly segregated when Ellington's career began. All entertainment industries, from movies, radio, and Broadway to recordings, concerts, and vaudeville, had different policies and/or company divisions geared towards whites and blacks. There existed very little recognition that the black and white races could enjoy any music or entertainment unless it originated in or culturally drew from their own race. Black artists like Bert Williams and James Reese Europe had established inroads in attracting mass multiracial audiences during earlier periods, but no figures could match their draw to white audiences by 1926.

Because much of his marketing centered on selling Ellington as a great composer, Mills also had to devise ways to overcome Eurocentric cultural prejudices against the notion of considering American, African American, and popular music as art forms. American music, art, and literature were still not widely taught in universities or respected as serious artistic contributions in the 1920s, and would not be until roughly World War II. Most popular music of the late nineteenth and early twentieth centuries had the reputation of being an exercise in flavor-of-the-month novelty. The notion of blacks creating music of a serious and lasting nature was even more far fetched than the idea of an American doing so. To thwart such long-standing and inaccurate cultural hierarchies, Mills devised a way for the public to accept Ellington as an important American composer, a figure far beyond the usual conception of popular or jazz musicians. The "hot" jazz for which the Ellington orchestra and other black musicians initially became famous had the additional problem of frequently being portrayed in the media as primitive. During their partnership, Ellington and Mills made essential contributions to eradicating these various prejudices, transforming American culture. By the end of the twentieth century, it was taken as common wisdom throughout the world that the best American jazz and popular music represented not just entertainment, but art of a high order. This notion had its first firm planting in the American and international consciousness during the trailblazing Ellington and Mills teaming.

Irving Mills was born on the Lower East Side of New York City in 1894, a second-generation Jewish immigrant whose parents, Sophie and Hyman, originally hailed from Odessa, Russia. Because of the family's poverty, Mills began working at the age of eleven in Shanley's Restaurant at Broadway and 29th, which provided his first exposure to the burgeoning theater and entertainment world of his home city. From there, he maintained a steady trajectory upward in the world, becoming a page boy at the Friars Club (where he knew George M. Cohan), and eventually getting started in the music business as a song plugger promoting songs to recording artists and orchestra leaders in about 1910. In 1913 he married Bess, the woman he stayed with for over sixty years, and by 1923 they had seven children, all of whom would eventually work in the music business. Mills worked sporadically in the 1920s as a recording artist himself, usually performing songs from the publishing company he founded with his brother Jack in 1919.

When Mills Music opened, competition among Tin Pan Alley publishers was crowded. "We found it very tough to get songs because all the big publishers had a staff of their own writers, and we had to get writers that were more or less amateurs and find the material," Mills recalled in 1975. In order to obtain its own profitable niche, the company focused on a burgeoning area of the music world where minimal professional rivalry existed: black music in the form of jazz and blues, an area shunned by most publishers. Such counterprogramming represented a trademark of the Mills brothers' business. "Finding themselves bucking the old line firms, [who] cater[ed] to bigtime acts, with $1,000-a-day song exploitation overheads, the Mills's strategy was to do something—anything—contrary to the current trend," *Variety* reported on the occasion of Mills Music's fortieth anniversary. "If Feist [a large competitor] was plugging a hot ballad, Mills whipped up a comedy song." The company also scored with novelty tunes, especially a million-seller rushed out after the death of Enrico Caruso entitled "They Needed a Songbird in Heaven, So God Took Caruso Away." Latching on to the generally unrecognized and growing market for black music proved the smartest move Mills Music ever made.

With the advent of the Great Migration, many white-owned businesses in major Northern cities began to realize the wealth that could be garnered from the black consumer dollar.[6] Blacks were increasingly working in urban jobs with steady salaries rather than sharecropping. They possessed unprecedented discretionary income. Over the next two decades, Mills employed strategies to capitalize not only on pleasing black consumers, but on giving all music consumers more of the black rhythm and sound that had proven popular for decades, and had influenced a new generation of American songwriters, such as George Gershwin, Jerome Kern, and Irving Berlin. If those composers could sell millions of copies of their songs featuring such African American musical devices as syncopation and ninth chords (just to name two), what would the market be for African Americans themselves, as musicians and composers? Mills sought to find out.

Another possible reason Mills decided to present and publish black music is that he knew that Jews were commonly discriminated against in business, and he felt that he could more easily gain a foothold in a profession where whites did not usually reside.[7] Since the 1880s, the publishing business in New York City teemed with Jewish-owned firms, which aggressively carved out a profitable and powerful haven from anti-Semitism. A 1930 history of Tin Pan Alley suggested that their motto could have been "Staff notes into bank notes." Kenneth Aaron Kanter argued that Jewish entertainment entrepreneurs chose their profession because success in this area particularly depended on results and satisfying a market, and their Jewish identities were less likely to be held against them in such enterprises. Similar explanations hold true for the Jewish movie moguls that ruled the film industry in Hollywood and the agents and bookers that enjoyed a large presence in the New York City–centered world of mass entertainment during the same period.

Like blacks, Jews in this period were victims of oppression, isolated from positions of traditional power in society, and shunned by many white Christians, though Jews rarely faced the threat of mortal violence that African Americans did. Both groups endured discrimination in employment, restricted housing covenants, and restricted college and professional-school admissions. Such situations inspired Jews to initiate their own opportunities by creating small businesses. Easier access to loans and capital allowed them to do this, an advantage they had over blacks.

Both Hasia Diner and David Levering Lewis have argued that, for Jews especially, black/Jewish cultural and political collaborations were "extremely beneficial." Jewish leaders avoided speaking out against anti-Semitism, fearing that "pushy" and "demanding" talk would invite more of the same treatment. So instead they led "a vicarious attack on a nation, which, they believed, had not lived up" to its own democratic ideals. "Through race issues," including stands for civil rights and equality, "Jews could show America how useful they were," commented Diner. Such actions coincided with long-standing Jewish traditions of human rights and philanthropy. Associations with and advocacy for blacks were not only potentially profitable, but also demonstrated the character of the Jewish people, and served as an invitation to view these mostly Russian and East European immigrants as ideal, moral, and equal citizens in a pluralist United States.

The artistic styles of many famous Jews in the entertainment industry, especially Berlin, Gershwin, Fanny Brice, and Al Jolson, among others, reflected their immersion and interest in black culture—but their white skin gave them entrée into the Broadway cabarets from which black entertainers were excluded. These artists received much more attention and compensation than their black mentors, yet they did widen the audience for black culture. "It makes sense that most of the pioneers who reclaimed the American vernacular for musical and theatrical culture in the 1910s and 1920s were Jews and blacks," according to Ann Douglas in her cultural study of Manhattan in the 1920s. "The claims of both groups to speak standard Anglo-American were half discounted from the start." The two groups had an affinity for each other, and some similarities, but much different opportunities. Mills belonged in this group of Jewish entertainment figures influenced by and trading in black culture, but he brought significant financial rewards to the major black artists he represented, and exacted a high price for his services to them.

Ellington wrote that by the early 1920s, Mills Music, at the corner of 45th and Broadway, had a reputation as "the last resort for getting some money by those who had been peddling songs all day without success," especially blacks. In the mid-1920s, the *Amsterdam News* asked its readers to imagine "the picture presented by a view of the [Mills] home office with its big percentage of Negro visitors, the race members of our group obtained an interview with the executives, and one begins to believe that . . . one liberal minded concern has opened wide the gateway for Negroes into a field that very properly belongs to us, yet under whose fence we have heretofore been obliged to crawl, if we would enter." In 1981, Mills recalled the reaction from his white peers in the publishing business:

> Everybody thought I was crazy in the early days . . . Who went for race records then? The black people. But I had to get the next best thing, anything that I could get that's easy . . . when I got into the black thing, I figured I might as well corral something so that I could have control of something, and these people are appreciative. So to build up that kind of a catalog, and a dollar don't care where it's from, whether it's black, green . . . So everybody looked down at me. They said, "Geez, he fools around with niggers. Nig-

ger bands." And just because I started this and it worked so good, all the other black people started to come around to me, all the best of them. Now I couldn't resist getting them, they were that good. If I found a good musician, I had to find a way to use him. And then I had so many [contacts with] labels that I was able to do it.

Many black writers sold songs to the company for immediate cash payment, opting for no royalties or copyright protection. Usually, this represented a good deal, especially for unproven songwriters, since few songs sold well enough to generate royalties. Songs obtained in this manner would usually have Mills's name on the credit, whether he contributed to the song or not, and soon Mills Music was regarded as the preeminent publisher of black music. Ellington recalled Mills in the 1920s bragging, "I own all the blues!" Ellington also recalled Mills "buying the same goddamned tune over and over so many times it wasn't funny" from down-on-their-luck black songwriters, who, after changing a line here and there, would be happy to sell such cannibalized material for the $15–20 Mills paid for each accepted submission. Still, for Mills, this policy constituted a good business move. It consolidated relationships with promising black talent, introduced him to Ellington, and, as Ellington noted, "a couple of times Irving would take these damn things and get them recorded and they would make money!"

Irving Mills had a sharp ear for a potential hit song; "I Can't Give You Anything but Love" and "Sweet Lorraine" were among his early successes. He also had a talent for knowing what type of lyric and arrangement would produce commercial success. A 1930 profile in *Metronome* magazine documented Mills's sense of his role:

> Mills does not know how to read or play music. He believes that a knowledge of these details would cramp his style, which is that of an orchestra director. He hears a tune that appeals to him and dictates it to a competent arranger, knowing just what he wants to do with it. He also knows just what he wants the orchestra to do with it. He can detect a *faux pas* in harmonization or orchestration instantly and that makes him a valuable orchestra man . . . He knows what the public wants [for their "hot dance numbers"] and gives it to them.

Mills's most important talent entailed being able to discover and promote budding songwriters. Helen Oakley Dance, employed by Mills in the mid-1930s as a publicist and the first female jazz producer, recalled that "an impressive collection of people frequented [Mills's] office because Mills, like Ellington, was alert to talents not always obvious to others." Among his discoveries and early signings were Harold Arlen, Hoagy Carmichael, Sammy Fain, Dorothy Fields, Irving Gordon, and Mitchell Parish. Mills claimed that an ASCAP (American Society of Composers, Authors and Publishers) representative once called to complain because he was sending "in more applications [for new writers] than all the [other] publishers put together." Tellingly, most of these songwriters did not remain with Mills Music for long; his habit of taking credit for songs he had no hand in grated on most of these writers. Also during this period, Mills helped secure a recording contract for Ben Pollack and his Park Central Orchestra, one of Benny Goodman's first bands, and served as an early manager for comedian Milton Berle.

Because of Mills's strong feelings about the band's own material and his hopes to cash in on Ellington's writing prowess, he insisted that Ellington record mostly his own works, which were published by Mills Music, Inc. This was a special policy; other Mills-managed artists did not record mainly their own material. Cab Calloway, Mills's main artist/client of the 1930s after Ellington, "was told what to record and he might have picked out some tunes," over which the Mills organization had veto power, according to Irving's son Paul Mills, involved in his father's business from the mid-1930s on. Mills, aware of the poor commercial results of Ellington's few pre-1926 recordings, knew Ellington would be more effective artistically and commercially, and would, moreover, represent something unique, with his own material.

As early as January 1927, trade articles concerning Ellington trumpeted the fact that he recorded only his "own compositions." This boast was not entirely true, as the band also recorded songs by other writers, especially those represented by Mills Music that stood a good chance at climbing the best-seller charts or getting placed in Hollywood films during the 1930s. Still, the majority of Ellington recordings featured songs with an Ellington writing credit. This policy helped Ellington develop and become known as a composer and, not incidentally, brought increased financial rewards to the coffers of Duke Ellington, Inc., a partnership with Mills formalized in 1927 or 1928. Previous biographers have reported that Ellington and Mills each owned 45 percent of the corporation, with the remainder going to Mills's lawyer, Samuel Buzzell. But, according to a certificate of incorporation dated 23 December 1929 recently found in State Department files, the shareholders were listed as Ellington, Mills, and Buzzell, with each holding an equal one-third share of Duke Ellington, Inc. Such percentages were normal for the time, although they would be viewed as unethical (especially

Mills's and his lawyer's take of the proceeds) in today's business environment. John Hammond, the famous recording executive and talent scout, worked briefly for Mills and Ellington in 1934. During that period, he said, "I found out how tremendously Duke was being exploited . . . Duke was not entirely the master of his own destiny and very few people in show business were in those days." But Hammond also appreciated the music business situation at the time: "In the early days [of the Great Depression], Irving Mills pretty much carried Duke. Irving Mills was not an ogre by any means, and Irving was really fond of Duke. Irving was really interested in these recording sessions because he published the songs and I think very often Irving paid the recording fees out of his own pocket because the record business was absolutely bankrupt, everyone, at the start of the '30s."

The terms of the Duke Ellington, Inc., deal en toto may never be known. Hammond felt that, out of Buzzell's share of the corporation, there were a "few other people being taken care of as well." Ellington's close friend H. Robert Udkoff and others maintained that the partnership also included a financial interest for Ellington in the career of fellow Mills client Cab Calloway. Mercer Ellington claimed that the deal included a piece of Mills Music for his father, which is hard to believe, and not corroborated by anyone else.[8]

The Duke Ellington, Inc., deal gave Mills an enormous stake in Ellington's future and the economic impetus to work as hard as he could to promote Ellington's career. He did. Shortly after their association with Mills began, the band's publicity in music business publications such as *Orchestra World*, *Variety*, and *Metronome* visibly increased. Ellington began to record for three major record companies under pseudonyms, a move that maximized Ellington's commercial presence since most retailers of the period were contractually limited to only stocking the products of one record label. In addition, the band gained unprecedented exposure in movies in the late 1920s and '30s and landed the coup of nightly national radio broadcasts at the Cotton Club from 1927 to 1931. These events marked the beginnings of Ellington's national reputation.

No high-powered management existed in the music business when Ellington and Mills's partnership commenced, though it became common during the Swing Era and afterwards, according to Hammond. In those days, Hammond maintained, "nobody compared to Irving Mills. He was the best. And he just broke his back for Duke, he really did. He made a lot of money doing it, but at the same time he did it." Ellington "knew he needed somebody like nobody'd ever had, he needed somebody with a vivid imagination, great nerve, untiring energy, great persuasive powers who could see, envision things, and who could accomplish things—and Irving Mills was just the man for him," argued Helen Oakley Dance, who affectionately referred to Mills as a "madman" in business who prided himself on only sleeping five hours a night, and expected his office executives to keep similar hours. "And Irving Mills made Duke Ellington, in the sense he made the name, he made the commercial product, and Duke delivered. Duke needed this slot to come to public attention, to reach the heights he was eventually to reach."[9]

Ellington and Mills seemed to have a genial professional relationship most of the time. They spoke daily over the phone, usually about business. Dance felt they "got along beautifully, because, of course, Irving admired Duke tremendously," while Paul Mills recalled that they were friendly with one another, but not "buddy-buddies." Looking back almost a half century after the start of their business partnership, Irving Mills called Ellington "a wonderful gentleman, a great arranger, great writer and a very appreciative man who liked what we were doing for him." Mills had the final word on all business decisions on behalf of Ellington and the band during the early period of their relationship, and no record survives of Ellington having a problem with the direction Mills set. The two men apparently felt a mutual respect for each other's musical and business acumen, and, according to Dance, tried to balance each others' needs in the relationship:

> There had to be a give and take with Irving, because of the fact that his background was as a song plugger, and so Duke was sensitive to Irving's interests there, and if [Mills] had to have certain pop tunes done and so on, Duke would do them. It was sort of fair play. But [Ellington] didn't like it. And so on the other hand, when [Ellington] wanted something done specially, he'd tell Irving "this is special" and then Irving would see it was done properly and that he didn't have any trouble about it.

Dance recalled that such "special" requests usually had to do with the recording or promotion of Ellington's compositions, because "Duke was always very serious about his writing." Mills viewed Ellington not just as a musician or songwriter, but as an important composer, and he treated him that way. In reminiscing about the early days of their association, Mills said in 1952, "I immediately recognized that I had encountered a great creative artist—and the first American composer to catch in his music the true jazz spirit . . . I never tried to persuade Duke to sacrifice his integrity as Duke Ellington, the musician, for the sake of trying to find a short-cut to commercial success." The Ellington/Mills relationship was mutually beneficial for most of the time that they worked together. Both men traveled to places they never would have without the influence of the other. "Irving was as much a genius in his field as Ellington was in music," Mercer Ellington stated in 1979. He added that Mills "was the first to demand that [Ellington] get the same [financial] consideration as the big white acts," which was far from common industry practice when their partnership commenced.

Besides the respect from financial rewards, Mills sought to endow Ellington and the band with a professional respect that few, if any, African American musical performers enjoyed. When longtime Ellington drummer and friend Sonny Greer was asked in 1979 what made the Ellington band so different from others, he credited, among other things, the influence of Mills:

> Well, the way we played. The way we looked and the class we had. They had never seen nobody like us. They had heard different colored aggregations that come through on a little ragged-ass bus or something like that, but we were the first band and the only band, white or colored . . . [that had] our own Pullman car, had our own baggage car, and when we was traveling, we had full possession of the diner . . . We were traveling heavy. We had our own lighting equipment, own stage . . . We never had to run to get no rooms [as other black bands usually had to do], we paid an extra fare to have our car parked in the station . . . That's the way Irving Mills made us travel . . . he was the tops. He was blue white diamond. He was the guy.[10]

The Mills organization (which included Mills Music and its various publishing subsidiaries, as well as Mills Artists, the artist management side of their business) promoted Ellington and his band on numerous levels. Much of what they did was indistinguishable from marketing normally done for popular artists. They placed ads and articles in trade publications. They increased public awareness of the band by forwarding press releases and caricatures of Ellington (by such artists as Al Hirschfield) to international columnists and newspapers. They also arranged bookings, and distributed press books filled with biographical information, photographs, sample press releases, and poster matrixes to help promote upcoming shows.[11]

But Mills employed a different tack than other managers of popular music acts. He brought principles of the new corporate advertising aesthetics of the 1920s to bear on popular music. As Roland Marchand has documented, corporations started portraying themselves as dedicated to serving the nation, rather than the cause of pure profit, to win the long-term support of consumers and to fend off potentially negative associations concerning the huge power these institutions wielded. They imbued their ads with a sense of history. They stressed respectability and long-lasting worth. Companies like Heinz associated moral and personal uplift with their products and employees in their marketing campaigns. AT&T stressed how their wiring of the nation via huge phone networks constituted a community service that connected people, enriched their lives, and saved money for consumers. These long-term campaigns succeeded in deflecting negative impressions of the monopoly they enjoyed in much of the country.[12] They were also remarkably similar to the messages Mills imparted to the public concerning Ellington's talent and significance.

The Mills organization's marketing of Ellington differed from that of other songwriters, performers, or bands, black or white, in its insistence on portraying Ellington as an important American composer and as a "genius." His work and demeanor were constantly associated with values of quality and respectability. The publicity maintained that Ellington uplifted as well as entertained audiences. Such strategies shielded Ellington and the orchestra from the degrading contemporary images of Jim Crow discrimination. Particularly from the early 1930s forward, the Ellington image served as a stark counterpoint to the buffoonish and decadent stereotypes that usually accompanied black careers in popular music. These marketing themes continued for the rest of Ellington's career. Cumulatively, they presented the impression that entering an Ellington show or buying an Ellington recording constituted an invitation to view popular music, African American music, and African Americans themselves in a manner considerably different than how they were traditionally viewed in American society and the mass media. Factors of social, artistic, racial, and economic significance were bound together in new and exciting ways.

No internal Mills Organization memos from the 1920s or 1930s survive to indicate whether Ellington directly participated in formulating this media strategy. But the way in which it dovetailed perfectly with the precepts of his Washington, D.C., background and his well-documented views on black and popular music strongly suggest that Ellington acted as a leading architect or, at the very least, the main inspiration for the plan. While Ellington always placed his primary focus on writing and performing, he clearly understood the long-term cultural and financial value of a dignified image.[13] Mills did a brilliant job in exploiting Ellington's character, music, and image, and obviously did the primary work concerning the elaborate marketing, but Ellington provided the substance behind the hype.

In the beginning of their association, Mills and Ellington seemed more concerned with establishing the orchestra as a top show business attraction than promoting Ellington as a serious artist. During his famous residency at the Cotton Club from 1927 to 1931, his music was often (though not always) denoted as "jungle" music or given a heavily African connotation in promotional announcements. The distinctive growling, shrieking, and moaning sounds of band instrumentalists Bubber Miley and Joe Nanton inspired this characterization, as did the club's penchant for presenting skits set in Africa, though the permanent décor of the venue purposely resembled a slavery-era Southern plantation (hence the name of the club). These skits, usually featuring scantily clad light-skinned African American women, often portrayed African Americans as being one step removed (if that much) from a jungle civilization, although Ellington and the band wore elegant tuxedos and were not part of the jungle tableaus. Howard "Stretch" Johnson, a Cotton Club dancer who later became a professor of black studies, remembered the routines:

> The shows were sophisticated, but they were cloaked in primitive and exotic garb. They were top-flight performers designed to appease the appetite for a certain type of black performance, the smiling black, the shuffling black, the black-faced black, the minstrel, coon-show atmosphere which existed . . . And while it wasn't stated as such, certainly the light color of the [female] flesh gave it a kind of exoticism and kind of forbidden-fruit quality.[14]

The venue's exclusionary policies and excessive prices barred blacks from the club, except for the rich and famous, and even those visits were rare. There existed a separate section for the black families of performers. "Harlem Negroes did not like the Cotton Club and never appreciated its Jim Crow policy in the very heart of the dark community," recalled Langston Hughes, who added that they also did not appreciate being gazed at by "slumming whites" as if they were "amusing animals in a zoo." Ellington's family and other African Americans found this exclusion insulting, and with his success, Ellington acted to ease the exclusion, according to writer Jim Haskins:

> Within a year Ellington had become such a prize property that the Cotton Club agreed to his request to relax the "whites only" policy. This is not to say that Ellington pushed for complete integration of the clientele, or that the club suddenly welcomed black patrons. But Ellington had hinted that it was a shame some of his friends could not enter the club to hear him and that the families of the other performers were not permitted to watch them. The management, aware of its stake in Ellington, had cautiously acceded, at least while he was at the club. But black customers were still carefully examined before being admitted. The complexion of the Cotton Club did not change radically; after all, there were not that many Harlemites who cared to patronize the new *semi*–Jim Crow establishment.

Greer remembered that George Gershwin coined the term "jungle music" to describe the Cotton Club–era music of the Ellington orchestra. According to Greer, Gershwin and Paul Whiteman used to be "in awe of the things Duke used to do, so they were sitting up at the Cotton Club and George Gershwin said to Paul, I know what that is, that's jungle music. And it stuck with us . . . but . . . they would never say that [to members of the Ellington band because] they were scared to offend a guy's feelings." Barney Bigard, Ellington's famous clarinetist, recalled that Gershwin wanted to collaborate with Ellington as "a partner" on songwriting while the band was at the Cotton Club, but Ellington refused the offer.[15]

Behind the footlights, however, the situation could be ugly. Johnson's descriptions of the Cotton Club's gangster owners, Owney Madden and Herman Stark, stressed their priorities of presenting the best in black entertainment while catering to some of the worst white stereotypes of blacks. They "recognized [the black Cotton Club performers] as, in their opinion, a more talented group of blacks, but generally they thought of us as niggers, like everybody else. They were a bunch of hoods, and they were using the club as a money-making operation . . . Sometimes, some of them would come backstage to look the [chorus] girls over, but generally they kept their distance and we kept ours." Yet Greer years later said he wished he still worked for them because they always made good on their word, and Ellington and his girlfriend Mildred Dixon used to play cards until dawn at the club with Stark and another gangster named Big French DeMange. The kitchen served them breakfast, and they went to their respective homes to sleep off the long night.[16]

The trappings of the Cotton Club seem wildly at odds with the Ellington persona of later years. "Jungle music," minstrel-show clichés, organized crime, a special valuation of black women with lighter-colored skin—how did Ellington reconcile this with the respectable vision of black music and history instilled in him by mentors? For one thing, he knew the difference between the show business hype and the realities, opportunities, and talents of Harlem residents. "The girl you saw doing the squirmy dance . . . in the middle of the floor, she was not in the throes of passion," Ellington said in 1964. "She was working to get that salary to take home and feed her baby, who sometimes lived pretty well. So, all of these things are much contrasted to what they seem to be or are reputed to be."[17] When Ellington gained more control over his career a few years later, things would be different. He would represent an unclouded image of black pride, beauty, and artistry decades before it became fashionable in the 1960s. But while paying dues and establishing a reputation, he and his band took up a profitable residence at the Cotton Club.

The Cotton Club, despite its unsavory stereotypes and backers, also bestowed a status on its performers that Ellington commented on in 1964:

> The Cotton Club, to begin with, was a place that commanded more respect from everybody than any place I've ever heard of. For instance, if somebody was performing on the stage, no matter whether it was the star or a secondary supporting artist, they demanded absolutely silence, and if you . . . started talking while somebody was singing a song, the first thing, the waiter would come over, and [whisper] "Madam, (or whoever it is) will you please be quiet," and then the captain would come over, and then the head waiter would come over, and then the next time, that cat would be, you know, beckoning for you to come on out, and out you went . . . There's never been anyplace like the Cotton Club before. On Sunday night, every celebrity in New York City was in the Cotton Club . . . to take his bow.

Those celebrities included Jolson, Fred Astaire, and the Marx Brothers, as well as literary luminaries such as William Faulkner, F. Scott Fitzgerald, and Carl Van Vechten.[18]

The Cotton Club engagement provided huge promotional and creative advantages for Ellington and his band, advantages no black musical artist had enjoyed before. The nightly coast-to-coast radio broadcasts from the venue delivered a large national audience and established Ellington as a popular international attraction. In contrast to other African American and jazz bands during the 1927–31 period, Ellington's band rarely left the New York City area. Most black bands and performers traveling on the jazz and vaudeville circuits did not have the luxury of dressing in tuxedos every night or, for that matter, changing into clean ones with every show. They traveled across the country on crowded, segregated trains, cars or buses, performing for often rowdy or drunken crowds whose priorities might have been to dance, talk, or drink alcohol, not to listen. They struggled against Jim Crow restrictions to find places to stay overnight and eat.

In addition, the Cotton Club stage presentations afforded Ellington a rare opportunity to write programmatic pieces, works in varied genres and experimental music. He could write and perform music for listening. Because of the presence of a radio audience, his acceptance did not entirely depend on whether he could musically satisfy a dancing crowd, as most black bands were expected to do—although he certainly did that as well. In 1927, the *New York Tribune* remarked how the band played great dance numbers, but when they played a waltz, listeners "wander off into a dream." The Cotton Club presentations placed him in close working proximity to experienced Broadway songwriters like Dorothy Fields and Jimmy McHugh. This provided an opportunity for Ellington to learn even more Tin Pan Alley and Broadway techniques—not just songwriting, but creating a sense of drama within musical structures and fitting compositions thematically into stage productions. At the Cotton Club, Ellington's signature style blossomed, encompassing progressive and conservative elements simultaneously, as Ted Gioia eloquently demonstrated in his musicological examination of the Cotton Club–era gem "Black Beauty." As Ellington recalled decades later, "all the other big bands in the world were imitating Paul Whiteman and paying big grandiose fanfares and all that sort of thing, and we had a very plaintive style and it sort of broke through."[19] Such qualities during the band's residence at the Cotton Club helped Ellington attract something rare in pop music then and now: an audience both wide and discerning.

Not only was Ellington able to write a wide range of music at the Cotton Club, he also received immediate national feedback concerning it, because of the band's late-night broadcasts from the venue. This represented unprecedented and exclusive promotion, the first time a black band was broadcast nationally on a regular basis. Philip Eberly, in his study of popular music on American radio, called the Ellington Cotton Club engagement "the first important national propagation of black music by a pop group" and argued that it was "the first encounter most white Americans had with black music." Fletcher Henderson and his orchestra were the only other black band airing regularly during this period, but his band, broadcasting on two stations heard mainly in the Northeast, did not score nearly the impact around the country that Ellington's did on national radio powerhouse CBS.[20] In a 1930 radio popularity poll for the *Daily Mirror* newspaper in New York City, listeners voted Ellington's band "the most prominent Negro broadcasters on the air . . . the only Negro broadcasting stars to receive a rating." The same clipping noted that "They are as heartily admired by the white as the colored people." A flyer designed to increase black attendance at a 1931 Chicago stand at the Oriental Theatre illustrated Ellington's power on the airwaves, especially among blacks: "'Now-a'days' when you turn on the old Radio, the first thought is Duke Ellington. When you don't find Duke— 'Well' you just turn it off again." As a paper in Tacoma, Washington— thousands of miles from the epicenter of the radio industry in New York City—wrote, "Of course, there are but few persons indeed who have not heard [Ellington] over the radio."

Radio provided more than mere notoriety; it represented the primary marketing tool for the music industry, and Ellington's Cotton Club engagement arrived just as radio's importance for popular artists and song-writers was becoming understood. Publishers used to promote a new song a year or two before it became a nationwide hit. With radio, that same process could take weeks, or days. As a widely syndicated 1931 feature trumpeted, radio concerts now signified "the elevator to success and 'big time'" for bands. And, as one fall 1931 ad featuring Ellington with a lineup of exclusively white musical radio stars asserted, and as Mills Music undoubtedly realized, "Famous Stars of the Ether [radio broadcasting] Help You Sell Sheet Music." Ellington's participation and ranking in the medium, unprecedented for an African American artist, marked the perfect launching pad for his future success, and proved essential in Ellington and Mills's efforts to bridge the segregation of the music industry. In an article from *Orchestra World* accompanying the first results of a 1931 nationwide poll deciding "the King of the Orchestra World," Ellington led. The magazine highlighted the fact that he received votes from a wide geographical spectrum, not just the New York area, and that this development proved the growing importance of radio and films (two mediums in which he was far ahead of his competition, thanks to Mills) in determining the popularity of bands. Among black bands, only Ellington's was competing at the highest national level on the radio with established outfits like Hal Kemp, Guy Lombardo, and Paul Whiteman.[21]

Ellington's band, however, possessed an advantage the other bands on the radio did not have. As seen in Cotton Club–era tracks like "Three Little Words" and "Ring Them Bells," the Ellington orchestra could play the melodious pleasant "sweet jazz" that ruled the airwaves and dance halls of the 1920s, famously practiced by two bandleaders Ellington admired, Lombardo and Whiteman. But Ellington also proved adept at performing hotter and more experimental jazz as well, lacing his music with exciting and still controversial African American musical devices like distortion (as seen in the "gutbucket" trumpet playing of Bubber Miley in the opening solo of "Flaming Youth"), dissonance (part of the main instrumental hook of "The Mooche"), radically shifting time signatures ("Creole Rhapsody"), and a funkier, bluesier rhythm than other big bands on the radio could muster ("Saturday Night Function"). This flexibility and mastery of a number of styles, often creatively juxtaposed in the same piece, enabled the Ellington orchestra to provide listeners with sounds they were used to, yet have them accept an increasingly African American–derived sound.[22]

While Ellington's music exhibited some characteristics of African music in the 1920s and 1930s, neither he nor any of his band members had ever spent any time in Africa, nor had they seriously studied African culture. His music resembled American jazz music more than anything else. However, the Cotton Club, with its white audience paying high admissions to watch black performers, stressed African stereotypes in attracting audiences to the venue. This tactic took advantage of the lucrative market for a "Negro infatuation" by whites who, during the Harlem Renaissance, wanted to expose themselves to the supposedly more licentious, primitive, and authentic culture they perceived African Americans to have.[23] Although jazz played outside the Harlem Renaissance, the Mills organization, for a time, utilized publicity tactics that catered to the "Negro infatuation" to increase Ellington's appeal to a white audience and start the process of breaking down the traditional segregation of white audiences from black songwriters/performers.

The Ellington orchestra's first press manual functioned as a bridge between the jungle-themed promotions of the Cotton Club residency, and the newer, more respectful marketing style that lasted for the rest of Ellington's career. Mills publicity manager Ned Williams designed the manual in 1931, months before the band left the Cotton Club to embark on cross-country and international touring. In an interview from the press manual, Ellington spoke of the "weird, queer effects of primitive Negro melodies." References to African cultural motifs were numerous. A press release claimed that "one hears the very quintessence of physical Africa moving in sinuous and suggestive rhythms."[24]

But, because they wanted to gain Ellington and the orchestra a lasting foothold in the white musical world, Mills and Ellington did not long adhere to this tactic of stressing "primitive" and "weird" effects in a manner somewhat reminiscent of minstrel stereotypes. For one thing, it did not resonate with the view of black music Ellington gleaned during his Washington, D.C., youth. It is difficult to imagine that he actually made the 1931 comment about the "primitive" qualities of "Negro music." Also, such descriptions hinted that the band resembled an ephemeral novelty act, rather than a serious unit with staying power. After the Cotton Club engagement allowed the band to make strides into the broad white market, "genius" supplanted "jungle" as the key marketing term.

The first page of the 1931 press manual presents an early stage of the strategy that defined the marketing of Ellington from then onward:

DUKE ELLINGTON and His Famous Orchestra is the correct billing for this organization. It is true that this organization won its reputation at the Cotton Club in Harlem, New York, but do not refer to it as the "Cotton Club orchestra," which is confusing. It is okay, however, to refer to the Cotton

Club engagement in stories or advertisements, not forgetting that Ellington and his band also were featured in Florenz Ziegfeld's musical comedy "Show Girl"; in the motion picture "Check and Double Check," with Amos and Andy, and with Maurice Chevalier in his first Broadway personal appearance. An excellent personal catch line of copy for Duke Ellington himself is: "Harlem's Aristocrat of Jazz." [25]

This excerpt suggested two important concepts. First, the eschewing of the "Cotton Club orchestra" moniker perhaps represented an attempt to allow the band to venture beyond the automatic African American connotation surrounding the club—a subtle notice of Ellington's appeal to all races and classes, not just a segregated rich white clientele. Elsewhere in the manual, Ellington is referred to as "the Rudy Vallee of the colored race" and that "he and his band have just as great and just as enthusiastic a following among the white people [as the black]."

Second, the citing of the band's successful and singular early forays into the white show business world (Ziegfeld, Chevalier, and films) and the term "Harlem's Aristocrat of Jazz" (which followed Ellington for decades) underlined the efforts of Ellington and his management to stress the values of quality and respectability in the band and its music. Chevalier, an internationally famous French entertainer, and Ziegfeld, one of the most successful Broadway producers of all time, represented the pinnacle of popular, classy, high-priced white entertainment. Ellington personally sought and secured these important gigs, which were unprecedented for black bands, apparently without the help of Mills. According to band guitarist Freddie Guy, Ellington secured the 1929 Ziegfeld engagement after Mills refused to attempt to do so because of his certainty that "they weren't going to have a Negro band in the [Ziegfeld] Follies." Mills was peeved upon hearing the news, and supposedly "cried real tears," though whether this emanated from the loss of face or the lucrative three months of commission is not recorded. Ellington trombonist and songwriter Juan Tizol recalled playing the Ziegfeld gig early in the evening, hopping in a cab to the Cotton Club and performing until 3:00 AM, and collecting $125 per week (almost $1,600 in today's dollars) during the engagement.

The 1930 two-week booking with Chevalier proved crucial since it marked the first time the band played for a seated concert-style audience, which brought new respectability to the band and its music. Mills reportedly fumed that Ellington procured this date, and not him, although it was probably Chevalier's interest in Ellington that brought the two of them together. In any case, Mills understood the significance of the band's appearances in the Gershwin-scored Ziegfeld show and the Chevalier production and promoted them for years afterward. The Ziegfeld show significantly increased the band's asking price, according to Mercer Ellington. Mills also made sure the Ellington orchestra received a listing in *Variety*'s Leading Orchestras Directory, a significant source of the most lucrative band bookings in the country, and a place where African American units were rarely featured.[26]

It was no accident that Ellington's first nationally distributed press manual appeared when it did. "Mood Indigo," the band's most popular single yet, had been released at the end of 1930. As Schudson has argued in his study of marketing, "sales cause advertising," not the other way around, as is sometimes surmised.[27] The Ellington orchestra had succeeded beyond all expectations during their period of test marketing from 1927 to 1931 at the Cotton Club and on national radio. With a national radio audience hungry to see the band in person, and the enhanced emphasis on artistry outlined in their 1931 press manual, the economic incentive now existed to take the band to the next level in terms of lucrative national and international tours, appearances in films, and increased recognition of Ellington's composing prowess.

Mills enacted this new marketing strategy stressing genius, respectability, and serious artistry through various measures in the early 1930s. In June 1931, the month Ellington recorded the eight-minute-plus "Creole Rhapsody," his first extended composition and probably the first original work by a popular composer to be issued on two different sides of a 78-rpm disc, Mills took out a full-page ad in *Variety*, a rarity for a black act at the time. Rarer still, the ad, rather than heralding the release of "Creole Rhapsody," instead heralded the vision of Ellington that Mills wished to present. It was image advertising, not product advertising, uncommon in popular music promotion at the time, but frequently used in corporate advertising. With its modernistic art deco design and tag line of "Duke Ellington: America's New Vogue (A Different Kind of Music)," the ad made the argument, as would dozens of ads from the Mills organization during the 1930s, that here was a popular music artist unlike any other, an artist whose talent would make fans and critics of popular American music revise their expectations of what the medium could deliver and encompass.[28]

Advertisements for Ellington songs tended to equate them with lasting quality, as if they were gems, explained Paul Mills. "Every song came 'from the pen of Duke Ellington' . . . it was promoted like 'another hit from this genius,' and that went on all the years that we managed and promoted his music." This sentiment is confirmed in period advertising in the years following the initial Cotton Club engagement. "Again!... the stamp of Ellington genius!" claimed a 1935 ad for the song "Solitude," while another from the previous year proclaimed Ellington as a "five star genius" (the five fields of Ellington's genius listed are "composer, orchestrator, conductor, pianist, showman"). Hovering over a drawing of a piano keyboard, an ad for "In a Sentimental Mood" heralded the song as "Duke Ellington's latest hit classic!" A Mills Music ad for numerous artists and songwriters lists a book of the *Duke Ellington Series* featuring "compositions from the prolific pen of this musical genius." No other artist in the full-page ad is described in such venerated tones. Benny Carter's offering from the Mills catalog is described as "dynamite" and Fats Waller's advertised song is hyped as being "torrid." While both of these black artists are viewed today as composer/arranger/bandleaders who approached and occasionally equaled the Ellington standard for excellence, their music and the images associated with it differed from Ellington's, and received the standard black marketing treatment.

In a four-page promotional ad from 1935 shaped like a 78-rpm disc, the unprecedented Ellington-authored four-sided composition "Reminiscing In Tempo" is promoted unabashedly as a serious work of art, and contains ten complimentary quotes from critics. In the realm of popular and jazz music marketing, it represented a distinctive and unique ad, aping advertising approaches used in the promotion of serious literature. No other popular music artist of the 1930s or 1940s was given such highbrow presentation. "Discussion means interest!" starts the ad copy, describing the mixed reception the work received upon release. "It is a fact... that only the important things in art and life merit serious discussion and create critical controversy ... Whatever your musical opinion of this latest work in the modern idiom created by Duke Ellington—trailblazer in the newest music—it will not be indifferent!"[29]

The positioning of Ellington's music and image as novel experiences in the musical marketplace proved a powerful selling point. Michael Schudson observed that "when a genuinely novel product enters the market, it sometimes has the power to establish a new criterion of judgment ... the first product is often taken to be the premier product."[30] Backed by Ellington and the orchestra's frequently astonishing musical achievements, this is the impression that Mills broached to the public starting in the late 1920s. But Ellington changed the paradigm: historically, the biggest successes in pop music were (and still are, to a large extent) evanescent novelties and dance crazes for young people, which sold prodigiously but also tended to fade quickly into obscurity. Ellington and Mills, however, wished for a larger and longer-term audience than that, and Ellington's music deserved a more sophisticated kind of attention. By identifying Ellington with a more exalted vision of what popular and American music could encompass, they not only established "a new criterion of judgment," but also established a precedent for the music to endure and evolve over time, allowing Ellington a great deal of creative flexibility. According to Schudson, advertisers find it particularly effective to work on products that have "ego involvement" intertwined with the purchase, "badge" products redolent of a refined sensibility that reflects status on the consumer.[31] Ellington and Mills created this kind of aura around the Ellington orchestra. In 1952, Mills recalled his marketing plan:

> For me, the development of Duke Ellington's career was an over-all operation consisting of much more than merely securing engagements for him or selling his songs. Anyone could have done that. My exploitation campaign was aimed at presenting the public a great musician who was making a lasting contribution to American music. I was able to guide Duke Ellington to the top of his field, a field in which he was the first to be accepted as an authentic artist, because I made his importance as an artist the primary consideration.[32]

The Mills emphasis on quality and respectability assigned special emphasis to visual image. During the Mills era and well into the 1940s, the band dressed immaculately on stage, sporting tailored and elegant tuxedos. "Everything was first class, every time you look around, [Mills] said 'I better get you guys another set of uniforms,'" remembered Greer. "Every time we opened up, we had boutonniere flowers. He was there to see everything was perfect . . . every show we had a different uniform from top to bottom . . . Irving Mills was a very shrewd man. And he knew that appearance was half the battle." The battle was for both profits and having respect paid to skilled African American musicians. "The moneys that I spent on Duke for photographs, for clothes, for publicity . . . I don't think that anybody ever spent on anybody what I did for Duke," recalled Irving Mills decades later. Mercer Ellington, Duke's son, wrote that this emphasis on a dignified appearance extended to the design of the band's elegant stage set. Paul Mills confirmed that such attention to detail was part of the marketing scheme to promote the band to as large an audience as possible. The Mills organization wanted the name of Ellington and his orchestra:

> to stand out—the sound of the band, the look of the band, immaculately dressed, uniformed on the stage . . . when [the band] was under Mills Artists, they were always almost like a military unit. They were precision musicians, and they all had the same uniforms. Good-looking tuxes, things like

that . . . satin, shiny tuxedos . . . those pictures [of the men in tuxes] . . . sold the band.[33]

The imagery pointedly deviated from the usual expectations associated with popular and black performers. As a young man growing up in Washington, D.C., during the 1930s, Billy Taylor, the jazz pianist and educator, made a point of catching all the black bands that performed at the famed Howard Theater, including Fats Waller and Earl Hines. But when the Ellington orchestra played the venue, a singular mood reigned:

> The thing that hit me immediately was how dramatic his music was. Everybody else would start off with a bright, snappy opening [with the lights up full]. When Duke played, before they went on, there was an offstage announcement: "And now ladies and gentlemen, the internationally famous Duke Ellington and His Orchestra." The curtains parted, it was dark, and the music started, a slow piece, like "Mood Indigo." There was a pin spot on the soloist, like Johnny Hodges, and the rest of the band would be in silhouette.

This dramatic approach to performance drew rave reviews during the initial years of touring after the Cotton Club, and required the presence of a fulltime electrician, Jack Boyd, and a separate electronic board because the presentation was too complicated for most technicians in theaters. A Memphis reviewer documented the scene at the Orpheum in 1933: "Ellington's swift fingers on the keys, the trim orchestra sharply outlined against the scarlet curtain, odd, pulsing music whose effects are heightened by skilful [sic] lighting—it is a good show and a rare one." The drama surrounding the band's stage presentation complimented the band's singular approach to music, according to the same Memphis reviewer: "Ellington has made a name for himself as composer and arranger, a thorough modern in feeling and method." Another critic commenting on the band's 1933 Southern tour noted that "The band's presentation is particularly well staged and lighted against colorful drapes of red and gold velvet." Mills and Ellington created a new standard not just for popular music, but for its presentation as well.[34]

This emphasis on appearance marked a common theme in Ellington bands since his Washington, D.C., days playing for official functions and the white elite in the 1910s. Music scholar Mark Tucker and Ellington himself reported that a "dignified image was important" in the pre-Mills mid-1920s gigs in New York City. Sartorial elegance, personal grace, and eloquence were hallmarks of Ellington's bearing long before and after his professional association with Mills. Cab Calloway reported that his band "dressed perfectly" before his professional association with Mills began in the late 1920s. But Mills seems to have taken both bands to higher levels in this sphere.[35]

Many sources confirm that Ellington needed no help in appearing dignified and urbane, but perhaps some members of his band did. Some others decidedly did not. Ellington recalled that Arthur Whetsol, who had been raised in the same Washington, D.C., African American milieu as Ellington, "would speak up in a minute on the subject of propriety, clean appearance and reliability . . . He was aware of all Negro individuals who were contributing to the cause by *commanding respect.*"

Dignified appearance and manners for black musicians signified more than show business propriety. They also symbolized a nonconfrontational but unmistakable subversion of the segregation that attempted to denigrate their character. This aesthetic had a long history in black culture. Jacqueline Moore, in her history of the Washington black elite at the turn of the century, documented how fine clothes and furnishings delineated status in Ellington's hometown, and Lawrence Otis Graham discovered similar findings in his studies of upper-class black collegians of the 1930s and 1940s. Both authors found that displaying such items separated the black elite from the black masses, acted as a protest to Jim Crow strictures, and served notice that, even if they were kept from many of the best opportunities and venues in American society, they still exuded an innate respectability, equality, and pride. Black jazz musician Jimmy Heath, speaking six decades later about an Ellington show he saw as a teen in the 1930s, never forgot the strong nonverbal message Ellington and his men transmitted to their audience. "Of course, I was also impressed with the elegance of Duke himself and his music," he recalled. "It was something to aspire to, looking at Duke and the uniforms they wore, their stage presentations."[36]

The emphasis on an image of respectability also provided a strong counterargument to critics who accused jazz, especially as performed by blacks, of being a musical genre that somehow imparted values of immorality and depravity. Mills respected Ellington's music, and realized that an elite visual image would help it cross over into the more profitable world of "white" music as well: an elegantly attired African American orchestra would appear less threatening to white audiences of the 1930s, who, told of "genius" and assured of "class," would be more likely to purchase Ellington sheet music, show tickets, and recordings.

The Mills organization also bridged music industry segregation by having Ellington and his orchestra integrate dozens of venues previously limited to white acts. Such shows not only represented a blow against Jim Crow, but also opened up new markets and audiences for Ellington and other black artists. They proved by example that black artists belonged in the classiest, most exclusive venues and situations. While Ellington started this trend with his securing of the Chevalier and Ziegfeld engagements, Mills continued the precedent across the country. In the 1930s, Mills booked the band as the first African American musical attraction to appear at venues such as: the Paramount Theater in New York City (1930), the Avalon Club in St. Louis (1931), the Academy Awards (1934), the Orpheum in Memphis (1937), and Colgate University (1940). This last date appeared in *Time* as "the first time that a major U.S. college had ever put a jazz band on its official college course." Sometimes Ellington paved the way not by integrating a white-only venue, but by being booked for an extended run, as Barry Ulanov described happening at the Chez Maurice in 1936, the first instance of a black band enjoying such a run at a "downtown spot" in Dallas. Cab Calloway recalled Mills being emphatic concerning the integrating of venues. He "pounded the doors and paved the way" to allow the Calloway and Ellington units to enter "white clubs that had never had a black band before."[37]

Recordings were another realm in which the marketing of Ellington emphasized a message of genius and respectability. Ellington's attitude concerning recording was more advanced than other artists of the period. According to Russell Sanjek, records were viewed in the 1920s and 1930s as fleeting documents used primarily to promote the live appearances of musical artists or the sheet music of the composers. Sheet music reigned as the primary moneymaker in the industry, and records were rarely played on the radio before the advent of disc jockeys in the mid-1930s. Some bandleaders avoided recording because they feared that competitors could study and duplicate their arrangements.

According to Paul Mills, a relaxed atmosphere existed in terms of making records. The priority was to "keep putting out material to meet the bulletin," a monthly guide every major record company put out to keep consumers aware of upcoming releases. Paul Mills reported that the record companies:

> had to come up with some releases, and . . . they were glad in those days if they got their money back, if they sold some, it was still worth putting out the record. Today, it's different, everybody just wants the number-one hit in the country. In those days, they worked on the basis that as long as they could keep their heads above water and get enough [releases] out so that the average [of the releases] was making money, they'd put 'em out. They didn't have the albums yet, so it was single records and [there] was always a market for

certain things, [records] that were not universally popular might have been really popular with a certain group of people. There were, in those days, the die-hard jazz people that couldn't wait to hear anything new, others didn't understand the music at all.[38]

Ellington, from as early as 1926, viewed recordings in a different manner. Imitators did not worry him. He knew that no band, physically or on paper, could copy his arrangements or the men who performed them. Most importantly, he took unusual personal care to ensure the quality of his band's recordings. When electric recording technology that captured the sonic portrait of an orchestra more accurately became available in 1925, Ellington's orchestra was among the first in the jazz field to utilize this breakthrough. Mills had a role in this as well, securing the band a contract with Victor, the company with the finest recording facilities in the country. A. H. Lawrence has argued, without citing his information, that in the late 1920s Mills wanted the sessions the band did under pseudonyms for lesser labels to serve as "workshops." When the band was ready to put down a final version of a composition, they went to Victor and recorded under Ellington's name.

But it wasn't just technology that made the Ellington discs of the period stand out among not only contemporaries, but also among recordings produced a decade or more later. Ellington's attention to detail, part of the professionalism and perfectionism that were hallmarks of his career, also differentiated his band's recordings. This was particularly significant, since the popularity of sheet music encouraged band anonymity. But Ellington, very early, was selling the long-term popularity and worth of his band and compositions through the quality of his recordings. He produced records designed to last. While other band recordings tended to carelessly blend the sounds of the orchestra into a flat, indistinct midrange, Ellington's 1926–33 output featured a wider dynamic range of sound and clearer delineation of the various instruments. The bass is prominent, the drums snap, even over the hiss of the technology of the time. On "Creole Love Call," the vocal by Adelaide Hall and the solos by Bubber Miley and Barney Bigard exhibit the fluidity and presence their instruments have in real life, a rare feat for 1927, and one that demanded careful engineering. These recordings make the 1920s seem like a less distant era.[39]

All accounts suggest that Ellington insisted on this attention to detail. Lawrence writes that during 1927 and 1928, Ellington and Mills paid close attention to issues of microphone placement, but sources from later periods do not confirm Mills's close involvement in this area with Ellington after the early 1930s. Mills generally stuck to his main area of expertise during his partnership with Ellington: marketing the artist and his songs around the world. In the recording studio, especially from the mid-1930s forward, Ellington was firmly in control of the content of his own recordings. Sonny Greer recalled Ellington standing back from the band and listening during sessions in the 1930s, making sure performances were flawless. He spoke about a chief engineer named Bob who also "demanded [that] we had to do it exact." In the studio, according to Greer, "it wasn't 'let's get this done and get this through.' No, babe, it had to be perfect." John Hammond, present at many Ellington sessions after 1932 as a producer and executive for Brunswick Records, wrote in his autobiography that "In matters musical, Duke was the boss and no one ever told him how the Ellington band should sound."

In 1981, Irving Mills claimed that, in the studio, "I told them everything. I created the balances. I cut out the arrangements." While this may have been true for the Ellington's orchestra's earliest recordings in the 1920s during the Mills tenure, all other sources do not agree with Mills's view on this subject. Louis Metcalf, a trumpeter for the band during the first two years of the Mills period, recalled Mills's contributions in the studio as distinctly unwelcome:

> During our recordings, we had our arrangements all made up the way we wanted to play them [from playing them live], they was perfect . . . For some reason or another, Mills always classified himself as a musician or something, and he always toned the arrangements down and changed them all around to his idea. He killed our spirit so many times. We had so much that we wanted to do and so many different stories we wanted to tell in music, but he put his 2 cents in because he was the boss and it kind of interfered with the job. I'm surprised that it sounded as good as it did.

Paul Mills reported that, although his father or someone from the Mills organization attended 1930s Ellington sessions, the business people "didn't pick and choose. Duke would record what he felt like," including songs suggested by Irving Mills that were published by Mills Music and/or utilized in Cotton Club productions. He also remembered Ellington's willingness to perform songs by other writers: Ellington "was always open for the right thing where it meant enough [commercially] . . . to the band." H. Robert Udkoff, who attended sessions as early as 1933, recalled Ellington being in charge of sessions throughout his career, but listening more to the A&R men and staff producers in the early to mid-1930s. "But then, as time went on, he knew what he wanted to do and then he took control," he added. "He didn't need a producer." Udkoff also reported that Ellington paid closer attention to recording playbacks than other artists and bandleaders of the time.[40]

Ellington's drive toward commercial success also had to counter the fact that the records of the 1920s that garnered the most airplay and sales were "exclusively white," and very Tin Pan Alley. African Americans had difficulty competing in this arena. According to a recent survey, black artists in the 1920–35 period claimed a total of nine number-one bestselling 78-rpm discs, two of them by Ellington and his orchestra. Of these nine top sellers, only two were written by African Americans; the others were Tin Pan Alley songs performed by blacks, or songs from movies. Ellington's first two number-one records, "Three Little Words" (1930) and "Cocktails for Two" (1934), were not examples of the trailblazing or danceable jazz for which Ellington is currently renowned, but were comparatively saccharine efforts produced for inclusion in feature films. They were not the band's most exciting efforts, but because most hit singles of the 1930s emanated from films, they did get the band before a mass audience during a period when blacks seldom enjoyed such a position.[41] The biggest commercial success for African American recordings in this period usually occurred when black artists appropriated the best-selling formulas associated with the white-dominated recording industry and the Tin Pan Alley style of songcraft and arranging, instead of using a recognizably African American sound. Because black artists were beginning to arrive on the record charts, it did not necessarily mean that black music was on the charts. It was, however, making its way into a more accepted place in the commercial mainstream. Ellington and Mills accelerated this process.

The marketing strategy for Ellington's recordings also reflected a striving for quality and respectability, and seemed reminiscent of an earlier age in the record industry. The most financially successful record company of the 1910s and 1920s, the Victor Talking Machine Company (later RCA Victor), "put major emphasis in their advertising and publicity on music that was good for their general image and also attracted customers of the 'better kind.'" Victor "Red Seal" releases by Caruso and concert-hall versions of Stephen Foster songs by Alma Gluck sold hundreds of thousands of copies and contributed to the high-class image Victor propagated. Premium prices of $2 to $7 were charged for these releases, which were obviously meant for a richer clientele.[42]

Ellington and his management tried to appropriate the high-class "Red Seal" aura to jazz and popular recordings. Mirroring classical artists who needed multiple sides to present the entirety of longer classical compositions, Ellington was the first among jazz and popular artists to utilize multisided 10-inch 78-rpm recordings to present extended original works, such as the nine-minute "Creole Rhapsody" in 1931. "We recorded it [first] on Brunswick, and just about got thrown off the label," Ellington recalled decades later. "The idea of using 2 sides!" The Ellington band also made an appearance in 1933 on a 12-inch record, a longer disc format rarely used in popular music. The recording, "Cotton Club Medley," enlarged the Ellington orchestra to two dozen pieces for the session, and was also notable because it was one of the first to feature black and white musicians together. Forty years later, Mills said that he was summoned to the Victor corporate headquarters in Camden, New Jersey, and "chastised" at a board meeting "for mixing the races" on the recording. Paul Mills recalled that Victor:

> fought it, only because they were scared. My father had to threaten to take Ellington off the RCA bulletin if they didn't put it out, and they wound up putting it out. The record was a seller. Twelve-inch records in those days didn't sell like 10-inch records. They were a little harder to produce, and there weren't that many. They were reserved more for classical music than for pop music.

A high-class ambience was also cultivated by Ellington's tendency to sign exclusive contracts with major record companies: Victor from 1929 to approximately 1934, and Brunswick/Columbia from 1935 to 1939.[43] Such actions probably helped records overtake sheet music as the center of the popular music business by the late 1930s. With sheet-music sales, the song was paramount, and the performers interchangeable. With recordings by the Ellington orchestra, an instantly recognizable performance, arrangement, and sound were guaranteed. They were products that could not be reproduced elsewhere, products that represented quality and class, challenge and fun.

Ellington's varied audiences and personal receptiveness to many kinds of music led him to record songs in more eclectic genres than his contemporaries. In the 1930s and 1940s, he wrote and recorded in an array of musical styles, some commercial and some challenging: frenetic New Orleans–styled jazz pieces; moody bittersweet ballads that, with lyrics attached, became Top Forty hits; extended pieces that drew from a trailblazing mixture of jazz, pop, and classical elements; songs written for films (not always by Ellington); Swing Era–styled riffing stompers; programmatic portraits of black cultural figures; big- and small-band pieces; blues-inspired compositions; vocal and instrumental recordings. Except for the hit singles, of which Ellington had more than any other black artist of the 1930s, most of these recordings were rarely heard on the radio.

This varied approach increased Ellington's reputation and enhanced his skills as a composer while also placing him in more marketing categories than the usual popular artist. One of the reasons for Ellington's longevity was that his versatility made pigeonholing his work difficult. Audiences never knew what he would come up with next; it was hard to dismiss him because he was always developing, experimenting with some new sound, genre, or concept. And some of the tracks he wrote and performed also featured a happily compromising nature as well, pleasant trifles earmarked for the best-seller lists. Sometimes new Ellington product could be brilliant and artistically rewarding, sometimes it moved hundreds of thousands of units, and sometimes it fell flat on both counts. But audiences learned that following Ellington's output represented an adventure, something outside the usual pop music experience. Yet the adventure was made easier by record company policies that strove only to have recordings break even economically. He did not encounter the pressure to produce a huge seller every time he waxed a recording, and could thereby utilize a more extended musical palette, with little commercial penalty. Also, as John Hammond pointed out, waxing numerous recordings made Ellington more money as well, since during the 1930s, like most artists, Ellington only received a flat fee for each recording, and earned no artist royalties for recordings sold in the United States.

The Ellington musical difference seemed readily apparent to both fans and Ellington's band members. "You could tell it was Duke's band the minute he got on the radio because it's a complete different style of arrangements and music, the way he had it all cut up and fixed up," recalled band clarinetist Barney Bigard, who admitted that he sometimes found it difficult to learn new Ellington pieces because of their unorthodox nature. Band bassist Hayes Alvis agreed: "You don't hear what you're accustomed to hearing from other groups, his balance is altogether different. The guy [playing] next to you, you're not hearing what you're accustomed to from other bands . . . it takes some time to acquire an ear for this kind of voicing." Bigard felt that this singular Ellington trademark allowed the orchestra to prosper during difficult times: "all during the Depression we were working while other bands were starving, because people wanted to hear that sound."[44]

The "genius" tag the Mills organization worked so hard to associate with Ellington allowed him more musical freedom than the average performer. Schudson argued that "advertising promotes or encourages quality products."[45] The more advertising done for a product, the more money invested in promoting its qualities, the more incentive exists to keep quality high, to live up to the hype surrounding the product, particularly one subjected to long-range marketing campaigns. Even before he and Mills forged their partnership, Ellington already was headed in the direction laid out in ads designed by the Mills organization. But the ads, and the overwhelmingly positive public reaction they helped generate, probably encouraged Ellington's resolve to develop as a composer, and to further challenge common presuppositions surrounding the consumption of popular music in America. The ads sold a new, more serious vision of American music and culture to the public.

Another gateway for listeners to discover the varied charms of the Ellington orchestra, too frequently ignored by modern-day scholars and fans, is the collection of recordings featuring lead vocalist Ivie Anderson. Perhaps their neglect comes from the fact that they were tailored for maximum commercial impact by taking advantage of the growing market for vocalists in this period. Some of the songs tackled are saccharine and forgettable ("Love Is like a Cigarette," "Kissing My Baby Goodnight," both from 1936), but Anderson's sultry, conversational vocals and the horn arrangements and performances, which slice and dice the main melodies of the songs in an exhilarating, almost postmodern fashion, transform them to a higher level. The best of the records featuring Anderson are prime examples of how Ellington was as accomplished in creating intriguing records that easily fit into commercial boundaries as he was in composing more esoteric efforts. His serious reputation sometimes obscures how zany and innocuous he could be, as heard in Anderson records like "I've Got to be a Rug Cutter" (1937) and "You Gave Me the Gate (And I'm Swingin')" (1938), both of which anticipate the manic aesthetic of the Louis Jordan proto-R&B records of the 1940s.[46]

Out of all aspects of the music business, vocal tunes represented the number-one priority for promotion. Hit vocal tunes sold sheet music. Gerald Marks, the songwriter who wrote the standard "All of Me," explained that for publishers and songwriters of the 1920s and '30s, sheet music "was all you cared about." Mills Music courted the largest possible pop audience by commissioning lyrics for Ellington instrumentals that contained the most promising potential vocal lines. When it came to lyrics, a crucial element in the appeal of vocal tunes, Ellington had minimal involvement in the 1930s, according to Paul Mills. "He might've voiced an opinion on a lyric, and have a change, but he was not a lyric writer by any means." In 1981, Irving Mills claimed that he titled all of Ellington's songs. The lyrics were done "almost always, 100 percent" of the time after the music was finished and recorded, sometimes "months and months later," the writing of them done by Mills Music lyricists. Paul Mills recalled that:

FIGURE 2. Duke Ellington and vocalist Ivie Anderson in Hollywood, 1934. The best of the recordings featuring Anderson, from the early 1930s to the early 1940s, are prime examples of how Ellington was as accomplished in creating intriguing records that easily fit into commercial boundaries as he was in composing more esoteric efforts. His serious reputation sometimes obscures how zany and innocuous he could be. Frank Driggs Collection.

Most anything that was singable was deemed to need a lyric because that sold so many more . . . records . . . [the Mills organization] automatically wrote [a lyric] to the things that wanted a lyric . . . sometimes the song already had a title. Duke himself might have had an idea of what he thought it would be, and the lyric was written around that. Most times he'd call up day after the sessions, and say, "What's the name of my songs?" He didn't know. He liked the tune but had no idea what the title should be . . . the Ellington band recorded a lot of instrumentals. There was no real picture in the song that led you into a particular title. They just had to pick things out of the air.[47]

Vocal tunes assembled in this manner were among Ellington's biggest hits of the decade ("Solitude," "I Let a Song Go out of My Heart") and were relatively rare examples of non-movie-related hit vocal songs during the decade. Ellington's jazz instrumental hits of the 1930s ("Caravan," "Clarinet Lament," "Echoes of Harlem") represented another genre, even more rare, of nonvocal and non-movie-related material on the bestseller charts. According to Paul Mills and other sources, the biggest profit came from plugging songs more than particular recordings:

> We would put all our efforts on a particular one to three songs that looked like they had great possibilities. And we'd go after every possible kind of artist to do the song in a different interpretation . . . in the old days, we used to get [interpretations by] an Artie Shaw, which was a swing band, and a Guy Lombardo, which was a sweet band, Bing Crosby for a male vocal, and Dinah Shore for a female vocal, or Boswell Sisters, or some other singing group and so forth because the more interpretations a song had, the bigger audience it would get to. There were people who were not jazz conscious, but if you sang "In My Solitude" or something like that—it didn't have to be a jazz thing if Guy Lombardo played it. It was just a pretty song, know what I mean? [Publishers] went after the widest possible coverage for everything, and then once it passed its peak as a plug song, we tried to get it enough performances to keep it going to make it a standard.[48]

It was rare for a black musician/composer to be involved in this Tin Pan Alley–dominated process that resulted in songs being covered by a wide variety of artists in different genres. But this was part of Mills's strategy in representing Ellington—black music represented a potentially popular market. Other firms' nearsightedness and prejudice provided an opportunity for Irving and Jack Mills to become major players in the publishing business.

Different subsidiaries of Mills Music (such as Milsons, Exclusive, Grand, American Academy of Music, and more) marketed Ellington songs to different audiences. Mills Music, like other big companies, hired independent song-pluggers to promote their songs to disc jockeys and music stores. Paul Mills insisted that they did not indulge in payola, but instead "did favors" to "find a way to get the plug, as we'd call it . . . by hook or by crook." His father agreed with this statement in a separate interview, adding that he would sometimes pay the studios to place the bands he managed in movies. Among contemporary African Americans, perhaps only Fats Waller (who had some of his copyrights handled by Mills) enjoyed the same advantages and presence in the songwriting marketplace that Ellington enjoyed during his tenure with Mills Music. Louis Armstrong had two songbooks dedicated to his work in 1927, four years before Mills published songbooks that collected Ellington material, but Armstrong's folios notated his famed "hot" instrumental breaks and were intended for trumpet players, not the mass commercial market at which Mills aimed Ellington's work.[49]

The Mills organization made Ellington sheet music available in multiple formats: as single copies, song books, piano solos, piano vocals, solos for the various instruments, orchestral/concert band arrangements, and big- and small-band arrangements, with separate publications for each kind of presentation.[50]

The marketing of Ellington's sheet music also represented a form of integration practiced by the Mills organization. Throughout his tenure with Mills Music, ads accompanying his sheet music featured cross-promotions with white songwriters and artists.[51] Such racial cross-promotion was rare in any facet of the music industry, and must have helped forward Ellington's work to a white audience. Conversely, such cross-promotion may have increased the sales of the white Tin Pan Alley–oriented songwriters at Mills Music. Ellington was a star as a songwriter as well as a performer, and it appears from the ads that Mills used this fame to cast a light on other Mills-managed performers and composers.

Ellington's extended pieces, which he began writing in 1930, proved to be one area in which economic motives did not mesh smoothly with artistic motives. Many reasons existed for the relative commercial failure of these pieces. First, until the mid-1940s publishers tended to refuse songs that lasted more than thirty-two bars, resulting in roughly three minutes of music. Not only were they too long for the standard 10-inch 78-rpm record format, but they also entailed additional pages in printed sheet music, which ate into profits and mandated a more expensive and less marketable product. An additional problem ensued because, even if the public bought sheet music for such extended pieces as "Creole Rhapsody" and "Reminiscing In Tempo," it would be difficult or impossible for most musicians to reproduce the intricacy of Ellington's arrangements and the unique timbres of his instrumentalists. Ellington wrote these pieces with his band's individual talents in mind, and those men were some of the best musicians in jazz history.

The major companies generally refused to issue popular and jazz recordings on the longer format of 12-inch discs, where pieces could be heard without the interruption of turning the disc over. In the 1930s, no other popular performers besides Ellington released such extended pieces, and exceedingly few did even in the 1940s. The fact that such pieces were deemed too long by radio programmers did not help their popularity either. Besides the technical and sales considerations, it is a possibility that the 12-inch record was also off-limits to popular artists for reasons of snobbery. Classical works needed the extra time on 12-inch discs to develop their musical ideas, while the supposedly lesser popular artists did not.

The segregation between pop and classical music in the 1930s and 1940s further complicated the longer pieces' immediate success. When Mills Music started publishing some classical folios featuring composers such as Mendelssohn, customers would not buy from the company because it sold pop music as well, even though Mills Music versions were less expensive and "had better engraving." Paul Mills's father-in-law, a conductor, used different names when he worked on classical radio programs and popular music programs. "You couldn't even use the same name playing two different kinds of music. It was that much of a difference," recalled Mills.

Ellington's extended works upset those segments of society that insisted on strict pop/classical segregation. Their relaxed and charming trouncing of the three-minute barriers of pop records and their unique straddling of pop, jazz, and classical genres established them as some of the freshest and most intriguing pieces in the Ellington canon, even decades later. Tracks like "Creole," "Reminiscing," and "Diminuendo and Crescendo in Blue" deserved the application of the 12-inch format, but instead were released on 10-inch discs, which meant that listeners could not hear them in their entirety without turning the record over. With their shifting tempos and unpredictable transitions, these pieces represented a musical adventure. They were and remain examples of the kind of emotional and carefully plotted-out music that rewards repeated listenings and careful attention, like the best music of any genre. In these longer works, Ellington demonstrated the myopia of segregation in the area of music.

Efforts were made to convince audiences to regard jazz and popular music as potentially serious and highbrow before Ellington and Mills's 1930s collaborations towards this goal. Paul Whiteman, the most popular bandleader of the 1920s, acted as a central figure in such efforts, and represented an important influence on Ellington's views concerning popular music. Ellington was a fan, both personally and musically, of Whiteman, despite the fact that decades of jazz critics have since derided Whiteman's widely publicized title of "King of Jazz" and described Whiteman's output as staid and unadventurous. But Ellington, as usual, was more attuned to music history than those critics. "Paul Whiteman was known as the King of Jazz and no one as yet has come near [to] carrying that title with more certainty and dignity," he wrote in his autobiography. "He 'dressed her in woodwinds and strings' and made a lady out of jazz." Indeed, Whiteman viewed jazz and pop in their finest incarnations as being as refined as symphony or opera. By emphasizing quality instead of novelty and by staging numerous concerts during the 1920s and 1930s that stressed the serious side of jazz and pop music, Whiteman purposely sparked a lively cultural debate that suggested a more highbrow vision of American popular music.[52]

No wonder, then, that in 1931, when Ellington released the second and best version of "Creole Rhapsody," his first original extended composition, on RCA Victor, he was featured with Whiteman in a photo and story that Mills distributed widely. In the photo, Ellington and Whiteman beam at each other, as Ellington hands Whiteman a copy of the score for "Creole," which Whiteman promised to perform with his orchestra. It seemed as if a baton was being handed from the scion of 1920s American pop music respectability to the man who would take the concept even farther in ensuing decades. Ellington and Mills were sending a message of Ellington's seriousness, but also of his blessing by the revered Whiteman. "Wild and barbaric as its rhythms may be, 'Creole Rhapsody' is musically correct in form and structure," assured the article adjoining the picture.[53]

George Gershwin was, at least for a few concerts in the 1920s, Whiteman's partner in his efforts to establish a respectability for popular music. Their February 1924 concert at New York City's Aeolian Hall, which premiered Gershwin's enduring piece "Rhapsody in Blue," marked the most significant of these events. Gershwin represented an ideal partner for Whiteman in these cachet-creating endeavors. He had combined successful Broadway songwriting with serious works since 1922. Gershwin, unlike Whiteman, did not view himself as a jazz musician, but instead insisted on the sobriquet of "American composer." Gershwin also shared with Ellington an impressionistic and historic approach to American song. In his longer pieces (such as "Rhapsody in Blue" and the 1926 "Preludes"), he tried to capture the flavor of the frenetic, urban American environment, as Ellington would later use his extended pieces as vehicles for celebrating black history and personalities.[54]

The messages Gershwin and Whiteman imparted concerning jazz and pop music bore striking similarities to the one Ellington received about race from his Washington, D.C., background. But unlike Ellington's African American precedents, Gershwin and Whiteman voiced these opinions and elicited critical comment from the highest reaches of the national media, where black voices and supporters seldom existed. And in this situation a predictable dynamic occurred: while Gershwin represented an exception to this, most of the white musicians extolling American jazz and pop as an art form tended not to recognize the black contribution to the medium. Whiteman's 1926 published history of *Jazz* and his 1930 film appearance as the *King of Jazz* ignored African Americans.[55]

Jazz and extended popular music composition became accepted as respectable during the 1920s, but only if executed by whites. During the 1930s, Irving Mills fought resistant record companies in order to release extended Ellington pieces such as "Reminiscing In Tempo," which Brunswick initially threatened to delete. Mills did this even though he felt that "Reminiscing" represented a "wrong direction" and "never should have been released." John Hammond, who supervised Ellington's sessions for Brunswick while also serving as the premiere American jazz critic of the time, believed the piece showed "Ellington had lost contact with his origins." The composition had its origin in Ellington's extended grieving following his mother's death, which probably explains much of its bittersweet quality. "I just lost my mother and it looked the end of everything . . . and I was on a long tour, and I was down, you know, I was way down," Ellington remarked decades later. "It was a matter of looking back . . . and I just kept writing it, and nothing else really mattered." G. E. Lambert wrote that Mills resisted Ellington releasing anything seen as "highbrow" because such music didn't sell.[56] If record company professionals with extensive experience in dealing with African American music such as Mills and Hammond had reservations about releasing one of Ellington's most exquisite recordings and compositions, it is easy to imagine the overall resistance in the music industry to a work like the thirteen-minute "Reminiscing." Yet Ellington insisted and Mills, with longer economic objectives in mind and an extensive long-term marketing campaign to live up to, stood by him.

While recordings of Ellington's long-form compositions did not become big sellers, they cemented Ellington's image as an artist apart from popular conventions, even as he simultaneously achieved unprecedented success as a black songwriter and bandleader on the sales charts. The multiple musical personalities that Ellington and Mills controversially put into play in the 1930s transformed into profitable synergy during the course of Ellington's career. They ensured that, for the rest of his life, Ellington would be able to write and release works that deviated from the usual pop and jazz designations concerning category and length. In addition to breaking down cultural and racial prejudice, this multiplying of musical identities allowed Ellington an eclecticism to express the full range of his musical talent, helping him to thrive and surprise audiences for decades in the notoriously fickle and faddish world of pop music.

Phoebe Jacobs attributed the resistance to Ellington's longer and more challenging pieces to racism and a disrespect for jazz and the music of African Americans: "People didn't accept the fact that there was a black composer who was turning out something memorable." Hammond believed, like many others at the time, that the primary goal of black music and jazz should be to get people's feet moving. "My biggest argument with him concerned his failure, certainly his inability, to get people on the floor to dance," lamented Hammond decades later in his autobiography, seemingly still bitter that Ellington refused to follow his advice in the recording studio during the 1930s.[57] Hammond and other observers, some well meaning, some racist, harbored no hesitation in imposing strict limitations on Ellington's and all African American musicians' growth and artistic freedom. People at Ellington's shows danced, but in contrast to audiences at other jazz and big band performances, they also enjoyed themselves immensely just watching and listening to the band. Somehow this kind of aesthetic appreciation of black music, though de rigueur in the classical field, signaled a failure to the mostly white jazz purists and critics of the period. Ellington, with Mills's help, created an audience considerably less constricted in taste and tolerance than the "experts" realized.

Mills's strategies also allowed Ellington to make a large amount of money, something most black artists were unable to accomplish. Mills secured financial returns for Ellington that no black artist had achieved previously, and that few white recording artists could achieve during the 1930s. He kept the Ellington band working and earning large amounts of money during the Great Depression, when the music business experienced dire straits, going from 100 million records manufactured in 1921 to 2.5 million in 1933. "Duke Ellington and Cab Calloway were making it [in the Depression]. No one else was," wrote Hammond. Hammond was mostly correct: in a 1932 article in *Variety* that chronicled plummeting Depression-era salaries for the eighty top show-business draws in America, Mills clients Calloway and Ellington each made $5,000 per week (more than $75,000 in today's money), easily landing them in the top 40 percent of the list. The only other black performers on the list, Louis Armstrong and the Mills Brothers, made $2,500 and $3,000 per week, respectively.[58]

When Ellington arrived on the national musical scene, African Americans were expected to enjoy only a fleeting career. In June 1930, *Variety* predicted that the Ellington orchestra's brief appearance in an Amos and Andy film would mark "the crowning point of Duke Ellington's career."[59] Mills's marketing strategies, particularly after 1930, set up Ellington, his music, and his orchestra for serious critical and financial success far beyond the parameters of the time in which Ellington initiated his career. None of the other "hot" big bands of the 1920s (such as Jean Goldkette, Fletcher Henderson, and Benny Moten) enjoyed a significant career in the Swing Era, and Mills's long-term marketing strategy represented one of the decisive factors in this durability. And Ellington, in his own way, followed this marketing path long after his association with Mills. For the rest of his career, he continued to sell himself and his music as something singular. He picked musical projects and shows that very few or no other artists in his field could duplicate. He radiated a refined sensibility. And he kept supporting his audience's expectations of good taste and musical adventure. Through this differentiated approach, Ellington, over time, helped create a new culture and identity around American music.

With the substantial proceeds from his work, Ellington also provided his family with a new, more financially secure, and luxurious existence, in which he reveled. In 1930, he moved James, Daisy, Ruth, his wife Edna, and son Mercer up to his apartment in Harlem. "My mother immediately discharged the houseman that Duke had because my mother said that nobody was going to clean her house or cook," Ruth remembered in 1964. "She had done it in a three-story house in Washington, and she could certainly handle a five-room apartment, so she fired everybody and began to cook and clean herself, and Duke was as happy as he could be." Ruth also recalled her brother coming in from the Cotton Club in the early mornings, kissing her and Mercer goodnight in a "very tender, very careful" way, and proceeding to work on new compositions, "softly on the piano" until it was time for Ruth to leave for school. Within his new living arrangements, Ellington found immense pleasure in attempting to spoil his mother as much as she spoiled him as a youth, according to Ruth:

> I remember my mother used to say to him [imperiously], "Edward, I don't want you wasting your money on me!" He was always giving her diamonds and furs and cars and chauffeurs. "No, I just won't take it!" . . . My mother was absolutely puritanical . . . I mean, she wore nose glasses and she didn't even wear lipstick because she thought a woman should not, it would be attracting another man . . . And so here he comes giving her white foxes and emerald-cut diamonds [giggles], so she says "I'm just not gonna spend all

your money, boy." And he'd say, "Mother, if you don't take these things, I'm gonna sit down. I only work for you. I won't work if you don't take them," you know. So she drove around with her white foxes and his diamonds, looking very elegant.

The move to New York did not work out as well for Ellington and his wife Edna—they separated about a year afterward, and Mercer mainly lived with his grandparents.[60]

While a policy of integration between the heavily segregated white and black segments of the music industry appeared to have been a priority in the marketing of Ellington, Paul Mills clarified what he viewed as the motives behind this strategy. Market share and increased profits formed the only motivator in his experience with his father's company, with no conscious attempts to promote equal rights for African Americans. "It wasn't a conscious move for integration, it was just creating a larger audience," said Mills. "There was nothing political, there was nothing racial intended, it was just getting the widest possible audience . . . to increase the variety and size of the audience."

However, it is also true that no black artists at this time were promoted as widely as Ellington in venues and formats usually dominated by white musical performers and composers. A few, such as Waller and Armstrong, enjoyed comparable marketing presence, but these acts were mostly viewed as entertainers, not as artists and leaders like Ellington. Marian Anderson hoped that her brief tenure with successful white concert manager Arthur Judson in the late 1920s would free her from relying on strictly "black auspices" for her engagements, but he proved unwilling to act as a trailblazer with Anderson in opening white markets to a black performer in the way Mills did for Ellington, and she left Judson's agency two years after she signed with him. Her switch to concert manager Sol Hurok eventually broke those barriers for her in the United States by 1938, years after Mills's marketing began.[61]

Ellington's image and music represented a new role for an African American in the emerging mass media, and the Mills organization did a considerable amount to strengthen this impression around the world, even if it did not connote their primary mission. For African American music, popular music, and the black community at large, the marketing emphasis on artistic genius and lasting worth, which instilled an image of racial pride and leadership around Ellington in the American mind, was trailblazing and important. And at least one person in the Mills organization focused on the

Ellington orchestra's achievements from an African American perspective: publicity chief Ned Williams, who detailed a list of "firsts" for black bands that the Ellington orchestra achieved (first in a major Hollywood feature, first to be selected by Ziegfeld for a Broadway show, etc.) in a letter he wrote to help the band win a music poll sponsored by the *Pittsburgh Courier* in October 1931.[62] The main motives in the promotion of Ellington were economic, but Mills and his subordinates were also aware that important precedents were being set, and that the band that gained such new ground would probably be economically rewarded and taken to heart by the black American populace, among other demographics.

Something else significant gradually occurred during the late 1920s and early 1930s, something beyond the goals of the Mills organization: Ellington became known as a "race leader." He did not speak out on civil rights issues or engage in protests. Few such activities existed at this time, and Ellington never required a soapbox to make an eloquent statement. His acclaimed music and dignified image, skillfully transmitted through the mass media by the Mills organization, signified a jarring enough statement in this period, when twenty or more blacks were still being lynched each year. Ellington provided a striking counter to the centuries of negative images of blacks in the United States. His national reputation as an accomplished artist represented something far outside the realm of the public perceptions of African Americans, and blacks and whites celebrated his special position as a leader in the field of race as well as music.

The "race leader" image surfaced in both the black and white media in the first years after the Cotton Club engagement, when the band started touring nationally. A story heavily syndicated among African American newspapers in 1931 entitled "Negro Race Produces Another Leader" hailed Ellington as "the greatest colored artist since the days of Jim Europe and Paul Robeson" and predicted that history would eventually confirm him "as a leader, musician, composer and shining light in the long list of negroes who have brought glory to their race." The *Pittsburgh Courier* lauded him as "a man of whom we should all be proud." A 1931 circular promoting an Ellington charity benefit in Chicago declared that Ellington's nationwide success proved the "theory that efficiency and higher class production can successfully eliminate the [Great] depression." In a syndicated story in black newspapers, a portrait of Ellington by an unnamed white artist hung at the prestigious Corcoran gallery in 1932 in Washington, D.C. A letter published in the *Pittsburgh Courier* in 1931 commented on the Ellington orchestra's status and the pride they brought to the community in comparison to their black musical competition. Admiring them because they were "not a band of 'clowning,' but true harmony, tone and rhythm," the woman declared that "Our race needs just that, and until we wake up to [that] fact we will not be in demand, for substitutes [for 'clowning' or minstrel-styled acts] can be made so easily."[63]

The large number of benefits performed for black-related organizations and charities also enhanced Ellington's reputation as a race leader. His sister Ruth recalled Ellington beginning long-lasting friendships in the 1920s and 1930s with civil rights leaders Thurgood Marshall and Walter White. Irving Mills recalled that Ellington gave away a considerable amount of money to black charities and the poor "because he was in a spot to do it" during a time when most blacks could not. "Whatever town he went to, there were people on his back for donations, and he helped everybody," according to Mills. "He spent more money than he was making." In a 1981 interview, Mills described Ellington as "very liberal" when it came to helping charities, and as having "the softest touch." Looking back, Mills seemed proud that no one in the band "got out of line" or "smoked weed . . . The only thing [was that] Duke would leave a town and we'd get a letter that he'd obligated himself for a charity. He was very charitable. He had no conception of money."

The band played numerous benefits for the NAACP, including two whose funds were earmarked toward the defense of the nine "Scottsboro boys." One of those benefits was advertised as "DUKE ELLINGTON's personal contribution to the defense."[64] The "boys" were nine young black men saddled with grossly inadequate counsel in their initial trial for raping two white women in 1931. Five of the nine endured long prison terms, despite weak evidence and the recanting of the charges by one of the women. The trial functioned as an important rallying point for civil rights activists of the 1930s. Besides his support for black organizations, Ruth recalled that, during the Great Depression, her brother was "very generous" and would sometimes stand "out at the corner of 124th Street and hand out money to whoever needed it." He also made himself available to "musicians and artists he knew . . . on Wednesday mornings . . . if he was around . . . giving them five or ten dollars" if they needed it.[65]

Sometimes Mills seemed alarmed at the money Ellington gave up in order to play these benefits. At a 1932 NAACP event in Harlem where Ellington's sister Ruth was crowned as "Miss Olympic" for the proceedings, Mills pulled a stunt that perhaps endangered the Ellington/Mills relationship. Though the NAACP had promised Mills a portion of the gate receipts (probably to cover costs, as was commonly done) at the end of the show, Mills, after seeing a crowd of four thousand waiting for the band, insisted on an upfront payment of $500. When the event organizers refused, Mills forbade the band to play, and they left. For a man as dedicated to his sister and family as Ellington, it must have represented an especially humiliating moment. "It was terrible, man, terrible, Duke was bullshit at Mills," Greer told A. H. Lawrence. "Ruth was standing there crying. If she hadn't been there, I think Duke would have punched him, that's how mad he was . . . I know Duke saw a lawyer to see if he could get out of the contract. He and Mills were barely on speaking terms until we left for Europe a year later."[66]

Nevertheless, the benefits kept happening, during and after the Mills years. Harlem was a central place for Ellington benefits,[67] although the band also played charity events in dozens of other places in the 1930s, including St Louis, Chicago, San Francisco, and Cleveland.[68] For a January 1934 performance broadcast live on national radio that benefited President Franklin Roosevelt's Warm Springs Foundation's efforts to build a pool for crippled children, the Ellington orchestra was the only black act featured, a rare circumstance for a presidentially affiliated event. In fact, the benefits became so numerous that Mills banned benefits for all of his managerial clients for a short time in the spring of 1933, claiming that his acts often got stuck with transportation charges for which they should have been reimbursed.[69] This edict did not apply for long to Ellington and the orchestra.

While Ellington did not usually speak out publicly about racial discrimination, he spoke out occasionally in private, especially concerning the presentation of his band and its music. In 1969, he recalled a situation that arose on the first day of "a nice four-week engagement" at a Philadelphia theater in the early 1930s, "at a nice juicy salary" during the time in which the band was commanding top money after leaving the Cotton Club. Ellington, watching from the wings, noticed that:

> Before we went on, they had a presentation there which I thought had some social significance and I objected to it. It had a cotton field scene, man, and they were singing some of them way-back songs. So I—this was opening day and I got four weeks to go—and I says to the guy, "this has to come out." I said, "We don't follow that. It has to come out of the show. Otherwise, we come out." And he took it out. You know, you put it on the line like that, man, without benefit of federal troops.[70]

The mainstream white media also provided coverage of Ellington that portrayed him as a race leader, though not yet to the degree that black newspapers did. Walter Winchell, the most popular and important syndicated columnist in the country, opened his 16 May 1933 column with a poem from a reader named Jessie Carter dedicated "To Duke Ellington and His Orchestra," which began with the following stanza:

Play on, you jazzmen, who have found your themes
Within the broken patterns of my race;
Reweave the straggling threads of faded dreams
And build a syncopation in their place.[71]

One of the more telling examples of Ellington's status in both the white and black worlds is a September 1932 feature in *Syndicate Broadcaster* magazine, a promotional publication for the Investors Syndicate, a firm that later became American Express Financial Advisors. The syndicate had the reputation as one of the few financial groups in the country that accepted money from minorities, which may be why Ellington appeared in the publication. "Ellington realizes the importance of anyone in his profession setting up a financial reserve," the article reported, adding that Ellington was in the process of building a $25,000 fund with Investors Syndicate. "He has seen many musicians who were earning substantial incomes when they were in the public spotlight end their careers in poverty and oblivion because they didn't have foresight enough to put away some of their earnings." While some famous show business personalities and musicians were profiled in the magazine, Ellington was the biggest celebrity written up during this period. The article's mention of the band's radio sponsorship by Lucky Strike also seems to allude to the band's cross-racial and corporate appeal.[72]

The image of a black man as a successful composer and businessman cautiously saving five-figure earnings in a major white-owned firm represented an exceedingly rare one not only in the midst of the Great Depression, but also in America during the first two-thirds of the twentieth century. As Juliet E. K. Walker documented in her history of black American business, a concerted effort arose in the 1910s and 1920s to institute African American–owned banks. Naturally, personal profit marked one motive for the growth, but the more important motive, inspired by the business strategies of W. E. B. DuBois and Booker T. Washington, was to create a separate black economy, since many major white-owned businesses, including banks, refused to serve blacks or provide them with equal services and benefits. DuBois and Washington felt such separation necessary to insure black economic self-sufficiency.[73] This kind of racial atmosphere pervaded in the business world when *Syndicate Broadcaster* featured Ellington. Among other things, Ellington was becoming a symbol of the power of multiracial appeal, the artistry and respect that blacks could earn, the money that could be made from the neglected African American market, and the possibility of a comfortable and mutually profitable meeting point between blacks and whites.

Despite the absence of confrontational political or moral messages, Ellington's image and work represented a significant promotion for the cause of civil rights, and helped change and expand American attitudes concerning blacks. Through Ellington, the black experience, replete with humanity, history, and artistry, filtered into millions of American homes as never before. Ellington, by the mid-1930s, had become a serious and respected figure, selling out concerts all over the world, featuring on network radio and in national magazines and newspapers, all the while contradicting the precepts behind centuries of American racial discrimination and decades of Jim Crow regulations. He did not need a placard to protest the racist trappings of the United States; his whole being and his achievements protested against them and maintained a campaign of covert subversion without having to utter a word of protest.

During the first half of the 1930s, Mills also was concentrating on establishing an identity as a "race leader" in a different fashion. Mills, having already capitalized on the underserved market for black entertainers at the highest reaches of show business, diligently worked to establish himself as an impresario of African American entertainment. This role was noted and celebrated in a 1931 story in the *Pittsburgh Courier:* "In an effort to build high class attractions with colored talent which hitherto has not developed because of mishandling or a lack of proper opportunity, Irving Mills . . . has placed a number of [black] artists under contract and is looking for more." For Mills, black artists' previous problems in reaching the top of the entertainment field were due to bad management, not race. The article further commented that Mills was held in esteem by "those who have the interests of the colored entertainer at heart" and that "he has already contributed in an indirect way to the advancement of many colored artists." A word like "advancement" in African American newspapers like the *Courier* signified far more than just financial advancement—it also connected Mills and his artists with advancement of the race. Three days later, *Variety,* the main show business trade periodical, a publication that rarely featured black entertainers until Mills made Calloway and Ellington fixtures in its coverage, concurred with the *Courier:* "Mills has done considerable to upbuild a new vogue of colored entertainment and music on the radio and stage."[74]

Beginning in 1932, Mills assembled a wide variety of black performers, not just bands, and made sure his name figured prominently in their promotion. A headline from February of that year in *Variety* announced a "New Duke Ellington Discovered by Mills." This "new and dynamic personality" who "now looms on the orchestra horizon as another Ellington or Calloway" was the black English orchestra leader "Baron Lee, melody's finest gentleman, and he waves a baton and sings with . . . polish." Soon after this story (which seemed ghostwritten by the Mills PR department) appeared, Mills accorded Lee headliner status with the Mills Blue Rhythm Band. A splashy full-page ad in *Variety* heralded the Mills Blue Rhythm Band as "a new Irving Mills presentation" as well as, a little lower on the page, "a Duke Ellington unit" with an "Ellington vogue setting the pace in modern music!" A Mills Blue Rhythm Band photo caption from the same month in the *Chicago Defender* bills the band in large letters as "New Ellington Unit."

Mills apparently hoped to find a way to franchise the Ellington magic and sense of black artistry, creating numerous bands to reap the rewards that the Ellington orchestra had found on the national concert trail. Perhaps Ellington, as a business partner with Mills, was given a piece of the action, or so it seemed in a widely syndicated story from the fall of 1931 entitled "Ellington Makes Way for Others." "It was Ellington impressed by the demand and craze for good musical organizations similar to his own in character who induced Irving Mills to put together and develop the Blue Rhythm combination which has met with quicker success than any band in jazz history," according to the article. Ellington, in the article, cited the Mills Blue Rhythm Band's "success as a confirmation of his confidence in the ability of Irving Mills, the sponsor whom he credits with his own success."[75] Aside from this example, which may have been concocted, Ellington never acknowledged any involvement with the band, and he appears in none of the pictures with them. The Mills Blue Rhythm Band did fairly well in the pop music marketplace, but at nowhere near the level of Mills stalwarts Calloway and Ellington in popularity much less artistry.

More Mills-manufactured black acts followed. In 1933, Mills Musical Playboys, a black band touted as having numerous composers within its ranks, immediately received a national radio hookup along with a stint at the Cotton Club. Also short lived was a national touring version of "The Cotton Club Revue" organized by Mills that summer.[76] Such bands and presentations burnished Mills's image as an impresario of black talent, took advantage of the craze for "hot" black bands, preserved Mills's hold on profitable club and radio venues, and served as farm teams for the more popular Calloway and Ellington bands. Bassist Hayes Alvis, for one, stepped up to the major league of the Ellington orchestra after a residence in these Mills-related groups.

Mills's efforts to establish himself as impresario of black entertainment went beyond the arena of music. In late 1931, he produced and put on the road a show entitled *Harlem Speaks,* whose main attraction was a bevy of Mills-picked black showgirls, usually displayed in various stages of undress in promotional photos. Mills felt he had discovered another facet of show business where black talent had not been fully exploited or appreciated yet. A widely syndicated feature described the situation: "Irving Mills, whose efforts on behalf of Duke Ellington, Cab Calloway and other stars have done much to raise the status of the colored musician and entertainer in the show world, soon will occupy the same relation toward beautiful girls of the colored race as do Ziegfeld, White and Carroll toward white beauties." Mills awkwardly insisted that *Harlem Speaks* was an event promoting racial equality: "There is plenty of feminine beauty and charm among members of the colored race and there is no reason why colored beauties should not be 'glorified' in the same manner that their white sisters of the stage are exploited." As two examples gleaned from period newspapers make clear, the atmosphere was not as inclusive as the above quotes intimated. Black reporter Ted Yates complained of a strict and unfriendly segregation policy at a *Harlem Speaks* performance in New Jersey that "ma[d]e us feel NOT at home." Despite the show being billed as a celebration of black women, only light-skinned blacks were featured in ads for the show, as was usually the case for the dancers in Ellington's stage shows as well.[77]

Mills indeed made efforts to promote black entertainment in new ways, with an amount of publicity money and media presence unusual for black entertainment, but with his clients besides Ellington, he also observed many of the limits society placed on the "colored race." Perhaps, due to social customs of the period, he was unable to avoid doing so. Mills used notions of equality in his publicity to bring in larger, more diverse audiences to see black artists, and earmarked some of the massive profits he personally earned toward promoting new black talent. But he still honored many of the traditions of discrimination in show business, including segregated shows, color prejudice among blacks, stereotyped film appearances by blacks, and taking credit and royalties for songs composed by blacks. He and the artists he chose to promote were careful not to rock the boat. His interests, and those of his artists, were more financial than ideological.

In some aspects, Mills and Ellington harbored different motivations in the promotional strategies they employed during the 1920s and 1930s. For Ellington, the effort to promote the dignity, creative possibility, and artistic freedom of blacks and their music was paramount, while Mills relished the financial possibilities of expanding the paying audience for black artists. Both visions succeeded spectacularly. By the end of the decade, Ellington established a presence on the airwaves that few if any composers, black or white, could match. In 1938, ASCAP (American Society of Composers,

Authors and Publishers) reported that more radio show themes were written by Ellington than anyone else, and, for the third time in five years, they named Ellington as composer of the year (two times he shared the honor with other composers). An article celebrating this achievement referred to Ellington as "the Joe Louis of song champions."[78] The broader economic and artistic strategy of placing Ellington's work and image in numerous genres and markets allowed Ellington's music to reach new intricacy in the long run and to be supported by a larger and more varied audience. By the mid-1930s, various hoary racial and aesthetic barriers were dissolving, thanks in part to new marketing strategies and technologies. Ellington was set to have a singular and very lengthy career as an American composer and performer.

3
SERIOUS LISTENING

Prelude

One night at the Cotton Club during a return Ellington engagement in the mid-1930s, after the club moved to midtown Manhattan, Ellington found Leopold Stokowski seated alone in a box above the stage, awaiting the start of the show. Ellington went to meet the white-maned conductor of the Philadelphia orchestra, one of the premiere American figures in the classical music world, and they engaged in a brief repartee of mutual admiration.

"I have always wanted to meet you and hear you conduct your compositions," Stokowski said. "Tell me, what are you striving for in your music?"

Two replies have been attributed to Ellington; both sound like expressions he made regularly at this point in his career and afterward. Barry Ulanov reported that Ellington explained that "I am endeavoring to establish unadulterated Negro melody portraying the American Negro." John Edward Hasse's biography of Ellington quoted him as saying: "I am trying to express American music as I hear it and know it."

Ellington programmed his concertos that night for Stokowski; they showcased black history, identity, and feeling, as well as the individual band members he wrote the pieces for: "Clarinet Lament," "Echoes of Harlem," "Trumpet in Spades," and "Yearning for Love." He added other compositions, spotlighting various timbres, speeds, and genres that, according to Ulanov, sampled "the moods and their manners of expression by the orchestra. Stokowski applauded loudly" and thanked Ellington when he returned to Stokowski's box after the set. "Mr. Ellington, now I truly understand the Negro soul," he enthused. "Perhaps you would honor me by attending my concert at Carnegie tomorrow evening." Ellington did, and Stokowski thereafter became somewhat of a champion of America's big band jazz and dance music, defending it against charges that it incited delinquency and did not represent worthy musical or American art.[1]

This exchange between a black composer/bandleader and a white classical conductor, quite rare for the time, illustrated a development that Ellington instigated in American culture for which he has not received adequate credit. From 1931 to 1935, Ellington provided a key precedent for international critics and audiences to view the music of Americans as serious and lasting, equal to that of Europeans, previously seen as the sole masters. Before classical American composers became internationally renowned, Ellington embodied a vision of American music as worthy of the highest appreciation.

Ellington's successes in the 1930s in getting audiences to listen to his music seriously were in part a triumph of that merit that is, in the American tradition, supposed to bring sure reward. Proving oneself by merit had served as a peculiarly American measurement of worth since the American Revolution when, according to Gordon Wood, many of the American rebels hoped to create a society in which people were judged according to their abilities, not their lineage.[2] Yet given the hostile preconceptions about the limitations of American, popular, and black culture, merit had to be abetted by a great deal of manipulation of public opinion that the Mills organization provided. Well before decade's end, without any open argument concerning the stereotypes he infiltrated and transformed, Ellington's talent had made him the exception that changed the rules of American racial and artistic perception.

The Ellington orchestra confounded previous expectations and guidelines concerning American music, black music, and race in the 1930s. During this period, American music, literature, and art were seldom respected as high achievements worthy of academic study, and blacks were rarely seen as three-dimensional human beings in the mass media, let alone as artists contributing enormously to American culture. Ellington, through his work, image, and behavior, inspired a reevaluation of these longstanding prejudices. Through his presenting listening as well as dancing music, cultivating a strikingly dignified image on film, and inspiring a tumultuous reaction during his orchestra's triumphant 1933 European tour, he transformed staid American cultural hierarchies.

For their first extended national tour in early 1931, the Ellington orchestra played the Publix Theater circuit, a first for any big band, black or white. During the usual engagement of a week, the band appeared in between showings of a feature film for about a half hour, three to four times a day. The audience was seated as they would be for a concert, vaudeville show, or movie. Though the option of dancing in the aisles existed, audiences did not usually indulge.[3]

Performing before a seated listening audience seemed an unusual concept to white commentators, who expected black bands to only perform music for dancing—but not to audiences or Ellington. Audiences had enjoyed the orchestra in the same manner for years at home, listening to the radio. Also, Ellington's musical mentors in Washington, D.C., viewed African American and popular music as music worthy of concentrated attention. Nearly four decades later, Ellington remembered the pioneering of the Publix circuit as one of the most significant barriers that his band broke, although subsequent scholars have mostly ignored it.[4]

Ellington's insistence on writing and performing music for listening followed an important trend in American songwriting that surfaced during the 1920s. As radios and phonographs became more affordable and popular, the ways in which Americans consumed music changed. Before efficient electric public address systems were available, Tin Pan Alley songwriters specialized in songs featuring big and brassy sounds and choruses, tailored to get attention on a stage or in a noisy bar. But with radio and records in more people's homes, a quieter and sometimes subtler music could be heard. Irving Berlin, in particular, pioneered a more intimate and introspective songcraft tailored for the more individualized mediums of radio and records. His series of bittersweet laments from 1924, "All by Myself," "What'll I Do," and "All Alone," reached out to listeners in a personal way, and they richly rewarded him for this new approach.[5]

This stylistic and technological shift provided impetus for American songwriters and their audiences to consider American popular song as a serious art form encompassing deep and diverse emotions. Intimate works by Berlin and his successors, many not nearly as talented, became fodder for the crooners who emerged in the 1930s. The individualistic viewpoint of the blues also influenced this new aesthetic. Ellington's music, which expressed more of a personal and consciously artistic viewpoint than any of his peers in the popular music world of the 1930s and 1940s, was in a good position to develop this new opening. He established a precedent for blacks and their music to be included in the new rubric.

Soon after his orchestra began touring nationally in 1931, Ellington made it clear that his ensemble played for both dancing and listening. In Cleveland in the summer of 1931, Ellington suggested how he saw his double role as artist/entertainer:

> There's method in my apparent madness. Of course, it's more satisfactory for me and the boys to appear in a theater like the Cleveland Palace, where we are received as artists by the large [seated] audiences that come to hear a vaudeville program. When we play for dances, we're just there as hired entertainers and we know it. But, do you know, it's a mighty good thing for the boys, this playing for dances, it keeps them on their mettle.[6]

While some critics were not ready for the Ellingtonian blend of listening and dancing music, audiences were. In an effusive 1931 article, the *Motion Picture Herald* observed that Ellington "has proven during his

18 week tour of Publix deluxe theaters, that a band famous for its syncopated dance rhythms can also bring patrons to the box office, not to dance, but to hear their concerts." This article and many others make it clear that the ability to skillfully present both dancing and listening music represented a rare achievement for any band, black or white. And audiences loved it: "In nearly every house in which this band has appeared, the house records have been broken."

The idea behind presenting bands as popular as Ellington's in between movie shows or in venues where vaudeville once reigned was to bring audiences back to theaters that had been losing money for months in the Great Depression.[7] The economic strategy worked, and other bands were soon booked on circuits similar to the Publix. But perhaps most importantly, reaction to the band on the Publix tour provided the clearest indication yet that the general public had accepted the dual image of serious and popular success by a black artist that Ellington and Mills wished to convey.

However, in reviews of Ellington's opening night at the Paramount Theater in New York City in April 1932, the two most influential show business periodicals offered contrasting views of Ellington's new aesthetic moves. Perhaps because the show marked the first time a black band played a "Broadway deluxer," Ellington prepared a quieter, moodier program than usual, with two of the three numbers in his first set eschewing the wilder Cotton Club sounds for which the band was still renowned at the time. *Billboard* felt that his versions of "Sleepy Time Down South" and "Mood Indigo" "plainly show the leader's desire to get away from the blaring Harlem type of music," although Ellington did finish with "Dinah," a Cotton Club stomper. The reviewer concluded that "both when playing sweetly and barbarically hot, this band still rates the top rung in the colored orchestra field." *Variety,* conversely, found the first two songs "lots slower and softer than is customary in colored dance music" and intimated that Ellington, in his new direction away from playing exclusively "hot" jazz, "may be overdoing it." Clearly, for some critics, even the top black orchestra in the country could not get away with deviating from the familiar approach associated with black musical artists.[8]

The dual dancing and listening abilities of the band were a major factor in changing critical impressions. Hundreds of bands made audiences dance. Few popular ones made audiences stop and listen. For perceptive observers, this signified something worth writing about. Gilbert Chase, who later became an important scholar of American music, saw the Ellington band as a young man in Paris in 1933. It appeared to enlarge his expectations of what popular music could encompass. "I have always maintained that jazz, because it is primarily dance music, and because of its stimulating effect on the muscular and nervous systems, should be taken actively, that is, as an incentive to the dance, and not passively, as though it were something simply to listen to," he wrote. "But I fear that last Thursday [at the Ellington show] I would not have maintained my theory with any degree of conviction."

Ellington's bearing underlined these impressions of quality. When he walked into a venue, the atmosphere changed. William S. Cunningham, a reporter at a 1932 Columbus, Ohio, performance for which Ellington overslept and arrived a half hour late, noted that the band, sans Ellington, got the crowd dancing for the first half hour. When Ellington finally arrived, the band finished a last number without him, and "the dancers applauded lustily, reluctantly left the floor." Sitting down to the piano, Ellington joked about how much the audience appreciated the band without him: "I'll never hear the last of that." But, in the first number with Ellington, half the crowd stopped dancing and drew up to the band to listen, to "better watch the work of this one man. It was an appropriate tribute to this truly great leader of popular music." Cunningham preferred to listen to the Ellington orchestra, yet "many fans danced and danced." In the end, he concluded that Ellington's could not be categorized as exclusively dancing or listening music—"it must be up to the individual."[9]

Ellington fought for his band to be heard and successful in both worlds, but cherished his listeners. Grover Sales, a later friend and publicist of Ellington, finally got up the nerve in the 1950s to meet Ellington after watching his shows in awe for two decades. Ellington immediately recognized him and "fixed him with a searching look." "I know you, you're from Boston," Ellington told Sales, smiling brightly. "You're a listener. I never forget listeners."[10] Ellington retained a special affection for these listeners, and tried to please them, especially since the music they usually clamored for were his newer, more challenging pieces, not the frequently played hit singles audiences commonly requested. In almost every interview, reporters asked Ellington to name his favorite composition. He invariably responded that his favorite was the one he was currently working on, or the one as yet undreamed-of piece that he might write the next day. For Ellington, his oeuvre represented an ongoing process. As much as he enjoyed playing old favorites for nostalgic fans, he could hardly wait to write and hear what emerged next from his ever-developing muse. The listeners in his audience shared this enthusiasm.

While scholars have cited the Ellington band's 1933 England tour as the start of serious highbrow appreciation of the band, evidence suggests that such praise actually began in the American press during the two years of touring following their 1931 exodus from the Cotton Club. Robert Darnell set the pace even before then, applying serious quasi-academic analysis to Ellington pieces as early as the late 1920s in the American magazine *Disques.* A January 1931 review in *Phonograph Monthly Review* extolled Ellington's "Dreamy Blues" (later to be retitled "Mood Indigo") as "a poignantly restrained and nostalgic piece with glorious melodic endowment and scoring that even Ravel and Strawinski [*sic*] might admire." Of "Jungle Nights in Harlem," a "hot" jazz number, the same reviewer commented that "Rimsky-Korsakov would rub his ears on hearing some of the tone colors here!" One month later, a writer for the *Chicago American,* although referring to them as "chocolate covered tunesmiths," opined that the Ellington "soloists were so eloquent, indeed, during the performance we attended that the audience would not stop applauding some of their numbers for many minutes." A 1931 Cleveland review linked Ellington's "Mood Indigo" with Gershwin's and Whiteman's efforts at pop music respectability in the 1920s: "This tune, we think, belongs in the group which includes the more ambitious 'Rhapsody in Blue.'"[11]

Perhaps the most prestigious pre-England Ellington rave emanated from Percy Grainger, director of the music department of New York University, a figure who did a lot to meld and extol popular and folk, as well as classical, music. He invited Ellington to speak on the subject of arranging and orchestration, an event widely publicized throughout the United States. Gilbert Swan, in a syndicated column, marveled at how Ellington was previously best known for such typical show biz achievements as his 1930 appearances in the Ziegfeld show and the Amos and Andy film, and now Ellington "winds up in the culture centers, teaching the young [the] idea [of] what jazz is all about." Two brief notices in 1933 New York City gossip columns hinted that the Ellington band would soon appear at Carnegie Hall, America's famed classical music venue, "to show 'em something about American music." Ellington would not actually appear at Carnegie for another decade, but the sentiment that American highbrow music was missing an important component of the American experience was on target. Columnist Louis Reid amplified this point when he reported Leopold Stokowski's dismissal of the idea of "high-brow jazz." Reid noted in 1933 that Ellington and Calloway "have no qualms about the word ['jazz']. They spell it with a capital J. With it they have raised torso-shaking to a fine art and garnered for themselves a soft seat in the hall of the mazuma."[12]

During Ellington's initial American tours, the press demonstrated a willingness to see a classic element in the orchestra's "concerts," but many of their articles betray an amateur quality, with their sensational writing style and clumsy references to classical composers. America did not yet possess a tradition of serious criticism of popular music works, as did England. Most American newspapers printed syndicated national columns concerning popular music geared towards glib promotion, rather than analysis and contemplation. The 1933 Ellington European tour, and the critical reaction it generated, played a crucial role in bringing more sophisticated popular and jazz music criticism to America.

Most American press coverage centered not on discussions of their artistic qualities, but on the sensational business the Ellington orchestra attracted in every corner of the country. Demand for the band had built for years through extensive radio exposure with no national touring. Their success in New York, even in the face of the Great Depression, brooked no equal. Mark Hellinger, in a February 1931 Broadway Episodes column, written just as Ellington left the Cotton Club engagement, noted that:

> Cabaret conditions are positively brutal at the moment. Things have been going from bad to worse in the past few years . . . Up in Harlem, there is a wailing and gnashing of teeth. With the exception of the Cotton Club—and possibly Connie's Inn—the rest of the black belt cafes have gone pretty much to the doggies. Ever since it opened with the music of Duke Ellington, the Cotton Club has been showing a profit. I think that, over a period of years, it is far and away the biggest cabaret moneymaker in all of New York.

On the road, the Ellington orchestra raked in large audiences and paydays, despite the country's economic calamity. A March 1931 *Variety* ad trumpeted the record crowds the band drew in the months following their Cotton Club exit. A few weeks later, after a thousand people waited outside while four capacity shows were being performed in Peoria, Illinois, the band, "the biggest sensation ever to hit the city in a theatrical way," agreed to do an unprecedented fifth midnight show. The Oriental Theater in Chicago served as the site of Ellington's most famous engagement of 1931. The band sold out six weeks at the venue over the course of the year, a feat that inspired a full-page ad in *Variety* ("of course we're proud!"). Chicago fell particularly hard for the Ellingtonians in 1931: in addition to the six weeks at the Oriental, the band enjoyed four weeks at the Lincoln Tavern, while a show at Chicago Stadium drew five thousand patrons. This kind of peak business lasted for years, all over the country. By autumn 1931, the band's asking price was a $6,000 guarantee per week, or $1,000 per night. Usually, booking contracts gave the band 50 percent of the gross, if that amount was higher than the guarantee. Given their consistent sell-outs, it is likely they received more than their asking price, although no records survive from the period. This was probably the Ellington orchestra's highest-grossing period, when adjusted for inflation. Even in the 1950s and 1960s, the band often earned the same amount ($6,000/week, $1,000/night) as they made in the early 1930s. In addition, their fees for radio work were astronomical: in February 1932, it was reported that they received $5,000 per hour for broadcasting nationally from New York City.[13]

Meanwhile, as Ellington discovered the extent of his appeal across the country, Langston Hughes felt that the Harlem Renaissance ended in the spring of 1931. "We were no longer in vogue anyway, we Negroes," he lamented in the first volume of his autobiography. "Sophisticated New Yorkers turned to Noel Coward. Colored actors began to go hungry, publishers politely rejected new manuscripts, and patrons found other uses for their money . . . The generous 1920s were over." The differences between Ellington's fortunes and those of the Renaissance writers were never starker. The support for his work blossomed and extended, as theirs, never large or national in scope, faded from the scene.[14]

The Ellington orchestra also gained unprecedented national presence with their numerous film appearances during the 1930s. Mills saw that Ellington and the orchestra were featured in movies earlier, more often, and in a more respectable light than any other African American musical performers of the late 1920s and 1930s (the major American film studios seldom portrayed blacks more respectfully until the late 1940s).[15] Ellington's appearances represented another essential way that he and his orchestra surmounted the cultural and racial hierarchies of their time.

According to Paul Mills, placing the band in a film did not differ significantly from obtaining an engagement for them in other media:

> My father . . . sold the band as he sold it for any other venue and medium . . . the film had to have an opening and a reason to have the band. It was just selling somebody on the idea that [Ellington's] presence in the picture would make the picture more popular. People would want to see it. They had heard this band, but had never seen them live. You know, if you didn't live in New York, or if you didn't get to the few places where they performed, there was no television or anything, you had no idea what they looked like, and [audiences] wanted to see the band . . . At the same time, the [film] producer . . . [wondered] "am I gonna run into trouble with having a black band in the picture?"

To judge by the Ellington orchestra's appearances in films of the 1930s and those of their competition, Mills and Ellington effectively fought the usual stereotyped portrait of African Americans.

The film sector represented the one area of the entertainment industry in which blacks had not done well at the highest level. Ellington was the first to make significant strides in changing that situation. Because of his personal bearing, and the multipronged Mills campaign, he could not be compartmentalized into the bumbling, decadent, or sassy stereotypes usually associated with blacks in major-studio films. Even Louis Armstrong, whose personality and approach to soloing and singing revolutionized music, could not escape being presented in a degrading fashion. Phoebe Jacobs commented on the difference between their cinema images:

> Louis's popularity was fantastic. If it was film, of course, they only filmed him as a stableboy, or something like that, a waiter. But with Duke—when Duke went into a film, Duke went into a film as a maestro, a conductor. They would hire him to write a film score, or perform because he brought to the podium, as a maestro, the discipline and the professionalism of a serious musician where everybody had thought about jazz as being "la-de-da, jazz is fun."[16]

However, Ellington proved far less successful breaking into the white market via films than by his music and live performances. He was someone depicted apart from the Jim Crow constrictions of the time, but, especially in the film world, he was still held back by those same constrictions, despite the efforts of Mills and sympathetic directors like Dudley Murphy. The popular narrative structures associated with feature films proved much less malleable than those found in the world of popular music. Blacks were literally visible on film in a way that they were not on vinyl. By featuring them in films, studios ran the risk of offending white Southern audiences or encouraging a boycott of their products. Movie studios, with their high fixed costs, found it more risky to take a chance with blacks than record companies did. Mass national success was essential to their profit, and cult success not as easily abided as in the music industry. But Ellington's image on film still represented a striking counter to how blacks were usually seen in American movies.

Mills arranged the movie deals for Ellington and the band, making sure their depiction coalesced with the image he had established. Management was key in this process, as seen in the career of Armstrong, whose manager Joe Glaser harbored "a desire to please" the Hollywood studios "at all costs," which resulted in Armstrong portraying a stable boy named Uncle Tom, a bumbling financially inept bandleader, and a musical seducer of white actress Martha Raye in his films of the 1930s. Armstrong biographer Laurence Bergreen has written: "moviegoers who thought they were seeing the 'real' Louis Armstrong on screen were mistaken; they witnessed only a distorted impression of the performer as he tried to fit into stereotypical 'darkie' roles." Bergreen argued that the movies represented the one area in Armstrong's career where he did not retain his "dignity" as a black artist.[17] Thanks in large part to Mills, Ellington did not endure such embarrassing treatment.

The Ellington orchestra's appearance in the film short *Black and Tan* (1929) marked one of the first by any black band in the age of sound films, certainly the first respectful portrayal of a black band. It was intended as a successor to a short devoted to Bessie Smith entitled *St. Louis Blues* (1929), which, as Klaus Stratemann in his exhaustive study of Ellington's film career has written, was "regarded by some as the earliest musical film that successfully depicted certain aspects of Negro life with a semblance of reality and dignity." *St. Louis Blues* did feature examples of blacks portrayed with dignity, and the music was assembled by some of the most important black artists of the period, yet the overall impression of blacks in the film is not positive. Throughout, blacks are pictured as either gambling or drinking, and Smith meekly accepts her boyfriend's misogynistic habits of throwing her to the floor, verbally berating her, two-timing her, and taking her money. Disturbing to watch, this scenario counters every depiction of Smith's character and personal strength in later biographies.[18]

Black and Tan, written and directed by Dudley Murphy (who performed the same duties on *St. Louis Blues*), provided a much more respectful portrayal of African Americans. While it featured a couple of humorous Amos and Andy–like bumpkins accepting a bribe of whiskey from Ellington and his girlfriend in exchange for not repossessing his piano, the portrayal of Ellington and blacks in general is quite naturalistic compared to other films of the era and beyond. Despite his role in the film as a black musician living in a precarious financial state, Ellington is dressed and groomed impeccably, and speaks with a rounded, almost British diction. At home and in performance, Ellington is serious about his music. Ellington and his girlfriend are clever, quick-witted, and devoted to each other, professionally and personally, in contrast to the common stereotyped, oversexualized or violent images of black romance in songs and films. The music in *Black and Tan* is rich, not watered down, as jazz usually was in most major films of the period, and it featured the stirring sounds of the Hall Johnson Choir, a black group dedicated to preserving African American music. *Black and Tan* represents the

FIGURE 3. The Ellington orchestra's appearance in the film short *Black and Tan* (RKO, 1929) marked one of the first by any black band in the age of sound films, certainly the first respectful portrayal of a black band. *From left to right:* trumpeter Arthur Whetsol, dancer/actress Fredi Washington, and Duke Ellington at the piano. Frank Driggs Collection.

only time Ellington played a dramatic role other than orchestra leader, and he acquitted himself well, making questionable the judgment of casting directors and film studios who never allowed Ellington another chance at dramatic presentation.

Black and Tan, with its then progressive portrayal of blacks, was made and released because its modest length and budget represented a small business risk. Perhaps it was seen as an experiment, along with the Bessie Smith short before it, to find out if films could capture some of the same lucrative sales in the black community that "race records" enjoyed in the 1920s. Much of the credit for getting the band on the screen in this fashion should go not only to Mills, but also to Murphy, who sold the RKO studio on the idea of film shorts dedicated to black music, and to Harlem Renaissance author and patron Carl Van Vechten, who purportedly helped with the project as an uncredited advisor. Indeed, with its level of cinematic flair and musical quality, *Black and Tan* outdistanced not only *St. Louis Blues,* but also the low-budget soundies and other short films used to promote black musical artists decades later in the 1940s and 1950s.

However, Stratemann documented how the lack of films featuring African Americans and the lack of venues that catered to a demographic that would enjoy such fare cost the short film initial popularity. Upon first release in 1929, *Black and Tan* was attached as an extra attraction to a Ruth Chatterton comedy and a Ken Maynard western—not ideal programming for the film.[19] Perhaps this is why Mills arranged for the next Ellington appearance to be in a feature-length production that could stand on its own and appeal to all races. Mills expanded the composition of Ellington audiences by giving him unprecedented exposure for a black artist on the radio and by booking gigs that integrated venues, but changing the complexion of the Hollywood studio and distribution system was beyond his grasp.

The Ellington band's appearance in the Amos and Andy vehicle *Check and Double Check* (1930), the first instance of any African American orchestra in a feature film, represented "a very exceptional distinction," despite RKO Studio's insistence on requiring two of the lighter-skinned musicians to wear blackface make-up, the first and last time the Ellington orchestra experienced this indignity. Perhaps unknown to Ellington, RKO took Ellington's name off the billing in Southern theaters. Previously only heard on radio, the white actors playing Amos and Andy also wore burnt-cork make-up, which, as Stratemann noted, probably accounted for both the large drop-off in box office sales among black customers during the second week of the film's run and the fact that, unlike Ellington, the duo never made another feature film appearance.[20]

The Ellington orchestra's music is mostly used as background in *Check and Double Check,* but in one groundbreaking sequence, the band's entire performance of the driving "Old Man Blues" is featured with no cut-aways to dialogue. Numerous close-ups of the individual members of the tuxedo-clad band are interspersed during the sequence, and, aside from trumpeter Arthur Whetsol's exuberant trumpet spinning, the musicians are portrayed in a serious fashion. There is no clowning, no hint of novelty or the usual clichés associated with the portrayal of most blacks and their music on film in the 1930s and 1940s. Moreover, the well-dressed upper-class white crowd at this prestigious gig watches the band with intent interest. *Check*'s placing of the Ellington orchestra in rarified surroundings qualified as an impressive presentation of African Americans and their music, one seldom duplicated in future decades by any black artist but Ellington.

The 1933 Ellington-centered short film *A Bundle of Blues* appeared next. While four years between film shorts may seem an extended time, such appearances by major black bandleaders were still limited to Armstrong (who starred in his own short the year before) and Ellington. At the same time, numerous white bands had several to their credit by 1933, including such currently obscure artists as Gus Arnheim, Vincent Lopez, and Leo Reisman.[21]

A Bundle of Blues makes the case, already forwarded by the Mills organization and by Ellington's tours, that Ellington and his orchestra existed in a category apart from most popular music outfits, black or white. The film's centerpiece, an extended version of "Stormy Weather," shows this most convincingly. Ivie Anderson, the band's vocalist, sings the composition calmly and movingly, with no vocal histrionics. She is presented as a serious artist, wearing a simple formless long dress at a time when when most black women appearing in musical films wore more revealing or ostentatious clothing that amplified their bodies and sexuality. Athletic black female dancers gyrate wildly and do the splits in short skirts during the film's concluding number, but Anderson is portrayed as someone apart from this hubbub. The "Stormy Weather" sequence, like the "Old Man Blues" scene in *Check and Double Check,* spotlighted numerous Ellington sidemen in close-up, allowing viewers to get a sense of their personalities. In most music shorts of the period, sidemen seldom received significant screen time, which was commonly devoted to bandleaders, singers, and dancers. This demonstrated how, in Ellington film appearances, the music and musicians were treated with unusual respect and took precedence over the dancing, novelty, and comedy that usually predominated in film depictions of popular music performers.

Perhaps the most striking element of *Bundle of Blues* is its portrayal of black life. Rather than the images of gambling, drinking, misogyny, and abandon that black music commonly inspired in film makers, Anderson is shown in a rural setting during a dream sequence, standing in a clean, just-swept small house, watching rain fall onto the countryside. It's a jarring contrast to the swank trappings usually accompanying popular musicians on film in the 1930s and 1940s. Over the course of his career, Ellington maintained that the media routinely overemphasized the decadent side of blues and jazz culture. For years, he demonstrated to attentive listeners and viewers a more diverse and truthful interpretation of blues and jazz culture through his music. In *Bundle of Blues,* he extended that vision to the film world. Knowing that Ellington would not tolerate and did not deserve the indignities heaped upon appearances by blacks in films, that they would hinder his music's profitability and contradict the vision of genius that he spent so much time and effort selling to the public, Mills made sure that Jim Crow trappings were minimized in Ellington's films.

The next major-studio excursions for the Ellington orchestra were their appearances in the 1934 Paramount features *Murder at the Vanities* and *Belle of the Nineties*.[22] Despite the Ellington orchestra's limited time on screen, never before and probably never after had a black orchestra been portrayed in such an elevated manner in mainstream Hollywood films. Both films depicted the band performing in high-class, yet somewhat decadent situations. Though they portrayed Ellington and his band in a more progressive manner than any other black orchestra in the first half of the twentieth century and integrated them into the plot to such a degree that Southern theaters would have difficulty excising their images, the overall impression imparted by the filmmakers was one of easy entertainment, with little overlay of art, far from the serious critical approval Ellington began to receive at this juncture of his career. Ellington budged, but hardly overturned Hollywood stereotypes.

In *Murder*, the Ellington orchestra is the only black act in an elaborate variety stage show, somewhat reminiscent of Ziegfeld's Follies. They appear in the second act ("The Rape") of a strange three-act piece entitled "The Rape of the Rhapsody." The first act ("The Rhapsody") featured the lead actor of the film as Franz Lizst sitting at the piano in period dress, singing new lyrics for his Second Hungarian Rhapsody, which express his wish that his composition be heard and enjoyed for decades to come. In the next scene, an orchestra dressed in nineteenth-century courtly costumes begins to play the piece, only to be interrupted every so often by horn riffs from the Ellington orchestra, who peek out from behind the orchestra to play brief parts, then hide behind the orchestra again. Quickly, the Ellington orchestra usurps the place of the old-fashioned orchestra, throwing the old Lizst music off the music stands and breaking into a swinging number based on the previously played Lizst rhapsody. After maestro Ellington good-naturedly refuses a request to halt the song and abandon his piano, the classical maestro breaks his sticks in two in frustration and storms off the stage. Ellington and the band look impeccable as usual in their tuxes, but their music elicits an obviously different effect than the original Lizst rhapsody. The Hungarian Rhapsody in the first act inspired dancers in pantaloons and ruffles to perform Viennese waltzes, while Ellington's "Ebony Rhapsody" is greeted by the sudden appearance of braless black female dancers shimmying suggestively. At the end of the number, the classical maestro returns and pretends to mow down all participants in the scene, black and white, with a real-looking submachine gun. The Ellington orchestra received numerous close-ups throughout the scene, which were interspersed with close-ups of white cast members, something rare in feature films of the period, and afterward. But there also existed a part-playful, part-serious intimation that such music represented a negative, hedonistic moral influence—as well as being a lot more lively than old Franz Lizst. Often in Hollywood films, the vigorously lowbrow triumphed over the pretentiously highbrow, but this scene appeared to be a displacement of the old by the new, however violently resisted.

The same juxtaposition of high class and decadence surfaced in *Belle of the Nineties,* written by and starring Mae West, who insisted on using the Ellington orchestra despite the studio's economic concerns. Even more so than in *Murder,* they were showcased respectfully and were "more integrated into the plot than any other black orchestra in Hollywood motion pictures before or since," according to Stratemann. The racially integrated close-up shots of African American band members backing up West's vocal performances were a first in Hollywood film history, especially because of the obvious ease between the band and West on screen. These artists, one white woman and ten black men, clearly held each other in high regard, a scenario that must have been threatening to some white audiences, though people did go to West's films expecting to be shocked, as she well knew. West was particularly inspired by the Ellington orchestra's presence, giving what were probably her best vocal performances in a film. A scene depicting a singing black revival service on the beach, which comforts and strengthens the character West plays, is tastefully done, with few of the Hollywood stereotypes usually attached to black culture. Some stereotypes were still present, but seemed more linked with West's reputation than with blacks.

Mae West, however, as was her custom, probably intended a subtler meaning behind the images of high class and decadence in *Belle.* The people that her script celebrates are not the usual Hollywood heroes. The character she plays sees through the sexual and financial shenanigans that the white, usually upper-class men try to ensnare her with, and ends up outsmarting them all. The only person with whom she can truly be herself is her black maid, Jasmine (played by Libby Taylor, her maid in real life). She is touched and inspired, too, by the Ellington orchestra and the music of the black revival service. A strongly stated view on the humanity and equality, or even superiority, of blacks was present for those who watched "between the lines."

While the inclusion of Ellington's orchestra in movies of the 1930s shows their place on the cutting edge of race and culture, they still could not avoid the financial indignities heaped upon black film performers of the time. Ellington's pay for the three films in which he appeared for Paramount in the mid-1930s amounted to half of what white bandleader Guy Lombardo received for his appearance in one Paramount film in 1934.

The singular 1935 film short *Symphony in Black,* also made for Paramount, was Ellington's best and most creative effort, the film project over which he exercised the most control. Perhaps the creative freedom in this film represented Mills's price to the studio for getting the orchestra to appear so cheaply in the other two films. The orchestra, clad in formal wear and shown in numerous close-ups, performed the Ellington-penned ten-minute, four-part musical suite that formed the only soundtrack of the film. The movie presented a varied and artful panorama of African American life without dialogue.

In *Symphony,* black life was conveyed with a naturalism reminiscent of the earlier *Black and Tan.* However, the scope of *Symphony* expanded to include a wider spectrum of blacks, not just musicians and their immediate community. The first sequence of Ellington's "symphony of Negro moods" featured a track entitled "The Laborers." After a spirited opening fanfare that creates the impression that the composition will be a swinging tune, the piece instead abruptly gives way to a forlorn Ellington piano solo, followed by the band executing a bluesy arrangement with a beat that suggests hard manual labor. Onscreen, the imagery alters with the changes in musical mood. Initially, the band is impeccably dressed on a glamorous set, with a similarly attired approving audience seated high above them. As the music shifts, the scene does as well, to shadowy dramatic images of black workmen dressed in rags, sweating as they labor, a tableau as removed from the glamorous Ellington orchestra as could be imagined. Similarly disquieting imagery occurs later in the film, as African Americans cry and wring their hands at a child's funeral in a dark church, a scene depicted with stark camerawork reminiscent of the WPA photographs that captured some of the worst suffering of the Great Depression. No other popular music act, black or white, offered such disquieting visions along with their music.

Ellington made a statement with *Symphony in Black,* a statement repeated throughout his career in various ways: he and his band did not simply entertain, but composed and performed works that emanated from real life, from situations of sorrow and adversity. Though Paramount changed Ellington's intended sequence for *Symphony* without his consent, substituting an upbeat finale for the child funeral ending that Ellington envisioned, it still represented an unprecedentedly African American–oriented and –conceived film from a major studio, and nothing like it at such a high artistic level would be attempted again for years.[23]

In 1937, the Ellington orchestra appeared in another feature, *The Hit Parade,* their last major film appearance of the decade. It was released by Republic, a studio that specialized in low-budget B movies. Though the production values are lower than in Ellington's other 1930s films, and the plot and acting unimpressive, the Ellington band is presented in a similar fashion to past appearances, playing before high society in tuxes. By 1937, the Swing Era reached high gear, and black bands experienced an even more difficult time than they had in the late 1920s and early 1930s in obtaining film appearances. As lightweight as *Hit Parade* was, the orchestra was probably lucky to get the assignment in this more restrictive atmosphere. Hollywood would not call for their services again until 1942, and even then, during the period of Ellington's greatest success on the Top Forty sales charts, the band's 1940s film oeuvre would not match the quality and respectability accorded to the band in the 1930s cinematic appearances that Mills arranged.

The typical depictions of black and white musicians on screen during the 1930s and 1940s demonstrate the uniqueness of Ellington's film persona. Film shorts featuring black artists almost invariably included numerous alcoholic, sexual, and other morally suspect references, with none of the impressionistic and dramatic renderings seen in Ellington vehicles like *Black and Tan, Bundle of Blues,* and *Symphony in Black.*[24]

In a 1934 film short for Warner Brothers Vitaphone, the Don Redman Orchestra, an African American big band, appeared on a set overshadowed by a huge roulette wheel, dice, and playing cards, and they performed novelty numbers for two of their three songs. "Nagasaki" consisted mainly of nonsensical scatting extolling alcohol and "tobacky," and crudely satirized Asian and African American speech. It was sung by Red and Struggie, two black comedians dressed in clown-like attire, with cheap hats, badly tailored clothes, and unpressed collars. For the last number, Redman, in a talking blues style, performed "I Get Everything That a Tall Man Gets," proclaiming his luck with women despite his lack of height. The band is dressed far more plainly than the Ellington orchestra.

In a short made the same year for the same company, Jimmie Lunceford and his Dance Orchestra, generally recognized as the finest black band of the era next to Ellington's, are introduced by a ludicrously costumed white Lucifer, speaking of sin and fire, and situated amidst flames of hell and superimposed visions of writhing, scantily clad women. When Lunceford and his band finally appear, the music they play sounds like typical conservative movie dance music of the period, not the well-arranged and irresistibly danceable jazz for which they were (and still are) most prized. Lunceford's band members are also depicted quite differently than those in the Ellington outfit. During one song, supposedly inspired by the irresistible spell of the music, two of them put down their instruments and dance, and two more beat their chairs with mallets. Throughout the short and the Redman one, much more attention is paid to the dancers and vocalists than to the band and the quality of its performance. The image of hell proved popular as a juxtaposition with black bands in the 1930s. In an undated clip from the decade entitled *Stomping at the Savoy,* the Erskine Hawkins orchestra is also introduced by Lucifer, who tells the band that if they acquit themselves well, they can avoid a trip to hell.

The image of black female vocalists did not improve in the decade following Bessie Smith's 1929 appearance in *St. Louis Blues.* Ethel Waters, singing the title track in *Underneath the Harlem Moon,* performed before a mute, comically nodding "Negro Senate." The lyrics mentioned Georgia gigolos, marijuana smoking, and "picking numbers." In the 1932 Warner Brothers Vitaphone short *Pie Pie Blackbird,* Nina McKinney referred to her young children as "pickaninies" and cheerfully sang of saying "yassuh boss" to her "master." Black music pioneer Eubie Blake and his band also appeared in that film, dressed like bakers, performing music so hot that the gigantic pie they're performing in explodes, transforming them into dancing skeletons. The 1936 short *The Black Network* found McKinney once again mouthing platitudes that could have directly emanated from nineteenth-century minstrelsy: "Only half of me wants to be good . . . one minute I'm singing 'hallelujah,' the next I want to go downtown." Throughout the short, the music performed by the stars of the film is as dull and formulaic as any anonymous Tin Pan Alley tune of the era.

But even most white bands of the period, though portrayed more favorably than most black bands, preserved little dignity in film. Mid-1930s shorts featuring white bands led by Ben Pollack and Freddie Rich showcased a scattershot approach to their music, designed to appeal to all audiences, aimed at the lowest common denominator. In *Mirrors,* a short devoted to Rich's band, a fast and jazzy number opens the film, followed by a corny romantic pop song (sung by a female vocalist clad in her underwear), a Hawaiian novelty song, and a barbershop-styled vocal number. A 1935 clip starring Isham Jones and his orchestra featured a song-and-dance number at the Toyland Club with the band dressed as toy soldiers and an uninspired jazzing-up of Rachmaninoff's Prelude in C Minor, replete with superimposed shots of the Soviet Union! The insipid eclecticism pervading these clips portended show business as usual, with heavy doses of a staid vaudeville aesthetic mixed in.

The most instructive comparisons to Ellington's film appearances, however, are those of Mills's other major clients. Right behind Ellington in popularity during the 1930s was Cab Calloway and his orchestra. Though they, like Ellington, sported shiny satin white tuxes, their approach and image differed. They were a party band whose most popular songs lyrically detailed abandon in the form of alcohol, marijuana, sex, and music. Calloway was a dynamic front man and vocalist, gyrating madly, or dancing gracefully, as called for by a particular song. The songs he performed (and occasionally co-wrote) were famous for their humor, their display of black slang, and their catchy, often nonsensical "jive" lyrics. In his performance of "Kicking the Gong Around" from the 1932 film short *Harlem Harmony,* Calloway openly sang of "cokies," and mimicked the actions of a cocaine snorter, scatting more manically after doing so. The film short *Reefer Man* features similar references. The 1935 Calloway short *Jitterbug Party* promised a "musical description of darkest Harlem" and followed it up with a series of images that emphasized poor boys, fried chicken, alcohol, and dice games. The Calloway persona lent itself easily to animation, as seen in *Snow White* (1932), one of a series of simultaneously delightful and somewhat disturbing Betty Boop cartoons that featured black jazz artists, including one featuring Louis Armstrong as an African cannibal chasing down Boop's friends. Calloway is a clown in *Snow White,* transformed by a witch into a ghost, and surrounded by images of cards, dice, and skeletons.

The Mills Blue Rhythm Band's film short from the period, like Calloway's, provided more evidence that other African American acts managed by Mills were positioned with far less gravitas in their film appearances than Ellington. Alcohol consumption is copious, and blacks appear unable to control themselves when music featuring supposedly primitive rhythms is played. At the rent party that ends the film, the black bartender briefly converses with one of the black celebrants: "Don't that remind you of the ole days in the jungle?" "It shore do!" At this moment, the clothing on the blacks dancing in the living room is cinematically transformed from hip urban dresses and suits to stereotypical African tribal gear, including grass skirts for the women, headdresses and no shirts for the men. While Mills disdained promoting Ellington's output as primitive, potentially immoral "jungle music" after 1930, he did not hesitate to pursue the same direction in a more concentrated and offensive manner with his other artists.

The fact that Mills accepted Hollywood's commonplace stereotyping in his promotions of other black artists shows that economics played a more important role than civil rights in the marketing strategies for his black artists. Mills was a businessman first; there were limits as to how far he would push the envelope of promoting black artists and, by extension, notions of black equality. Ellington emerged as the exception to this rule. Artists like Armstrong, Blake, and Lunceford clearly deserved promotion that emphasized the full dimensions of their artistry. But they did not have, at the very least, a manager like Mills to implement that vision.

The Ellington orchestra's 1933 tour of England and France was a watershed event that epitomized the sentiments expressed in the marketing of Ellington. "Spike" Hughes documented the tour and commented on its importance at length for the British music periodical *Melody Maker*. He led the charge, echoed in large and small newspapers throughout England, that trumpeted Ellington as "the first essentially American composer, the first composer to produce music that was *really* American in its idiom." In a preview of the tour, Hughes predicted correctly that "Duke himself will be surprised to see how famous—and how deservedly famous—he is among musicians and critics, and a million other people who appreciate beauty and originality in music when they find it."

An aura of anticipation arose in England well before Ellington's arrival. Mills spent time in England the year before, investigating potential venues and the English music scene. Also, according to numerous sources, a budding English jazz community of listeners and musicians had surfaced in the years before Ellington's arrival. They were inspired by the availability of Ellington recordings, but especially by an editorial turnabout by the *Melody Maker*. According to Max Jones, a longtime writer for the paper, when the *Melody Maker* was founded in 1926, its writers argued for the supremacy of white musicians, referring to blacks in derogatory, colonial-derived terms such as "wogs" and "blackies." By about 1930, writers such as Spike Hughes and their American correspondent John Hammond led a change in editorial policy that not just praised, but exalted African American jazz musicians. By the time Ellington stepped ashore, the English, according to Helen Oakley Dance, who attended one of the 1933 shows, "were really a little jump ahead, in that they were not only interested in jazz, but they were wildly enthusiastic about it, and nothing was too minor for them to know or think about." Earlier 1920s tours by African American classical vocalists Marian Anderson and Roland Hayes also helped pave the way for Ellington's reception.

English musicians attempting to duplicate the jazz they admired on Ellington's records laid part of the groundwork for Ellington's ecstatic UK welcome. Spike Hughes, a bassist and an authority on Mozart, was one of these musicians, as was Max Jones. Jones recalled playing in a band just be-

FIGURE 4. Duke Ellington (*right*) and his manager/publisher Irving Mills (*center*) arrive in Southampton, England, in June 1933 for the start of the Ellington orchestra's fabled first European tour, which played a key role in breaking down longstanding prejudice against American culture being viewed as serious art. *On the left:* British bandleader and impresario Jack Hylton. Frank Driggs Collection.

fore the Ellington tour that labored for weeks trying to transcribe Ellington pieces such as "Rockin' in Rhythm" from recordings, which they had to play at a slower pace because it was the only way, with their limited abilities, they could perform the piece "correctly." These people were in awe of the speed and grace of the Ellington musicians, and they followed their recording history with near-obsessive fervor.

Throughout their tour, Ellington and the orchestra found English fans not only treating them with the utmost respect, but peppering them with questions of technical and artistic aspects that they almost never received in their home country. Cootie Williams, the band's long-serving trumpeter, laughed when he recalled arriving at their hotel in London: "everybody knew you, the same as in America. They knew you better than the people did in America. And they would invite you to their home, and they had all your records. Knew when you were born, what was the first record you ever made." In an interview during the tour, Ellington remarked: "I must say that it has been positively embarrassing at times to be asked the most analytical questions [in England] about work I have nearly forgotten by now." Then there were also the people who "clung to the limo as he drove away from the venue," in a precursor to the Beatlemania of the 1960s. "Never have such scenes of enthusiasm been witnessed over any visiting band . . . the various dance and concert halls where special performances have been given have been packed to suffocation," reported *Metronome*. "He hadn't found a level of appreciation back home that he found here," remarked Jones, a friend of Ellington's for decades, in 1989.[25]

In later years, Ellington and band trombonist Juan Tizol recalled their initial shock at English audiences bestowing upon them the kind of reception usually accorded to classical artists, including ovations of five to ten minutes before the band played a note. They had never experienced anything like that in America. In 1959, Ellington still seemed amazed by the reception of the band's opening number at their first show in England at the London Palladium:

> We got ten minutes of applause. Actually, we weren't certain that it was applause because their idea of applause was hand-clapping, foot-stomping, whistling, cheering, and booing—everything but the Bronx cheer. And if you have never experienced it, let me tell you that this can be very confusing. After it was all over, we realized it was applause. It was too late because everybody on stage was terrified.

European critics and audiences enthusiastically placed the music of Ellington into the center of a spirited academic debate about the artistic value of jazz and popular music. Unlike most American observers, they had no trouble crediting Ellington's African American heritage as a significant source of his musical inspiration and genius as a composer. To quote Hughes, Ellington "refused to study [formal] composition, for he felt that as a Negro he had something essentially Negro to express in his music, something which European musical culture and methods would stifle rather than encourage."[26] In 1934, the classical composer and critic Constant Lambert favorably compared aspects of Ellington's work to Ravel and Liszt and proclaimed him "the first jazz composer of distinction," a widely quoted accolade in Ellington's subsequent publicity, but a sentiment that would not be generally accepted in America for a decade or more.[27] During the 1933 tour, the musicians were feted as serious artists performing "true works of art" in twenty-four-page concert programs. Nothing this elaborate would be done for Ellington in America until his Carnegie Hall concerts in the mid-1940s, and even those programs did not contain the detail and superlatives featured in the earlier English examples.

Underscoring this artistic respect, English audiences and critics took Ellington to task in his initial series of shows at the Palladium for playing too many commercial songs and not enough of the works they deemed more serious, such as "Blue Tune" and "Creole Rhapsody." The latter, Ellington's most accomplished extended composition to date, did not sell in America anywhere near as well as his more commercial tunes of the early 1930s, despite lavish Mills-generated publicity on its behalf. In England, audiences clamored for such material. After the orchestra's first concert, one *Melody Maker* reader lamented that "we couldn't hear Ellington, the composer in all his moods." Another went so far as to suggest that admission prices should have been raised to keep out the supposedly lower-class audience that enjoyed Ellington's less challenging, more commercial material. His other recommendation, if the first proved unfeasible: "give tickets only to those who pass the ordeal of a stiff questionnaire" concerning Ellington's music! John Hammond, in *Melody Maker*, insisted that "Ellington is not entirely to blame" for "the unadulterated tripe he served during his first concert." Hammond instead pointed a blaming finger at fickle American record companies and audiences who craved the "hottest" acts instead of the best. "Therefore, in order to make money [Ellington] has to rely on showmanship and effects, singers and dancers and such," Hammond complained. "In other words, Duke isn't used to having his own music appreciated" in America. Probably part of the reason Ellington programmed a revue-styled show was because he was the closing act on a thirteen-act vaudeville bill that evening.

Ellington satisfied the more discerning fans by scheduling two extra *Melody Maker*–organized concerts at the 4,300-capacity Trocadero. Max Jones called the shows "a tremendous innovation," comparing them to the 1924 Gershwin/Whiteman Aeolian Hall show because he could recall no popular or black act playing a concert in England without any other opening acts in such a large cinema venue. Ellington played a program on "a big cinema stage" consisting almost entirely of his own compositions, including the full nine-minute "Creole Rhapsody" and an eight-minute extended version of "Sophisticated Lady." Always attuned to the desires of an audience, Ellington switched to faster numbers at the close of the show when the Troc crowd "got a bit restive during the slower pastel numbers." The columnist "Mike" in *Melody Maker* pronounced the proceeding "altogether admirable," although he complained that the crowd proved too adoring and lengthy in its applause for soloists, which detracted from his enjoyment of the compositions in their entirety. The young art of jazz music criticism had reached the environs of classical snobbery.

The seriousness accorded to the Ellington orchestra's music translated to the venues where they were asked to perform: concert and stage show settings, not the nightclubs, vaudeville stages, movie theaters, and dance halls the band usually played. The advertisements for the shows were strikingly different from those employed in the States, featuring a simple and dignified font along with expressions like "personal appearance" and "gala dance" instead of the sensationalistic cartoons and typesetting that typified American ads for Ellington.

Also, the way the band was treated behind the scenes stood in contrast to the treatment accorded to African Americans in the United States. As Sonny Greer recalled decades later:

> We stayed in the biggest hotels. Irving Mills had our accommodation in front . . . the American flag was flown on the hotel. In honor of us. Just like they fly a flag if a diplomat come and stay in the hotel, they flew the American flag for us. We carried the flag and the prestige of my people. I am an American Negro . . . We carried the flag for the dignity of the American all over the world. We were treated with the utmost respect.[28]

While this was true, Mills probably also realized that such treatment served as effective promotion, advertising the band and underlining its special position among popular artists and African Americans. To further personify American dignity, the band opened their English shows with "The Star Spangled Banner."

A sense that Ellington and African American jazz represented some kind of turning point in music history pervaded many of the clippings from the 1933 tour. An essay entitled "The Art of Duke Ellington" compared Ellington's innovations to the twelve-tone methodology of Arnold Schoenberg, which drew considerable controversy among audiences when premiered, yet was "applauded by the musical diletttanti." *Sound Wave* magazine argued that Ellington had instilled an "impressionism" into the art of dance music "far and away in advance of his contemporaries." The critic for *Dancing Times* stressed this historical significance in an American context: "Ellington, the first real composer of jazz, will perhaps do for modern music what Wagner did for the modern school—he is only just beginning—and his mastery of modern acoustic rhythm reflects American industrialism on a basis of 'jungle rhythm,' as few other composers have done." A writer for the *Huddersfield News* compared Ellington's "hot jazz" songs to Elizabethan madrigals of the 1600s, which, according to the author, also presented somewhat primitive, discordant, and rule-breaking material that eventually was recognized to have important and lasting value, especially in terms of rhythm.[29] This writer oddly insisted that Ellington lacked melodic skills (which he compared to an equally fallacious example of Bach's supposed lack of rhythmic complexity), but more importantly he, like other writers and observers, viewed Ellington and his music as part of a continuum of hundreds of years of music history. Unlike their brethren in the United States, these European critics and audiences possessed a longstanding tradition of viewing music, even popular music, as an art form, and they exhibited avid intellectual curiosity concerning how Ellington fit into their system.

Some reviewers adopted the African imagery that Mills initially used to promote the Ellington orchestra at the Cotton Club. The reviewer for the *New Statesman* viewed Ellington as simultaneously an artist and a primitive:

> His jazz is complicated by all the refinements of modern orchestration; but this music, which is at once a challenge, an invocation and an exorcism, evokes the jungle, the heavy foliage, the night cries of preying or preyed-on beasts, the hovering spirits of the ancestors which must be propitiated, the darkness round the torch-lit spaces, the throbbing rhythm and wild zest of life . . . Once when the composer turned on his piano stool and sat brooding in the shadow of his soloists, a vague smile on his lips, one could have sworn his soul was back where no doubt his body has never been, in the square of an African village.[30]

Intellectuals and critics were not alone in assessing Ellington's significance; his music and manner also profoundly affected English musicians. Greer recalled that, among the audience at the Trocadero, "half the people [in the audience] were musicians." Spike Hughes, writing in *Melody Maker* nearly four weeks after Ellington had left England, presented a four-part series concerning "The Technical Lesson of Ellington," which sought to summarize "the free education to all dance musicians recently offered by Duke and his band" during their English tour. While not especially insightful, the lengthy articles included musical notation and examples, and mused over the role and technique of each orchestra member, a level of detail not seen in America until the 1940s.

"Duke has made us [musicians] all think," commented "The Rambler" in his monthly column for *Tune Times.* For him, "the sheer sound of the Ellington band was something never heard before in this country," and it proved conclusively that "jazz is not all noise." He provided a picturesque description of Ellington's aftereffect among musicians: "In small variety halls they sing 'Mood Indigo' with blue lights and blue notes; arrangers sigh for six brass every time they make an arrangement for a society gig." Max Jones recalled that "all of the professional bands, I mean even to the rather straight bands, all had an Ellington number or two" following the Ellington tour. Drummers obtained elaborate drum kits like Sonny Greer, and the "doo-wah doo-wah" of "It Don't Mean a Thing" became an arranging staple. "Ring Them Bells" marked a particular favorite of English bands, Jones recalled, and if English bands could afford it, they imported the same bells Ellington featured on the recording, which the musicians referred to as "Ellington chimes." Sid Phillips, in his monthly column The Saxophone Team for *Rhythm* magazine, urged English musicians to emulate the discipline and passion exhibited by the "perfect sax team" of the Ellington orchestra. "Throughout my experience in recording, broadcasting and show production, I have been forced to the conclusion that English saxophonists in general have the habit of just playing the notes and, having done so, are satisfied that they have played their part and earned their money," he opined. "This is a great pity."

Peter Rush, in *Tune Times,* also insisted that English musicians had a lot to learn from Ellington:

> The music of Ellington is elusively clever and the playing of it by his band is provocatively so, and I am going to be rash enough to say that it was "over the heads" of the audience. It was too advanced for our immediate consumption. Breathing space was required to digest it, so to speak. For my part I would have liked the score in front of me and to have closely followed the theme . . . Ellington has shaken up the English musicians and caused them to put on their thinking caps. Let us hope that when the thinkers have finished with their wet towels they will take action, and the sooner the better in the general interests.[31]

The formation of numerous record clubs in the wake of Ellington's English tour represented an extraordinary example of how the Ellington sound inspired fans, as well as critics and musicians, to take jazz and popular music more seriously. These were not fan clubs, but organizations that sought to bestow serious amateur attention upon the music of Ellington and other jazz bands. Lectures on the history of jazz were presented, and "recitals" of recordings occurred, followed by group discussion and comment. Some even featured musical instruction. Six weeks after Ellington's exit from England, a Mr. Crabtree of the "Hot Record Circle" in Colne in Lancashire previewed "an All-Ellington Record Recital, which is to be held in Bracewell Hall, Yorks." The subjects of the weekly meetings of the forty-strong Liverpool Ellington Society were previewed in *Melody Maker* in November 1933. An address for the curious Ellington fan was included, since "a few more students would be welcomed as members."[32] Only in the late 1950s, with the creation of the Duke Ellington Societies, would there be similar serious music appreciation organizations on behalf of a popular music artist in America.

The influence of the Ellington tour lasted in England. Months later, letters commenting on the band's visit were still appearing in musical periodicals, and clubs analyzed and attempted to duplicate the band's style. A letter to *Melody Maker* published in November 1933 tirelessly argued the merits of Armstrong versus Ellington, declaring the former superior. Paragraphs of evidence are presented, including a detailed accusation that Ellington and his band appropriated instrumental breaks from Armstrong. Nearly a half year after Ellington's last English concert, the columnist known as "The Rambler" complained that "not even in Wales can I get away from Ellingtonism."[33]

Popular music artists who had toured in England before Ellington had not been rewarded with the same critical reaction. British audiences enjoyed Guy Lombardo, Rudy Vallee, and Paul Whiteman before 1933 and they did good business, but none were accorded the kind of acclaim Ellington received, nor were any thought worthy of comparison to him. The *Kansas City Call,* one of the major African American newspapers, made a comparison between Ellington and the American bands that went to Europe before him in their headline celebrating the tour: "Duke Ellington's Trip Abroad Answers European Plea for the Best in Jazz."[34]

The one American artist continually compared to Ellington in the English press was Louis Armstrong, who toured Europe the year before. According to biographer Laurence Bergreen, Armstrong ventured to Europe to escape troubles with gangsters who ran jazz clubs and kept him from working in Chicago and New York. Armstrong felt his life, as well as his livelihood, threatened by this situation. For Ellington and Mills, however, the European tour signified financial opportunity, increased record sales, and a useful foreign chapter in their long, elevating campaign. In fact, Mills threatened to cancel the Ellington tour when English promoters initially experienced difficulty securing the band's usual $5,500 per week. Conversely, Armstrong's "drunken" manager Johnny Collins booked gigs at fees far below what Armstrong should have been earning and worked him "like a dog," which led to a split lip and a forced convalescence for the trumpeter.[35]

While financial conditions differed between the Armstrong and Ellington tours, the marketing and critical reception surrounding Armstrong's tour proved even more instructive. Armstrong was portrayed in ads as a monkey in stylish tux and tails, and, though the more sophisticated critics at *Melody Maker* praised Armstrong's performances, most followed the precedent set by the promotion. An article in *Rhythm* magazine entitled "The Armstrong War" rounded up the more hateful critical barbs: "ugliest man," "untrained gorilla," and, perhaps most astonishingly, "dreadful babyish singing." A Glasgow paper could not decide if he epitomized "the last word in syncopation and rhythm" or "something akin to musical savagery." The *Scotland Sun-Mail* reported that Armstrong elicited "the greatest controversy in London for years" and wondered if he represented "an insult to music hall patrons." Perhaps in reaction to such vitriol, *Rhythm* featured an interview with Paul Whiteman entitled "What I Think of Louis Armstrong," which seemed to intimate that the approval of a respected white bandleader like Whiteman should assure skeptical British fans of the worth of Armstrong. Even *Melody Maker,* the British champion of jazz music, made no mention of Armstrong's artistry in their initial article on the tour, championing instead his "electric personality," "showmanship," "good humor," and the fact that he "is on the move the whole time" on stage. Weeks later, the periodical extolled him as a "colored genius . . . far ahead of his time," the point of view that music historians and fans generally agree upon today.[36]

Overall, the reaction to Armstrong was positive, but often puzzled and sometimes mean. For most observers in the press, the tour represented a strange phenomenon that they attempted to explain, and perhaps enjoy. With his famously gregarious stage presence, Armstrong did not carry himself as a serious artist, and his ads and his manager certainly did not intimate such status, so he was mostly treated as an entertainer. Journalists Max Jones and Stanley Dance recalled that they knew, from 1920s recordings such as "West End Blues" and "Weatherbird," that Armstrong was an artist of the highest caliber, but they and other audience members were initially put off by Armstrong's "eccentric manner," running around the stage and "mopping his brow." They felt his reception was particularly impaired by the fact that he brought a small band of pick-up musicians from Martinique and

France instead of his crack American band. "For people interested in jazz, it was a disappointment," Dance remembered. "But Duke was better in person than on records because . . . the sound was better . . . the [phonographs] in those days and the recording techniques did not give you the full spectrum of sound that they could project in person. So when the brass opened up [in the Palladium], it kind of knocked you back on your heels if you'd never heard that sort of thing." Jones added that Ellington's more "Europeanized features" and his ability to "address people in a way that was very civilized for a black man" also contributed to the positive reception for Ellington in England.

The reception behind the scenes differed for the two artists as well. Armstrong could not be booked into "a class hotel" in 1932, but Ellington received accommodations at the "snooty" Dorchester Hotel in London, although the whole band did not gain admission (and were overall treated less elegantly than Ellington, though better than in most parts of the United States). Ellington felt a "loyalty" to the Dorchester because they took him in on his first visit, and stayed there every subsequent time he was in London.[37]

Not everyone waxed rapturously about Ellington in England. Resistance to his artistry arose in the press, some of it racially inspired. *Pearsons Weekly*, in an article subtitled "Negroes Invade Our Theaters," seemed threatened by positive interpretations of black musicians, a point of view that existed only in the distinct minority of British press coverage. Citing recent tours by Armstrong, Ellington, and Robeson, the writer lamented that "England's theatrical agents seem to have developed a negro complex" and wondered if this meant that "negroes will eventually capture the [British] theatre?" The article seemed to disdain the fact that white audiences exhibited unbridled enthusiasm in demanding encores of African American musicians. He sought to remind the "colored stars" that "a hundred years ago they would have been working in the cotton plantations with a white man cracking the whip over them." A small minority of audiences at the Palladium for both the Armstrong and Ellington shows "expressed derision" by throwing pennies on the stage as if they were "buskers," or street musicians. Some walked out. Max Jones believed such audience members probably came for the vaudeville acts and were not expecting American jazz.

The harshest common criticisms among the deluge of approval for the Ellington tour protested less his music than its overpraise. One Ellington fan, writing to *Melody Maker*, decried "the dilettantes and musical snobs" who urged that Ellington release 12-inch long-playing 78s, as classical orchestras commonly did. The reader predicted that "the Philadelphia and Berlin Philharmonic may spread themselves on to a 14-inch record just to keep their honor unspoiled." Ellington, he wrote, "is a composer of note, but he is not, and never can be, a Beethoven." "There can be no doubt at all now that the attempt to foist hot music and hot styles of playing on the public has failed," declared a letter in *Sound Wave*. "It is true that a great fuss is often made for a few days or weeks over the visits of artists like Duke Ellington, the Boswell Sisters and so on, but, apart from a handful of fans, the majority of the British public still likes melody and simpleness, just as their fathers and grandfathers did before them." Over a month after the Ellington orchestra left England, Ralph Hill in the *Music Lover* severely criticized its music and the significance accorded to it by magazines like *Melody Maker*. But in his writing, Hill also exhibited respect for the orchestra's work and its success in England, amidst his disgust at the more enthusiastic encomiums:

> And what did it all amount to? Nothing more nor less than the bursting of a bubble filled with the most evil smelling gas that has ever issued from the foul tenements of Tin Pan Alley. It is said that Duke Ellington is the only composer of jazz music that musicians take seriously, which only goes to prove the kindly tolerance of musicians and what poor composers the Duke's competitors must be . . . Their passage work is Kreisler-like in accuracy, smoothness and agility, and their ability to play long sustained notes pianissimo at the top of their instruments is undoubtedly a remarkable *tour de force*. But this is not music: it belongs to the *genre* of acrobatics, trick cyclists, trapezium antics, etc. . . . Ellington has proved conclusively that "hot" jazz may provide an admirable turn for the music hall and circus, where the acrobat is welcomed, but to talk of it seriously as if it were a legitimate branch of musical art, is the publicity bunk of a gang of vulgar ignoramuses.[38]

Upon returning home, Ellington knew that while English critics and audiences placed high cultural value on his music and his place in musical history, American audiences had proved much slower in this regard, despite Mills's aggressive marketing. A few articles in the English press even expressed pride that English audiences recognized the worth of Ellington's artistry before Americans generally did.[39] Racism certainly played a part in this American reticence, as well as the notion expressed by John Hammond and others that black music was somehow only capable of serving entertaining and dancing purposes. But it was more than that.

In their efforts to make Ellington's music both popular and acclaimed in the United States, Ellington and Mills faced not just prejudice against blacks and against the merits of popular music, but also long-term American prejudice against the worth of American art. "As a nation we have often been hesitant and apologetic about whatever has been made in America in the vernacular tradition," observed John A. Kouwenhoven in his classic 1948 study *Made in America.* "Perhaps the time has come when more of us are ready to accept the challenge offered to the creative imagination by the techniques and forms which first arose among our own people in our own land." Since the first American universities were founded in the seventeenth century, American culture was deemed unworthy of study. Instead, "classic" works by Europeans dominated curricula, a trend that continued, for the most part, until World War II. For most of the nineteenth century, despite Ralph Waldo Emerson and Mark Twain's urgings in *The American Scholar* and *Innocents Abroad* to ignore the pervasive influence of European works and concentrate on creating an American aesthetic, American college students read only ancient Greek literature, and even these works were not read for themes, grammar, or structure, but to inculcate a sturdy "mental discipline." At the end of the century, after acrimonious academic battles, some British literature began to be taught in American universities, although even the teaching of Shakespeare drew controversy in some academic circles until the 1930s.

American literature endured a surprisingly slow and tortuous route to academic respectability. In the 1920s and 1930s, according to Lawrence Levine, "American universities offered as much graduate work in Chaucer as in all of American literature." Even on the eve of World War II, only 20 percent of English department courses taught American literature in the United States, which was not surprising since teaching the subject in the 1920s was viewed as "professional suicide" for professors seeking to establish themselves.[40]

A homegrown disrespect for American culture manifested itself in music as well. Leonard Bernstein noted the exclusion of any study of American music from the American college curricula of the nineteenth century. Charles Ives, the noted American composer, recalled that in the New England of his youth during the 1870s and 1880s, and at Yale, the axiom that "the only good music was European music" went unquestioned. John Philip Sousa, probably the most popular musician in the world at the turn of the century, insisted that disproving the widely accepted premise that American musicians and composers could not be as skilled as those from Europe served as a major inspiration in his writing and performing. Joseph Horowitz chronicled how celebrity conductor Arturo Toscanini brought a calcified, old European aesthetic to the American classical music scene in the first half of the twentieth century, creating a national atmosphere where "American composers had no fixed place in a musical community modeled after German norms."[41] Ragtime and jazz also faced resistance in being seen as serious music in the first third of the twentieth century.

Perhaps the primary explanation for the resistance to the study of American culture in the United States lies in the lack of cultural antecedents, as outlined in the 1930s by cultural historian Constance Rourke. Ellington (and other American composers already mentioned) experienced similar problems of acceptance as American nineteenth-century writers like Hawthorne, Melville, and Poe, as described in Rourke's book *American Humor.* She argued that because "the American strain [of literature] was new, recognition was not easy . . . Through the interweaving of the popular strain with that of a new expression on other levels a literature has been produced which, like other literatures, is related to an anterior popular lore that must . . . be called a folk-lore."[42] The American writers of the nineteenth century utilized uniquely American traits, styles, and subject matter with roots in a singular American folklore. They did not employ the standard European trappings that previously characterized exemplary writing. Largely because of this, European and American critics of the nineteenth and early twentieth century had difficulty realizing their artistry. Rourke also noted that this lack of cultural precedent, along with racism, kept critics and society from recognizing the contributions of African Americans to American culture. The problem of the acceptance of American and African American culture was discussed outside of academic circles. It was a vital issue of the day, inspiring vigorous debate in the *New York Times* in the months after Ellington began his professional relationship with Mills.[43]

Surmounting these cultural hierarchies entailed a far more difficult struggle for black American composers than for white composers. The irony of this situation resided in the fact that much of what would eventually be hailed as groundbreaking as well as financially profitable in American music could be traced to black sources, both American and African. Perhaps no one understood the implications of this situation for blacks earlier than W. E. B. DuBois, who first recognized the lack of respect for American art in the 1890s as a student in Germany, a country then regarded as the academic paragon. "Even I was a little startled to realize how much I had regarded as white American was white European and not American at all," he reported. "The Americans have no art, said the Italians; America's music is German, the Germans said; and their literature, remarked the English, is English." In *The Souls of Black Folk,* written at the dawn of the twentieth century, DuBois referred to African American music, specifically "Negro folk-song," as "the sole American music." But as much as he rhapsodized about the historical and emotional power of black music as first voiced by

American slaves, he viewed its importance as more than musical. "Through all the sorrows of the Sorrow Songs there breathes a hope—a faith in the ultimate justice of things," he wrote. "A faith that men will be judged someday by souls, not skins."[44] For DuBois, music made the case for black equality better than any speeches could. In the final chapter of *The Souls of Black Folk,* he seemed to present a vision of black music and culture as the most effective bridge and uniting force between the races. And when one views the history of American music in the twentieth century, one can see that DuBois was dead-on prescient. Black music and culture represented an important, perhaps the most important, meeting ground for blacks and whites in the twentieth century.

The Ellington orchestra's fabled 1933 European tour helped break down this long-standing prejudice against American culture being viewed as serious art—if European critics and audiences could hail Ellington as an artist worthy of serious attention, the point was more likely to be accepted stateside. But this process also set up an intriguing and ironic conundrum for Americans concerning Ellington's acclaim. After centuries of Americans disdaining American artists' abilities to produce serious art, what did it mean when a black American composer, a member of a race accorded at best second-class citizenship, was hailed by critics in Europe as the first serious composer the United States had produced? The situation both confirmed and flew in the face of some of the noblest and most controversial of American ideals. The marketing of Ellington as a serious artist marked the first major instance of Americans and the rest of the world coming to terms with this significant contribution and the contradictions it represented.

The European tour also brought Ellington and his orchestra the most concentrated and widespread American news coverage they had yet received. It was not an entirely unprecedented situation. Black artists such as Roland Hayes and Paul Robeson had visited Europe previously, but they were performers who worked in the traditional recital format, and not composers. Like Ellington, their European sojourns changed their standing in the United States. In his essay "Criteria of Negro Art," DuBois wrote about Hayes in the 1920s, a generally unrecognized figure before his European tour. "It is not simply the great clear tenor of Roland Hayes that opened the ears of America . . . a foreign land heard Hayes and put its imprint on him and immediately all of America with its imitative snobbery woke up," he snorted. "We approved Hays because London, Paris and Berlin approved him and not simply because he was a great singer."[45] The approbation of European audiences and critics could do wonders for an American's artistic reputation, even a black American.

Prompted by the Mills organization, newspapers in every corner of the United States triumphantly parroted the praise English critics showered on Ellington. Such coverage proved more effective than Mills's previous efforts: an ad was more easily dismissed than a news story from Europe. "Six famed English music critics gave whole columns to Duke Ellington and his music," wrote the radio columnist of the *Omaha News.* One English columnist quoted extensively in the American press was S. R. Nelson of the *Era,* who was "not ashamed" to admit that he cried during the performance of "Mood Indigo," referred to Ivie Anderson's singing as "high art," and imagined that Wagner "would have hailed this music as [one of] the most significant phases of modern musical art." Ellington himself praised British audiences more than critics: "The British reacted much quicker to most of our programs than the Americans do," he told the *Boston Transcript.* A month of extra dates, booked because "Irving Mills . . . was swamped with offers of additional engagements," was widely noted in the American press. So was the Ellington orchestra's achievement of nabbing the highest fee ever paid a band to broadcast on the British Broadcasting Corporation, and the interesting sidelight that "when B.B.C. officials found that Ellington was using 'Mood Indigo' only as a closeout fading signature, they extended the [broadcast] period five minutes, cutting into the next program to permit him to play the number in its entirety." The BBC also interviewed Ellington at length live over the air, discussing "Duke's music and his musical aims," not the innocuous celebrity chat usually heard during Ellington's brief American radio interviews during broadcasts of the band.[46]

George F. Frazier, Jr., writing in *Playhouse* magazine, an entertainment-oriented publication in Boston, used arguments that, in making a case for Ellington as the best representation of American music as art, echoed those of Constance Rourke. Few if any popular or jazz artists of the period could have inspired such a discussion of cultural history and identity as Ellington did here:

> Of the music that is America's, the question arises as to how much of it is truly hers. How much of it is strictly a native idiom? How much of it is free from indebtedness to models of origin that are both alien and classical? And the answer must surely be, that beside negro jazz there is precious little music of genuine American stamp. Mr. Gershwin's celebrated "Rhapsody in Blue" was for a time highly acclaimed as a notable achievement in the native strain. But upon closer inspection it reveals itself as stemming from something of more remote origin. The one person who more successfully than any other has given voice to America in terms of music is Edward Kennedy (Duke) El-

lington, the young negro composer . . . It is a truism that prophets are ever without honor in their own lands . . . Ellington had to take his orchestra abroad before his genius received its due acclaim. The British and the French publics realized that here was American music undiluted, music unblemished by foreign tinctures, music that had come, many generations past from Africa to New Orleans and Harlem.

A Cleveland newspaper columnist noted that "Duke Ellington and his aggregation have been giving the people of the world's metropolis something that makes them think they have never heard jazz before." Other black groups were considering going to Europe, the writer mentioned, but thought "some of them might well remain on this side [of the Atlantic] . . . They won't give [Europeans] what Duke Ellington gives and that's what people are liking."[47] Lots of bands could entertain and cause dance floors to shake, but who else could also deliver the highbrow goods?

The American press generally changed their tone in writing about the Ellington orchestra in the year following the European tour, employing rarified language not usually garnered on popular or jazz musicians, and increasingly comparing Ellington to classical composers. The *Youngstown Vindicator* offered a headline of "Ellington to Show Piano Art at Appearance Here." Though dancing and comedy also figured as part of the program, "Ellington cannot be catalogued as another 'fast' colored combo," the paper reported. "The Duke has been praised for his new notes in semi-symphonic music, his dreamy waltzes and unique style." The *Columbus Dispatch* predicted Ellington would "edify" his audience. Another Columbus newspaper referred to Ellington as a "versatile" artist "just back from European triumphs," who could play both a concert and a dance on the same stage in the same evening, utilizing his "many manuscripts" of original music. The *Memphis Scimitar* wrote that Ellington's "unorthodox, frenzied jazz" earned him the sobriquet of "this negro Stravinsky." A Dallas paper likewise called Ellington "the African Stravinsky," claiming that his music "is not butterfly jazz with three months life." Another reviewer hailed Ellington as a "black Wagner, creating new and startling forms of jazz drama." This style of review spread. Cab Calloway, in the same article, was compared to "a Harlem Lizst, the rhapsodic interpreter of the new musical voodoo."[48] These were strange and awkward comparisons.

Ellington himself never emphasized such platitudes. He had little use for fawning and ahistorical classical comparisons outside of the promotional opportunities they presented. His music illustrated the feelings and impressions of his own existence and identity. In "words bearing a slight London accent," Ellington told the *Hollywood News* in 1934 that "I want to be independent. I want to do what I want. I want to break away from European traditions."[49] Despite international inclination to classical comparisons by various critics, this is what Ellington's music had done all along.

Not all American critics adorned their columns concerning the Ellington orchestra with highbrow pretensions. Many combined descriptions of this aspect of the band's activity with depictions of how primitive, fast, and sensuous their dance numbers were. Such descriptions were not surprising, as Ellington shows contained compositions that featured raucous as well as more tempered aspects of the band's personality. A Detroit reviewer speculated that Ellington's music may exist within Sigmund Spaeth's definition of "permanent music" and name-checked Beethoven and Elgar, but he also predicted that "even an African savage" would find that the band's "'hot' numbers" were "barbaric to the point of savagery." The *San Francisco Examiner* acclaimed the Ellington orchestra as "the most accomplished jazz orchestra" and praised two of their numbers as "outstanding examples of abstract jazz," but also commented on the "aboriginal voodoo throbs" in the music.[50] Besides highlighting some racial stereotyping, such juxtapositions showed Ellington's resolute refusal to be corralled into any category, high or low. A performer accepted on many levels, Ellington and Mills knew, could attract more bookings and afford Ellington increased freedom as a writer as well as a performer.

Ellington encouraged the highbrow emphasis after Europe by changing the nature of the shows the orchestra played. Continuing to tour movie-theater circuits, Ellington made sure there were segments of each show in which the band performed extended works to seated audiences—usually "abstract jazz" compositions like "Mood Indigo," "Black and Tan Fantasie," and "Sophisticated Lady." Dancers still accompanied the orchestra on tour, drummer Sonny Greer continued to perform brief comedy bits between numbers, and "hot" danceable songs and hit singles were still prominently featured, but the shows emphasized the music, especially Ellington's own compositions. Critics noticed the difference, particularly in comparison to the band's competition. "More than any of the negro shows that have been on local stages in recent weeks, Ellington places the burden of entertainment on the music," commented the *Akron Beacon Journal.* "And surprisingly, he has turned his band away from the swift syncopations of the radio to a concert style that is as much more entertaining as it is radically different." H. Robert Udkoff, a longtime friend of Ellington's, recalled seeing Ellington for the first time as a teen in the 1930s after the 1933 European tour: "I remember seeing Cab Calloway also, and even though Cab Calloway had a very explosive sound and presentation, I recognized they were not in the same league musically, because Calloway's was more of a contrived stage show and he was jumping around and tossing his head around, and Ellington was so elegant, you know, walking, and leading his orchestra." Ellington also changed the song list nightly, a big shift from the stationary song lists of the initial post–Cotton Club tours, and of other traveling acts.[51] Many Ellington scholars and fans date Ellington's first formal concert as a 1937 show at UCLA,[52] but the Ellington orchestra had actually been performing similar shows to seated crowds in England in 1933 and throughout the United States in the vaudeville movie-theater circuits for years preceding the 1937 UCLA concert.

This post-European concert aesthetic at Ellington shows probably also reflected Ellington's growing control over his music and the orchestra. During the Cotton Club engagement, Mills's office resided an easy taxi ride away from the venue, and on the tours immediately afterward, Mills was often present and perhaps evinced some kind of control over the set list of the band. At the Cotton Club in particular, the Ellington orchestra song selection was mandated by the stage presentations, not Ellington, and featured numerous non-Ellington compositions. But after Europe, with Ellington's talents encouraged by unprecedented critical respect, and with Mills's time increasingly taken up by a much larger roster of artists, Ellington appears to have enjoyed a freer rein in deciding which numbers to present. Saxophonist Otto Hardwicke, who left the Ellington orchestra in 1928 and returned in 1932, said that the band atmosphere changed significantly in four years, becoming "less of a collective" and more of "Ellington's band," especially in matters of composition.[53]

Mills scheduled the orchestra's first Southern tour less than a month after their return from Europe. Ellington and the orchestra had previously resisted lucrative offers to tour the region, unwilling to deal with Southern racial attitudes and violence. "The South? God-damn, no!" formed the consensus opinion of the band during the Cotton Club years, according to Barry Ulanov. "I won't go south, I don't care what they offer me," Ellington told Mills on many occasions.[54] But Ellington's changed image in the wake of the European tour, the money, or the measures Mills took to insure the safety of the orchestra eventually changed their minds. The shows were, as always in the South during this period, racially segregated in various forms,[55] but the Ellington performances made Southern newspaper writers, and audiences as well, reconsider their perceptions concerning the capabilities of blacks.

Ellington's first Southern tour received a much different reception than other black bands that preceded him on the same circuit. In 1931, Earl Hines and his orchestra "were the first big Negro band to travel extensively through the South." Hines referred to it as an "invasion" rather than a "tour." Between a bomb exploding under their bandstand in Alabama ("we didn't none of us get hurt, but we didn't play so well after that, either") and numerous threatening encounters with the police, the experience proved so harrowing that Hines in the 1960s recalled that "you could call us the first Freedom Riders." For the most part, any contact with whites, even fans, was viewed as dangerous. Finding places to eat or stay overnight entailed a constant struggle. The only nonmusical "victory" that Hines claimed was winning the respect of a clothing store salesman who initially treated Hines with derision until it became clear that Hines planned to spend $85 on shirts, "which changed his whole attitude." Louis Armstrong, who grew up in New Orleans, also endured numerous instances of trouble, the worst being when he and his band were thrown into a Memphis jail after a local bus driver, not knowing that the band he agreed to transport would be black, refused to transport them. Armstrong and the band, who were regularly involved in business relations with gangsters who ran jazz clubs in New York City and Chicago, did not meekly submit to the authority of the driver or the summoned police, a transgression which landed them in the slammer until the club they were scheduled to play that night freed them on the proviso that the band would perform a free radio broadcast for the club. Visiting black entertainers had endured such treatment in the South for decades. Bert Williams encountered a crowd in El Paso in the mid-1890s that forced the entire troupe he was performing with to take off their clothes, "which were too good for them," and don burlap sacking instead. Williams never returned to the Deep South.[56]

Nothing resembling those events would occur on the first Ellington Southern tour. There was too much at stake for Ellington and Mills, financially and artistically. If Ellington and the band had experienced the indignities that greeted Armstrong and Hines in the South, it would have represented a contradiction of the Mills organization's careful and expensive marketing around the concepts of respectability and artistry. So, Mills and Ellington took precautions to minimize risk and ensure that the Ellington orchestra members were treated as great American artists, even in the South.

The main precaution taken, noted in some of the ads for their shows, was the hiring of three well-apportioned Pullman train cars, with the band's name painted on the outside, to ferry the band around. The band had hired out train cars for nonstop cross-country trips before, but it usually used buses between gigs.[57] As Ellington recalled in 1956, the Pullman cars yielded a combined premium of safety, economy, comfort, and status:

> In those days the charter[ed cars] were very reasonable, it was cheaper than room rent . . . with two drawing rooms you had a lot of sitting space, it was clearly good living. And the baggage car—we had a whole lot of trunks and scenery and platforms. And [band member] Billy Taylor was the cook in the band and he would set up a stove, [you'd ask him if] you want some soul food . . . A lot of fun, a great experience. Private cars were a priority then, because it would come from the top, the headquarters of the railroad. You get to a town, and they switch you over on a siding, the last track on the station, and connect you up with steam, water, sanitation, all that service.

The Pullmans had significance beyond the fact that they ensured, as Ellington described, that the orchestra "had a minimum of trouble down there" in the South. The way that the Ellington band traveled sent an unmistakable message to blacks and whites. Drummer Sonny Greer's memories, as usual, were colorful on the subject of the logistics of the Southern tour:

> They never seen nobody like us. Down South, you know, confliction, segregation . . . We pull up, baggage car in the yard and pay extra to park it. We didn't have to go through that junk—colored over this side, white over this. Our guys in the morning, we didn't have to dress. We'd keep our pajamas and robes and stay in the car, relax all day until the time to work. And if we wanted something in the morning, we would put a order in and have the guy deliver it to us. When we went to the gig, we have a fleet of cabs waiting to take us, bring us back . . . The average one of them crackers down south, they never been inside a Pullman car, never saw it, and them porters used to put on the dog, them cats would put on them beautiful starched uniforms and the step to come down [off the train] they would lay it [down for the men in the Ellington orchestra] . . . [white people had] never seen that. They would come down out of curiosity. Ofays and everybody would come down, we were travelling like kings. That's how Irving Mills had us travel.[58]

No band, black or white, had traveled through the South in that manner before. They also represented a nonaggressive, yet pointed statement concerning the inanity of the racial mores of the South, and how they could and should be subverted. "It turned out to be a great thing . . . a very good symbol, more or less," Ellington told a television interviewer in the mid-1960s. "Because the President travels around in private cars in the same way, I just figured it had to be something of some importance, and I think, commanded a certain amount of respect, and you know, we respect everybody else, so there's no reason why they shouldn't [respect us]." Aside from two minor hassles in which individual white audience members briefly challenged Ellington and trombonist Juan Tizol offstage, Ellington's 1933 Southern tour went off without a hitch. "Everything was terrific," recalled Irving Mills a half century afterward. "We had no trouble at all." Mills later mysteriously added in the same interview that he "always had protection" for the band during the tour.[59] Whether he hired strongmen or was referring to the demonstrative fashion in which he had the band travel through the South was unclear.

Numerous articles covering the Ellington orchestra's 1933 Southern tour referred to the luminous praise the band received in Europe, with special attention paid to Ellington's reputation as an American composer: "Recognized as the jazz leader of the day in America, he is considered by European music critics to be the outstanding figure in American music and the only contributor to music that this country has produced," extolled a writer for a Dallas paper. In another Dallas article entitled "Higher Development of Jazz Expounded by Duke Ellington," journalist J. R., Jr., insisted that Ellington's compositions "erase the color line between blue and chromatic music" and that they "deserve . . . first place in patronage." He predicted a long life and significance for Ellington's songs and praised the musicians. The Ellington oeuvre "can and probably will be performed whenever you can find musicians to play it," he commented. "Whether such musicians exist outside the dark ranks of the Ellington band is doubtful."[60]

But, as was often the case during his five decades in the music business, the Ellington significance carried beyond musical appreciation in the South. Reviewers not only praised the music but some saw it, as Ellington did, as an expression of black identity. M. C. C., an Amarillo newspaper reviewer, detailed an argument that mirrored Constance Rourke's insights concerning the precedents for African American artists:

> It is perhaps the sincerity [of Ellington's music], which most impresses. At no time is there any effort at imitation, the musicians know they have something inimitable, and they make the most of it. The simple, familiar folk song of the southern negro is ignored, since it takes on much of the section which gave it birth and the traditions of the slavery days which were its locale and its inspiration. The Ellington music is . . . blaring, bewildering, primitive, deafening, and again it is searching, appealing, haunting.

Such Southerners glimpsed that Ellington's approach outlined a new, more urbane identity for African Americans, proud of both their postslavery urban roots as well as their preslavery African roots. Ellington's American audiences, even in the South, began to realize that he and his band represented black artists who defined themselves on their own equal terms, and not as whites viewed them. The Ellington orchestra implicitly rejected the Jim Crow vision of blacks not through words (which would have been dangerous) but through deeds, images, and actions.

For many American whites, especially those in the South, Ellington's stature and seriousness came as a shock. "Tomorrow night a well-built, suave-mannered negro seated at a piano (which will do things you never thought it could) will bring a show to a Majestic Theater capacity audience that will be worth anybody's price of admission," a Dallas paper reported. The article stressed the historic nature of the event: "Yet our grandfathers would have given any odds as to the improbability of his appearance." Indeed, any Southerner viewing the event—a formally clad, internationally renowned, locally acclaimed black orchestra selling out a white venue for weeks in the middle of Texas—knew that the times were definitely changing. The same writer viewed Cab Calloway as a "bleating, shrill-voiced" performer and Louis Armstrong as "muggle-smoking," but "Ellington is an earnest, all-round musician and composer as well as a master band-man." Words like "earnest" and "master" were seldom associated with blacks in the Southern media. But, as Barry Ulanov pointed out, the same white newspapers in Texas that praised Ellington refused to print his photograph, only featuring caricatures of him, usually a respectful one by Al Hirschfield provided by the Mills office. Omar LaGrange, a black newspaper reporter, described the surprise of some white Amarillo audiences when exposed to the Ellington orchestra: "The patrons, many of them sons and daughters of ranchmen and cowhands, never having seen a leading Negro orchestra in action, could hardly dance for watching the Duke and his musicians dispense their hot numbers, and believe me you they were certainly scorching." *Variety* reported that Paul Short, manager of the Majestic Theater, the Dallas venue where the Calloway and Ellington orchestras played in 1933, "in taking a chance on the two bookings has presumably demonstrated that parts of the South will accept Negro talent."[61]

Whites were not the only ones to have their attitudes challenged because of the presence of the Ellington orchestra; the band also evinced a profound effect on blacks. Blacks in the South could not hope to evade Jim Crow constrictions in the regal manner of the Ellington orchestra, but the mere presence of well-dressed, world-renowned., and accomplished black men, who attracted white paying audiences as well as black, made a lasting impression on blacks living in the "beleaguered segregated communities" where Ellington, Armstrong, Calloway, and Hines played and stayed. Such bands provided a contrasting vision of life for blacks in the South, the great majority of whom endured economic conditions as harsh and nonremunerative as those attending Reconstruction in the 1860s and 1870s. During the Great Depression, most Southern blacks still labored as farmers, mostly as share-croppers or tenant farmers. Only 20 percent of Southern blacks owned their own land, and their yearly wages seldom exceeded $200 (approximately $3,200 in today's dollars).

Ralph Ellison, who saw the Ellington orchestra as a teen in the South during the 1930s, remarked decades later that "they were news from the great wide world; an example and a goal; and I wish that all those who write so knowledgeably of Negro boys having no masculine figures with whom to identify would consider the long national and international career of El-lington and his band, the thousands of one-night stands played in the black communities of this nation." Famous black bands who toured the South in the 1930s "arrived as heroes, as proof that life outside Jim Crow could lead to success," according to historian Burton W. Peretti. "Generally black Southerners embraced jazz as an embodiment of progress."[62] Southern movie distributors edited out scenes featuring black actors and musicians in Hollywood films, and books by Harlem Renaissance writers were seldom available for sale below the Mason-Dixon line, but Ellington and his orches-tra offered living proof of the achievements of African Americans during a period in which Southern blacks were mostly denied a vision of an equal and secure existence.

Shows for exclusively black audiences seemed special occasions for the Ellington orchestra and its promoters, with associations made and emotions expressed that clearly went beyond the usual stage show. A "Special Dance for Colored Only" in Dallas labeled Ellington as the "KING OF JAZZ" (usu-ally Paul Whiteman received this accolade in the mainstream white press of the 1920s and early 1930s) and carried a message of uplift at the bottom of a promotional poster:

> Mr. Ellington is the undisputed originator of Jungle Jazz; which in no way shadows the fact that his band is composed of all educated highly trained musicians. The Duke and his Band are acclaimed by all Americans as one among the very best. Particularly should the race be proud of this Band, its reputation is an emblem of good will . . . You will miss a big event if you fail to hear the Duke, recently returned from Europe with Royal praises.[63]

According to black newspaper reports, Ellington and his orchestra seemed aware of their extramusical importance to the black population, and treated segregated black concerts, including those at black colleges, as especially significant occasions. The band performed at the Houston Colored Junior College on the 1933 tour, where it was noted that Ellington spent extra time talking with numerous students. They also appeared at Tuskegee and Alabama Teachers College when they returned to the South in the spring of 1935. Ralph Ellison attended the show at the former venue and wrote about it decades later. "When I was a student in the music department at Tuskegee, I shook his hand, talked briefly with him of my studies and of my dreams," Ellison remembered. "He was kind and generous even though harassed (there had been some trouble in travel and the band had arrived hours late, with the instruments misplaced and the musicians evil as only tired, black Northern-based musicians could be in the absurdly segregated South of the 1930s), and those of us who talked with him were renewed in our determination to make our names in music." As Omar La-Grange reported in 1933, Ellington established it as a priority that the band played before black as well as white audiences in the segregated South. Though the orchestra became the "first colored attraction to play a [exclusively white] Panhandle Theatre" in Amarillo earlier in the week, Ellington and a local black community leader ensured that the black population was served as well:

> Our people never had a chance to see the band in action until the last night of their engagement here, and that mainly at a midnight show mainly through the efforts of Matthew-Bones-Hooks, Pioneer Negro cowboy, and leading citizen in this part of the country, and when the Duke learned of the situation, he used his influence with his traveling representative . . . with the result that colored people had the entire main floor of the Paramount to themselves. This was not a great deal to brag about for many people resented the fact that they had to wait until the last night and, too, for a mid-night show at that, but it was the best that could be had, and is victory in itself even though small, as Negroes had never before been inside the Paramount Theatre as patrons until the coming of Duke Ellington and his company.
>
> At the mid-night show, they tried to out-do themselves for our people and what a great show . . . Duke dedicated a number to Matthew Hooks, in honor of his tireless efforts in fighting for a chance for us to see and hear this attraction . . . if there is ever a great Negro symphony orchestra, Duke Ellington will have it . . . [his compositions] belong to the classical.[64]

On the 1933 Southern tour, Ellington and Mills devised ways of presenting black music with dignity, as they had done in the North and in Europe, but as had never been accomplished in the South. In keeping with the Mills organization's focus on financial as well as artistic success, the Ellington orchestra garnered significant receipts at the box office, setting a precedent for future tours by African American bands. The tour also succeeded in another key Mills priority: attracting the biggest multiracial audience possible.

Ellington's music and its critical acclaim from 1931 to 1933 acted as a major catalyst for serious critical appreciation of American popular music. Before the mid-1930s, most newspapers featured syndicated columns covering popular music, usually "promos" praising the music purely as entertainment. "Of the many American writings on Jazz, both pro and con, few are knowledgeably critical, none of any instructive value," lamented Roger Pryor Dodge, one of the few academically trained musicians to write about both classical and jazz music, in 1934. "There are magazines and articles in Europe with an attitude toward Jazz as serious music that we [in America] haven't approached."[65]

Down Beat and *Metronome* took up the challenge of coming up with an American answer to the more scholarly approach of the English critics who praised Ellington on his European tour. They also included a generous dollop of social activism in their pages, especially on issues of racial equality. *Down Beat* premiered in 1934, headed by young, mostly upper-class whites like John Hammond and Helen Oakley, who schooled themselves in black music and culture at a time when no serious books were yet extant. As music historian David Stowe pointed out, no previous magazine accorded so much attention to black music. Besides music reportage, they also took pride in promoting racial harmony and racial mixing, on and off stage. In the pages of *Down Beat,* wrote Stowe, "Music was depicted as the ultimate American melting pot," an area where "talent alone" was the basis of critical judgment, "not the color of one's skin." Until the 1930s, the decades-old *Metronome* magazine had been a humdrum publication emphasizing classical music and the more saccharine forms of popular white music until jazz enthusiasts Leonard Feather (yet another Brit), George Simon, and Barry Ulanov (Ellington's first biographer) took it over and focused it upon the big band scene. Feather bragged that the firm anti–Jim Crow stands of both magazines threatened a public backlash and loss of sales, but that the policy would not be withdrawn.

While both *Down Beat* and *Metronome* were owned and written by whites for an audience of mostly whites, they still represented a signal phenomenon. In their pages, artists like Ellington, Count Basie, Lunceford, and Armstrong were celebrated as they had rarely been elsewhere in the United States, with witty, intelligent, and argumentative prose. The birth of *Down Beat* and the revamped *Metronome* also provided a more powerful role for American critics. Before, record companies and radio stations alone controlled the flow of music and decided which artists received the most airplay, promotion money, and store display. After the emergence of the two new publications, critics weighed in as well, bringing a more artistic aesthetic to bear on the popular-music marketplace. But many times, extended discussions in the magazine also revolved around which band was the hottest, or which band inspired more abandon in dancers—not every popular record or group could be intellectualized; most could not withstand the scrutiny, or had no interest in doing so. By the late 1930s, most newspapers featured their own critics, who at least attempted to imitate the intellectual spin on popular and jazz music that proved so popular and influential in *Down Beat* and *Metronome.* As music professor Joseph McLaren has pointed out, several post-1933 books also adopted the new, more serious critical aesthetic concerning jazz music.[66]

The music, marketing, and manner of Ellington set into play a jarring and long-needed shift in the cultural hierarchies that exalted European classical music as high art and disdained popular American and African American forms. Before Copland and Ives rose to national prominence,[67] Ellington inspired a reevaluation of American and black music, fueling schools of music criticism on both sides of the Atlantic in the 1930s. By 1936, *The Gramophone Record Shop Encyclopedia of Recorded Music,* which did not usually cover nonclassical artists, found it proper to compare Ellington's "orchestral ingenuities" with those of Strauss and Rimsky-Korsakoff. In the same year, Copland cited Ellington—his first public acknowledgement of a jazz musician—as part of a lecture on the use of tone color in a course he taught at the New School for Social Research in New York. In a 1938 review, he praised Ellington as a "composer" and "the master of them all," speaking in terms of the big bands of the day.[68] Old stereotypes and hierarchies, cultural and racial, still stood, but on increasingly shaky foundations.

In the last few decades, some scholars have argued that the bebop musicians of the 1940s first transformed jazz, in the eyes of the musicians and their audiences, into an art form.[69] Certainly, many bebop musicians were accomplished artists. But more important for these scholars, many of them took on modern and stereotypical attributes of artists: the rebelliousness, the avant-garde aesthetic, the self-destructive substance abuse, the overtly political, the noncommercial, the insistence on a generational newness, among others. A prejudice often surfaces in American culture that entertainment and high culture cannot coexist. Because Ellington never denounced the role of entertainer for the role of artist (and in fact seemed to relish both), because he never embraced an avant-garde or self-sacrificing

artistic identity, because his disposition was consistently genial and upbeat, many observers have taken him less seriously as an artist, in his time
and in our own time. But when one examines the work, the influence, and
the history behind Ellington's achievements, little doubt can exist as to the
originator of an artistic aesthetic in jazz at the popular international level.
Numerous bebop musicians and their critical advocates have championed
Ellington in this role.[70]

Even more important, Ellington forwarded and proved American music as worthy of serious appreciation and study. With painstakingly gathered folkloric evidence, Constance Rourke convincingly suggested in 1930
that African American culture represented the central and most significant
American cultural contribution. Ellington, through his work and his carefully cultivated image, represented that vision to the world in a tangible and
affecting form that could not be denied. Ellington offered convincing evidence that American music could offer something original and lasting, even
though earlier works by composers such as Anthony Heinrich, Ives, and Joplin, among others, should have tipped off critics years before. But those
artists did not have the marketing tools and access to the mass media that
Ellington enjoyed. Following World War II, American music, along with
American literature and art, would be more frequently and seriously studied and reviewed both in the United States and abroad. Ellington's work
in the 1930s proved significant in presaging and inspiring this cultural shift.

4

CREDITS/ EXIT MILLS

Duke Ellington and [fellow Mills client] Cab Calloway are owned body and soul by Massa Irving Mills . . . The avenue crowd conjures up fancy lives on fat bank rolls for the members of these two outfits.

The truth of it is that . . . Duke Ellington is just a musical sharecropper. He has been drawing [an] account . . . At the end of the year when Massa Mills's cotton has been laid by, Duke is told that he owes them hundreds of thousands of dollars. He owns the monicker [sic] of Vice President of Mills Inc. and is entitled to a percentage of profits. However, his lawyer and accountant happen to be Mills personal employees. When they finish totaling, there ain't no profits left . . .

The Negro has sharecropped too long. Independence, even if it means straining, is the only way out. The boss who puts his arm around you and says you're just like a son to him may not burn a pin in your back, but he burns a permanent bite in your salary check. We don't want any more paternalism in our jobs, we want a chance and a fair wage and we'll take care of the rest. REV. ADAM CLAYTON POWELL, JR.,
famed Harlem political figure, 1936

Duke was a very much exploited man in [the 1930s] . . . Duke got pretty bad treatment considering the amount of money he made for other people . . . even though he was being treated very badly financially, [Ellington] still considered himself lucky. This gives you a little bit of the idea of what show business was like in this country, although Duke got as much social recognition as any band had gotten. JOHN HAMMOND, 1965 interview

We dissolved our business relationship agreeably, and in spite of how much he made on me, I respected the way [Mills] had operated. He had preserved the dignity of my name. Duke Ellington has an unblemished image, and that is the most anybody can do for anybody.

DUKE ELLINGTON, from his 1973 autobiography[1]

Various problems and conflicts emerged within the Ellington/Mills partnership during the 1930s before it finally terminated amicably in the spring of 1939. Mills's increasing power and contacts especially helped his newer clients, but their significance for the already established Ellington and fellow Mills client Cab Calloway was probably more mixed. In the fall of 1933, Mills became talent scout, advisor, and record producer for RCA Victor Records. Almost immediately, he secured and signed RCA recording contracts for Calloway, Ellington, and the Mills Blue Rhythm Band. Mills retained competing financial interests in the deal as the manager, publisher, and recording executive in charge of the acts. A glaring conflict of interest existed. How could major artists like Calloway and Ellington ensure that they received the best deal their reputations deserved when their manager received percentages of their record company royalties and fees, as well as executive compensation from the same company? Mills had loyalties to all parties in the transactions. A year later, Mills switched his record company loyalties to Brunswick, taking all of his artists with him.[2]

Mills tended to make the record deals for his artists in bulk, making his position with both the artists and the companies paramount, giving him even more financial and artistic power. But he also may have compromised the already weak bargaining positions of his black recording artists in the process. With Mills wielding ultimate power in the deals, a Mills artist probably had little choice but to accept Mills's choice of company and terms. Still, considering his record in making black artists successful, such risks were offset by the outsized chances for success he brought to the table. Being their manager, his artists' successes were tied to him anyway. But throughout his career, Ellington preferred to be viewed and dealt with as an individual and a top priority in any managing or recording situation. Mills's dealing en masse with his clients may have seemed too pedestrian of a treatment for Ellington, aside from the economic and ethical problems.

More than any other manager of the period, Mills made sure his name was linked in trade publications with the artists he managed. It marked a concerted effort to establish himself as the leading source of the most exciting artists from the world of black entertainment. Both Mills and his firm were usually conspicuously mentioned in major Ellington ads in trade publications like *Billboard* and *Variety*. His name appeared as prominently as Ellington's in the credits for the 1929 film short *Black and Tan*. In clippings from 1930, Mills, not the Ellington orchestra, received mention in headlines for brief stories concerning the band's activities on the West Coast. A 1931 review of a new Ellington release described it as "a characteristic Irving Mills recording." Mills was mentioned repeatedly in gossip column reports as accompanying Ellington on his return from Europe in 1933. In an article previewing the Ellington orchestra's upcoming Southern tour, the *Dallas News* filled up most of the latter half of the story with an account of Mills's career, even including a sidebar in letters twice as large as the font used in the piece that advertised "Irving Mills Management." "Thus has Irving Mills charted cleverly the career of his negro protege," the article concluded. "The success of it is a tremendous testitmonial [*sic*] to the impresario's judgment. Ellington's ability to deliver is, however, also worth mentioning."[3]

Mills's most visible presence in the mass media came during his role in a 1933 Paramount short featuring promotional snippets of his three most famous bands. In the short, Mills introduced segments of (in order) the Mills Blue Rhythm Band and the orchestras of Ellington and Calloway. Though the band performances take up most of the four-minute, fifteen-second running time, Mills seemed to have been viewed as the film's main attraction by both Paramount Studios and gossip columnists. According to Klaus Stratemann's research, the studio, in its paperwork for the production, titled the segment "Irving Mills." And Nat Presser, in his syndicated column, previewed it by saying that "Irving Mills, head of the artists bureau bearing his name, will appear in a Par[amount] short."[4] Mills did not exude star quality in his film appearance and looked nervous, awkwardly relying on a cue sheet on his desk. But the clip clearly portrayed Mills's wish to be viewed as a black-entertainment impresario. In dozens of hours of promotional films for 1930s and 1940s popular and jazz music performers housed in the Ernie Smith Film Collection at the Smithsonian, one never sees any other manager on screen besides Mills.

For Ellington and the rest of the stable of Mills artists, Mills's notoriety and power within the industry guaranteed maximum coverage for their careers. But, after a while, especially for an artist as serious and individual as Ellington, being seen as a Mills "protégé," at least in the eyes of the music industry, meant that he was not seen as his own person, apart from the Mills personality and publicity machine. Also, Mills seems to have been less able to visualize and promote careers like Ellington's that did not adhere to the usual show business formulas. These are probably two of the largely unspoken reasons Ellington went off on his own at the end of the decade.

Despite the many positive attributes of the Ellington/Mills partnership, one major negative aspect existed, though Ellington never expressed dissatisfaction about it in public, and possibly it did not bother him at all. According to most sources, Mills took unwarranted writing credit for Ellington compositions. During his tenure with Mills, Ellington generally wrote only instrumentals (though he would pen some of his own lyrics starting in the 1940s). When a tune showed commercial promise, Mills provided a lead sheet of the melody to one of the stable of lyric writers under contract to Mills Music. Sometimes he gave the lyricist credit, but often he claimed it for himself.

According to Steven Lasker, an Ellington scholar and archivist, a particularly divisive conflict occurred between Mills and Mitchell Parish, who wrote the lyrics to the Ellington classic "Mood Indigo." Mills received the credit for them, along with substantial royalties over the decades. Herb Jeffries, a vocalist with the band in the late 1930s and early 1940s, worked for Mills Music in the mid-1930s. He left when Mills tried to buy him out of a composition, "I Left a Good Deal in Mobile," that Mills felt had commercial promise. "I wouldn't go for it, and so he took it and published it, but he put his name on it, and he never wrote nothing on it at all." Jeffries recalled that Mills "did that a lot. He would change one word in it. Instead of 'so,' he would put 'that,' or whatever, you know, and change it, and say 'I don't like this' and change it, so then he'd put his name on it, that made him co-writer"—in Mills's opinion, not in Jeffries's. Writers outside the Ellington circle harbored similar complaints. In a 1980 interview, Nat "King" Cole's wife Maria said that Nat called Mills "a thief" for giving him $50 outright and no royalties for his 1944 hit "Straighten up and Fly Right," to which Mills made no creative contribution. Cole brought a lawsuit against Mills to regain ownership of his song later in the decade, but it went nowhere.

Such arrangements were viewed as common practice, especially with a publisher as well connected and powerful as Mills. Numerous sources feel, however, that Mills was more liberal in assuming such credit than any one else in the business.[5] Parish, a contracted songwriter at Mills Music in 1930, received a regular paycheck from the company. If Mills decided not to give credit to Parish for a lyric written while Parish was under his employ (technically called a "work for hire"), no legal stipulation existed to prevent him from doing so. According to songwriter Gerald Marks, who co-wrote the standard "All of Me" in the 1920s, publishers placed their name on songs they did not compose for "the advice" given to a songwriter or for the privilege of having one's song placed with a powerful publisher that could bring the tune national attention. Not only publishers, but also bandleaders like Guy Lombardo and vocalists like Al Jolson engaged in such practices. "Al Jolson, when he died, left a tremendous catalog of songs with his name on them in ASCAP, and I doubt if Jolson ever wrote a word or a note, but he did get that credit for singing the songs, usually for introducing them, and making many of them hits," recalled Marks. "That's the way [Jolson] got paid off by the songwriter, was by having his name on the song." "Irving always had his name on [almost any composition published by Mills Music], and without Irving, nobody would get any royalties at all," Helen Oakley Dance stated in 1989. She added that Mills underwrote recording sessions for many of those same songs. Marks suggested that this assumption of authorship occurred more frequently with African American writers since they experienced more trouble breaking into the industry than whites, and therefore had to be more willing to give up some royalties in exchange for obtaining a foothold in the business. However, most of the lyricists who have claimed lyrics for which Mills officially took credit—including Parish, Irving Gordon, and Edmund Anderson—were white.[6]

Perhaps what Mills took could be termed as an "editor's credit"—less a literal authoring than an essential role in the process leading to the finished song that emerged in the marketplace. In 1981, he claimed that he titled all of Ellington's songs. "I'm sure they [Mills and Ellington] must have had some kind of arrangements," Paul Mills surmised. "I can't tell you for a fact what they were, but I know that my father wrote a lot of the lyrics, not only with Duke, but with a lot of other people. Duke himself acknowledges that [Irving Mills] was the writer, so who is anyone to say he's not?" It should be noted that none of the sources consulted in this study, including Paul Mills, recall seeing Irving Mills actually writing lyrics for Ellington songs or being on the "commercial floor" at Mills Music with the other songwriters working on lyrics. There exists no record of Ellington verbally giving credit to Mills for lyrics written for his songs or recalling Mills's lyrical contributions. Irving Mills also took writing credit for some of the most lucrative Ellington instrumentals of the 1930s (including "The Mooche," "Rockin' in Rhythm," and "Braggin' in Brass," among many others), which, as with the situation concerning lyrics, no source directly confirms, and is highly dubious.

Yet it should be noted that Ellington never disputed Mills's credits. Helen Oakley Dance wrote that Ellington "defended [Mills's] views on the subject [of song credits] and was not among his detractors." To her, people like John

Hammond and Rev. Adam Clayton Powell, Jr., were underestimating the intelligence and insight of Ellington when they aggressively told him to extricate himself from a situation that was supposedly cheating him:

> Duke was never taken advantage of, in his life, as far as I know. He always knew the score and he could always maneuver so the score was suitable. He needed an Irving Mills. That's what people don't realize . . . John [Hammond] went [to Ellington] and said "My dear Duke, you must disengage yourself from this bloodsucker," and so on. Duke didn't appreciate unsought-for advice from anybody.
>
> You see, Duke was a very sophisticated man and a very knowledgeable man. In the end, he broke from Irving [because] he was so launched that he could make it on his own. He had performed miracles for Irving too, which Irving knew. Irving had a music company which was chock-a-block full of Ellington compositions which would last him his lifetime . . . So when people all came to Duke and said "You're being taken advantage of," Duke just smiled because it was a mutual affair. He needed Irving . . . It was just an ironic smile on Duke's face, people were talking about things that they didn't know what they were talking about. He wasn't being taken advantage of at all.[7]

To the end of his life, Ellington never complained or said anything publicly concerning the arrangement. For decades after leaving Mills, he praised Mills's guidance and actions as invaluable to his career. Maurice Lawrence enjoyed a close personal friendship with Ellington beginning in the late 1930s, and was called "number two son" by Ellington. Because of their twenty-year age difference, Lawrence looked to Ellington as a mentor. In the 1950s, Lawrence asked the maestro about his relationship with Mills because he felt surprised that Ellington was "not disgruntled" about it. Lawrence, with anger rising in his voice, asked Ellington, "'Why in the devil, when you found out what was done to you,' Mills coauthoring all his compositions, drawing royalties, plus also simultaneously drawing an agent's fee, double dipping, and I says, you know, 'why didn't you blow the whistle?'" Ellington replied that he could have blown the whistle, but then he "would have been blackballed in Tin Pan Alley." Lawrence said that what Ellington meant was that once he betrayed Mills publicly, the tastemakers and power players of the music industry

> would literally destroy you with rumors and innuendo in the press. Instead of getting favorable reviews, everything would be downhill after that. Remember the time, you know, everything was vicious. Competition was keen between whites and blacks . . . what [Ellington was] saying then, is that he

could have come and out and announced 'I've been had,' and blah blah blah, but then when they got through doing a job on him, I don't think he would have been the person he is today.

With five words, "it wouldn't gain me anything," Ellington summed up for Lawrence his position on the so-called controversy and why he had no desire to out Mills. Instead, Ellington used what Mills had taught him about the business for the rest of his career. Lawrence said the situation with Mills inspired Ellington to "start assembling a new library. That's when he did all that prolific writing between him and Strayhorn" during the next stage of his career.[8] Complaining and whining were never part of the Ellington palette; instead, less than two years after leaving Mills, he began his own publishing company, ensuring his future songs showed proper credit, and earned him more money than ever.

The situation described by Dance and Lawrence provides a valuable glance into the inner workings of a man who usually only displayed a warm smile and standard public-relations patter to the world, and rarely expressed deep personal feelings or anger. Though his relentlessly upbeat manner doubtless reflected happiness and satisfaction in playing his music, the smile also had a protective function. It helped keep the public focus on the music and away from the divisiveness, prejudice, and violence that had historically marked associations between blacks and whites. Becoming publicly angry would not have helped Ellington recover the millions of dollars in royalties Mills garnered in his name, but it easily could have marred Ellington's image and kept him from being supported by the public and the industry. White bandleaders Benny Goodman and Artie Shaw regularly shot off vituperative public ripostes at the allegedly greedy and overcommercialized powers-that-be in the music industry, but Ellington's position, despite his international fame, was more precarious because of his race. Any anger he expressed could be turned back against him in a much more brutal and unforgiving manner. Ellington's situation was not unlike Jackie Robinson's: Branch Rickey, in 1947, picked Jackie Robinson to integrate baseball's major leagues because of the strength of his character, his extensive experience and comfort with whites, and his ability to control his temper in the face of taunting racists.[9] Unfortunately, such prerequisites were necessary for blacks wishing to attain significant public careers in the United States before the 1960s.

Black celebrities in the 1930s and 1940s who angrily denounced American racism, such as Josephine Baker and Paul Robeson, found that their ability to have a career in the United States dropped precipitously, forcing them to base their careers in Europe.[10] Ellington existed on the front lines of a racist society, moving against its strictures in his own way, openly celebrating and documenting black culture and history. His activism was cultural, artistic, and significant, but it was not overtly political. A few members of the black community protested bravely and made political statements in this pre-1955 period; Ellington, Robinson, and writers like Langston Hughes, by contrast, skillfully represented what blacks could contribute to the world, their undeniable humanity. Both roles were essential to the African American struggle for equality, and both roles extended the possibilities for blacks in American society.

Robin D. G. Kelley, among other historians, has pointed out the need for historians to look beyond "mainstream" civil rights organizations such as the NAACP and the Urban League in order to depict the complete picture of black resistance to discrimination and violence. Ellington's brand of activism, based on his black middle-class Washington, D.C., upbringing, demonstrated that those who were quiet on political issues could also push the boundaries of racism and black participation at the higher reaches of society and culture. Ellington's approach was infiltration and circumvention, not confrontation.[11]

Because of widespread prejudice and stereotyping, businessmen and advocates like Mills were needed as intermediaries for African Americans (even more than they were needed for whites) to help them navigate and become successful within the burgeoning mass media. Fletcher Henderson, Ellington's main black competition in New York City in the late 1920s, had become a virtual nonentity in the national music scene by the early 1930s, mainly because he refused to hire a manager. Unlike Ellington, Henderson had no advocate to push for his development and creative freedom in the music industry. When Henderson wished to write and perform waltzes and other nonrace material, he was denied the opportunity because such genres were not within the "hot" and "torrid" standards that the music business expected from black artists, and he had no one to back him up. Ellington was well aware of the essential advantages of aggressive professional representation. In a 1965 article, he reminisced about a talented pianist in the 1920s named Stephen Henderson (unrelated to Fletcher Henderson), also known as "The Beetle." "He never played anywhere in particular, he didn't play regularly, or in other words he didn't have good management, like some of us have been lucky to have," he wrote. "A whole lot of great talent has been channeled down the drain, you know, because of lack of management."

As the Henderson experiences (both Fletcher and Stephen) illustrated, few blacks broke through to national prominence in the pre–civil rights era without the assistance and muscle of white entrepreneurs. Because Mills handled the recording, film, and booking deals for Ellington, the musician never had to deal directly with the racism of the industry on the managerial level. This not only represented relief from an ugly burden, but it also freed up time for Ellington to spend on music-making. Mills shepherded and protected Ellington through the highest levels of the music business, where blacks had rarely traveled previously. Rickey provided roughly the same function for Robinson in baseball in the 1940s, as Joe Glaser did for Louis Armstrong in the 1930s, and as Carl Van Vechten did for Langston Hughes in the publishing world of the 1920s. These black men yearned for and deserved the largest multiracial audience possible, and they realized they could not achieve such fame unless they had, as Armstrong biographer Laurence Bergreen put it, a "white protector."[12]

Mills played an essential role in establishing Ellington as a world-famous celebrity, the first African American to be marketed as a serious composer in the mass media, and "the best paid ASCAP Negro composer in America." No wonder, John Hammond wrote, "Duke had a great feeling of loyalty to Irving Mills." He added that "I think Ellington felt it was his business and nobody else's that he would go along with whatever it took to repay Mills." Mills also helped create a situation that allowed Ellington to transcend the usual constraints African Americans faced in the business world. According to historian Juliet E. K. Walker, "the history of black business in America is primarily one of small enterprises" because of blacks' long-term inability to access large amounts of credit and capital due to discrimination. This forced blacks to rely on "the self-help tradition" to initiate business enterprises, thereby limiting their size and growth potential. In contrast, the reputation Ellington made during the Mills era would aid him in his future business and music endeavors. By 1939, Ellington possessed advantages that most other black businessmen could only dream of: ready access to banks, lawyers, and the ability to fund his business projects with a steady income stream of royalties instead of having to raise capital in a difficult business environment.[13]

The issue of song credits also became controversial between Ellington and some of his band members during the 1930s. Many people point out, including several Ellington band members, that Ellington sometimes took primary credit for arranging, embellishing, or completing a brief musical phrase originally thought out by an Ellington band member, who sometimes received credit and sometimes did not.[14] "A lot of the things that Ellington had his name on [in the 1930s] started with one of the [band members] who worked with Duke," recalled Paul Mills. "Duke was in a position to get it recorded, so Duke's name went on it. He made the arrangement and all, but the original idea was [by] one of the sidemen. So, it was not uncommon for that to happen."

In the earliest days of the band, from roughly 1925 to 1935, the band was very tight, personally as well as musically, and ideas flowed freely. Many contributed to writing and arranging new pieces, encouraged by Ellington. Louis Metcalf, a band member during the 1927–28 period, recalled the band working especially hard because of the musical competition they felt from Fletcher Henderson's band across town. "Sometimes we'd have a rehearsal after working 'til three, three-thirty," Metcalf said decades later. "Then we'd go get a drink and have a sandwich, and 'Man, let's go back and straighten out those numbers.' Sometimes Duke would say, 'Man, I've got a date with a chick,' and we'd say 'Come on, it won't take long' . . . and that's the feeling the band had toward one another." In 1933, *Metronome* observed this scene: "After the last show is over, the band reassembles in the rehearsal room, if the theatre has one, and if not, on the stage. If Duke Ellington has an idea for a tune, the men sit in with him until he finishes it, accepting criticisms and suggestions from each." Helen Oakley Dance, who witnessed and produced many Ellington recording sessions during the 1930s, described a typical session:

Nothing was written. Nothing was even approached before you entered the studio . . . Nobody had any idea what they were going to do. Probably not Ellington either . . . that's why I say those days . . . were fruitful, creative. And so, what Duke would do, you see, he called on, without calling by name, he called on his special guys. Now you could always call on [Johnny] Hodges [on alto saxophone], 'cause Hodges was an absolute song factory. You know, he just floated out . . . those beautiful phrases and concepts . . . Duke—there was always his idea, you couldn't praise people. You couldn't afford to praise people, because they'd up their money, you see. You'd have to pay ten dollars more. Barney [Bigard, on clarinet] was like that, too. They were all like that. And so, Duke wouldn't bat an eye. You know, you got to know Duke, so when that nothing face was on, you knew that he was already inside . . . And so, he'd grab some Hodges there, eight bars and repeat, then the middle would be, possibly Tricky [Joe Nanton, the trombonist]. And, of course, Tricky always had his bottle by his side, and he wouldn't have cared if you stole [his idea] outright from him, you know.

Several Ellington orchestra members from the period felt that Ellington's supposedly liberal taking of songwriting credit spoiled the camaraderie of the band that existed in its earliest days. Cootie Williams, who played trumpet for the band throughout the 1930s, recalled everyone feeling free to pitch in with the writing in the earlier part of the decade. "It was a pleasure, you know, to have the band play your song . . . that's the reason we did it," Williams said in 1976. But "people stopped doing things like that because they weren't paid for them properly." Long-time band trombonist Lawrence Brown described "Sophisticated Lady" as "one of those where everybody jumps in and helps out," particularly himself and Otto Hardwicke. Barney Bigard and Sonny Greer held similar memories of the song's genesis. "We didn't even care. We were just doing something that we wanted to do," Brown remembered. Brown and Juan Tizol both mentioned that several Hodges melodies were transformed into hits by Ellington (such as "Don't Get Around Much Anymore" and "I Let a Song Go out of My Heart"), who didn't always assign credit to Hodges. For decades, when such songs were played on the bandstand, Hodges would roll his fingers at Ellington, making the universal sign for money, nonverbally complaining about the lack of royalties on his creation.

But a close examination at the wealth of oral history on this subject paints a more nuanced portrait of the Ellington orchestra's songwriting credits. With "Sophisticated Lady," according to Bigard, "Duke made a tune out of . . . [Brown and Hardwicke's] fooling around in the dressing room. He didn't give the guys credit . . . for what they did . . . [Ellington] composed some good numbers too. Give him that credit, but give the boys credit for what they did." Clark Terry, a band member from the 1950s who is friendly with band members from all generations of Ellington personnel, also spoke about Ellington's talent in this area:

> This thing that Barney Bigard used to play, [Ellington] made a tune of that, "Mood Indigo," that Barney used to warm up [his instrument] . . . And Cootie did [hums melody of "Do Nothing 'til You Hear from Me"], Cootie warmed up on that. [Ellington] took these things and made tunes out of them. A lot of guys get the wrong idea. They say, 'Well, he stole from these guys.' But these guys, that's as far as it would have ever gotten, [the melody just] would have been a tune-up. He didn't know where to go from there . . . it was a great facility [on Ellington's part] to make something out of what would possibly have been nothing.

In separate interviews, Terry and baritone saxophonist Harry Carney called Ellington a "great compiler" of ideas. Brown called Ellington a "compiler" as well but not in the same positive light. He called compiling "the basis of the operation" in the band, particularly during the 1930s, and when Brown, who had a tempestuous relationship with Ellington, called Ellington a compiler more than a composer in this period, Ellington's "ego boiled over."

Though the band members generally give credit to Ellington for having the talent to transform their instrumental fillips into hit singles, the financial details still rankled. Ellington had learned the ins and outs of the publishing business from Mills and applied them to his dealings with the band's melodic contributions. "I wrote a couple of things and sold them outright [to Mills] too, real early. That was before the '30s when I sold. I didn't sell anything in the '30s," Ellington recalled, laughing. In the 1930s, Ellington band members received cash up front for their contributions, usually $25 or $50, forfeiting potential royalties and sometimes songwriter credit. According to Bigard, band members were initially satisfied with this financial arrangement, "and then Irving Mills would have his name on it and he didn't write the first note or nothing." When some of the songs they signed away royalties for became hits, "the boys . . . began to get wise, and then there was a different story altogether," but by then "it was too late," the hits were written, registered for copyright, out in the marketplace, and earning thousands. "That was pretty smart, you know, because nobody else did ever do things like that," Bigard mused decades later. "Duke studied all his men." In 1978, Bigard claimed that he wrote the first part and the bridge of "Mood Indigo," that Ellington gave him $25 for his contribution, and that Bigard did not get credit and royalties until twenty-eight years later when he threatened to sue. Bigard didn't blame Ellington and Mills "because that's their business," yet he also felt that "they tricked me."

Juan Tizol initially received $25 for contributing the main melody of "Caravan," one of the band's most enduring hits. "Later in years, [Ellington] decided to give me a percentage on the composition," Tizol said in 1978. "Because I sold it outright [to Irving Mills], I didn't have no business getting nothing." Yet Tizol also recalled that Ellington wrote the bridge for "Caravan" and arranged the tune for the orchestra, and that Ellington did the same work for other Tizol songs. Songs Tizol contributed to were usually credited to him during the 1940s. Cootie Williams shared a similar experience with "Concerto for Cootie," a 1940 composition and recording regarded as one of the band's all-time best. Ellington bought the main melodic hook from Williams for a $25 flat fee after he practically begged Ellington to, and Williams felt it wouldn't be right to ask for royalties after that. When a lyric by Bob Russell was added to the song, it became "Do Nothing 'til You Hear from Me," one of the band's biggest singles ever. Williams saw none of the royalties. He sounded aggrieved in a 1976 interview, yet he also acknowledged that Ellington wrote the verse, the bridge, and arranged it. The original version of the song represented a finely tailored solo vehicle for Williams, showcasing his talent and range as perhaps no other piece ever did. It made Williams's reputation as a premiere soloist in the jazz world. Ellington took a lot from his band members, but he gave them things they could never have come close to achieving without him. As Bigard maintained, Ellington closely studied his men, not just so he could garner songwriting ideas, but also so his arranging would compliment their prodigious talents.

Should Ellington have been more generous in assigning credits? Perhaps. But everything he did in this regard fit snugly within the context of the music business of the time, and, according to the available evidence, band members often preferred guaranteed money upfront than a potentially big score down the line, and sometimes they paid the price for that gamble. Just as Mills extracted a price in taking unwarranted publishing credits from Ellington in exchange for managing him and bringing him to mass popularity, so did Ellington extract a price from his band members for his ability and power to fashion lasting excellence from tossed-off musical phrases. Tizol showed Ellington everything he wrote while he was in the band, and felt "thankful" that Ellington could get his work recorded, despite the fact that he felt financially slighted by Ellington's assigning of credits during the 1930s. Without Ellington, the men of the orchestra would probably not have reached the musical heights and international popularity they enjoyed, even jazz legends like Bigard and Hodges. The situation was certainly not fair, but Ellington and Mills knew that any of them could ultimately be replaced (and were replaced over the years), and the band would continue to achieve and soar. But there was no replacing Ellington and the myriad gifts he brought to the fore. Ellington's writing partner and close friend Billy Strayhorn, who joined the band in the late 1930s, provided the most eloquent take on this situation when asked in 1962 about the rumor that Ellington relied more on band members' castoffs than original composition:

But how do you explain the constant flow of songs? Guys come in and out of the band, but the songs keep getting written, and you can always tell an Ellington song.

Anyway, something like a solo, perhaps only a few notes, is hardly a composition. It may be the inspiration, but what do they say about 10 percent inspiration and 90 percent perspiration? Composing is work.

So this guy says you and he wrote it, but he thinks he wrote it. He thinks you just put it down on paper. But what you did was put it down on paper, harmonized it, straightened out the bad phrases, and added things to it, so you could hear the finished product. Now, really, who wrote it?

It was ever thus.

But the proof is that these people don't go somewhere else and write beautiful music. You don't hear anything else from them. You do from Ellington.

Though they each spent significant time away from the Ellington orchestra during their careers, Bigard, Brown, Hodges, and Tizol never wrote a hit song apart from the ones that Ellington turned into full-fledged arrangements and songs. Except for Hodges, none of them made attempts to write songs. During World War II and afterward, Ellington composed in a more solitary manner with far less input from the orchestra.

There are many stories surrounding the end of the Ellington/Mills partnership in 1939. Most accounts center on the fact that Ellington felt he no longer received the same amount of attention from Mills.[15] The stable of talent at Mills Artists had grown considerably since Ellington became the first client of the company in 1926, and Mills spent far less of his time with the Ellington band than in past days.

Indeed, by 1939, the Mills organization that engineered the worldwide fame of Ellington, his orchestra, and his compositions had changed drastically. Mills delegated key decisions and functions concerning the Ellington orchestra, preferring to concentrate on building a multifaceted empire of publishing, film, recording, and management deals. In addition to the stable of black artists he managed, in 1935 he also began promoting the careers of European artists such as Bert Ambrose and West Indian composer Reginald Foresythe. None became as successful, artistically or financially, as the Ellington orchestra. Ned Williams, the main force behind the 1931 press manual that established Ellington's more serious post–Cotton Club image, left Mills's employ in 1935, causing publicity surrounding Ellington to lose much of the zip and consistency it once had. In 1937, the Mills organization ceased booking dance dates for its acts, outsourcing them to Consolidated Radio Artists, who, in return for the business, allowed Mills to record CRA artists for his newly instituted labels Master and Variety, which were funded and distributed by the American Record Company (ARC). The deal included Mills's own recording studio in New York City, and seemed constructed to take advantage of the burgeoning record sales of the Swing Era and to create a recording-business empire to complement Mills's publishing and managing interests. Within weeks of the announcement of the CRA,

Master, and Variety deals, Mills had supervised over thirty artists recording 165 songs, including the initial sessions for an ongoing and delightful series of Ellington small band recordings produced by Helen Oakley Dance.

Though Ellington's success made much of Mills's industry power possible, Mills could not be expected to concentrate solely on one client, particularly on a client whose interests over time were not as unified with his as they were years before. According to a *Down Beat* article detailing the Ellington/Mills split, Mills had sold back his stock in Duke Ellington, Inc., in 1937, giving Mills less financial impetus to work on furthering Ellington's career.[16] Mills's profits on Ellington's publishing from the 1926–39 period, however, were guaranteed and continue to this day for his heirs.

Dance also recalled that Mills hired an accountant named Charlie Weintraub at this time, whom she called "the first" of the "bottom-line men" who came to occupy the major music business organizations of the Swing Era. Weintraub knew nothing of the music and concerned himself solely with cash-flow issues, vetoing any project that did not look like a moneymaker in the short term, although Mills had final say. The Ellington small band sessions that Dance produced serve as an excellent example of the limitations of the "bottom-line" economic philosophy applied to the music business. Weintraub immediately tabled the idea when it came up at a Mills Artists meeting, knowing that such sessions were not commonly done and would probably not produce a huge seller. But Ellington immediately liked the idea, according to Dance, from an artistic standpoint and a financial one, and so did Mills, who was looking for material to release on his new Master and Variety labels. With one exception, the eighty-eight tracks recorded produced no hit singles, but they are among the most charming of Ellington recordings, showcasing what Ellington and the band could pull off in an impromptu setting. They sold steadily, but not spectacularly, for decades, adding to the coffers of Mills Music, Ellington the songwriter, and the record labels involved. The "bottom-line" short-term thinking of men like Weintraub may have led to better quarterly reports for a time, but that formulaic, conservative approach also probably helped speed the artistic and financial demise of the Swing Era. The impulses that inspire the public to support certain musical artists are not as predictable as those that dictate sales of consumer products, like refrigerators. The onset of such conservative business thinking at Mills Artists probably provided another reason Ellington sought more artistic freedom than he enjoyed with Mills. Ellington always found ways to balance artistic and financial concerns. Both needed to be addressed in order for Ellington to enjoy success on the terms he wanted. According to Dance, he "was never governed by the 'make money' bit, but he was only too glad if [money] came in under one of his musical ideas."[17]

There were various tensions in the Ellington/Mills relationship that seemed to come to a head one afternoon in the late winter or spring of 1939. Ellington, according to the Barry Ulanov biography, explained diplomatically that he went into Mills's office, asked to examine some of the accounting books, and then walked out, never to return as a Mills client. Long-time band member Otto Hardwicke told Maurice Lawrence that Ellington "asked to see the books unannounced, and he spent several hours [with them]. And when he got through, he got up, took a heavy sigh, and said 'oh well,' shrugged his shoulders, and put that camel hair coat across his shoulders, and walked out." H. Robert Udkoff, Ellington's close friend for almost four decades, provided more details:

> One day, Ellington just walked into [the Mills office] and wanted to look at the books. His mother had passed away [four years] prior to that and . . . he was very devoted to his mother . . . and he asked Irving to buy the most expensive casket available, and that's what he wanted his mother buried in. It was many years later that he found this out. Anyway, Irving told him that he had paid $5,000 for the casket, and Ellington found when he examined the books . . . that he paid $3,500, and that stuck in his mind, and he didn't trust him from that point on. That is the gospel truth as to why he split with Mills. There may have been other motivating factors, but that was the prime one.

Record producer Brad McCuen and Mercer Ellington have surmised that Ellington's examination of the books may also have revealed the true extent of the enormity of Mills's profits from Ellington's career, which may have accelerated Ellington's desire to strike out on his own with management that owned less of his career proceeds. Both McCuen and Mercer Ellington recall having conversations with Ellington in which he noted how "shocked" he was by how much more Robbins Music, his publishing company following Mills Music, paid him in royalties compared to Mills. Robbins did not assign song credits to company executives who had no role in the writing of a song.[18]

While a loss of trust contributed to the Ellington/Mills split, issues of musical direction were almost certainly involved as well. In a 1952 article, Mills claimed that "when I withdrew from my managerial relationship with Duke [all other sources portray Ellington as the one withdrawing], it was because I sensed that Duke had fallen into a different attitude toward his music, and was taking off in what I thought was a wrong direction." This direction, characterized by extended, less commercial works such as "Reminiscing In Tempo," was, as Hammond and Mills argued, supposedly making Ellington lose touch with audiences that wanted dancing music, not "the concert works to which he has practically confined his writing in recent years."

This difference in opinion also cropped up in the recording studio. Brooks Kerr, a pianist and friend of both Ellington and Hammond, has related how publishers and record company executives wanted melodies plainly stated on recordings so that the average music fan could easily hum them. Ellington's challenging arrangements, featuring dissonant harmonies and unique instrumental and melodic voicings, altered melodies more than was customary in the Tin Pan Alley tradition. Mills often tried to curb this tendency in Ellington during recording sessions, usually to no avail. Ellington's "music was always too heavy" and "overarranged," Mills complained in 1981. One day in the recording studio in the late 1930s, when Hammond was advising Ellington to adhere more strictly to the melody in an arrangement, Ellington replied, "John, you're getting more like Irving Mills every day." [19]

As the 1930s progressed, Ellington increasingly stretched and broke such rules, which largely accounts for the fact that his recordings sound fresher than those of his competition. But for Mills, such experimentation likely restricted sales in the Swing Era. While Ellington issued some recordings seemingly tailored to the big band craze, most deviated from the formulas that characterized hit records during the period.

By 1938, it was clear that Ellington, armed with his successes of the past twelve years, committed even more strongly than before to producing work that often fell outside the usual popular music experience. Rather than recycling the catchiest riffs clothed in the same musical phrasing throughout a recording, Ellington's main themes are often subtly developed in a way that moves them forward through the piece without overt repetition, rewarding the attentive listener with varying shades and nuances. The songs and arrangements are designed as if they are telling a story with a beginning, middle, and end, rather than calling attention to the fact that a potential hit record is being presented. They betray the touch of a composer, as well as that of a songwriter and arranger. The lengthy intervals Ellington used in his melodies (as especially seen in "I Let a Song Go out of My Heart" and "I Got It Bad and That Ain't Good") also favored a composer's or instrumentalist's aesthetic, as they made these songs more difficult for singers to perform than the usual pop song. Most non-Ellington cover versions of "I Let a Song Go out of My Heart" give the song a happy lilt, but the Ellington orchestra's original version is a more bittersweet affair, especially in its minor-key bridge and in some of Johnny Hodges's and Barney Bigard's counterpoint surrounding the melody. While most Swing Era bands aimed for the profitable youth demographic, Ellington, at least ten years older than most of his bandleader peers, often reflected a more adult sensibility in his love songs that recognized both good and sad times, sometimes simultaneously, instead of sugarcoated imagery of love.

During 1938, the last year of the Ellington/Mills relationship, there are numerous examples of Ellington recordings that deviated from commercial guidelines.[20] "Steppin' into Swing Society" opens with three simple and fetching horn riffs that could have appeared on a recording by someone like Kay Kyser, a more conservative bestselling bandleader of the day. On most Swing Era discs, those riffs would constantly repeat over the course of the three-minute record, with solos grafted on top. But following the first minute of "Swing Society," Ellington's arrangement deconstructs the opening theme to a nearly unrecognizable degree, transforming it at one point into a riff that seems to laugh at the listener hoping for more predictability in the piece. Other bridge sections follow, none explicitly tied to the original riffs, including a slightly disconcerting minor-key section that lends a momentary darker tone (a favorite Ellington device). Finally, with thirty seconds remaining, the opening motif returns. "Swing Society" is highly enjoyable, but was obviously not a ringer for airplay on *Your Hit Parade*. "Braggin' in Brass" shows off the speed and accuracy of the Ellington brass sections, but the tempo is too fast and furious to make it a typical swing dance tune, unless the dancers possessed the abilities of the legendary black dancing duo the Nicholas Brothers.

Sometimes Ellington also released recordings that approximated the smoothly propulsive, pleasant, and predictable midtempo swinging sounds of most hits of the era. "Riding on a Blue Note," "Dinah's in a Jam," and "Love in Swingtime," all from 1938, are examples of this, some written by Ellington and some not, all published by Mills Music. But none of these pleasurable recordings caught on with the public. Perhaps, by 1938, Mills had realized that, despite his occasional attempts to steer Ellington toward the more commercial ends of the Swing Era spectrum, the public tended to embrace Ellington when his music ventured outside (but not too far outside) the usual popular music trends. Mills's marketing of difference might have worked better than Mills wished.

Ellington, with his commitment to African American and popular music being considered art and his insistence on pushing musical and cultural boundaries and perceptions, was developing in a direction that Mills was unwilling or unable to help promote or even understand. Mills knew how to spot talent and make a hit record. He was a superior businessman. But his expertise did not encompass the direction that Ellington increasingly wished to go. Mills willingly helped Ellington expand his audience in the white pop music market, but it appears he did not want to risk Ellington's popular appeal for a foothold in the market for serious music. He did not have confidence in Ellington's ability to release popular and serious music simultaneously and still have it supported by the public. Perhaps he felt Ellington would not be successful if he strayed too far from what audiences perceived as his strongest talents. Maybe he was afraid of what could happen should Ellington move too far beyond the range of talents attributed to African Americans. In short, he was attempting to protect his client and his bankroll. Supposedly, in 1937, Mills had "scoffed" at Ellington's suggestion that he play Carnegie Hall, and Ellington was angry when Goodman played at the venue the next year.[21] Mills felt that, in order to continue the lucrative activities of the Ellington orchestra, they needed to focus on short, memorable, rhythmic hit singles, the kinds that won mass radio exposure and ASCAP awards, as "I Let a Song Go out of My Heart" and "Caravan" did in the late 1930s.

For Mills to have previously bragged that his contribution to Ellington was to present him as an important American composer, and then later to criticize him for increasingly moving in that direction seems hypocritical. But Mills was not wholly wrong. By the late 1930s, it was clear that longer, more ruminative Ellington tracks like "Reminiscing," despite extensive hype, did not sell well and were not going to achieve any radio presence. Ellington would pursue his own priorities in a more intensified manner in the decades ahead without Mills.

Mills was not a major player in the Swing Era and never would be again in the music business. By 1941, he moved his operations to California to break the association his business had in the industry as "a colored office" that only booked black acts. In 1964, he also cited unidentified health reasons for the move, although Mills did live to a ripe old age of ninety-one. The Mills's publishing enterprise grew exponentially during the 1940s and 1950s, establishing offices around the world, generating millions of dollars in royalties, and eventually being acquired for $5 million in 1964 (more than $33 million in today's dollars). But Mills never again introduced a major artist or songwriter, and only a very few hit songs, to the public after the 1930s.[22]

In 1939, Ellington left the Mills organization and Brunswick Records for the William Morris Agency and RCA Victor Records. The next six years would prove to be one of the most financially and artistically prosperous periods of Ellington's career.

5
SWINGIN'

FIGURE 5. Billy Strayhorn and Ellington in 1946. During the Swing Era, when airwaves and ballrooms were filled with predictable, anonymously arranged music and whimsical vocal songs performed by crooners, it was telling that Ellington brought into the center of his organization an arranger and composer with classical training who specialized in dense musical statements. From the time of his arrival in the band in 1939, Billy Strayhorn and Ellington quickly became lifelong musical partners and close friends. Frank Driggs Collection.

Prelude

During the height of the Swing Era, in the late 1930s, George Avakian, the producer of many important Ellington sessions in the 1950s, first met his long-time idol on the night of a show the orchestra played at the New Haven Arena. Professor Marshall Stearns, who led seminars on the subject of jazz, invited Ellington to dinner at the Yale University dining hall. Some of his students, including the young Avakian, attended, prompted by the chance to converse with one of the main subjects of Stearns's lectures. Over sixty years later, Avakian retold the story—with a palpable air of horror—of what happened that evening:

> We walked in with Ellington and some of the musicians and one of the students got up from the table, threw down his napkin, and loudly stated, "I don't eat with niggers." And he had two friends with him at the table; the three of them got up and walked out. It was a dramatic moment. I damn near died. I thought, this is the most horrible thing imaginable to have this happen at Yale University. He was a big tall guy. Everybody saw him, and he shouted it loudly enough. I looked at Duke, who was just ahead of me, and he didn't bat an eye, and he turned around when we stopped walking to our table, and sort of half-smiled, and said, "Gentlemen, let us enjoy our repast." That's all he said, and he sat down, everybody sat down, nobody said a word.

Avakian felt angry and outraged. His first thought was, "What are we going to do with this guy [who insulted Ellington]?" He recalled Ellington "actually said something [to me] later on, I don't think it was that same day. He said, 'Look, it doesn't mean a thing. It happens all the time. Pay no attention to it. It doesn't get to me, and it shouldn't get to you.'"[1] The mindsets of hateful people could not be altered with idealistic arguments of brotherhood or threats of violence. One could only show them, through deeds and attitudes, the ignorance of their behavior. Ellington viewed reacting to prejudice, especially on an individual basis, as an ineffective strategy, one that deviated from the instructions he received during his Washington boyhood on how to deal with racism and attain status. He refused to lower himself to the foul-mouthed student's level by reacting to him or addressing him. He carried himself as an equal, or above equal, personage and refused to recognize people who did not treat him with respect.

Despite years of success, Ellington still found himself facing prejudice on an everyday basis. During the Swing Era, from 1935 to 1945, when

African American–inspired jazz had its largest commercial impact, Ellington and other black acts found themselves locked out of the biggest monetary rewards of the period, their past advances reversed. Eventually, by the mid-1940s, Ellington and his orchestra conquered much of the prejudice of the music industry and regained the top spot among big bands and the jazz scene. They did this while highlighting black culture and identity in their music and presentation more aggressively than ever before.

✳

The heyday of the Swing Era brought unprecedented profits and attention to jazz music. Recordings by swing bands led by Benny Goodman, Artie Shaw, Woody Herman, and others spanned the radio airwaves and animated dancers in ballrooms nationwide. Even though, as Ellington and others pointed out, swing had been originated and performed by black jazz musicians at least a decade previously,[2] white bandleaders and their ensembles dominated in media exposure and enjoyed the biggest hit records, especially before World War II. No longer were dancing troupes, movies, or comedians needed as opening acts to assure a turnout as in the first half of the 1930s—big bands were the main attraction.

The Swing Era should have represented unequivocal boom times for Ellington and his orchestra, since they were key originators of the sound, along with Fletcher Henderson. Moreover, Irving Mills's marketing campaigns brought the Ellington orchestra unprecedented respect and renown for both their artistry and dance music. All this should have allowed them to capitalize on the mushrooming market for swing music. But the Ellington band was unable to participate at the highest levels attained by the most successful bands of the 1935–40 period in terms of bookings, record sales, and radio and print exposure. Increased discrimination in the music business made conditions more difficult for black acts during the first half of the Swing Era. This included the formerly top-grossing Ellington band.

The challenges for Ellington, however, went deeper than box-office receipts and public relations. The success of Goodman and other white big bands in attracting millions of new fans changed the music business. Larger firms dominated the managing side of the business. More dollars were being earned and more capital was at stake. Consequently, the band scene in the Swing Era became more competitive and formulaic in the rush to fulfill and extend consumer demand. Despite the occasional efforts of artists like Goodman and Shaw to steer the music toward more challenging pursuits, an avalanche of songs adhered to the strictures of proven hit singles by big bands: thirty-two-bar structures centering around simple and catchy riffs, innocuous vocalists and predictable horn arrangements, along with pleasant but unremarkable solos. The acts that followed proven formulas and gave audiences what they expected had the best chance of airplay and ballroom booking, and were the ones on which the powerful managing agencies lavished most of their attention. Nothing was inherently wrong with jazz music becoming a fad—in many ways, it represented a boon for the music itself, aside from the cash flow. But the fad, like most popular music fads, also brought, as Ellington termed it, a "stagnancy." Ellington, with his commitment to the progress of his writing and his race, as well his insistence on writing in numerous genres at various lengths, did not fit the new music-business mold.

Ellington, in many respects, set himself apart from the publicity hubbub surrounding the Swing Era and constructed his own path to transcend and subvert its public expectations and limitations. While the additional money and publicity gravitating to the band business represented an opportunity, he also recognized that the hype often overpowered the music, and stifled it at times. During his career, Ellington almost never made negative critical public statements. But the swing fad inspired him to make exceptions to this policy on several occasions. In 1938, speaking to the *Cleveland News,* Ellington declared that "swing is stagnant and hasn't a future." He compared most swing records to "the monotonous rhythmical bouncing of a ball. After you hear it so much, you get sick of it because it hasn't enough harmony and there isn't enough to it." Five months later, in one of a series of articles Ellington wrote for *Down Beat* in 1939, he declared that "nothing of importance, nothing new, nothing either original or creative has occurred in the swing field during the last two years." Ellington retained a diplomatic front by not naming names, but it was clear that he laid much of the blame for the situation on businesspeople:

> As is so often the case, the sweeping wave of popularity lost sight of the genuine values of its popular hero, and much that is false came into prominence. On fire with the new craze, writers, faddists, bandmanagers, night club proprietors, entertainers, and newspapermen entered the field with a vengeance. Genuine values became distorted and false ones set up in their places.

Ellington believed in balance between artistry and business. Too much emphasis on the art, especially when weighed down by self-indulgence, greatly diminished the commercial rewards needed to produce that art. But too much attention paid to commercialism, which Ellington referred to in one of his 1939 articles as "the most flourishing and potent evil to be combated in our field of endeavor," could crush the art. The swing fad was fleeting, Ellington argued, and his work and orchestra represented something more enduring. "Easing his six feet and 200 pounds of body into a black silk dressing gown," Ellington declared to a reporter in 1938 that:

> There is something lasting, however, to be obtained from the Negro idiom of music. I predict that Negro music will be alive years after swing is dead. Negro music has color, harmony, melody, and rhythm. It's what I'm most interested in. Let the others whirl and jerk like 'ickies' and 'jitterbugs' on swing, and let me sit back and drink in the music.

In one of his 1939 *Down Beat* articles, he expounded on how his band differed from his Swing Era competition. "Our music is always intended to be definitely and purely racial. We try to complete a cycle," he wrote, hinting at a vision of black history and the crucial role of music within it. "Those things which we have to say, we try to express musically with the greatest possible degree of freedom of inspiration and individuality."[3]

The Swing Era presented problems and opportunities for jazz artists and the people who managed them, and Ellington and Mills both moved to take advantage of the new conditions. Ellington followed a dual track: in 1939, he left Mills and signed with one of the largest management agencies and with the most successful record company of the Swing Era. He also incorporated his own publishing company, shaping it as a uniquely African American business. By 1944, the strategy worked resoundingly. In his own subtle musical and personal style, without preaching or protesting, Ellington transcended the artistic limitations, racial discrimination, and public expectations that characterized the early years of the Swing Era, while evincing a subtle activism on behalf of racial equality. He enjoyed his biggest string of hit singles ever, regained a regular radio-show billing, and increased his reputation as a serious black composer by presenting two successful long-form works, one a Jim Crow–bashing Broadway musical in Los Angeles, and the other a programmatic panorama of black history presented at Carnegie Hall. Ellington's activities during the 1940s further ensured the establishment of a singular and stable niche for himself among multiracial, multigenerational audiences that would endure long after the swing craze evaporated following World War II.

The band business underwent rapid changes during the Swing Era, and the spoils were increasingly going to the biggest corporate entities. This success marked in part the achievement of Music Corporation of America (MCA). Started in 1924 with $1,000 in capital, Jules Stein and Billy Goodheart, Jr., built MCA out of the proceeds of big band and jazz music, which other large entertainment agencies previously avoided. Like Mills, they discovered an underserved niche and built it into impressive music-industry power. By 1938, with the swing craze in full bloom, MCA had developed or put under contract two-thirds of the name bands in the country, including Goodman, Guy Lombardo, Tommy Dorsey, and Harry James. Along with two other agencies, General Artists Corporation and the William Morris Agency, MCA dominated the big band business at its height, managing bands and controlling the premiere hotel ballrooms that offered the coast-to-coast radio wires crucial for promotion. These agencies did booking and publicity and paid all bills and taxes for band members. They often owned a piece of the band (though not nearly as much as Mills did), and received 10 percent of the gross. The record business also underwent consolidation during this period. The dozens of labels extant during the 1920s, including many freelance and independent labels specializing in jazz, blues, and country music, were whittled down by the Great Depression to just three or four major labels during the Swing Era. The publishing business also became more streamlined as music became increasingly central in sound films. As a result, Hollywood movie studios bought up most of the major Tin Pan Alley publishing houses to increase profits through vertical integration.

These larger corporations were able to meet burgeoning national consumer demand during the Swing Era. By 1938, seven hundred thousand swing records left store shelves each month, and in 1939, Shaw's "Begin the Beguine" became the first million-seller since the 1929 crash, an auspicious sign that the Depression was waning. The earning potential of top bands skyrocketed. In 1940, Kay Kyser grossed a million dollars (almost $15 million in today's dollars), Tommy Dorsey made $79,000 in one week, and Chesterfield cigarettes paid Glenn Miller $250,000 for delivering three broadcast performances a week, in addition to his proceeds from other shows and recordings. Jazz became big business like never before, and not just in major urban areas like New York City.[4]

Historians and commentators have attributed a great deal of social and political significance to the swing-music phenomenon, some justified and some needing closer examination. Lewis A. Erenberg and David W. Stowe viewed the Swing Era as bringing a "democratic" and "egalitarian" nature to American popular music, echoing the more idealistic sentiments behind President Franklin Delano Roosevelt's New Deal. But the idealism and the reality often represented two different situations. While FDR and his New Deal programs were perceived at the time as being more sympathetic toward African Americans, inspiring a long-term shift in support by blacks from the Republican to the Democratic Party, actual policies indicated a different story. Despite First Lady Eleanor Roosevelt's occasional statements and appearances centering on problems African Americans faced, the Roosevelt administration usually met civil rights issues with silence, or with a worsening of the situation. The discriminatory practices of most New Deal organizations, Roosevelt's banning of black reporters from the White House, and Roosevelt's refusal to consider a much-needed antilynching law were typical. According to Kenneth O'Reilly, FDR possessed a "political instinct that told him not to waste any capital on black America's behalf or otherwise antagonize southern Democrats. 'I just can't take the risk,' he said repeatedly."[5]

Neither could most of the music business during the Swing Era. At the end of 1940, *Down Beat* openly wondered in a banner headline, "Are Colored Bands Doomed as Big Money Makers?" and declared that "Negro Leaders Could Make More Money Running a Rib Joint." The article mentioned how the top black bands, including the Ellington, Calloway, and Basie groups, were "fighting a losing battle" in obtaining the best radio and stage bookings. All found their "pay checks chopped" in recent years, compared with the money they made during the first half of the 1930s, and compared with the money white bandleaders made in 1940, which, according to the article, amounted to twice what Louis Armstrong and other black bandleaders could command.[6]

Black bands faced a significantly more intolerant and discriminatory musical marketplace, and they were not able to follow through on the economic successes engineered by Mills. They were systematically barred from the most lucrative portions of the Swing Era business, which were reserved for bands led by whites. Otis Ferguson, writing in 1941 in the *New Republic,* noted that "since [Ellington] is a Negro and all Negroes—as his father knew and told him sadly and quietly long ago—get shoved around, he can be on top of the heap and still be bilked on occasion (and still do $250,000 where a white band with the same drawing power would more than double that)." The best hotels of the country, equipped with cross-country radio hookups, were off-limits to blacks. No radio shows focused on the black audience, except for Amos and Andy, which featured "two white men in blackface." Radio generally shunned black bands during the prewar Swing Era in favor of the romantic, often bland Tin Pan Alley ballads presented by white big bands and their crooners, which were thought to capture the demographic sought by advertisers. Also, black bands found it difficult to secure national airtime because Southern stations complained about their presence on the radio. Advertisers and stations, mindful of their bottom line, heeded their complaints silently. The new source of exposure for bands during the Swing

Era, jukeboxes, also followed dictates of segregation, with black bands on jukeboxes in black establishments only, with few exceptions. Such musical discrimination extended into the armed forces of World War II: record producer Brad McCuen recalled "rednecks" during his training in Alabama that objected to his playing records by Ellington and other black artists on the company jukebox. Musicians' unions also discriminated against blacks, lessening the money they could earn.

Record companies gave black artists fewer releases and less valuable contracts, the best example being Basie's initial contract with Decca in 1937, which made the national reputation of the band through superior jukebox coverage, but only paid $750 per year, with no royalties on some big-selling singles. They also limited the artistic freedom of most blacks, insisting they only wax the "hot" kinds of records that the companies believed people expected from black artists. Black songwriters, even those with hit singles under their belts, also faced discrimination in joining ASCAP, which, according to the *Chicago Defender,* held up the membership of qualified blacks, hiding their reasoning behind secret committee deliberations. It meant that black songwriters missed out on major portions of the proceeds of their successes. "In fact not until a short time ago was Duke Ellington admitted despite the great songs he had turned out," the *Defender* reported. "His business partner, Irving Mills, was a member however, and records show that songs written by Mills were—well you tell it." Basie and vocalist Ella Fitzgerald broke through to fame during this period, but not on an equal basis with white acts, as Ellington and Calloway did earlier. Progress occurred, but it usually represented a limited step forward, often a backwards step for blacks, and did not always "embody the American melting pot," as argued by Stowe.[7]

Helen Oakley Dance recalled that such racial disparities in the commercial realm inspired tension between black and white musicians, which she noticed especially on the day in 1937 or 1938 when she introduced Ellington and Goodman to each other. Before the two met, Dance thought it would be "touchy" since Goodman at the time was highly successful performing music that Ellington had performed "since Benny was in knee-pants, probably." Dance, who knew both the business and artistic sides of the music industry, explained that Ellington was:

> drawing the people, but getting a very moderate salary. And here is Goodman, starting on a career, where he would have incredible returns, and was being called the King of Jazz ... So, neither one is going to embrace the other. However, Benny had to respect Duke, he had great respect for Duke ... and

of course Duke was amused to meet Benny. He knew he was a marvelous clarinetist, and he was amused to see how a group like that could easily jump into the big time, when it would take him about a half-lifetime if he ever did it, and he had an irony and a wit and everything, and he accepted it in good spirits. And so they met and they were cordial.

Dance also described how, in her role as a publicist and producer for Ellington during this period, she needed to always call ahead to clubs in New York City that Ellington wished to visit (not perform in) to make sure there would be no racial problems connected to his presence. Al Celley, Ellington's road manager starting in 1943, also reported having to perform similar reconnaissance regularly.[8]

Another argument forwarded by historians is that the success of jazz during the Swing Era forced Americans to face their indebtedness to black culture and helped unite the races in an unprecedented way. Stowe cited Benny Goodman's 1938 Carnegie Hall concert and the subsequent show late that night at the Savoy in Harlem as principal evidence. The shows did break "color lines" uptown and downtown, onstage and in the audience, but they represented one-time-only events in the most cosmopolitan city in the United States. What effect did it have among the majority of Americans? How much mixing really went on across the country? Until World War II, Swing Era sales charts and media coverage focused on white bands and on formula and novelty hit records, not the more sophisticated sounds of acts like Goodman, Basie, and Chick Webb, which held the spotlight that night in New York City in January 1938. White audiences still tended to support white bands with their cash and their votes in national magazine polls, reflecting the segregation of American society.[9]

Also, while newspaper and magazine columnists increasingly noted the influence of black culture in American music, the definition of African American music often entailed a loaded and exclusionary exercise. John Hammond, in a piece previewing the December 1938 "Spirituals to Swing" concert he produced at Carnegie Hall, insisted that "the authentic music of the American Negro" was not characterized by "the highly publicized Negro jazz bands, some of whom have made serious concessions to white taste by adding spurious showmanship to their wares" or by "magnificent trained soloists" like Marian Anderson and Paul Robeson. Instead, his article and the concert championed "artists who, for the most part, have had no formal training of any kind, cannot read musical notations, and have never played before white audiences or in any formal way before colored audiences." Hammond, who had earlier protested in the studio and in public against Ellington's efforts to write more serious pieces in addition to his danceable hit singles, seemed to be attempting to exclude Ellington (and all others fortunate enough to have received some education) from the definition of African American music.[10] By the end of the Swing Era, Ellington would make a convincing musical and verbal case for a more inclusive and far richer vision of what black music could encompass.

But, despite these drawbacks, scholars Erenberg and Stowe are correct in asserting that swing, with its background in African American culture and the insistence by many of its adherents that it represented an "art music," did provide a barrier-breaking focus for discussion in the media and probably in living rooms, ballrooms, and offices nationwide. When Goodman, the most famous musician in the country, extolled African American music and maintained that the Basie and Webb bands were "the real swing bands,"[11] his comments were widely disseminated because of Goodman's unprecedented popularity and the increased reach of the 1930s mass media. When white and black bandleaders such as Goodman and Henderson integrated their bands, it spotlighted an on-stage interracial cooperation and camaraderie mostly unprecedented in American music, sparking comment both about the controversy of the practice as well as how it exemplified American ideals of equality.

Upon leaving Mills in 1939, Ellington took steps to increase his autonomy and further elevate how the public and the industry viewed his band and his music. The first step was signing with the William Morris Agency (WMA). In business since 1898, the firm enjoyed the reputation since the 1920s as the agency that represented show business giants and "the more classy . . . attractions." The WMA client list of the 1930s boasted most of Hollywood's biggest names: Jimmy Cagney, Judy Garland, Al Jolson, Mickey Rooney, Mae West—the list went on and on. When swing music started showing huge profits in the mid-1930s, WMA executive Abe Lastfogel decided that the most powerful talent agency in the world should attempt to grab a piece of the lucrative big band market. He hired away top MCA booking agent Willard Alexander, who brought with him former MCA client Count Basie, to start up the new WMA band department.

Institutional problems arose quickly. The executives at WMA, except for Lastfogel, treated Alexander as an outsider. The company as a whole, used to dealing with white Hollywood and Broadway musical performers, had no experience concerning the history or character of big band and jazz music. Alexander felt isolated in an adjunct department not supported by most of senior management. He even felt uncomfortable eating lunch at the restaurants where WMA agents from other departments congregated. The long-run prognosis for the new division was not auspicious.[12]

Harold Jovien, a columnist for *Billboard* and the *Chicago Defender* during the 1930s and early 1940s, and a band booker from the mid-1940s on, recalls being initially slightly mystified concerning Ellington's move to WMA:

> William Morris was a very "uppish" kind of agency ... [and] I wondered why Duke went with William Morris, to tell you the truth ... And I'm sure they must have gotten him ... a lot of important booking ... But he was getting away from what he had built his whole reputation with ... I don't think the William Morris Agency had the feel for Ellington's greatness ... I feel that their people were much more commercial ... and maybe Duke felt that was going to be more helpful to him. They didn't have a sensitivity to ... jazz music. [The Mills organization] had the sensitivity, had the feeling. Sure, there was materialism, everybody's involved in making money to some degree. [But Mills] didn't have what the William Morris Agency represented. William Morris was the oldest booking agency. They had stature, William Morris people could go in to the highest level [of the show business world], and I'm sure Duke went in there with great purpose that they would be able to do bigger and more important things for him.

Probably Ellington wanted to be treated as a giant in the music-business world (or at least be welcomed at its highest level) and saw the William Morris Agency as an entree to that kind of respect. He could have signed with Joe Glaser's American Booking Corporation, which handled Armstrong and various big bands; or with General Artists Corporation, where Woody Herman and Nat Cole established their careers; or big band behemoth MCA. Perhaps his lifelong aversion to categorization made him wish to stand apart from the agencies that were known for only booking big band and jazz music. As his late 1920s and early 1930s associations with Chevalier and Ziegfeld demonstrated, he wanted his music and image associated with the top names in the white entertainment world. For a composer who saw his music as singular and strove to be considered an artist no matter what society in general thought of his race or the worth of the musical genres he wrote in, the William Morris Agency represented a logical choice on many levels.

Artistically, the William Morris Agency afforded Ellington more freedom than he had enjoyed previously. Cress Courtney, the primary agent assigned to Ellington, unlike Irving Mills, possessed no artistic or musical background and had no creative input on recordings or songwriting. No longer would Ellington be asked to simplify his arrangements to make sure that the melodies appealed to the lowest common denominator of musical consumer. No more would he receive automatic resistance to his longer pieces. But perhaps the most dramatic change for Ellington at WMA was his economic situation: Ellington's royalty checks for his post-1939 compositions would not be lessened by Mills's taking credit for them, and the company only took a 10 percent commission on the proceeds of his career, rather than the more exorbitant percentage taken by Mills.

For those close to him, the move to WMA signaled Ellington's desire to take "more control of his own career." Paul Mills recalls that Ellington generally approved bookings by the Mills organization, but according to H. Robert Udkoff, the process usually entailed that "Mills would make these deals and tell [Ellington] that he made this deal." With WMA, Courtney discussed booking strategy with Ellington before securing the dates. According to his sister Ruth, the move made Ellington "happier."[13]

From 1940 to 1945, WMA placed the Ellington orchestra on more important radio shows than they had been on previously. The clout of the agency paid dividends to Ellington in his attempts to surmount the discrimination of the Swing Era music business. As Mercer Ellington, who worked for the band during this period, put it, Courtney negotiated lucrative "white deals" for Ellington and the orchestra in the early 1940s and refused to knuckle under to the discrimination of the music business.

Starting in late 1942, Ellington enjoyed his most extensive radio exposure in years as the major networks began airing more black bands. Rocky Clark, African American syndicated columnist, took partial credit for this development. He had needled the networks on this issue for months, using a patriotic argument that became a common tactic for blacks arguing for equal treatment during World War II. "For some reason, the networks as a whole have been neglecting colored bands this season," he noted. "It's too bad because their music is extremely popular with the lads at Army camps who depend on radio for their entertainment." The Ellington orchestra's 19 November 1942 performance on the Coca Cola *Victory Parade of Spotlight Bands* marked their first commercial national appearance on radio in years, and the first on East Coast radio in months. They were the second of four black bands to appear on the series in a matter of two months, returning to the show numerous times during the war. Ellington appeared on national radio quite often during 1943, including a 19 June guest shot on the NBC *Million*

Dollar Band program, which invited a bandleader every week to supervise and solo with a thirty-four-piece studio orchestra. Ellington was the first "colored bandleader" featured on the show.[14]

At the same time commercial radio began yielding back air time to black performers, the federal government stepped in to do the same, hoping to curtail any "black disillusionment" in the military. According to historian Lauren Sklaroff, managers in the Office of War Information in 1942 "committed to pronouncing egalitarian rhetoric in the face of Nazi aggression" and intolerance "untangled some of the constraints that had previously prevented blacks from securing a national radio presence." The Armed Forces Radio Service network's *Jubilee* program, broadcast only to U.S. military bases, became the first "all-Negro variety show" to "reach a popular audience and remain on the airwaves for almost a decade." While some black newspaper columnists complained that the show only reinforced "the jim crow system" of the war that relegated blacks to inferior and sometimes degrading nonleadership positions, Sklaroff demonstrated that *Jubilee* provided a platform for a nonthreatening and humorous airing of issues that inspired racial tensions in the army. It brought a large and regular multiracial audience for black performers unprecedented in the history of American radio. Ellington appeared on the program numerous times, along with noncelebrity black servicemen, black luminaries such as Lena Horne, Eddie "Rochester" Anderson, and Art Tatum, and occasional white guest stars such as Bing Crosby and Frank Sinatra.[15]

In terms of their 1940s film output, the Ellington orchestra was not utilized as respectfully as in the 1930s, despite the WMA's influence in Hollywood. Since the late 1930s, the Hollywood studios increasingly placed bands in movies, realizing that they amplified box-office revenue. But during the Swing Era, exclusively white bands received this promotional opportunity; the respectable appearances of the Ellington orchestra among white stars during the first half of the 1930s were not duplicated in the late 1930s or the 1940s.

WMA did secure them a role in MGM's *Cabin in the Sky* (1942), the first all-black Hollywood studio film in years, and only the third in history aimed at a multiracial audience. It represented a partial response to a directive from the Roosevelt administration that "explicitly encouraged Hollywood to produce films with black casts" to stress interracial unity in movie theaters during World War II, even though such images did not often occur on the streets or, especially, in army barracks. In many ways, the situation in front of and behind the camera resembled President Roosevelt's World War II armed forces, where whites exclusively commanded black regiments and blacks could rarely rise above the more menial jobs of the military. While *Cabin* sported the glossy, big-budget look of an MGM musical, whites assumed the writing and directing chores, and critics then and now have vilified its stereotype-ridden vision of African American life. Ramona Lewis, writing in the *Amsterdam News* in 1943, called it "an insult masking behind the label of folklore," while Donald Bogle in a study of black films rued that "once more . . . ersatz Negro culture was passed off as the real thing." While director Arthur Freed took public pride in the fact that *Cabin* featured no black domestics on screen, the film did contain an uncomfortably large share of plantation imagery and clichés, in between some excellent musical performances. Ellington and the band were well showcased in their main number, "Goin' Up," written especially for the film and featuring an extended call-and-response-style solo from trombonist Lawrence Brown. But in a subsequent number, "Shine," Ellington seems reduced to an anonymously smiling background figurehead, the music (adorned by an MGM-supplied string section) and the image a marked contrast to his 1930s film appearances, which portrayed him as a maestro and composer at the center of attention in almost every scene in which he appeared. The song, which Ellington did not write, has a decidedly minstrel tone to its lyrics.

The Ellington band was also featured during this period in "soundies," promotional musical short films shown as movie trailers or in nickelodeon-like machines. They did not compare with Ellington's groundbreaking 1930s film appearances, but they were charming in spots and demonstrated, especially in *Jam Session* (1942), that the Ellington orchestra could be as fun or innocuous as any other swing band. In that short, the band presented a somewhat different image, performing in casual clothes (not the usual tuxes) and stylish hats in a run-down, mostly empty basement club, vying for the attention of three beautiful black women. Ellington, in all four "soundies" from the period, plays an upright piano rather than his usual imposing grand. The Ellington orchestra was among the last of the major bands to appear in soundies—they were not on the "cutting edge" as they were in previous 1930s movie incarnations under Mills. The 1943 three-song short *Duke Ellington and His Orchestra* brought the band back in tuxes (although Ellington sported a more casual coat). It resembled other big band shorts with its lavish piano-motif set, but it also sharply differed from them by keeping its focus on the music and soloists of the orchestra, eschewing the dancers, gags, travelogues, or other paraphernalia that littered the short films of other Swing Era acts, including the 1942 Ellington soundies.[16]

*

The William Morris Agency also continued the Mills legacy of placing Ellington in contexts that did not usually feature black artists. This included integrating venues, though it appears that they did this less often than Mills Artists. Some examples include a date at Colgate University in 1940, for which *Variety* and *Down Beat* proclaimed that Ellington's would be "the first name band to play a college jazz concert." Not only was the venue packed to the rafters, but the concert was also part of a series that featured Paul Robeson and the Philadelphia Symphony. Other examples of venues integrated by the Ellington orchestra include the Hurricane Club, New York City, in 1943, the "swank" Hollywood nightclub Ciro's in 1945, and Texas Southern University in 1948.[17] The band regularly played before interracial audiences during the WMA period, even down South in cities such as Chattanooga (4 July 1940) and Houston (16 April 1941). A 1940 "all-colored affair" in Atlanta featuring Ellington drew "the largest crowd in the dance history of the city" with seven thousand patrons overall, including a thousand white spectators, and more than half that milling around the building, unable to enter.[18]

Perhaps WMA pursued this strategy because more racial integration existed in Ellington audiences than in those of his competition. According to Wilma Cockerell, a columnist for the African American newspaper the *California Eagle,* a primarily black audience attended Count Basie and Jimmie Lunceford dance shows during the late 1930s and 1940s. In the same theaters, Ellington shows drew a more "mixed crowd," even at the Elks Club situated at the corner of Central Avenue and Jefferson Street, a predominantly African American neighborhood that served as a famous center for black entertainment in the 1930s and 1940s. Attendance at stage shows in theaters also proved more racially mixed for Ellington shows, though blacks were prevalent on the weekends. Ellington "had more of a following among whites" than Basie, Lunceford, or Chick Webb, certainly in California, and, according to Paul Mills and evidence from the venues in which Ellington played, in many other parts of the country as well. It was rare for black bands to cultivate a cross-racial audience as Ellington did. Cockerell observed that "the other bands never made it with a wider white audience like Duke did."[19]

The move to RCA Victor exemplified yet another way Ellington gained increased artistic control and freedom in the post-Mills era. Ellington's 1940 contract stipulated that his orchestra would be the only African American big band on Victor, RCA's highest-priced record label, a similar situation to his deal at Brunswick in the late 1930s, one that stressed the high-class and exclusive image of the band and its music, and one that recognized Ellington as a preeminent African American hit-maker. Other black artists recording for the same label were distributed on the lower-priced Bluebird label, and, later in the 1940s, Lionel Hampton could not record his big band for Victor because of the Ellington proviso.[20]

Leonard Joy became the staff producer for Ellington's Victor sessions. Herb Jeffries, the band's primary male vocalist from 1939 to 1943, described Joy's role as minimal and supervisory. "Joy was looking over Ellington's shoulder as far as producing was concerned," recalled Jeffries. "Ellington had the preconception of a successful record because he . . . found out what the public felt about [the song being recorded] by doing shows beforehand . . . Any successes from these records were first analyzed by Duke. The producers would say afterward: 'We'll take that take—is that OK, Duke?'" Harold Jovien, a close friend of Joy's, added that "Joy was an easy fellow . . . he had great, great respect for Duke and the last thing he would want to do was force him to do something he didn't want to do. Leonard Joy was very proud to have the band on the label . . . and gave Duke all the authority in its totality."[21] This contrasted greatly with the situation at Mills Artists. Nobody at his record company could tell Ellington what Ellington music or black music should or should not encompass.

Claire Gordon, a secretary and occasional publicist for Ellington's publishing company, recalled going to dozens of recording sessions in the early to mid-1940s. "As far as I could tell, either he liked [the recording take] or he didn't, and that was it," she reported. "And I don't think that I ever recall anybody else ever coming out and saying 'that's a take' and Duke looking unhappy and saying 'that's not' . . . He was always the final decider of whether the sound was what he had wanted." Others observing Ellington during the 1940s concurred: Harold Jovien felt that Ellington had more control than other artists he saw record, and columnist Wilma Cockerell recalled Ellington as more active in the studio than other artists, including Count Basie:

> He did a lot more of ordering people around . . . I remember once he went back into the booth while the band played through one whole song and then he came out and sat at the piano and did the [final] recording with them [Basie did not do this] . . . Duke always gave you the impression, not only of just control, you had the idea, you know, that he was second place only to God up there . . . I remember him asking the band questions, and people in the band questions: 'What about this, or this?' And they'd say something,

and he'd say "OK." So there seemed to be a give and take there. But . . . the basic plan . . . he'd already decided about that. They just went from there.[22]

RCA Victor promoted Ellington's image and music in a more far-reaching and splashy manner than ever before. A 1943 RCA Victor advertising campaign on behalf of Ellington, featuring notes by the promotion people who assembled it, is preserved in its entirety in the Smithsonian's collections. It demonstrates the immense promotional apparatus at RCA Victor's disposal during the 1940s. At least a half dozen publications regularly published by the record company promoted its artists and releases to every conceivable customer and dealer constituency, including the *Victor Red Seal Record Supplement* and the *Victor and Bluebird Popular Red Supplement,* which each went out to over a million people monthly, according to the company. In addition, RCA Victor also sent out the standard promotion items to newspapers, including short features describing Ellington-related events, and press releases that included glowing reviews of new Ellington recordings that could be reprinted verbatim by newspapers and magazines.[23] With the combined marketing muscle of show-biz behemoths RCA and WMA in the 1940–45 period, Ellington enjoyed a more elaborate and widespread promotional presence in the United States than during any other period in his lifetime.

Ellington used this newly gained artistic freedom and marketing power to produce one of the greatest extended periods of creativity in the band's history during 1940 and 1941. The "happier" mood that Ruth Ellington observed in her brother resulted in artistically important works and in some of the orchestra's all-time bestsellers (the melodies for "Don't Get Around Much Anymore" and "Do Nothing 'til You Hear from Me" were composed during this period), high art that often landed on the sales chart. Most compositions were written or co-written by Ellington, as usual, but he also had extensive help from his writing partner and eventual close friend Billy Strayhorn, brought into the Ellington organization in January 1939. The numbers not composed by Ellington or his associates were of a higher quality and better matched for the orchestra than in the 1930s, when the majority of covers were by Mills Music clients and probably pushed onto the band by Mills.

The 1940 and 1941 Ellington recordings represent an amazing combination of simultaneously challenging and pleasurable sounds, with a stylistic eclecticism no ensemble at the time could match.[24] They refrain from inundating listeners from the outset with their most memorable fillip. They are unafraid to build slowly and evince a cumulative effect, as heard in "Dusk," but they can also hit the listener with an immediately alluring melodic hook, as does "Concerto for Cootie." Ellington recorded few of the out-and-out riffing swing tunes that usually reigned during the Swing Era.

In these 1940–41 sessions, Ellington cut his own path. "Conga Brava" combines unexpected musical mood and time changes, ranging from Latin exotica to hard-driving swing riffs. In the hands of another band, a resourceful listener could imagine how "Blue Goose" could become trite, its creamy and romantic main theme duplicated and sweetened ad nauseum. Instead, in the third A-section of Ellington's recording, the horns restate the melody with light dissonance creeping around the edges, complicating and transforming it from something comforting to something vaguely unsettling, another instance of the more adult-themed statements Ellington made in the popular music marketplace. "Across the Track Blues" is, to use a pet Ellington phrase, "always in a state of becoming," a constantly molting three-minute composition with new riffs and ideas emerging every few seconds to twist numerous permutations onto the allegedly simple structure of a twelve-bar blues. Like many Ellington works of this period and afterward, it is not designed as a hit song, but as an absorbing musical journey.

Industry disputes over the growing popularity of music on the radio facilitated a wider selection of songwriters contributing to the Ellington orchestra during this period. ASCAP, the performing rights organization for songwriters and composers, banned the broadcasting of its songs at the start of 1941 because they felt that radio stations should compensate its writers for airing their material. Ellington, an ASCAP composer since 1935, could not broadcast his songs during the ban, so the band relied on non-ASACP writers like Strayhorn, band trombonist Juan Tizol, and Ellington's son Mercer to provide material for the band. As Strayhorn recalled, "there was a big scramble to write a new catalog." Strayhorn and Tizol contributed many pieces that became Ellington orchestra perennials ("Take the 'A' Train," "Bakiff"). Compositions attributed to Mercer Ellington during the 1941–43 period also became Ellington evergreens ("Moon Mist," "Things Ain't What They Used to Be," and several more). However, contemporary scholars who have extensively examined the enormous collection of Ellington orchestra sheet music at the Smithsonian have concluded that the songs attributed to Mercer are in his father's hand and probably were not written by Mercer. In a 1980 interview, Mercer described the songs he wrote during this period as having originated as "lessons" in composing and orchestration from his father, who would correct his mistakes and tell him to rework the material. Perhaps, as occurred with band members, Ellington took his son's bare melodic ideas and rendered them into full songs. Perhaps this arrangement signified Ellington's way of contributing to the band secretly when new material was scarce, while his ASCAP membership kept him from overtly contributing during the ban. Throughout his career, Ellington employed many ways to funnel the proceeds of his career to close family members, and this may have represented another reason for giving Mercer authorship and royalties on the songs. The fact that Mercer Ellington never again wrote anything close in quality to the songs attributed to him in the first half of the 1940s also adds doubt as to whether he deserved sole credit or any credit for the songs.[25]

Another mark of the Ellington determination to succeed on his terms during this era was the celebration of black culture that figured prominently in his writing and recording. Over the course of Ellington's career, this represented nothing unusual, but it was particularly risky for Ellington to stress those themes at a time when black bands were doing so poorly because of Swing Era discrimination. "Sepia Panorama," with its musical foundation resting on the pioneering bass playing of Jimmie Blanton, served as the band's theme for a few months in 1940 and 1941, until "Take the 'A' Train," a Strayhorn song whose lyrics feature directions to Harlem, took its place for the rest of Ellington's career. "Harlem Airshaft," according to Ellington in a *New Yorker* profile, musically documented the smells and sounds of an African American community in a Harlem apartment house. "A Portrait of Bert Williams" and "Bojangles (A Portrait of Bill Robinson)," like "Black Beauty" (1928) before them, programmatically honored important figures in black culture.[26] In the latter, various band members and sections, from bassist Blanton to the trumpets, take turns imitating the dance steps of Bill Robinson. Such pieces served notice that Ellington continued to place black culture in the popular music marketplace as no one had quite done before.

The hiring of Strayhorn heightened the band's singularity. At the moment when airwaves and ballrooms were filled with predictable, anonymously arranged swing tunes and tightly structured whimsical vocal songs performed by crooners, it was telling that Ellington chose to bring into the center of his organization and his life an arranger and composer with classical training who specialized in dense musical statements. Strayhorn was drawn into the fold in an unusually intimate way; he stayed in Ellington's New York City penthouse apartment with Ellington's lover, sister, and son shortly after he arrived from Pittsburgh in 1939. While Ellington toured Sweden in the spring, Strayhorn studied Ellington's scores in the apartment. "I couldn't really arrange, but that didn't make any difference with him," recalled Strayhorn, referring to his first assignments of doing the arrangements for small band sessions. "He inspires you with confidence. That's the only way I can explain how I managed to do those arrangements." Strayhorn is probably being modest here, as his biographer David Hajdu has documented that Strayhorn penned arrangements in musical productions in the Pittsburgh area before joining with Ellington.[27] But Ellington saw and developed a potential for artistic greatness in Strayhorn that no one previously detected. The arrival of Strayhorn represented another example of Ellington's willful veering away from the most reliably profitable sounds in popular music—and the sensibilities of Irving Mills. It's possible that the move constituted yet another factor in the breaking of the Ellington/Mills relationship, which occurred just three months after Strayhorn's arrival.

By 1940, Strayhorn's brief period of penthouse hibernation immersed in Ellington manuscripts ended, and the twenty-five-year-old prodigy was regularly turning in stunning contributions to the band and occasionally taking the piano chair during recording sessions. Besides providing his own compositions, one of Strayhorn's main assignments was fashioning vocal song arrangements for the orchestra. He bestowed upon them a new level of class and distinction. Working with somewhat corny, romantic crooners' ballads such as "Flamingo" and "What Good Would It Do?" Strayhorn crafted a vision of the pop vocal single as a high artistic statement, partly by using tenets of classical composition. As Mark Tucker has observed of "Flamingo," "the rich modern harmonies of the introduction betray the taste of someone who has admitted a fondness for Ravel and Debussy." The piano flourishes and horns dart in and out and between Herb Jeffries's vocal with a level of activity and dexterity rarely seen on a pop single of the period. Before the main instrumental section and at the end of the piece, Jeffries's forlorn falsetto cries fade into the distance of the recording, swallowed up by more of the modern and offsetting harmonies of which Tucker wrote, programmatically replicating the restless searching set out in the lyric and vocal performance. Sometimes silky, sometimes dissonant and disturbing, "Flamingo" and "What Good" incur a sense of dreamy suspension, of a musical movie played out on a three-minute record, an uneasy mix of Tin Pan Alley and the art-song tradition. Pieces that in other hands could easily have turned out hackneyed and unremarkable were transformed by Strayhorn into profound, breathing productions that hinted at adult emotional pain amidst the youth-oriented squeals of the Swing Era.

Strayhorn's gifts were evidenced in his own compositions ("Chelsea Bridge," "After All," and many others) as well as those of others that he transformed into dramatic curios. Ellington recognized these gifts. He cherished and praised "Swee' Pea" nightly from the stage and in numerous quotes given to journalists for the rest of his career. "The orchestration he did on

'Flamingo' was, in my opinion, a turning point in vocal background orchestration, a renaissance in elaborate ornamentation for the accompaniment of singers," Ellington noted in his autobiography. "Since then, other arrangers have become more daring, but Billy Strayhorn really started it all with 'Flamingo.'" He also gave Strayhorn financial rewards that symbolized his worth to Ellington and the orchestra. By January 1942, Strayhorn's weekly salary was $75, higher than anyone in the band except for its leader and star soloist, Johnny Hodges. By the fall of 1943, his salary reached $125 weekly ($1,500 in today's dollars), and publishing royalties pushed his earnings higher.[28] Strayhorn was valuable to Ellington not only in bringing highly individual pieces to the band and in assuming arrangement chores that allowed Ellington more time for his writing, but in being a partner with Ellington in the creation of the longer and more conceptual pieces that would increasingly concern him for the rest of his career.

But, thankfully, not all of Ellington's 1940–41 recordings radiated artistic seriousness. He could compete on the basis of musical pleasure and fun, as seen in the scatting-happy "Bli-Blip," the fanciful "Chocolate Shake," and "Jumpin' Punkins." During this period, Ellington's lighter side is readily apparent, especially in the lyrics he penned himself. None boast the sophistication of an Ira Gershwin piece, but they have a humor and earthiness that perfectly fits their musical backing. The imagery of "Rocks in My Bed," while not spelled out entirely, presents a more honest and adult impression of sexual loneliness than most Swing Era lyrics. The last lyrics in particular, with Ivie Anderson expressing being "underloved, overfed" appear to emanate from a conversation Ellington overheard between two female friends concerning their lack of romantic luck. "I Don't Know What Kind of Blues I Got" betrays a theatrical bent at the outset with its hushed dynamic that slowly escalates, creating the image of the sun rising on a brand new and depressing day for someone who suffers from the blues. The trumpets that answer Herb Jeffries's first vocal section form a jagged riff, quite different from the smooth backing preceding it in the song, hinting at anguish beneath the surface of the light-hearted lyrics. For relief he plans to solicit the advice of "Snake Mary," but the closing fanfare, first insistent and then dismal, hints that the visit will not be satisfactory.

The difference that the Ellington orchestra brought to the Swing Era could also be seen at live shows. According to Wilma Cockerell, "mainly, the kids came to the big band shows to dance, but for Ellington, very often, the audience was just sitting and listening." She and other observers could not recall this happening with such regularity or at such length during shows by other bands, white or black. "Oh, some people in the background would be dancing. But not the biggest part of the crowd. The kids all stood in front of the bandstand or we sat on the dance floor and we just listened." For Basie shows, for Jimmie Lunceford's band, for the Chick Webb orchestra, "everybody tried to dance." Yet, at Ellington performances, for much of the time "everybody was very attentive, like you were at a concert." The shows that Cockerell and other sources described happened before the mid-1940s Carnegie Hall shows that formally established the Ellington orchestra as a major concert attraction.[29] In 1964, Ellington recalled the same transition:

> The audience gradually became a listening audience rather than a dancing audience. Way back, as far back as 30 years ago, we used to feel complimented if you had a single line in the front of the band, and then it grew to be a double line, and then the line was probably 20 deep, and it got to the point where there was very little room left for the dancers, you know. And this just grew of itself. People actually felt they were musically mature enough to listen, and feel that they were enjoying it just for the listening, rather than having to dance.[30]

Cockerell, as a fan and a reporter, tried to discern the reason behind such behavior. "It was really funny. I used to say it to a lot of my friends. I'd say, 'Why don't we dance at Duke?' 'I don't know [they would say], I'd rather listen.'" In retrospect, Cockerell and her friend Henrietta Livingston believed that the character of the Ellington orchestra's music prompted this audience response. Basie, Goodman, and others tended to perform excellent, though predictable, arrangements with a steady 4/4 dance beat. For Cockerell, the Ellington arrangements featured a unique "intricacy." "Even though you might not have been a musician, you knew there was something special going on." Separately, Livingston, also a nonmusician, concurred: "It was a wonderful sound to hear, to hear a little dissonance, you know, instead of what I had been accustomed to hearing . . . I don't want to say that I didn't hear anything unusual [in the other bands], but . . . [the Ellington sound] was much different."

In press reviews, dancing at Ellington shows was not stressed. At one 1942 California show, Ellington "talked of culture, citing ex-singing waiter Joe Turner's blues chanting, and he threw in a few slow-measured rhythms for art's sake. But it was no use," according to a reviewer. "Everything he served up seemed only to excite his worshipers the more, with an increase of foot-tapping and shoulder-swaying," not dancing. At a hotel ballroom in Chicago, Ellington reportedly was "held nightly in the rapt stare of his youthful admirers who are exuberant in their applause before and after but who are caught in rigid silence during the music." "Heard the Duke last week, and as usual, the Ellington 'ork' is in a class by itself," raved a *Pittsburgh Courier* columnist, who in the same article reviewed a Basie show that attracted 3,000 "jump happy" souls. "[Ellington's] music is definitely not for the 'jitterbugs' nor 'platter-brains,' rather it is for those who favor the transition between 'boogie-woogie' and the staid old classics. I would call it 'jazz symphonics' and let it go at that." Not all observers were pleased with Ellington's wider approach. In Philadelphia, a *Billboard* reviewer complained that a 1942 show did not feature "the speed, punch, and spontaneous enthusiasm one expects to find in a sepia [African American] show ... While it is all excellent in the Ellington tradition, the musical perfection and instrumental wizardry on display hardly passes off as entertainment here." The Ellington orchestra could and did inspire dancers, but also engaged a larger palette and more varied musical goals than other bands, as evidenced in this 1940 Chicago newspaper piece: "For early evening dancing, Ellington manages a similarly restrained output of danceable swing ... It is not until the midnight show that Duke cuts loose, to the unalloyed joy of the jivers."[31]

In another move that signaled the growing control he exerted over his music and career after he left Mills, Ellington incorporated Tempo Music, his own publishing company, in New York City on 23 December 1940.[32] During Tempo's initial two years, Ellington's compositions were contracted to Robbins Music Corporation by previous arrangement, but Tempo immediately began publishing works by Strayhorn, Ellington orchestra personnel, and non-Ellington songs covered by the band such as Edward Anderson and Ted Grouya's "Flamingo," waxed just five days after Tempo's incorporation. For the rest of Ellington's career, Tempo insured that he would earn the publisher's share of his songs' royalties (and those of the writers contracted to Tempo), as well as the songwriter's share. The creation of Tempo was a business move that greatly aided the survival of Ellington's band and his music during the decades that followed.

The problems of mistrust and the lack of attention that Ellington felt in his later years at Mills Music were solved at Tempo. By establishing Tempo, Ellington gained more autonomy and set an important precedent for African Americans and all jazz artists controlling their own publishing. Historically, publishing represented the most lucrative area of the music business, usually controlled by businesspeople, not the artists who created the revenue-producing compositions. No major popular music figure, white or black, had created his own publishing company since Irving Berlin in 1914.[33]

More than a decade later, John Coltrane and Charles Mingus followed Ellington's lead.

Many important changes separated the marketing of Ellington at Tempo from his previous affiliation with Mills Music. Published mass-marketed sheet music for Ellington's compositions largely disappeared for Ellington's new songs, especially after World War II. While Mills and Robbins published Ellington's music in numerous and varied editions, Tempo did so more rarely, and concentrated on selling band arrangements and cover versions more than sheet music intended for home use. Of the dozens of pieces of Ellington sheet music in the Smithsonian's DeVincent collection, only two ("Flamingo" from 1941 and "Carnegie Blues" from 1945) were published by Tempo. This policy followed a general trend in the music industry. As John Edward Hasse pointed out, reduced musical literacy in America brought about a gradual downturn in sheet-music purchases. By the 1940s, recordings superseded sheet music as the dominant market for music purchases. "The public decreasingly made its own music (or did so without reading music) and increasingly relied on professionals—through records, radio, and, soon, television—for its music," reported Hasse. From this point forward, the role of publishing companies changed. They were now less concerned with activities that increased sheet-music sales and instead assumed new roles as gatekeepers, guardians, and facilitators of performance rights and royalties.

Ellington's sister Ruth served as president of Tempo, assisted during this period by her husband Dan James and Claire Gordon, among others. Ruth possessed little if any experience in the music business, and in fact had recently graduated from Columbia University with a degree in science, planning on a career as a doctor or biology teacher when her brother asked her to head the new company. She felt "shocked" but agreed to do it because, in the Ellington family, "everything was for Edward," and she usually did whatever her brother asked. Also, her new position did not require her to be an expert in the music business. She found herself "surrounded with lawyers . . . and they knew what was right and regular."

According to her son, Michael James, Ruth "never liked" working at Tempo, and viewed it as "a family obligation . . . an assignment out of loyalty" to her brother. Gradually, she also "realized that [Duke arranged her position at Tempo to ensure] a certain amount of security for herself." Business records from the 1960s indicate that Ruth controlled 90 percent of the stock in Tempo, with Strayhorn holding the remainder. By 1969, her holdings were valued at $900,000 (more than $5 million in today's dollars), and that amount was probably conservative. Part of the reasoning behind the stock assignations was probably linked to tax issues—under this arrangement, less of Tempo's royalty income would be taxed as Ellington's personal income. Rather than enlarging his own bank account, Tempo was designed primarily to benefit his family and retain control of the proceeds from his writing. In the 1950s and 1960s, Ellington's son Mercer and his nephews Michael and Stephen James also worked for Tempo. According to Michael James, the incorporation of Tempo accomplished "several things at once" for Ellington. "Being independent of publishers, and taking care of his sister . . . He would feel that it was something his mother wanted him to do . . . It's all connected . . . The last connection with his mother was his sister."

After he left Mills, Ellington made moves to ensure a congenial business environment, and also to ensure that the people he cared most about, such as his sister and his close friend Strayhorn, were well taken care of. From their offices in the General Motors Building, Ruth, the lawyers, and the staff at Tempo reviewed incoming contracts and copyrighted Ellington's music as well as the songs of Ellington-related writers, including his son Mercer, band members such as Johnny Hodges, and Strayhorn. According to Ruth and Claire Gordon, Tempo purposely represented a place where Ellington felt comfortable. When he arrived at the office, it seemed as much a social occasion as a business one: "He'd just give me [Ruth] some kisses, look around, and visit, and leave." He did not want to hear about day-to-day recording or publishing business, but did wish to be appraised of the largest or most important deals. Ellington's management companies supervised recording deals, but Tempo handled rights for his music in all aspects: radio, recordings, movies, foreign. Like Mills Music, Ruth and the staff at Tempo placed ads in music trade publications for Ellington's songs, and went to nightclubs and record companies in order to get Tempo's songs covered by other artists. Ruth, along with her husband, often did the latter personally.

Tempo's casual atmosphere represented a stark contrast to the noisy and cutthroat Tin Pan Alley ambience of Mills Music. Claire Gordon recalled her work for the company as rigorous, but also noted that she often improvised the parameters of her job, much to the benefit of Ellington in one instance:

> I noticed that when I got the list from ASCAP of the music Ellington had written that [the list] was not complete . . . so I did the best I could to kind of [collate] all the music he'd written, all the things I could find . . . and then I sent to ASCAP all the missing music that I knew of, and I got him a double raise in ASCAP [royalties]. I didn't know if he ever knew that I did that. I don't think I ever told him, he was away at the time . . . it was [at] the end of '43.

With his sister overlooking the operation, presenting a friendly face to clients, and promoting his songs to artists and music-business representatives, he felt absolute trust and security concerning the handling of his music.

African American companies, because of the unique challenges they faced in the marketplace and in American life, often viewed men and women in different ways than nonblack businesses, according to historian Angel Kwolek-Folland. Tempo followed many of the patterns she documented. "In African American companies, ideal male figures contained all the elements of both manhood and womanhood: company rhetoric presented executives as strong, rational, business-like and professional, but also nurturing, tender, and benevolent toward employees and clients," she observed. "This combination constituted a sort of 'benign patriarch,' perhaps modeled on the black upper-class mode of patrician race service." The description dovetails well with the Ellington personality, the passive yet firm way he led his band, as well as the insistent teaching of his father in matters of manners and grooming, which his father absorbed from his years in the kind of service Kwolek-Folland described. Even Ruth's role, as the public face of the company, mirrored the different roles African Americans assigned to women in their companies. Kwolek-Folland found that black female workers often "embodied the refinement and class status the companies wanted to project."[34] Ruth Ellington's position presented a rather interesting balance in this regard: with her semicelebrity status and the furs and fine clothes she was known for sporting around town, she embodied "refinement and class" much like her famous brother. But whereas most female executives or managers of the period were viewed as unwomanly because of their power in a male-dominated business world, Ruth never seemed to have that problem. Yet, she also, by her own admission, was not a full executive—though she possessed the title and the stock accorded to her position, she functioned more as a figurehead than as one running all facets of the company. The lawyers took care of most of the details concerning contracts and setting royalties. The atmosphere at Tempo and other Ellington business enterprises could be homey and comforting at times, but the lack of fiscal discipline and professional management would cause Ellington financial problems, particularly during the last fifteen years of his life.

Ellington's creation of Tempo Music also reflected African American business trends and priorities. In her history of black business, Juliet E. K. Walker found that, starting in the 1930s, African American businesses were written about and promoted as "more than a mere enterprise to make profit for the owner . . . From the standpoint of both the customer and the owner it becomes a symbol of racial progress." Because blacks were frozen out of the best opportunities by discrimination, preachers and business people extolled the concept of the "double duty dollar" to maximize economic power in the black community by encouraging blacks to patronize black merchants. The Chicago Metropolitan Assurance Company provided an example of this kind of thinking when, in the mid-1930s, after a successful first decade of business, they erected their own building, even though renting space would have represented a less risky alternative. The company used the occasion to construct an edifice that graphically illustrated the success of the company and the fact that blacks could excel in the white-collar business world. In addition to office space, they added on the Parkway Ballroom, one of the premiere stage facilities in the country (Ellington played there), which proudly lacked a separate Jim Crow seating area. The ballroom did not return a regular profit, but the CMAC board did not object. They were more concerned with the facility's public-relations value in Chicago's black community.[35]

Ellington favored such economic "statements" concerning race. His views mirrored not only those of Booker T. Washington and W. E. B. DuBois, who both argued at the turn of the century that successful black business could act as a "springboard for racial toleration," but also African American columnists of the 1930s and 1940s, such as William Bell, who argued that blacks would receive more respect from whites if they wielded more spending power. Such thinking was reinforced by the first African American consumer boycotts in the 1940s against companies who advertised their products with racially offensive ads. Apologies and reversals by the companies followed, outcomes that some scholars believe set the stage for more ambitious civil rights protests of future decades. In the days before widespread marches and protests, when lynchings and police brutality were common, business was used as an arm of the civil rights cause, projecting pride, service, and solidarity, as much as financial gain.

Ellington believed in this philosophy, although he rarely spoke of it publicly. "You own one hundred million dollars, you go and demand something, you're somebody, you're somebody of substance," Ellington said in an unreleased interview from 1964. "You don't walk in and say 'I represent twenty million people,' you say 'I represent one hundred million dollars.' It has a different image." Ellington "felt the solution was economic," recalled his son Mercer in 1990. "His philosophy toward race was the achievement of financial support in order to go about these things legally."[36] In other words, it took money to litigate and overturn Jim Crow segregation. Polite pleas alone would not impel racists to back down from policies of exclusion. Building up African American economic power and independence seemed to many at the time to represent the most effective way of engendering respect and forwarding civil rights for blacks.

Also, the possession of economic power proved the intrinsic worth of a person in a peculiarly American way, or at least the worth of the work they did. As his Washington upbringing emphasized, Ellington believed that by achieving excellence, a person's work would be recognized, no matter their skin color. To this way of thinking, blacks deserved equality not just because of high-minded principles concerning equal rights, but because they held essential talents and insights that contributed to America and the world. As his sister Ruth remarked in 1936:

> I grant that we have got to combat a certain amount of prejudice, but race prejudice is more an inculcation than a color-psychosis. Color may make one's objective more difficult to attain, but color barriers melt more easily when we have accomplished. It's largely a matter of application. We need more zeal.[37]

Ellington continued to exhibit barrier-breaking zeal during the Swing Era with his African American "revu-sical" *Jump for Joy,* staged for eleven weeks during the summer of 1941 in Los Angeles.[38] It represented an "attempt to correct the race situation in the U.S.A. through a form of theatrical propaganda," recalled Ellington in the 1970s. "A show that would take Uncle Tom out of the theatre, eliminate the stereotyped image that had been exploited by Hollywood and Broadway, and say things that would make the audience think." In 1972, Ellington told the BBC that *Jump for Joy* emerged from the fact that

> We were very social-conscious and many things had to be said. And I was out in the neighborhood of California for about a year and around Hollywood and a lot of those intellectuals, some of them were labeled communists. And 15 Hollywood writers and I, we did *Jump for Joy,* which was supposed to bury Uncle Tom. As a matter of fact, we had him on his death bed in the opening, and his children dancing around clapping hands said he lived a good ripe old age, let him go, God bless him, you know. That was the opening originally. It was a great show, said a lot of wonderful things.

The production, with its combination of hit songs ("I Got It Bad and That Ain't Good") and politically pointed material ("Uncle Tom's Cabin Is a Drive-In Now") represented, in Ellington's words, "the hippest thing we ever did."

But for those who participated in the production, *Jump for Joy* transcended mere hipness. Despite the comic nature of the material and staging, the deeper mission lurking behind the gay costumes and swinging tunes resonated among the players as well as audiences. "I was more proud to have been in that show than any show I have ever done in my life," stated Alice Key, one of the dancers, in a 1999 interview. "We probably would have done it for free," said Avanelle Lewis Harris, another dancer. "The importance of its message caused a wave of enthusiasm throughout the cast, which was well aware of its controversial impact." Harris called *Jump for Joy* "uplifting" because "it was so different for us to sing about our people and what we were doing." In his autobiography, Ellington expressed pride reminiscing how the African American comedians "came off stage smiling, and with tears running down their cheeks" because they were able for the first time to perform without burnt-cork make-up (some initially resisted, skeptical of their ability to get laughs without it). Ellington also remarked on the class diversity of black audiences who saw the show, but noted that all shared the same reaction by the time of the nightly final curtain: "The Negroes always left proudly, with their chests sticking out."

The black press in Los Angeles shared a similar reaction. The *California Eagle* proclaimed the show "a home run" and a "daring satire of white society by a dusky brother." A month later in the same paper, Gilbert Allen tried to define what he viewed as the singularity of the production:

> At certain intervals, Duke Ellington stops playing and talks lectures in musical forms to the audience. He stands before his piano as if it were a pulpit and prates his message in music.
>
> What are you trying to say, Duke? The whole show, "Jump for Joy," seems to be a search for a new form. It is the democratic form of many minds, ideas, writers and races. "Jump for Joy" is not a happy show. There is too much double meaning in the jive lines.
>
> We laugh, but we are just Pagliaccis, because our hearts are filled with doubts, fears, hopes for a better America, wondering if our dreams of Democracy will crumple . . .
>
> "Jump for Joy" is a symbolic show with a political message. Duke Ellington is the head man, the voice in the wilderness crying to a troubled world, playing, directing, guiding, speaking the mind of oppressed Americans.

Within the guise of entertainment, Ellington again infiltrated his music and presentation with messages radiating race pride and scorning race prejudice. The sentiments expressed might have caused an angry backlash if printed on editorial pages, but the venue of the off-Broadway musical provided liberties not easily available elsewhere for blacks in American society. In 1967, Ellington explained his approach:

> *Jump for Joy* was well done because we included everything we wanted to say without saying it. Which is the way I think these social significance things should be handled, if it's going to be done on stage. Just to come out on the stage and take a soap box and stand in the spotlight and say ugly things is not entertainment.

Instead, the message was conveyed through the lack of Jim Crow stereotypes and the humorous but pointed lyrics, in which, according to one cast member, "every word meant something." The title song, its gospel-quartet feel welling up from the low-end choir of baritone saxophonist Harry Carney in harmony with the trombones, tweaked white Southern culture. The lyrics celebrated black culture, defied the way blacks were portrayed in stereotypical films such as the plantation-glorifying *Green Pastures* (1936), and subtly bragged about the death of Jim Crow. These were three qualities never seen in any other Swing Era big band recording.

Newspaper readers also realized something unusual was brewing when they read about how both black and white celebrities collaborated on and financed *Jump for Joy,* including Hollywood stars John Garfield and Mickey Rooney and the Broadway producer Sid Kuller. Charlie Chaplin and Orson Welles offered to direct. Harlem Renaissance poet Countee Cullen visited, and Langston Hughes contributed a lyric for a song in the production. In 1964, Ellington spoke about the nightly postshow conferences that shaped the content of *Jump for Joy:*

> I understand [issues of discrimination and stereotyping] more than anybody else because I was in *Jump for Joy,* where we had 12 weeks of discussions every night after the show concerning the Negro, the race, what constituted Uncle Tom, what constituted chauvinism, what constituted everything. I mean, we'd change a sketch practically every night. Fifteen cats would sit up and discuss it and *prove* in their discussions *why* this thing, where it appeared, where it was very, very funny, and it appeared to be legitimate, but actually it was a form of Uncle Tom because there was a compromise there. And it was, you know, done on a very high level. Pinpoint fine. You sit there and do that, and by that time, you get to see these things from all these different examples.

In a 1972 interview, Ellington detailed one of these late-night postshow sessions:

> Some of the best material had to come out, I mean not the best material, but most successful audience-wise material had to come out . . . it was a little chauvinistic here and there for instance. I remember one big [act] that was absolutely a riot. A comedy number with three black boys at one table sewing, you know, in a tailor shop and they were singing this Jewish song [Ellington sings in what sounds like Yiddish]. Well, this had to come out. Because you know what you're doing, you're doing what you're saying we don't want somebody to do to you. These were brilliant people, absolutely brilliant people [working on the show], none of that [racism] . . . You didn't do anything you didn't want somebody doing to you. And that's the way it had to be, clean.

The unusual cross-racial show business power that united to make the show possible, along with the discrimination-bashing nature of the material, made some whites uncomfortable. Tension resulted: one cast member was beaten, bomb threats were issued. The latter supposedly caused the removal of "I've Got a Passport from Georgia (and I'm Going to the U.S.A.)," one of the more controversial songs, in which a protagonist yearns for a town where the signs on businesses at noontime read "Out to Lunch" instead of "Out to Lynch." Cast members recalled that the song inspired a visit from a contingent of young men from the Glendale, California, Ku Klux Klan. They demanded the song be excised and hinted that violent action would be taken if their orders were not followed.

On two occasions, Ellington and the cast found that, even among the fairly liberal production staff, they still had to fight Jim Crow stage tradition. Though an early production decision had been made to ban dialect from the show, later on in the run, one director tried to insist on using it, inspiring a victorious cast rebellion. Herb Jeffries had a messier run-in with film star John Garfield, who, after the show had opened successfully, invested $10,000 in the production (a significant portion of the overall investment of $52,000) and assumed a "directorial" role, intent on making changes to help bring the show to Broadway. One night before the show, Garfield entered Jeffries's dressing room; it was the first time they had met. "I don't want to offend you," Garfield told Jeffries, a light-skinned African American. "But you know, your skin is very light against these people and your eyes are very blue." He suggested dark-skin make-up, and Jeffries acquiesced because of Garfield's "finance and influence" in the show: "OK, Mr. Garfield, whatever you want." Jeffries remembered clearly what happened when he stepped on stage:

> Ellington looked up at me, he was mortified . . . he was directing [the band in the orchestra pit] and he kept looking at me . . . he's following me across the stage and I'm wondering if something's wrong with my apparel. Maybe my pants are unzipped or something . . . I became very conscious. So the show went on. When intermission came on, Ellington was in my dressing room,[39] and his voice went way up high . . . [I'll] Never forget it. "Who do you think you are, Al Jolson?" I said, "No, buddy, Mr. Garfield." "Mr. Garfield?!? Mr. Garfield put that on your face?" I said, "No, make-up man did it. Mr. Garfield told him I was too light, I didn't look Negro." Boy, he flew out of that dressing room, and in about two minutes after that, make-up man came right back in, man, I think the audience thought I was two different people from the first half of the show to the second half of the show. See, these little things show you the philosophy of Ellington.

The various controversies, small bouts of self-censorship, and the constant reworking of the show by an unwieldy team of fifteen writers did not obscure the fact that *Jump for Joy* represented an unprecedented undertaking for black artists. A week and a half after *Jump for Joy* opened at the Mayan theater, a traveling Broadway production of *Cabin in the Sky,* with a larger budget and celebrity-ridden cast, opened in a more "swank" theater six blocks away. A local black weekly, the *Inter Church Tribune* compared the two: "*Cabin in the Sky,* expertly produced Broadway hit, nightly regales audiences with the white man's conception of the black man's conception of the eternal verities. Those Negroes cavorting about the stage know that their actions bear little resemblance to Negro life . . . that they are pandering to the white man's liking to Negrocaricature." Almena Davis, writing for the African American newspaper *Pittsburgh Courier,* had similar criticisms concerning *Cabin* and agreed with the *Inter Church Tribune* about the difference represented by Ellington's show:

> "Jump for Joy," gawky and as unaware of its real charm as an adolescent, is new and exciting. It's a new mood in the theatre, reflecting truly the happy-satire of colored life. In "Jump for Joy," Uncle Tom is dead. God rest his bones.

Initially, *Variety* pronounced the show "a tremendous hit, drawing a full house every night." When it closed, over a hundred shows later, the final performance sold out amid news reports that "the show is at last [being] readied for an Eastern tour, primarily Broadway." Reports were premature: despite excellent ticket sales, financing could not be secured for a national or New York run. In the late winter of 1942, Chicago newspapers carried word of a national tour that never coalesced.[40]

There are many theories why *Jump for Joy* never enjoyed a national or Broadway run. Racism no doubt played a role. The Ellington-written music was either hit material ("I Got It Bad") or hit-worthy ("Bli-Blip" as well as the title track). WMA possessed the resources and the financial interest, with Ellington as one of their main musical clients, to underwrite the production. Most likely, they and other potential investors calculated that it represented too much of a financial and/or social risk to present a musical portraying African Americans with equality on a national platform in 1941. It was one thing to assemble *Jump for Joy* in Los Angeles, where it was, according to dancer Avanelle Harris, "the first legitimate show to be created and produced on the West Coast." But to move the production east, where ingrained practice and discrimination had prevented the staging of all-black shows at top-level Broadway venues since the early 1920s, probably represented an impossible task for the time, despite exalted reviews and the fact that Ellington and the writers made sure it resembled entertainment far more than propaganda. Mercer Ellington felt that his father's race was not a factor in his career, except in the area of Broadway acceptance, where he argued that "there is a basic concept that they do not want a mixture of races on the stage." The fact that *Jump for Joy* stood alone for decades in its position as a major all-black show satirizing racism probably did not help matters. Light-hearted, well-scored shows highlighting controversial political points were viewed as failing economic propositions on the Great White Way since the Gershwins' World War I profiteer-bashing *Strike Up the Band* went belly-up upon opening in 1927, becoming a hit only when mostly sanitized of critical commentary three years later. When it came to the Carnegie Hall concert of January 1943, WMA and RCA backed Ellington's lyric-less extended composition *Black, Brown and Beige,* which programmatically documented African American history, with the biggest publicity campaign ever accorded an African American artist until that time. But they and other investors balked at the sentiments, however true and humorously expressed, found in *Jump for Joy.* By engaging in a production that openly revolted against the traditional signposts of prejudice in American entertainment, Ellington traversed farther than most of the country would allow him to go, despite the cultural capital he accumulated over the years.

The second major problem was a lack of expert management. As Norman

Granz, the future jazz entrepreneur who attended the show several times, pointed out, the *Jump for Joy* brain trust and financial backers were a group of enthusiastic, well-off Hollywood executives and stars who felt that Ellington deserved his own show and that it would be fun to put it together. They were not experienced Broadway producers and did not take proper preparations to maximize the chances of a successful run. With a cast of sixty, the payroll kept the show from profiting even when the theater sold out. No back-up financial reserve existed that could assume the exorbitant union costs a Broadway move would incur. Herb Jeffries recalled that, behind the scenes, "there was beaucoup confusion," much of it centering on the problem of "too many chiefs and not enough Indians. It suffered because it didn't have a single director." The fifteen investors always felt free to throw ideas into the pot, a situation that produced the late-night conversations Ellington savored, but it did not represent an optimal environment for assembling a successful Broadway production.

Other observers offered additional reasons for the failure of *Jump for Joy* to reach a national audience. In his autobiography, Ellington blamed the World War II drafting of performers for their inability to open in venues besides Los Angeles, but the 1942 Chicago articles indicated that the main members of the original cast were available for the never-realized productions. Mercer Ellington felt that his father was "too prolific" and "gave people too much" in all his Broadway projects, refusing to reprise material throughout a musical, as most composers would. Many have also noted that the 1941–42 ASCAP ban kept the Ellington songs from being played on the radio during the run of the show, denying them the hit status that might have inspired more financing and public interest. Some latter observers, including Granz, felt *Jump for Joy* failed as a social contribution as well, its lack of militancy and confrontation ensuring that the production only preached to the converted. "I'm not so sure that what it did had the impact that they had hoped it might have had initially because the people who went to see the show already felt that way," he said in 1989. Granz's viewpoint seemed to judge the proceedings by the standards of modern America, a milieu in which *Jump for Joy* would be viewed as timid. But compared to the usual images of African Americans that Americans received via film, music, and theater, it represented a huge difference, and probably any 1940s American would have recognized it.

During the Swing Era, when African American–derived music made untold amounts of money while African American bands faced tough racial barriers, no other major band or composer of the Swing Era made such a direct musical statement concerning the racism of American society. *Jump for*

Joy represented only the first of numerous failures by Ellington to initiate a successful Broadway show, the one area of show business he did not conquer in his lifetime. Musician and friend Brooks Kerr reported that Ellington regarded the show's closing without a national run as his greatest professional disappointment. "That killed me," Ellington told Kerr in the 1960s.

The Ellington orchestra's benefits for black causes and organizations, fairly common in the 1930s, were mostly usurped by benefits on behalf of the armed services and other war-oriented causes during World War II, such as the Joint Anti-Fascist Refugee Committee at Carnegie Hall in May 1944. His numerous domestic dates for servicemen were usually performed gratis and sometimes included postshow visits to VA hospitals. Like most bandleaders, Ellington became a fervent promoter and frequent purchaser of war bonds, and beginning in April 1945 did a series of dozens of radio shows sponsored by the U.S. Treasury Department that promoted bonds. He did this even though the USO remained "largely segregated during the war" and kept black bandleaders like Ellington from performing for troops overseas. Perhaps because of this hypocrisy, Ellington used his voice whenever possible to highlight the participation and sacrifice of blacks in the war. No black bandleader of the day, and very few white ones, established a stronger presence in performing and promoting on behalf of the war. But in interviews he made it clear that his strong support of the war, and the support by African Americans in general, was founded in political purpose as well as love of country. "We were freed and as before, we fought America's wars, provided her labor, gave her music, kept alive her flickering conscience, prodded her on toward the yet unachieved goal, democracy—until we became more than a part of America," Ellington said in Los Angeles during a sermon he gave based on Langston Hughes's poem "I, Too, Sing America." "We—this kicking, yelling, touchy, sensitive scrupulously-demanding minority—are the personification of the ideal begun by the Pilgrims almost 350 years ago."[41]

As Stuart Nicholson's research revealed, some of Ellington's war efforts placed him on the FBI's radar screen for the first time. Ellington allowed himself to be named as a sponsor for benefits set up by organizations that the FBI deemed later to be communist fronts: the American Committee to Save Refugees (10 November 1941), the Artists' Front to Win the War (16 October 1942), and American Youth for Democracy (2 April 1944). Ellington attended the latter benefit, a "tremendous, spontaneous demonstration of interracial unity" held at Carnegie Hall, and was photographed saluting patriotically with a white male dancer and a black female actress. At a

May 1944 Carnegie Hall benefit for the Joint Anti-Fascist Refugee Committee, an organization secretly "cited by the Attorney General of the United States as Communist," Ellington played a few numbers sans his band. The benefits and associations described by these FBI files were common during the war, when the strategic pairing of the United States with the Soviet Union inspired many domestic communist sympathizers to initiate fundraising to help the beleaguered Soviet Union. Also, as Lewis A. Erenberg noted, African American musicians occasionally supported Communist Party–related events "because the party acknowledged their national aspirations and their desire for inclusion in American life" much more than most organizations did, especially the federal government. No sources, including the FBI, considered Ellington a communist, or close to it, but they kept an eye on him throughout the 1940s and 1950s. In January 1944, the FBI filed a report concerning his mailing out 1,500 letters "on behalf of the National Committee to Abolish the Poll Tax." "The committee had been receiving money from the people Ellington contacted," they noted. One of these letters is preserved in record-company executive Goddard Leiberson's papers at Yale University. Ellington called the drive to abolish the poll tax "the most important issue since Abraham Lincoln freed the slaves" and argued its elimination would help "defeat Axis [Nazi and Imperial Japan] propaganda." A handwritten note on the letter indicates that Leiberson sent a check. As biographer Arnold Rampersad reported, FBI brass were particularly offended by the racially mixed audiences Langston Hughes attracted during the war;[42] since Ellington's shows and his social life were often similarly diverse, this probably gave the FBI another reason to loosely follow his activities.

Despite a lessening of public activities on behalf of black causes, Ellington was still viewed as a prime representative of African Americans. At the end of 1937, *Life* named him as one of "the 20 most prominent Negroes in America." In 1942, the Schomburg Collection of the New York Public Library announced that Ellington was selected to be part of a yearly list of twelve blacks and six whites "who have done the most to improve race relations." The Honor Roll of Race Relations also included George Washington Carver, Captain Hugh Mulzac ("for becoming the first colored captain of a U.S. merchant ship"), Paul Robeson, and Wendell Wilkie. The Schomburg's curator explained that these people were honored because "they strengthen morale and quicken the faith of the whole American people in the democratic ideal" by helping to "secure the rights of all of the people."

Sometimes Ellington also participated in actions, such as the letters advocating abolishing the poll tax, that were not picked up by the media. Claire Gordon recalled a time in 1943 when some "rich Jewish ladies" who knew of her association with Ellington tried to convince her to ask Ellington to attend a private benefit they were organizing to abolish the poll tax. When Gordon asked the Ellington orchestra road manager Jack Boyd about it, he "grumbled" that "Ellington doesn't want anything to do with that." She then asked Ellington herself, somewhat naively telling him he needed to do it because "your people are being disenfranchised." Ellington came to the benefit "resplendent" in a white suit, said he was happy to do it, played the piano, and "charmed all the ladies."[43] Through various public, private, and musical efforts, Ellington put blacks in a positive public light in the 1940s in a different, slightly more aggressive fashion than he had during the preceding decade.

Ellington's attitude on race becomes clearer with the evidence from this period. In private situations, he acted aggressively, as seen in the examples of the rejection of the plantation tableaus in his 1932 theater engagement, the resistance to minstrel make-up and dialect in *Jump for Joy,* or the various benefits he performed at and supported in the late 1930s and early 1940s. But in public, especially at musical events, Ellington shied from direct confrontation or statements. This policy led to tension with Ivie Anderson, the band's vocalist until 1942, because, as Ellington told Max Jones, "we found her bawling out white guys" during the band's Southern tours. Herb Jeffries, a person close to both Ellington and Anderson, confirmed the story:

> Oh yeah. Being a woman, naturally, she felt that she could get away with things and that no one would harm her or would hit her. And of course, when she was in the South, you had to be very careful with her, if you got out of line with her, she'd tell you off, you know, she'd tell a redneck off in a minute, especially if he used that word, you know, I mean she didn't care. And it was dangerous. Because . . . being raised in California, she didn't understand, you know, that you had to just sorta disregard it. But she didn't. She was on the soapbox. She'd fight any kind of discrimination . . . It didn't make no difference where it was, on or off the stand, or wherever. If . . . somebody would holler up and say "Hey girl, can you sing . . . " "Wait a minute, what do you mean 'girl?' I'm a lady." Very dangerous . . .

Ellington told Jones that he told Anderson "that had to stop," citing issues of "discretion and personal safety." It also increased the possibility of bad publicity for the band, which could eclipse the message Ellington carefully honed concerning black artistry and respectability. No matter how justified Anderson's individual struggles with hecklers, Ellington felt there existed more powerful and lasting ways of making a statement.

Jeffries, who traveled with the band for years, and whose Smithsonian oral-history interview featured numerous examples of how the Ellington orchestra found food unavailable for traveling black musicians of the 1940s, summed up Ellington's attitude on these issues in this period:

> Duke Ellington was a diplomat. You see, if the door is closed, you get nobody's ear. If you got your foot in the door, somebody might hear you. See, Ellington, as much as I can remember, and let me tell you something, it's a good philosophy in a way, he said he never did any freedom riding, he did freedom walkin' ... Ellington knew he was getting in with his music, and everybody heard him. You have to be very careful; it's very dangerous to be political and musical. If you're musical, you can get anyplace. If you're political, a lot of doors will get shut on you. One doesn't always have to voice his feelings in order for him to find a way to have an effect.

Jeffries recalled a miserable night in the particularly prejudiced town of Moline, Illinois, in the early 1940s, where the band had to stay on their Pullman train and experienced more difficulty than usual obtaining a meal. Jeffries asked Ellington why he even bothered to play such places. Ellington replied:

> The accommodations you're having on a Pullman right now are far better than the funky hotels in Moline, Illinois, whether you realize it or not, plus the fact that I am here to keep my men employed. Maybe you can't go into a hotel and stay here, but when you go backstage there'll be a line of these [white] people out there getting your black autograph. That is far more effective than fighting this thing [when it] is not the time to fight it.

Ellington walked a delicate line, writing and talking about black history and culture at every opportunity, yet participating in the system of segregated venues and accommodations in many American cities, not just the South. Jeffries recalled that it was "very painful to be living with men [with whom] you are making your living, men who are your constituents, men who you are living with like relatives, like family, [and see them] subjected to this kind of indignation." Ellington would never make a similar statement in his lifetime, though he must have seen countless examples of the "indignation" Jeffries described. Instead, he chose to present himself as someone unaffected and untarnished by racist attempts to belittle and take status from black Americans. Also, he made the decision that his priority was his music as well as his ability to share his creative gifts in the very expensive way that he preferred, with a big band of fifteen musicians. Music served as the platform for his main statements on race in America, not only because his mentors did the same, but also because he knew he did not possess the force to institute significant changes by making a stand. Such a stand—against segregated shows or Jim Crow discrimination—would only undercut his ability to write, record, and perform at a high level in the public eye, as very few blacks could. H. Robert Udkoff, an old Ellington friend, recalled an early 1940s Ellington show at the Trianon Ballroom in Los Angeles, where management told Ellington that they had a "problem" because a "bunch of colored kids" wanted to enter the ballroom and "you know, we can't have that." Ellington volunteered to talk to them, and Udkoff accompanied him. "I know how you feel, they won't let you in, [but] this is not the time," Udkoff remembered Ellington telling the six to eight young black men. "If you make any trouble, there's gonna be 15 guys [in the Ellington orchestra] ... Negroes, they're gonna be out of a job, and they're the ones supporting the NAACP." Ellington "talked them out of any problem, and sent them on their way."

From his years of traveling with and befriending Ellington, Jeffries learned that people who thought and acted like diplomats in the civil rights struggle, "who don't get up and fight it, and close the door," were needed in addition to the more vocal and political protesters. "Ellington didn't want to close any doors," Jeffries concluded. "He didn't close any doors, he opened a lot of them. Of course, again, we have to realize this is the history of our country being made."[44]

By the closing years of the Swing Era, Ellington had finally conquered the music-business discrimination characterizing the era and grabbed for himself and his band a part of the greatest commercial bonanza that the jazz world would ever experience. But he did it in his own way, further establishing a reputation that allowed him to enjoy a career that flourished long after Swing Era fads and bands faded into the historic distance. His path through the Swing Era was particularly characterized by his presentation of an African American image of eloquence, power, and achievement that brooked no equal in the American media. As the 1940 publication of author Richard Wright's violent and disturbing *Native Son* and labor leader A. Philip Randolph's 1941 threat of a black march on Washington hinted at the waxing willingness of African Americans to wage conflict to achieve equality, Ellington presented a focused, though highly differentiated, argument for equality. In an essay accompanying the 1989 edition of *Native Son,* John Reilly argued that the book showed that "violence is a personal necessity for the oppressed" person and that "defiant rejection of society is the only independent action society has left him."[45] Ellington had demonstrated, and would continue to demonstrate, that direct confrontation on a mass level, or on the individual level that Bigger Thomas unconsciously struggled with, did not represent the only—or even the most effective—counter to the virulently racist American system.

But nothing exemplified the singular path Ellington trod through the Swing Era and World War II more than the Carnegie Hall premiere of *Black, Brown and Beige.*

6
BLACK, BROWN AND BEIGE

It is only in his music, which Americans are able to admire because a protective sentimentality limits their understanding of it, that the Negro in America has been able to tell his story. It is a story which otherwise has yet to be told and which no American is prepared to hear . . .

The story of the Negro in America is the story of America—or, more precisely, it is the story of Americans. It is not a very pretty story: the story of a people is never very pretty. The Negro in America, gloomily referred to as that shadow that lies athwart our national life, is far more than that. He is a series of shadows, self-created, intertwining, which we now helplessly battle . . .

This is why his history and his progress, his relationship to all Americans, has been kept in the social arena. He is a social and not a personal or a human problem; to think of him is to think of statistics, slums, rapes, injustices, remote violence; it is to be confronted with an endless cataloguing of losses, gains, skirmishes; it is to feel virtuous, outraged, helpless, as though his continuing status among us were somehow analogous to disease—cancer, perhaps, or tuberculosis—which must be checked, even though it cannot be cured. In this arena the black man acquires quite another aspect from that which he has in life. We do not know what to do with him in life; if he breaks our sociological and sentimental image of him we are panic-stricken and we feel ourselves betrayed. When he violates this image, therefore, he stands in the greatest danger (sensing which, we uneasily suspect that he is very often playing a part for our benefit); and, what is not always so apparent but is equally true, we are then in some danger ourselves—hence our retreat or our blind and immediate retaliation.

JAMES BALDWIN, 1951

Duke sometimes thinks that it is good business to conceal his interest in . . . American Negro history. He doubts if it adds to his popularity in Arkansas, say, to have it known that in books he has read about Negro slave revolts he has heavily underlined paragraphs about the exploits of Nat Turner and Denmark Vesey . . . New acquaintances are always surprised when they learn that Duke has written poetry in which he advances the thesis that the rhythm of jazz has been beaten into the Negro race by three centuries of oppression. The four beats to a bar in jazz are also found, he maintains in verse, in the Negro pulse. Duke doesn't like to show people his poetry. "You can say anything you want on the trombone, but you gotta be careful with words," he explains. RICHARD O. BOYER, *New Yorker,* 1944[1]

It was, as of that date, the biggest and most publicized night of Duke Ellington's career. On 23 January 1943, the Ellington orchestra appeared in its first concert at Carnegie Hall before a racially mixed, celebrity-filled SRO audience that included first lady Eleanor Roosevelt, conductor Leopold Stokowski, soprano Marian Anderson, poet Langston Hughes, and academic Alain Locke. In the weeks preceding, stories about the event ran prominently in several national publications. The highlight of the evening was the premiere of Ellington's longest extended work, the forty-five-minute *Black, Brown and Beige: A Tone Parallel to the History of Negro in America*—a composition in three movements meant to illustrate the story of black Americans, from their abduction from Africa to their role in World War II.

With this event, Ellington used the music business power at his disposal as well as the patriotic sentiments swirling around American engagement in World War II to place the subject of black respectability, pride, and history into the national consciousness even more fully than he had done before. The concert further solidified his reputation as a serious composer who created works outside of the usual popular music experience and as a historical figure whose journey evinced a transformative effect on America's racial and cultural landscape.

Benny Goodman and John Hammond had brought jazz and black music to Carnegie in the late 1930s, but under far different circumstances. In terms of repertoire and arrangements, Goodman's 1938 Carnegie appearance resembled a typical show with his band, although guest musicians did appear (including moonlighting Ellington band members). Hammond's 1938 "Spirituals to Swing" Carnegie program took pride in presenting musicians unversed in the music business, without musical training or note-reading skills, arguing that such attributes signified a more authentic version of black music. Conversely, Ellington brought an entirely different, more serious vision of popular and black music to Carnegie in 1943, and did it amidst skillfully applied maximum corporate marketing and national media coverage. It was an event where issues of business, art, and race were conjoined uniquely, stimulating a national discussion on a larger scale than ever before about the history and meaning of black, popular, and American music.

What the audience did not hear that night was Ellington's impassioned explanation of what this music was all about. They were unaware that Ellington had also written a verbal narrative—a uniquely personal window into how he viewed black history and his role within it.

Ellington voiced his intentions to write a musical panorama celebrating black history since the early 1930s. A 1930 interview in the *Christian Science Monitor* served as the first hint of the project in the media. "The tragedy is that so few records have been kept of the Negro music of the past," Ellington mused. "It has to be pieced together so slowly. But it pleases me to have a chance to work at it." In interviews from 1932 and 1933, he described the project-in-progress as a five-part "symphonic saga of the African race . . . from the time of his life in the African jungle to present-day Harlem." Ellington indicated that the fifth movement would demonstrate "the great enlightenment [Ellington] envisions for future generations of his people." A Dallas reporter, in a 1933 article entitled "Ellington Composing," quoted Ellington on the "negro suite . . . which has been in the process of composition for several months." By late 1933 or 1934, at least one live review from an Omaha newspaper revealed that the Ellington orchestra was playing "snatches from [the] 'African Suite.'" The pageants Ellington attended as a youth in Washington, D.C., that celebrated "Negro life and music" and history inspired him, especially W. E. B. DuBois' *The Star of Ethiopia*. A few black theater and Broadway productions and black composers presented themes of black history in individual songs and tableaus during the 1920s and early 1930s.[2] But none strove to present as serious and historically accurate a picture of black history as *Black, Brown and Beige*.

By 1939, the "negro opera" had not reached completion, but Ellington still tinkered with it and talked about it, perhaps hoping to build interest in the project. During his 1939 tour of Sweden, he spoke of the "almost completed" piece to two reporters and remarked that "the Rockefellers" were interested in backing the production. By 1941, Ellington told a journalist that he had completed a libretto and the music, and that he viewed his work as a kind of corrective to the more academic musical visions of black history supplied by composers who followed classically oriented rules of composition. "I wrote it because I want to rescue Negro music from well-meaning friends . . . All arrangements of historic American Negro music have been made by conservatory-trained musicians who inevitably handle it with a European technique," Ellington stated. "It's time a big piece of music was written from the inside by a Negro." During a 1942 interview conducted in the balcony of an Illinois theater amidst the "gun play, fist fights, and auto wrecks" of a gangster movie, Ellington once again brought up his five-part "opera," now titled *Boola*. "The title, Mr. Ellington explained, is significant because Boola means a negro who has performed an outstanding deed or made a noteworthy contribution to the history of his race," reported columnist Belle Ayer. "Five of the 10 years which have gone into the writing were put in on research, and the other five years were required to write the book and the music." "All I need now," Ellington told Ayer, "is the cash to put it into production."[3]

Even after having hinted at his project for over a decade in the media, Ellington could not procure a backer for *Boola*. As he found when trying to mount a national Broadway run for *Jump for Joy,* backers (or, as they were referred to at the time, "angels") for progressive black productions were difficult, if not impossible, to find. Despite the interracial and international fame and financial power of the Ellington name, America was still highly segregated, and not just in the South. When Ellington mused to reporters about African and African American slave history in a fairly accurate if truncated manner, it was a rare instance of black history being discussed in the mass media. To put such views on display in the national context of a major Broadway show or opera was unthinkable—not even Ellington could pull it off. Producing a major black Broadway show was easier and more common at the turn of the century than during World War II, when no major black shows had been produced for two decades on Broadway. Ellington's work on *Boola* and *Jump for Joy* indicated that, by World War II, he felt the time had arrived for him to address issues of discrimination and black identity in a more direct and verbal manner. But the backers, interested more in noncontroversial, glamorous investments that brought a return, evidently did not agree. *Boola* was never finished or produced, but many of its ideas were evidently incorporated into *Black, Brown and Beige*.

The events of World War II offered new opportunities to present themes of racial equality, which Ellington took advantage of in *Black, Brown and Beige*. While unity and patriotism were stressed in publicity promoting the American war effort, racial tension and violence erupted in urban areas and within the ranks of the armed services, whose policies not only segregated black troops but forbade them leadership roles and mostly relegated them to noncombat service positions. In the midst of Nazi and Japanese propaganda pointing out the hypocrisy of Jim Crow laws and violence in a supposed democracy, the United States government and media were eager to portray a front of united diversity, even though such a view represented a distortion of reality.[4]

Ellington used this wartime yearning for unity and patriotism as a way to inject views of black identity, culture, and equality into the national media. Such perspectives were more welcomed than usual on the home front. Ellington's focus on the black contribution to American wars throughout history in the piece promoted unity and patriotism, but it also highlighted the fact that blacks still had second-class citizenship after exhibiting first-class bravery on behalf of their country for over a century. Ellington and other black spokespeople of the 1940s hoped that their support of the American war effort would lead to a long-postponed improvement of their social and political situation. The largely nonverbal *Black, Brown and Beige* did not feature bald satire concerning Jim Crow, like *Jump for Joy,* or a graphic illustration of the pain of slavery, as *Boola* promised to, but it presented a vision of blackness rarely acknowledged in the American mass media. It also served as another example of how music served Ellington as an ideal, nonconfrontational medium to transmit messages about character and identity that defied stereotypes and took an obvious, though subtle, stand for black equality.

Most sources agree that William Morris, Jr., was the prime instigator in pushing for Ellington to play Carnegie Hall for the first time, although an Ellington appearance there had been rumored at various times during the previous decade, and two sources report that Ellington had been offered a Carnegie concert in 1937, a year before Goodman's concert there, but Irving Mills rejected the idea because "there wasn't enough money in it."[5] "Ellington was very fond" of Morris, recalled his nephew Michael James, because of his support of ambitious and potentially controversial projects like *Jump for Joy* and *Black, Brown and Beige.* Morris "had the class, the education and he knew the business too. He was sophisticated enough to understand what Duke was . . . [he] saw Ellington in Carnegie Hall, and that says a lot about him." In 1964, Ellington recalled that after an extended period on the West Coast in 1941 and 1942, the orchestra returned to the East Coast in the fall of 1942. Because they'd received little promotion in that area in recent months, "we had a hard time getting proper money going into the Apollo [Theater, in Harlem], so I didn't take it, so William Morris says to me, 'What you need is a Carnegie Hall concert.'"[6]

Ellington's memory of events may be faulty here on one count, as Klaus Stratemann's research indicated that throughout 1942 and on both coasts, the band did extremely good business—sometimes even record business. In addition, Ellington won top honors in *Down Beat*'s annual All Star Swing Poll at the end of 1942, wresting the crown from Benny Goodman, the holder of the title for four of the previous five years. *Metronome* named Ellington's band the best of 1942, and of the entire preceding decade.[7] But Ellington's intimation that the Carnegie show was meant to spruce up bookings was also correct. One possible reason for the show was to provide publicity for the Ellington orchestra during the Petrillo ban, which, because of a union dispute, kept bands from recording from 1941 to 1942 and reduced the Ellington orchestra's presence in the popular music marketplace.[8]

Ellington threw himself into the work. "I think I started writing *Black, Brown and Beige* on the 19th of December, we were playing the [State] Theater in Hartford, and Frank Sinatra was the extra-added attraction ... I was writing it all the way down from Hartford down to Bridgeport, on out to Detroit and various other places," he recalled twenty years later. "I was always writing in the hotel, in the backstages of theaters, Columbus, Ohio." In Hartford, Ellington remembered composing the piece backstage behind the curtain as his band was taking a break, writing the notes down on manuscript while the co-billed Sinatra performed and the movie *Cat People* was showing. He joked that he wasn't sure which of the two influenced him more.[9]

WMA threw its promotional machinery into high gear supporting the Ellington orchestra's first Carnegie concert, promoting and presenting Ellington in a manner that suggested his status as one of the giants of the show business world that they commonly represented. "National Ellington Week" was proclaimed, inspiring stories in *Time, Newsweek,* and the *New York Times.* A lavish spread in the national pictorial magazine *Look* was the first ever dedicated to an African American band. Numerous radio broadcast tributes, arranged by WMA, were aired. WMA sponsored a half-page ad in *Variety* featuring a portrait of Ellington and a short essay ending with these lines: "His concert at Carnegie Hall this Saturday evening will be a fitting climax to twenty years of brilliant achievement ... and will mark the beginning of a new development in the career of a great creative artist."[10]

The hype surrounding the January 1943 Carnegie concert marked the height of the WMA's marketing of Ellington—nothing this elaborate, creative, or involved would be attempted again by the organization on his behalf. It also represented a continuation, at a more advanced level, of the Mills-era strategy to stress values of quality and respectability in the marketing of Ellington and to have the public view him as an important composer, as well as a hit-maker. This strategy was particularly exemplified in an ad the company designed, along with RCA Victor, to coincide with the Carnegie concert. "Ellington Music is never dated!" roars the banner headline. "Two-thirds of the records made by Duke Ellington for Victor and Bluebird labels during the *last fifteen years* are available and being sold today—including four numbers waxed on his first date in 1927!" bragged the ad copy. "No other recording dance band can make that statement!" The ad also touted Ellington's setting of "new theater marks in recent weeks" in four major cities, his recent film appearances, and the upcoming Carnegie concert. Two more slogans completed the pitch: "America's Most Original Exponent of Orchestral Technique!" and, one plagiarized from the Mills campaigns of the early 1930s, "Creator of a New Vogue in American Dance Music!"[11]

RCA Victor also pulled out all the stops in promoting the 1943 Carnegie debut, stressing Ellington's identity as an artist who merged highbrow and popular sensibilities. Three different advertisements refer to Ellington as a "genius of jazz" or as a composer who performs concerts at Carnegie Hall, America's premiere classical music venue, including one featuring a cartoon image of Ellington clad in a tuxedo, baton in hand, looking like a classical conductor. As Joseph Horowitz documented in his cultural history of classical music in America, celebrity conductors such as Arturo Toscanini and Leopold Stokowski had, by the late 1930s, superseded composers and performers as the premiere archetypes of classical music. For RCA, record company home to Toscanini, to present Ellington in this role was a prescient and significant move. In the weeks surrounding the concert, more direct appeals were sent to RCA's dealers and their best customers around the country, praising Ellington's work as "unadulterated American Negro music" beyond the scope of "ephemeral Tin Pan Alley tunes."[12] The extensive marketing tactics undertaken by WMA and RCA mirrored Ellington's long-held ideas that popular music and black music should be taken seriously.

It was rare to find popular musician-songwriters, black or white, being marketed in this manner. A 1946 study by Harold H. Kassarjian demonstrated that these images of Ellington were in marked contrast to how blacks were usually depicted in the mass media. Kassarjian found that out of every 1,000 magazine ad pages, only 5.83 featured drawn or photographed African American models. Seventy-eight percent of those ads featured blacks performing menial labor or service jobs. Fifteen percent of them featured blacks as entertainers and sports figures. Only one out of the tens of thousands of ads Kassarjian examined pictured an African American in a white-collar occupation. He hypothesized that the ads depicting "the 1946 Negro" posed little threat to the middle-class whites who were the primary supporters of these magazines.[13] The concentrated efforts to picture Ellington as an avatar of American culture whose best works earned long-term artistic significance were a challenge to the status quo of American racial life as portrayed in the American media.

Ellington used the occasion of the unprecedented national media exposure to expound upon black history and character, subjects rarely broached in such quarters. "I always say that there are more churches in Harlem than cabarets," he told the *New York Times Magazine*. "The Negro is not merely a singing and dancing wizard but a loyal American in spite of his social position. I want to tell America how the Negro feels about it." The article also spent a long paragraph describing Ellington's vision of black history as expressed in *Black, Brown and Beige,* including the "sorrows" of slavery and "Jim Crowism" after the end of slavery. A lengthy piece in *Down Beat* included more detail on this subject, and Ellington argued that his band was uniquely situated to tackle the topic. "The things we use are purely Negroid—we want to stay in character," he said. "We are, in the final analysis, the only serious exponents of Negro music." Ellington also expounded on the modern-day importance of education for African Americans: "Without enough food, with no clothes at all, with hardly a roof over his head, even the poorest sharecropper struggles to put his kids through school." Perhaps with such quotes in mind, the *Harlem People's Voice* proclaimed in their review of Ellington's Carnegie Hall debut that "he is the articulate spokesman for the existence of a new Negro with a new point of view." In the months after the Carnegie Hall debut, Ellington continued his focus on black history on national radio broadcasts by performing "Barzillai Lew," a new medium-tempo swinging instrumental named after a black military hero of the American Revolution.[14]

Record reissues represented another area in which images of Ellington as a trailblazing and historically important figure were emphasized around the time of the initial Carnegie Hall concert. The big band craze and various *Down Beat* and *Metronome* articles celebrating the history of pre–Swing Era jazz helped fuel the market for reissues, making record companies realize that older recordings, at least the better ones, retained commercial value. This represented quite a change from the 1920s, when companies and bands viewed recordings as disposable artifacts. Ellington had always viewed his recorded work as having long-term impact—and now his views were being confirmed in the marketplace. Since the 1943 Carnegie show was partially promoted as a way to mark Ellington's first two decades in the music business, looking back at his past achievements proved a natural and irresistible potential financial bonanza for record companies. Both RCA Victor and Ellington's label before that, Brunswick, released four-disc, 78-rpm "albums" of Ellington evergreens in the weeks surrounding the concert. A serious artistic and historical aura characterized the packaging and marketing of these compilations. On RCA Victor's *A Duke Ellington Panorama,* which surveyed eight recordings ranging from 1927 to 1940, dates and musicians for each track were listed, along with "commentary" by "an authority on Ellingtonia" that stressed Ellington's "unorthodox" approach to music.[15]

Such nostalgic collections became common in future decades. The practice kept significant older recordings in circulation, adding profits to the coffers of record companies, performers, and songwriters without incurring new production costs aside from packaging and promotion. Such sets also received plenty of publicity from journalists who enjoyed opportunities to expound on the subject of music history in magazines like *Down Beat* and *Metronome.* But reissues evinced a negative effect also, especially on a restless, adventurous artist like Ellington. They created a situation in which Ellington, for the rest of his career, had to compete with his younger self. After the Swing Era, as his audience aged and became less active in following the music scene, he continued to develop as a composer and explore new musical areas. When faced with the choice of purchasing new and unfamiliar Ellington material or well-known hits from decades past, audiences often took the less risky route. As part of Ellington's future record deals, labels often required him to record new versions of older hits such as "Mood Indigo" and "Solitude" so that, even after Ellington left their employ, the companies retained familiar consumer-friendly Ellington product in their catalog that they could sell for decades. Ellington's last session for Brunswick in 1939 featured such material, and it represented the start of a pattern in his recording history. These sessions made Ellington money, especially as a songwriter, and helped finance his band, but they also ensured less attention for his finest and most demanding works of the 1940s and beyond.

Ellington's Carnegie debut benefited Russian war relief, a cause that added to the patriotic and urgent mood of the proceedings. The concert sold out twelve days in advance, and "an overflow crowd of about 2,000 persons milled about the sidewalks and lobby of [the 3,000-person capacity] Carnegie Hall Saturday night in the hope of securing tickets." One of the more astute critics and observers of the music business, Irving Kolodin, predicted that Ellington could have filled the venue for at least one more night, "yielding that much more to the Russian War Relief program . . . [and] show[ing] how long this appearance of Ellington in a formal concert has been overdue here." It was viewed as more than a musical event, particularly by black newspapers. "We won't wait until the concert is over. All the bigwigs will be shouting then and you may not hear us," wrote one on the eve of the show. "That [Ellington] will make good goes without saying." The *New York Post* predicted that "the Carnegie performance will be the most important milestone in the Duke's career."[16]

All accounts described the unique atmosphere surrounding the arrival of the Ellington orchestra at Carnegie. The *New York Post* assigned two reviewers to the show, their "swing analyst" and their classical music critic. The latter set the scene vividly:

I must say that to a regular concert-goer Carnegie Hall didn't seem like Carnegie Hall Saturday evening. As a rule one knows the faces, if not the names, of half the people there. Week after week you see the same white-haired dowagers in ermine, the same rakishly mustached man about town, the same gentleman with a Vandyke beard and monocle who looks more like the popular conception of a music critic than any music critic of my acquaintance.

None of these showed up Saturday. Their places were taken by a horde of glamorous strangers, who came to hear Duke Ellington make his debut in this historic auditorium. Celebrities were practically hanging from the chandeliers.

The *Washington Afro-American* reported that bandleaders Count Basie, Jimmie Lunceford, and Benny Goodman attended, with Goodman picking up the check for the concert proceeds of $5,000 on behalf of Russian war relief. Mills Music, Inc., and Irving Berlin, Inc., bought $100 boxes, and Frank Sinatra left his engagement at the Paramount to visit backstage, posing arm-in-arm with Betty Roche, the black vocalist who did a stellar job with "The Blues" section of *Black, Brown and Beige* that evening. Ellington made it a point to pose for pictures that night with noncelebrity black servicemen. A headline in the *Washington Afro-American* touted how the occasion of Ellington at Carnegie caused "Jitterbugs and Millionaires [to] Rub Elbows" within the hallowed American venue of classical music. The younger jivesters and jitterbugs were also visible onstage, where "the overflow" of paid customers necessitated the presence of "almost 200 [patrons] seated on the stage. A sideshow were a couple of hyper-enthusiastic jazz savants whose peckin' antics [hand percussion], in tempo with the Duke's rhythm, made for a visual obligato to the basic tempos," according to *Variety*. Columnist Elsa Maxwell noted that the mixed nature of the crowd was de rigueur for an Ellington performance:

> The spirit of his audience, made up of equal parts of black, brown, and beige listeners, is always magnificently infectious . . . Duke never has a typical American concert audience, attending for "cultural" reasons and carefully applauding in the "right" places. We his listeners are more like Italians at their local little opera houses, enthusiastically singing their favorite Verdi arias along with the singers on the stage . . . It occurred to me that here is **our** native music being given the audience it deserves.[17]

The diverse crowd heard a program carefully constructed by Ellington to demonstrate the merit and personality of the band and its material. None of their current hit singles made the set list, nor were any pop vocals part of the program.[18] Each of the compositions carried an implicit artistic statement, either as a programmatic portrait of events and personalities in black history or as an Ellington-designed tribute to the skills of an outstanding individual in the orchestra. The show began with "The Star-Spangled Banner," probably meant as a reminder of the war but also as a signal of Ellington and the orchestra's loyalty towards the United States. Despite the fact that he would spend much of the ensuing evening celebrating black culture and history, Ellington made it clear from the outset that he harbored no radical or unpatriotic intentions. Without any spoken introduction, Ellington and the band then began "Black and Tan Fantasy," the song that first brought them national attention in 1927. But the version played this night demonstrated the maturity of the band's musical vision and prowess in the intervening years. Extended to twice its original length, and following a more languid, bluesy pace than the original, the piece allowed extra room for the soloists' eloquent restatements of the bittersweet melody co-written by Ellington and Bubber Miley. Throughout the evening, older compositions were endowed with new dynamics, entirely rethought by Ellington ("Portrait of Florence Mills" represented another example of this), making clear how pronounced the difference was between his aesthetics of 1927 and 1943. Next, the band tackled two compositions attributed to Ellington's son Mercer, the first of which, "Moon Mist," in its meticulously rendered detail and beauty, may have represented the band at its finest form that evening. Preceding the premiere of *Black, Brown and Beige* were, in the words of Ellington from the stage that night, "our portraits": programmatic tributes to black cultural figures Bert Williams, Bill "Bojangles" Robinson, and Florence Mills.

Ellington's spoken introduction to *Black, Brown and Beige* is uncharacteristically awkward with incomplete sentences and faulty grammar. Usually, in dozens of performances recorded over the decades, he is consistently eloquent. But, on this night, he stumbled on his verbal presentation in introducing the first movement. Perhaps this indicated how important the evening and the composition were to him, or perhaps it reflected the last-minute preparation and revisions of the piece that went on backstage in the hours and days before the Carnegie concert. Trombonist and copyist Juan Tizol recalled receiving shots from Ellington's physician and close friend Dr. Arthur Logan to keep them awake while extracting the score since, according to his wife Rose, "a couple of days and nights without any sleep" preceded the Carnegie premiere.[19]

To this day, *Black, Brown and Beige* is not an immediately penetrable work, either musically or in its attempt to document black history. Numerous listenings are required for its ideas to instill their intended effect. Part of the reason for this is its strictly programmatic, nonverbal nature (although "The Blues" section in *Brown* does feature a lyric). Ellington commonly wrote in that kind of style, but for *Black, Brown and Beige,* he also wrote a scenario that rendered, in both rhyming and free verse, the images he captured through music. There is a sadness and a frustration expressed in the unpublished scenario that he never voiced in public. The reception of the work would have definitely been altered had critics possessed the document upon its premiere. Perhaps the reason it never came out was that, by 1943, Ellington had already witnessed the lack of financial support given to projects that overtly (if humorously) challenged Jim Crow and celebrated little-known African and African American history. The scenario for *Black, Brown and Beige* did both in a thought-provoking way rarely seen in the mainstream media or the historical profession in the 1940s. Today, the historical facts referenced are accepted and even conservative; in 1943, the script probably would have aroused resistance, controversy, and criticism. Ellington sought to avoid such reactions.

The *Black, Brown and Beige* script is a fascinating document, polished and surprisingly poetic, proof of Ellington's research.[20] It lends credence to his 1944 claim that he had educated himself by amassing an eight-hundred-volume library of books about "Negro culture and its evolution."[21] Mercer Ellington recalled that his father started assembling the collection in a more serious fashion immediately after the band's 1933 European tour. Billy Strayhorn also inferred that *Black, Brown and Beige* was linked to that tour, and felt sure that the composition "would not have seen the light of day if Duke hadn't gone to England that first time. He used to tell me [that] when [he] found out his music was talked about in the press just like Stravinsky and Ravel, [and] he realized they considered him a real composer and took his music seriously, it gave him the strength to go on." In an unpublished 1956 interview, Ellington said that the title of *Black, Brown and Beige:*

> has to do with the state of mind, not the color of the skin. Because when [Africans] arrived, everything was real black, you know. The Negro thought that when he was being brought here from Africa that he was being brought as food, because he was a very delicious thing, and they expected to be eaten. And when they got here, they found all they had to do [was] the work, it lightened. It lightened. It got to be brown with the entrance of the spiritual,

which was later . . . So gradually it got lighter. In *Black, Brown and Beige,* of course we went on up to [the color] cream and so forth, and various other degrees, but it never got quite right. There was still a little jazz in there [laughs heartily].

In Ellington's *Black, Brown and Beige* scenario, he claimed with obvious pride that the "seeds of the first civilization known to man" as well as innovations such as glassmaking, bronze-smelting, and Grecian art arose from blacks on the African continent:

> In the kingdom of Songhay
> There flourished a system of agriculture, law,
> Literature, music, natural sciences, medicine,
> And a schooling system, too. As early as the
> Eleventh century you were weaving cotton . . .
> In the Sudan!

He seemed to tease the white historical establishment who, until that time, had largely ignored the spoken histories of Africa as voiced through the generations by griots: "How many scholars know the 'Epic of the Sudan,' / To measure the classics of any land?"

Ellington's portrait of Africa differed vastly from the primitive, third-world visions (or worse) usually presented in the media, and aligned with heroic portrayals of history practiced by nonacademic black historians of the nineteenth and twentieth centuries such as William Wells Brown, Frederick Douglass, J. W. C. Pennington, and, most famously during Ellington's lifetime, Joel A. Rogers. Their intensively researched books were ignored or belittled in the white media and in the historical profession, but were common items in black households of the 1940s and before, and continue to be so today. In their works, sometimes sold as pamphlets on street corners to reach the widest audience, the authors strongly contested the notion advanced by bigots that Africans had never invented anything worthwhile or contributed to human progress.[22] They represented a kind of historic and scientific arm of the civil rights movement, bringing solace and strength to American urban black communities.

Some of Ellington's evidence evidently came from academically accepted scholars such as Franz Boas and DuBois,[23] but Ellington adopted the more heroic tone of the nonacademic black historians. DuBois, in *The Negro,* featured a Boas quote: "Neither ancient Europe, nor ancient western Asia, nor ancient China knew the iron, and everything points to its introduction from Africa." In his scenario, Ellington wrote: "Neither ancient Europe nor

Western Asia / Nor ageless China knew about iron . . . But you [black Africans] did!" Ellington further proclaimed that "Buried in the dark, uneasy conscience of Man / Lies the bright and glorious Truth / About your heritage." By casting Africans as the progenitors of modern civilization, as Ellington did, it is easy to see why promoters and financial backers blanched at presenting this controversial, if arguably truthful, portrait to American audiences.

Black, Brown and Beige's written scenario closely resembles Ellington's earlier outline for *Boola,* starting off in Africa before slaves were brought to North America and describing the harshness of life during the Middle Passage. In Ellington's handwritten early draft of the scenario, the violence and deprivation of the Middle Passage is rendered in gorier and more disturbing detail, including a story of mutilation of the Africans by the whites in charge of the slave ships.[24] The final scenario seems to indicate that Ellington originally wished *Black, Brown and Beige* to follow the same historical trajectory, using a character named Boola, a black Everyman who represents blacks throughout the centuries in North America. However, from Ellington's comments at the concert and in news stories, it appears that the final version of the musical piece begins with blacks already arrived from Africa and living in the American colonies as slaves.[25] Still, the opening drum motif, repeated throughout the piece and representing the "Work Song" portion of the *Black* movement, probably symbolizes the African origins of American slaves. The opening image of the script details "A message . . . shot through the jungle by drums. BOOM! BOOM! BOOM! BOOM! Like a tom-tom in steady precision." A steady tom-tom pattern opens *Black, Brown and Beige.*

The first movement, *Black,* revolves around two main themes that Ellington believed most characterized the life of the black American slave: the work song and the spiritual. "The two are very closely related," Ellington told the audience at Carnegie Hall. "There are different work songs—those for the Negro who labored in the fields and those for the one who worked in the house," Ellington explained to an interviewer on the eve of the piece's premiere. "The latter is lighter, freer."[26] Within the "Work Song" themes, Ellington's penchant for not acquiescing to negativity is in full effect. The tom-tom-led rhythm and trumpet calls are for the most part proud, charging, and swinging, echoing Ellington's sentiment in the scenario that the work song was "Not a song of triumph . . . Not a song of burden." In the music and the written scenario, Ellington allowed no anger at the injustice of enslavement and its theft of the livelihood of millions of blacks for more than two centuries. Instead, he focused on the character and fortitude that the experience built in black Americans:

1700
Boola put down his heavy load and gazed about.
He'd been looking at this tree-swept land
Reclaimed by steady swinging of his ringing axe,
And was proud of what he saw there. Honest toil
Was not without reward. Had not this toil
Restored those steel-y muscles rippling
'Neath the black satin smoothness of his skin?
Had not the sun erased the mark of cruel, cold hate
That etched his face the night they brought him
To this strange and friendless place?
... WORK! WORK! WORK! WORK!
But to work was to grow strong, and he knew
Weak men could not survive this test
Of worthiness to be free!

But Ellington also noted that the "work song" served a dual purpose as a smokescreen to comfort the white slavemasters and to conceal feelings that may have provoked a violent response:

Boola sang while he worked ...
Boola danced away from a boot in the britches ...
A song eased his master's conscience ...
Boola reasoned: "I'll sing ...
And hide my thoughts from him ... "
A silent slave was a brooding slave ...
A brooding slave was a dangerous slave ...
    Too many masters found dead
    Or not at all ...
So! SING, you black bastards ... SING! ...
A song eased the lash. The whip fell
Less frequently across his weary back.
Boola sang. His master smiled. His slaves
Were happy. He complimented himself on
His great philanthropy.

This simply rendered, yet psychologically complex view of the push-and-pull of the slave/master relationship and the acknowledgement of the perspectives of both blacks and whites in the situation would not become common in American historiography until the 1950s and afterward. Like his rendering of blacks in the shaping of world civilization, Ellington's representation of the dynamics of slavery espoused a view of black history and agency not commonly accepted in 1943. Even DuBois, in his chapter dedicated to the slaves' "Sorrow Songs" in *The Souls of Black Folk*, focused on the "weary at heart" sentiments they embodied, their hope and "faith in the ultimate justice of things" rather than the "revolutionary potential" of African American music that later academic historians like John Blassingame and Eugene Genovese detailed in the 1970s and Ellington hinted at in the 1940s.[27]

The sadness and pain of the slaves is expressed musically in the "spiritual" section of *Black*, where such feelings can be subsumed and lifted by the peace religion brought. In his scenario, Ellington wrote that "Boola was irresistibly drawn / To that pretty white house with the steeple." Hearing the church bell ring (a sound included in *Black*) and the songs sung by the congregation attracted the blacks and roused their curiosity, but they were not allowed to worship in the same building:

> Came Sunday. With all the whites inside
> The church, their less fortunate brothers
> Emerged from everywhere to congregate
> Beneath a tree. Huddled there, they passed
> The Word of God around in whispers . . .
>> When the whites inside lifted voices
>> In joyous song . . .
> The blacks outside would hum along,
> Adding their own touches . . . weaving melodic,
> Harmonic, rhythmic patterns.
> Thus the spiritual was born.
> Highly emotional worshipping of God
> In SONG.

Ellington's description of the birth of the spiritual brings particular poignancy to the delicate hushed backing provided by the rhythm section and reeds behind Johnny Hodges's heavenly recital of *Black*'s main spiritual theme of "Come Sunday," which does resemble humming in the distance, possibly out of range of the hearing of the people within the church. While no documents exist that confirm Ellington's vision of how the spirituals originated, his story accurately portrays how, according to modern-day historians, the spirituals represented an African American–created amalgam between black and white cultures.[28] As DuBois suggested in 1903, culture, especially music, represented an important meeting ground for the races, a place where they could acknowledge each other's humanity and transcend stereotypes. But where DuBois mostly cited whites becoming attracted to the black spirituals, Ellington correctly suggested that the process worked the other way around as well. The music that Boola hears emanating from the white church is so beautiful and "strange" that it beckons him closer and makes him think that "Maybe the master is not a bad man, either . . . Maybe he just doesn't understand." In Ellington's slightly different hand-written early draft of the scenario, the slave master is deluded by the singing of his slaves in the fields, which he believes demonstrates that they are "content." "That gave him the feeling of a great Philanthropist," Ellington wrote, describing what later academic historians would more sentimentally term as paternalism. "He had done a Human Being some good—He was Eligible to Wash—Comb His Hair—Put on a tie + Come Sunday Go to Church + Pray, Pray to the good God Who Had given him the Strength—that he was putting to such an Evil Cause."[29]

Ellington's scenario for the "spiritual" section of *Black* also included a passage in which a white woman notices Boola's hunger for knowledge, and offers him the gift of a Bible. "Take it then and read it. It will help you," she tells him. "But do not let your master know!" As Ellington hints here, religion represented another point of convergence for blacks and whites throughout American history, a place where, at times, prejudice and segregation was relaxed and some interracial unity practiced. It not only provided a gateway to reading for some blacks, but also functioned as a launching pad for many important black leaders.[30] This represented another area in which Ellington adopted a more confrontational and cynical tone in his earlier handwritten draft, arguing that literacy also distanced blacks and whites, at least slave-owning whites. "The Reading of the Bible Was the Beginning of the Negro's Education," he wrote. "The More Educated [he became] the More Unbearable His Slavery—Good Souls Praying + Singing Faithfully without a Word of Bitterness or Revenge—'I forgive thy Past Suffering, Just let My People go.'"[31]

Ellington, from the 1940s forward, increasingly tried to find common ground between whites and blacks within his musical works. Though committed to portraying and representing black history, Ellington's was not an exclusionary vision. He presented a glorious vision of black history, but also realized that the history of American blacks and whites, however ugly at times, was intertwined, through the land, the religion, and the founding documents they shared, as well as the realization that they needed to find some sort of peace to live in a common democracy, especially one faced with the threat of destruction from without during World War II. In future compositions, Ellington would note and expand upon other intersections of black and white cultures—in his programmatic celebrations of Shakespeare, John Steinbeck, and in the Sacred Concerts, among other works.

But Ellington made it clear in *Black* that he recognized the more disturbing chapters of race relations, particularly as expressed within the realm of religion:

Thrilling, puzzling, strange it was . . .
They spoke of love of all mankind . . .
What then was this? Did they not hear:
"A false balance is an abomination to the Lord;
But a just weight is his delight." . . .
"When pride cometh, then cometh shame;
But with the lowly is wisdom."
"The integrity of the upright shall guide them;
But the perverseness of transgressors
Shall destroy them."[32] . . .
The master carried his fear with him . . .
Clutched to his bosom, into the haven of love.
Boola sang his way into the gallery of the church
He could sing . . . yes . . .
But he couldn't sit with the worshippers
Of the Christ who said: "Peace on earth,
Good will toward men." Boola sat upstairs,
The "Crow's Nest"! Did they not realize
He was above them—closer to that Heaven
They were shouting about?

In Ellington's historical vision, work strengthens the character of slaves while religion alerts them to the discrimination they face under slavery, its immorality, and why it should be overturned. In the last minutes of *Black,* its two main motifs of the movement, representing work and spirituality, mesh within each other, sometimes speeding or slowing or becoming inverted, swirling around each other in imaginative and unexpected ways, suggesting their intertwining in the black American character. Ellington's scenario invoked the Bible against slavery, much as slaveholders used it to justify slavery. He also portrays blacks as having a pronounced Christian temperament, more in tune with the Sermon on the Mount than prideful slavemasters who preached brotherhood on Sundays, but treated their slaves in a subhuman manner the rest of the week. The blacks in Ellington's scenario have insight into the emotional lives of their white masters, while the whites possess no such insight of blacks. They have sympathy for the tribulations that went on in the souls of their masters, even though such tribulations and hypocrisies lay at the core of the pain and stolen opportunities they and their kin endured in the course of being slaves:

> Poor master! Why must he crush his soul
> With fear? Why he must he live a lie
> Of inequality? Why must he force his lie
> On others? Why must he pick clean the bones
> Of the silver-throated thrush
> The golden lark
> And leave the crow to rasp alone?

Ellington's vision on this issue in 1943 also coincided with the research of recent historians indicating that blacks knew far more about the inner lives of whites than whites did about them.[33]

Ellington's scenario for the second movement, *Brown,* begins with a lengthy episode only slightly hinted at in the music as premiered at Carnegie Hall. Just as the African experience described at length in Ellington's scenario became reduced to a tom-tom motif in *Black,* Ellington's five pages (almost half the libretto for *Brown*) on African American participation and frustration in the Revolutionary War is similarly summed up in a brief snippet of "The Girl I Left behind Me," a song associated with the war, played on clarinet in a fashion reminiscent of a fife. Ellington stressed the willingness of blacks to fight alongside white soldiers in the war for freedom and against British oppression, even when given no guarantees for their own freedom or equality. Taking his lead from the writers of African American popular history, Ellington once again took standard histories to task for their exclusion of blacks from the Revolutionary War. "Gone from the pages of history," he wrote. "Names of black men who made us free."

The first of the three parts of *Brown,* "West Indian Influence," celebrates the participation of seven hundred free black Haitian soldiers in defending the city of Savannah from the British during the Revolutionary War. In the scenario, Ellington salutes Christophe, the little-known leader of that attack, and Touissant Louverture, the famous black statesman of Haiti following the successful slave revolt he helped engineer in the 1790s. "[Boola's] black brother from across the sea," Ellington rhapsodized. "Had come to fight for *his* liberty!"[34] The Latin American beat of the piece saluted that culture's influence "150 years later" on the birth of jazz, according to Ellington's early handwritten draft.[35] It probably also meant to highlight the Pan-American cooperation of the Savannah battle. Thanks to the efforts of American and Haitian blacks, Boola felt that "Surely, now he'd get his due... The war was won ... *Where* was HIS liberty?" As Ellington noted, the answer could be found in the Declaration of Independence, but not in the everyday existences of most African Americans:

> *"All men are created equal ..."* A noble document...
> But to Boola it was sheer hypocrisy...
> A mockery of men's souls.
> Four million blacks wanted to be free!

After the "West Indian" segment follows the "Emancipation Celebration," but before that segment begins, an out-of-tempo transitional thirty-second passage occurs. As Brian Priestley and Alan Cohen pointed out in their masterful musicological study of *Black, Brown and Beige,* Harry Carney's clarinet plays "Swanee River" in a minor key, producing a mood far from the usual jaunty nature of the song, followed by a brief response by the trumpets quoting "Yankee Doodle."[36] The section finishes with a tired and dispirited duet between clarinet and tenor sax. This brief interlude before "Emancipation" seems to suggest the period between the Revolution and Emancipation, which Ellington dealt with at length in his scenario, but not in the music of *Black, Brown and Beige.* The themes Ellington developed in his scenario for this section reflect how the American dream of freedom had been turned inside out for African Americans, just as Ellington had turned those two American standards inside out. The scenario describes blacks trying to escape to freedom after the Revolution: "Pursued by blood-thirsty men and beasts ... Hunted ... Tracked down like wild animals ... Still fighting / Tho' the battle had been won!" It hailed the black heroes of the first half of the nineteenth century, such as Frederick Douglass. But Ellington spent the most space saluting blacks who headed violent slave rebellions and a black woman who found fame as a determined liberator of Southern slaves. Like Douglass in his historical writing, Ellington found much to admire in these slave rebels and hinted that they were truer to the ideals of freedom than many whites of the period:[37]

> Out of this welter of broken bodies ... blasted hopes
> And shattered dreams ... Arose mighty men
> Of action! Nat Turner ... Denmark Vesey ...

The Gabriels . . . The Catos . . . The Toms!
The greatest of them all
A black woman . . . HARRIET TUBMAN!

This section of Ellington's scenario finishes with a condemnation of the slaveholders who "erred" and became "Unbalanced by their dreams of power" and their "ease" with "whipping black men to their knees." This section, more than any other in the scenario, deviated from the upbeat and patriotic atmosphere that he projected most of the time at Carnegie. As he reminded his readers, blacks again fought in a war for freedom, helping the Union win the Civil War.[38]

Ellington clearly underwent a change of heart concerning how he wished to portray Emancipation. As played at Carnegie in January 1943, the "Emancipation Proclamation" spans roughly two minutes, its buoyant mood led by Rex Stewart's joyful trumpet, Sonny Greer's cowbell accents, and a melody reminiscent of "Don't Sit under the Apple Tree." But in Ellington's scenario, Emancipation is barely touched upon, and it is steeped in sorrow and frustration. "Boola jumped for joy," Ellington wrote, but he soon realized his freedom "was shrouded / Now in uncertainty and insecurity." This represented quite a change from his original handwritten draft that described at length "Happy People Drunk with Freedom."[39] In his onstage remarks at Carnegie, Ellington explained that, in addition to the celebratory main Emancipation melody, he included a theme in this section to illustrate the fate of the older slaves "who had earned the right to sit down and rest on someone's property and of course their song was a very plaintive but tragic one." His scenario is more graphic:

They had earned the right to finish out
Their sorry lives unworried and at ease . . .
What now? "You must go . . . You're trespassing here."
"Get up and go!" . . . But where?
. . . Nobody knows but Jesus . . .
    "They set us free . . . but left us alone
    To starve . . . to freeze . . . to die."

From there, Ellington's narrative quickly moves on to "brave black men" who, "when danger threatened their country again," went off to fight in the Spanish-American War of 1898. Despite playing a key role in helping the United States achieve victory, Ellington makes it clear that blacks came home and found disappointment again. "Elation, frustration, joy and sorrow," he wrote, "Got all mixed up in the hearts of these black souls / Set free."

Though he does not spell it out, the disappointment Ellington referred to probably consisted of the effects of living under the rules of Jim Crow society. After shedding blood for their country, black soldiers came home to find themselves with a status worse than second class, with few rights, haunted by lynchings conducted with impunity, which sent a message to blacks who dared to challenge the system or succeed within it, especially in the South. It was therefore appropriate that Ellington followed his musical descriptions of Emancipation and his written description of black participation in the 1898 Spanish-American War with a theme entitled "Mauve," or, as it is better known, "The Blues." Historians and musicians have identified the birth of the blues as roughly concurrent with the rise in racial violence, discrimination, and loss of black voting rights at the turn of the century. As Robert Palmer stated in his history of the blues tradition, "black American music as it was sung and played in the rural South was both a continuation of deep and tenacious African traditions and a creative response to a brutal, desperate situation."[40] Ellington's scenario seems to intimate that discrimination and prejudice formed the basis of the sorrow he describes:

> And marching home a hero came
> Who learned to play the white man's game
> Was to suffer the loss as well as the gain,
> And the joy of the victor was turned to pain.

The lyric for "The Blues" (the only vocal portion of *Black, Brown and Beige*) follows, its words oblique enough to suggest the alienation at the end of a love affair, or the alienation and fear that Jim Crow brought upon blacks:

> The Blues . . .
>   The Blues don't . . .
>   The Blues don't know . . .
>   The Blues don't know nobody as a friend
>   Ain't been nowhere where they're welcome
>   back again . . .
> Sighing . . . crying
>   Feel just like dying . . .
> The Blues is a one-way ticket from your love to nowhere
>   The Blues ain't nothin' but a black crepe veil
>   Ready-to-wear.

For all the celebrations of victory in the American Revolution, Civil War, Emancipation, and the Spanish-American War invoked in *Brown,* the movement pointedly closes with dissonant and disembodied stabs and moans from the brass section, darting in between Betty Roche's vocal lament as it fades away. There is no relief, no spirited reprise of the tonic chord at the end of "The Blues," as many big bands would finish a blues song. The overt message Ellington made was muted, subtle, and mostly confined to his hidden libretto, but the feelings of alienation and disappointment were plain.

The scenario for the final movement, *Beige,* is more vague and impressionistic and less historically plotted than *Black* or *Brown.* The musical themes are more varied, less unified, giving the movement a restless, searching quality. According to Ellington's scenario and Ellington associate Leonard Feather, *Beige* documented the modern urban lives of American blacks, particularly in Harlem, and saluted the African American influence in Europe. Musically, the piece seems to celebrate the diversity within the black community: Sonny Greer's drums pound loudly through the first section (according to the scenario, this signifies the black influence spreading across the country and the world), Ellington's solo piano abruptly quiets the proceedings, time signatures keep changing throughout, a waltz is featured, as well as a patriotic fanfare that resembles "My Country 'Tis of Thee," followed by a swinging, optimistic finale, capped off on a high note emitted by trumpeter Rex Stewart.

In introducing *Beige,* Ellington, for the first time during the evening or in the numerous press interviews he did for the event, hinted at the dissatisfaction with and ramifications of the unequal status African Americans faced. Though no press accounts picked up on his words, they evinced a strong, if respectful and patriotic, message concerning the modern situation of African Americans:

> The first theme of our third movement is . . . the veneer that we chip off as we get closer and find that all these people who are making all this noise and responding to the tom toms, there are only a few making a living . . . many don't have enough to eat and a place to sleep, but work hard and see that their children are in school . . . And it develops until we find ourselves today, struggling for solidarity, but just as we are about to get our teeth into it, our country is at war and in trouble again, and as before, we, of course, find the black, brown, and beige right in there for the red, white, and blue.

As usual, Ellington's libretto featured more explicit prose regarding the same subject, especially in his depiction of Harlem, which equally stressed its soul as well as its deprivation, its decent people as well as its exploiters.

The anger expressed in the passage and Ellington's sadness at the prospect of broken lives and lack of opportunities he saw in his own city is evident:

Harlem! For all her moral lurches
Has always had
LESS cabarets than churches!
Who draped those basement dens
With silk, but knaves and robbers
And their ilk?
Who came to prostitute your art
And gave you pennies
For your part . . .
And ill-repute.
Who took your hunger
And your pain
Outraged your honor
For their gain?
Who put the spotlight
On your soul.
And left you rotting
In the hole
These strangers dug!
Who brought the dope
And made a rope
Of it, to hang you
In your misery . . .
And Harlem . . .
How'd you come to be
Permitted
In a land that's free?

A questioning of his personal motives and dedication concerning the race emerged at the end of Ellington's scenario. In a poem that appears to have no relation to the music, he seemed to wonder whether his actions have lived up to the examples he painted of Boola and other black heroes, and whether he should be doing or saying more. It's a rare moment of self-doubt and reflection expressed by Ellington, and suggests that *Black, Brown and Beige* represented some kind of watershed in his thinking about his role as a prominent black citizen. For the only time in the scenario, he is not talking about Boola or black people, but instead appears to be talking to himself, and about the frustration he felt with the constraints, both imposed and internalized, on his political expression:

And so, your song has stirred the souls
Of men in strange and distant places
The picture drawn by many hands
For many eyes of many races.
But did it ever speak to them
Of what you *really* are?
Did it say to them
"The joy I'm giving,
Is the foil I use to lose my blues
And make myself an honest living?"
How could they ever fail to hear
The hurt and pain and anguish
Of those who travel dark, lone ways
The soul in them to languish?
And was the picture true
Of you? The camera eye in focus . . .
Or was it all a sorry bit
Of ofay hocus-pocus?
How then, this picture
They have drawn?
It can't be true
That all you do . . .
Is dance and sing
And moan!

Ellington wondered if delivering the message about the need for equal rights exclusively through the medium of music was sufficient, given the scale of the problems and suffering he had witnessed and endured. He apparently also struggled with the issue of how effective the messages were that he placed programmatically and emotionally within his compositions. Was he being too timid? Did his insistence on staying within the musical realm only play into old stereotypes that viewed music as one of the few areas in which blacks were skilled? Had he had penned musical tributes to Bert Williams and Bojangles, rather than the more radical, political, and violent blacks championed in his scenario, such as Frederick Douglass, Nat Turner, and Harriet Tubman, only to keep his position in society? With *Black, Brown and Beige,* which encapsulated his lifetime interest in black history, Ellington seems to have arrived at a personal crossroads, and at the end of his scenario, he appeared concerned and somewhat haunted that he may have chosen the wrong path. Maybe this explains the strange hesitancy in most of his comments at Carnegie that night—was he mulling over whether he should have spoken his mind in a more forceful manner?

On the scenario's final page, Ellington seems to question some of the very underpinnings of the evening at Carnegie Hall. Not for the first time, his scenario criticizes greed, materialism, and profit, especially when they get in the way of principles. He uses the example of Dr. Charles Drew, who he knew from his adolescent years in Washington, D.C., as a paragon of moral behavior, and argues that Drew's "endless toil and searching [for blood plasma] / Was for knowledge . . . *not* for power!" He reminds his audience, or perhaps himself, to

Seek not for honor
Nor for gain
But rather for the joy of doing . . .
For credit is an empty thing
Unless accomplishment's derived
From a burning, aching need for giving.

One wonders if Ellington felt that he was giving enough in presenting his forty-five-minute opus to black history, or whether he felt that the glory of the moment, performing in America's most refined concert venue before some of the most famous people on the planet, was too self-serving. At the very end of the scenario, he also privately questioned the wisdom of black American participation in the war:

Once more you've heard your country call.
Patient . . . wond'ring, . . . you give your all . . .
Altho' the livid, vivid "why" evolves within
        your brain
You know that right or wrong . . . your homeland
        will remain

The *Black, Brown and Beige* scenario allows a momentary glimpse behind the Ellington veil, a hint of the "twoness" that DuBois argued all blacks felt living in an unequally segregated society, but that rarely surfaced on Ellington's usually impeccable, self-confident exterior. Expressing angry discontent, however justified, about the exploitation of blacks past and present and questioning the wisdom of blacks fighting for a country that did not accord them full citizenship probably would have cost Ellington his preeminent media status if he had publicly released his scenario in 1943. *Variety* reported that Ellington would release the score of *Black, Brown and Beige* along with an accompanying text, but the book never materialized. Zora Neale Hurston, though not nearly as famous as Ellington in this period, also decided to excise her more scathing comments on the subjects of American racism, slavery, and European colonialism from her 1942 autobiography.[41]

The explanation behind Ellington's reticence to directly challenge the foundations of American racism in a verbal and political manner were probably similar to the reason he declined to "blow the whistle" on the exorbitant percentage Irving Mills exacted from the proceeds of his early career. Such objections would have been portrayed in the media as complaining and nonconstructive—they would not have changed the system or gained anything tangible and would probably have caused the forfeit of the influence and power he assembled over the years. Ellington judged, probably correctly, that he could more powerfully affect race relations by achieving at the highest levels and performing music that celebrated the African American contribution than by getting involved in political controversies and spats in newspapers. For weeks preceding and following his first Carnegie concert, Ellington expounded upon the history of African Americans to reporters. Though he did not supply the details that African American popular historians like J. A. Rogers provided to their black audiences, Ellington established to a multiracial audience of millions that American blacks had a long and honorable history that deserved close scrutiny. DuBois rued that his production of *The Star of Ethiopia* played to tens of thousands, yet was "given by Negroes for Negroes . . . the white American world hardly heard of it."[42] Ellington, whose scenario shared several major themes with *Ethiopia,* spread the message far wider than DuBois had three decades previously.

Michael James, Ellington's nephew, recalled author and theorist Albert Murray in the 1960s getting upset when some observers argued that Ellington did not participate in the civil rights struggle. Murray replied incredulously that "they expect you're going to take your greatest composer and have him on a picket line, that any other black professional, anybody else can do, when he can do the one thing that no other person can do?" "You don't put Beethoven on a picket line," James summed up. "He's working on a different area." James placed Ellington's approach in a larger, long-term context:

> If you asked the civil rights people, let's have [Dr. Martin Luther] King and all of them write *Black, Brown and Beige* and all of that, do they make those kinds of contribution to history? No. Their whole thing is tied up in justice, that's what their whole careers are about. But somebody's got to be there to

produce something, you know what I mean? [In the future, people will ask] Well, what did the black people do? Well, they fought, and they complained, and then they got this law—but what did they contribute? The final analysis, what history looks at, when you look at ancient Athens, you're looking at that achievement, culturally. In America, we get these things confused . . . In the end, the culture is your strongest statement for who a given people are, and Duke understood that fundamentally.[43]

Ellington's *Black, Brown and Beige* scenario, and the strong emotions and opinions it betrayed, never became public and never had a chance to influence the public debate one way or the other. In an interview with the BBC in 1972, Ellington seemed to regret the loss of this opportunity when he publicly acknowledged the existence of the scenario for the only time in his career. "Of course, the script itself is more interesting than the music," he stated. "I think the music's pretty good," the interviewer replied. Ellington chuckled and quietly said, "Yeah." He sounded disappointed, an emotion he rarely indulged in when speaking to the media.[44]

The commentary following the Carnegie concert focused solely on the events that transpired onstage. "As one man the audience applauded the great piece of Ellingtonia," reported the *Washington Afro-American*. "Impeccable in full-dress attire, the Duke, and his musicians in pearl-grey jackets, trousers of almost midnight blue and magenta cummerbunds stood to acknowledge the tremendous wave of tribute which swept the rafters of Carnegie, eddied and burst forth again." By almost all accounts,[45] *Black, Brown and Beige* received a tumultuous response from the crowd assembled that night at Carnegie. The critical reaction to the concert as a whole, especially its significance as a marking of the twentieth anniversary of Ellington's involvement in the music business and his continuing historical and musical legacy, was also overwhelmingly positive, unqualified by reference to skin color. "There's no doubt of his importance to American music," concluded Henry Simon in *PM*. "Ellington is the most creative spirit that has worked this field," said Irving Kolodin in his review for the *New York Sun*, which referred to the concert as "a milestone in the history of popular music in this country."[46]

But when it came to *Black, Brown and Beige* itself, critical reaction was divided, to say the least. *Variety*, usually concerned more with business than art, proclaimed it "a bit self-conscious, as these tone poems usually are, but it never bored, even though running a bit fulsome with its 45 minutes." The more serious critics delivered sharper cuts. The *New York Post*'s classical reviewer commented that "Mr. Ellington had set himself a lofty goal, and with the best of intentions he did not achieve it." "It was a let-down," declared Dolores Calvin. "A big let-down from way up." Paul Bowles, in a widely reproduced review for the *New York Herald-Tribune,* pronounced it "formless and meaningless . . . The dance parts used some pretty corny riffs, too."[47]

Two common themes emerged among those critical of the piece. First, some critics questioned and felt threatened by Ellington's diversified approach to rhythm. To once again quote Bowles:

> Between dance numbers there were "symphonic" bridges played out of tempo. This dangerous tendency to tamper with the tempo within a piece showed itself far too many times . . . If there is no regular beat, there can be no syncopation, and thus no tension, no jazz. The whole attempt to fuse jazz as a form with art music should be discouraged. The two exist at such different distance from the listener's faculties of comprehension that he cannot get them both clearly into focus at the same time.

Other influential and powerful white jazz critics and businessmen agreed. "The conclusion that one can draw from this concert is that Duke is dissatisfied with dance music as a medium of expression and is trying to achieve something of greater significance," commented John Hammond, who evidently did not pay attention to the numerous shorter dance pieces that evening. "My feeling is that by becoming more complex he has robbed jazz of most of its basic virtue and lost contact with his audience." Magazine editor and future jazz producer Bob Thiele weighed in on this theme as well, insisting that jazz is "hard music, beat out for hard dancing." "*Black, Brown and Beige* is not true jazz. Louis Armstrong improvising the blues is real jazz," he argued.[48]

For these critics and music business representatives, Ellington's deviance from the traditional 4/4 jazz beat and his adventuring into the realms of 5/4, 3/4, and free-floating tempos transgressed the boundaries of jazz and public artistic expectations of blacks. They found it hard to accept that Ellington could work in several genres at once, not just those genres associated with African American participation. It was small wonder that, after 1943, Ellington and Strayhorn took pride in refusing to use the word "jazz" in their discourse, insisting they created in a milieu that existed beyond category. For years, Ellington had produced longer pieces such as "Creole Rhapsody" and "Reminiscing In Tempo," which broke the industry's three-minute barrier for popular and jazz recordings and featured tempos that varied. Ellington wanted and needed to create danceable hit material, but his artistic vision also ventured beyond those parameters. Besides, as many scholars have subsequently pointed out, in African musical traditions, personal expression mattered more than form, and rhythm was viewed as a means of sophisticated communication.[49]

Ellington communicated eloquently with rhythm as well as melody, in his own manner, in a genre of his own, mixing various influences. Especially for a work such as *Black, Brown and Beige*, which attempted to convey hundreds of years of black history under shifting circumstances, Ellington needed a wider musical palette than he normally employed. The schematics of Swing Era hit singles were highly predictable and not particularly challenging, especially for restless, envelope-pushing artists like Ellington and Strayhorn. Record albums were still half a decade away in 1943, but the duo increasingly created works to fit that format in the mid-1940s. The varied musical and programmatic construction of *Black, Brown and Beige* proved that blacks could create in any musical genre and even devise new ones beyond jazz, blues, spirituals, and other commonly accepted black-associated categories.

The second common criticism of *Black, Brown and Beige* implied that Ellington needed conservatory training in order to produce extended, multimovement works. "One can only conclude that the brilliant ideas it contained would count for much more if scored for a legitimate orchestra, augmented by the sole instruments indicated for certain specific passages," remarked Kolodin. Ellington "needs to acquire more resources if he is to venture so far from home." Robert Bagar, like other reviewers, complained that Ellington's transitions between themes were too abrupt. While praising the main musical themes, he mused that "they would have to be properly exploited, developed, and all the other classroom technology, in order to constitute a piece of music that is sequential."[50]

What these critics did not realize, though Ellington had been clear on the subject for years, is that Ellington harbored no intention of composing in the traditional European classical manner. Indeed, he actively resisted doing so and insisted that he created in the entirely different "Negro idiom." The unorthodox and abrupt transitions in *Black, Brown and Beige* were employed purposely to communicate certain programmatic statements concerning the lives and histories of black Americans. These musical and historical ideas had served as a staple of Ellington's interviews for decades. "I have always been a firm believer in musical experimentation. To stand still musically is equivalent to losing ground," he confided to a Washington, D.C., newspaper in 1934. "Music must keep satisfying the public taste—even, in some cases, it must educate the public taste so that gradually it will learn to know, like, and call for this new type of jazz, this 'sophisticated jazz.'" He told the *Hollywood News* in 1934 that he wished to "break away from European traditions." As he told a Portland newspaper in 1934:

> You can't stay in the European conservatory and play the negro music . . . Negro music is what we are working on. Not as a component of jazz, but as a definite unadulterated musical entity . . . You know how the negroes are. They pass quickly from the extremes of joy to gloom and back again. There must be the same quality in pure negro music. If you hear a group of negroes singing on the levee or in a cotton field you know there is something that cannot be expressed exactly in notations on a staff. We are trying to capture that quality. The negro spirituals, as they have been given to the world, are the true negro melodies, but they have been formalized in the writing . . . We are trying to express the experiences and the thoughts and feelings of the negroes in music. When I want a certain effect, I feel around until I think I have found it. It probably won't be orthodox, but even if three or four half-tones are bungled together, if the effect expresses the desired thought, it stays in.[51]

In the months preceding the *Black, Brown and Beige* premiere, Ellington reiterated this commitment to the "Negro idiom." Just because he was finally billed at Carnegie Hall did not mean he would practice the kind of music usually performed there. As he had proclaimed for over a decade, he was establishing a new tradition for African American music, and American music in general. On the eve of the Carnegie show, Ellington insisted that "conservatory theories can't be applied" to the "Negro idiom." "You've got to realize that the Negro is emotionally different," he explained. "He makes extreme and sudden transitions of mood and you'll find that in the music" for *Black, Brown and Beige*.[52]

Ellington picked the perfect musical aesthetic to help illustrate his scenario for *Black, Brown and Beige,* with its mix of struggle, achievement, and patriotism. "When one comes to ask what are the distinguishing qualities of the work as a whole, one of them is very definitely the use of contrast and surprise, balanced as it is by an unshakeable sense of forward movement," summed up musicologists Priestley and Cohen. The story of American blacks is indeed one of abrupt starts and stops, and mixed emotions, especially during the crucial moments Ellington focused on, such as the Revolutionary War and Emancipation, when initial hopes led to disillusionment.

Priestley and Cohen's analysis of Ellington's score points the way toward various subtle indications of black history occurring within the orchestrations. Ellington originally penciled in a return to the loud and joyous main trumpet melody of "Emancipation Celebration" at the end of the section but then decided against doing so. Instead, he "sketched it in gently on piano *during* the last repeat of [the] C [section of the 'Emancipation' piece]," using it as a muted counterpoint.[53] Ellington's decision at the end of the section to only hint in a barely perceptible way at the mood of celebration that began the section nimbly suggested how the joy of emancipation quickly dissipated after the Civil War. It also eschewed the customary rules of popular and classical arrangement, which tend to conspicuously reprise major and memorable themes. The change of arrangement also made programmatic sense in establishing the transition to the section that immediately follows, "The Blues," with its alienated tone. Contrary to many critics' charges, *Black, Brown and Beige* did feature form and continuity, but not the kind learned in a conservatory.

A few years before, in 1937, Langston Hughes had crafted a play entitled *Don't You Want to Be Free?* that tracked the course of black history in a manner that, in its attempt to adhere to a distinctive "Negro idiom," departed from traditional theater style. "It was . . . improvisational . . . montage-like rather than static . . . strongly lyrical and rhythmic in a linking of intense moments of Langston's own poetry, and with music—black music—blended into its tissue as an essential element," detailed biographer Arnold Rampersad. "Its major criteria . . . came not from the white stage but from Hughes' sense of the distinguishing features of modern, urban black culture and his own poetic gifts." The play did good business and inspired the formation of radical black theater groups in at least four cities. But, like Ellington's experience with *Jump for Joy,* Hughes failed to find backers to mount a national touring production. Hughes's plays and Ellington's *Black, Brown and Beige* had much in common. For the rest of his career, Hughes built plays differently than most playwrights, employing loose, unorthodox structures and ambivalent endings that frustrated critics who expected convention. As Rampersad put it, Hughes "was at first unable, then finally unwilling to change his apparently wayward method of composition," a term that Ellington's harsher critics might have adopted as well.[54] Both men were ahead of their time in presenting a vision of black history and culture to a multiracial national audience and in asserting that such presentations required a new artistic aesthetic that deviated from traditional European forms.

Though some of the critical jabs aimed at *Black, Brown and Beige* were harsh, a few critics grasped the piece insightfully. Leonard Feather and Mike Levin, the latter writing for *Down Beat,* the magazine that Ellington's 1930s emphasis on artistry in popular music helped inspire, praised the piece and defended Ellington. But they had the privilege of listening to acetates made at Carnegie that would not be officially released until the 1970s. Part of the reason behind the contemporary critical barbs might be traced to the fact that popular music reviewers, used to examining much shorter songs, only heard the complex *Black, Brown and Beige* once, and it is not a work that reveals itself in one hearing. Feather, an Ellington employee at the time, could always be counted on to provide an insightful Ellington rave, which was not yet seen as a conflict of interest in the music business. Columnist Elsa Maxwell unearthed old clippings that initially lambasted the 1924 premiere of Gershwin's *Rhapsody in Blue*, a piece widely viewed as an important American work by the 1940s, using much the same criticisms employed against *Black, Brown and Beige*. Billy Rowe, a black journalist writing in his weekly *Variety* column, particularly understood the historic and patriotic underpinnings Ellington sought to elaborate:

> Duke Ellington was in his element last Saturday night in Carnegie Hall where the famous of music have long since been immortalized. For his debut there he played a living music . . . His wasn't just the music of a great composer whose notes fitted the men in his band, nor the thing which we call Modern Jazz or Negro Syncopation, but the anguished cry of a people calling to the Gods of our time for fair play . . . each note meant something. Each bit of lyric sang, not a song of happiness or despair, but the words of Lincoln, Booker T. Washington, Fred Douglass and all those other great Americans whose lives were built upon the pulpit of freedom for all people and all lands.

The critic that best summed up *Black, Brown and Beige*'s significance for American music was Nina Naguid, writing in the *Chicago Musical Leader*: "There's a new word needed in the English language, it's a word to describe the kind of music played by Duke Ellington," she began. "Anyone familiar with it will recognize it instantly just as one does Bach or Beethoven, yet one can't apply the same standards to it that are applied to art music because Ellington writes in no established form." Since she reported for a magazine rather than a daily newspaper, she was able to read and comment upon the notices that immediately followed the concert, and compare them to her own impressions:

> most of the New York reviewers concerned themselves with [*Black, Brown and Beige*]. Because it lasts forty-five minutes, they fell into the error of thinking that it had to be judged according to formalistic rules. Apart from its rondo-like third movement, the work follows no definite pattern, and judged by established rules of technic, it is diffuse and aimless. However, it is programmatic, and for sheer wealth of ideas, melodic and rhythmic ingenuity, and creativeness, the work is an artistic phenomenon. This reviewer . . .

sat through the forty-five minutes without a moment's boredom, and judging from the ovational response of the audience, she was not alone. I bow in humility to the opinion of the majority, and can only say that in spite of the lack of discipline and unorthodox progressions, "Black, Brown, and Beige" is the beginning of a new American music which has its roots right here and cannot be judged from European standards of composition. Its historical and sociological backgrounds put it into the category of "heart" music, or folk music if you will, and out of the super-sophisticated, intellectualized realm of art music.[55]

It was appropriate that Naguid used the term "heart music" to describe Ellington's achievement, since the term was a favorite of Walt Whitman, who, nearly a century earlier, similarly introduced innovations that established American poetry as a distinct and vital art whose forms and concerns differed greatly from European antecedents. When Whitman used the term "heart music" as a newspaper columnist, he bestowed it upon mid-nineteenth-century popular artists like the Hutchinson Family and Stephen Foster, who, in Whitman's estimation, presented a music that featured a simpler, more personal, less formal aesthetic that reflected American values and served as a welcome contrast to the "affected, super-sentimental, kid-gloved, quavering" music from Europe, which stressed technique over feeling. In an 1855 column, Whitman openly yearned for an American music "underlain by . . . American realities."[56] Quite unconsciously, Ellington's *Black, Brown and Beige* embodied that request.

Though he never spoke of it publicly, several close friends attest that Ellington felt profound disappointment over the criticisms that greeted *Black, Brown and Beige* and the fact that it was never fully available to the public during his lifetime. At the band's next appearance at Carnegie Hall eleven months later, they played only brief excerpts from the piece, preceded by these comments by Ellington: "We thought we wouldn't play it in its entirety tonight because it represents an awfully long and very important story and in that I don't think too many people are familiar with the story, we thought it would be better to wait until the story was a little more familiar until we did the whole thing again." That moment never came during Ellington's lifetime. The orchestra played shorter versions of the main themes of *Black, Brown and Beige* intermittently until Ellington's demise, and he did rerecord various parts of the composition during the 1950s and 1960s, but these were truncated versions of the original, and the 1960s rerecordings were not released during Ellington's lifetime. Ellington's sister Ruth felt that the initial critical reaction to the piece affected her brother. "At that time, I think he sort of withdrew, was very quiet, I think at that point he was very influenced by critics," she said in 1960. "When they stated something like that, he would withdraw and kind of think it over." Brooks Kerr has said that Ellington considered it the second greatest disappointment of his professional career, while H. Robert Udkoff recalls that "inwardly, it hurt him. I don't remember Ellington ever discussing [the criticism], but I know he felt it . . . I don't think the criticism deterred him. No, he wouldn't allow that." Yet Ellington would never again attempt a musical work on the scale of *Black, Brown and Beige* and seemed to have made no efforts to release the entire work, even after long-playing record technology became common in the early 1950s.[57] Ellington released numerous multipart suites and pieces roughly ten to fifteen minutes in length over the next three decades, but he would never come close to issuing a similarly complex extended composition that continued the potential shown on *Black, Brown and Beige*.

But, when examining the scope of the reviews of the piece, critical reaction was not nearly as negative as some have portrayed, particularly if adopting a national perspective, giving less weight to the New York critics Ellington probably read, and who largely dismissed the piece on the Monday following the premiere. One of the outgrowths of the wealth of publicity that surrounded *Black, Brown and Beige* is that, soon after the concert, critics and columnists across the country lavishly praised the composition, including many who almost certainly did not hear the complete work. The unexpurgated piece was performed in only two concerts in the month following the Carnegie premiere.[58] Due to the critical drubbing it received, as well as the limitations of recording technology, the full piece was never made into a studio recording. Instead, *Black, Brown and Beige* was recorded in 1944 and subsequently performed as four smaller, edited segments lasting four and a half minutes each. When reviewers outside of New York wrote about the piece, they were probably basing their opinions on hearsay, hype, and the import of the occasion rather than the music itself. In 1944, the *Cincinnati Enquirer* called *Black, Brown and Beige* one of Ellington's "successful attempts to fuse jazz with art music." The local newspaper in Minneapolis, where Ellington had yet to play a concert, mentioned the work as evidence that Ellington "has ventured into the realm of more serious music with like success."[59] Through widespread marketing and publicity, *Black, Brown and Beige* significantly added to Ellington's reputation as a serious composer, despite the onslaught of negative reviews in New York, and even though relatively few people heard the piece in the 1940s.

Whatever critics thought of Ellington delving into new artistic territory, the 1943 Carnegie concert represented a huge success in business terms. The evening's proceeds went to Russian War Relief, but the economic benefits to Ellington and his orchestra were palpable following the show. *Variety* observed that:

> The Duke should cash in plenty henceforth. His stature among maestros now approximates the [Paul] Whiteman tradition . . . Among band business people . . . there was no other subject of conversation . . . Whether or not the concert was an artistic success, it is agreed that the comment it created was invaluable to Ellington's future.[60]

With the 1943 Carnegie show, the Ellington orchestra pioneered the profitable trend of jazz and popular music artists playing concerts, in addition to the usual venues of night clubs, dance halls, and the like. Ellington had performed sporadic concerts in classical venues as early as 1933 in England and 1937 in America,[61] and Goodman, Fats Waller, and James Reese Europe had previously played Carnegie Hall, but the Ellington band's yearly 1943–48 Carnegie concerts brought this phenomenon to a new level of mass popularity and artistic purpose. Each of the 1940s Ellington Carnegie concerts featured the premiere of a new extended work as well as rearrangements of older pieces. Following each performance, the Ellington orchestra performed the same program at other concert halls throughout the country in subsequent weeks, usually promoted by the phrase "direct from Carnegie."

The concerts served several purposes in the marketing of Ellington. They gave him a venue to showcase his extended works without alienating the segment of his fans that mainly wanted to dance to his music. They allowed Ellington's artistry and his reputation as a serious composer to grow and develop without hurting his commercial reputation and sales. They enabled the band to reap a bountiful harvest of publicity with every Carnegie Hall concert. WMA issued a huge foldout poster-size ad that heralded Ellington's January 1943 "SRO" concert engagements and reminded bookers in tall capital letters that "America's foremost concert personality—conductor, composer, pianist . . . [is] now on the concert stage."[62] Also, concerts carried a larger admission price and made significantly more money than the average show. By 1947, an article in *Variety* titled "Wham Coin for Jazz 'Longhairs': Concert Payoff on the Upbeat" reported that "the jazz concert field is rapidly becoming one of the most profitable outlets in live entertainment" and that Ellington "this year plans to do 100 longhair type recitals." Jazz, folk, and popular artists were described as taking in anywhere from $5,700 to $15,000 per show for such performances.[63] No won-

FIGURE 6. With its 1943 Carnegie Hall debut, the Ellington orchestra pioneered the profitable trend of jazz and popular-music artists playing concerts in addition to nightclubs, dancehalls, and the like. Each of the subsequent Ellington Carnegie Hall shows, from 1943 to 1948, featured the premiere of a new extended work as well as rearrangements of older Ellington pieces. Here (*left to right*), Duke Ellington, Ben Webster, and Jimmy Hamilton rehearse for the 1948 Carnegie Hall concert. Frank Driggs Collection.

der the Ellington band, which usually earned a base salary of roughly $1,000 to $2,000 per night in 1944, wished to step up their number of concert recitals.[64] Once again, marketing decisions proved beneficial artistically as well as economically.

Perhaps most importantly, Ellington utilized these 1940s Carnegie concerts to further establish and expand an African American artistic and historic vision. The extended pieces Ellington premiered tended to be programmatic pieces relating to the black American experience. In December 1943, the band premiered "New World A-Comin'," a ten-minute piece inspired by an optimistic book about black Americans written by Roi Ottley. *The Deep South Suite* (1946) attempted to musically illustrate African American life in the South. The black Liberian government commissioned *The Liberian Suite* (1947) in honor of the centennial of the country's birth. In an interview given a few weeks before the *Black, Brown and Beige* premiere, Ellington told *Variety* that the presentation of black music and history was important for the edification of blacks as well as whites:

> The trouble is that in a place like Harlem, a place where they have a chance to give impetus to original Negro compositions and an idiom already established, they turn to accepted Tin Pan Alley creations. Listen to any Harlem jukebox and you'll find the latest Hit Parade tunes, with an occasional song that details Negro musical expression. That doesn't mean that Tin Pan Alley doesn't put out good music. It does, as everyone knows. Rather, it means that until the time comes when the colored race takes its own music seriously, Negro music will remain undeveloped and for the most part unearthed.[65]

Ellington's actions as a black spokesman through the medium of music mirrored the efforts of other African American spokesmen and authors during World War II. Like Ellington, these authors stressed loyalty, patriotism, and the cause of victory in the war, while serving up a uniquely African American brand of nationalism and history. Roi Ottley's *New World A-Comin': Inside Black America,* published soon after Ellington's 1943 Carnegie debut, was an upbeat and breezy take on black history and life, detailing and celebrating a wide array of African American activities, personalities, and groups, and finding ways to link them all to a common purpose. Despite its generally positive tone, the purpose at the core of Ottley's *New World* was firm. "Negroes are no longer in a mood to be placated by pious double-talk—they want some of the gravy of American life," he argued. "Today, the vast majority of Negroes are omitting no activity, or opportunity, to make the war the vehicle for rolling equality into American life." He assured white Americans that blacks would gladly give their lives to fight fascism, but warned that without "concrete safeguards of their rights," blacks in America and elsewhere "will lose faith" and there will only be "a brief interlude of peace" after World War II before a domestic war erupted for equal rights. *New World A-Comin'* was hopeful and inclusive, but not naïve. Ellington found himself so impressed by it that he named his next extended piece after the book. Ellington reprised "New World A-Comin'" throughout his life. His searching and delicate solo performance of it at the Whitney Museum of Art in 1972 may be its most poignant rendition.[66]

What the Negro Wants (1944), edited by history professor Rayford W. Logan, featured a wide political spectrum of the best-known black writers. Using solid historical evidence, the authors discussed their ideas for the proper postwar treatment and strategies for blacks. Most of the contributors pointed out that World War II had inspired a heated national multiracial discussion on the subject of equal rights unparalleled in recent memory, and that the book meant to take advantage of that opportunity in fashioning an ideal response to the clamor. DuBois unsurprisingly viewed education as the remedy for discrimination, for whites as well as blacks. In a largely autobiographical piece, he noted how prejudice and lack of funding stood in the way of his studying and documenting black history in the late nineteenth century. Unless such situations were rectified, he predicted that "race prejudice in America will linger long and may even increase."[67]

The Carnegie Hall debut was tied to huge successes for the band on numerous levels. In the year following the show, the Ellington orchestra claimed seven chart appearances, their best showing since 1936. But the achievement was even more impressive because the 1936 charters were mostly vocal and novelty numbers seldom reprised or even available today, while the 1943 hits were among Ellington's best loved and most lasting, including "Don't Get Around Much Anymore," "Perdido," "Bojangles (A Portrait of Bill Robinson)," "Sentimental Lady," "Do Nothin' 'til You Hear from Me," and a reissued "Take the 'A' Train."

According to Klaus Stratemann's research, the Carnegie Hall publicity appeared to have raised the band's draw on the road for at least the next year, though exact figures are difficult to procure since the band's bonuses on top of their guarantees often went unrecorded. The band's extraordinary twenty-five-week stand at the Hurricane Club in New York City, which included a live national broadcast six nights a week, is but one piece of evidence indicating the band's elevated popularity in 1943. During this engagement, the singularity of the Ellington sound amongst its Swing Era competition was underlined by weekly *Pastel Period* broadcasts on Sundays, which concentrated on "some of the more introspective music in the Ellington repertoire." While most Swing Era bands used radio appearances to plug their biggest hits, the *Pastel Period* broadcasts concentrated mostly on obscure tracks from the Ellington catalog, often over three minutes long, that produced, according to the program's announcer, "a musical mood that is at once happy and sad, sorrowful and serene." The theme for these shows was the beguiling "Moon Mist," rather than the band's signature "Take the 'A' Train." The *Pastel Period* programs featured very little talking or show-business patter, almost exclusively consisting of moving, bittersweet music with an adult sensibility. It showcased the utter singularity of the Ellington approach and his continuing ability to please listening as well as dancing audiences. Radio broadcasts following the *Black, Brown and Beige* premiere often highlighted this distinction, boasting that some Ellington orchestra pieces featured a "strictly-for-listening treatment."[68]

Looking back in 1964, Ellington also seemed particularly proud of the fact that, armed with increased financial and celebrity power from his Carnegie premiere, he and the band were able to begin the process of breaking down segregation in Broadway clubs of the 1940s. As was his custom, Ellington dealt with the matter privately:

> The Negro in Harlem, who sought entertainment, why, of course, they were closed out of their entertainment in Harlem [because of the Great Depression and fallout from prewar Harlem riots], so they started coming downtown and getting turned away from various places on Broadway until 1943, [when] we were playing at the Hurricane, 49th and Broadway. And Dave Wolper was the owner of the place, and I found that I had to go to him one day, and say "Dave, you know, some of my friends have been coming here, and the head waiter is telling them that the place is sold out, there's no reservations. And if this continues, I can't stay here, because I'm embarrassed before my neighbors." And so with that Dave went to the door and raised hell with the head waiter, and the head waiter says "Oh I certainly did not." He said "Well it happened 2 or 3 times." So we actually caught him doing it, and this was the beginning of Broadway opening up, as far as nightclubs on Broadway was concerned. This was the absolute beginning of it. Shows how simple these things can be accomplished.

Or, at least, how easily such things can be accomplished when one has sufficient leverage. As was often the case in the Swing Era, the band lost money during the Hurricane engagement, as Ellington recalled in the 1960s, but its extensive national radio presence ensured that "when we went back on the road we could charge five to ten times what we could before that"—which added up to "$4,000 a night, $10,000 in the theaters," more than twice what the Ellington orchestra charged per night during most of the 1960s.

Ellington and the orchestra's singularity was also marked by the kinds of attention they received. Two months after *Black, Brown and Beige*'s premiere, the English and music departments at Harvard invited Ellington to discuss the work and give a lecture, which he entitled "Negro Music in America." Bela Bartok and Igor Stravinsky had recently presented similar lectures.[69]

Most importantly, the power of *Black, Brown and Beige,* and the issues it raised, allowed Ellington to establish himself as a unique force in the American musical scene, a focus for American and African American pride and achievement, a figure of commercial strength and historic importance who, more than any other musician at the time, could stretch out in almost any artistic direction he wished. Through his portrayal of himself in films, concerts, and numerous interviews during the Swing Era, Ellington provided an active and eloquent counter to media images of blacks in America. Herb Jeffries surmised that this represented a calculated strategy. "He decided to be articulate and not talk in an uneducated way with black slang . . . He wanted to portray an image." Perhaps the image that mattered most to him, as reflected in *Black, Brown and Beige,* was the recognition and elevation of black history, culture, and music. Ellington, even with his mix of black and white cultural influences, resolutely referred to his music as "Negro music" in this period and maintained that it represented a long tradition separate from, yet deserving as much respect as, the European classical music tradition. In 1944, he commented on this issue:

> When I sit down to compose or arrange a piece of my own, the striking of a few chords does not conjure up in my mind visions of Duke Ellington as a maestro of the old school.
>
> Frankly, I prefer to regard my compositions as strictly, "yours truly," as does any creative musician . . . If anyone finds Schoenbergian "images" in "Solitude," "Mood Indigo" or any other of my compositions, they should charge it to subconscious activity. I did not intend them and in all probability they do not exist anywhere but in the minds of self-important, over-sophisticated musicologists who like to make an occasional comparison.
>
> That I owe a debt to the classical composers is not to be denied but it is the same debt that many composers, for generations, have owed to Brahms, Beethoven, Debussy and others of their calibre . . .
>
> If I seem a little shy about being displayed on a critical platform with the classical big shots, let me also dispel the notion that I hesitate to put the jazz medium in a top musical category.[70]

Despite the artistic and economic glory earned in the first half of the 1940s, by 1946, Ellington, Strayhorn, and the orchestra faced a serious problem that would dog them for the next decade: where could they go from the pinnacle they had reached? They were proven hit artists, but the market for big band swing was plummeting. They had established themselves as serious artists and composers in the public consciousness as no popular or jazz composers before them had, but their best and most interesting pieces, such as *Black, Brown and Beige* or *The Perfume Suite* (1944), were either impossible or unwieldy to present on existing technology, and had no chance of radio airplay in their complete forms.

For the next ten years, they would learn how to survive in an increasingly unfriendly commercial environment. The new niche they eventually created in that environment would allow Ellington to continue developing in new and exciting ways until the 1970s, creating works at times that rivaled if not equaled the greatest achievements of the first half of his career. In addition, Ellington, with Strayhorn's help, maintained the band's commercial and artistic relevance in a way that none of his peers of the 1930s and 1940s would match. But first, Ellington and the orchestra would have to endure some hard times.

7

POSTWAR STRUGGLES

Prelude

In the summer of 1948, for the first time in nearly a decade, Duke Ellington returned to Europe to play a five-and-a-half-week slate of shows. In addition to repeat performances in London and Paris, he played in new locations such as Antwerp, Brussels, Zurich, and Geneva. Strict postwar union regulations kept the entire band from crossing the Atlantic, so he toured as a "cabaret act" with a British rhythm trio and two vocalists from his band, Kay Davis and Ray "Floor Show" Nance. The latter, as usual, also performed on violin, trumpet, and "stole the show" with his comedy bits. Reports from most performances documented large audiences and profits greeting Ellington. But for Ellington personally, Europe, with less racist audiences who appreciated him as an artist even more than American audiences did, once again represented a reconnecting with his reasons for being a composer. "I wanted to get back to Europe for a while. It's good for the morale," he told Down Beat. "It gives you the kind of adjustment of mind you need in this business. Over there [in America] you get too used to the *Hit Parade*. You know it means nothing, and yet after a while, you start paying attention. That's bad for your music."

Yet, despite the successful and memorable shows, the moment that remained clearest four decades later in the mind of Max Jones, who covered the tour and interviewed his friend Ellington for *Melody Maker*, existed separately from the music and its reception. He stood alone with Ellington on a "veranda looking over this beautiful bay" in a "high-class" suite at the Bournemouth Bay Hotel in the south of England. "He talked to me quite a bit, you know he'd drift off in conversation," Jones recalled. "Are you happy, Mr. Jones?" Ellington asked. "You see, I'm looking out here on the veranda." Ellington paused, and then made an exceedingly rare admission: "You know, I love this place. I don't know if you realize this, but I have the utmost difficulty staying in a hotel like this in the United States."[1] Usually, his prideful and refined manner never acknowledged that racism caused him pain or regret. Ellington almost always moved forward, refusing to publicly recognize negative factors, be they racism or overcommercialization, refusing to grant them any power in his highly productive life. Yet he deeply felt and despised both.

For all the achievements and status earned in the twenty years since his initial Cotton Club engagement, Ellington remained constricted by both racism and the American music scene. Oral histories from the Ellington orchestra indicate that racial violence and resistance against them worsened during and after the war. The situation mirrored the mood around the country: black bravery and participation in the war effort did not bring the first-class citizenship blacks hoped for. Numerous incidents—on the streets, in courts, and in legislatures—demonstrated that most whites felt more determined than ever to deny such rights to blacks. Though Ellington carefully distanced his image and musical identity from the most egregious commercial trappings of the Swing Era, the demise of the big band scene made economic survival difficult for him and the large orchestra he preferred. By 1948, he was probably already dipping into his publishing royalties to underwrite his band, which he continued doing for the rest of his career. It was a new era for blacks, and for American popular music. Gains from previous decades did not necessarily translate to the postwar era. Once again, Ellington and, to some degree, all black Americans had to formulate new strategies to deal with the struggles of earning a living and gaining a more equal status.

✳

The financial and artistic success stoked by Ellington's 1943 Carnegie debut continued through most of 1944 and 1945, even though a strike by the American Federation of Musicians kept them from recording during most of that period. The AFM's two-year-plus ban on commercial recordings lapsed in November 1944, and in the next year the orchestra waxed and released dozens of pieces, including "I'm Beginning to See the Light," their last major hit single. In the spring of 1945, Ellington opened a four-week residence at the 400 Club in Times Square, reputedly the best-paying and most prestigious club in the United States. Ellington's $3,500 weekly guarantee mirrored Tommy Dorsey's just prior to Ellington's appearance, another reminder of the parity Ellington finally achieved with white bandleaders in the mid-1940s. The engagement also provided nightly national broadcasts for the orchestra.[2]

Years before the advent of the long-playing record, such compositions as the swirling, dissonant, and emotionally complex "Strange Feeling" (from *The Perfume Suite,* premiered in 1944) pointed the way toward future possibilities for jazz and popular music. The adult alienation and paranoia expressed within it is reminiscent of the protagonist who exists under the streets in Ralph Ellison's novel *Invisible Man* (1952). Musically and lyrically, it's a disturbing piece, as far from the love songs of the 1940s radio show *Your Hit Parade* as could be imagined:

This strange feeling is seeping through my blood
This strange feeling is sleeping somewhere cuddled up inside of me

I know it will guide me
To I don't know where . . .
I walk, I try to do so without reeling
I talk and someone answers
From the ceiling
This strange feeling is rapping like a knife
This strange feeling is snuffing out my life
But I can't stop this savage ravaging, no
This strange feeling

The unsettling nature of those last three words is punctuated by the halt-ing, off-time crescendo of chords Ellington and Strayhorn place under-neath Al Hibbler's vocal. No further words are offered during the last half of the record; no resolution or happy ending emerges. It ends with a despon-dent marching figure and dissonant horns fading away. Ellington ardently searched for hit singles and music that younger audiences would embrace during the 1950s and 1960s, yet his influence (and Strayhorn's) proved in-strumental in establishing an adult sensibility in popular music that became increasingly common in rock, jazz, and country circles during those decades. However inspiring such works were, their distance from traditional popular music forms began to trouble RCA Victor when the recording ban was lifted: *The Perfume Suite* remained unreleased until the early 1950s, though the or-chestra performed it on live radio broadcasts. Ellington and Strayhorn's best work increasingly fell outside record industry categories and markets.

Ellington's prominence at the end of World War II was also signified by the 1945–46 weekly series, *Your Saturday Date with the Duke,* an hour-long radio show sponsored by the U.S. Treasury Department that aired live across the country and on discs for troops in Europe and Asia. The selling of war bonds marked the program's main mission, and Ellington usually is-sued three personal scripted appeals each week, sometimes supported by Strayhorn on piano. An astonishingly eclectic selection of Ellingtonia went out over the air. Hits were juxtaposed with lesser-known historic Ellington pieces that rarely or never received radio exposure, such as "Reminiscing In Tempo," "Harlem Airshaft," "Blue Serge," "New World A-Comin'," *The Per-fume Suite,* and a seven-minute reconstruction of "Frankie and Johnny," an African American folk song from the previous century that the announcer referred to as an accepted example of American culture. The show served as a platform for Ellington's newest works, many unrecorded and unreleased: "Blutopia," "Esquire Swank," "Air Conditioned Jungle," and many more. Most programs also featured an extended thematic set that highlighted segments of the orchestra's repertoire with no equivalent among their peers: Billy Strayhorn compositions, jazz "concertos," the "blues cluster," "three tunes in the blue mood," and several assorted groupings of eight separate pieces from *Black, Brown and Beige*.[3] On *Your Saturday Date with the Duke*, the world heard the extent of the Ellington and Strayhorn palette, something that never transpired on television during Ellington's lifetime. Though Ellington continued developing memorable works for the next quarter century, this show sadly marked the last time that a wide audience regularly heard the latest creations fresh from the Ellington workshop. It would not, however, mark the last time the United States government asked Ellington to reach audiences it wished to influence.

Another mark of historic distinction for Ellington and the orchestra in this period was their unprecedented role in the national mourning of President Franklin D. Roosevelt in April 1945. Roosevelt's funeral fell on the day of one of Ellington's Saturday night treasury-sponsored radio shows. The regular show was cancelled, but Ellington assembled a program of bittersweet original pieces along with rearranged black spirituals for the occasion. Klaus Stratemann reported that "it was the only broadcast by a dance or jazz orchestra following the president's death, when solemn classical music dominated the airwaves." As radio personality and jazz expert Rob Bamberger insightfully remarked, "the point here is that, while the old [classical] masters dedicated some of their works to death and immortality, they bore no particular cultural relevance to the times in which Roosevelt lived, or to a grieving black public." Ellington did, and the difference was remarked upon at the time. "No other dance band could have filled the spot without arousing criticism," commented *Variety*. Once again, Ellington made inroads on behalf of American music, and highlighted the patriotism and centrality of black Americans to the United States and American culture—without having to utter a word about it. John Edward Hasse discovered that Ellington wrote a letter to the Roosevelts in 1934, attempting to make arrangements to perform at the White House for them, but was rebuffed and informed that the president did not plan to view any entertainment that week. Three years previously, President Hoover chose not to meet with Ellington after agreeing to do so. In 1944, despite the brush-off, Ellington allowed his name and photo to be part of ads and articles that collected celebrity endorsements on behalf of Roosevelt's last election.[4] During the April 1945 radio broadcast, Ellington finally got his wish to play for Roosevelt.

World War II had provided a wedge for black Americans to use in combating and improving their status. NAACP membership increased tenfold to half a million, and the Congress of Racial Equality (CORE) began its work of nonviolent direct action. Black labor leader A. Philip Randolph secured a presidential directive that forbade discriminatory practices in government-related war employment, and blacks in labor unions doubled to 1.25 million. Army officer training became integrated, while industrialization and war mobilization brought better-paying non-farm-related jobs to millions of blacks. By 1950, a million Southern blacks could vote—four times more than in 1940.[5]

But these gains, for Ellington and other blacks, were sometimes fleeting and illusory. American victory in the war trickled down few long-term benefits for American blacks. Wartime appeals for interracial unity and tolerance dissipated quickly after the surrender of Germany and Japan. The legislation against job discrimination did little for blacks after the war, as "hate strikes" by whites became a common tactic to deny blacks the industrial jobs they enjoyed during the war, an antilynching bill was still deemed beyond political achievement by both major parties, the South still denied 75 percent of its black population the right to vote, and the blacks who moved north to take advantage of war employment usually were relegated to ghettoes instead of reaping the benefits of middle-class suburbia. In addition, the Red Scare unleashed by the cold war undercut civil rights activism and progress by insisting that such efforts threatened American unity and were communist-supported and inspired.[6] With no significant civil rights legislation (other than President Truman's desegregation of the U.S. armed forces) passed to consolidate the small gains made by some blacks during the war, conditions deteriorated, and working blacks, including those in the Ellington orchestra, found racial resistance just as strong after the war, and perhaps even stronger, as racists tried to thwart any perceived progress.

While reports of bigoted resistance appeared worse in the South than in the North before World War II, afterwards, the Ellington orchestra and other traveling black entertainers reported that conditions were just as bad if not worse in the North. "The worst place was the Bible Belt, that was worse yet than the South . . . the Dakotas, Iowa, and all those places up there," recalled Al Celley, the band's road manager from 1944 to 1963. Producer and promoter Norman Granz concurred, remarking that "no laws in Michigan" existed that barred blacks from dining establishments, but bands on the road in that state and others nearby, such as Illinois, Indiana, and Ohio, "couldn't go in and eat." Ellington vocalist Joya Sherrill remembered Ohio as a "particularly prejudiced state," as bad as or worse than any state in the South.[7]

But the Ellington orchestra experienced trouble in the South after the war, too. They traveled the region in Pullman cars until the late 1940s, but even so, much of the respect and ease they experienced in the 1930s seemed to have evaporated, particularly after the war. Cress Courtney, the band's William Morris Agency management representative, was "almost killed" on an Ellington orchestra Southern tour when shots were fired at the phone booth he was using. His wife, not present at the time, said that Courtney, a white man, believed "that he was shot at because he was down there in the South representing a black band." Celley and longtime Ellington sideman Jimmy Hamilton both recalled an incident in 1947 when the band was chased by police out of a private restaurant dinner hosted by a "well-off" white fan who sought to pay a personal tribute to the band in Georgia. Joya Sherrill remembered many tour stops where black cooks gave the band food out of the back door of a restaurant, and that in Mobley, Missouri, the band was told that no food could be secured for them anywhere near the town. A 1944 *New Yorker* profile of Ellington detailed a stop in St. Louis where black band members could not secure a taxi to take them to their hotel before the show, were denied sandwiches ordered from a café after the proprietor learned they were for a black band, and only received food during intermission when they complained to the theater manager "that if the band was to work it should be allowed to eat." "Duke tries to forget things like that," summarized Richard O. Boyer, the author of the piece. "And if he doesn't quite succeed, he pretends he does." Celley and Granz recalled that, when touring in the South, Ellington and the orchestra were unusually punctual, arriving at the gig at the last moment and ready to leave immediately afterward. "It was one thing in the South, I never had trouble with the band getting out of the places we worked," Celley remembered, laughing. "Any other place, they'd loaf and wait, we had the band packed up and ready to go, and we can't find this one [band member] or that one. Any time in the South, they were ready to go."[8]

The South and the Bible Belt held no monopoly on discrimination during this period. Sophisticated urban venues on both coasts also engaged in discriminatory practices. In 1945, the Ellington orchestra became the first black band to play Ciro's, a "posh nightclub" in Hollywood. According to band members Harry Carney and Sonny Greer, the management objected to the band's between-sets socializing with white movie stars such as John Garfield and George Raft (who the band had known since the Cotton Club). "The help [is] not allowed to socialize with the guests," Ellington was told. Raft, outraged by the management's suggestions, set up a table in the alley outside the club so that "we won't disturb your guests and Sonny and Duke are going to have a sip."[9]

Methods were devised to secure safe and respectable places to stay and eat in difficult environments. Often, these methods created precedents for the integration of facilities. Hamilton recalled standing up in the front of the tour bus with Celley as they entered "very prejudiced" Salt Lake City one morning in the 1940s, after driving all night. "'Cause we always had to live in this beat-up hotel where we used to stay [because blacks were not accepted anywhere else in the city], I say, 'Hey, Celley, when you going to break this thing down, you know?' He says, 'OK, we gonna try it.'" Four decades later, Celley explained his strategy:

> You had to play it cagey at that time. I would call the hotel up, and say "I'd like to make a reservation." They'd say, "For how many?" I'd say "Twenty-something," or whatever it was. They'd say "Fine." [I'd] Make [the reservation] under my name . . . I'd get into town, the bus would drop me off, I'd go in the hotel and sign everybody up . . . I'd sign the register, once I signed the register, it was OK because I had the reservations, understand? Then I'd come marching in with the band, understand? That's how I'd get them in. It was all right all the time that way.

In Salt Lake City, Hamilton recalled the hotel manager asking Celley to "tell [the band] not to come downstairs [to the lobby] and eat." "So we got room service," Hamilton said, chuckling at the memory. "But, you know, from then on, it was cool. Come downstairs, eat, do anything we wanted to do after that. That had never happened before." Celley and Hamilton reported that these methods usually cleared the way, in the long run, for the band to stay in better hotels and receive better treatment in many previously discriminatory stops on the Ellington tour itinerary. Ellington's close friend and long-time baritone saxophonist Harry Carney felt such gratitude that he offered to buy a gift for Celley to reward him for securing improved accommodations. In the North and South, according to Hamilton, "we broke down a lot of that [racism]" by becoming the first blacks staying at certain hotels. "We did things that had never happened before."[10]

But such challenges, no matter how successfully met, prompted a stressful everyday existence for everyone in the band's entourage, black and white. Norman Granz, who managed many black artists during this period and afterward, and accompanied them on tour, observed the conditions Ellington and others faced on and offstage:

> Duke was . . . royal in his attitudes, if you like, with how he conducted his lifestyle and the way he wanted people to regard him. And that's fantastic if you can pull it off. He was also able to come to terms, at least outwardly, with the prejudice that existed all around him . . . it's pretty difficult to come

to terms with America 52 weeks a year if you're a traveling band doing one-nighters. You have the first problem of housing. You have the second problem of playing before segregated audiences . . . or worse, playing in places where there was a de facto segregation, where the blacks would sit upstairs and the whites downstairs. It would seem to me, standing on the stage and seeing that, that it would be an awfully difficult thing to accept without getting an ulcer. But it was also a fact of life in America.

Ellington refused to allow Jim Crow conditions to give him an ulcer or distract him from his most important priority, his writing. He acknowledged the presence of Jim Crow conditions on the road, but refused to cede them power in his life. "You have to try not to think about it, or you'll knock yourself out," he said in 1944.

Ellington was internationally renowned, but not immune from the dangers and inconveniences blacks faced in the United States. As Granz pointed out, there "was nothing that [Ellington] confronted that was dramatically different from what the average black person who went to work each day, except that black person lived at home, and went to the same office, or got the same job, and in the sense didn't have to face up to new problems and new obstacles." But Ellington, and those who toured with him, had to seek out and deal with those unpredictable and potentially hazardous adjustments on a daily basis. Celley carried a gun on tour in the 1940s, mostly because he held so much cash (the orchestra disliked payment by check and Celley had been robbed once while working for another band). But, with shots fired in manager Courtney's direction in the South during this period, it's probably a safe bet that additional reasons for carrying a firearm were also taken into consideration. Ellington also carried a gun in the 1940s, "a .38 snubnose," according to Celley: "he used to carry it . . . in case he got on the elevator [at his home in Harlem and was threatened by an intruder]. You had to always carry it, you know, 'cause he was afraid that way . . . but he would never use it." Just the same, Celley maintained, Ellington "would know how to use" the gun and had the permit renewed yearly, as did Celley.[11]

An important part of the services provided by these white managers was protection of their black artists not just from physical harm, but from the worst aspects of racism on the road. In the less confrontational tour stops, such as New York City or Philadelphia, the band made their own arrangements for eating and lodging. But in the more restrictive and hateful environments of Iowa and Omaha (which, according to many of the oral histories, represented one of the worst cities for touring black bands), Celley assumed this role. "On the road, it was very hard eating. In other words, when we make a stop, I had to go in and ask . . . and make sure, because we didn't want to get thrown out . . . before we got halfway in," Celley recalled. "I'd go in, tell 'em who I got, we want to come in for dinner, and they'd say 'OK,' or 'go on in.' . . . We didn't want to go where they didn't want us." Celley approached these situations cautiously because he felt protective toward Ellington. Not only did he need to guard him physically, but he wished to spare him any involvement or psychological discomfort with discrimination on the road. "I would never let it get to him, you know what I mean?" Ellington also did not wish to go anywhere he was not wanted: "he'd be scared, he'd want to run right out" if they entered a restaurant that did not accept blacks in the 1940s.

Over time, Celley, Ellington, and the band assembled a network of trusted places, which eased life on the road: "we'd travel so long, in and out of these towns all the time, we always knew our spots too, we always kept them reserved for ourself, you know what I mean?" Granz called it "the grapevine" and argued its existence was especially important during the second half of the 1940s:

[Ellington] knew that it would be a hassle to get a room in Birmingham. But the grapevine always worked, and he knew there was a reverend who took in people, and the reverend's wife was a great cook . . . The word was out where to stay. I remember Duke and I having a big discussion where he said, "You know, you really oughta ride up where you can get some great ribs. Now I know a great place in Cleveland. Put that on your list." And of course cats would say "This is a good place to eat, and it's cool, it's straight. You can eat there." . . . Unfortunately, there weren't enough of those places, and also there weren't that many reverends to pass around for 16 members of the band.

Granz, recalling the 1940s, and Robert L. Jones, recalling the 1970s, reported that Ellington possessed uncannily intimate knowledge of seemingly every road in North America and Western Europe, including where the best and most accommodating restaurants were located. In the 1944 *New Yorker* profile, Ellington provided a page-long spoken treatise on his preferred dining establishments, from Biloxi to the Hague, and from Toronto to San Francisco, providing a list of his favorite dishes, which are every bit as eclectic as his music: octopus soup, chow mein with pigeon's blood, and cinnamon rolls, just to name three examples.[12]

Harsh racial conditions were only one of the barriers the Ellington orchestra faced during the postwar era. The 1943–45 period represented a new peak of exposure and celebrity for Ellington, but by the time the *Saturday Date* series ended in October 1946, the economic and artistic landscape of the popular music market had altered significantly, making survival far more difficult. The mid-1940s marked the formal end of the big band era.[13] During the winter of 1946–47 alone, bands led by Benny Goodman, Woody Herman, Artie Shaw, Tommy Dorsey, Les Brown, Harry James, Jack Teagarden, and Benny Carter ceased performing. "The music business was last seen going thataway," wrote Michael Levin in a front-page *Down Beat* story in late 1946. "That at least is the summary of the laments heard throughout the land . . . Business is unquestionably off." Two years later, in an unsigned editorial titled "Dance Band Biz Needs Stimulus," the situation seemed worse—*Down Beat* editors advised bands to invent new dance crazes to stave off the economic doldrums, claiming that it was the first time since the days of James Reese Europe that some dance fad had not captured the country's youth, spurring sales of records and ballroom admissions. Another article advocated "funny hats," comedy routines, novelty songs, and adopting a "give-the-customer-what-he-likes motto."

Throughout this precarious period, Ellington kept his orchestra working fifty-two weeks a year, the only big band to do so continuously, but for the first time he dipped into his sizeable song royalties to offset losses. Tempo Music, his publishing company, went on a three-year hiatus. Sponsors canceled radio shows highlighting big bands. The generation that grew up with the big bands was not going out to dance and drink as frequently. The arrival of television and mass-produced suburbs like Levittown took a toll on the existence and popularity of nightclubs. "All luxury and entertainment business is 'off,'" *Down Beat* reported, not just the music business. The venues that could support a band like Ellington's for a profitable week's run were few and far between by 1947, necessitating a seemingly endless string of one-nighters for the band for the rest of its career. "Everything shrunk, the hinges fell off," Celley recalled. "It had its days, sometimes it'd be good, some days it wouldn't be, weeks, months, too . . . you played a lot of one-nighters . . . that's what we had to do [to survive]." Profitable and even record-setting engagements for the Ellington orchestra, especially in larger cities and on the West Coast, occasionally occurred during the postwar period up until 1950, when conditions seemed to worsen.[14] The economic trend for Ellington and other big bands headed relentlessly downward.

Carrying an eighteen-person band plus vocalists and support personnel entailed a high fixed cost during a period of falling profits. Famous vocalists, such as Frank Sinatra and Patti Page, accompanied by a small band of anonymous sidemen made much more economic sense on the road and ruled the airwaves as well. From 1940 to 1945, most number-one pop records were by big bands. From 1946 to 1955, vocalists and small groups (such as the King Cole Trio and later Bill Haley and the Comets) attained a virtual lock on the spot, though big bands Kay Kyser and Count Basie held the top position for a combined nine weeks between 1946 and 1948. The Ellington orchestra enjoyed no charting singles from 1946 to 1955, let alone a number-one single, according to a *Billboard* chart survey.[15] Statistics from the era also suggest that black bands as well as more artistic musical approaches represented particular economic liabilities during this period, as they did during the mid- and late 1930s. A December 1948 *Down Beat* editorial reported on the bands that still drew good business in certain areas. All were white and most adopted a conservative and nostalgic approach: Vaughn Monroe and Sammy Kaye ranked at the top, followed by Stan Kenton (a more musically adventurous band), Guy Lombardo, Tommy Dorsey, and Spike Jones ("more of a theatrical than a band attraction").

In the midst of this musical stagnancy, a younger generation of music listeners and dancers latched on to the vibrant genres of bebop and rhythm and blues, both of which featured smaller, more economically viable ensembles. As Scott DeVeaux argued, the shaping of the bebop aesthetic was grounded in blacks' musical frustration at being consigned to the margins (or worse) of the Swing Era. They reshaped boundaries of artistry and employment to ensure their participation and primacy in the new music. The groups were smaller, four to six men, which allowed a flexibility big bands could not match. New ideas and improvisation were incorporated quickly, without a need for charts. With smaller overhead, bands frequented friendlier urban locales where Jim Crow practices were rare, instead of relying on unpleasant and dangerous tours in the South and Bible Belt to meet large payrolls. In addition, smaller nontouring groups, by staying close to urban centers, were less affected by the wartime rationing of gasoline and tires that helped speed the demise of the big band era. (The Ellington orchestra was excluded from many of these restrictions because of their involvement in the U.S. Treasury–sponsored shows).

Having smaller ensembles and avoiding national touring meant that bebop groups were less reliant on satisfying national commercial tastes. The major record companies, with their generally conservative emphasis on proven formulas, had little interest in bebop initially, which opened up a market for independent labels. These companies surged after World War II, picking up artists with small and dedicated audiences like Charlie Parker that the majors avoided. Having hit records and making dancers happy meant much less to the bebop groups, allowing them to push beyond current commercial norms. They adopted the jam session as a central component of their live performances, with a creativity that 78-rpm records could never fully capture—you had to see virtuosos like Dizzy Gillespie live in order to experience their full effect. Boppers ignored the romantic Tin Pan Alley songs at the core of the Swing Era repertoire, except to speed them up, turn them inside out, and sample their chord structures and melodies for source material in new compositions. Parker did precisely this in 1946 with "Ornithology," his reimagining of "How High the Moon."

For the most part, the highbrow aspiring critics at *Down Beat* and *Metronome* initially dismissed bebop and portrayed it as detrimental. A younger generation of black musicians, brandishing a new set of rules formed in opposition to many of the precepts of the big bands, appeared threatening and somewhat incomprehensible to the old guard. A few of that older crowd, however, did recognize the import of bebop early on, especially Ellington associate Leonard Feather. Ellington found in the coming years that his more innovative material, especially works that bypassed swing band norms, were given similar critical treatment in the trade magazines as bebop's pioneers, at least initially.

As bebop became increasingly accepted in the 1950s, scholar Ted Gioia found that, among many of the rising jazz generation, "a wide audience was now a sign of having 'sold out.'" *Down Beat,* in one review, characterized "commercial" as a "nasty word." But Ellington knew that entertaining was paramount in the music business. The ability to satisfy audiences supported the music and brought in audiences who came to appreciate the art as well have a good time. For critics, Gillespie's clowning or Ellington's parade of nondescript vocalists may have seemed like empty gestures and facades, but such diversions were fun—an often essential goal in the musical marketplace. Besides, just as in the Swing Era, Ellington and Strayhorn demonstrated in this period that vocal records could be as sophisticated in their underpinnings as accomplished instrumental compositions—"I Like the Sunrise" from 1947's *Liberian Suite* offers the best example of this from these years. Ellington refused to relinquish the role of entertainer for artist and in fact seemed to relish both roles, which frustrated some critics, younger performers, and audiences. Michael James, Ellington's nephew, confidante, and close observer of the New York jazz scene, explained the dichotomy:

> The beboppers didn't understand what Duke understood, [and] that's when you go off and cut yourself off, when you have that break between the mass audience and jazz became a connoisseur's art form, you're relegated. Or as Jo Jones [a drummer with Count Basie] used to sarcastically say about the

young guys, "Mike, they never played anywhere! All they know is these shit-houses in the Village, where they pay off in pussy and cocaine, you know?" So [Ellington] felt that he came from an era of more class, where they had to [appeal to a wider audience in nicer venues] . . . [Ellington] understood that you don't have to give any [audiences] up. You keep 'em all.

Ellington would be pushing ahead in his art long after most boppers left the scene, either by drug overdose or lack of music business success. And his embrace of jazz as an art form, and his example of the black jazz artist as a symbol of seriousness and respectability were key influences among the bop generation, whether or not they admitted it (most of them did). Ellington supported the best of bebop, eventually recording with Gillespie and Max Roach, among others. Albert Murray recalled that Ellington paid attention to the new sounds and incorporated them into his work, as seen in *The Tattooed Bride* (1948). Ellington also recognized bebop as part of jazz history, its controversy sealing its significance. "Why be surprised bop is ridiculed?" he mused in 1950. "Jazz and swing got the same treatment in their early days, too."[16]

Like bebop, the genre of rhythm and blues, another source of music business competition for Ellington, represented a reaction to wartime rationing and big band economics. As with bebop, independent labels moved to publicize R&B after major labels mostly ignored it. It also resembled bebop in its appeal to younger, almost exclusively black audiences, its simpler orchestration, and the way its best recordings captured a personal intimacy that most Swing Era bands could not match. With fewer people on stage, no charts to follow, and opportunity for instantaneous give-and-take with the audience, "you could move around more, swing more," according to Jack McVea, who assembled a five-piece R&B outfit in 1943 in Los Angeles after leaving Lionel Hampton's orchestra. Like Ellington, many of these R&B artists wrote their own material, which seemed to emanate from a more personal place than a Tin Pan Alley assembly line. The widespread application of the electric guitar in rhythm and blues represented another signature musical shift from most bands of the Swing Era. Guitars frequently assumed the melody lines and solos previously assigned to horns and proved much less expensive than hiring and providing charts for a horn section. And they sounded more modern and exciting. Where Ellington drew upon trumpeter Bubber Miley in the late 1920s to produce a distorted, stinging tone that simultaneously embodied a new urban sound and the old South, Muddy Waters, T-Bone Walker, and many others used the electric guitar to produce a similar effect for the postwar generation. It was an instrument Ellington never adopted, which helped tie him to a previous era, despite the frequent updating of his sound and writing.

Ellington, with his celebrity, his need to tour nationally, and his desire to score a hit single, had little use for the smaller independent labels that specialized in bebop and R&B. He needed national exposure to keep his band afloat and his music before the public, and he had already graduated to the premium labels of the major companies, a status exceedingly few blacks retained and one that he hung onto for most of the 1950s. Ellington's music and position within the American music industry was mainstream, free from the usual separate, less respectful identity placed on black Americans, but it was hardly a safe position, as became increasingly obvious during this period.

Ellington also felt the cold wind of the cold war on his shoulder in 1950. The *Daily Worker* reported that Ellington had signed and personally promoted the Stockholm Peace Petition (*Newsweek* called it the World Peace Appeal), a "communist petition" indicating opposition to the atom bomb. Stuart Nicholson's research revealed that the FBI closely watched Ellington's reaction to the allegation. He recalled being asked to sign the petition while in Sweden on tour that year, but "Ellington denied signing the paper and the individual had departed." In addition, he wired the *Daily Worker* this message: "Strongly protest use of my name in connection with petition I never signed." Later in the year, in a story entitled "No Red Songs for Me" from a magazine called the *Leader,* Ellington threatened legal proceedings if his name was not removed from the petition and lashed out against people who were "trying to defame my name and reputation." "I've never been interested in politics in my whole life and don't pretend to know anything about international affairs," Ellington stated, adding intriguingly that "the only 'Communism' I know is that of Jesus Christ. I don't know of any other." He also noted his multiple appeals for Americans to buy bonds during World War II, and vowed to do likewise the next time any country threatened the security of the United States.

Nicholson documented that the FBI kept files on fourteen "innocuous" events (including stands against the poll tax) that Ellington participated in from 1938 to 1950, none of which contained a shred of evidence that Ellington harbored communist leanings. From 1950 to 1960, Ellington took no actions the FBI thought worth recording. Still, until the 1970s, they circulated his file with decades-old information in response to "enquiries," along with the proviso that "the foregoing information is furnished to you as a result of your request for an FBI file check and is not to be construed as clearance or non-clearance of the individual involved." Any concern by the FBI on this issue was misplaced. Ellington's antipathy towards communism and loyalty to his country and its democratic government was strong, and it was expressed frequently in the last decades of his life. Such beliefs were especially evident in his many efforts on behalf of the Voice of America and the State Department. In 1956, he recorded a public service announcement for Radio Free Europe, a network of stations in Europe sponsored by the U.S. government. "One thing is sure: jazz leaves lots of room for individual expression, and in the Communist-dominated countries, jazz and individual expression are two things that are not wanted," he stated, probably reading from a script. "When people behind the Iron Curtain tune to Radio Free Europe for a jazz program, they are getting two things at once: the music they want to hear and a little exercise in individual freedom." After the first take, Ellington bantered with the engineer. "Is that all right?" he asked. "Sure," the engineer replied. "You agree?" asked Ellington. "I agree." "You suppose [President] Eisenhower will agree?" ventured Ellington. "Yes he will." "All right," concluded Ellington, sounding satisfied.[17]

Despite the initial potential for unprecedented exposure, the television industry did not live up to the hype predicted for it by the music business and press, especially for an artist like Ellington. Bandleader Tony Pastor predicted that audiences, especially younger ones, would not be satisfied by images on a small screen and would venture out to see in person what they saw on television. Cab Calloway agreed and offered his own experience as evidence. "Frank Bunetta's presentation of [my] band on *Cavalcade* [*of Bands*, an NBC-TV program] was the greatest audition we could have given," Calloway gushed on the front page of *Down Beat*. "[The] response was so unbelievable that we had set up our entire Midwestern tour within a week of the two telecasts." By late 1951, however, patterns of popular music on television were coalescing, and they proved bland and conservative. For the most part, a safe, vanilla, vaudeville-style aesthetic prevailed. "Where are the new singers, new bands, or other musical units discovered on and built up by television?" *Down Beat* asked in an editorial. "You've still got the Fred Warings, the Wayne Kings, the Vaughn Monroes, the Paul Whitemans, the Sammy Kayes . . . This is new music?" The bands that enjoyed the most successful television careers were those that adopted an anonymous style that embraced well-known standard songs, such as Lawrence Welk and Spade Cooley. "Cooley, when he launched his TV career [in 1951], dropped all but the suggestion of the western music style with which he was originally identified," reported Charles Emge in 1952. "His band is now a standard dance combination of brass, reeds, and rhythm, comprised largely of competent musicians with radio and studio backgrounds."[18]

Ellington continued his interest in pioneering emerging technologies in his courting of the medium of television during the 1950s. Two advertising agencies approached him in 1950 with offers to underwrite a monthly "high-budgeted all-Negro revue" and a presentation of his musical *Beggars Holiday*. Ellington eventually rejected both because the deals did not provide enough artistic freedom for his tastes. He voiced disdain for the medium itself and the programming it generally featured: "This [artistic] freedom can not exist where imagination is lacking," he stated in 1950. "The light entertainment programs, without exception, are content to slip into the variety show format." He also expressed concern about the limitations of space, lighting, and camera flexibility inherent in television's early years. He told columnist Ben Gross that he was holding out for doing a "secret" project of his own devising that "would be broad in scope and sophisticated, a concept that is more than musical." Such a production, according to Ellington, required "independence of action and freedom from censorship," two qualities still rare on network television. Television proved to be a mostly confining and stifling environment for Ellington. With very few exceptions over the quarter century following his 1949 TV debut, Ellington's hundreds of American TV appearances were usually limited to one old hit song, or a medley of them, with no opportunity for playing or even talking about new material or projects. Sometimes he appeared as a celebrity, playing no music, on shows like *What's My Line* and on *Masquerade Party*, where he dressed as an Arab in order to emulate his old hit song (co-written with Juan Tizol) "Caravan." Television built a safe, static image for the bandleaders of the Swing Era, encasing them in nostalgic hits and preventing them from changing with the times. For most of these artists, like Calloway, that represented an accurate picture, but Ellington's commitment to composing and evolving made television a liability in some respects, a medium that only presented an out-of-date, one-dimensional image with the edges shorn off. Yet such appearances were necessary to keep his name before the public.[19]

Younger competition, the end of the big band era, the beginning of the television era, vague FBI harassment, and racism on the road did not constitute Ellington's only hurdles during this period. The business connections that served him effectively in the first half of the decade, enabling him to prevail over the discrimination of the Swing Era, began to fray. In December 1945, Ellington asked for a release from RCA Victor records, even though eleven months remained on the contract. *Variety* reported that his motives were grounded in "acute dissatisfaction with the way he has been handled by the disk company and the tunes that have been assigned to his band to record." Six months later, while still on Victor, Ellington elaborated on the reasons, singling out an influential RCA Victor executive and producer:

> For one thing, the return of Eli Oberstein to Victor as recording director meant tremendous pressure in choosing material. In the main, we played what we wanted. But we were forced to make concessions. The payoff came when Victor failed to release 17 of our best sides. Only our pops reached the public. Not that there's anything wrong with pop music as such. Don't rule out a ballad like "Flamingo" or "I Ain't Got Nothing But the Blues." They're as satisfying musically as anything else.

Strayhorn, in the same article, discussed how under Oberstein's reestablished tenure at Victor, "we were not able to record and release" more challenging, less "pop" material. "*Black, Brown and Beige* was distributed but was seriously cut. However, the material that *did* get on *BB&B* is great," he explained. Drummer Sonny Greer recalled a "big fight" between Victor and Ellington over "recording the pieces from *Black, Brown and Beige.*" Similar struggles probably ensued over the four-track, eleven-minute *Perfume Suite,* one of Ellington and Strayhorn's most important works of the 1940s, which was recorded in 1945 but not released by Victor until 1952. Long-time Ellington band member and close friend Harry Carney told A. H. Lawrence that Ellington also felt dissatisfaction with the promotion the company gave his recordings: "All he wanted was the same kind of publicity they gave Tommy Dorsey's records. He never felt he got that." Strayhorn told *Down Beat* that it was "especially unfortunate that our album of new arrangements of 10 old Ellington classics was never put on the dealers' shelves."[20]

Those ten RCA Victor sides provide clues concerning Oberstein and Victor's reluctance to release them. From the 1940s onward, companies frequently reissued Ellington classics, either the originals from the 1920s and 1930s or recent recordings that resembled them. Most of the ten Ellington evergreens the band recorded for Victor in May 1945, however, were extensively revamped. They contained familiar melodies, but most of the sides altered the arrangements, as seen in the extra dissonance applied to the hook of "Caravan," complicating the roundness of the original melody, or the shifting time and setting changes underneath "In a Sentimental Mood" and "Mood Indigo." The results were enjoyable, but did not provide effortless listening, as the band's hit singles of the period "I'm Beginning to See the Light" and "Don't Get around Much Anymore" did. The new method of popular and jazz orchestration Strayhorn introduced in the early 1940s, with its grounding in classical sources and a baroque sensibility, was being applied to the older Ellington sound. In at least one instance—the joyously building new version of "It Don't Mean a Thing," graced with tripartite female vocal harmonies—Oberstein may have missed an opportunity to release another hit single for the band.

New evidence indicates that the overarching conflict between Ellington and RCA Victor centered more on the way he was "handled by the disk company" than on the material recorded. A racist slur uttered by Oberstein created an untenable working situation and led to Ellington leaving the company as soon as could be legally arranged. Brad McCuen, an RCA producer and executive in the 1950s and 1960s (who worked on several Ellington projects), made it a personal practice to befriend older engineers at the company, and he heard the full story of the incident from engineer Lou Layton, who was present in the studio that day. McCuen's account follows:

[Oberstein] was a New Yorker, and brusque, and possibly crude. In the old days . . . The producer, or the A&R man, had his own little room next door with his little window looking out into the studio. There was also a window from the producer's room that looked sideways into the control room. And the communication, the walls were all soundproof, was by a series of microphones and talkbacks. The engineers would meet early, the band would come in and set up, they'd test each microphone, an engineer would push his talk-back [switch], as long as he depressed it, he could talk to [band members]. Duke came in . . . and was going through the music with whoever the copyist was. Eli came in to the control room where the engineers were. What Eli didn't realize, what the engineers didn't realize, the last time they had talked to the musicians, the toggle switch, that had a spring on it . . . when he took his finger away, the toggle switch should have flipped back to "off." It didn't, it stuck, I guess the spring was weak. And so that mike remained open, and Eli was there, and he says "OK boys, you ready for a little Saturday night nigger music," or something to that effect. Well, that went right out into the studio and everybody in the Ellington band just kind of looked up and it was not exactly what they were used to hearing, and they all looked in the control room, and Lou said from that moment, he knew that it was tragic. And Duke, you know, turned slowly back and said to the band, "Gentlemen, pack up." He shuffled the music, gave it to [the copyist], went and put his coat on, and Eli went into the studio . . . but what could he say? Duke ignored him, and Duke walked down the hall at 24th street, and on out . . . There was a real mess . . . [Ellington's contract] had 2 years to go . . . The compromise was Duke would finish out that contract, but Eli Oberstein couldn't set foot near the studio, and that if he saw Eli there, he would pull the men off, and the deal would be off . . . Some of the recordings were just stock arrangements . . . the arrangements were absolutely nothing, the value of them were the solos of course. It was a dreadful thing for Duke.[21]

It was also a dreadful situation for RCA Victor. From 1943 to 1945, the Ellington orchestra released nine top-selling singles. Most of the band's final recordings for Victor were, as McCuen related, rather lackluster, perhaps on purpose. Between November 1945 and July 1946, the band took an unusually long recording hiatus: the negotiations for the remainder of the contract were probably being completed during this time. Of Ellington's last twenty-one recordings for the label (from July to September of 1946), eleven were by songwriters with no direct connection to the band, an unusually high proportion. Of the forty-one Ellington RCA Victor recordings preceding those, thirty-seven were by Ellington, Strayhorn, and/or one of his band members. Eight of the very last fifteen songs were judged to be of such poor quality that they were not released until decades later.[22] The recordings were not terrible; most of them just lacked the vitality and originality of Ellington's initial four years of discs for the company and sounded like any big band could have waxed them. Perhaps another reason that none of Ellington's last sides for RCA became hits is because they did not wish to aggressively promote an artist that they knew would soon be heading to a competitor.

After working to extricate himself from RCA for months, Ellington signed with Musicraft in May 1946, six months before the Victor contract expired. They were a postwar independent label with a promising amount of capital (rare for such companies) and a reputation for granting "unprecedented [creative] freedom." The contract would not take effect until the RCA contract terminated. According to *Variety*, Ellington's Musicraft contract represented a deal "probably unequaled by any other Negro band in the business, and one that's the equal of many deals between top white bands and major firms." The three-year contract promised $100,000 in royalties a year to Ellington. Unfortunately, such numbers never materialized. A year after Ellington joined the label (which also featured Artie Shaw and Sarah Vaughan), it folded, as did many of the more ambitious independent labels of the period, a situation that led to a congressional investigation and hearings chaired by the Anti-Monopoly Committee. The "Big Four" labels (Victor, Columbia, Decca, and Capitol) accounted for almost 90 percent of the market and were netting "two to four times better than the previous year," while even indies stocked with talent like Musicraft were "wobbling" and forced to refinance or close, claiming that their troubles stemmed from the major labels' stranglehold on retail and radio. Ellington accepted a $25,000 bailout from Musicraft when he probably could have held out for more because it was more important for him to start recording again immediately for another label.[23] In an uncertain economic and artistic atmosphere, he had tried an independent label, knowing that such labels had produced hit singles in the R&B field and were hailed as havens for those who wished to avoid the conservatively commercial route of most majors. Such labels were more effective for new artists or artists in genres that the majors tended to ignore, such as bebop, blues, and gospel. But the approach did not work for Ellington, who needed the largest exposure possible to fund the continued existence of his music and large band. In an ironic twist, Eli Oberstein ended up buying the Musicraft catalog in 1953, releasing Ellington reissues from the Musicraft sessions for decades at cut-rate prices, and competing with Ellington's newer work.[24]

The end of the big band era also brought about the demise of the William Morris Agency's band department in early 1947. Ellington and Ellington acolyte Charlie Spivak stayed on at the company until the spring of 1949, even though Willard Alexander left WMA two years before and the bands had been offered the services of General Artists Corporation, a company second only to MCA in terms of band bookings.[25] Perhaps Ellington did not wish to professionally reside where everyone else in his wing of the business tended to congregate. Throughout his career, he seemed to prefer the special attention that often comes with being in a category of one's own.

However, while WMA represented the classiest and biggest stars, and served Ellington particularly well in the first half of the decade, Ellington had been promoted in a pedestrian fashion since at least 1945 by WMA and continued to be treated that way by subsequent publicists and managers until the mid-1950s. A 1946 WMA publicity manual for Ellington contained the same typeface and most of the same stories as a Mills publicity manual of the mid-1930s. Some 1940s photos were substituted for those of a decade earlier and changes in record and management company affiliation were noted, but otherwise the document is largely unchanged. Thirteen of twenty-three features in the 1946 WMA press manual are used entirely, or in large part, in the 1949 WMA press manual and in the 1953 and 1955 press manuals issued by Associated Booking Corporation, Ellington's booker for most of the 1950s. Seven of the twenty-three features either copy or are strongly reminiscent of the 1930s Mills press manuals, and half of the "punch lines" suggested to describe the band (including "Harlem's Aristocrat of Jazz" and "music no other band can play!") correlate between the two manuals.[26] Perhaps this forms another reason why the band's popularity descended in the post-1945 period: how could anyone have expected the media to become excited or generate coverage for a performer whose story had been told in largely the same way for over two decades?

Ellington never mentioned how he felt when his associations with the top recording and management companies foundered, when his nearly two-decade run of hit singles stopped, or about the shifting economic and artistic environment he found himself facing by early 1947. He rarely made negative comments publicly or privately, or dwelt on any setbacks. But it must have been disconcerting to find himself financially supplementing his band out of his own pocket and facing racism that was probably worse than what he saw in the 1920s and 1930s—on the road as well as from a top executive at his own record company. In the coming years, Ellington would once again have to reinvent his art and how it was promoted and establish new business relationships and patterns.

8

REINVENTION AND NADIR

Reputation Shredded, Duke Should Disband, [Critic] Claims

Headline in *Down Beat,* 1949

NAACP Plans to Boycott Duke Ellington

Headline in *Richmond Times-Dispatch,* 1951

Maestro Says 'We Ain't Ready Yet':
Duke Ellington's Views on Jim Crow Shock Nation

Headline in *Baltimore Afro-American,* 1951

Selected Down Beat *1955 Reader's Poll results for best dance band:*
Les Brown (first place), 1,905 votes; Lawrence Welk, 85 votes;
Duke Ellington, 52 votes.

As these headlines demonstrate, the 1946–56 period featured some of the more frustrating and dispiriting times in the history of the Ellington orchestra. Yet, alone among their big band competition, they soldiered on without a break through money-losing gigs, record contracts, and projects, financially buoyed by Ellington's royalties. Racial controversies and poor recordings shook his reputation as never before. Ellington persisted nonetheless, creating memorable works as well as some of his least distinguished, keeping the band working during unprecedented bad business conditions, and laying the foundation for the stunning and surprising artistic and business

FIGURE 7. The story of Mercer Records, an independent label mostly run by Ellington's son Mercer and journalist Leonard Feather, provides another example of how Duke Ellington and his associates developed creative and aggressive ways to keep his name and work before the public, refusing to be relegated to the periphery of the rapidly shifting postwar music business that claimed so many of his peers. This photo captures a Mercer small group session from the early 1950s, with (*left to right*) Lloyd Trottman, Duke Ellington, and Oscar Pettiford. Frank Driggs Collection.

successes he engineered from 1956 until the early 1970s. In the postwar era, American culture, especially African American culture and attitudes toward civil rights, was changing. A new generation was emerging, and it took time for Ellington to adjust to and finally master these new realities.

Beggar's Holiday, Ellington's first attempt at a Broadway musical, represented one of the disappointments during this postwar period.[1] It was based on John Gay's classic *Beggar's Opera* of 1728, updated with a plot that revolved around a gangster and his "three molls," but true to the original's theme of "the bourgeois and the criminal share the same vices and are, essentially, identical," according to theater historian Daniel C. Caine. The prognosis looked promising, with John Houseman as director, Alfred Drake, fresh from the hit *Oklahoma!* and the then-unknown Zero Mostel in the cast. John LaTouche, successful in writing for Hollywood musicals, contributed the book and lyrics. Publicists vaunted the fact that it represented Ellington's first full score for a major Broadway production. Like many of Ellington's own works of the period, it attempted to bring a more adult sensibility to the Broadway musical, a reaction against the "optimistic claptrap" that characterized most Broadway hits of the period.

But *Beggar's Holiday,* which opened at the Broadway Theater on 26 December 1946, drew mostly negative reviews. The *New York Daily News* provided the most positive assessment, calling it the best musical since *Porgy and Bess* and touting Ellington's refusal to follow Tin Pin Alley tradition in his score. The *New York Times* praised Ellington, the dancers, and the production's attempt to do "something different," but most critics, including nationally syndicated columnist Walter Winchell, dismissed the songs and the show. The main positive legacy of the production, cited by *Down Beat* and subsequent biographers, was the liberally integrated casting. "This is the first time whites and Negroes have been used on a musical stage with complete indifference to their colors, merely cast according to capabilities and treated onstage as characters of their parts, nothing more," wrote Mike Levin in *Down Beat.* The main gangster was white, and the chief of police was black, a reversal of accepted racial roles at the time. Integration occurred behind the scenes, as well, with Perry Watkins, one of the few African Americans working on major Broadway productions, serving as production designer and contributing impressive sets to the show. This enlightened liberal perspective on race emerged from a cast and staff that, within a few years, with the exception of Ellington, would mostly be listed in *Red Channels* as communists or sympathizers. Many of them were victims of the blacklist starting in the late 1940s. The premiere for *Beggar's Holiday* benefited Paul Robeson's Council on African Affairs, soon to become "a favorite target of the House Un-American Activities Committee investigations and red-baiters everywhere," according to Caine.

Composing a hit Broadway musical marked the one major professional goal unachieved by Ellington in his lifetime, and many factors explain this. For starters, the show faced immense competition, playing opposite the initial runs of *Annie Get Your Gun, Carousel, Finian's Rainbow, Brigadoon,* and *Oklahoma!* More importantly, chaos reigned backstage. Distrust mushroomed between Houseman, the alcoholic and unreliable Latouche, and Ellington, who, despite receiving a sizeable advance, refused to put his orchestra on hiatus to concentrate on *Beggar's Holiday.* Many great lyrics and songs were dropped from the show, which kept changing radically during months of preproduction. Houseman and star Libby Holman were fired just before the premiere. The new director, George Abbott, wanted to return to the original script, but no one could find a copy of it, which led to Abbott's quitting and young assistant Nicholas Ray, soon to be a successful Hollywood director, receiving last-minute credit as director. Financial problems plagued the production; somewhere between $350,000 and $500,000 was spent before the premiere, a sum two to three times larger than that spent on *Oklahoma!* before its premiere. This ensured that the show would experience extreme difficulty becoming profitable, and it only opened when producers found a wealthy investor, literally "a drunken angel," to underwrite previous expenses and, eventually, take the loss.

Like *Jump for Joy, Beggar's Holiday* was probably also harmed by the prominent black presence on stage, a rarity on Broadway previously and for years afterward. Both shows broke barriers, but such actions, however laudable, stood in the way of greater success. Ellington viewed this as the main reason for the show's quick demise. "It was just ahead of its time . . . I think, the audience, the critics, nobody could understand why anybody would have an integrated show where it was practically half white and half colored. And not have them opposite each other, or calling each other names," Ellington said in 1964, two years after *West Side Story,* which shared similar themes to *Beggar's Holiday,* won the Oscar for best picture. His son Mercer also listed race as the leading factor behind his father's Broadway failures.

Another reason was that Ellington, with *Beggar's* and subsequent attempts at musicals, refused to spend months solely concentrating on the work, as successful Broadway composers usually did. "I never saw Duke Ellington, never worked with him," stated Abbott, who felt that more work and songs were required. "Billy [Strayhorn] took care of whatever I asked for. He sat down and wrote it right there when it was needed."

In the same year that *Beggar's* opened on Broadway, so did *Street Scene,* with songs by Kurt Weill, Elmer Rice, and Langston Hughes. It was the first musical put together by blacks and whites in decades (though such integration did not occur onstage, except for a black playing a janitor), and it became a critical and commercial hit, giving Hughes the first fleeting financial independence he had enjoyed in his professional life. But, Hughes found, the fine tuning of the show, the seemingly endless reworking of music and lyrics, the attendance at rehearsals, and the search for backers took months of his time. "Shows, I do believe were designed to bring authors to an early grave!" he lamented. Ellington never made it to the final rehearsals, or perhaps any rehearsals, for *Beggar's,* and the show suffered for it. His later attempts at Broadway success, such as *Pousse Café* (1965), shared similar fates.

Another problem emerged from the fact that Ellington's musical style did not adapt easily to a Broadway aesthetic. The best and most popular Broadway songs featured instantly singable and memorable choruses. Most Ellington melodies were more insinuative, taking effect slowly and subtly in the listener's consciousness. Ellington's commercial successes had always challenged the rules of popular songs: "Mood Indigo" (1930) and "I Got It Bad (and That Ain't Good)" (1941) were bereft of traditional refrains but became hits regardless. Also, Ellington tended not to repeat common themes, which Mercer Ellington viewed as his father's "perhaps only compositional limitation." He "was too prolific, wouldn't reprise material through a musical, like most [Broadway] composers would." Lastly, the *Beggar's* songs, at least the ones that survive, are mostly subpar. Latouche's lyrics are riddled with clichés and contain no memorable turns of phrase. Ellington turned in some of his most pedestrian songs ever, perhaps because he worked from the lyrics first. Houseman recalled Ellington recycling old unused song ideas rather than starting afresh. "Who needed a score with a melodic stockpiler like Ellington around?" he complained. Ellington's most successful pieces usually emanated from his muse or were inspired by the character of his band members. His penchant for composing material better suited for an instrumentalist than a vocalist is vividly illustrated by comparing the graceful, emotionally moving 1959 version of "Brown Penny" (from *Beggar's*) by the orchestra with Johnny Hodges on alto sax to Kay Davis's painfully awkward 1947 attempt to sing the song. The melodic intervals of the song were difficult to navigate, even for someone with the huge range of Davis. Only five of the dozens of *Beggar's* songs were recorded; if these represented the pick of the lot, the show was probably in trouble from the start.[2]

The *Beggar's Holiday* experience also marked the first public sign of growing frustration Strayhorn felt at the lack of recognition for his creative work in the Ellington organization, a rift that continued for nearly a decade. According to Walter van de Leur, who has extensively examined Strayhorn's music manuscripts, Strayhorn wrote some of the music for the production, including "Brown Penny." Strayhorn's partner, Aaron Bridgers, recalled that "he gave [the show] everything he had in him." Strayhorn biographer David Hajdu quoted many cast and staff members who remembered Strayhorn writing for the production, although one of them, Luther Henderson, a close friend of the Ellingtons and of Strayhorn, told different stories to Hajdu and the Yale Oral History American Music project. "Strayhorn really did a lot of the exposition in *Beggar's Holiday*. But all the tunes were written by Ellington," Henderson told the Yale interviewer in 1981. As usual, it proved difficult for outsiders to determine who wrote what since Ellington and Strayhorn did much of their work in private and on the phone. In any case, Strayhorn believed he deserved more credit. When he arrived at the premiere and saw that the program credited him for "orchestrations," with "music by Duke Ellington," Strayhorn "reportedly walked out of the gala party thrown in honor of Ellington, on the night of the show's Broadway opening." In the years to follow, the situation between Strayhorn and Ellington worsened, and it is telling that the eventual artistic and commercial rebirth of the Ellington orchestra in the mid-1950s did not occur until Strayhorn was guaranteed proper credit for his significant contributions.

Some of the advice Ellington received during this period, privately and in the press, encouraged him to dismantle his band and find different ways to write and perform his music. Norman Granz described his attempts to put together a deal with Ellington in the late 1940s:

The [Ellington] band wasn't doing too well, and I had begun touring my package [of Jazz at the Philharmonic] and though it wasn't very successful in the beginning... I had a feeling that it was a question of time before people would begin to accept the concept of having jazz in a concert hall where you had classic music... Anyway, I met Duke backstage on one of these things and I said "Why don't you give up the band and I'll pay you a weekly salary, at that time it was commensurate with what Duke would net after paying the band... and anytime we get ready to tour, well then you can hire the cats and you can pay them more, and be sure to get them, then the rest of the time they'll find other gigs to do. And you can devote your time to writing." Because it came up that he felt that he didn't have enough time really to sit down and write something . . . Economically, it made a lot of sense, of course. But I'm not sure Duke ever entertained the idea . . . He said no, he really wanted to keep the band together . . . It was obvious when I was smarter about the band that he needed that band just for his compositions, to hear what they sounded like. That became one of the Ellington clichés of the future: "that's my instrument," the band. Well, of course, it made sense.

Michael James recalled Ellington "always fond of talking" about Sol Hurok's attempts in the late 1940s to wrest Ellington from his band in order to stage the kind of lavish international concert tours he had produced for decades for Marian Anderson, among other classical music stars. "Sol Hurok, he wanted me to go legit, you know," James recalled Ellington telling him. "Yeah, he told me, 'Look, let me book you. I'll have you play nothing but the greatest concert halls all over the world. No dance halls, no nightclubs, all of that's out.'" While Ellington appreciated Hurok's offer and the respect it symbolized, he told Hurok that "he couldn't do that."

James explained what he viewed as the reason for Ellington's rejection of Granz and Hurok, even though such offers promised an easier life than the fifty-two-weeks-a-year, grinding existence with his band: "Duke understood that that would cut him off, 'cause he meant it when he said that he liked the idea of playing a concert tonight, a dance tomorrow night, a nightclub the next night . . . [such performing conditions] allowed him to move through the whole society." For classical artists like Van Cliburn, exclusive venues and tours were fine. But Ellington used everyday American life and people as one of the main sources of inspiration for his writing. As an American popular and jazz musician, he felt that he could not afford to get too far away from his audience and subject matter. The road and the people he met while traveling on it inspired him, as Richard O. Boyer of the *New Yorker* witnessed while riding in the band's Pullman car in 1944:

> [Ellington] looked out the window at a drab village through which the train was speeding. A woman stood on a porch, holding a tablecloth which she seemed about to flourish. Before she completed her motion, she was out of sight. "I'd like to write something about that," Duke said. "You know, people moving on a train, other people standing still, and you see them for just an instant and then you rush on forever. Sometimes you look right into their goddam eyes. Seems for a minute like you know them. Then they're gone." He kept staring out the window.

In the same article, Ellington spoke about how "Eerie Moan" (1933) and "Harlem Airshaft" (1940) were written based on the sights and sounds of

New York City, and how "In a Sentimental Mood" (1935) was inspired by an incident that happened while the band was on tour in Durham, North Carolina.[3]

At the same time, *Down Beat* began criticizing the Ellington orchestra as the big band era faded, and even recommended its termination in 1949.[4] The jibes revealed as much about the current scene and the critics as they did about Ellington and the band. While praising Ellington's past contributions as unparalleled in American music and crediting him as the premiere bandleader around, these critics found fault with Ellington "slipping" or "fail[ing] to top himself." The high expectations Ellington had met in the past brought a harsher critical judgment upon him. Ellington's main competition, they argued, was himself, and, in strikingly personal terms, various writers for *Down Beat* between 1946 and 1949 wondered if Ellington was letting them down just as the music scene needed a boost. They appeared to view Ellington as a saviorlike figure during troubled times, which may explain the mood of betrayal in some of their writings. "More important than whether or not the Duke is better than Woody [Herman] is the question of whether or not the Duke, circa 1946, is better than the Duke, circa 1942 or '38 or any other time in the past," wrote Bill Gottlieb under a banner headline that read "'I'm Not Slipping'—Duke Ellington." As an Ellington band member told *Down Beat,* it seemed as if "Duke is expected to compete with an illusion . . . to surpass an idealized memory of his past." In a review of Ellington's two 1946 Carnegie Hall concerts, Mike Levin noted their financial success (sold out a week in advance) and the audience's enjoyment, but mentioned in his opening sentence that the band received a "luke-warm reception by local music critics" because the show did not "take off" and "become a real musical event" as expected of Ellington concerts. "Artistically, if anybody else but Ellington had given [the concert], everyone would have been raving," concluded Levin.

The Gottlieb article took the band to task because of its loss of key members (a widespread big band problem, though less so for Ellington) and the fact that its recent recordings relied too heavily on pop tunes and vocal "ballads" instead of supposedly more serious jazz-oriented material, a situation that reflected RCA Victor's whims more than any decision made by Ellington. As an Ellington band member commented when discussing "Transblucency," Ellington and Strayhorn's approach to vocal tunes could be just as innovative as their instrumentals. Besides, vocal tunes held the possibility of large potential paydays for the band and its composers, which they particularly needed in this period. Recordings featuring Al Hibbler such as "I

Ain't Got Nothing but the Blues" (1944) and "I'm Just a Lucky So-And-So" (1945)—both charming and both derided in Gottlieb's article—seem, to some degree, to represent attempts to tap the lucrative market and younger audience recently developing for R&B. Ellington's simultaneous embrace of serious art and pleasurable entertainment and his catering to multiple audiences bothered some fans and critics.

The height of *Down Beat*'s criticism of Ellington appeared in the 17 June 1949 issue, in a front-page article entitled "Reputation Shredded, Duke Should Disband, Mix [Mike Levin] Claims." The story began with a bang:

> Isn't it about time the Ellington orchestra was disbanded before what was left of a great reputation is completely dragged in the muck? Much has been written about the oldtime men in the organization, what a wonderful creative past the Ellington band has had, and what it will do in the future. Little is said of the cold cash attitude of many of the sidemen and of the frightful trash the band has been turning out for the last three years.

The bold headline and lead paragraph, along with a call by an anonymous classical critic for Ellington to "quit," made news and shaped reaction to the story, but the story itself, particularly near the end, featured a more sympathetic portrait of the predicament Ellington faced during this period. Levin felt that "Ellington himself seems unsure, uncertain as to which direction he should turn musically" and suggested that his peers, who all owe Ellington a creative debt, pool together $25,000 for Ellington to take a year off from the road (and, noting Ellington's overgenerous reputation, from supporting his various family and friends), "then let him return to work in whatever way he feels best." Levin worried that Ellington's reputation as well as that of American music was being harmed by Ellington's alleged decline and confusion. He did not reconcile his views with the fact that *Down Beat* had named Ellington's as the best band for three years running (1946–48), with many of his sidemen and Strayhorn listed at the top of their categories. In 1949, the band did move down to second place, behind Woody Herman's band, which had disbanded by the time the awards were handed out.

Two issues later, Ellington's many defenders sounded off in the pages of *Down Beat*. Foremost among them was fellow bandleader Charlie Barnet, a longtime admirer who viewed Ellington as comporting himself as well as could be expected during bad times, and who painted Levin as a journalist behind his typewriter unaware of business realities:

> You're right that Ellington sounds dispirited and tired a lot of the time these days. But who the hell doesn't? Do you have any idea what it's like, night after

night, playing to sparse crowds and unenthusiastic ones at that? How many places like Bop City you think there are now where a band can sit down [for an extended run instead of playing endless one-nighters] and even catch its breath . . . The things I admit are wrong about Ellington, just as you do, are a reflection of the whole business today, not just Duke. And don't forget for one minute, if Duke goes down, the whole horse show goes right down on a toboggan with him . . . Ellington may not be causing any comment this year, but neither is anybody else.

Barnet correctly pointed out that Ellington faced a more difficult situation because he "has a Negro band, which from the road standpoint makes it twice as hard on him and his men." Like Levin, he also referred to "the horde of parasites that use [Ellington] for a living," but asserted that Ellington's royalties contributed more than enough to stave off economic ruin or anything close to it. Fans, writing in the letters column, reported discussing Levin's article with Ellington, who shrugged it off by saying, "I've had worse reviews by better people." Two issues later, Ellington wrote his own letter to the publication, which landed on its front page. He dismissed Levin's calls for additional discipline and punctuality in the band by replying that applying "tin soldier discipline" would only produce a "manufactured music" (and leave him less time for composing). His men were professionals and adults, if sometimes fallible or lazy, and he intended to treat them as such:

> I don't believe in telling people who are grownups to do things they should have learned when they were about six years old. To me it seems a waste of time. If I didn't like the way this band plays I wouldn't pay so much to listen to it and write for it. Our band is operating at a loss now. We haven't cut salaries since the wartime high, but I can get everything played I want played with this band.

His musical priorities, as usual, were composing and pleasing audiences, two goals not contradictory for Ellington. "When I write I want to give Billy Strayhorn a tickle and when he writes he writes with the same attitude toward me. If I started worrying about people who didn't understand . . . " Ellington paused without completing that sentence. His next sentence was a typical and revealing Ellington quote: "We're always looking to the future. The past and now are over, it's the future that counts."

Alongside the Barnet letter, *Down Beat*'s front page on 15 July 1949 also featured a report of an interview with Strayhorn held on critic Leonard Feather's New York City radio program, *Jazz at Its Best*. An exchange from that show illustrated the vast differences between the priorities of the critics and the artists. "Hibbler does a nice juke box vocal," Strayhorn commented. "But we don't look to Ellington for juke box records," Feather replied. Such closed-mindedness blinded critics to the skill and charm Ellington, Strayhorn, and Hibbler brought to vocal tunes. It also represented an unrealistic attitude. Ellington's orchestra needed the support of the widest audience, and vocal tunes dominated the charts during the postwar period. And Ellington obviously enjoyed and was successful creating such material. Ellington and Strayhorn knew that their extended and less pop-oriented pieces, while admired by certain segments of the public, stood little chance of radio exposure, and record companies resisted releasing them. But this did not stop them from writing and performing such material.

Ellington made room for all facets of his musical identity in his shows and recordings, and from this point forward, this quality differentiated him even further from his bandleader peers. Goodman, Herman, and Lombardo, among many others, occasionally left their self-imposed semiretirements in the late 1940s to embark on tours as late as the 1970s, but they rarely premiered new material. When they did, it usually did not deviate significantly from their music of the 1930s and 1940s. Ellington provided nostalgia, too, and plenty of it, but he was the only Swing Era bandleader to treat jazz-oriented big band music as an ongoing artistic movement after World War II. His compositions kept developing, adapting new concepts and sounds as the decades went by, as if Ellington refused to recognize that big band music no longer occupied the center of attention in American music. Ellington had effectively balanced commercial, artistic, and financial concerns since the early 1930s, but now, in the late 1940s, as jazz was becoming more universally viewed as a significant art form, many people, especially critics, wished to see and support only Ellington's more artistic side.

Was Ellington's 1946–49 output "frightful trash," as Levin termed it? Certainly many of his last RCA Victor recordings made after Oberstein's slur were subpar, as he acknowledged. The Musicraft recordings did not enjoy the distribution or presence in the market that RCA Victor, the biggest recording company in the country, could muster. Breaking off with Victor in 1946, even for good reasons, denied Ellington maximum access to the mass media at a difficult juncture in music business history and probably enhanced the image of Ellington's decline in the public eye. Musicraft's studio capabilities paled next to Victor's, giving many of Ellington's recordings on that label an echoey quality at times, with less dynamic range. But the songs themselves were often musically enjoyable, though usually not groundbreaking. The chord structure and melody of "The Beautiful Indians—Hiawatha" resembled that of "It Don't Mean a Thing," yet its hushed and swinging backing and tenor saxist Al Sears's joyous performance radiated pure pleasure. "It Shouldn't Happen to a Dream" featured a more challenging and sweeping melody (co-written by Johnny Hodges) than the usual vocal song, and perhaps if Don George's syrupy lyric did not so closely resemble the concept for Sammy Cahn and Jule Styne's recent hit for Sinatra, "It's the Same Old Dream," one could imagine it landing on the pop charts. "Green, Pink, and Plaid" verified that the current orchestra could still acquit itself admirably in a "jam session" situation. The Musicraft tracks did not boast sustained brilliance, but they demonstrated that Ellington was still operating in a realm far different than most popular or jazz artists. And sometimes, in tracks like "Magenta Haze," another in a four-decade series of soaring romantic vehicles for saxophonist Hodges, and "Happy Go Lucky Local Parts 1 and 2," Ellington and the band produced work at Musicraft that could stand among their best.

Many of the more successful steps Ellington took toward reinvention occurred at Columbia Records, where he signed a contract in 1947, following the Musicraft buyout. According to Harry Carney, Ellington only joined the label after assurances from Count Basie that John Hammond, the recording executive who attempted to squelch Ellington's more ambitious works in the 1930s, was leaving the label. Klaus Stratemann maintained that Basie's exit from Columbia also paved the way for Ellington's entry: when Ellington left Victor, Basie left Columbia (along with Hammond) and assumed Ellington's place at Victor. Ellington eventually took Basie's "spot" at Columbia. The terms that Stratemann used, which are featured in *Variety*'s report of the label switch as well, seem to imply that only one "spot" existed at each major label for a black big band.[5]

By the time Ellington arrived at Columbia, they had perfected the process of creating long-playing albums (LPs) in 10-inch and 12-inch sizes, which played for twenty-seven and forty-five minutes respectively at 33 1/3 rpm. By the late 1940s and early 1950s, the company earned notoriety within the industry for "revolutionizing" the recording process with the addition of multitracking (Les Paul played a major role in this) and engineering pop records that sounded like classical records. Columbia represented an ideal place for Ellington, a perfectionist who enjoyed writing and recording extended pieces. Other companies resisted and protested the LP format at first, some offering their own alternatives at 45 rpm, but by the early 1950s, the LP had earned a place as a popular and universal recorded-music format.[6]

Ellington's extended compositions had previously chafed at the limits of

78-rpm recordings. The longer format would theoretically allow Ellington and Strayhorn to release the full extent of their output. But in the beginning they found themselves stymied out of longer formats. Major labels like Columbia initially limited music on LPs to classical artists and pop vocalists like Rosemary Clooney and Dinah Shore. This could have been because the new technology was initially expensive: a new RCA 33-rpm portable player retailed at $166 in 1947 and did not accommodate competitors' discs. RCA shelved a planned ten-song album of rearranged Ellington classics in 1946, and *Down Beat* noted Musicraft's reneging of its stated intent to release *The Deep South Suite* in album-length format the next year. Musicraft also abandoned plans to release a *Beggar's Holiday* album. It's hard to tell if record executives felt that Ellington fans could not afford the technology or if the decisions were based on some sort of discrimination.

The music press noted the lack of black or jazz artists on the LP format. The first 101 LPs released by Columbia, according to *Down Beat,* included no jazz (though they termed Les Brown and Harry James "near-jazz"). "We believe Columbia has missed a faithful block of record buyers by not including some good jazz in their initial inventory," George Hoefer argued, ending his article by asking Columbia for some Ellington on LP. A year later, Columbia announced a new Dance Parade series of discs that included Benny Goodman, Woody Herman, and several other bandleaders, none of them black.[7] The list of initial Columbia LP releases shows that, perhaps in order to establish and test the new format, Columbia tended to limit LP content to reissues at first instead of releasing new material. Their first Ellington LP, *The Ellington Special,* released in the summer of 1947 and consisted of mostly unreleased Ellington small band sides from the 1930s. The aforementioned Goodman, Herman, James, and Brown releases also featured older recordings.

Before the Ellington orchestra was allowed to premiere new material on LPs at Columbia, they recorded a bevy of songs that ranged the musical gamut, many obviously waxed in hopes of scoring a hit single. In a brief three-month period, they completed at least forty sides, an unusually prodigious effort. The flurry of recordings resulted from the imminence of another recording ban by the American Federation of Musicians, set to take effect at the close of 1947. Labels stockpiled as many discs as possible to release during the strike, which ended up lasting fifty weeks. Ellington waived his usual advance so the company could accumulate plenty of Ellington product to release during the strike. "We would record almost anything at all, we were going a mile a minute in those days [before the ban]," recalled George

Avakian, Ellington's main producer at Columbia during this period and the executive in charge of the pop-record division. He remembers several studios always running at once, while he dashed around New York City trying to keep track of all the sessions for the label. "It was a merry-go-round, great fun . . . It wasn't the best possible attitude really . . . get the artists in the studio, do something." Avakian, a longtime jazz fan who started his career assembling and writing liner notes for record reissues in the late 1930s when he was barely out of his teens, had admired Ellington for over a decade before he became his producer.[8]

The rush to record gave Ellington and Strayhorn a lot of freedom, and they recorded some exciting new material. But it also resulted in some of the orchestra's all-time worst recordings, including two songs annoyingly calculated to try and take advantage of current music fads: "Cowboy Rhumba" and "Boogie Bop Blues." "Don't Be So Mean to Baby" and "Antidisestablishmentarianismist," attempts to forge a sound for the R&B market, fared the best. The latter, with its lyrics awkwardly attempting to link a woman who refuses a romantic invitation with a political protester, marked yet another in a long series of painfully cornball lyrics supplied by Don George (one of three songs he penned that week alone). Ellington and Strayhorn did in fact sound lost, or perhaps they were listening to the label too much.

In New York, with Avakian, output improved, but some dross still emerged. Particularly troublesome to the critical establishment was a trio of Tin Pan Alley standards the band recorded on 14 November 1947, including "Singin' in the Rain," cited as one of the main inspirations for Mike Levin's characterization of recent Ellington output as "frightful trash." Even Charlie Barnet, in defending Ellington against Levin's harsher criticisms, referred to the single as "dreadful." But such material was chosen, or at least brought in, by Ellington. "We were not assigning songs to Duke," Avakian explained. With Sinatra or Dinah Shore, for example, the company's producers or the vocalists themselves solicited "push songs" from publishers, trying to discover a potential hit song. Ellington knew Columbia wanted a large number of tracks, and he prepared to fulfill the need. Songs like "Singin'" were "available to be done while the ban was going on. They went so 'bang, bang' [quickly] that I had no recollection [years later] of recording 'Singin' in the Rain.' It was like a throwaway." From the sound of it, perhaps stock arrangements were procured. Though critics viewed the recording as a new low for Ellington, the record should be viewed in a wider perspective. Charles Allen, manager of the Rhythm Record Shop, wrote to *Down Beat* to complain of the dismissal of "Singin' in the Rain." He concluded: "This happens to be the best-selling instrumental record [in my shop] released by the Duke in the last two years. Pardon me, fellows, if I sound so commercial, but aren't we all in this business to make money?"[9]

During the Great Depression, Ellington proved willing to use a non-Ellington song if it meant more money or exposure for the band. Apparently Ellington decided to follow this strategy again during another uncertain period in the music business. Also, recording forty original tracks in three months, even for the prolific Ellington and Strayhorn team, represented a tall order. Meeting Columbia's demand for product before the ban ensued required some scrounging.

Yet, within those last three months of 1947, the seeds were planted for another Ellington renaissance. Columbia took eight of the best tracks recorded in New York and put them on the first Ellington 10-inch album of originals, *Mood Ellington*, released in August 1948. It previewed the approach that Ellington and Strayhorn would apply to long-playing records. It was a cohesive conceptualized package of material; moody, as the title promised, and, with one exception, not swinging. The anonymous arrangements were gone—no doubt existed that this was the Ellington orchestra that was playing. "On a Turquoise Cloud" was an eerie aural painting featuring Kay Davis and co-writer and trombonist Lawrence Brown in tandem. "New York City Blues," a track concocted in the studio by Ellington, functioned as a beautiful jazz miniature, full of personality, redolent of a late-night cab ride past Central Park up to Harlem. Perhaps most impressive and historically important was "The Clothed Woman," which John Edward Hasse referred to as "probably" Ellington's "foremost composition for piano." *Mood Ellington* served as an early template for the concept album, a grouping of songs meant to evoke certain moods. During the 1950s, Ellington and Strayhorn and other artists, especially Sinatra, would refine and improve the idea, but *Mood Ellington* showed the artistic possibilities for the new LP format. Hit singles continued their importance in the business, but albums became an important artistic canvas and financial mainstay for recording artists, especially those who appealed to a more adult sensibility.

From this point forward, Ellington and Strayhorn's most successful albums were united by concepts, some solid, some more amorphous. This convention made economic sense as well as artistic: concepts were used as marketing totems to draw attention to the band's latest LPs. It made a new release seem more like an event. A catchy hit single would no longer be the only way to hook new listeners. Ellington and Strayhorn used the album format for the rest of their careers to demonstrate the difference of their sound and approach.

The next Ellington orchestra 10-inch Columbia album was the twenty-four-minute *Liberian Suite,* commissioned to celebrate the centenary of Liberia and premiered at Carnegie Hall in 1947. Though recorded at the close of 1947, it remained unreleased for two years, which probably reflected company reticence concerning the project. It consisted of five separate "dances," as well as "I Like the Sunrise." Unfortunately, the last three "dances" were not as interesting as the first two. Avakian felt that "it took some real prompting from Duke to get it released" since there was "no great interest" at the company to release a project like that, and no one, including Ellington, felt it would sell in large amounts. But it received glowing reviews and helped update the image of Ellington as an artist who brought a different and more serious perspective to popular music.[10] Besides, as recent experiences with tracks like "Cowboy Rhumba" demonstrated, if the Ellington orchestra wished to continue to prosper as a vital unit, they needed to claim territory of their own apart from the usual popular fare, even if it was not the most commercial or profitable ground. They would not and could not survive by doing what dozens of other bands could do as well or better. They had to play to their considerable strengths and differences in a very competitive market.

Ellington's emphasis on concept albums featuring challenging new material at Columbia in the late 1940s and 1950s bucked a profitable music business trend. As Joseph Horowitz documented, the advent of the LP and television broadcasting significantly increased the audience for "serious music." In 1934, classical music brought in $750,000 in record sales and gate receipts; twenty years later, it represented a $70 million-per-year enterprise, with more admissions and a higher gross than Major League Baseball. Millions of Americans watched conductor Arturo Toscanini's weekly NBC-TV broadcasts. While such statistics made the classical music industry seem healthy, Horowitz argued the opposite. Only a strict, small list of accepted works, mostly forwarded by Toscanini, were showcased. The emphasis rested on celebrity and a rigorously guarded canon: new music, American music, and twentieth-century classical music were almost completely ignored. Such strategies, while profitable in the short run and pleasing to Toscanini's sensibilities, proved deadly to the long-term viability of the classical market. Without the encouragement and promotion of vibrant new works and composers, the audience dwindled over time, and an enduring image was constructed that painted classical music as a non-evolving highbrow enterprise with little relevance to modern times and younger audiences. Aaron Copland, seeing this problem developing in the 1940s, recommended to his colleagues that they reach beyond "the concert audience" and seek out nonclassical listeners with "simple" and "direct" music, "fresh in feeling" that "in no sense [was] capable of being interpreted as a writing down to the level of the public."[11] Copland's peers and the business people in the classical world did not heed his warnings. Ellington and his most talented compatriots in the jazz and rock worlds followed that recommendation in the 1950s and 1960s instead.

The initial pop and jazz releases for Columbia's LP division consisted mainly of familiar artists and compositions. *Down Beat* and *Metronome* regularly heralded jazz as important American art, but most jazz releases on major labels and on the airwaves were just as static as Toscanini's canon of nineteenth-century Italian and German works. Both served as perfect examples of the kind of culture that Dwight Macdonald described in 1960 as "midcult": "high culture diluted for mass sales and consumption." Such trends also directed public appreciation and sales toward the accustomed and away from the adventurous. Ellington straddled both sides of this divide. While he released many albums during the last quarter century of his career that aimed to take financial advantage of commercial trends and fads, none of them achieved large sales. Perhaps the image of Ellington as an artist who deviated from the commercial norm was too ensconced in the public imagination. Ellington's best recordings of the late 1940s and 1950s—and there are many, far more than most critics then and now have acknowledged—fought against the "midcult" strictures of the popular marketplace, which is why so many of them sold disappointingly and why Columbia had "little interest" in releasing *Liberian Suite*. TV ratings and profits accruing from Toscanini's appearances paled next to most shows in the early 1950s. But his presence and sanctified national reputation were viewed as invaluable in enhancing the image of the NBC-TV network.[12] Ellington bequeathed a similar prestige to the companies and venues where he recorded and performed.

During his 1947–53 tenure with Columbia, Ellington found his newest Columbia material competing in the market with leftover sessions done years previously on Musicraft and RCA Victor. Often, Ellington's prior labels timed the releases of older sessions to coincide with the promotion of new Ellington product. Such releases flooded the market and probably contributed to Ellington's commercial troubles during this period. With the arrival of the concept album, the Ellington orchestra tended to only record and release material for individual projects, leaving fewer extra sides that could be released later without Ellington's permission. Starting in the mid-1950s, and for the rest of his career, Ellington recorded numerous sessions at his own expense, apart from whatever record company his band was af-filiated with. These sessions, known as "the stockpile," became the arena in which he did much experimenting in the studio, and they remained mostly unreleased until after his death. They served as a creative outlet since Elling-ton and Strayhorn composed and arranged more material than most com-panies were willing to release. But they also probably were used as a form of control over their work.

With big bands failing, lucrative offers to tour as a solo act, new record for-mats becoming available, and (premature) calls for retirement streaming in, numerous options were open to Ellington, but he elected to remain with his orchestra. For one thing, it represented the ideal and perhaps only vehicle for Ellington's composing. Not only did his creative spirit feed off and tai-lor itself to the individual talents of his players, but, as Granz pointed out, it would be difficult to imagine Ellington having much of a commercial im-pact without them. "I can't see [a bandless] Duke writing an arrangement, and then going to [a band leader such as] Tommy Dorsey and saying 'Would you like to play this new thing I wrote?' or his publisher doing it," reflected Granz. "Offhand, I think he [also] needed the band as a guarantee of satisfy-ing his ego. I mean, standing in front of the band, and playing, and being all dressed up . . . I think that the fact of the public recognizing the great Duke Ellington leading a great band, and Duke was obviously the most imposing of bandleaders, I think that was necessary to satisfy his ego." Bob Udkoff, a close friend of Ellington's, felt that of all the professional roles he assumed, Ellington most enjoyed that of "showman." "He loved, maybe not the grind of it, but the [reminders of] days of vaudeville, he loved coming out, and having that spotlight," Udkoff recounted. Granz agreed that Ellington rel-ished the role of "entertainer," and offered a more business-oriented spin:

> Sometimes you call an artist, jazz or otherwise, an entertainer, it's almost an insult by certain standards. It denotes commercialism, it denotes compro-mise, and other things that the writers [in the press] feel are beneath the art-ist. [Such people would say that] the artist should really starve and not do anything that's commercially acceptable, which is nonsense. There was no compromise. He did what he did. But I think he was very knowledgeable about that because Duke was very intelligent in looking at the ways that you get to the public and succeed. His whole deportment on stage. He dressed in an exaggerated way. Like he would have, I don't know, six-inch cuffs on his trousers, and the trousers themselves were two inches above the shoe line,

so you could see his stockings, which were red or some outlandish color . . . It was all part of [the show], you see. He knew how to make people look at him. You always saw Duke. Duke loved show business.[13]

And, as had been true since the early Mills era, Ellington's priority remained the development of his composing. "It's the only excitement I need," he enthused in a 1948 article entitled "Composing Still Thrill to Ellington." In the same piece, he credited Strayhorn with helping steel his creative resolve during this difficult career period when unnamed persons were encouraging Ellington to "go commercial." "Sometimes they'd tell me to write for current modes and not for myself," Ellington explained. "I'd get the feeling that maybe I ought to listen to them and then sit down and talk with Billy. He'd convince me all over again that I ought to write what I felt. That's what I've done." Also, as Ellington repeated numerous times for the rest of the career, he had grown addicted to and, to some degree, was spoiled by hearing his new compositions immediately, a privilege enjoyed by few composers in any genre: "My band is my instrument even more than the piano. Tell you about me and music—I'm something like a farmer. A farmer that grows things. He plants his seed and I plant mine. He has to wait until spring to see his come up, but I can see mine right after I plant it. That night. I don't have to wait. That's the payoff for me."

Mercer Ellington, who was intimately involved in business and creative matters with the band for the last thirty-five years of his father's life, explained the economic consequences of this decision: "When the jobs became few, he kept the band organized so he didn't care where he had to get the money from, whether it was royalties or whatever . . . The thing that sets him apart from most of the bandleaders and composers . . . [is] sooner or later, they let economics get in the way of creativity. Ellington never did. He knew that we could switch from steak to beans, or whatever, that we were behind him, and that's where we went."[14] Conditions never deteriorated to the point where the Ellington family suffered economically, and throughout his career, Ellington's proclivity for downing one to three steaks per day attracted wide coverage in the entertainment press. But the margin of profit, already thin during the orchestra's best years in the Swing Era, must have dropped considerably during the decade after the war, though no financial records survive to corroborate this. Ellington's composing supplied the secret weapon, a steady stream of royalties from his two decades of hit songs that no other bandleader possessed. It proved essential to the band's status as the only organization to survive through the postwar period without an extended hiatus.

*

George Avakian at Columbia proved an excellent partner for Ellington in his commitment to musical development.[15] The "huge success" of the album division he headed at Columbia allowed latitude most record executives did not enjoy. "The albums sold at an even more profitable rate [than singles] in terms of dollar volume," Avakian recalled. "Singles were listed at 99 cents, albums at $3.95 . . . so a million-seller album was like a 4-million seller single [a rare occurrence], and therefore . . . the album department brought in far more money than anybody suspected." By 1953, the LP format that Columbia introduced brought in over $200 million per year (over $1.5 billion in today's dollars) for the record industry. Besides doing well in America, albums opened up the European market to American record companies like never before, providing additional revenue and creating more justification for signing jazz artists like Ellington, Louis Armstrong, and Erroll Garner, who usually sold better in Europe than domestically. This situation, and Avakian's long-term love and respect for Ellington's music, led to a large amount of artistic freedom. "Anything he wanted to do, I was all for, even though I would sometimes feel, well, [this particular song] doesn't have a chance [to be a hit single]," Avakian explained. "Hell, give the man a shot, he's earned it. [If] Duke Ellington wanted something, I salute[d]."

Another advantage for Ellington at Columbia was Avakian and the company's commitment to building a strong long-term catalog. Putting a varied "catalog" of band performances on tape had marked an Ellington priority long before his tenure at Columbia with Avakian. Ted Wallerstein, president of Columbia, appointed Avakian as head of Popular Albums in 1947, asking him to ensure that Columbia's albums radiated a different identity than their singles. Avakian felt "delighted" to take the position because "the single record business [headed at Columbia by Mitch Miller] was a business of novelty hits and it didn't interest me too much." Popular 10-inch albums previously were vehicles for enhancing revenue for a hit song by affixing seven other recordings next to it and raising the list price. As a result, Columbia's initial output of LPs was "dull as dishwater," according to Avakian and the contemporary music press. The emphasis on building a diversified, long-lasting catalog changed that to an extent. Rather than cranking out attempts to succeed on fickle Top Forty radio, the Popular Album Division's mission became releasing quality albums encompassing a diverse variety of styles to satisfy every kind of music customer. They wanted albums that sold steadily and returned profits for years, no matter what evanescent trends roosted on the pop charts. "A company survives on its catalog, it does not survive on its hits," Avakian said in a statement as true in today's music business as in the 1950s. This long-term viewpoint marked a sea change from RCA Victor executive Eli Oberstein's resistance to releasing extended excerpts from *Black, Brown and Beige* and the *Perfume Suite* in the mid-1940s. More enlightened executives now viewed music, properly recorded and marketed, as an important cultural treasure that spanned generations and sold for decades. The companies began to realize this when they first released reissues of classic older jazz and popular recordings in the late 1930s. This represented an improved commercial atmosphere for Ellington and Strayhorn and other more ambitious recording artists.

Together, Avakian and Ellington produced two of Ellington's best albums, *Masterpieces by Ellington* (1951) and *Ellington Uptown* (1953), both of which focused on extended pieces. Avakian explained the process behind those projects:

> With Ellington, it was a matter of planning, with him, a mixture of his product so that his appeal would be as widespread as possible, and Ellington was very conscious of that. He was always trying to get a hit single, and he usually failed, as we all know ... His particular strong desire was to build a catalog of works that would endure, that would be works of stature. He didn't think in terms of "Well I'm a composer and I have to compose big long works in the way that classical composers did in the preceding centuries." But his greatest interest was in his longer compositions, not in the short pieces. So, during the time that we worked together, which was not a long time ... both of us had that thought in mind. I was lucky in one regard ... in that Duke had written some longer compositions and had not recorded them because nobody was particularly interested in doing so at the time ... And that's the way we got around to recording, say, "The Tattooed Bride" and "A Tone Parallel to Harlem." And [they were] intermixed with the short 3-minute works which he recorded, some of which he was hoping might hit.

On both albums, Avakian served as the producer of note for Columbia, but under today's definition of a record producer, Ellington would have been credited as coproducer at least. As the producer, under the definition of that time, Avakian represented the executive in charge of the Columbia division for which Ellington recorded, and he was responsible for the sound and marketability of the released album. "You had to know ... the acoustical properties of a studio and ... [have] a pretty good idea of what the engineer was able to do so you could ... get the sound that you wanted," Avakian explained. Producers at Columbia, according to Will Friedwald, had the reputation of taking care of the technical studio details while leaving the artists and band arrangers to deal with aesthetics, especially when dealing with accomplished and creatively involved people like Ellington and Frank Sinatra. Avakian described himself as a "conduit," helping Ellington achieve what he wished in the studio, providing technical and sometimes artistic ideas when Ellington asked for them.

Under today's definition of a record producer, Ellington would have certainly qualified. He decided on which material to record, provided the major conception of the track, had it arranged beforehand or arranged it on the spot, frequently not letting Avakian know what would be committed to tape until Ellington cued the band to begin. As in the 1930s and 1940s, Ellington paid special attention to playbacks, insisting on approving final takes in the control room. "Ellington was so involved with sound, to a degree that almost no one else was," Avakian stated, adding that Ellington was also willing to experiment with editing and effects if they could improve a track.

Another significant difference between record producers then and now rested in the matter of compensation. Avakian received no royalties for albums he produced for Columbia between 1947 and 1958, including many by Ellington, Louis Armstrong, and Miles Davis that moved millions of copies over the years. Producers had to be "music fans" in those days, Avakian argued, because "they weren't interested in money, there wasn't any money to be made in the business particularly. In fact, everyone in the business was badly underpaid for what he did and for the results that the company gained, if they were successful." In addition, according to Avakian, executive salaries were "very low," especially compared to the mid-1960s and afterward. So were artist royalties during the period, and for years afterward. The contract Avakian drew up with Ellington gave him 5 percent, the highest royalty rate then at Columbia, which translated to about fifteen cents per album sold at a four-dollar retail price, after deductions for breakage, among other costs. Ellington's publishing royalties added more, but for the rest of his career, Ellington almost certainly made more from his recording advances for each project he undertook than from royalties. The royalties were fairly puny and were not awarded until they reached a level above that of the advance.

From the title to the cover to the contents, *Masterpieces by Ellington,* the band's first long-playing 12-inch album, signified an unusual way to promote and present African Americans and big bands in 1951. The forty-seven-minute LP consisted of just four tracks in, as the cover boasted, "uncut concert arrangements." A highbrow mood prevailed on the cover, which pictured Ellington in a tux with tails next to an upright piano. The same mood surfaced in the liner notes with their talk of "edification" and the "finest Ellington scores," as well as their detailed comparisons of Ellington to Gershwin, Stravinsky, Debussy, and Respighi. On the opening track, a fifteen-minute reimagining of "Mood Indigo," the sound is clearer and truer than most recordings of the era. The composition loses none of its power or bittersweet quality when quintupled in length. The alluring, continually varying backgrounds provide aural changes of scenery that suggest that Strayhorn is operating much like the skillful editor of an unfolding narrative film rather than as the song's arranger. The track proceeds in a relaxed and unhurried fashion, solos by Russell Procope and Johnny Hodges giving way to a soaring and drastically different orchestration of the main melody by Strayhorn, who proceeds to offer perhaps the most beautiful solo he ever committed to tape. With the *Masterpieces* and *Uptown* albums, the Ellington orchestra took full advantage of the opportunity to stretch out on a long-playing record like no popular or jazz act had previously. Three Ellington compositions from the first half of the 1930s, along with the new eleven-and-a-half-minute "The Tattooed Bride," make up the whole of *Masterpieces,* but it is no nostalgic enterprise: the songs are recast for a new era and new technology.

Masterpieces and *Uptown* also clearly indicate Ellington and Strayhorn's intentions of forwarding the artistry and traditions of the American big band, even as their peers fell back to duplicating sounds of earlier eras. Both were "event albums" that promised to showcase perspectives of the Ellington orchestra never heard on vinyl before. *Uptown* featured the recorded premiere of *A Tone Parallel to Harlem (The Harlem Suite),* a fourteen-minute programmatic tour of Ellington's home city replete with aural references to its churches, Latin neighborhoods, traffic, and dancing women, among other features. Mark Tucker called it "Ellington's most successful extended work," and it signified yet another, perhaps the most distinguished, example of Ellington's lifelong efforts to depict and document black American culture in his music. Ruth Ellington was especially proud of the piece because even though Toscanini commissioned it, her brother wrote about black history, not European subject matter. Avakian "got a little criticism for recording so many of [Ellington's] long works, because they didn't sell, you know." Despite "some grumbling from salesmen" for Columbia, he was able to fill Ellington's first two 12-inch LPs with numerous extended pieces "because I had carte blanche, we were making gigantic profits on the popular albums and anything I wanted to do, I didn't have to ask [executives] any questions."

Not every track on these albums evinced a serious or reverential tone. Avakian remembered being dismayed in June 1952 when Ellington told him they would be recording the band's well-known theme "Take the 'A' Train," written by Strayhorn and a major hit in 1941 and 1944. With his philosophy of building a diverse catalog, Avakian felt averse to the band recording copies of songs already famous and recorded numerous times: "I almost said 'Gee, Duke, do you want to do that *again*?' But I didn't say a word." Ellington ran through the first couple minutes of it in the studio, stopped the rehearsal, and said, "Let's make a take and see what it sounds like." Years later, Avakian recalled that he was "knocked for a loop" when he heard the full eight-minute revamped "'A' Train" in Columbia's 30th Street Studio in Manhattan that day, and he noted that "it was a record that had a lot of impact" on the music scene. It opens with the rhythm section adopting an easygoing swing feel, more akin to the Nat Cole trio than the charging beat and brassy surges of the original. Along with Betty Roche's understated and sexy vocals adorned by bebop scat, the remake made it clear that the Ellington orchestra had moved on from the Swing Era but still knew how to create a party atmosphere. The middle dreamy section, with its reduced tempo and lush backgrounds, features a Paul Gonsalves sax solo that beautifully deconstructs the melody, providing an image of Harlem in the wee small hours, when the streets are lonely and empty and its denizens are in bed. The tempo doubles after that, and Gonsalves, a new member of the band, lets off an extended biting second solo, spraying numerous notes in a short time as skillfully and exhilaratingly as any bop player. For those listening, new instrumentalists like Gonsalves and trumpeter Clark Terry, replacing older and cherished members of the band who left in 1951, and new tracks like the 1952 "'A' Train," announced that the Ellington orchestra still existed in a state of aggressive development, experiencing no lack of imagination.

The *Uptown* album achieved further success because of its links to the growing trend of "high fidelity" phonograph equipment. The track "Skin Deep," written by Louis Bellson and featuring an expansive drum solo by him, became a popular choice among dealers at hi-fi shows for demonstrating the range of the best sound systems. After sending a copy of the song to a speaker manufacturer, Avakian recalled, "Skin Deep" "caused a sensation among the people in the audio field, the word got out immediately to our New York distributor that Ellington's 'Skin Deep' track was turning everything upside-down at the hi-fi show, and the distributor sent a couple of their salesmen to hear it . . . and they immediately went out and campaigned among record dealers that this is the sensation of the New York high fidelity show." The publicity caused a national "chain reaction" of sales, moving twenty thousand additional copies, according to Avakian. Eventually, the album's title changed to *Hi-Fi Ellington Uptown* to highlight the connection.

From all accounts, Columbia seemed happy with Ellington's performance. Avakian recalled that he could count on any 1950s Ellington LP automatically yielding at least thirty to thirty-five thousand in sales, "which was good," particularly when viewed alongside the idea of creating a catalog at Columbia. The Ellington albums were repackaged over the years and sold to new generations for decades. In the 1950s, when smaller groups led by Dave Brubeck, Miles Davis, and the Modern Jazz Quartet scored the biggest economic successes in jazz, "Duke's was the only orchestra at the time that was doing anything" saleswise, even if his overall album sales did not approach those artists. But Ellington seemed unhappy with the performance of the company. In the spring of 1953, just as *Uptown* was released, Ellington asked for his release from Columbia, received it, and immediately signed with Capitol Records, a decade-old major label known for its success in promoting hit singles. He issued a terse press release: "I signed with Capitol because this firm is doing an excellent job of presenting all its artists, particularly as it concerns exploitation."

Neither side revealed details about the temporary break (Ellington returned to Columbia three years later), but various clues exist. Columbia released only two 12-inch Ellington albums in his last four years at the label, when the company customarily released two albums per year from their most successful artists. Most importantly, the lack of advertising for those two albums in *Down Beat* and *Billboard,* despite their groundbreaking appeal, must have irked Ellington. There existed plenty of intriguing angles for ads, but none materialized. From a pure business perspective, this made sense. As the trade papers made clear, Avakian's Popular Album Division brought in extraordinary and ever-increasing profits, but not with artists like Ellington. Less than a month before the release of *Masterpieces, Billboard* published their annual music record programming guide, featuring popularity charts for artists of every genre and previews of releases for the coming season: Ellington's new LP was not mentioned or advertised. The week before the arrival of *Masterpieces, Billboard* reported on the profitable "youth movement," an area in which Columbia outperformed its rivals; their recent successes—Tony Bennett, Rosemary Clooney, and Guy Mitchell— were all touted. Ellington was fifty-two years old. Columbia's "weekly check list of best sellers for dealers, operators and jockeys" in *Billboard* did not feature either *Masterpieces* or *Uptown* or any singles from them in the months surrounding their releases. There was no place to put Ellington: the 1951 ads featured popular, folk, R&B, and children's singles, but Ellington did not fit in these categories. The 1953 version of the weekly ads added a bestselling album section, but no sign of Ellington or any other jazz artist surfaced.

Avakian, in a 1953 article for a special hi-fi issue of *Down Beat,* averred that the jazz artists represented his favorite portion of the Popular Album

Division, and he lauded *Uptown* in his opening paragraph. But the company did not yet share his affection. The main money in contracts and promotions went to Doris Day, Sammy Kaye, Liberace, Paul Weston, and the aforementioned "youth" artists, mostly specialists in conservative chart- and radio-bound material, without much support for jazz, except Benny Goodman, who, in 1953, moved significant copies of his 1938 Carnegie Hall concert. These Columbia artists regularly received full- and half-page ads in *Billboard* during this period, but Ellington never did, even on the eve of major album releases.[16]

When *Down Beat* produced a lavish Ellington tribute issue for the twenty-fifth anniversary of the opening of his Cotton Club engagement, the impetus came from Irving Mills, his son Sidney, and Leonard Feather, not Columbia.[17] Columbia seemed satisfied with the thirty-thousand-strong performance of Ellington albums. Perhaps they felt additional sales unlikely, especially because of the emphasis on longer pieces. Ellington justifiably felt that more could be done to bring his work to a wider audience and that he was not being treated as a special and individual artist, a common concern of his in relations with those who represented him in the music business.

Avakian expressed sympathy both for Ellington and for Capitol's situation, despite his sadness at seeing Ellington go:

> My recollection is that Duke didn't even discuss [his] offer from Capitol, he just simply made the switch. My feelings did hurt, but on the other hand, I had so much respect for the man that when we saw each other and he said he was switching to Capitol, because he felt that they would give him exposure that he hadn't gotten at Columbia, my reaction was . . . "I thought we gave you fine exposure." He said "Yeah, but you know, they need me more than Columbia does, and I think I will be better off" . . . I could understand that, I mean Ellington was not one of our top [selling] artists by any means . . . Ellington's sales were relatively modest. They were profitable, we were delighted to keep him on from the dollars-and-cents point-of-view, but we didn't need him.

With the possible exception of Nat Cole, no one could outshine Ellington at Capitol in the spring of 1953, and he immediately would assume "top dog" status at the label, with all the attention and promotion that arrived with it. Also, Capitol's reputation rested on hit singles, which Ellington hungered for, while Columbia relied on the album, soon to become the main industry moneymaker. Ellington's first Capitol single, released less than six weeks after he signed with them, inspired a full-page ad in *Billboard* that pictured Ellington beaming as he edged himself around a door that had his name, Capitol Records, and a star emblazoned on it. The difference between Capitol and Columbia, at this early juncture in the Capitol contract, could not have been plainer. Dave Dexter, Ellington's A&R man at Capitol recalled Ellington telling him, "I want a hit, Dave. Other bands make hits. I want to hear Ellington records in the jukeboxes, and on the radio, and playing over the p.a. systems in shops and markets."[18]

During the Columbia years, Ellington sought to diversify his business and creative efforts by acting as the main and probably sole investor in Mercer Records, a label run by Mercer Ellington and Leonard Feather.[19] The label, initiated in the summer of 1950, served many purposes for Ellington. Feather acted as general manager, and Mercer Ellington is mentioned in press releases as "head" of Mercer; both of them appear to have handled daily business and creative decisions. Ads and press releases trumpeted Mercer's executive and artistic contributions to the label. Yet, two surviving pieces of business correspondence written by Feather make a convincing case for Duke Ellington's central contribution. In one letter, Feather asks Duke's permission to issue a new slate of six Mercer sides and threatens to leave Mercer Records "altogether" if not allowed to make decisions "in the interest of the company." In another, Feather stresses the fact of Duke's financial investment in an Al Hibbler project for Mercer that Atlantic Records wanted stopped because they argued that they had Hibbler under contract. Feather indicated Ellington's willingness to meet with Atlantic vice president Ahmet Ertegun personally to work things out "amicably." The distribution of incorporated shares in Mercer Records went as follows: Duke had thirty, Strayhorn had twenty, and twenty-five each went to Mercer Ellington and Feather.

Mercer Records seemed to have been created as a venue for Duke and Mercer Ellington, as well as Strayhorn and Feather, to compete in the independent label market for small group jazz and R&B. In the months before the label's creation, *Down Beat* reported that Mercer Ellington had scored some success with a small group performing "convincing . . . bop and shout-jazz" that featured "shuffle guitarist and blues howler" Sticks McGhee, who scored a top-five R&B single in 1949 with "Drinkin' Wine Spo-Dee-O-Dee." He obviously knew something about the new market. Many Mercer sides featured Ellington sidemen in impromptu small band sessions resembling in form the late 1930s small band sessions produced by Helen Oakley Dance. The Mercer recordings sported intriguing combinations of musicians from Ellington orchestras past and present, as well as multigenerational jazz virtuosos like Benny Carter and Max Roach. Duke was frequently involved, sometimes contributing new material. Strayhorn signed as a solo artist, fronting his own orchestra, an all-star Ellingtonian group, and, in perhaps the most significant sessions for the label, playing piano in a trio for eight songs with Duke Ellington and alternating bassists. Strayhorn also wrote, arranged, and performed on various sessions, earning his minority stake in the company.

Mercer Records appeared to be part of an attempt at vertical integration for Ellington and his associates, maximizing potential sources and outlets of financial revenue and artistic expression. The reactivation of Tempo Music at roughly the time of Mercer's incorporation bolsters this observation. Ellington was now involved in multiple facets of the music business: publishing, recording, performing, big bands, small bands, and introducing new talent. Columbia still exclusively released the seventeen-piece Ellington orchestra's recordings, but Mercer Records served as a workshop in small band experimentation. The projects probably bolstered the egos of Ellington sidemen, offering them increased opportunities to showcase their talent and build their names outside of the orchestra.

Both Tempo and Mercer were also probably designed to provide income for Ellington's family and closest associates, a chief concern and pattern throughout Ellington's career. Trade papers reported Mildred Dixon, Ellington's romantic partner during most of the Mills era, named as Tempo's manager, while Ruth Ellington James, Ellington's sister, remained president of the company despite her lack of expertise. While Ruth manned the Tempo office for decades, Dixon's name or contributions cannot be found in any Ellington business records housed at the Smithsonian. It is highly likely that Dixon and, to some degree, Ruth were employed on the books largely for tax purposes, to justify to the government the money paid them. During the 1960s, Ellington frequently claimed money paid to friends and families as salaries instead of gifts in order to avoid paying extra taxes. This would become one of the many sources of his IRS troubles during that period. The available evidence suggests a similar situation occurred with Tempo Music and the Mercer label.[20]

Despite its promising array of artists, the Mercer label folded sometime near the beginning of 1952. An accounting of royalties paid Tempo Music between 1950 and 1953 showed that, while one Mercer release sold over twelve thousand copies (a single featuring Ellington teamed with bassist Oscar Pettiford), the rest did not approach that level. Half the releases sold a thousand copies or significantly less. The effort failed financially, but artistically and in terms of promotion, and perhaps even as a tax write-off, the label met with some success. The story of Mercer Records provides another example of how Ellington and his associates developed creative and aggressive ways to keep his name and work before the public, refusing to be relegated to the periphery of the rapidly shifting music business that claimed so many of his peers.

Two events occurred during 1951 that harmed Ellington's previously stellar reputation among blacks. The events demonstrated the tensions beginning to form between older, more conservative blacks and the newer, more aggressive tactics being employed by a younger generation of blacks in order to gain civil rights in the postwar period.

On 28 January, the Ellington orchestra was scheduled to play a segregated concert at a venue called the Mosque in Richmond, Virginia. The local NAACP chapter, headed by Dr. J. M. Tinsley, had recently called for a boycott on such shows by black artists as part of a campaign to overturn state segregation laws. The first boycott occurred less than two weeks before Ellington's show when Marian Anderson performed, playing to a house less than half full, with blacks picketing outside. The management reserved and segregated the best center seats for blacks, hoping to quell the protest, but to no avail. Ellington cancelled his appearance at the last minute, but, in the press, "flayed" (as *Down Beat* reported) the local chapter for instigating the "vicious" (Ellington's word) situation that forced his hand. Ellington pointed out that the boycott warning came less than a week before the event, "long after the contract had been signed," and that "nobody wants to cross a picket line and get hurt; it just isn't the thing to do." Though Tinsley said the policy was directed against Virginia law and not black artists, Ellington recalled playing segregated concerts in Richmond for years and noted the hypocrisy of only targeting events featuring black artists. "What do they do the rest of the year when Negro artists do not go there? This only happens when they come," he said in a "disgusted" manner. "They don't boycott Tommy Dorsey and the symphony, and the Negroes are allowed to attend [in segregated seating]." Ellington explained the economic situation that led him and other black entertainers to accept such conditions:

> I don't know why they pick out a Negro's investment and destroy it, but not the whites' . . . I don't agree on anybody's segregation . . . This thing was an investment of $4,000 for one night. Times are bad. This band is an outfit of the highest paid musicians in the world, nobody gets loot like my men. Just think of paying the railroad fares for all of the group, including entertainers, dancers, etc. They should have some system set up for these sorts of things,

and people should be warned in advance. It has happened before, it is nothing new, and is very costly.

Ellington noted his numerous activities and benefits for the NAACP over the previous two decades, including a benefit a week earlier at New York City's Metropolitan Opera House that Ellington claimed brought anywhere from $9,000 to $10,000 to the national office of the organization. He also criticized the priorities of the Richmond NAACP for going after people like him and Anderson when there were "old [black] people living their lives in filth and dirt. What about the toilets and water fountain[s] in colored waiting rooms, why don't they do something about that? Why pick on entertainment investments?"[21]

Other areas of discrimination had greater impact on local communities, yet attacking segregation at entertainment events became increasingly common during this period. Such efforts grew out of the successes that performers, especially Ellington, had achieved to increase the status and respect accorded black Americans in the wider American society. When celebrities were involved in attacks on segregation, publicity for the cause increased. Ellington had worked for years to create a new kind of respect for himself, his race, and his music; activists of the postwar era wished to broaden that respect to encompass all blacks and, increasingly, were willing to take more risks and demand that others make great sacrifices to achieve their goals. The wartime and postwar civil rights promises from the White House amounted to little by the early 1950s. President Truman desegregated the military and met with a few blacks at the White House (including Ellington), but the calls for reform he made during the first ever presidential speech at an NAACP gathering—for a permanent Federal Equal Practices Commission and antilynching and anti–poll tax laws—were abandoned. Despite honorable military service in World War II and Korea, and despite skyrocketing rates of black consumer spending ($3 billion in 1940, $11 billion in 1950), the average black American saw little or no improvement in civil status.[22] Frustration mounted, eventually coalescing into the more protest-oriented civil rights movement of the late 1950s and 1960s.

The Richmond NAACP was not the first to look toward the entertainment industry to jumpstart the process of gaining equal rights. In the mid-1940s, Norman Granz first pushed the idea of nonsegregation clauses in contracts for black jazz performers. In 1947, he wrote more than thirty bandleaders, including Ellington, pointing out how thirty-six leading members of Actors Equity recently "either pledged or promised to investigate the possibility of pledging themselves to a clause whereby they would never be forced to play a segregated theatre," and he asked them to do the same. The bandleaders supported the idea in theory, but they would not, in the late 1940s or for most of the 1950s, sign the pledge, which required integrated audiences and mandated that the promoter would lose the deposit if they insisted on Jim Crow conditions. "I went to Duke," Granz recalled. "Duke wouldn't sign that. No way." Like Basie and Goodman, Ellington told him he would sign it "if everyone else does." Granz knew that lesser-known bands, such as Lucky Millinder and Erskine Hawkins, who were forced by economics to tour the Jim Crow South, could not possibly support the segregation clause, "but I felt with Duke and with Basie," the two most popular black big bands of the 1940s and 1950s, "I had a shot." Artie Shaw signed the pledge, "but Artie didn't have a band then, so it was academic." For Granz, obtaining better race relations through music represented a more important priority for him than the music itself. Since the 1943 zoot-suit riots in Los Angeles, he aggressively used jazz and benefit shows as vehicles for promoting racial harmony and antilynching legislation, and he tried to enlist influential musicians such as Ellington and Basie in this cause. But, as a businessman who viewed the discrimination of the road in midcentury America firsthand, he also understood why black musicians had difficulty following his lead:

> [Ellington] probably would have argued that the band was scuffling as it is, and he had to take those Southern tours, cause they all played the South, and they all played the South under the conditions that the South invoked . . . I'm not being critical that they didn't do it. I mean, I don't think it's fair for anyone to say "Well, the hell with it, Duke should have sacrificed the band, or Basie, or whatever." I don't think it's a realistic position to take, because you really have to understand their problems.[23]

Like Ellington, Marian Anderson felt that confrontation would not solve the problems incurred by Jim Crow. Both were pioneers in changing impressions and conditions for blacks in the music world and the mass media in earlier times, but changing circumstances and attitudes in the 1950s were undercutting their reputation and achievements. Since the early 1940s, Anderson, to much acclaim, insisted on "vertical seating"—still segregated, but at least not placing blacks in the back of the venue. Yet at the same time, Paul Robeson refused to perform for any segregated audience. In 1952 and 1953, Anderson performed precedent-breaking integrated shows in states such as Florida, which listed no segregation laws on the books. Still, she received criticism in the black press, even from Mary McLeod Bethune, for not doing enough. During the 1950s, Ellington came under similar attacks. Most black and white observers sided with them in the Richmond NAACP boycotts, but also felt that change was needed and that perhaps a tougher stand would improve the situation. Joseph V. Baker, writing in the *Philadelphia Inquirer,* noted how Ellington and Anderson had never been labeled as "crusaders" in the political sense for the civil rights cause, and he intimated that such a role might prove necessary. P. L. Prattis, in the black newspaper *Pittsburgh Courier,* recommended that musical artists more aggressively pressure bookers and promoters to back off segregation practices, but he gave no indication of allotting them help in doing so, and he demonstrated no knowledge about the current ways of the music business.[24] Ellington and Anderson had projected images of pride and achievement unparalleled among black musical artists, but neither was willing to pursue commercially suicidal paths.

The worst damage to Ellington's reputation among African Americans resulted from an interview by Otis N. Thompson, printed in various black newspapers in November 1951.[25] Thompson's original article contains mostly sentence fragments from Ellington, usually the most incendiary ones, with very little context. In the lead paragraph, Thompson quoted Ellington as saying that "we [black Americans] ain't ready yet" for integration and that efforts toward integration were "a silly thing . . . it's something that nothing can be done about." Thompson reported Ellington as "somewhat aroused" by the subject as he changed into "one of his many suits" before getting onstage: "This thing is in the legislation . . . we can't do anything about it," he said. Ellington questioned the "good it's doing us" to (as Thompson wrote) "get one or two people in a few white schools or certain jobs." He also characterized "this thing about sitting anywhere they want to" as (Thompson's phrase) "so much bunk." "What does it get us?" Ellington said, according to Thompson. "If you go South, don't you have to sit in the rear of the streetcar?" In his last paragraph, Thompson wrote that "Ellington maintained that there are so many arguments against us that our efforts are futile." "No, we ain't ready yet," Ellington told Thompson, according to the article. "Get together one hundred million dollars and then we can do something."

Ellington replied in a letter and telegram sent out to the *Baltimore Afro-American* on 1 December 1951; it was published two weeks later, almost a month after the original story. "A number of stories have been circulating in the colored press attributing to me the statement that colored people 'ain't ready' to fight segregation," he began. "I categorically deny having made any such statement. I further assert that what has been published is the exact opposite of what I actually said." Ellington asserted that Thompson took no notes during the interview (Thompson claimed he did, but could not keep up with Ellington's "verbosity"). Thompson, in an accompanying article, claimed that such words accused him of being "an out and out liar," but Ellington made clear in the rest of his statement that his main complaint rested not with Thompson's honesty, but his taking statements out of context:

> I told Thompson that I thought fighting segregation was not a part-time proposition, but a full time one and that little could be accomplished by working spare time.
>
> Thompson wrote that I said colored people were making no headway. But I can see nothing wrong in admitting that colored people are not doing all they can to abolish segregation, and that much more can be done. I stand by that contention.
>
> I then ventured a specific suggestion. If the breaking down of segregation is a full-time job, I said, then it required the full-time services of many more leaders than we have.
>
> Now, obviously, people can't be expected to work fulltime on race problems without compensation. But if each one of us contributed $1 apiece three times a year, in two years we'd have almost $100,000,000 and then be able to go out and do a real job.
>
> Thompson wrote that I advocated doing nothing until we raised that sum. What I actually said was that this money would enable us to do far more than we're doing.
>
> As an example, I pointed out that segregation is sanctioned by law in the South, and we'd have to have new legislation in every state before segregation is completely abolished. That, I pointed out further, takes money.

As Ellington knew from firsthand experience, resistance to integration and equal rights loomed large in America. First-class citizenship for blacks could not be achieved by brave and prideful statements appearing in black newspapers with limited readership—they entailed serious investments of time and money, as later events made clear. Thurgood Marshall's victory in the 1954 *Brown vs. Board of Education* Supreme Court ruling was built on four years of legal work, encompassing scores of lawsuits, reams of research, and hundreds of hours of lawyers' fees, paid for by years of fundraising by the NAACP Legal Defense Fund. Dr. Martin Luther King spent the bulk of his time fundraising in the 1950s and 1960s to pay for the infrastructure that staged the protests he led.[26] An article in the *Baltimore Afro-American* referred to Ellington's comments on raising $100,000,000 as "the old and hoary gospel that has been preached by conservatives and reactionaries alike for generations," but it represented a more realistic perspective than many realized in 1951.

Ellington defended his actions in an incident in Atlanta that Thompson described in which numerous black patrons ripped up their tickets for a package tour featuring Ellington when told they had to enter through a separate side entrance. Ellington explained that he signed on only for the Northern leg of the "Biggest Tour of 1951," with an option to tour the South under a separate contract. Unbeknownst to him, his booking agency signed the Southern contract. After expressing his refusal to play segregated gigs (mandated by most Southern venues) and engaging lawyers to negotiate a way out of the agreement, he was told that he could be sued for breach of contract, so "I had no choice but to observe the terms of the contracts," Ellington explained. "In the light of what has since been written about me, what I have related above is only one of the more recent proofs that I have consistently fought segregation and have not changed one bit from the position I have always taken." The "Biggest Show of 1951" marked the last bookings made for Ellington by the Moe Gale Agency. In July, Ellington moved his account to the Associated Booking Corporation run by Joe Glaser, ex-gangster and Louis Armstrong's longtime manager and friend. His anger over the problems with the Southern tour may have precipitated the switch.

Thompson did not seem to be aware of the economic exigencies that existed for black musical artists in the 1950s. With little television exposure and even less radio and film presence than they enjoyed in the 1930s and 1940s, black musicians had to rely on records and touring for their promotion and paychecks. Many of them endured Jim Crow conditions when they performed, a fact that civil rights organizations and black newspapers detested. But it remained a fact of life. Ellington sought to avoid segregated shows, and for the most part did, though he did not publicize this fact. From 1950 to 1955, aside from the "Biggest Tour of 1951," the Ellington orchestra played the South for only six dates, and never in Deep South states.[27]

Ellington never spoke to the press about the hardships of the road during the first half of the 1950s, the cities that tried to ban white drummer Louis Bellson from playing with his black band, the Thanksgiving when the men could purchase no better food for dinner than sardine cans. But band members like trumpeter Clark Terry later filled in the details. Dealing with such conditions "made a lot of people just dig in and [perform] better, rather than just to get angry and succumb to the tactics of the enemy." Terry felt that Ellington orchestra performances offered an opportunity for blacks and whites, audiences and band, to observe each other and interact, even in highly limited Jim Crow situations.[28]

Ellington's defense also centered on his "sadness" that Thompson (and those who seconded his outrage) ignored his two-decade-plus "devotion to the fight for first-class citizenship." Thompson responded that "he didn't preach anything to me [that day] about his record of fighting segregation," but perhaps Thompson should have done more research. A piece published a week after Thompson's initial story entitled "Duke Ellington's Views on Jim Crow Shock Nation" repeated Thompson's charges for the third time in the *Baltimore Afro-American,* but concluded with a summary of Ellington's record on fighting discrimination. It cited his past efforts at integrating dozens of venues, his mid-1940s appeals to raise money to fight the poll tax, his insistence on "a mixed cast" for *Beggar's Holiday,* his numerous benefits for black-oriented causes, and his lifelong efforts to document the emotions and history of blacks, especially in *Black, Brown and Beige.* In addition, just nine months earlier the Ellington orchestra became the first black band to headline a major Las Vegas nightspot, during which Ellington was the guest of honor at a local NAACP banquet.[29]

To some extent, Ellington had himself to blame for the swipes at his devotion to the civil rights cause. He insisted on primarily voicing his opinions through his music. Had he, for example, released his 1943 scenario for *Black, Brown and Beige,* his commitment to black history, identity, and equality would have been more obvious to the media and the public. "I am not the sort who makes speeches—or even statements of this kind," Ellington wrote in his response to Thompson's article. "Instead, as always, I stand on what I have done and will continue to do." Ellington cared about musical progress as much as civil rights progress and in some ways viewed them as one and the same. Starting in the 1950s, such views were less accepted in the black community. He had amassed an exemplary record for his time, but times were changing, and a new standard for activism in the public sphere was evolving. Rising 1950s jazz star and composer Charles Mingus constantly railed against racism with harsh and confrontational language onstage and in *Down Beat,* using his music as a "platform to address the world."[30] Artists like Ellington and Anderson belonged to an earlier generation that espoused different standards on speaking out. They would be held accountable and sometimes found lacking by the new standards of the emerging civil rights revolution.

The outcry in newspapers against Ellington lasted a month and a half. Despite Ellington's letter explaining the context of his remarks, the coverage by and large misrepresented Ellington's views and tarnished his long reputation as a race leader in the black community. By the time Ellington's defense hit newsstands, numerous writers had already hammered on Ellington. The reaction in the weeks following the original Thompson story was predictably harsh. A front-page editorial featured a cartoon picturing Ellington at the piano with a piece of paper on his music stand reading "I ain't ready yet" with a dollar sign next to it. Above him were placards of satiric and fictitious quotes attributed to him inspired by the original Thompson article, all of which he did not actually say: "we'll always have Jim Crow . . . fight for rights silly . . . may as well stay in your place . . . fighting gets us nowhere . . . money's everything . . . we've made no progress . . . what good is protest?" It made for a damning display and a memorable image. An unsigned front-page editorial seemingly represented the collected opinion of the *Baltimore Afro-American* staff: "The great Duke, an expert on music, but obviously a babe in the woods in the matter of what America stands for, has reached the absurd conclusion that 'we ain't ready yet' . . . sinking deeper in the mire of his own ignorance." It further argued that Ellington's financial success, especially as signified by his fine collection of clothes, had blinded the "money-grubbing bandleader" to "the struggles of his own people to achieve first-class citizenship" in matters of voting, housing, schooling, and public accommodations. "It's a shame that anybody with his talent should be so stupid," the editorial concluded.

The barrage continued inside the paper with two lengthy articles. James L. Hicks excoriated Ellington for claiming that his 21 January 1951 benefit at the Met donated $13,000 to the NAACP. Hicks claimed that only $1,500 made it into NAACP coffers, mostly because of exaggerated expenses from the Ellington organization, which he accused of viewing the benefit as a profit-making opportunity. Hicks's figures were wrong all around: Ellington claimed in press accounts that $9,000 to $10,000 had been donated, not $13,000. Also, Hicks did not include $5,600 in profit that, according to his numbers, the NAACP brought in on ticket sales, quoting only what the Ellington organization had handed over after their expenses were met. By Hicks's numbers, over $7,000 was donated to the NAACP from that night's concert, but he stressed only $1,500 in the article's bold headline. The accounting figures supplied by the NAACP, printed in an obscure corner of the *Baltimore Afro-American* two weeks later, proved that both Ellington and Hicks were wrong. NAACP publicity director Henry Lee Moon recorded a "net profit" of $3,129.89 after total NAACP/Ellington expenses of $12,262.55.[31] Moon added: "Mr. Ellington promised a contribution of $3,000 in order to reach the anticipated net of more than $6,000 for the NAACP."

More attacks appeared before the publishing of Ellington's rebuttal. Columnist Josephus Simpson wondered if Ellington "has at long last succumbed to . . . 'moneyitis,' a disease that makes one think money is everything," and further wondered whether he had allowed his royal nickname to go to his head. One reader felt that Ellington "did millions of trampled upon colored people a distinct and definite disservice." "I deplore such utterances," wrote another. Future letters columns featured another dozen readers on the subject, including many written and printed after Ellington's rebuttal. Except for one, all criticized Ellington. One proclaimed that he would never see Ellington again even if offered free admission, another said Ellington "deserved" the accusations leveled against him. Others argued that Ellington "has let us down," needed mental help, and referred to him as part of a group of "the hypocritical, double-dealing back-stabbing bandleaders."

In looking back at the "We Ain't Ready" incident, Mercer Ellington and trumpeter Clark Terry, who had recently joined the band when the fiasco erupted, felt it marked the beginning of an Ellington retreat from making statements on race to the press. "That almost clobbered him," Terry said about the Thompson story. "One of his viewpoints about that whole scene is that the less he had to say from that point on, the better—because anything he said would only multiply and be taken out of context." Ellington was reticent to comment on racial issues before 1951, but the incident only increased his hesitancy. "He was very discreet about it, because he knew if he tipped his lip too much, it could be detrimental to his performance, his career, his life, really . . . so he couldn't be too vehement about it," explained Terry. "But he was the first one to respond when it came to support for causes, black causes, we played for the Urban League, NAACP . . . he was always eager to respond." This was true before December 1951, and it would recur in the spring of 1956, but in between those two dates Ellington played no benefits, according to Klaus Stratemann's account of Ellington's daily activities and the clippings scrapbooks housed at the Smithsonian. One wonders if the hiatus on benefits was inspired by the challenging of the proceeds from the NAACP Met benefit. Perhaps Ellington felt embarrassed having the financial affairs of a benefit concert laid out in such bare fashion, even though the pattern he followed at the NAACP Met benefit was normal for such occasions. Ellington went without pay, as the NAACP noted, but he could not expect his band members, copyists, or arrangers for the event to do the same. The fact that *A Tone Parallel to Harlem* premiered that night, perhaps his most noteworthy musical chronicling of the black experience, probably further embittered him, if he looked back on that at all.

Ellington certainly felt betrayed by the black press in late 1951. "The most bitter experiences we've ever had with race have been as a result of the blacks. It's stupidity on the blacks' part," Mercer Ellington recalled, though he did not clarify whether the "we" represented him and his father or the Ellington orchestra. Duke Ellington's ideas concerning the civil rights cause remained "very consistent" from the 1940s until the end of his life, according to Mercer, but he rarely spoke about them further in public.[32] Ellington possessed insightful views on race and equal rights, views grounded in black history, the discrimination he witnessed and endured, and an enduring sense of black identity. To lose his voice for the most part during the crest of the civil rights movement represented a tragedy of sorts for him and for the movement.

The Thompson story accelerated the trend of Ellington's declining presence in black newspapers and probably in the black market for jazz as well, especially among young people. From the late 1940s onward, the *Baltimore Afro-American* and *Chicago Defender* covered the new R&B artists far more extensively than jazz performers, especially those in big bands. The *Afro* featured no notice or ads concerning Ellington's two Columbia albums of the early 1950s, *Masterpieces* and *Uptown*. Ellington's draw at the Apollo in Harlem steadily deteriorated from 1949 to 1955, a 1953 engagement with Pearl Bailey representing the only exception. R&B acts and vocalists like Ella Fitzgerald were gaining ground on big bands like Ellington's at the Apollo just like they were in the black media. From 1953 to 1955, during three separate stands, owner Frank Schiffman noted in his personal business files that the Ellington band "still lacks drawing card power," merited a "mediocre draw," and inspired the "usual unprofitable business." From September 1955 to September 1958, the Ellington orchestra did not play the Apollo, the venue that signified the American center of black musical entertainment.

Perhaps Ellington fell victim to the same trends in the black community that biographer Arnold Rampersad viewed Langston Hughes as experiencing during this period. Both of them were from the same generation and concentrated on similar themes, especially in their dedication to depicting black life in all its guises and classes. Hughes felt that, in the postwar era, especially the Eisenhower 1950s, racial pride was on the wane and that the whispered, ultimately hollow promises of integration, along with postwar opportunity and prosperity, lulled many middle-class blacks to a political sleep. New and encouraging signs of black progress were emerging: in 1950, the first blacks won the Pulitzer and Nobel prizes, blacks attended college at four times the rate they had in 1930, and nearly one-third of them owned their own dwellings, another huge increase from decades past. But significant and dangerous challenges still lay ahead. Many of these upwardly mobile blacks were, according to Hughes, "ashamed of their heritage" and wished only to hear modern and optimistic stories of progress. According to Rampersad, Hughes's "harping on blues and jazz and the beauty of black folks was an archaic position many were eager to repudiate in the [supposed] dawn of integration."[33]

Another significant piece of bad news emerged during this period for the Ellington organization, though few knew it at the time: the relationship between Ellington and Strayhorn reached its lowest point during the first half of the 1950s.[34]

For most of his nearly three decades with the Ellington orchestra, Strayhorn lived an enviable life, artistically satisfying and challenging with lots of international travel. "Strayhorn lives the life I'd love to live," Ellington once said. "He is the pure artist." Strayhorn got paid more money per week than any Ellington band members during this period and also enjoyed royalties from Tempo Music. While the band slogged it out on the road night after night, Strayhorn usually did not accompany them, remaining in New York City and Paris for long stretches, living an openly gay lifestyle (a rarity in the African American and jazz social worlds), doing his writing, and always being on call for Ellington when he needed help composing and arranging. According to band members, his lifestyle afforded him a "$5,000 piano" in his apartment and a car, even though he didn't particularly want a car in New York City. Even more gratifying, he had become the close friend and working partner of the man who had been his "favorite musician" when he was growing up in Pittsburgh.

Strayhorn did not yearn for fame. Marian Logan, the wife of Dr. Arthur Logan and a close friend of Ellington and Strayhorn's, recalled that "Strays never cared about the limelight. He just liked to hear the music played and if it was done well and the band understood it was Strays' [work] . . . that was enough for Strays." Band member Milt Grayson characterized Strayhorn as "very quiet, did not want anything to do with the spotlight" and recalled that he would perform with the band only rarely, after "great coaxing." In the early 1960s, Strayhorn told his nephew Gregory Morris his views on why he avoided the trappings of celebrity. At the time, André Previn was "making his play" to get into "the national limelight," and Morris felt that his uncle was "every bit as competent" as Previn and should do the same. Strayhorn replied:

> That's not for me . . . What's it going to get me? . . . Oh yes, a lot of fame, a lot of publicity . . . a lot of ulcers . . . All that money you end up making, then

you end up paying it either to the doctor or you give it to a shrink trying to get your head back together because you're trying to keep up with too many things . . . No, I'm really happy with the kinds of things I'm doing. And I'd rather be kind of behind the scenes where I can be kind of creative, I can work at my own pace . . . I'm not dangling on the end of someone's string.

Strayhorn did not wish to occupy center stage or grace the covers of magazines, but he did want his sizeable contributions recognized. Walter van de Leur, the preeminent expert on Strayhorn's published and unpublished sheet music, argues that while Ellington gave Strayhorn credit, particularly from the stage, other forces in the Ellington organization did not always do so. Tempo Music did a terrible job with copyrights, especially Strayhorn's, and credits were missed or misapplied. Van de Leur's analysis indicates that Strayhorn's composing work in Ellington pieces often went uncredited during the 1940s and 1950s, while Ellington's contributions to Strayhorn's pieces were always credited. Van de Leur maintains that a few of the most famous Ellington pieces of the 1940s were partially written by Strayhorn without attribution, including "C Jam Blues," "Rocks in My Bed," and "Sepia Panorama" (all copyrighted solely in Ellington's name). Van de Leur handles his evidence skillfully and carefully, and he is probably correct in his conclusions, but how can we be certain that Strayhorn's writing on particular scores was not dictated or directed by Ellington? As van de Leur indicates, Strayhorn did more arranging than composing for the band during the 1940s, and band members have testified that Ellington directed or at least had a hand in the assignments given to Strayhorn.

Starting in 1947, Strayhorn experienced further alienation. After his evident unhappiness at the *Beggar's Holiday* premiere and having almost none of his original compositions used by the orchestra in 1947–48, Strayhorn started backing away, privately archiving his new compositions rather than allowing the band to perform them. Strayhorn could have been upset by Ellington's frequent wholesale cutting of his scores, sometimes "ruining their effect," according to van de Leur. A conversation during this period with arranger and pianist Lennie Hayton, the husband of Strayhorn's close friend Lena Horne, continued this trend. Hayton felt "alarmed" that Strayhorn had no written agreement with Ellington and that he "had no idea how much his arrangements and compositions might be worth on the open market. Hayton urged him to be more attentive to the business side of his career." "That was the beginning of problems with Strayhorn," Mercer Ellington remarked decades later. "We didn't see much of Strayhorn for a while." Aside from his arranging and performing contributions to the *Masterpieces*

LP, Strayhorn is largely absent from the band's recordings from 1948 to 1953. After Ellington took out sections and reshuffled the order of some of Strayhorn's new works at one of the first sessions for Capitol Records in April 1953, Strayhorn contributed almost nothing to the band for the next two and a half years.

The financial considerations and the incorrect copyright registrations did not seem to bother Strayhorn as much as Ellington's cavalier treatment of his work. On stage, at the microphone, Ellington nightly lavished praise on Strayhorn's talents, and they were the closest of friends, but behind the scenes, when his work was reassembled without his input, Strayhorn seemed to feel disrespected as a composer. According to van de Leur, Strayhorn gave "serious thought to other professional and artistic options" during the 1953–55 period in which he largely abandoned the band. It is probably not an accident that Strayhorn's absence coincided with the artistic and commercial nadir of the Ellington orchestra. Ellington would not regain his artistic and commercial success until Strayhorn returned full force and received full credit and respect for the work he contributed.

Despite its auspicious start, most of the Ellington orchestra's nadir coincided with their two-and-a-half-year sojourn with Capitol Records from 1953 to 1955. No hit singles resulted. Though "Satin Doll" was the B-side of his first single, it did not become a standard until years later. Some of the most crassly commercial music of Ellington's career was recorded at the label, none of it attaining the target of the *Billboard* charts. Goaded by Capitol producer Dave Dexter, he tried to cash in on the mambo craze started by Perez Prado with the "Bunny Hop Mambo," and he even released something called the "Tyrolean Tango." Many old hits were re-recorded (in high fidelity but with less fire) at Capitol, and one project featured non-Ellington songs made famous by Ellington in the past, a rather dismal album concept. Ellington pulled out one gem during his Capitol tenure, a piano-trio album entitled *The Duke Plays Ellington* (now called *Piano Reflections*) recorded mostly during his first month at the label. It showcased a member of the Ellington orchestra whose musical chops rarely received their just acclaim: the piano player. Alternately delightful and meditative, the album is divided between older rearranged songs and new compositions, some of which were surprisingly melancholy. On a 1955 NBC broadcast, Ellington described the session: "It happened out at Hollywood in the Capitol Studios late at night, it must have been 3 or 4 o'clock in the morning... Dexter dimmed the lights and we were striving for the type of atmosphere that usually comes with what they call piano jazz, you know, where there's no preparation, no music, no orchestration, no nothing, just let your heart beat and keep time with it."[35]

A short contract with Bethlehem Records in late 1955 resulted in two mostly desultory albums, one featuring yet another waxing of Ellington chestnuts and another featuring the orchestra's take on Tin Pan Alley standards. The three years following the recording of the Capitol piano-trio LP marked the longest period in which Ellington did not record a significant new composition or track; it was the low point of his career. Ellington's standing in the press dropped precipitously as well. Stratemann reported that, for the first time ever, Ellington completely disappeared from the trade papers during the summer of 1955, and his showings in the *Down Beat* annual critics' and readers' polls for 1953 to 1955 were his worst ever. In the 1955 readers' poll, Ellington took fourteenth place in the "dance band" category, garnering a bit more than half the votes Lawrence Welk did. In the critics' poll of that year, neither Ellington nor any of his band figured in the voting.[36]

One gig particularly symbolized Ellington and the band's nadir, according to some observers. "For six weeks in the summer of 1955, Ellington was reduced—undoubtedly out of financial necessity—to the demeaning role of accompanying a water show with ice skaters, called the Aquacade, in Flushing, New York, during which he played only a medley of his hits, then was excused while another conductor led his band, augmented by strings," wrote Hasse in his Ellington biography. "For the duration of the engagement, he had to let four players go because they were not members of the New York City musicians' local," a deed unthinkable in earlier, more lucrative times. "It was a condescending area . . . He must have been in dire straits," recalled Clark Terry. "It seemed like a stupid, senseless gig, but it was regular employment." Avakian stopped by one afternoon and found the Aquacade a "hokey" but pleasant setting in which the audience was not there to see Ellington. But not everyone viewed the engagement so darkly: Jimmy Hamilton, clarinet and sax player, viewed the gig as "a high spot for me" because he had a short drive home to his family every night for a month and a half (an anomaly in the life of an Ellington band member) and he worked with interesting older musicians.[37]

Ellington utilized his down time during the Aquacade run to finish an original play, *Man with Four Sides,* which he shopped to producers unsuccessfully for years. Ellington's prospectus for potential investors described the work as "mostly about the woman from various perspectives." The action almost exclusively focused on the Lanes, a middle-aged African American couple. Mrs. Lane is a puritanical, inhibited, snobby woman who refuses to let Mr. Lane smoke a pipe, chew a toothpick, or listen to blues music ("base slithering vulgarity") in their home. Through the course of the play, she is transformed into the kind of woman Mr. Lane prefers. A pique of mistaken jealousy when Mr. Lane does not come home one night and a chance encounter with blues music makes her realize that her haughtiness has kept her from enjoying life. From then on, she adopts a more sensual and relaxed attitude, especially in matters of sex, music, and food.[38] Ellington imbued the material with an earthy Langston Hughes–like feel and wrote songs to accompany it, though most of the play is dramatic, not musical. His depictions of femininity veer between visions of misogyny and extreme respect and love for the power and soul of women, especially in the lyric for "Streamline." *Man with Four Sides* questions the conservative family values and materialism of 1950s middle-class black America, somewhat mirroring the way Jack Kerouac and Allen Ginsberg did the same for whites at the same time. Ellington seemed to argue that a life of American middle-class domesticity is not as healthy or soulful as life outside its boundaries. With Ellington's rootless, mostly homeless existence, nominally single status, sexually promiscuous lifestyle, and freewheeling artistic attitude, *Four Sides* may have represented a revealing, though still masked, glimpse into Ellington's personal life and values. But it did not represent a way of life that had much resonance in 1950s America, especially among middle-class blacks, probably a major reason it never saw the light of day. With various projects of the 1960s, especially his Sacred Concerts, Ellington would continue to question and mock the excessive consumerism and lack of soul he felt existed in the more uptight elements of society.

Somehow, through ingenuity and an ability to deal productively with unpleasant times, Ellington and the orchestra emerged through their toughest period as the only big band to tour and record continually through the postwar era without an extended hiatus. Numerous factors consigned them to peripheries and precipices of the music business, yet they survived—and sometimes did much better than that. Ellington weathered this uncertain chapter and was poised to make a huge comeback that set the pace for another seventeen years in the spotlight, accompanied by an orchestra that often matched or exceeded past ensembles, ready to bring to life whatever composition he had dreamed up the night before.

9
REBORN

FIGURE 8. Duke Ellington on 16 February 1965 in London, indulging in his constant daily obsession: composing. Photograph by Val Wilmer.

Ellington's interviews from the period and afterward document a man nearly obsessed with his writing, rearranging his life and his sleep patterns to accommodate the creative process. "You write when you're sleeping, eating, walking, showering," he explained in 1962. "Sometimes you may just be riding along in a car and a melody comes to you. But don't trust it to memory. Jot it down. Otherwise you'll lose it." Stanley Dance, who often traveled with and wrote about Ellington during the 1960s, reported on this proclivity:

> Whenever he was long enough in one hotel, a piano had been moved into his suite. At Camden, it hadn't been possible, and he had worked alone in the hotel's empty ballroom, all lights on, until dawn. Here in Boston, the piano was conveniently located opposite the TV and near the doors of adjoining rooms. He could step out of the shower, play a chord or a phrase, and step back in again.

Fans and band members remember Ellington composing on the bandstand, scribbling down an idea for new material on manuscript paper while keeping track of the band performing an entirely different song at the same time and contributing his parts to the live performance.[1]

Ellington's devotion to composing served as the main motivator in his hectic existence. "I like to have [writing] problems [to solve], otherwise everything gets routine, and I get lazy," he told the New York Post in 1961. Most Ellington interviews over the years featured a preponderance of repeated boilerplate expressions, which hint that Ellington's mind often resided somewhere else during encounters with journalists (perhaps working out a melody in his head). But when the subject of composing was broached, particularly in the late 1950s and throughout the 1960s, he usually contributed passionate and personal testimonials to the primary love of his life. Because composing occupied a defining role in Ellington's personal and professional existence, it is useful to examine a chronological gallery of his quotes on the subject, ranging from 1956 to 1967:

> I don't knock myself out working, you know. I'm not a slave to this. Music is my first love actually. When I do go after it, of course, I go after it real wholeheartedly, with everything that I've got. I may sit down and write and write and write, without any sleep for a week, you know. And if I do go to bed, get up in the middle of the night, or after a couple hours sleep, and come

back with an idea, and complete something. But then when I go away from it, there's no telling when I'm coming back to it because I don't like to force things. I write when I feel like writing. When I'm riding. Bus, train, automobile. [These] things help me. Long stretches.

This is my writing period. I must have written more in the last two years than I've written in my whole life. But it keeps coming and there's no good in saving it up.

[When asked "Does it . . . drain you physically to write so much and with such consistently high quality," Ellington replied:] None of it takes it out of me. It gives me more than it takes. When I hear what I wrote I receive the type of physical and emotional reward that money can't buy. For me it's a stimulus.

To me, music is a hobby. That is why I have to have a band. It is a sort of vanity. As soon as I hear a piece, I have to hear it played . . . People say my music has "progressed" or "matured." Maybe it's like getting food and adding pepper and curry—you add musical ideas and spice. People enjoy music like a good meal. Say, what rhymes with "compatible"? That's what's been bothering me.

It's this thing you keep chasing. This melody. You are always looking for it. Then a bit of it comes to you, you bite a piece, and it tastes sweet. Then you go back and reach for a bit more. It's still "this melody," but it's a different one now. If you're lucky you get it again—a new one. This tree has got a lot of different fruit on it . . . A composition may make some money for me, but I don't care about that. I just want to hear it.

You know how it is with the up-and-coming musician. Always trying something new. We like to have our dreams; we like climbing mountains. My life is all music; there is complete commitment. I have no other definitive interests. You could say I'm addicted to music, that I have a hungry ear that consumes sharps and flats. I'd have to be totally involved to keep the band together 52 weeks a year.

[Ellington apologized for being late to an interview:] You know how it is, you go home expecting to go right to bed, but then on the way in you go past the piano, and there's a flirtation. It flirts with you. So you sit to try out a couple chords, and when you look up it's 7AM.[2]

Expressing and satisfying that drive, hearing his newly born compositions hours after their completion, became the consuming focus of his later years.

In fact, he authored so much material during the last eighteen years of his life that, fifteen years after his death, "new" Ellington compositions were still being released.

After 1956, with the rise of rock and roll, R&B, and other genres geared to younger audiences, Ellington realized that he no longer would enjoy the kinds of hit singles that afforded him and other artists maximum power and money within the music industry. Instead, he used the possibilities of festival concerts, media appearances, and long-playing records to demonstrate his continuing creativity. Though he never had a bestselling album or single after 1956, such efforts kept his name in the media and gave him a relevancy that carried beyond the nostalgia market. His love of composing and hearing his newest works performed immediately by the band of his choice made up for the fatigue of one-nighters on the road, the constant financial binds that touring with a big band placed him in, the hassles of dealing with bookers who did not always have his best financial interests in mind, and the responsibility of supporting a large retinue of family and friends. One does not get a sense of desperation from Ellington in these circumstances. Rather, it seemed that, as long as he lived the daily life he wanted, centered on his writing and performing, the rest of his supposed problems existed in a separate area that did not usually trouble him.

✳

For Ellington, it was as important to grow artistically as to sell records and tickets. While he clearly loved playing his old hits for audiences, and needed to do so financially, he simultaneously refused to rest on his creative laurels. For decades, he had built a popular music audience that, among other things, looked to him for something beyond the usual commercial product. In this aspect, he resembled the rising generation of more freeform jazz artists like Ornette Coleman or John Coltrane, who emerged during this period and spent much of their careers exploring musical boundaries without great concern that such wanderings stood little chance of topping the sales charts. The artistic journey mattered most, and these artists were skilled and intriguing enough to attract an audience, even if they and the rest of the jazz community were not experiencing interest or sales anywhere near those seen during the Swing Era. One never exactly knew what to expect from each new album by artists like Coleman and Coltrane, but their work and their gifts were usually worth the time it took to understand their new direction. Ellington had trailblazed this path for them decades before, providing aural landscapes for contemplation, such as "Reminiscing In Tempo," "Transblucency," and *Harlem*.

Ellington came to stand for the way in which the aging process could be a developing process. No one else in his generation, or perhaps any other generation of American artists, tried so intently to grow and take on new sources at his age. Even such skilled and significant artists and composers as Louis Armstrong, Aaron Copland, Miles Davis, Dizzy Gillespie, Frank Sinatra, and Muddy Waters were mostly reprising earlier successful styles and formulas as they approached their fifties, rather than releasing innovative work that ranked among their best contributions, as Ellington did well into his seventies. Word of a big band revival kept surfacing in the press during the 1950s and 1960s, probably planted by publicists. Previous Swing Era idols hit the road for a few weeks at a time, but almost all of them confined their repertoires to what originally brought them success in the 1930s and 1940s. Consequently, with few new ideas to update their sound, the much-predicted revival never arrived. Ellington, on the other hand, with the significant help of Billy Strayhorn, incorporated literary sources and international influences into his writing, and began composing for films, classical orchestras, and dance companies. He pushed the creative evolution of the big band sound almost singlehandedly, and he kept his band working fifty-two weeks a year, surrounding himself with a younger generation of musicians when older ones bowed out. Ellington created a new precedent of innovation and vitality for a popular artist advanced in years that has never been equaled in American music.

In a country that liked to define its artists early with one overarching image, and then encase that image in stone, Ellington insisted on establishing an artistic rhythm difficult to pin down in his new works. He proved a soul of constant musical reinvention, while still adhering to his decades-old mantra of creating Negro music. No wonder Ellington kept trying to revise his age or deny it being released to the public, all the while insisting he had been "born again" at the 1956 Newport Jazz Festival. The pop and jazz marketplace, especially during the 1960s, favored the young and beautiful. Ellington was no longer young in age, but his recordings of the 1950s, 1960s, and beyond demonstrate that he was often young in thought and still quite beautiful.

Even before their 1956 Newport appearance, signs pointed toward a rising profile for Ellington and his orchestra. According to Ellington, an upward trajectory started just after the Aquacade engagement. "It began to appear that I was back at my peak or something like that," he recalled, though he never explicitly acknowledged a decline in the band or himself. "That's when Johnny Hodges came [back] in [to the band], and his wife called up, wanted to know if I wanted an alto [sax] player. I told him yeah [chuckles], he came back, and [drummer] Sam Woodyard came in the band. We had a real good drive, you know. Jimmy Woode was playing bass, it was a good-sounding foundation, we were playing some nice-sounding things." Young players recruited earlier in the decade, such as trumpeter Clark Terry and saxophonist Paul Gonsalves, were now comfortably ensconced in the band, set to make crucial contributions and claim their place as some of the most important players ever to work for Ellington. Private "stockpile" recordings that Ellington produced in March 1956 (unreleased until the 1980s) document a band fiery and inspired again, augmented by new and intriguing three-minute miniatures composed for them by Ellington, such as "Feet Bone," "Discontented," and "Short Sheet Cluster." Others noticed an upswing in the band's power even before the mass media trumpeted the Newport performance. In March 1956, *Down Beat* proclaimed his the "most underrated band in the country." "It has become rather fashionable in recent years to fob off Duke Ellington," commented Whitney Bailliett, one of the most respected jazz critics, in May 1956. "Yet, the truth is that Ellington inescapably remains after almost thirty-five years as a professional the richest figure in jazz as well as one of the most inventive, original minds in American music . . . he has been consistently ahead of the music he has done so much for."[3]

Billy Strayhorn's return to fulltime duties with the orchestra at the end of 1955 also augured well for their future. Like star saxophonist Johnny Hodges, who also left the band for much of the first half of the 1950s, Strayhorn found that it would be more artistically and commercially rewarding to remain with Ellington. Also, unlike Hodges, Ellington and Strayhorn were the closest of friends. When Strayhorn returned fulltime, "Ellington sought better ways to accommodate him," according to Strayhorn scholar Walter van de Leur. "Not only would they share the credits to all the future suites . . . but, more important, Ellington encouraged Strayhorn to initiate his own projects." When Ellington re-signed with Columbia later in 1956, Strayhorn "was promised more artistic freedom, as well as full credit for his work," even his arrangements.[4] This situation set the stage for perhaps the best album-length examples of their mutual composing: *Such Sweet Thunder* (1957), *The Nutcracker Suite* (1960), and *The Far East Suite* (1966).

From its inception, the Newport festival emphasized the view of jazz as a serious American and African American art form that highlighted the best strands of American culture, a viewpoint Ellington had maintained and promoted for decades. The purpose of the festival, as set by Newport Jazz

Festival, Inc., in 1954, was "to encourage America's enjoyment of jazz and to sponsor the study of our country's only original art form." George Wein, who headed the festival throughout its history, taught a course in jazz at Boston University and played respectable jazz piano in addition to his duties as a major booker of talent in the New England area. "They want to give the festival a kind of academic flavor," *Down Beat* editor Nat Hentoff, who worked for the festival, told the *New Yorker*. On Sunday afternoon of the 1954 festival, a panel on "The Place of Jazz in American Culture" convened. Over a thousand attended. Four college professors spoke: an anthropologist commented on the links between jazz and African music, composer Henry Cowell compared jazz and classical music, and Marshall Stearns, probably the most famous academic teaching and writing about jazz at the time, also spoke and took questions.

The academic approach continued in the years following. Two racially integrated panels featured at the 1955 festival, one with academic "social scientists" and one with a combination of musicians and journalists. Ellington contributed an essay to the program entitled "The Future of Jazz," which showcased his usual studied approach to discussing the history and identity of the music. He advised jazz musicians and lovers not to worry whether their music fell into jazz, classical, or folk categories: "Let's just say that what we're all trying to create, in one way or another, is American music." The 1956 festival also included two panels. One featured Strayhorn, among others, discussing "The Future of Jazz," while Langston Hughes joined a panel of mostly academics and authors in exploring "Jazz as a Communication." At the latter, Wein blamed the public for the conservative musical approaches of artists like Louis Armstrong and Dizzy Gillespie in the 1950s, since they responded to novelties and gimmicks instead of "great music." A well-intentioned highbrow snobbery accompanied the opening years of jazz's first annual multiday event.[5]

Despite his insistence that the public needed to champion the more challenging jazz artists, Wein "favored the venerable Louis and Ella and Duke over younger, more experimental cats" in his programming, which helped build support for the festival among jazz fans and among the aristocratic enclave of Newport, where some of the richest Americans had summered since the Gilded Age. Initially, many residents feared and resented the intrusion of jazz and its plebian fans upon their island of sprawling ubermansions. But, by 1956, the *Wall Street Journal* reported that "after a couple of years of decided coolness to the show, Newport came around and provided full cooperation this summer." *Variety* added that "the Newport cream and the visitors, pro and audience, are now homogenizing nicely," even though many festival-goers slept in sleeping bags or in their cars in the exclusive neighborhoods. The festival started attracting an international crowd, according to the *Boston Herald*, which noted "the medley of . . . accents" heard at the site. The Voice of America broadcast the show to an international audience, and Columbia Records recorded the event for release, the first time jazz artists were recorded at a festival. The 1956 Newport festival demonstrated the rising commercial power, international reputation, artistic respectability, and social interaction accorded to jazz, but, apparently, any "desegregation" of the exclusive summer colony was mostly in terms of class, not race. Langston Hughes felt surprised that the twenty-five-thousand-strong audience comprised almost exclusively whites. In his column for black newspapers, he noted the irony of the fact that mostly black artists were being celebrated by a white audience on an island that previously served as a center for the slave trade.[6]

Wein and George Avakian, who was trying to lure Ellington back to Columbia, helped to spur Ellington's commercial and artistic rebirth at Newport. Wein wished to create a reputation for the Newport festival as a not-to-be-missed annual event where musical surprises regularly occurred. He felt that he could count on Ellington, who had delivered on many historic and artistic occasions in the past, to present material that met such expectations. Wein wanted Ellington to "not just play the medley, you know, in other words, I didn't want him to just go through the motions, particularly at festivals, where critics were analyzing every note that was being played. I felt that he had to come up with something different, something new, that he hadn't been playing at his regular concerts. So I told him, 'Here I am, working my fingers to the bone to perpetuate the genius that is Duke Ellington,' I talked to him like he talked to me, 'and I'm not getting any cooperation.'" Wein believed this approach inspired Ellington to arrive at Newport armed with both new material and freshly reworked older, lesser-known material.

Avakian took a similar stance when he produced Ellington in the early 1950s at Columbia and again urged Ellington in the same direction, suggesting that he pen a suite dedicated to the festival. "He was not under contract to us at the time, but we were talking about having him come back," Avakian recalled. "Duke came back eagerly, and signed a new contract and all that, and I don't know that he came back just because I suggested that, but . . . it just worked out perfectly because the mere fact that I proposed he write a new composition was something that was very dear to his heart."[7] Capitol and Bethlehem released few significant new Ellington compositions between 1953 and 1956, even though Ellington completed the ambitious seventeen-minute, three-movement *Night Creature,* scored for a combined jazz orchestra and symphony orchestra, at the end of his Capitol tenure. The piece, besides presenting an unprecedented challenge for him, proved to be one of his most successful and appealing longer works, yet it remained un-recorded and unreleased for a decade. Ellington was probably happy to re-turn to Columbia, a company that encouraged challenging as well as com-mercial projects.

The evening did not start well for the Ellington orchestra. At showtime, four band members, including the bass player, were absent and probably in-toxicated. Three of them were featured soloists in the new suite, which made it useless to continue, and the band left after playing a scant twelve-minute, three-song set that included the national anthem. Ellington and the orches-tra were then forced to wait three hours backstage until they went on again. Ellington disliked going on so late on the last night of the festival and knew that the situation endangered his dream of using the premiere of a major new piece to initiate a comeback. "I said to George Wein, 'What are we—the animal act, the acrobats?'" Ellington told *Down Beat* a few months later. "By the time we got on, we'd be playing just exit music, because a lot of peo-ple have to get over that bridge by a certain time, or make curfew, or catch a suburban train." According to Avakian, Ellington already felt more anxiety than usual because he

> was very very worried that if he couldn't get a good performance of the suite, it would be a career disaster for him for various reasons ... he said it on the telephone [on the Friday before the show], the words are quite memorable. He said, "Look, we've got to be ready to do something to protect this com-position because I can't afford to not have it come out, I can't afford [for it to] come out in a bad version, and the guys are simply not prepared." ... [El-lington] was nervous about any performances of [new] long works ... he was actually traumatized, I would say ... because he was so tired, as he said, of "having the John Hammonds of the world tell me I should stick to three-minute songs."

Such worries over his image and reputation were exacerbated by the fact that Ellington knew that *Time* was planning a cover story on him, and that the assigned reporter, Carter Harman, was in the audience.[8]

The rustiness almost always present at premieres of Ellington extended pieces (Ellington often wrote until the last minute, giving the band little time to rehearse) surfaced during the *Newport Festival Suite,* especially in the opening and closing minutes of the third section, "Newport Up." Slight mistakes led Avakian and Ellington to re-record almost the entire suite in a studio the next day for release as a long-playing record, an option that they had discussed before the concert.[9] The studio recording, with its canned applause, pales before the original concert tapes, but Ellington refused to issue what he viewed as an imperfect performance. Overall, the suite, while contributing no indelible melodies to the Ellington canon, serves as excellent music for a summer festival. The writing is lively, warm, and inviting, especially in the first two sections.

While the new suite was well received, it was the performance of "Diminuendo and Crescendo in Blue" that nearly ignited a riot at Newport and prompted journalists to declare the Ellington orchestra as "once again the hottest thing in the business," as *Time* reported. This piece, originally waxed on two 78-rpm sides in 1937, was road-tested by Ellington and the band in recent weeks and, according to Clark Terry, it went over well. The biggest draw of the performance, however, was not Ellington's writing, but the steadily building, six-minute, twenty-seven-chorus tenor saxophone solo by Paul Gonsalves, which, as can be heard on the tapes, put the crowd into a frenzy, changing the course and fortunes of the Ellington orchestra. Gonsalves's solo did not resemble the stratospheric, existential extended solos that fellow saxophonist John Coltrane made popular during the 1960s. It was a nonflashy, blues-based solo that skillfully aimed to accentuate the swing and excitement of the rocking beat and get people to move, a solo that unleashed a spirit of joy and abandon. Witnesses unanimously recall a blonde woman in the front of the audience breaking free from the crowd to dance, inspiring others to leave their chairs on the field and do the same. Wein called it a spontaneous "happening." Ellington saw this unfold and did whatever he could to ratchet up the band and the crowd. "Duke was really out there, doing it, you know, he was almost dancing, he was doing his thing, [moving] side-to-side, shuffling, hand-clapping, [bellowing] 'ah-HA!'" recalled Terry, and the recording bears him out.[10] "Higher!" Ellington called out to Gonsalves at one point, and Gonsalves obliged. The audience roared when Gonsalves finished his marathon solo, aggressively signaling their desire for more. The band responded in kind, turning in an especially fierce and driving conclusion to the piece.

After that performance, and for the rest of the band's set, the crowd sounded insistent, almost angry, audibly shouting at Ellington and the band for the soloists they wished to hear, imploring them not to stop. *Time* reported that "festival officials began to fear that something like a rock 'n' roll riot was taking place." Ellington brandished one of his most powerful weapons to calm the horde, Johnny Hodges. After a shaky start, Hodges featured on two numbers, including an exquisite, languid version of "Jeep's Blues," with some particularly tasty and subdued interplay between Hodges and Ellington in a performance that deserves more notoriety. But the crowd still was not sated, and assuring them repeatedly that "We got a lot more," Ellington kicked off "Tulip or Turnip," a silly and swinging novelty number featuring Ray Nance on vocals.

By this time, 12:30 had come and gone, and the crowd grew even more aggressive in calling for requests and encores. Partly under pressure from the police, Wein had signaled since the end of "Diminuendo" for the band to stop, but Ellington, fearing an uncontrollable melee and wanting to prolong his band's triumph as long as possible, kept the band going, trying to calm the crowd with music. Wein protested this approach that night, but in later years complimented Ellington on his crowd-control tactics. Finally, by the end of "Tulip," Wein's patience seemed to have snapped. He yelled "That's it" into a microphone, without consulting Ellington. Loud, angry booing and pandemonium ensued. Wein and Ellington then had a testy conference onstage, partly within range of the microphones. "You can't . . . I mean it . . . that's it . . . no! No! No! I mean it now," Wein asserted, an edge of fear and tension in his voice. "Let me tell 'em good night," Ellington countered. "Can I tell them good night?" Wein allowed it, but did not sound happy about it. Ellington took the opportunity to thank the crowd again and, much to their delight, launched into "Skin Deep," a ten-minute song adorned by a lengthy and pounding drum solo. Afterward, Ellington finally said good night to the strains of "Mood Indigo" and walked offstage, the crowd protesting the band's departure.[11]

The frenzied Newport crowd reaction to Ellington was reported widely in the media, depicting the Ellington orchestra as a vital unit that, three decades after their Cotton Club opening, could still provoke crowds and cause a sensation. The event was a publicist's dream, spotlighted in feature stories about Ellington for the rest of his career.

Langston Hughes felt particularly moved by the intensely emotional, not cerebral, reaction whites had to the jazz played by blacks that weekend. Such reactions were common when white musicians and fans embraced black musical and dance styles in the Swing Era, and a similar dynamic seemed on the rise again. The embracing of black culture by whites with the new popularity of rock and roll may have represented part of the reason for the uproarious Newport response. With easy-listening exceptions like Nat King Cole's sumptuous ballads, blacks had mostly disappeared from the top of national sales charts from 1945 to 1955, relegated primarily to the segregated black charts. Starting in 1955, black rock artists Chuck Berry, Little Richard, and some vocal doo-wop groups scored Top Forty hits on the pop chart. A new, more economically independent generation of American teenagers embraced black music in a manner somewhat similar to the previous generation during the Swing Era. Part of the roots of this transformation arose from the slowly increasing acceptance of black R&B music by whites in the years before Chuck Berry's "Maybelline" became a top-five single in 1955. Artists like Ruth Brown and Nellie Lutcher began drawing both black and white fans in the postwar period, along with substantial coverage in *Down Beat,* for producing music more overtly sensual and danceable than the antiseptic hit parade of the day. Still, these performers scored their hit singles mostly on the black R&B charts, which accounted for only 10 percent of the record business.[12]

Perhaps more important in assessing the precedents for the reaction to the Gonsalves solo was "the honking tenor sax craze" during the first years of the 1950s. As Jim Dawson explained, it was "inspired by the earlier pyrotechnics of [1940s jazz saxophonist] Illinois Jacquet, began with Big Jay McNeely's #1 [1951] R&B hit, 'Deacon's Hop,' and led to riotous late-night Battles of the Tenor Saxophones attended by screaming, blissed-out, black, white, and Chicano teenagers." A memorable photograph from the book *Central Avenue Sounds,* which documents the jazz and R&B scene in Los Angeles, depicts black tenor saxophonist Big Jay McNeely lying on his back onstage, beads of sweat glittering on his forehead, soloing as whites crowd around him, howling into the air, pounding their fists on the stage, and shouting encouragement. Once again, as they had during Ellington's 1927–31 Cotton Club engagement, whites were heading to clubs in black neighborhoods during the early 1950s to enjoy and embrace black rhythm and culture that respectable society and their parents often did not accept.[13] A few years later, an even more frenzied and widespread reaction by teenagers of all races greeted black rock and roll pioneer Little Richard, who employed a tenor saxophonist, Lee Allen, whose honking, anguished solo style sometimes resembled McNeely. The spirit of abandon and personal expression that many associated with jazz was being transferred by a new generation to R&B and rock and roll.

This transition resulted in a renewal of the fortunes of the previously backsliding music industry, which in the period from 1953 to 1954 saw record sales drop 5 percent, a continuation of the postwar trend of declining platter sales since 1945. In 1956, the first full year of rock and roll's reign as a national craze, the record industry enjoyed sales increases of 40 percent over the previous year.[14] Rock and roll was hot, in more ways than one.

Ellington was aware of these trends. In a 1955 article for "the teen page" of the *Detroit Times,* Ellington commented on the increasing market for R&B, rock and roll, and black gospel music, arguing they were all connected to American "folk music" created by both blacks and whites. He claimed he was "up to my ears in all of it" and name-checked Ruth Brown, Ray Charles, Sister Rosetta Tharpe, and Muddy Waters (though his listing of Frank Sinatra and Perry Como as rockers showed his lack of knowledge of the category at this time). Mercer Records, the label Ellington financed for his son Mercer, featured recordings that attempted to tap the R&B audience in the early 1950s. According to business documents, Ellington was directly involved in Mercer Ellington's attempt to revive the label in 1956 with a black doo-wop group called the Enchanters. In a 1956 interview, Ellington spoke about the origins and business aspects of rock and roll and defended it against those who accused it of corrupting the morals of youth:

> Rock 'n' roll is nothing more than the folky rhythm and blues music that people have been playing all along. Its naïve folk quality makes it easy to understand and thus easy to promote to a large number of people. As for producing any excessive sexual excitement, rock 'n' roll is no more guilty than a lively country dance, which is actually its derivative form. Mind you, I'm talking of the music, not what some performers do with the music. As a matter of fact, the most sensual music is the waltz. I think Strauss wrote some of the sexiest music there is. There's something censorious about [the resistance to rock and roll]. Personally, I think the only criterion for music is whether it sounds good. Music is music. If it sounds good, it is. If it doesn't, it isn't.

In this quote, Ellington proved more astute about American music history than most observers of his time. Recent scholars have agreed that rock and roll emerged as a product of earlier American folk music made by blacks and whites, including blues and country music influences. Ellington's mentioning of the waltz as a sensual musical form was ironic because, in the mid-nineteenth century, the waltz emerged as the subject of the first American attempt to censor popular music. Many in the 1850s urged its banishment since it required couples to grip each other tightly, gaze into each others' eyes at close range, and refuse to share dancing partners or even acknowledge other dancers on the floor. Worse yet, as Thornton Hagert reported, "the hypnotic effect of the unrelenting and mechanical turning, turning of the early waltz was thought to summon up uncontrollable passions that would surely lead to ridicule or even dishonor, disease and pregnancy," a litany of charges resembling those inveighed against early rock and roll, without the racist trappings that often accompanied efforts to censor that music.[15]

Either Ellington or his promoters and handlers made occasional attempts in the months before and after Newport to affix the marketing term "rock and roll" to the Ellington orchestra, even though their music hardly resembled the genre. Ellington wrote "Rock and Roll Rhapsody" and "Rock City Rock" in 1956, and the latter was performed on the road. Neither were recorded. Ellington, along with Nat King Cole and Lionel Hampton, artists usually identified with jazz, were featured in a film entitled *Rock and Roll Riot,* according to 1956 clippings, though the film was probably culled from other sources (perhaps illegally) and retitled to take advantage of commercial trends. Film clips featuring black R&B and rock performers Ruth Brown and the Clovers were also used in the film. Klaus Stratemann, in his exhaustive study of Ellington on film, made no mention of the project.[16]

As he had during the 1920s and the Swing Era, Ellington positioned his band to take advantage of the commercial trend of whites—the majority of the population and the biggest market for music—embracing black music. The hubbub over the Gonsalves solo resembled the reaction to R&B and rock and roll genres. It was an unplanned connection, yet it resonated. Even though Ellington did not belong in the rock and roll camp, the Newport 1956 festival offered young white audiences a chance to celebrate a true pioneer of the African American music they loved, a sophisticated antecedent to 1950s rock and roll. The association with rock and roll was a fleeting and minor trend in the marketing of Ellington, abandoned by 1957, but it represented the first of numerous gestures and strategies by Ellington seeking to portray himself, his band, and, particularly, his writing as modern and developing, even as he neared his sixties.

In the press, Ellington began to express impatience with fans and reporters that always mentioned his age and dwelled upon past achievements. Such sentiments increased as he grew older. Behind the scenes, Ellington attempted to discourage overly nostalgic media depictions of himself and his work. Patricia Willard, a publicity agent who worked with Ellington on projects from 1949 to 1974, recalled Ellington asking her to find a way to make *Down Beat* cease mentioning his age in the lead paragraphs of stories about him. He adamantly wished not to be seen "as a relic" and felt it unfair that the ages of other artists were not reported. Willard addressed a letter to the "47-year-old" editor of *Down Beat,* who got the message and stopped the practice, at least temporarily.

Starting in the mid-1950s, Ellington often asked for a new biography to send out in publicity kits, highlighting recent achievements. He also refused to provide set lists in advance, despite insistent pleas from promoters who told Willard that "we always have a program." Willard speculated that Ellington wished to demonstrate that he was still the boss and an unpredictable artist, not just a popular performer. Also, many sources and concert tapes demonstrate Ellington's skill at gauging the moods of audiences and coming up with unexpected musical choices to make them happy. This unpredictability also kept the band on their toes. Sometimes Ellington reluctantly listed twenty-five to thirty compositions for Willard to bestow on particularly persistent promoters for use in a program. "Are you really going to play these?" she asked him more than once. "I don't know," he replied, "but it'll shut them up!"[17]

Ellington knew that following a more musically challenging path could make it more difficult to attract and retain an audience. "This is a push-button age, and people don't want to try too hard to understand anything. Musically, they are geared to hotel band music, which doesn't tax their imaginations," he told the *Cleveland Press* in 1956. "Our job is to figure out a way to 'get' to them." Ellington constantly tried to prompt his audiences to expect the unexpected from him, in addition to the generous supply of Ellington classics he provided at each concert. "People keep saying 'that doesn't sound like Ellington' when we play something new," Ellington noted in May 1957. "This is a compliment, because Billy Strayhorn, who works with me, and I try to create and to be creative means that when we get something done it must be something new."[18]

By training audiences to expect new and challenging material from his pen and orchestra, Ellington enhanced the market for discs featuring his newer works. Columbia Records, his label from 1956 to 1962, often touted Ellington's new works in ads during the 1950s as "the sound of genius." A 1957 Columbia ad in the *New Yorker, Harpers,* and *Saturday Review,* among other venues, linked Ellington's newest album of originals with the most prestigious classical figures on their roster: Leonard Bernstein, Aaron Copland, and Bruno Walter. All were noted as "geniuses," while most jazz artists in Columbia ads of the period were characterized as "great" and "the greatest." In the Smithsonian's collections, no other ad from this period compared classical artists with a jazz or pop artist in such exalted fashion.[19] Ellington's emphasis on composing prompted Columbia to market him in more categories than the average artist. Classical, pop, nostalgic, and jazz audiences were considered potential purchasers of Ellington product, and he reached for these audiences and more to keep his musical operations solvent. Columbia and Avakian's emphasis on the long-run strategy of constructing a varied catalog continued from Ellington's first tenure on the label and probably also represented a welcome respite after his experiences with Capitol and Bethlehem. Even though Columbia executive Avakian produced no further albums by Ellington following the bestselling 1956 *Newport* collection (Avakian left the label in 1958), a similar aesthetic seems to have been followed by his replacement in the studio, Irving Townsend.

The later Columbia albums also revolved around concepts, casting each Ellington release as a separate new event, enhancing marketing possibilities. No longer did Ellington hope for a hit single; jazz had not existed on the pop charts for years. His embrace of and success with the album format marked him as more contemporary than his generational peers. Ellington fit in well with the Columbia stable of much younger, forward-moving, best-selling jazz artists like Dave Brubeck and Miles Davis, particularly the latter because of Davis's chameleon-like abilities (largely learned from Ellington and Strayhorn) to change styles and aggressively develop new sounds and concepts with each release. For the next six years of his Columbia contract and for most of the rest of his career, each album Ellington released bore little resemblance to the one preceding it, other than the fact that it featured Ellington's name on the cover. In an unpublished excerpt from his 1956 interview for the *Time* magazine cover story, Ellington voiced trepidation to reporter Carter Harman about focusing too extensively on past glories. "I think it'd be better for you, well, for me too of course, if we don't get too historic, if we don't emphasize the history point of view," he told him. "It's all right for you to have [quotes from Ellington about the 1940s], but for this particular project, it would do me a helluva lot more good, if the reason for the goddamn thing has to do with *now*."[20] Ellington mostly got what he wished: *Time*'s cover story enthused about his illustrious past, but most of the first and last pages of the five-page feature dealt with 1956 events and optimistic prognostications for his future.

One of Ellington's most interesting and misunderstood projects of the Columbia years was *A Drum Is a Woman*, the basis for an hour-long nationally broadcast CBS-TV special sponsored by U.S. Steel.[21] It was his first album following the hugely successful *Ellington at Newport* release. The idea had its genesis in the early 1940s, when Orson Welles hired Ellington for twelve weeks as a consultant for a film outlining the history of jazz. "Then there never was a movie, but I never forgot the theme," Ellington told columnist Bill Ladd. Ellington and Strayhorn purposely assembled the album with hopes for staging it on television: "We tried to do something that would visualize," Ellington told *Newsweek*.

A Drum Is a Woman marked another project in which Ellington confounded expectations of his various audiences in an attempt to present an experience unique in the world of entertainment. "This is not written for jazz addicts, and it isn't written as a history of jazz," he warned in interviews.

"It's a fantasy and a play." It was probably unprecedented that exclusively black talent appeared during an hour of prime national network TV time designed by and starring a black artist. It represented "TV's first attempt at a serious dramatic jazz hour," according to Anne W. Langman in the *Nation*. She compared *Drum* to CBS-TV reporter Edward R. Murrow's successful news feature program *See It Now*. Both programs were an "invention of the medium" that capitalized "on the special qualities of television to develop a new way of exploring a place or a situation." In other words, Ellington did not give the predictable television variety appearance that musicians generally provided or translate his usual show to the small screen. Ellington, as he had done previously in radio and records, hoped to wield a pioneering artistic and musical influence in an important new technology.

Drum was a breezy, fairytale-like tour of the history of jazz from the Caribbean jungle to the American urban centers of New Orleans, Chicago, and New York. Historic points were mostly made by extensive dancing, percussion, and fanciful music and lyrics, not scholarly attribution or examples of the best in jazz. It was a slick show-biz production, yet full of black culture. It implicitly portrayed music as a historical and cultural link between African, African American, and Latin American peoples, and implicitly argued for a Pan-African unity. The music reflected this: Ellington and Strayhorn's compositions explored calypso, rhumba, bop, Dixieland, and other American and non-American genres. In a less serious fashion than *Black, Brown and Beige, Drum* took viewers on a tour through international black culture. Nothing like it had ever been on national television before.

The show revolved around Madame Zajj ("jazz" spelled backwards, sort of), who, in her travels through the jungle, falls in love with the conga drumming and dancing of Caribee Joe. But Joe is too committed to following his music and refuses to leave the jungle for her, so she leaves, flying through the air with her mysterious power, searching for an environment as attractive to him as to her, where he can practice his music and they can live happily. The songs are as corny as the premise, but if one suspends disbelief, *Drum* is a delightful and, between the lines, instructive hour of television. Ellington hoped to capture a mass audience with his first major appearance on television, not the sophisticated demographic he and Strayhorn reached for with their extended and more serious pieces.

Zajj's first stop is Barbados, where she inspires an impromptu calypso number during which attractive blacks of all hues kiss and hug, a sight rarely if ever seen elsewhere on American television in the mid-1950s. Next, she disappears (literally) and lands in New Orleans just in time for Mardi Gras, complete with authentic costumes and a fictionalized appearance by the leg-

endary, never-recorded early jazz trumpeter Buddy Bolden. Off-camera, Ellington exhorts him and repeats the fanciful legends of his life: "Born on the
afterbeat . . . Buddy played the horn before he could talk . . . When Buddy
tuned up, you could hear him across the river!" Zajj continues on through
the urban environments of 1920s Chicago and New York, still in love and
restless, continually developing and in search of innovation, just like jazz itself in this period. Though jazz had become sophisticated, Ellington hints
that it never fully abandoned its more primitive origins, an unsurprising
sentiment from a composer and bandleader who regularly told his band
members to "get in the gutter" when performing a bluesy solo. "Though her
past was shady, Zajj was a lady," Ellington says in his role as the jive-inflected
principal storyteller on the TV special. "They dressed her in woodwind and
strings, and golden dulcet lush things, she was seen and heard in the company of kings, but still spoke her mother tongue fluently." For "The Ballad
of the Flying Saucers," Zajj even travels to outer space. Finally, after evocative shots of jungle trees with jewels hung on them, black couples dancing
amidst fog in formal 1890s dress, and a beautiful ballet segment featuring
a harpist and saxophonist Johnny Hodges, Zajj and Joe find a place to coexist in love within an environment somewhere between jungle and urban
milieus.

Apart from the historical significance, *A Drum Is a Woman* may have had
further personal resonance for Ellington. "A drum is a symbol of jazz, and
that's why we use it in the title," Ellington explained to the *Boston American*.
"We call it a woman because musicians sometimes become as close to their
musical instruments as they do to their wives. We know musicians who'll
send their wives out to the movies just so they can be alone some nights with
their musical instruments." Speaking to *Hue* magazine, a monthly aimed
at black Americans, Ellington made similar comments in more colorful
language:

> Any real jazz cat is in love with what he plays. A cat says to his wife, "Here's
> $2, chick, go out and have a ball." He says it so he can be with what he loves,
> his horn or whatever it is. Why you can hear those hot romances up the air
> shafts in the night . . . a sax cat standing there all alone in a lonely room, blow-
> ing against a wall just to hear the sound bouncing back. Maybe he doesn't
> drink or gamble or play around with the chicks. But he can be real dirty and
> mean when he gets alone with what he's in love with. He's a schizo. That's
> why a drum is a woman.

Besides depicting the history of jazz, perhaps *Drum* also reflected the obsessive hold of music upon Ellington, and the price it exacted. For decades,

Ellington's own devotion to music, especially his composing, had kept him from a traditional family life. The *Time* cover story from nine months previously featured a photo of "The Duke & Family." Neither his wife, separated from him for over three decades, nor his partner of two decades, Evie Ellis (sometimes referred to as "Mrs. Ellington," though they never married), were present. Instead, Ellington surrounded himself with his son Mercer and daughter-in-law, his sister Ruth (her husband was not pictured), and his writing partner and close friend Strayhorn who, in the jazz world, was openly homosexual. Not exactly the average 1950s nuclear family. Perhaps, to some extent, Carribee Joe, who had trouble leaving the "jungle" of the music world and settling down, was a representation of Ellington himself. While Ellington came home from touring to Ellis and their apartment in Harlem for a few weeks a year, multiple sources concur that Ellington engaged in sexual relations with numerous women on the road, many of whom sought him out. The life he had chosen to lead as a year-round, intensely committed bandleader and composer (and sexual raconteur) closed off any opportunity to sustain a typical domestic married life. In a private 1964 interview, Ellington further detailed the relationship in his life between family, love, and music. The interview provides further evidence of Ellington's questioning stance toward traditional American middle-class values. Ellington told Harman that music was his life, "the big romance," and Harman asked what mattered to him after that. Ellington replied:

> Well, I mean, it's the people you love, your foundation which goes all the way back to your beginnings and the family, and your romantic encounters, which are sometimes sustained, and others are not sustained . . . There's a tendency in the romantic set of love which has to do more with possession and demonstration, and this has nothing to do with love. You can't just love somebody because you possess them, or you can't go love somebody just because they behave well . . . The minute it becomes conditional, then it's no longer love, so far as I can see. If love is a kind of behavior, then what's that got to do with love?

The view of women in *Drum* is also complex and two-sided. Elements of misogyny are present—for example, in the idea that a woman can be ably replaced by an inanimate object such as a drum, in the many women seen as temptresses, and in Ellington's last, almost leering comment at the close of the show: "Whose pretty little drum are *you*?" Yet, at the same time, Zajj is a strong, independent main character who chooses her own destiny, is highly cultured, dances splendidly, and accepts no guff from anyone. Ellington's personal and sexual life and views lie mostly beyond the purview of this study, but *A Drum Is a Woman* and comments made in private and public offer clues about the subject.

Television critics greeted *Drum* with mixed reviews, with the more influential New York scribes weighing in negatively. It marked such a departure from the usual treatment of music and African Americans on television that critical resistance and befuddlement were not surprising. But in the black political and cultural communities, the show received extravagant praise, with observers noting the historic dimensions of the program. "I appreciate very much indeed the effort Mr. Ellington is making to popularize news of our contributions," commented Dr. Channing Tobias, chairman of the NAACP board. "While listening intently as the drums sounded and the calypso music ran along, it seemed to me most appropriate that this music—if it is to be exploited—was finally being exploited by the people who created it." NAACP public relations director Henri Lee Moon, Urban League chief Lester Granger, and baseball retiree/corporate executive Jackie Robinson all praised CBS-TV and U.S. Steel (as well as Ellington), arguing that their corporate sponsorship of national programming featuring blacks "established a healthy precedent" and "is significant and should be encouraged."

Artists also chimed in. "It was wonderful that the towering talent of so fine a composer and musician was made available to the nation via television," remarked Langston Hughes. "I hope that other talented people in our American segment are now going to get a chance." Marian Anderson and her husband were "enthused" and declared the show "better than anything which has been done by a Negro on television." Mahalia Jackson sent a telegram to Ellington: "Thank God you were the one chosen to show what we can do if given a chance."

The TV program and the massive publicity buildup orchestrated by CBS and Batten, Barton, Durstine & Osborn, Inc. (one of the top ad agencies), placed Ellington squarely in the spotlight of the national media during the spring of 1957, generating hundreds of articles. But aside from that, the career impact on Ellington from the special was limited. The music on *A Drum Is a Woman,* not Ellington and Strayhorn's best by a long shot, was too explicitly tied to the visuals to artistically succeed or sell significantly as an album.

In a *Newsweek* interview conducted before *Drum* aired, Ellington expressed his hopes for doing further television in the style of *Drum.* "What happens with this TV show will make several decisions for us. I have a couple other shows in the back of my mind," he mused. "If I do TV regularly, I wouldn't want to pattern it on any other show. I like being creative . . . you shouldn't throw rocks in your own bed by limiting yourself to one set thing."

The networks did not offer Ellington or other black entertainers a similar opportunity for years. Nat King Cole hosted a show for a year on NBC starting in November 1956, a traditional musical-variety program, but lack of a sponsor caused it to fold prematurely, despite generous network support, good ratings, and excellent critical notices. No advertisers wished to alienate racist customers south or north of the Mason-Dixon Line.[22]

As for Ellington, his television appearances for the rest of his career, with exceedingly few exceptions, returned to the bland and predictable patterns established earlier in the 1950s. The pay for nationally televised appearances was excellent, five to six times what the band made for a typical show, and Ellington insisted through his booking agency on a minimum of $7,500 for such appearances, with $1,000 more for the band, if they were requested. The exposure, of course, was valuable as well. But the sense of artistic adventure seen in *Drum* rarely resurfaced again. For the star-studded *Standard Oil 75th Anniversary* special, which aired in October 1957, he and the orchestra performed three brief and unsatisfying snippets from *Such Sweet Thunder* in less than three minutes, along with a short medley of hits. Two months later, live from the Blue Note in Chicago on the Timex All-Star Jazz Festival, Ellington and the band did a truncated, solo-less song from *Drum*, another from *Such Sweet Thunder*, and they also backed a vocalist. "That was crazy, Duke," Steve Allen, the host of the show, exulted. "Thanks very much, Steve," he replied. "Band sounds just as great as ever," Allen countered. "Oh, thank you. Well, we try," Ellington said nonchalantly, then he paused, adjusted his coat and the handkerchief in his pocket, eyed Allen, and told him, "Wait 'til next year."[23] For Ellington's television career, "next year" would never arrive.

Such Sweet Thunder (1957), a tribute to the plays of William Shakespeare, ranks as Ellington's premiere achievement on Columbia Records. Ellington and Strayhorn, impressed by the performances they witnessed on a 1956 visit to the annual Stratford Shakespeare Festival in Ontario, Canada, wished to contribute in their own fashion to the following year's festival, and the company commissioned a suite from them. Several sources recalled that the composers went through "all" of Shakespeare's plays in their preparation, outlining passages and discussing the personalities and motives of the principals in the plays. In a Toronto interview, Ellington said the idea had been gestating in his mind since he visited Stratford-on-Avon during his 1933 British tour. *Such Sweet Thunder* is a delightful and dramatic jazz chamber suite, an unorthodox interpretation of the immortal bard consisting of twelve thematically but not musically linked short pieces.

Ellington and Strayhorn did not intend any literal references to Shakespeare plays within the compositions. The pieces function more as colorful musical vignettes that hint at the personalities of fictional characters and tableaus. "Half the Fun" provides a panoramic ride down the Nile with Anthony and Cleopatra. "Up and Down, Up and Down" traces the romantic peregrinations of the fickle lovers in *A Midsummer Night's Dream,* concluding with trumpeter Clark Terry playing Puck and "speaking" the famous Shakespeare line "Lord, what fools these mortals be." As Ted Hudson reported in his examination of the literary sources in Ellington's oeuvre, a "strong-willed Shakespearean lady is depicted in 'Lady Mac,' which begins with a rather regal waltz tempo, changes to 4/4 [a typical jazz tempo], and to support a Clark Terry trumpet solo, changes again to 3/4 [waltz tempo], then ends on a dark chord. Ellington usually introduced the piece with his observation that although Lady Macbeth was of noble birth she had 'a little ragtime in her soul.'"[24]

The album warranted further, perhaps unintended, significance. For decades, Ellington had crafted compositions celebrating and documenting the black American experience. Projects like *Thunder,* and Ellington and Strayhorn's reimagining of Tchaikovsky's *Nutcracker Suite* and Grieg's *Peer Gynt* (both from 1960, and both signifying the first time Ellington dedicated an entire album to a composer besides himself), established the precedent that African American artists could also interpret the finest in highbrow Western culture, and imbue it with a black aesthetic. With these releases, Ellington issued a charming and unspoken reminder that blacks were unlimited in the art they created. When Ellington repeatedly spoke of jazz as representing a uniquely American freedom of expression and of his commitment to making music "beyond category," he meant racial as well as musical categories, seeking to ensure that black artists were not ghettoized in purely black categories and were free to roam anywhere in the musical universe. Albums like *Thunder* were part of a series of subtle statements made during Ellington's career that implied the intertwined relationship between racial equality and artistic freedom.

The unique conceptual slant of *Thunder,* along with the quality of the music, led to some of Ellington's most positive critical notices since World War II. It demonstrated that, since the long-playing record had become increasingly accepted and popular during the 1950s, Ellington did not have to land a Top Forty single in order to secure media attention. The *New York Times* proclaimed *Thunder* "the best work that Mr. Ellington has done in a decade," while the *Louisville Times* termed it "in many ways the best thing Ellington has ever done." *Down Beat* offered "triple congratulations" and their highest five-star rating, musing aloud that the album should make reviewers "ashamed to think of all the relatively trivial releases on which five-star ratings have been squandered" in the past.[25]

At the same time Ellington experienced success with more artistically ambitious projects at Columbia Records, an increase in the serious appreciation of his work was brewing around the world. Two books with a scholarly slant were published concerning Ellington and his work in the late 1950s, both in London: Peter Gammond's *Duke Ellington: His Life and Music* and G. E. Lambert's *Duke Ellington*. They divided his oeuvre into periods, provided biographies of Ellington's most significant sidemen, listed discographies, and, in Gammond's book, included essays by numerous critics and scholars. In 1958, an organization called the Duke Ellington Society formed (originally called the Duke Ellington Jazz Society, but Ellington frowned upon the extra word), in which admirers gathered, usually on a monthly basis, for amateur study of the Ellington phenomenon. By 1960, chapters existed in twenty-five countries, and the New York City chapter initiated a recorded series of group interviews of Ellington musicians, friends, and family that has been used extensively in this book. On 10 March 1959, Ellington dropped in unexpectedly to a meeting of the Hollywood chapter of the Society, regaling the members and serving them ice cream (one of Ellington's favorite foods) until 2:30 AM. This seems to have been the only time Ellington dropped in on a meeting. While he appreciated the interest, and particularly enjoyed meeting society members as he toured foreign countries, he did not want to be too closely aligned to people studying his past; he still had a over a decade of musical progress to achieve and document. He asked his sister Ruth to keep in touch with the chapters of the society because "he's very enthusiastic about this, and very pleased . . . very flattered." But he eschewed any personal involvement for the most part.

The serious recognition was overdue and would only grow as the decades passed; as columnist Murray Kempton pointed out in 1960, which other figures in American culture from the 1920s were still working and relevant in the present day besides William Faulkner and Robert Frost?[26] Yet it wasn't a fair comparison since Faulkner and Frost were already years past their best work, while Ellington still had a decade of musical invention, and some of his best releases were yet to be crafted.

For the remainder of their Columbia tenure, Ellington and the orchestra swayed between varying genres, styles, and concepts. He followed *Such*

Sweet Thunder with *Ellington Indigos* (1957), an album of slow and romantic ballads, older standards written by Ellington alongside well-known chestnuts like Rodgers and Hart's "Where or When." The LP required no careful listening in order to appreciate it, and bore no resemblance to the complex *Thunder*. "For [vocal] soloists to record ballad collections, including current pop songs, is acceptable, but if a big band, even one so distinguished as Ellington's, does it, the automatic response of many listeners and most reviewers is to regard the product as tainted with commercialism," observed Eddie Lambert in the most detailed study of Ellington's musical output. "In fact, *Ellington Indigos* is an LP of superb music-making."[27] Ellington once again was creating sophisticated art out of a very commercial setting, just as he and Strayhorn previously did with Ivie Anderson's vocal sides of the 1930s and 1940s.

Ellington's next album was *Black, Brown and Beige,* a truncated version of the forty-five-minute salute to black history he premiered in 1943. The LP, which featured Mahalia Jackson, the most famous gospel vocalist of all time, mainly utilized themes drawn from the *Black* movement of the work, and critics such as Nat Hentoff complained that Ellington had "unaccountably not taken the opportunity to do the work in full." Such sentiments did not seem to reflect Ellington's intentions, despite the fact that the complete *Black, Brown and Beige* needed and deserved a full recording. His priorities on this not wholly successful project revolved around taking advantage of Jackson's seemingly unlimited vocal range and emotional capacity and reprising two of his most evocative musical themes concerning black history, "Work Song" and "Come Sunday." The latter performance, as Ralph J. Gleason wrote at the time, "resulted in one of the most magnificent recordings either of them [Ellington and Jackson] has ever made, a performance of such tremendous force that this listener had difficulty listening to it dry-eyed." Ellington veteran Ray Nance reported two decades later that he cried when he first heard Jackson sing the song at rehearsal. The album cover and the music reaffirmed Ellington's early and continuing involvement as a musical artist immersed in black history during a time when civil rights protest swelled in the United States. The Mahalia Jackson–accompanied "Come Sunday," one of the most nakedly emotional performances Ellington ever committed to tape, sent a message not just about the history, but also the humanity of black Americans. Such timing and sentiment, arriving on the heels of the televised violence visited upon black students in the 1957 Little Rock incident, probably was no accident. On a late 1957 radio broadcast, Ellington mentioned he had "several requests" for a "re-do" of *Black, Brown and Beige.* "It would be a wonderful background to put on a tremendous pageant," he mused—a goal he would partially realize in 1963 with the *My People* stage show in Chicago.[28]

Diverse concept albums continued throughout the Columbia tenure. *At the Bal Masque* (1958) arrived next, a "satiric set of pop performances" inspired by the collection of masks in the supper room of the Americana Hotel in Miami Beach. *The Cosmic Scene* (1958), whose title celebrated the launch of the first American satellite, was a small band album, made up of a select group of Ellington sidemen called the Spacemen. Neither found favor with record buyers or critics. *Newport 1958* collected a batch of recent and often challenging jazz-oriented works by Ellington and Strayhorn. *Duke Ellington's Jazz Party* (1959) delivered as advertised: enjoyable, easy-going Sunday afternoon jazz with simple song constructions designed to show off the band's soloists, not the band's composers, as *Newport 1958* had done. Still, Ellington and Strayhorn could not resist adding surprise ingredients to the stew, including a team of nine symphonic percussionists on two tracks (on mallet instruments such as marimba and xylophone, which had not appeared on an Ellington session before or since), Basie blues vocalist Jimmy Rushing on one track, and Dizzy Gillespie on two tracks.

Ellington's devotion to composing was particularly illustrated by the story behind the creation of *The Queen's Suite* (1959).[29] On a 1958 European tour, Ellington and the orchestra participated in the first festival of the arts in Leeds, England, where he was presented to Queen Elizabeth. Various reports confirm that they charmed each other. She asked when he first visited her country, and Ellington diplomatically replied "1933, Your Majesty, years before you were born." She expressed regret concerning her inability to attend his concerts on the tour, at which point, according to *Melody Maker,* Ellington's "face puckered into a huge smile." "In that case, your Majesty, I'd like to write a very special composition for you—a real royal suite." The Queen said she would be "delighted," and Ellington set to work.

The six-part *Queen's Suite* resulted, one of the most gorgeous selections in the Ellington canon. It is pastoral jazz adorned with delicate orchestral colors, which, according to Ellington's commentary, sought to compare Queen Elizabeth's beauty and grace to that found in nature. "Sunset and the Mocking Bird" was based on a birdcall Ellington heard in Florida at twilight. "Northern Lights" sought to reflect the beauty of "the greatest display" of the phenomenon he had ever beheld, which happened one night while driving in Canada with his usual traveling partner in the band, Harry Carney.

"Le Sucrier Velours" represented "the name the French have for a bird whose song is as sweet as sugar and who feels as soft as velours," while "Apes and Peacocks" referred to the gifts of the natural world that the Queen of Sheba bestowed upon King Solomon in the Old Testament. "Lightning Bugs and Frogs" sonically illustrated another transfixing scene Ellington witnessed on the road:

> We came out of Cincinnati late one night, took a road to the east on the south shore of the Ohio River, and got lost while searching for the country club we were supposed to play. We ran into an area where the sultry moon was half-hidden by the trees it silhouetted. We stopped short, for there in this huge arena, with the trees as a backdrop, were, it seemed, millions of lightning bugs, dancing in the air. It was a perfect ballet setting, and down below in a gully, like an orchestra pit, could be heard the croaking of frogs.

"The sixth movement, 'The Single Petal of a Rose,'" Ellington explained, referring to one of the most beautiful melodies he ever composed, "represented wonder."

Ellington recorded the *Queen's Suite* at his own expense, separate from his Columbia contract, pressed one copy, and shipped it to Buckingham Palace. He refused to allow its release in his lifetime despite numerous entreaties, though he performed sections of it live with his band, and "The Single Petal of a Rose" became a frequently requested solo piano piece. The royal association in the creation of the suite and its exquisite quality probably would have ensured a larger amount of publicity and sales than usual for an Ellington release, but he forbade this. In his autobiography, just as in the *Queen's Suite,* Ellington used images of nature and divine power to stake out a strong personal position concerning the influence of money and commercialism in art, presenting his feelings about creativity within a spiritual cast:

> There is hardly any money interest in the realm of art, and music will be here when money is gone. After people have destroyed all people everywhere, I see heaping mounds of money strewn over the earth, floating on and sinking into the sea. The animals and fish, who have no use for money, are kicking it out of the way, and splattering it with dung. Money and stink, the stink of dung, the stink of money, so foul that in order for the flowers to get a breath of fresh air, the winds will come together and whip the sea into a rage and blow across the land. Then the green leaves of trees, and grass, will give up their chlorophyll, so that the sea, the wind, the beasts, and the birds will play and sing Nature's old, sweet melody and rhythm.

Such images, with their questioning of societal mores and their espousal of nature and art, could just as easily have emanated from the pens of Walt Whitman, Allen Ginsberg, or Ralph Waldo Emerson.

Next on the continually surprising Ellington Columbia release schedule was Ellington's first film soundtrack, for Otto Preminger's Oscar-nominated *Anatomy of a Murder*.[30] According to *Ebony,* it marked the first time an African American contributed the score for a major film. It followed recent trends of directors using "crime jazz," by black jazz performers Miles Davis and John Lewis in smaller independent and foreign films, and by white film arrangers Johnny Mandel and Elmer Bernstein in mainstream Hollywood fare. Ellington also had a small part portraying Pie-Eye, a jazz musician at a local juke joint performing a brief piano duet with Paul Biegler, the film's main character, played by Jimmy Stewart. Ellington appeared a tad nervous and stiff in his first fictional film role since his promising debut in the 1929 short *Black and Tan*.

Jazz critics mostly frowned on how the music was used for the film, hoping for jazz to infiltrate the Hollywood world in a more forthright fashion. "I had to absorb the atmosphere of the picture," Ellington told a UPI columnist, which is exactly what he did. Ellington's main themes and the ways he reprised them in alternating musical circumstances were not textbook jazz, but they complimented Preminger's determination to keep audiences guessing about the true character and intentions of the protagonists throughout the film. As is true in most soundtracks, Ellington and Preminger did not want the music to stand out. It was designed to blend in and hint at the hidden dark and violent emotions within the outwardly pleasant Michigan town in which the film is set. Movie critics noted and appreciated Ellington's skill at enhancing the film's "mood." Ellington, in responding to the negative reviews of his first crack at a soundtrack, used the critical controversies to underline the reputation he set for himself as a still-developing artist. The sixty-year-old composer told columnist Ralph J. Gleason that "the next [soundtrack] will be better. I'll try another one and I'll show them. I'm young. Give me a chance!" Ironically, the *Anatomy* album brought Ellington his best night ever at the Grammys. He took home three of the statuettes, but few other film scoring opportunities surfaced in ensuing years. Both *Paris Blues* (1961) and *Assault on a Queen* (1966) were lesser projects in terms of film and soundtrack quality. The main reason for the dearth of Ellington film projects probably resided in his unwillingness to interrupt his band's touring for the time required on the set to compose a soundtrack.

"I'll never do anything memorable with film scores, [they're] too restrictive," Ellington said in 1966, after the Frank Sinatra vehicle *Assault on a Queen* tanked at the box office, and no demand arose for an album release of Ellington's music for the film.

Ellington's efforts to build a varied catalog, construct numerous musical identities, and reach disparate audiences with his Columbia albums continued into the early 1960s. *Blues In Orbit* (1960), a collection of relaxed miniatures recorded between midnight and dawn, with melodies and rhythms that burrow into the subconscious, is one of the most criminally neglected albums in the Ellington catalog. Most of the tracks are grounded in the blues, but they are Ellingtonian and Strayhorn-esque blues with appealing quirks that hint at an urbanity and mystery not usually present in blues or big band recordings. The title track featured Ellington contributing trebly stabs of blues piano meant to resemble a satellite's signal against beautifully layered soft horn riffs. Strayhorn's two contributions to the album were particularly excellent: "Sweet and Pungent" was titled perfectly, and "Smada" memorably brought a tangolike feel to the orchestra. Both were simultaneously gorgeous and emotionally painful, a Strayhorn specialty.

Ellington and Strayhorn's playful yet respectful jazz reconstruction of Tchaikovsky's *The Nutcracker Suite* (1960) followed *Orbit*. With its mix of jazz, classical, popular, and holiday elements, along with a strong sense of humor, it had appeal that spanned across the generations. Its novelty status and its quality made it commercial, yet, because of its singular nature in the jazz and pop world, alternative and challenging, a willful blurring of many boundaries. In a year that also saw the release of Ornette Coleman's purposely noncommercial and confrontational *Free Jazz* album, the *Denver Post* reviewer argued that Ellington and Strayhorn (pictured on the cover together) "prove[d] once again that jazz does not have to be obscure to be art."[31] A collection centering on Ellington's piano, *Piano in the Background* (1960), was issued next on Columbia.

A few months later, another 1960 Columbia LP paired Ellington and Strayhorn's take on Grieg's *Peer Gynt,* done in a similar spirit to *Nutcracker,* with their new four-part *Suite Thursday,* another original piece based on literary sources, this time the Cannery Row novels of John Steinbeck.[32] In a lengthy interview about the suite, Ellington demonstrated a familiarity with the books. As in his play *Man with Four Sides,* Ellington seemed drawn to earthy but decent characters who did not follow the dictates of middle-class American mores. He is also clearly attracted to the bittersweet quality of the Steinbeck books, a key component of Ellington's own best work:

The characters, judged by conventional standards, are a lot of social misfits . . . Steinbeck brings them alive and the mood evoked here is, I would say, gay and funny, sad and tragic, conveying through simple people and incidents the essence of human nobility touched with the ridiculous, which give it reality . . . Doc [a marine biologist, the main character] has a theory that the octopus changes color according to its moods, emotions, etc. Now I'm just pulling this out of my head, but we sort of feel the people in Cannery Row change their colors, too. You look at a man, you think he's a bum, but it turns out he's a real angel. Or you think he's a horrible guy, but inside he's—well, dress him in some clean clothes and you find he's a real right guy, and so forth.

Judging people by their souls, instead of clothes or possessions also represented a key theme in Ellington's Sacred Concerts later in the decade.

Reviewers for *Time* and *Metronome* were unimpressed at the premiere of *Suite Thursday* at the 1960 Monterey Jazz Festival, yet six months later, upon its release as an album, most reviewers rhapsodized over it. The *New York Times* termed Ellington "still the pioneer" in its headline, and called *Suite Thursday* "one of his more completely realized extended compositions." Thirteen years later, in his autobiography, Ellington remembered the critical turnabout: "The critics at the festival didn't dig the suite too well, but when the record finally appeared there were a lot of reversed opinions. It wasn't the first time we had experienced that kind of thing!" Like most of Ellington and Strayhorn's more ambitious and satisfying compositions, time and concentration were required for the charms of *Suite Thursday* to assert themselves.

No similarly challenging pieces would be recorded again for Columbia. Ellington's last projects for the label were a piano trio album, a gimmicky *Battle Royal* between his orchestra and that of Count Basie, an adaptation of the Broadway hit *All-American,* and a set of mostly non-Ellington compositions celebrating Paris. From this point forward in Ellington's career, record companies tended to release only recordings that courted this "commercial scene," and they resisted Ellington's more ambitious projects, making him search out one-time licensing deals or forcing him to agree to record what companies deemed more saleable in return for the release of projects they felt possessed little commercial potential. Ironically, neither approach produced a bestselling Ellington album in the 1960s, but the more ambitious and challenging works brought long-term sales and profits to the record companies for decades following their release. As of this writing, *All-American* and *Midnight in Paris* are out of print on Columbia and have never been domestically issued on compact disc, while *Such Sweet Thunder* and *Suite Thursday* are commonly available.

Ellington's contract with Columbia lapsed in mid-1962, and neither party moved to renew it. His recent releases for them were lackluster and overtly commercial, with none of the artistic fervor of earlier releases. Ellington also expressed unhappiness with their lack of promotion, a concern that marked his earlier exits from record labels. Long-time Columbia Records reissue producer Frank Driggs recalled that Columbia executives were not happy with him either. In the last years of Ellington's contract, they refused to send engineers to record significant Ellington concerts, such as his rare solo piano concert at the Museum of Modern Art in 1962. At such times, Columbia insisted Ellington "was over his recording budget," according to Jerry Valburn, an engineer and obsessive Ellington music collector whom the Ellington organization asked to record shows when Columbia or other record companies refused to oblige. According to Driggs, each of the early 1960s Columbia albums sold about seven thousand to ten thousand copies in their initial release, which not only was only a third of his sales performance in the early 1950s, but "did not begin to pay for the cost of the recording." During this period, Clive Davis, the chief executive of Columbia Records, indicated that he wanted no records released that sold less than fifty thousand units. Ellington "was being subsidized to an extent," Driggs said in 1977. "Well, that stopped after a point. Cause Clive Davis sure as hell wasn't going to subsidize him. That was the end of Duke Ellington at Columbia. They just went around saying, 'Duke doesn't sell records.' But they really didn't try to sell them," as Ellington realized.[33] Ellington left Columbia and promptly embarked on one of the greatest years of activity and creativity in his career.

This banner twelve months began with a series of one-off deals for Ellington albums recorded with famous jazz personalities. For the rest of his career, except for his tenure at Reprise Records from late 1962 until 1965, this kind of business arrangement characterized his usual relationship with record companies. He would lease his services, or already recorded or conceived albums, to companies for an upfront advance, often for one album at a time. No longer would he be asked to sign record contracts for his exclusive services over a certain period of time, where he could record anything he wanted. In some ways, this demonstrated his declining power in the music business, but it also allowed him the freedom to negotiate among companies to release what he wanted, instead of being contractually obligated to produce albums for a company that might demand more commercial or less challenging products than he wished to produce, as probably happened with Columbia, and later, Reprise.

In this economic environment, the recording advance paid to Ellington became all important because he and the companies knew that he would probably never earn enough royalties to recoup royalties against his advance. For example, the contract for his album recorded with Charles Mingus and Max Roach for United Artists in 1962 awarded Ellington a $6,000 advance, with the proviso that $4,000 of that "shall be deemed an advance against royalties which may become payable hereunder." At roughly the same time, Ellington signed a deal with the independent jazz label Impulse for two similar albums that paired him with John Coltrane and Coleman Hawkins for what was probably a similar advance of roughly $12,000. Three years after the release of these albums, despite uniformly good reviews, Ellington had seen no royalties after his advance, and needed to earn over $7,500 in royalties in order to earn back his advance and start actually receiving his royalties, which almost certainly never happened within his lifetime.[34] This is not to say that the companies cheated Ellington; he received good money for his advance, and they received an Ellington album for their catalogs that returned revenue for decades with little additional investment.

The three albums recorded in the fall of 1962 for United Artists and Impulse were musically delightful, and historically significant. One could not imagine another member of Ellington's generation coexisting so comfortably and creatively with the most innovative young lions of the jazz world. *Money Jungle,* recorded with Mingus and Roach, is, at its best, raw, spare, and adventurous, with unexpected flares of bebop surfacing within old Ellington compositions, alongside new Ellington ideas quickly and specifically composed for the occasion. *Duke Ellington and John Coltrane,* while sometimes a little stiff, offered a chance to hear two of jazz's primary iconoclasts and innovators finding common musical ground, despite their thirty-year age difference. *Duke Ellington Meets Coleman Hawkins* may rank as the best of the three, a warm excursion between what seemed on the record to be two relaxed old friends along with a small band of Ellington veterans. In actuality, Ellington and Hawkins, despite emerging in the New York jazz scene at roughly the same time in the mid-1920s, had never played together.

On 28 November 1962 in Chicago, at what *Billboard* called "easily the loudest, swingingest, brassyest, most-sought-after and most-crashed cocktail party of the year," Frank Sinatra, flanked by Sammy Davis, Jr., and Dean Martin, announced the signing of Ellington to his new label, Reprise Records. The prognosis for an artistically and financially fulfilling relationship looked good. Reprise's billings doubled in the last quarter of 1962, which bode well for future Ellington recording budgets and promotion. Also, Ellington signed as an artists-and-repertoire (A&R) executive as well as an artist, able to sign and produce other artists for the "Ellington Jazz Wing" at Reprise, an industry position never accorded to an artist before, and given to exceedingly few blacks. (A few days afterward, Atlantic Records offered a similar position to John Lewis of the Modern Jazz Quartet, a successful act on their label.) "I thought it would be a very good idea to be contracted to some company which is controlled by an artist rather than a businessman," Ellington commented. In an interview with *Jet,* Ellington said he signed with "Frank because we're trying to do the same thing—improve America's musical taste. We also believe in the same thing—a country free of bigotry." Ellington mentioned Sinatra's efforts speaking out against racism, which earned him a special award from the Academy of Motion Picture Arts and Sciences in the mid-1940s.[35]

The Reprise years did not live up to their advance billing for the most part, but the first three months of the contract produced superlative work. The first release, *Afro-Bossa,* was part of Ellington and Strayhorn's continuing exploration of internationally inspired sounds. Layered percussion along with mysterious and lovely muted-horn arrangements combined to create one of Ellington's best albums of all time, modern yet sometimes faintly reminiscent of the "jungle jazz" of the Cotton Club days. Reviewers almost uniformly praised it as another example of Ellington refusing to rest on his laurels, and many surmised that its quality had been influenced by the fact that Ellington was fully in charge of his sessions at Reprise.[36] Ellington also recorded *The Symphonic Ellington,* an album that paired his orchestra with several European symphony orchestras and provided the long-overdue opportunity to record the symphonic version of *Harlem,* as well as the three-part, seventeen-minute *Night Creature,* both premiered with symphony orchestras in the mid-1950s. Another excellent album, *Duke Ellington's Jazz Violin Session,* was waxed in February 1963. Recorded in Paris, it consisted of Ellington's rhythm section (with Ellington on piano), along with three violinists, Ray Nance (from the Ellington orchestra), Svend Asmussen, and Stephane Grappelli. It was a joyful and surprising meeting, and nothing quite like it exists in the Ellington catalog.

Subsequent Reprise albums proved less impressive. The band recorded two albums' worth of big band classics made famous by other bandleaders. Many of the Strayhorn and Ellington arrangements recast old favorites in daring and emotional new ways, but some also coasted listlessly, and they did not reach the commercial audience they aimed for. Two more albums,

Ellington '65 and *Ellington '66,* featured the Ellington orchestra waxing the pop hits of the day, something that they frequently did during the 1930s. Hearing the band interpret the Beatles and hoary hit songs such as "Danke Schoen" was amusing, but broke no new artistic or commercial ground, and seemed disposable. The band's 1964 recordings of songs from the *Mary Poppins* soundtrack were better, but mostly in the same category. More problems seemed to lurk behind the scenes: Ralph J. Gleason reported that Reprise refused to release the *My People* album, an album celebrating black history. At least half of the albums Ellington produced for the label by other artists sat in the vaults, and he did little if any A&R work in the last half of his tenure with them. *Duke Ellington's Jazz Violin Session* and many of the best of the big band retreads were inexplicably not released until after Ellington's death.

Even with an artist as sympathetic to Ellington as Sinatra at the helm, the market could not be found by a large record company to present Ellington in the way that he desired. In retrospect, the result was not surprising: before Ellington arrived, Reprise was mostly filled with middle-of-the-road artists such as Martin, Davis, and Rosemary Clooney, who did not fit in with the rock music dominating the music business. In the months after Warner Brothers bought Reprise for $3.5 million in the late summer of 1963, the jazz artists were gradually moved off the label, perhaps as a measure of consolidation instituted by Warners limiting Reprise to the market that it knew and served best. "What happens to Duke now?" asked *Jet.*[37]

But the first three months of the Reprise deal marked the site of an enormous amount of varying and satisfying creativity, adding to one of the finest years in Ellington's career. From September 1962 to September 1963, Ellington produced the albums with Mingus and Roach, Coltrane, Hawkins, *Afro-Bossa, The Symphonic Ellington, Duke Ellington's Jazz Violin Session,* and *My People.* Not bad for a man a few months away from Social Security eligibility.

10
MONEY

In good business practices, the first thing that you do is that you know what the thing will pay, the average, I mean what bands normally are getting, and if you have a hot record or a medium-hot record, you're worth so much money, or if you're not hot, you're only worth so much, and if somebody needs you bad enough, you're worth so much money, or something like that. I mean, Fridays is probably the biggest day in the week, Saturday's the next, Sunday's the next, and the rest of them you can't give away, you know. But the good way to [do] business is, first, you have to adjust your budget . . . first of all, the leader has to have this amount of money each week. Now, how much can we afford to spend for a band? How much can we afford to spend for arrangements? How much can we afford to spend for transportation out of this? And then you always figure that according to the net, after the agent's commission. This is sound business practice. But the way we operate just doesn't make sense, and a lot of people look at me like I'm an idiot, and maybe I am. As a business man, I certainly must be.

DUKE ELLINGTON, 1964[1]

Previous chroniclers of Duke Ellington's life, as well as Ellington himself, referred to him as a poor businessman. What the Ellington business records and various interviews reveal is that he was actually successful in achieving his goals, which mirrored the priorities of other black entrepreneurs of the period. While he made a lot of money over the course of his career, he did not accumulate wealth in the classic Andrew Carnegie fashion, extracting profit from each division in the most efficient manner and amassing a fortune—though with the high amount of royalties pouring into Tempo Music and Duke Ellington, Inc., he certainly could have. Instead, he sought to support friends, family, and community, the fulltime touring of his orchestra, and, perhaps most importantly, his composing and his ability to hear his work immediately. On his own terms, helping those he loved and keeping his five-decade streak of creativity going strong, Ellington proved extraordinarily successful in wielding his economic power.

Ellington had a steady income even without performing. His annual songwriting royalties alone in 1964, the first year in which near-complete figures are available in his business papers stored at the Smithsonian, were at least $100,000.[2] Recording royalties brought in further, though smaller, proceeds. Ellington's total royalties from 1964, according to tax documents, were $133,802.57. In today's dollars, that would be about $900,000 annually in royalties, and the succeeding five years listed in the same document show that rate holding steady, averaging about $123,000 per year in royalties.[3] If Ellington had stayed home and composed during the 1950s and 1960s, he and his family could have lived a financially comfortable existence.

But carrying an orchestra filled with gifted players, many of whom could have enjoyed solo careers and needed to be compensated commensurately, ensured an economic struggle. "The payroll I've got is criminal, I have 24 guys on my payroll," Ellington told a reporter in 1959. "They're [paid the] equivalent to about 100 workers employed by a small plant."[4] The numbers in the Ellington business papers, though incomplete in spots, tell the story. Duke Ellington, Inc., operated at a loss four of the seven years from 1953 to 1960, according to their annual statements of operations. The three years of profit (1956, 1958, and 1959) brought in just $9,984.18, $8,510.71, and $1,393.21 of profit, after income and royalties of roughly $350,000 to $400,000. The numbers may be somewhat incomplete or cooked (the IRS certainly thought that deductible expenses such as tips, alcohol, and

FIGURE 9. Duke Ellington and his son Mercer in the mid-1960s. After financial improprieties occurred on the road and probably at the offices of Duke Ellington, Inc., Ellington asked his son in 1964 to assume the jobs of road manager and trumpet player, duties
that Mercer fulfilled until his father's death a decade later. Mercer had unimpeachable
loyalty to Ellington and ensured that such improprieties ceased in the Ellington organization. Frank Driggs Collection.

flowers were), but booking contracts, road expenses, and band salaries are fairly well documented. In 1956 and 1960, salaries for the band, vocalists, and staff each year ran about $190,000, with Ellington's salary as bandleader adding $20,800, and $25,000, respectively. These expenses ate up more than half of the income and royalties accruing to Duke Ellington, Inc. Travel expenses in 1956 and 1960 ran to $51,288.62 and $78,861.93, respectively. Various federal, state, local, and union tax charges and disability insurance payments on behalf of employees added $5,298.31, and $10,047.01, respectively. Already, the above expenses accounted for over three-quarters of the income and royalties coming in to Duke Ellington, Inc. Additional expenses such as retaining a lawyer and accountant, telephone and telegraph services, office rent, advertising, music copying, and photographs contributed to a situation in which half the time from 1953 to 1960, Duke Ellington, Inc., did not make a profit, according to its records.[5] The financial situation did not change appreciably during the 1960s and 1970s.

Ellington acknowledged the economic bind his band put him in, but did not seem to mind. He welcomed it and constantly bragged to reporters about the financial inadvisability of carting around a big band fifty-two weeks a year. "They get the money, and I get the kicks!" became a mantra of his. "Man, if it wasn't for kicks, there would be no point. If you don't get a kick out of music, it'll whip you," Ellington told the *Detroit Free Press* in 1963. "There's not enough money in the big band business. To stay in it is not sound business, but it's enjoyable and I don't have any ambition to quit."[6]

Duke Ellington, Inc., and Ellington's entire life centered on the pleasure, the addiction, the intimate relationship he had with music and composing. When asked in the mid-1960s if a possible big band revival would increase his fortunes, Ellington scoffed that he never spoke or thought about trends, popularity, and other trappings of the business end of music. "I'm not interested in business. I'm not a business man," he said in a radio interview. "I have a thing with music . . . it has nothing to do with money . . . the way I do [music] there isn't much chance of making any." Ellington told Carter Harman in 1964 that "it's impossible" to enter the big band business until one has decided "whether or not you want to make money or play music, I think. I don't think in terms of posterity, or anything like that, you know, I don't give a shit about it. But I do believe in the idea of enjoying what I am doing. I think this is a helluva healthy thing." Ellington knew the price he paid for these decisions and mused about them to Harman: "I'm not very material minded, I don't think, considering. If I did, I'd have a million dollars or more. A couple million."[7]

Money was not for amassing, in Ellington's view, it was for using immediately, while alive, to take care of what he loved: composing, family, friends. When those items were taken care of, he did not wish to even speak of money. "Money didn't mean nothing to Duke. He wouldn't let that worry him," recalled Al Celley, the band's long-serving road manager. "Yeah, he spent it, but he . . . wouldn't let it come in the way of any happiness or dishappiness with him. He'd say to me, 'That's your problem.'" Clark Terry, along with other band members, recalled that once Ellington hired a musician, he never discussed money with them, leaving salary negotiations to Celley after Ellington made clear to Celley how he wanted the matter handled. Terry said he stood "totally aloof from all the business garbage." Celley and Ellington vocalist Herb Jeffries testified that this had been the case since at least the early 1940s. As Ellington put it in 1964, when some band members were demanding more money during a European tour: "I can't waste my strength bullshitting somebody for a hundred dollars . . . the doctor's bill oughta be about $10,000 trying to get back what I lose in the argument." Wherever possible, Ellington shielded himself from the stress that money could create to preserve his stamina and health for composing and touring, but he kept close track of the salaries of the orchestra.[8]

From the early 1950s, George Wein hired the Ellington orchestra hundreds of times for dates around the world. He provided many interesting insights concerning Ellington and money. "You have to understand Duke Ellington's attitude about money. It didn't exist for him," he told the Smithsonian in 1991. "Duke didn't want to know, and didn't want to be bothered. He really did not care about business. He was concerned about music, and the business would take care of itself." In Wein's experience, Ellington left all business details to others in his organization. Whenever Wein, a fellow pianist as well as a promoter, brought up something even peripherally related to business, Ellington charmingly reprimanded him: "George, when two artists are talking, we should never discuss money or business, we should only discuss the music." Wein was convinced that Ellington did not care for money as a means to profit. But he did pay attention to money as a marker of respect:

> I had one fight with Duke Ellington once, and it wasn't a fight that I knew of, it was a betrayal of a confidence . . . Duke worked a lot for me, worked all my festivals, worked the clubs, worked concerts. I think I paid him for one of the concerts at Newport . . . maybe $6,000 a night for the band. And Benny Goodman, who didn't have a band, I put together a special band for him, this might have been '59—it was costing me $10,000 a night . . . Columbia Records, 'cause they were recording the programs . . . would. . . . give the festival the equivalent of what we were paying the artists. So, I told them what we

were paying Ellington, I told them what we were paying Goodman. So, we got that money from Columbia Records and they recorded [the shows] . . . this [Columbia] executive told Duke that I was paying Goodman more than I was paying him. And Duke didn't care what I was paying him, he probably didn't *know* what I was paying him, but [now that] he knew, his ego was such [that he was thinking], why was I [Wein] paying Benny Goodman more than I was Duke Ellington? And Duke gave me a freeze for 2 years. So I went to him one day and I said, "Duke, what's happening, you and I used to have [a good relationship]." He says "Well you pay Benny Goodman more." I said, "Is that what you're mad at me about? I can't believe it. I use you 20 to 30 times a year, I use Benny Goodman once, I put together a special band, and you hold *that* against *me*?" We straightened [it] out after that . . . It shows you the attitude of artists. It's the status that was more important than the money, in many cases.

In the same vein, Wein told stories concerning Ellington's insistence on always having top billing, a detail he showed much more concern about than the amount of his paycheck. "He was very, very concerned about that. He had respect for these other people, but he had a lot of respect for himself, and the years he put in to develop his name and of course they were all children compared to him," Wein said. Ellington always won billing conflicts with "currently hot" stars like Lena Horne, Mort Sahl, and Mel Tormé. He threatened on at least two occasions to leave a gig rather than accept a lower billing. Bookers and acts backed down before that occurred. Wein pointed out that "the fact that they might have been more popular at a given moment did not mean anything to Duke. He might have been getting less money than they were on that bill, but the status was very important to him, and the recognition and respect. And he deserved it, of course. I always backed it up. I never would put anybody over Duke Ellington."[9]

Ellington was also concerned that he possessed the money to live in a certain style on the road. Starting in the 1950s, he usually had his own room, often in a separate and better hotel than the band. Friends and associates recalled that he wanted privacy, for composing and for his personal life, more than he wanted luxury and that he "loved" life on the road. Clark Terry said that Ellington referred to himself as a "chronic tourist" and that "he thrived on it, absolutely. He's not a person who has a luxurious layout as far as acreage, swimming pool, he didn't care anything about that." "I'm a hotel man," Ellington said in 1956. "I like being alone, you know. I don't know why." Wein recalled that, unlike other artists he dealt with, Ellington preferred to pay his own way. To be able to entertain in a grand style was important to him: "You'd go to Duke's room to say something to him, and if he was eating, he says, 'Sit down and have dinner.' He'd order room service, a steak dinner, and he would pay for it. He was lavish in his generosity, as far as that kind of generosity."

Ellington's wardrobe was another area in which he splurged. Not only did he need to look his best on stage, but immaculate and stylish clothing had functioned as an Ellington trademark since his Washington days. Ellington could also engage in profligate spending when abroad, buying souvenirs and expensive items he rarely saw again, according to H. Robert Udkoff, a close friend. "When I was in Europe with him in '58, he bought a set of service for 18 in Royal Copenhagen sterling, and then he bought dishes . . . and shipped it home," recalled Udkoff. "When he lived with Evie in Central Park South they had one room . . . absolutely crammed with boxes of things that he had purchased that had probably never been opened up." [10]

After composing, the most important financial consideration for Ellington was to ensure his ability to support a large number of family and friends. [11] Some of this activity is reflected in the Ellington business records, and some of it was off the books (perhaps to conceal such activity from the IRS), but remembered by those close to him and in the band. The priorities he exhibited resemble other black business priorities of the period. Business in black communities was not usually viewed as a strictly-for-profit, financially enriching personal enterprise, but as an endeavor designed to reflect well upon the black community as a whole and support friends and family. [12]

"He operated like the father of a big family," commented Stanley Dance, a journalist who traveled frequently with Ellington during the last fifteen years of Ellington's life, and who also did occasional jobs for Tempo Music. "He protected, looked after [his son] Mercer, his sister [Ruth]." According to Phoebe Jacobs, an Ellington family friend and publicist, Ellington regularly signed off on luxurious purchases for Ruth including numerous mink coats. Jacobs recalled a man coming to a club she was involved with, Basin Street East in New York City, in the 1960s and asking for $3,000 for the mink coat he had in a box for Ruth. Jacobs called Ellington, who calmly replied, "Well, give the man what he wants." She remembered Ellington as "very gracious" with his family. Mercer Ellington recalled that his father supported his extended family "to the greatest extent that was possible. He supported everybody in it. He could have had so much more for himself . . . He supported his mother's sister Flossie [Florence Hartgrave], 'til she passed away. And any obligations that would come along he took care of. There's only one time I know of that he didn't take care of me." Ellington bought two buildings on St. Nicholas Avenue for his sister and son to live in, an investment managed by J. E. Daisy Corporation, an amalgamation of his parents' names.

Ruth Ellington still ran Tempo Music in the 1960s, as she had since Ellington set up the publishing company in 1940. Some close to Ellington felt that Tempo "never properly exploited" Ellington's music to yield its full financial potential. While the company hired song pluggers to promote Ellington and Strayhorn's work to various artists and bands during the 1940s, no one did such work in the 1960s except for Ruth, who also had to look after paying Ellington's bills, registering his copyrights, and the day-to-day business of running a publishing company. "It wasn't really very efficiently run," recalled Stanley Dance. While Ellington probably would not have had hit singles in the 1960s even with better promotion, more aggressive song plugging could have resulted in more covers of his songs in the burgeoning MOR (middle of the road) market of the 1960s, represented by artists like Tony Bennett, Vicki Carr, and Andy Williams.

Despite his obvious devotion to his family, Ellington seemed to be happiest alone. The situation represented a dichotomy that a few people commented upon. "I know at certain times he liked having family around and he appreciated the times we were together at parties and he'd be over at Ruth's," his granddaughter Mercedes Ellington recalled in 1980. "But it was still out of his realm. I really do think he felt more at home in a hotel room with his piano." Irving Townsend, a Columbia producer and a close Ellington friend, commented on the arrangement Ellington created for himself:

> There was no large city, no small town in the country where an old friend or an old girl or both did not wait for the next one-night visit. These friendships too were for life, but they suited Ellington best because they were renewed, enjoyed, and suspended again, usually within a twenty-four-hour period. The secret of Duke's security was constant movement . . . A thousand hotel rooms, a thousand room-service waiters ready to push his breakfast table in on cue, a thousand loyal friends waiting to handle any local problems he might have: these made up the Ellington ménage. Except for daily calls to Billy Strayhorn or to Arthur Logan or to his sister, Ellington was out of town to most of his friends and family. Still, I believe Duke Ellington was the most sentimental family man I have ever known. He kept in touch with all of us and never lost one of us . . . We also knew that every now and then the phone would ring between six P.M. and six A.M. A dark, sleepy voice, "Good morning. Did I wake you? I'm so sorry. What time is it anyway? What's happening?" Duke was back.[13]

Old friends and band members depended on Ellington, receiving substantial help from him over the years, particularly in the 1950s and 1960s. Though no records in the Smithsonian's Ellington collections confirm this, numerous sources confirmed that drummer Sonny Greer was paid regularly by the Ellington organization for years, and probably decades, after Greer left the band in the early 1950s. "Of course, Sonny never felt like he got enough," recalled Udkoff, laughing as he told a story that illustrated Greer's notorious sense of humor. "I remember Sonny coming in to [Ellington's] dressing room . . . I think it may have been in the Rainbow Grill [in the 1970s], he came in and he says [to Ellington], "You [motherfucker], you stole my band!" You know he's talking about the Washingtonians [in the mid-1920s]."

Ellington's nephew Michael James, who accompanied him on tours, did odd jobs for Ellington and his businesses, and sometimes advised him on potential musicians for the orchestra in the 1960s and 1970s, described Ellington's attitude on aiding old friends and musicians:

> There was a guy on 129th Street [that] I took a check to a couple times. A guy that took care of Duke when he first came to New York . . . he let [Ellington and Greer] stay in his apartment when they ran out of money and work, know what I mean? Took care of him for the rest of his life . . . Duke didn't forget anybody. People that had contributed, that had helped him at different stages of his life, turning points that were key. And so when he got in a position where he was better off than they are, that would be his way of thanking them. And then Sonny Greer would be more like a family member. Sonny had been with him since the beginning . . . he had been closer with Sonny than almost anybody else. Came to New York together, lived together. So he'd want to look out for Sonny and his wife. And there was always people he was giving money to irregularly, out-of-work musicians, you know. All musicians in the jazz world knew that you could go to Duke if you were uptight. Duke don't ever say no . . . He'd tell 'em to go by the office or something to get a check, or he'd call and tell them "So-and-so is coming by." 'Cause Duke very rarely carried money on him in later years, he might ask me for a pack of cigarettes or something! [laughs][14]

Ellington also pursued a very liberal policy in granting loans to band members, particularly the bigger stars, and then forgetting about those loans. Accounting ledgers from 1960 to 1964 show most band members with loans of several hundred—and sometimes several thousand—dollars, with no indication of any of it getting paid back. According to Al Celley, Ellington's attitude on the subject was "Keep your band happy. What's the matter?

Don't fight your men. Let them have what they want." He also reported that the money lost from the loans came from the "corporate funds" of Duke Ellington, Inc., and that Ellington signed off on all IOUs. These financial patterns perhaps suggest something telling about the Ellington personality, something intertwined in his need for an audience as well as his love for being alone and in his propensity for doing financial favors for people he rarely saw. Perhaps in addition to expressing affection for these people, Ellington's financial giveaways also meant to keep some of them at arm's length and to allow more time for composing or whatever he wished to dedicate his private time to doing. George Wein expressed shock at the economic structure of the band and Ellington's cavalier attitude toward money:

> Ask Jimmy Woode [Ellington bass player in the 1950s and 1960s] about finances in Duke's band; ask Jimmy Woode how much he owed Duke Ellington when Duke let him go because he was always borrowing money from Duke. Most of the musicians did that. Paul Gonsalves [star Ellington sax soloist as well as an alcoholic and drug user], he never got a week's pay, they just carried him. Because whatever money he got, he would drink. No band in the world ran like the Duke Ellington band. If [Ellington] needed money, he would call somebody and say "I need 10, I need 20, I need 50, I need 100," and somebody would give it to him, on an advance against work, off an advance against songs, or whatever the case may be. I don't know the details, I just know that they were always in debt.

The 1960–64 Duke Ellington, Inc., accounting ledgers also show thousands of dollars in loans to Evie Ellis, including over $25,000 in 1961 alone. There are no indications in later ledgers that it was paid back.[15] The loans were probably used as a way for Ellington to support his long-time romantic partner without having to report such gifts to the IRS.

Ellington also extensively drew cash from his account at Associated Booking Corporation (ABC), his booking agency. Throughout the 1950s and 1960s, he constantly owed them money for advances forwarded him. In 1965, these debts totaled over $67,000. Starting in 1964 and continuing until at least 1968, Ellis was also regularly paid from the ABC account, usually $1,000 to $2,000 per month, even while she still had loans on the books from Duke Ellington, Inc. There are records of Ellis receiving money from Ellington's ABC account in the five years before that as well, but not as regularly. Sometimes Ellington would assign other debts and expenses to be paid through the account, including clothing, medical costs, publicity, and, one time, $1,000 that Joe Glaser said Ellington owed to a "number's man." In an April 1960 letter to William Mittler, the accountant at Duke Ellington,

Inc., Glaser notes paying $3,312.50 in medical expenses to Ellington's doctor and close friend Arthur Logan: "I am sure you know the situation with Duke's account, and I do hope he tries to live within his means." It seemed that he probably did not: in the last six months of 1960, Ellington asked for and received at least $8,500 in further advances from ABC.

These longstanding loans and advances not only placed Ellington and his organization further in debt, but they also gave ABC and its abrasive, tough-talking, ex-gangster founder Joe Glaser an amount of leverage and power in Ellington's life that often made Ellington uncomfortable. Wein was aware of these issues and claimed that Ellington at one point in the early to mid-1960s was "feeling me out to see if I could be his manager" because of his frustration with Glaser:

> The structure of an artist is sometimes such that he needs money. And Joe Glaser was always quick to lend out his money. And when you owe a man money, you're more or less bound to pay him back, one way or the other. And the way you pay him back is by staying in his stable. It's sort of a plantation philosophy . . . I mean, Joe Glaser was a business man, and if he could control people by money, he controlled them by money. He did a lot of good, he didn't do any bad, but I mean he certainly controlled a lot of artists' lives the way he wanted to control them. And Ellington, for a while, was under his yoke.

During the same period, Udkoff, Ellington's friend as well as a successful business man with connections in the entertainment business, offered negotiating and financial help to Ellington to absolve his debt to ABC, but he said Ellington felt the problem was too "overwhelming."[16]

Ellington's generosity, his live-and–spend-for-today attitude, and his insistence on carrying a large band weren't his only economic impediments. The big band business was difficult and declining. Despite constant touring, some excellent albums, and more media coverage than almost any other jazz act during the 1956–63 period, the Ellington orchestra was still making basically the same amount of money per night and per year they were making in the mid-1940s, without adjustment for inflation.[17] The Ellington band was doing very well for a full-time big band working fifty-two weeks a year. But they were the only such band in a marketplace that had changed dramatically since the Swing Era's halcyon days. Basie's band worked most, but not all, of the year; bands led by veterans like Woody Herman and Stan Kenton worked less; and the new big bands of the 1950s and 1960s, such as the one led by Thad Jones and Mel Lewis, assembled for short tours and recording sessions. With a freak exception like Basie's "April in Paris" (1955), these bands did not enjoy radio or chart hits. The most popular jazz acts of the mid-1950s and onward, on the charts and on the road, were smaller, less economically taxing combos of four to six men like the ones led by Dave Brubeck (the most popular jazz figure of the 1950s) and Miles Davis. The Ellington and Strayhorn influence was abundant in this new generation of successful jazz artists. To name just three, the Modern Jazz Quartet (MJQ) and arrangers Nelson Riddle and Gil Evans filtered the elegance, sophistication, and artistic formality of the Ellington/Strayhorn sound through their own profitable musical ventures.[18] But the MJQ toured with just four people, not the fifteen-plus musicians, along with vocalists and assistants, that Ellington carried. Riddle and Evans utilized and extended the lush and sophisticated arranging styles of Ellington and Strayhorn in albums for Frank Sinatra and Miles Davis, respectively, which outsold Ellington heavily in the 1950s. Both Davis and Sinatra rarely played live with orchestras of the size they recorded with, while Ellington always did.

Ellington's name and image were often seen in the media, but his box-office reputation was declining, especially in the largest urban areas where the band faced substantial entertainment competition. Phoebe Jacobs recalled how Ellington fared at Basin Street East during that period:

> Ralph Watkins [owner of the club] would hire Duke Ellington, and I think that if his partners could, they would have shot him. Because you could run deer through the place, ten people would be here. He never did business, never. In the Rainbow Grill [a venue at the top of Rockefeller Center that catered to a swankier crowd in the late 1960s and 1970s], yes, he did business, but in Basin Street, maybe Saturday night he was busy, or if he did a dance, [but] other than that, no. Louis Armstrong, there were lines around the block, you'd have to get the ropes out. We would pay Duke Ellington $8,500 [a week] for 14 men, you'd pay $12,000 for Louis Armstrong with 5 men . . . Duke had the same kind of electricity [as a personality and a celebrity that Armstrong did], it's just that he wasn't as commercially successful in those days . . . I mean, Billy Eckstine was famous and good, because he was a singer, as was Nat King Cole, or Ella Fitzgerald . . . Duke Ellington was strictly music.

George Wein found that, in order to be successful with Ellington performances, one could not book him as just another jazz or popular act. He usually was a lucrative act under special conditions that recognized his status as an artist who created works beyond usual categorizations. "Ellington was always perceived as a genius, and he had nothing but respect, [but] he was never the box office success that he should have been," Wein recollected. "Ellington was a risk when you bought him, you weren't sure to make money with Ellington . . . Packaged correctly, like I did at some of my festivals, I mean he was the biggest possible star you could have. But he was not a pop artist."[19]

As the band's economic fortunes on the road declined, so did onstage discipline, the fancy staging and lighting schemes, and the band's habit of dressing in uniforms and the finest outfits. Part of the reason for this rested in the relaxation of formal clothing standards in America throughout the 1950s and 1960s, but some of it was probably prompted by the lesser fortunes of Duke Ellington, Inc. Most observers in the band's universe suggested that the Ellington of the 1950s and 1960s, no longer seen as a top hit act, cared only about his music and whether it was played well. Reviewers sometimes castigated Ellington for allowing band members to stumble onstage late, or occasionally fall asleep or (more rarely) fight during shows. "As long as they played music on the bandstand, he didn't care" what the band members did the rest of the time, Celley recalled. "That's how he kept them together, he didn't get into their fights, see, he let 'em go . . . they'd be on the bandstand with their backs to each other" in anger, but if they played well, Ellington did not bother them. Clark Terry said that Ellington believed the musicians he hired were adults who should discipline themselves, and play with discipline, without him having to remind them. "I'm not a disciplinarian," Ellington regularly told the band. Michael James explained the psychology behind the seeming lack of discipline among Ellington band members on stage:

[Ellington] understood human beings so well, men in particular. That's why he was able to handle his men in a way even musicians marveled, [and] the other band leaders . . . There were these watering holes where [famous jazz musicians] would all stop in after their business was finished and they would congregate . . . and they would all ask me, "Look, who's *running* that band?" Cause they couldn't understand: "I went to see Duke and Johnny Hodges got up and went to the bar to get a drink, so-and-so went to the bathroom and come back [in the middle of a show]." Most musicians would be threatened [by such behavior], like a challenge to their leadership, where Duke was never threatened . . . never afraid of his men . . . partly because he understood that he was doing something none of them could do. So there was no competition. He was not another instrumentalist [he was the leader and composer].

He had a Shakespearean understanding of human beings. That if you're going to keep men, talented, gifted men, with you for 30 years, 40 years, you're not going to be able to hold them with tight regimentation, like a Lunceford, a Tommy Dorsey . . . what Basie did [in the 1950s and afterward] was get a bunch of solid, professional musicians, and they weren't like Prez [Lester Young, jazz legend and Basie sax player of the 1930s and 1940s] and those [kinds of] guys, they weren't individualists. When you're dealing with creative unique personalities [as Ellington continued to do], you got to allow for the eccentricities of the man. It's all tied up with that uniqueness that's in the music. So, Duke respected that, you know, being a genius himself. So he could understand that that's a given with [such gifted] human beings. And he also appreciated some of it, some of it he was even amused by, you know what I mean?

Norman Granz, the jazz entrepreneur, recalled Ellington going on stage more than once during this period with only three or four musicians with him on stage, while the others were late or off carousing somewhere in the venue. "He made it very clear . . . certainly to me, that there was only one indispensable person in that whole orchestra, and that was Duke," Granz commented. "If nobody else showed up, that's OK, I'm the one."[20]

Ellington was not alone in his economic problems; most jazz figures of the period shared them. At the beginning of 1959, *Metronome* reported that only three jazz performers (Armstrong, Basie, and Brubeck) acted as "loss leaders" for jazz clubs across the country. The editors of *Metronome* further argued that the jazz that did well in clubs was "jazz with strings attached . . . the new audience was more conservative than the usual jazz listener." This audience gravitated toward acts that provided "*excitement,*" received national magazine coverage, and performed recognizable material "just like it was on the record," with little experimentation or new improvisation.[21] Ellington could and did satisfy this market in his shows, and seemed happy to do so, but he harbored other priorities as well.

Despite his reputation as a serious composer, Ellington recognized the dangers of becoming too snobbish toward his music or audience. "People will not come into places where jazz enthusiasts congregate if they are going to be made to feel ignorant," he said in 1960. "They may be afraid to buy a ticket and sit in the audience because the man next to them might look down his nose at them, so to speak, with a flatted fifth." Ellington released baldly commercial albums and regularly played older tunes and hits medleys. He usually did well in the Midwest, where big acts came more rarely and where he still retained a sizeable number of Swing Era fans that wanted nostalgia more than innovation. He didn't mind providing that for them, albeit with some newer material mixed in, as various reviews from the period demonstrate. With every night and every new record, Ellington tinkered with a precarious balance between going forward and providing nostalgia, between pushing the envelope and pulling in crowds, between making money and making art. "It is not that Duke wants to forget the past," Wein wrote in a 1957 article. "It is just that his experience has been that every time he has taken a step in a forward direction he has met with only reluctant acceptance, even by his most ardent fans."[22]

The economics of the 1950s and 1960s jazz scene made effective booking even more important than usual. The large booking agencies that emerged during the Swing Era for big bands mostly folded when the Swing Era did. In 1951, Ellington signed with Associated Booking Corporation (ABC), headed by Joe Glaser.[23] Armstrong biographer Laurence Bergreen chronicled Glaser's sordid past in the 1920s and 1930s, when he worked in Chicago jazz clubs run by gangsters and, at the very least, ran prostitutes and received a conviction on a rape charge and an indictment for receiving stolen liquor during Prohibition. By the mid-1950s, Glaser had seemingly shed most of these unsavory associations to assemble one of the more impressive music booking and management companies of the period. But, as admirers of Glaser such as Avakian, Wein, and Village Vanguard owner Max Gordon said long after Glaser's death, Glaser was "obscene," "coarse," "threatening," and often lied in his business dealings. He specialized in black and jazz performers, such as Lionel Hampton and his primary client and very good friend Louis Armstrong, but he also worked in other entertainment branches, managing and booking Barbra Streisand, among others, during the 1960s. Armstrong was especially loyal to Glaser, from 1935, when their professional relationship began, until the end of his life in 1970, calling him "Daddy" and entrusting him with all his money and financial decisions. Armstrong's wife Lucille and Bergreen suggest that Glaser took an astonishing 50 percent of Armstrong's earnings during his career and may have overworked Armstrong and unnecessarily weakened him physically, particularly in later years. Armstrong, however, expressed nothing but accolades for the man who pulled him out of his mid-1930s career slump: "He was the greatest for me and all the spades he handled," he declared upon Glaser's death in a private letter from 1969.

Ellington believed, along with his closest business advisers, that no one but Glaser possessed the expertise and muscle to secure fifty-two weeks of work for a big band in the 1950s and 1960s. Because of this, he stayed with ABC even though bitter disagreements regularly erupted during their long relationship. Ellington was also dissatisfied because he knew his account would never rank as the priority at ABC, a status he preferred to have in all business associations. Armstrong was Glaser's number-one priority and always would be, since Glaser acted as his manager as well as booker, and received a much higher percentage on the proceeds of Armstrong's career, whereas Glaser received only 10 percent of Ellington's booking guarantees. Armstrong and Glaser were also very good, if not best friends, while the Glaser/Ellington relationship was founded only on business and constantly fraught with tension. At ABC, Ellington ranked as number two or worse. The fact that he put up with this relationship and status represents another indication of how difficult his economic situation had become during the 1950s and 1960s.

Business records attest to Ellington's constant displeasure with ABC's bookings, perhaps because they often did not cover band expenses. Wein remembered booking the Ellington orchestra through Glaser during the 1950s at prices that he knew could not possibly pay for the upkeep of the orchestra. Ellington also made clear his preference for more "sit-down dates" lasting several days and concert dates. The former were more restful for the senior-citizen bandleader and his men, and the latter usually more lucrative and prestigious. Ellington, by the mid-1950s and for the next two decades, regularly delayed signing contracts for future bookings until the last minute, registering his displeasure with the worst deals and hoping to gain an advantage by threatening not to work, pressuring Glaser and ABC to come up with better offers. Dozens of business letters over the years, boomeranging from ABC to William Mittler, the accountant at Duke Ellington, Inc., during most of the 1950s and 1960s, illustrate the angry and contentious emotions such tactics caused. "Bill, I don't want to get involved in any situations with Duke as it is getting to [sic] hard and I am getting too old to beg and plead with Duke to take certain [show] dates as Duke is of the opinion we are working against him . . . [and] that people are out to get him," Glaser wrote Mittler in February 1961. "I definitely cannot understand why you hold up contracts, although I know you have a tough situation with DUKE ELLINGTON," wrote ABC agent Bob Bundy to Mittler in the fall of 1961, in a typically frustrated letter. "We are certainly not the only booking office in the country, and we certainly have competition, and even if I say so I think we are getting very good money for ELLINGTON with what business he does." The last sentence in the letter seemed a not-so-veiled threat: Ellington "alone can verify the business he has been doing and this news spreads like wild fire."[24]

The tensions between Ellington and Glaser/ABC seemed to come to a head in late 1963. In December, Glaser declared he would stop loaning money to Ellington after he found out that some of the band's 1963 State Department tour money was being paid to Ellington directly, bypassing Glaser's commission. Perhaps Ellington arranged matters in this manner because, being unhappy with the price Glaser negotiated from the U.S. government, he had sent in Wein to negotiate further, and Wein doubled the band's asking price. Even the State Department in their internal communications noted the palpable "animosity" between Ellington and Glaser. In December, Glaser also suggested that Ellington give ABC an additional 10 percent of his bookings until his debts were paid (this apparently never happened). Ellington may also have been in more of a financial bind than usual since the State Department tour ended one month early because of Kennedy's assassination, and the government initially balked at paying Duke Ellington, Inc., the balance of what they owed them. Ellington, displaying a rare anger and frustration, wrote a letter in longhand that broke off his relationship with Glaser and ABC. The document demonstrated the economic pressure, never betrayed in his genial public image, that Ellington felt during this period:

> Our association has been one of many . . . hostile clashes for one reason or another—mostly or mainly because of money, ever since I have been with ABC I have been in the red because of . . . sometimes careless booking—you know because I have many times told you of my minimum [financial] obligation at which point it might have been better for both of us to discontinue this association . . . you don't like to loan money and I don't like to be in position to have to borrow it especially when is not for my personal enjoyment—though you don't need it you have made a profit as my agent and on the other hand the period the entire period of 13 years has been a total loss [to me] financially—I have been advised badly by your people and in many instances they have decided to put a ceiling on my asking price [for shows] and many other acts not in my interest—Obviously I am a nuisance and an unnecessary addition to your kennel—and so to rid us both of this unhappy union I think it would be a good idea to discontinue our association immediately
>
> With great respect to a gentleman successful [unreadable word] in the industry—I am [Duke Ellington][25]

This letter, however, was never sent, and the contentious Ellington/Glaser relationship continued, along with Ellington's running debts to ABC, for the rest of his career.

In 1965, Ellington, having recently left Reprise Records, needed to find a new record label. Releasing his *First Sacred Concert*—a long-form, religiously themed work—and getting it to as many people as possible marked his main priority in this endeavor. Brad McCuen, RCA Victor producer and A&R executive, recalled getting a call from jazz producer and entrepreneur Norman Granz, who was acting as Ellington's personal manager for a short period during this time. "How'd you like to be responsible for Duke Ellington coming back to RCA Victor [after a two-decade absence]?" Granz asked him. "Duke isn't money-hungry. Heck, [he'll take] $12,000 an album, how many albums do you want at 12?" That figure was higher than McCuen usually allotted an artist, "but for Ellington, my feeling then was, and it's even more so now, he's going to continue to sell forever, so if we don't make it the first year, we're sure gonna make it eventually, and that's been borne out." The contract specified four albums over three years with an unlimited extension upon approval of both parties. But Ellington soon found that, despite McCuen's being an avid Ellington fan, he had to execute a distasteful tradeoff to record the music he most wished to release. McCuen described the deal:

> It was obvious talking for five minutes with Duke that [recording the *Concert of Sacred Music* LP] was of paramount importance. Acting like a typical company man at this point, I said, "I can't envision this as being one of your best-selling albums." It certainly is one any Ellington collector would want, but a mass sale, you know, I was a little skeptical. Victor had an experience with Paul Horn [doing a religious album] . . . I do know it didn't sell . . . A deal that Duke and I made, kind of verbally, was he wanted to do things and obviously, I needed to have a couple of albums that would sell, really sell, big. So I said the best example would be [an album of re-recorded Ellington oldies eventually titled] *The Popular Duke Ellington*, which he didn't fight it, but his face fell every time the subject came up. What I wanted was his greatest compositions done in the Victor fad at that time . . . Dyna-Groove . . . it was a commercial [high fidelity] gimmick . . . This album was a trade-off. You know, the deal that Ellington and I had is that, OK, we would do one of the projects that he wanted to do [if Ellington recorded an album of oldies].

McCuen put together a similar deal as a quid pro quo for agreeing to record and release *The Far East Suite* (1966), Ellington's best album of the last decade of his life and a consistent seller on RCA ever since. Upon hearing the *Far East* compositions for the first time, McCuen told Ellington that they "didn't sound like a *Billboard* chart album."

Ellington's albums on RCA Victor presented a telling problem for the sales staff. According to McCuen, they were used to albums that sold well for a few weeks while the marketing campaigns ran strong, and died soon thereafter, a circumstance especially prevalent with rock albums. Ellington's LPs, however, "were typical of [his] old things, they just kept on going, and the younger distributor people, expecting the same pattern as in the old pop albums, constantly had to [re]order." The staff was not used to such drawn-out sales patterns in the mid-1960s. *Concert of Sacred Music* and *The Far East Suite* both made the RCA sales department "very happy" at the time, won Grammy awards, and sold even more in decades to come. *The Popular Duke Ellington,* however, sold two to three times more than either of them in the short run.[26] Releasing artistically challenging material proved to be as much of a struggle for Ellington in the 1960s as it was in the 1930s, despite his track record of providing solid catalog sales over the decades.

Starting in 1964 and continuing for the next five years, Ellington rid himself of some of the old managers and accountants he had been loyal to since the 1930s. These people, particularly road manager Al Celley and accountant William Mittler, were inhibiting his ability to compete in the modern music business of the 1960s, and the extant business records give the impression that they probably were skimming Ellington and his organization as well. By relying on longtime associates (such as Glaser and Mittler) who had not adapted sufficiently to the modern music business, Ellington did not receive maximum income from the contracts and deals made on his behalf, particularly during the 1950s and 1960s.

Celley began working for Duke Ellington in June 1944, in his words as "a road manager, collecting receipts on the road, transportation, payroll, paying the men off, making the [accounting] statements out and sending them back to Mittler."[27] The band worked almost exclusively on a cash basis; almost every gig paid off in cash, which kept the orchestra payroll steady as they traveled over long distances. As Celley testified in his lawsuit against Duke Ellington, Inc., in 1966, "you have to always work with cash on the road. You have to pay off 20 men, 22, 23 people traveling." Celley also covered Ellington's hotel rooms with Duke Ellington, Inc., funds and occasionally some meals for the band, although usually food and lodging were the responsibility of individual band members, which is why they insisted on cash payment of their salaries and rarely accepted checks.

The break between Celley and Ellington occurred in February or March 1964, soon after the band's first State Department–sponsored international tour in late 1963. According to Celley's 1966 lawsuit testimony, the main issue centered on the accusation that Celley had stolen about $10,000 by getting U.S. embassies in Ankara and Beirut to cash his personal checks to meet band expenses and then stopping payment on the checks, leaving the embassies and, ultimately, Duke Ellington, Inc., in the lurch. The fact that several cancelled checks from the period are missing in the Ellington business records indicates that this might have happened. Celley insisted that Ellington ordered the checks written even though there were not sufficient funds. Ellington's lawyers also seemed to view Celley's accounting procedures over the years with suspicion. So did at least one band member. Longtime Ellington trombonist and songwriter Juan Tizol recalled that Celley "used to do a lot of strange things," including charging "the most exorbitant rates of interest you ever heard of" on loans to the band and "ask[ing] me to sign double receipts when he paid me . . . that meant that Celley had accounted for twice as much money as he paid out."

In a 1978 interview, Tizol recalled Celley disappearing for good during their 1964 European tour with $40,000 in band money; Michael James recalled the sum as three weeks of the band's payroll. In a 1966 interview, Ellington talked about bringing on his son Mercer as the band manager because "the managers I used to have had a habit of running off with $30,000 when we were in Helsinki." Such accusations are not mentioned in the legal documents housed in the Smithsonian. In investigating this matter, Duke Ellington, Inc., went so far as to hire a private detective to check if sudden income spikes due to impropriety could be found in Celley's accounts. However, since most of the band's transactions on the road were in cash, embezzlement could have been easily concealed, if it occurred. Celley, on the other hand, started the lawsuit by suing Duke Ellington, Inc., for $20,000 in back pay and loans owed to him by the corporation.

From the evidence in the Smithsonian's files, it appears that the financial records for the band were so confusing and the week-to-week accounting so convoluted that Celley could not be convincingly cleared or convicted of any dishonesty in his role as road manager for the Ellington orchestra. In transcripts from the proceedings, Ellington's lawyer seems unable to understand how business was transacted in the band, even with Celley present and attempting to explain how his accounting system worked. The records show that the Ellington organization represented a maze of debt and borrowing that no one person had a handle on: band members' wages were constantly delayed or carried from week to week if the band failed to make enough money on the road that week to pay them; most band members were in permanent and growing debt to the band, a situation Celley supervised; Celley sometimes borrowed from the band's ABC account to meet band expenses, transactions which required approval from both Ellington and Mittler; and Ellington personally was hugely in debt to ABC and Glaser. Ultimately, Ellington's lawyers settled the Celley case for $6,000 in 1968.

William Mittler, the main accountant of Duke Ellington, Inc., had originally started working in the music business with Irving Mills in the early 1930s.[28] He acted as assistant treasurer of the corporation during the Mills years and then became the treasurer for Duke Ellington, Inc., after Ellington left Mills. He performed similar duties for Cab Calloway, another former Mills act.

The Ellington/Mittler relationship came to an acrimonious end in 1965, inspiring another lawsuit against Duke Ellington, Inc., in 1966. Mittler sued the corporation that he had served as an officer for $9,000. As with Celley, it's difficult to assign ultimate blame because of the anarchic state of the records, but several people in the Ellington organization felt Mittler conducted shady, if not unethical, practices. In his resignation letter, Mittler said he was leaving Duke Ellington, Inc., because Ellington arranged for his royalty checks and deposits on engagements to be sent to himself or his son instead of directly to Mittler, as had been done for decades prior. In a 1991 interview, Mercer Ellington said he thought Ellington did this because he was "onto Mittler" and his supposed deceptions: "Mittler was furious when that change was made because he would always be able to have access to the ASCAP moneys in order to offset debts . . . when there was a hole in the band financially . . . this was the initial step to precede the break with Bill Mittler." Mittler also said he left because he claimed Ellington was using "trust monies" from band members' Social Security and New York state withholding taxes to shore up the band's finances. Among the government's many audits and penalties assigned to Duke Ellington, Inc., over the course of the 1960s and 1970s, only once, in 1969, did they accuse Ellington of not turning in these kinds of funds on time. Although after Ellington's passing, two band members complained that the organization's nonpayment of unemployment taxes over the years left them unable to collect unemployment benefits.[29]

Duke Ellington, Inc., disputed Mittler's accusations and added many of their own against him. They accused him of "unauthorized and excessive monthly charges for rent" for their office, since Ellington only used it approximately three weeks a year when in New York City, while Mittler used it year-round. They complained that in addition to working for Ellington, Mittler's wife Sarah worked for Mittler and Cab Calloway from 1956 to 1964, but her yearly wages were paid by Duke Ellington, Inc. In Mittler's deposition, he mentions her by her maiden name many times before admitting that he was married to her. Ellington's lawyers also accused Mittler of failing to audit Celley's weekly financial reports from the road (which were often late) and of failing to obtain an independent audit of the Ellington books. Mittler's failure to audit Celley's reports particularly intrigued

Ellington's lawyers, since the private detective's report on Celley showed that Mittler remained his accountant two years after he left the Ellington organization. In an oral interview, Mercer Ellington insisted, without evidence, that other irregularities existed that did not make it into the legal proceedings:

> We found many flaws in his regime after he departed . . . for instance when Pop bought a building, Mittler handled the insurance on the building, and without any appraisal from the fire marshal or anything like that, put this terrific value on the properties in order to have it insured. Had some catastrophe occurred at that particular time, the building probably would have only probably been able to collect maybe 30% of the face value of what the policy was, and this exorbitant amount was, of course, paid into a insurance company, which was basically owned, or in the major interest of Bill Mittler. There were these little things underlying the business. It wasn't like issuing double contracts, or anything. Everything was very logical the way it was done. Kickbacks from travel agencies and things of that sort.

In the end, however, documents at the Smithsonian indicate that Mittler ended up receiving a settlement of $9,000.

The legal struggles with Celley and Mittler were costly, but in some ways may have been worthwhile. They made clear the fact that the band's finances had to be more carefully managed. They also rid Ellington of influences that seemed to be draining his organization. As Ellington friend Robert Udkoff recalled, "Duke said that was the best $10,000 he ever spent because he got rid of Celley." Michael James called people like Celley and Mittler "nightmare characters . . . part of the necessity of the business. If you go on the road, or anything like that, you're gonna have these people handle the 'day to day' for you. Ellington couldn't do all that, you can't do all that and be a musician . . . and concentrate on [your] work. But he was aware that people did all these [unsavory] things." But what the legal documents do not discuss is that these incidents probably evinced an emotional toll on Ellington. He had known and trusted Mittler for thirty-five years. Over the course of two decades of travel together, Ellington had often shared a room with Celley while on the road, and, as can be ascertained from various oral histories, Celley seemed to be his closest confidant in terms of band business. The seeming betrayal of these close associates must have been somewhat painful.

Celley was eventually replaced by Mercer Ellington, someone with unimpeachable loyalty to Ellington, and problems of the kind experienced with

Celley never recurred. Mercer said he took the job as road manager and trumpet player as a favor since his father needed the help and because his father had helped him financially during the Great Depression. Mercer previously had a lucrative job as a New York City disc jockey (which his father helped secure for him), and he expressed his dislike for the manager job. He explained that he took it primarily to improve his trumpet skills and protect his father's legacy and economic wellbeing. He also hoped to do some writing with the band, but his tasks as manager ate up his time.

After Mittler left, a lawyer named Benjamin Starr handled the business end of Duke Ellington, Inc., along with help from Ruth Ellington. They signed the booking contracts and streamlined the operation as best they could. In this period in the music business, lawyers like Starr increasingly represented artists and their companies, and it seemed to be a beneficial move for the Ellington organization. The booking correspondence indicates that Starr seemed more attuned than Mittler to protecting Ellington's rights, guarding his image, and exacting the maximum financial rewards for deals he struck. Starr insisted on "no taping" clauses on Ellington's booking contracts since he felt bootlegs were cannibalizing record sales. He also insisted on higher fees for Ellington's endorsement deals, and Ellington signed more such deals than usual in the last years of his career, with such companies as Zenith, Olivetti, and Hot Shoppes restaurants. Starr rejected many other deals that failed to offer adequate compensation or, in the case of an outside proposal for the development of a company called Duke Ellington Foods, enough guaranteed equity in the company.[30]

In April 1967, Ellington's new accountants, led by Steven A. Burn, initiated a meeting with Duke, Mercer, and Ruth Ellington concerning cleaning up the confusion and abuses surrounding the financial practices of Duke Ellington, Inc. The agenda stated that "Despite the fact that the orchestra is constantly performing at what is considered a reasonable rate of compensation, the corporation is constantly short of funds." To remedy this situation, the accountants insisted that better coordination had to be instituted between the corporation, ABC, and the road manager; receipts needed to be saved and suitably cataloged for tax deductions; and withholding moneys needed to be "properly reserved and paid when due."[31] As will be seen, these directives were not always followed, but at least figures like Burn and Starr were trying to force some institutional discipline on Duke Ellington, Inc. Ellington's business documents housed at the Smithsonian seem to change during this post-Celley and post-Mittler period, reflecting a more modern and professional approach in dealing with the music business. But out in the real world, Ellington still tended to follow his own priorities, which often did not coalesce with sound business practices.

The biggest and most important change was the return of Cress Courtney as Ellington's personal manager in February 1968.[32] Courtney, an old friend and admirer of Ellington, had previously represented Ellington at the William Morris Agency during the 1940s. Unlike other old associates, Courtney still seemed to have a dynamic and aggressive edge in business negotiations. When Courtney returned, he immediately doubled and sometimes even tripled the band's asking price. Venues usually accepted the price hikes, which suggested that Ellington's gigs had been undersold and badly managed for a long time. Promoter George Wein recalled several times when Courtney insisted on thousands more dollars and transportation fees as a condition for booking Ellington and, when told it wasn't possible, said, "You're going to get more or you're not going to handle the band." "So I told my office we can't function unless we get more money," Wein said, and the deal got done. The booking correspondence shows that Courtney and Ellington goaded ABC constantly for higher booking fees and were extremely unhappy with them. However, just as Ellington and Mittler found in previous years, Courtney felt that no one else could secure the year-round bookings Ellington needed besides ABC.

Unlike previous handlers of Ellington, with the exception of Norman Granz, Courtney understood the cultural importance of Ellington and sought to use it to advantage. He saw that, with Ellington's sterling artistic reputation and advanced age, promoters would pay more to secure his appearances at their engagements, knowing they may not get many more chances to book a legend like Ellington. In 1970, Courtney explained his duties as Ellington's personal manager:

> I see that things are at least going toward a goal. In Ellington's position, my goal is to immortalize him as fast as I can while he's alive. This is a point of reaching a major portion of the public who don't appreciate what I believe should be considerably appreciated by all sections of the public. Also, the thing I must do is get enough money to pay everybody involved... I have to see that the money improves every year as prices and terms go up. However, I have one thing that goes for me: Mr. Ellington has such great faith in me that he very rarely knows where the hell he's going. He'll call me and say "Where am I next week?" ... It's a responsibility I can't take lightly.

From the business documents at the Smithsonian, it also seems that Courtney was more aware of the financial holes and problems within the Ellington organization, and he maximized compensation to try and resolve those difficulties.

Courtney tried to align business interests so they dovetailed with Ellington's composing and recording regimen. He liked to book Ellington for long runs in Las Vegas because Ellington "gets a lot of writing done." In the heyday of the big band era, numerous clubs across the country booked Ellington and the band for a week at a time or more. In the 1960s, Las Vegas represented the only location where Ellington could enjoy "sit-down," multiweek engagements. Courtney reported in 1970 that, during the band's last engagement there, Ellington finished editing more than one record album release for a six-album deal that Courtney had negotiated with Fantasy Records, which resulted in "a lot of money" coming into the band. With the lapsing of Ellington's recording deal with RCA Victor, Courtney secured the new deal with Fantasy in 1968 because, at the time, they had "all the money in the world . . . because of [their recent chart success with the rock band] Creedence Clearwater Revival." This fact proved important, since Ellington was unlikely to produce big record sales, but could bestow prestige upon a company, especially a relatively new independent label like Fantasy. As Courtney said, "we got a good deal for those 6 LPs, but I don't think the money will make up for the cost of producing those albums," especially because if Ellington heard "one bar he didn't like" during a song after it was recorded, he would return to the studio for hours to correct the mistake, no matter the cost of recording time and band union fees.

Most importantly, the Fantasy deal that Courtney brokered allowed Ellington to release some of the most important albums of the last years of his life without the commercial compromises McCuen exacted in the 1965 RCA deal. Ellington released all new material on Fantasy (including *Second Sacred Concert, The Latin-American Suite,* and *The Afro-Eurasian Eclipse*), not rehashings of golden oldies. Courtney summed up the situation he felt he had created for Ellington: "All he has to do now is think about what he's writing, what he's doing. Of course, I'm always riding on him" to come up with new releases.

Ellington's most serious financial problems during his last decade were with the Internal Revenue Service, which gave him a hard time over his business priorities of providing for his family, friends, and community. In a tax examination of 1964 by the IRS, it claimed that Ellington had underestimated his royalty income from Tempo Music during the 1957–60 tax years, owing $97,151.17 in back taxes, not counting penalties. In a protest to the IRS, Ellington's accountant Burn argued that Ellington's sister Ruth owned 90 percent of Tempo's shares (Strayhorn had the remaining 10 percent) and was therefore eligible to receive the publisher's 50 percent cut of all Tempo song income. Also, since Tempo had not been "consistently profitable," Ellington was temporarily deferring his composer royalties (the other 50 percent of song income) during the 1957–60 period until a time when Tempo could afford to pay him. Burn asked the IRS how Ellington could be taxed on royalties and publisher income he never received. The Ellington team justified their actions by the "fruit-tree doctrine" instituted by the Supreme Court case *Lucas v. Earl*, which, as Ellington's tax protest states, "established . . . that the taxpayer can avoid the tax if he assigns the *income producing property* [ownership of Tempo Music, in this case], rather than the income itself." The IRS disagreed and elected to count the disputed 50 percent take of publisher income as Ellington's, not Ruth's.

Furthermore, the IRS found Ruth's compensation from Tempo excessive and characterized it as a ruse on Ellington's behalf to avoid being taxed on his actual income by allowing large amounts of it to go to a family member as earned income. The IRS even questioned Ruth's credentials for such a high salary and executive responsibility. In the 1964 tax protest, and in a testimonial from a music business lawyer, the Ellington accountants reviewed her qualifications for the job including her quarter century of experience in the position and made the case that Ruth's compensation matched that of other executives running large music-publishing concerns. But the IRS had a point. Ellington gave ownership of Tempo to his sister to take care of her financially and to keep her close to him, as their mother Daisy asked Ellington to do on her deathbed. During her college years, Ruth studied biology, and she only learned the music business when handed the reigns at Tempo. Even then, Ellington's lawyers and representatives made most important decisions for the firm, according to Ruth.[33]

The IRS had further problems with Ellington's tax returns during the 1960s. On his 1965–67 tax returns, he claimed between nine and ten exemptions, including five Ellington cousins and an aunt in the first two years. The IRS eventually rejected them all except for Florence Hartgrave, Daisy Ellington's sister. Ellington also tried, unsuccessfully, to write off medical expenses he paid on behalf of these family members. These exemptions and medical expenses represented another example of the extent to which Ellington took care of his family and friends through his businesses. Hartgrave was particularly important to Ellington—for him, she was the last living link to his mother, and Hartgrave's daughter Bernice Wiggins recalled that Ellington "worshipped" her. When Ellington returned from the airport after overseas trips during the 1960s and 1970s, according to Wiggins, even "if it was 2:00 in the morning, he would never go home until he'd come and just sit by her bed for almost an hour and so tired he could hardly keep his eyes open, but he would come and see his aunt Florence." Wiggins and her daughter Juanita Middleton both worked for Tempo Music. From the days of his Washington, D.C., boyhood, Ellington was taught to protect and support the women of his family, and he kept that legacy until he died. Ellington tried to write off some of these family-related expenses, but even when the IRS rejected the deductions, there is no evidence that he ever ceased playing a patriarch role.[34]

Another problem resulted from Ellington's inability to save receipts for expenses, a problem that extended across all of Ellington's businesses. "Duke used to deduct $100 a day for expenses, which was probably justified," recalled H. Robert Udkoff. "He was a very generous tipper . . . he was very aware these guys had to make a living and he felt that he wanted to contribute, a guy carries his bag, he'd give them $10 [about $65 in today's dollars], cab drivers, bell hops . . . but he couldn't prove it. He didn't have any receipts." The government would not take Ellington's word on these matters, and when Duke Ellington, Inc., could not produce receipts for very reasonable everyday music business expenses such as piano rental and musical periodical subscriptions, they disallowed them as business deductions, adding to Ellington's already swollen tax bill. The "cash and carry" business philosophy that Ellington successfully practiced during the 1930s and 1940s was rejected by the IRS during the 1960s and 1970s.

As Shirley Courtney, Cress's wife, recalled, Ellington's IRS problems came about "because people were spending too much money" and not keeping proper records. Just to take a few examples out of many, Ellington regularly paid Evie Ellis's IRS tax bills and, in 1969, nearly $1,900 in back taxes and penalties on longtime band member Harry Carney and his wife's 1966 and 1967 tax returns. "There will be a further 1968 liability" on the Carneys' taxes, warned Steven Burn. "Frankly, I can't understand this arrangement." A normal business would not underwrite an employee's tax mistakes, but Duke Ellington, Inc., did so, especially for close friends like the Carneys. In one folder at the Smithsonian, a series of nine letters from 1973 ask charitable organizations such as the Southern Christian Leadership Conference and the NAACP to investigate and send documentation of Ellington's contributions to the organizations during 1962 and 1963 because no receipts could be found, and the IRS demanded proof for deductions. Juan Tizol, longtime band trombonist and composer, recalled Ellington sending him $1,000 when his wife Rose needed an operation. "He figured that [if it] was gonna cost more than that it'll break me," Tizol said in 1980. "He'd do things like that and I could always get money out of Duke anytime." Even with Ellington's lucrative royalty income and half a million dollars a year or more in bookings during the 1960s, Ellington supported too many people and skirted too many IRS rules to keep in the black.[35]

Starting in the late 1960s, the IRS showed up at certain Ellington shows to seize Ellington's payment from the promoter. "For months on end, he never got paid from the Rainbow Grill," recalled Phoebe Jacobs. "I had a notice from the U.S. Government that the money had to be turned right over to the IRS." In 1969, over Ellington's protest, ASCAP allowed $3,030.79 of Ellington's royalties to go directly to the IRS. Stanley Dance recalled finding Ellington, a famous late sleeper, awake earlier than usual one morning during this period:

> He'd got the sheets up like a tent to keep him warm and he had various bits of paper where he was adding up sums. I said, "What the hell are you doing?" He said, "I'm trying to see where we can get some money from to pay the bus company." . . . I mean [an] enormous amount of money went [into his organization] but it was siphoned off in all sorts of places.

When asked if the strain of the constant debt and IRS harassment ever showed on Ellington's visage, Ellington's nephew Michael James replied: "Not to the point where it's going to interfere with the music." James also remembered Ellington feeling that his "country was taking advantage of him" and that Ellington once thought aloud about becoming an expatriate to rid himself of the IRS hassle. "But how serious he was, I don't know," James added.[36]

Ellington's business papers make it clear that staying on the road with his big band was, in many respects, a stressful and economically disastrous course. His problems with the IRS exacerbated the situation, leaving hundreds of thousands of dollars in debt and penalties to be paid by his estate after his death. The return of Courtney to the fold in 1968 improved the financial picture, but Courtney could not erase previous debts and abuses, or stop Ellington's generous financial outpourings to family and friends. Ellington probably knew that no windfall of money from record sales or other sources would bail him out of his situation. And if he was even concerned about his financial situation, he could have sat home and let the money roll in with little effort. So, why did he put himself through it? The answer is simple. "With me it's some kind of basic, primitive, impetuous need. If I write a piece of music today, I've got to hear it played tonight. This is the problem with me," he said in 1966. Also, as Britt Woodman, a trombonist in the band for most of the 1950s, put it, Ellington lived exactly as he wished:

His hobby was with people in his room, talking on the phone. He could stay one night in a hotel and he spend around $300–$400 calling long distance. No windows open. The windows closed. He don't like air at all. And every room he got to have a piano and so that was his hobby and his life was on a bandstand. Waiting for that night on the bandstand with the people. That's why he was content and the person he was. He was doing everything he wanted to do, he could do it . . . you know, have somebody bring his chicks in and everything. He lived like a king. His life was beautiful. That's another thing too, you see. All these things that you think about. How to find yourself. And the average person go through life never really find themselves, what they want, they's always being led to a certain extent, pleasing someone else and not what you want to do . . . he lived his life.[37]

11

MY PEOPLE

"[Ellington taught me] that you don't always have to run around being vocal to get people's attention, just go ahead and do what you think is prudent, the right thing to do at the moment, and let time take care of the rest of it. You don't have to always get on the soapbox . . . Some of the civil rights organizations criticized [Ellington] during the civil rights struggle. But his concept was, he didn't have to wear a badge on his shoulder to advertise what his feelings were. He [communicated] them in a quiet way, unheralded in many instances . . . his way was by doing. I guess he felt this way, if I can paraphrase: 'I don't have to go advertising what I do, if it's a benefit, it'll eventually come out anyway.'"

MAURICE LAWRENCE, Ellington friend

"Ellington's songs may have given him the kind of social freedom that fellow Negroes are still struggling for, but they have longed to confine him to the jukebox world of jazz . . . He has established, thank goodness, that winning equal rights on the white man's podium does not mean giving up the precious musical heritage of the black man."

CARTER HARMAN in Life magazine, 1965[1]

While Ellington's economic situation remained difficult, the nationwide struggle by black Americans and their nonblack compatriots to overturn segregation and gain civil rights for blacks traveled on an upward, though by no means assured, trajectory. By the late 1950s, an increasingly aggressive approach to fighting discrimination became more accepted among black Americans. Marches, boycotts, and other forms of organized protest gained support and headlines in the United States and, eventually, around the world. The effectiveness of the Supreme Court's 1954 *Brown v. Board of*

FIGURE 10. Duke Ellington performed and appeared hundreds of times on behalf of African American organizations, from the 1920s to the 1970s. In 1956, with baseball great and businessman Jackie Robinson (*left*) and NAACP executive secretary Roy Wilkins (*center*), Ellington attended the ceremony for the Spingarn Medal, the NAACP's highest award. Ellington won the award, given to the person who made "the highest or noblest achievement by an American Negro during the preceding year or years," in 1959. Library of Congress Serial and Government Publications, NAACP Records.

Education decision was weakened by their enforcement decree, known as *Brown II*, which set no firm date for integration of schools and thereby allowed school districts to stall integration efforts. This kept black children in second-rate schools or worse and impelled civil rights leaders to take to the streets since efforts in court were not proving effective. During the first half of the 1960s, Ellington also became more aggressive concerning the fight for civil rights—participating in a sit-in, enforcing antidiscrimination clauses in his performance contracts, producing the show *My People*, and other activities—but he did it within his own style and strategies, reflective of the concerns of his generation and his upbringing. By 1963, if not before, his reputation as a "race man," tarnished since the 1951 "we ain't ready" controversy, had been rehabilitated and burnished.

As confrontational protest became more common, the NAACP's decision to bestow their most prestigious award, the Spingarn Medal, upon Duke Ellington in 1959 rekindled the passions of those who felt that Ellington either did not do enough, did nothing, or even harmed efforts to gain civil rights for African Americans. The Spingarn went to the person who made "the highest or noblest achievement by an American Negro during the preceding year or years." Those who castigated Ellington for his 1951 "we ain't ready" comment again questioned his commitment. The *California Eagle*, a black newspaper, printed a syndicated editorial that insisted the award should only go to those "who have been active in civil rights, to the exclusion of all other claimants" and strongly hinted that Ellington did not fit the criteria. The *Los Angeles Tribune*, the *Eagle*'s local black competition, accused the NAACP of giving the award to Ellington only because he raised so much money for them over the years. They also argued that the NAACP cheapened the award by giving it to him. "Lord knows, we love his music, but its sexy growls and moans have never moved us to go out and register to vote, or bowl over a bastion of prejudice," the unsigned editorial said. The *Chicago Defender* noted Ellington's decades of financial support for the NAACP but made a point of noting that "the Spingarn Medal is being awarded in recognition of his outstanding musical accomplishments," not because anyone thought that he made a contribution to the fight for equal rights for blacks.[2] The old idea that jazz music somehow represented an immoral social force also permeated these editorials.

Some black columnists praised the NAACP's choice. The *Detroit Chronicle* noted "the interrelated identification between his musicianship and his race" and the intensity of "Ellington's awareness of the color and race problem in America," as seen in his music, personal appearances, and ambassador-like role on behalf of blacks and Americans in general. The *Pittsburgh Courier* argued that entertainers like "Ellington, Cab Calloway, Earl Hines, to mention a few, have received only an iota for what they've given" to the black community, and urged its readers to spend their money on the companies that sponsored television shows featuring black artists. "We know what a powerful weapon talent is," the paper said, in a column that did not mention the Spingarn specifically. "We are ready, willing, and able to use it. We're determined that our children will not face a world with the cards stacked against them as we did."[3]

This schism did not take into account the gains Ellington made on behalf of blacks without resorting to explicitly political comment or actions: the music he wrote, the interviews he gave, the image he invoked that spoke, with and without words, of black pride, history, and identity. Such contributions were not quantifiable. They did not produce headlines, but evinced a subtle, long-term effect, and demonstrated during a period of Jim Crow denigration that blacks could contribute at the highest levels of humanity and artistry. Such actions changed how Americans and the world viewed black Americans as well as American culture and society as a whole. In accepting the Spingarn, Ellington gave a short speech that linked his art and the cause of civil rights with American ideals of democracy and freedom. Like Dr. King often did in the 1960s in order to show his loyalty to his country and gain wider support, Ellington introduced cold war issues to drive home his point of the importance of what he and the NAACP were striving to accomplish. Ellington argued that jazz meant not only freedom, but also peace "because peace can come to mankind only when man is free." He added that Soviet premier Nikita Khrushchev would soon arrive on American shores to visit and "I feel deeply encouraged to know that he will come to a land where there is an NAACP which . . . is on the front line in the struggle for human equality and has earned the support of all freedom lovers."[4]

For Ellington, issues of artistic and racial freedom were inextricably connected. His vision of progress was more than just racial: he also wanted to push his art, especially his composing, and American music forward. Ellington viewed creativity as a kind of freedom that transcended borders and brought the whole of humanity to new heights. Yet the African American component in his work remained fundamental. When he spoke in public upon receiving the Spingarn, he voiced only pride and optimism. But, speaking to a trusted journalist, Ellington expressed hurt over the criticism concerning his supposed lack of a public stand on civil rights matters. "They've not been listening to our music. For a long time, social protest and pride in black culture and history have been the most significant themes in what we've done," he told Nat Hentoff. "In that music we have been talking for a long time about what it is to be black in this country." "Duke was a historian," Dizzy Gillespie argued.

Ellington often spoke about his commitment to documenting and celebrating the black experience in America, but mostly he let his actions and compositions speak for him. Sometimes the media and certain audiences did not pick up on the nonverbal communication. Decades later, in 1998, the astute historian Brian Ward still had not picked up on these cues, denigrating Ellington's contributions to the civil rights cause by concentrating on his reluctance to join the 1963 March on Washington because of his "sore feet," a quote Ward reproduced from a largely discredited and undocumented book by occasional Ellington lyricist Don George. As Ward demonstrated, the black pop stars of the period usually steered clear of participating in the protests, musically or with their feet. A quote from the same page of George's book more accurately reflected Ellington's views on the subject. "You know I'm not a marcher, I'm a lover," Ellington said, according to George. "If there's any kind of sweet sounds you want to make for this event, you can call on me and I'll make sure I'm in the neighborhood. But you know I never did care for walking a lot. You can do more for the people if you're the best at what you're doing and you conduct yourself admirably." Ward credited John Coltrane, Charles Mingus, Max Roach, and Sonny Rollins for their jazz works in this period that directly addressed civil rights issues, but ignored the contributions Ellington made in the same vein from the 1920s to the 1970s. Sometimes Ellington tooted his own horn on the subject. "I'd love to see *Black, Brown and Beige* staged on Broadway as an opera or pageant," he told the *Springfield (IL) State Journal* in early 1961. "*Black, Brown and Beige* means just as much today as when I wrote it. It's the history of the Negro with no cringing and no bitterness."[5]

Perhaps reflecting the values of his generation, Ellington put particular emphasis on "conduct[ing] yourself admirably," and in a 1964 private interview, he commented on a related subject:

The responsibility of not embarrassing the Negro as I travel . . . is very important . . . you're playing a college, any college in the United States . . . the University of Indiana, Michigan, even down South where you have two or three Negro students there. Our number one responsibility is not to embarrass those colored kids there. And this is a responsibility that is very, very serious . . . you get up to tell a story and instead of telling it in a Negro dialect, you tell it straight. And this doesn't impress some of the [white] audience, you know. They say "What the hell, he's putting on." They just don't know. And this is something you got to live with . . . instead of you falling back into that clichéd category [where] they want you . . . you play it straight [onstage], just [use] American English.[6]

Such behavior voiced and represented racial equality without having to get into political specifics.

The uproar over Ellington's 1951 "we ain't ready" quote made it clear that gains made by blacks in the postwar period had created a racial situation of stronger white resistance and, consequently, growing black pressure on Ellington's strong but quiet approach. Helen Oakley Dance, a lifelong Ellington friend and business associate, felt that his work provided an essential contrast and adjunct to the work that civil rights political activists did:

> Not only was [most of his longest and most significant work] devoted to race, but, I mean, it's going to live. Other people made gestures, or did this or that, and tomorrow it's forgotten, and next year it never happened. But his music lives on, it's permanent, and it's there for black people to hear and know, and nobody else could do it, and there wasn't anyone else doing it. I mean his actions on behalf of race were of mammoth proportions in comparison with other people and things. People like Martin Luther King knew it . . . people who really knew and were active, they all knew it. But unhip writers or people who weren't sufficiently aware of things, or hadn't the intelligence to really think it out, they're the people who [gave Ellington a hard time for not] marching . . . Music first, foremost and last. I mean, always music. So, any statement he wanted to make, he made it with music . . . So that on the score of what did he do for race, did he care for race? He cared enormously. He said, he committed himself several times, that nothing had the same importance for him that his people had. He was black, and proud to be black, and proud to have a talent which he could devote to the expression of black beauty. I mean, when was it first spoken? If you just give a little thought to it, if people do, you'll see nobody had a contribution to make like he did, and he made it.[7]

Like Dr. King, a man Ellington admired even though he disagreed with some of his methods, Ellington tied the cause of civil rights to issues of religion, patriotism, and the democratic underpinnings of the United States' founding documents. "Most of the Duke Ellington family (including our children) are NAACP Life Members because the NAACP is the equivalent of the front line in the fight for democracy," Ellington told the *Amsterdam*

News in 1960. "We have love and faith in America to such a high degree, that we would be failing in our duty as citizens if we did not help her achieve the freedom to which she has always been dedicated."[8]

An unpublished 1957 Ellington article entitled "The Race for Space" provides a glance into Ellington's thinking on these subjects at the time and shows that, even if he was not directly involved in the civil rights movement, he kept close track of the events within it. Written just after the Soviets launched their *Sputnik I* satellite, setting off a cold war–inspired furor in the United States that criticized the lack of similar American accomplishment and urged increased science training in schools, Ellington's article blamed racism for needlessly taking Americans' minds away from weightier matters:

> When you stop and think of the way southern congressmen and senators tie up Congress with filibusters and delaying tactics against the passage of civil rights measures to protect minorities from persecution, when you think of the lost time and effort President Eisenhower spent trying to settle the Little Rock situation; in fact the time being lost all over the South as well as places in the North over the school desegregation issue ordered by the Supreme Court in 1954, you'll get an idea of how and why the Russians may be having breakfast on the moon by the time you read this . . .
>
> We're not going to get much done so long as discrimination keeps 16 million [black] Americans looking at the game from knotholes. Everybody has to get in the game if we are playing to win . . .
>
> So this is my view on the race for space. We'll never get it until we Americans, collectively and individually[,] get us a new sound. A new sound of harmony, brotherly love, common respect, and consideration for the dignity and freedom of men.[9]

Though the article appeared to be written for a magazine, no published record survives. Like his 1943 scenario for *Black, Brown and Beige*, Ellington allowed some of his more forthright views about race, America, and politics to remain hidden in his personal files. Perhaps Ellington feared that the patriotism underlying his arguments would be ignored or twisted, as happened with his 1951 comments, and decided not to issue his article. No entertainment figures released such reasoned and potentially controversial statements at this time, and Ellington may have figured that adverse reaction was the probable result. Such decisions kept Ellington's passionate feelings about the subject hidden from view, but they also coalesced with his commitment to keep his public and private life focused on the music.

In this matter, Ellington also had to consider audience issues. According to numerous observers, Ellington's audience during this period and afterward was usually "95%" white. This bothered some major black entertainers of the time, though Ellington left no record on the subject. "I think Louis [Armstrong] was very bruised when his own people wouldn't come to hear him [during the 1950s and 1960s], and I think it was the same for Duke," commented Phoebe Jacobs, a friend and associate of both men. Sammy Davis, Jr., was particularly vociferous on the subject. "If I had one wish it would be that Negroes would support other Negro entertainers," Davis told a black newspaper in 1956. "Most Negro performers with anything unusual don't get any support from their people. Take Duke Ellington. It's a shame. The man's a genius, but who supports him? Whites." Journalists came to similar conclusions about black audiences of this period, and seemed as upset as celebrities like Davis. Nat Hentoff, one of the most respected jazz-affiliated writers of his time, commented on the situation, which he argued was particularly acute in the jazz field:

> The majority of American Negroes characteristically continue to be uninterested in and uninformed about jazz, even though most of the major protagonists, orthodox and heretical, are Negro. A critic once asked drummer Art Blakey about the importance of Charlie Parker as a symbol to "the Negro people." Blakey looked at him as if he had just come upon a new and unprecedentedly large species of square, and said, "Hell, the Negro people never even heard of Charlie Parker."
>
> There is not only no Negro jazz critic on any general magazine—an absence that could be explained in some cases by Jim Crow hiring practices—but there are practically no writers on jazz in the Negro press ... by and large the Negro jazzman usually gets what small space he is allotted in the Negro press more by reason of his having become financially successful than through any appreciation or understanding of his musical achievements. Or conversely, he'll win space if he gets picked up on a narcotics or alimony rap ...
>
> The opposition to jazz—not just apathy—among middle- and upper-class Negroes is about as old as the music.

The same article featured jazz pianist and educator Billy Taylor's observations that only white schools and colleges carried courses on jazz performance and history, and that black clergy nearly uniformly stood against the music, as opposed to white religious figures such as Father Norman

O'Connor, who often cohosted the Newport Jazz Festival during the 1950s and 1960s, as well as a television show and newspaper column dedicated to the music.[10]

Going too far out on a limb on civil rights issues with his predominantly white audience might have further endangered the Ellington orchestra's already precarious economic existence. It was a situation analogous to that experienced by the black R&B and pop stars of the period described by Ward. They, too, avoided direct involvement with the civil rights movement, not wanting to alienate their majority white audience or to be subject to violence. Most black musical stars were not financially secure, nor were their fans, though their success and "spirit-raising" on the national charts did connote a significant contribution, argued Ward. Black Hollywood stars (especially Harry Belafonte) and white folk musicians (such as Joan Baez and Bob Dylan), both more financially secure and insulated from violence and fan backlash, were far more involved in movement activities than the black R&B and pop stars or Ellington.[11] But that same white audience that Ellington had cultivated for more than three decades, and the respect they accorded him, also afforded him opportunities to address them about issues of black history and identity, which he did within his music, his interviews, and more baldly in various incidents from 1960 to 1963.

A sit-in attended by Ellington on 22 February 1960 in Baltimore marked the first of these incidents that signaled Ellington's willingness to engage in a more forthright style of resisting discrimination.[12] According to historian Harvard Sitkoff, sit-in protests began sporadically in the South during the late 1950s. But they did not receive national media attention until 1 February 1960, when four black freshmen from the North Carolina Agricultural and Technical College, tired of being humiliated at various Southern businesses, staged a sit-in at a Woolworth's lunch counter in Greensboro. No civil rights groups prodded or organized them. After purchasing some school supplies in the store, they sat down and demanded service, drawing immediate and intense attention. Within the week, 1,600 students joined them in their cause, and similar protests flared across the country. As the *Brown* rulings showed, as well as the limited reform that followed in the wake of the Montgomery Bus Boycott, attempts to end segregation by appealing to the forces of law and politics had limited and often no success. But protesters soon found that disrupting the profits of a national corporation like Woolworth's elicited much quicker results. Within six months, the Greensboro Woolworth's lunch counter allowed blacks to sit and enjoy a coffee, dozens of other businesses in the South and North were integrated, and by August 1961, "more than 70,000 blacks and whites had participated in sit-ins and three thousand had been jailed. It was a watershed," wrote Sitkoff.[13]

Three weeks after the first Greensboro sit-in, Ellington played a show on the Johns Hopkins University campus in Baltimore as part of a celebration for "Brotherhood Week." Since at least 1958, a small group of students and activists staged small protests and a benefit jazz concert to draw attention to the fact that the small number of black students at Hopkins were often forbidden to eat and shop at the businesses surrounding the university. According to Wally Orlinsky, one of the students with Ellington that evening and later a prominent Baltimore politician, Jim Crow in Baltimore "was gentlemanly and all of that, but it was real," and it was directed against Jews as well as blacks, both in a nonviolent way. Orlinsky recalled that students "didn't want to have to call in for a pizza. They wanted to be able to go out and if their buddy was black and with the group, they wanted that person to be able to go with them . . . There were rallies and all the usual kinds of things, in a much lower key than we are accustomed to today." The students tested the businesses around the campus for their hospitality to blacks, occasionally helped and advised by Dr. Chester Wickwire, head of the YMCA, and Ruth Fegley, head of the Fellowship House, both of whom had ties to civil rights activists and organizations.

The students wanted to use Ellington to test the most adamantly Jim Crow restaurant in the Hopkins area, the Blue Jay, on St. Paul Street, but had no one to provide an entree. According to Orlinsky, the proprietor of the Blue Jay, a Greek American named Fred Paxenos, told him that he would serve a "proper nigger" such as Ellington, and Orlinsky and the students wanted to test Paxenos's boast. Bob Watts, a black judge in Baltimore who served as the students' "legal advisor," advised Orlinsky that if anyone could get to Ellington to ask him to enter the Blue Jay, it was Fegley, who had met Ellington and the band during their local stands in the last few years. "The students decided it was important to them," Fegley recalled. "So I said, OK, let's see what we can work out."

Fegley and Orlinsky spoke with Ellington backstage during the intermission at the Hopkins show. Fegley explained why she and the students wanted Ellington to be involved. His first reaction was "No, I don't want to be bothered." But after some "jocular chit-chat" (according to Fegley) and asking whether entering the Blue Jay would be "important," Ellington agreed to it, providing Fegley came along and that the enterprise would not take long, as the band had to drive to Philadelphia that night. "Once it was clear to him, Ruth said it and I said it was important, there was no 'Oh, goddamn it, I'll do it' [reluctance from Ellington], it was 'Let's go,'" according to Orlinsky. "He was very good about it . . . certainly willing." Orlinsky said that the students "had no appreciation that he was doing something that was very new for him. It was very new for us!"

Directly after the show, Fegley got on the band bus and directed it to the Blue Jay. A reporter and photographer from the *Baltimore Afro-American* and two or three policemen were waiting, called ahead by the students to provide security and publicity. Thirty-five students, five of them black, had attempted to eat together at the restaurant earlier that afternoon, but were ordered to leave. Newspapers placed Ellington's bus at the restaurant somewhere between 11:45 and 11:50 PM. According to Fegley:

> The bus pulled up, and of course the bus is very obvious, all the banners on the outside, "Duke Ellington," it was no sneaking-in, you know [laughs]. He and I got off . . . as soon as we opened the door and went in, [the owner of the Blue Jay] turned the lights off and said "We're closing." They used that as an excuse. They were about as subtle as a brick wall, I mean they were not going to say "We're not going to serve you." They just simply used the excuse that "we're closing." We didn't make an issue, we just left, the *Afro* took pictures, the Duke left.

Usually, the restaurant closed at one in the morning. "I accomplished my mission to get the Duke there," Fegley concluded, adding that she put no pressure on him to do anything else, nor did the students. Ellington said nothing during the occasion, but the photo from the *Baltimore Afro-American* spoke volumes: he is pictured looking dapper and imperious, hair perfect and shining, in a dark long coat, talking to a white student who is exiting the restaurant as a policeman is coming behind him, ushering them away from the restaurant. Another white student in a suit holds the restaurant door open for Ellington, while Fegley looks on a couple yards away. A respectable-looking mixed-race group of five to fifteen students (news reports varied on the number), along with one of the most famous black Americans on the planet, was being refused a postconcert cup of coffee. Paxenos refused to tell the *Baltimore Sun* whether he refused service to blacks in the Blue Jay, saying only: "I'm a citizen. I pay taxes. I'm in business. I'd like to stay in business."

The sit-in was short and relatively noneventful, but in the context of the time, it drew a large amount of notice across the country. It was rare in this early era of sit-ins for celebrities to join students in protest, and, as the dozens of national clippings in the Ellington Scrapbooks at the Smithsonian testify, the newspaper media, aided by syndicated wire services, pounced on the story. "Duke Can't Eat," screamed an inch-high headline in the *Phil-*

adelphia Afro-American. Black newspapers tended to cover the story in more detail, but many major white papers, including the *Washington Star* and the *New York Times*, also featured articles about the incident. Ellington's name was usually featured in each headline, as seen in a clipping from *Newsday*: "Duke Ellington Joins in as Bias Protests Grow." Orlinsky, examining the news coverage forty years later, was shocked, and wished he had known the extent of it at the time. "I didn't even know there were clippings," he marveled. "I imagine that if we had known about this at the time [and locally publicized the national media coverage], it would have had even more impact because the university, the faculty, trustees would have been horrified."

The coverage of the sit-in in black newspapers was quite complimentary to Ellington. An editorial in the *Amsterdam News*, perhaps the most significant black newspaper in the country, seemed to signal a change of mood about Ellington and his connection to the race issues of the day:

> Mr. Ellington knew that the restaurant had twice refused to serve Negroes earlier in the afternoon.
>
> But we are happy that Duke Ellington saw fit to go into the restaurant and be refused.
>
> We are happy because when the restaurant refused Mr. Ellington, it had turned its racial bias full circle.
>
> Earlier, it had refused the little average "nobody" Negro. But Duke Ellington is not a "nobody." Duke Ellington is a "somebody" Negro. His name is almost as well known at Buckingham Palace as it is in Baltimore . . .
>
> We point this out because Negroes are often divided by the fact that sometimes white people give certain Negroes "privileges" which they do not allow other Negroes to enjoy. Thus, we often find that certain "good Negroes" are allowed to slip in the side doors [of white establishments] . . . All of this is nonsense, we don't want our civil rights based on personalities. We simply want the law to apply across the board.

Two nights after the sit-ins, the Blue Jay was the scene of a fire that destroyed the restaurant. Baltimore fire investigators conducted an arson inquiry that "failed to turn up any evidence of an incendiary nature." The fire began in the basement, where no cooking facilities were located, shortly after the restaurant closed and "burned through to the restaurant's first floor." Aside from a firefighter who suffered smoke inhalation, no one was hurt. Student leader John Katz, in the *Baltimore Sun*, called it a "horribly dreadful coincidence" that "had absolutely nothing to do with anything we tried to do in terms of trying to do away with discrimination." Orlinsky, years later, harbored his own unproven conclusions about the incident. "I have no way of knowing, but I would think it was [a] self-inflicted [fire]," he said. Paxenos "knew that he was going to suffer a serious boycott [by Hopkins students]. By then, he had realized he had thrown out Duke Ellington. But maybe it wasn't [self-inflicted] . . . whatever it was . . . it was suspicious." The Blue Jay never opened again.[14]

Another sign of Ellington's changing with the times was his decision to stamp all of his booking contracts with a nonsegregation clause starting in 1961. The contract rider read: "It is mutually agreed and understood between all parties concerned, that the artist or artists have the prerogative of canceling this contract, if in any instance an audience is segregated because of race or color." Since the early 1950s, he had avoided segregated venues, and backed out of some, but this marked the first time legal language was added to his contracts that forbid such situations. Several times during 1962, Ellington's accountant William Mittler actually returned contracts that left off the clause to American Booking Corporation, Ellington's booking agency, even insisting on the nonsegregation clause at a private club in Missouri in late 1962. In 1964, Ellington agreed to two segregated shows at private clubs in Texas and Virginia as long as they were not publicly promoted and "strictly" restricted to club members.[15]

The installation of the antisegregation clause was probably partly inspired by events that occurred at shows during September 1961. Ellington cancelled a Little Rock date after being informed by the NAACP that it was segregated. "Mr. Ellington telephoned Mr. Bates [NAACP field secretary] and expressed appreciation for calling the discrimination to his attention and added that his contract was misleading," reported the *Baltimore Afro-American* in a story widely reproduced in black newspapers. For dates during the same week in Houston and Dallas, Ellington insisted on integrated audiences in venues both called the Music Club, the first time they housed such audiences. The *Houston Press* referred to Ellington's insistence as "this new policy" of an "unpublicized campaign for integrated audiences." This stand caused Tucson club owners to integrate a previously segregated Ellington date scheduled for 16 September. Dorothy Kilgallen, in her nationally syndicated column, called Ellington a "pioneer," noting that there were "no untoward incidents and unanimous cheers for the Ellington group" when they played what she called the first integrated concerts ever in Houston and Dallas. The *California Eagle* published a short editorial that applied the philosophy behind the sit-ins to Ellington's new policy. "Southern devotees of popular music are going to have to choose between their love for Duke Ellington's band and Old Jim Crow," it wrote. "If our experience is any indication, lovers of popular music are a persistent lot. They know what they want. Maybe they can desegregate public auditoriums faster than the courts." Two months later, jazz columnist Ralph J. Gleason praised Ellington's refusal to play segregated audiences as "exceptional" and reported on Norman Granz and John Hammond's efforts to get all booking agencies to adopt a similar policy.[16]

After Ellington affixed nonsegregation clauses to his booking contracts, however, he did not always boycott gigs when asked to by civil rights organizations. In 1966, with only one day of warning, about thirty-five black and white protesters from the local NAACP picketed an Ellington show in Milwaukee. They objected to the fact that Ellington was playing a ballroom whose owner also had a whites-only club next door to the ballroom. Ellington explained that he had played the venue since 1931 and that his contract was not with the building owner, but with two brothers who leased it from them, and that his concert was integrated. The show's attendance accordingly suffered. "We don't play to segregated audiences. All my contracts have had anti-segregation clauses for 20 years," Ellington said. "The situation in Milwaukee is mild. This is nothing, a little thing that is a matter of confusion." Ellington's figure of twenty years was wrong, though it is true that the band had generally avoided playing segregated shows for two decades. The next year, in Baltimore, Ellington also refused to accede to "a last minute plea [to cancel a show] from the local chairman for the League on Human Rights, who protested that the symphony organization's president, an apartment builder, discriminated against Negroes." Ellington felt aggrieved by these protests, particularly by their last-minute nature. His financial situation was always shaky, and it was risky to refuse to play gigs at the last minute, especially after contracts had been signed and publicity disseminated. An Ellington quote from Milwaukee seemed to hint at his frustration in the matter: "Civil rights is a highly specialized subject that should be handled by specialists who know something about it."[17]

Discrimination was still palpable on the road. While Jim Crow had eased, it still existed. Bill Berry, a trumpeter with the band for most of the 1960s and usually the only white person in the band during that period, remembered getting off the bus numerous times and ordering fifty hamburgers to go because restaurants refused to serve his black bandmates. "The guys couldn't get off to go to the toilet," Berry said in 1977. "And this is Duke Ellington, you know, a genius." Berry also experienced resistance renting in a new building on the east side of New York City because the landlord thought he must be black since he played with the Ellington orchestra. Berry also recalled a "big confab" occurring between Ellington and some ad producers as the band was filming a concert advertising Goodyear tires in 1962. The ads were targeted at countries other than the United States and Canada. "I found out later that the producers when they saw me in the band they said this was going to [apartheid-era] South Africa, we can't have this," according to Berry. "And Duke said, as only he could . . . 'What a shame, we had so looked forward to working with you on this project.'" The film was completed, in color, with Berry in the band. A few months later, South Africa banned *Anatomy of a Murder* because of Ellington's appearance in the film.[18]

Ellington's newfound willingness to engage in the issues and images of the modern civil rights movement, in his own fashion, was best illustrated in *My People*, a show he designed and performed in Chicago during the summer of 1963 for the Century of Negro Progress exhibition, the only national celebration of the centenary of President Lincoln's Emancipation Proclamation. Twenty-one major American corporations, from AT&T to Pepsi-Cola, sponsored exhibitions that traced black history from Africa to modern America, a subject Ellington had delved into often. In the July press conference announcing the show, he called it a "swinging thing about my people," but *My People* clearly represented more than that simple description. One clue he provided that day, ignored by those who later criticized the work, was that he meant the work to appeal to children, "mainly Negro, who have not been taught Negro history," as well as adults. Up to nine thousand spectators, including thousands of children, saw the show daily for six weeks. It was Ellington's chance to address black children, as he had been addressed in historical pageants a half century before in Washington, D.C. Ellington thoroughly enjoyed himself during the production, and veteran Ellington vocalist Joya Sherrill recalled that she had never seen him more excited and that "he felt he was making a racial contribution." A year later, he told Carter Harman that "I enjoyed this as a challenge, because I was the lyricist, the composer, the orchestrator, I directed it, I produced it, I lit the show, I did everything, and it was just a ball." As Ellington's son pointed out, Ellington even helped paint the sets, perhaps reliving the interest in painting that earned him a scholarship as a young man to the Pratt Institute, which he never fulfilled.[19]

In interviews, Ellington downplayed the "social significance" content of the show. "I've only got about one minute of social protest written into the script because while this aspect warrants notice, it unfairly tends to overshadow the continuing contributions of the Negro to American life," he told *Variety*, underlining his lifelong efforts to stress accomplishment over complaint. "*My People* is definitely not political. It has social significance, but the emphasis will be on entertainment." This was true, but its focus on diverse areas of nonpolitical black achievement gave the show a subtle political message in the weeks before the March on Washington. In the civil rights era, speaking about black history was inherently political. Ellington used such methods twenty years before in *Black, Brown and Beige* to make a strong point about the black contribution to America, and now an entire exhibition was built around that idea. To stress that point even further, Ellington used parts of the earlier *Black, Brown and Beige* in *My People*, specifically the spiritual, work song, and blues themes. "*My People* depicts the Negro in every walk of American life," noted the *Chicago Defender*. "It specifically states that there are Negro doctors, lawyers, businessmen, nurses, teachers, telephone operators, policemen, and housewives, but for the most part, *My People* points out that the past 100 years has been a century of swinging the blues."[20]

Social significance existed in the show in many forms, including that of an Ellington parable that encouraged listeners to examine themselves in areas beyond color and cautioned about giving in to hostility:

[*My People* was] based on the cultural contribution of the Negro, the foundation was built on the sweat, blood of the Negro. We went on for an hour and twenty minutes and never mentioned the word "color" . . . On the subject of color, we had a little girl tell the story of the green people and the purple people . . . who fought and fought till they both won and lived in a state of monotony since they both felt they had won an empty victory. So they both fought until they both lost. They were all dead, and there was blood everywhere, no purple blood, no green blood, it was all red. After the little girl finished telling her story, we had Joya Sherrill come out and say, "We finally got on to the subject and we're sorry. We tried to hold it back as long as we could so we're going to discuss color now." And then we had her sing [the Ellington song] "What color is virtue, what color is love" . . .

We send them out of the hall, the theater, on our closing number "What Color is Love, What Color Is Virtue?" which is a big question. If you answer the question, it says everything you want to say.

In the title monologue of the show, Ellington took on the persona of a "soap box speaker" as he listed black values and achievements in an impassioned preacher's cadence. Ellington's script for *My People* directed him to speak "loud . . . driving home every point with tremendous force":

My people—singing—dancing—praying—thinking—about freedom. Working—building America into the most powerful nation in the world.

Cotton—sugar—indigo—iron—coal—peanuts—steel—the railroad—you name it. The foundation of the United States rests on the sweat of my people. And in addition to working and sweating, don't forget that my people fought and died in every war.

My People also included the most outwardly political statement and song of Ellington's life, "King Fit [Fought] the Battle of Alabam," his personal interpretation of the April 1963 confrontation between police forces and thousands of black demonstrators trying to desegregate the department stores of Birmingham, Alabama, led by Dr. King. Eugene "Bull" Connor, the city's commissioner of public safety, used police dogs, high pressure hoses, and electric cattle prods to disperse the crowds, which mostly consisted of young black people and children. The sight was captured on national television and changed many Americans' minds about the need for equal rights. It obviously lit a fire under Ellington. In May 1963, he let loose some harsher comments than usual, telling a journalist that racial troubles such as Birmingham "must lose a million friends and get a million enemies every day for the United States . . . It's too bad that civilization doesn't bring with it some wisdom." He further noted that "I had my fights 20 years ago" in various Southern states "without any newspapermen around." Ellington sang "King Fit the Battle of Alabam" himself at jazz festivals in the summer of 1963, something he had never done before (*Jazz* magazine proclaimed that "it should be recorded and played in Congress at regular intervals during the civil rights debates"). A choir performed it during *My People*:

> King fit the battle of Alabam—Birmingham . . .
> And the bull got nasty—ghastly—nasty
> Bull turned the hoses on the church people . . .
> And the water came splashing—dashing—crashing
> Freedom rider—ride
> Freedom rider—go to town
> Y'all and us—gonna get on the bus
> Y'all aboard—sit down, sit tight, you're right . . .
>
> Little babies fit the battle of police dogs—mongrel police . . .
> And the dogs came growling—howling—growling . . .
>
>> And when the dog saw the baby wasn't afraid
>> He turned to his Uncle Bull and said
>> That baby acts like he don't give a damn
>> Are you sure we're still in Alabam?

In the show, the "King Fit the Battle" sequence finished with a "parade" of placards celebrating black Americans who had achieved, who had a made a difference in the world, each one recited and displayed to the audience: Dr. King, George Washington Carver, Dr. Ralph Bunche, Dr. Charles Drew, Bill Robinson, Booker T. Washington, Paul Lawrence Dunbar, Frederick Douglass, Thurgood Marshall, and more. Once again, Ellington seemed to reference *The Star of Ethiopia*, W. E. B. DuBois' staged pageant of black history, which Ellington saw as a teenager, and *My People* also featured banners proclaiming the "gifts" African Americans had presented the world.[21]

King and Ellington met for the first time during the Chicago exposition. It was a joyous meeting. "Martin is sitting in his limousine and he looks up and he sees Edward [Ellington] and jumps out of the car, and he runs over to him and they embrace like they were old friends," recalled Marian Logan, a civil rights activist and the wife of Dr. Arthur Logan. Ellington recalled the way that King commanded respect as he traveled. "In order for him to say hello to me, he had to have his chauffeur stop this long Cadillac. An aide got out and opened the door, and two motor policemen in front and two more behind had to stop so that he could shake hands with me," Ellington recalled later. "This is the way the man lives and travels who represents the oppressed race." Ellington suggested to King that they go together to where Strayhorn was rehearsing *My People*. Strayhorn had met King before as a result of his close friendship with Lena Horne, and he would in a few days be a member of "the inner circle" around King at the March on Washington. When Ellington and King arrived, Ellington asked the company to perform the song he had written about King. "Martin was very moved," Logan reported years later. "Very impressed—very proud . . . tears came down and Edward was delighted." Later that day, at the exposition, King awarded Ellington a plaque celebrating "his contribution to American society through music. Ellington, in turn, gave him a manuscript of a song from . . . *My People*."[22] One suspects the manuscript was "King Fit the Battle of Alabam."

But, as Ellington repeated many times to the media, politics and "social" comment were not the main themes of *My People*, though they were more present than he admitted. "There is one theme that runs through the production: love," *Down Beat* accurately reported. Love is viewed from many angles in *My People*. The theme is constant in the extensive spiritual section. "Lord, dear Lord, above, God Almighty God of love," the section began. "Please look down and see my people through." Love was explored in the ballet performed by Alvin Ailey's dance company during the "Work Song" (from *Black, Brown and Beige*), which depicted a young and passionate couple picking petals off a flower. The stormy and jealous sides of love were explored in the blues sections of *My People*. Ellington's new blues songs were simplistic and sophomoric, but *Down Beat* reported that they were "humorous" on stage. Most importantly, love was key in Ellington's achingly beautiful new song "My Mother, My Father (Heritage)," a tribute to the loving culture in which he was raised. Ellington sympathetically portrayed the civil rights movement in *My People*, but with this song he also stressed the importance of family tradition and good character in facing not only the struggles of life, but also in being able to appreciate and hand down the best things in life. From what is known of Ellington's early life and how he felt about it, it can be safely surmised that "My Mother, My Father" represented one of Ellington's most personal songs. Perry Watkins, who worked on the earlier *Beggars Holiday* as well as *My People*, recalled that Ellington had tears in his eyes when he first described the song to him:

> My mother—the greatest—and the prettiest
> My father—just handsome—but the wittiest
> My granddaddy natural born proud
> Grandma—so gentle—so fine
> The men before them worked hard and sang loud
> About the beautiful women in this family of mine
> Our homestead—the warmest—hospitality
> In me you see the least of the family tree personality
> I was raised in the palm of the hand
> By the very best people in this land
> From sun to sun
> Their hearts beat as one
> My mother—my father—and love

"That's everybody's song," Ellington told a Canadian TV host a year later. "Everybody feels the same way."[23]

My People and the Century of Negro Progress exhibition as a whole did not do as well as hoped. Early reports forecast eight hundred thousand attendees over eighteen days, but only one hundred thousand went through the turnstiles. Still, that number was more than usually saw Ellington live during a comparable period of time, and the exhibition provided valuable positive publicity for black Americans during a time of intense civil rights furor. Later observers, such as Stuart Nicholson and Klaus Stratemann, have argued that *My People* did not attract large audiences because it was "out of tune" with the prevailing aggressive mood among blacks concerning the reform of racial inequalities. Yet, except for a review of the exhibition as a whole in *Variety*, none of the dozens of media reviews or features concerning the show share this sentiment. *My People* received uniformly positive notices. Mercer Ellington instead blamed disappointing audience numbers on the lack of publicity and support for the exhibition in Chicago.[24]

With *My People*, Ellington made an important statement of long-term significance for him and his career. He exhibited for a new generation, as he had in previous decades, a strong and multifaceted commitment to the issues of the black struggle and black history. From this point forward, he received no serious challenge from the black press or any other media representatives concerning his personal and political commitment to "his people" and their desire to overturn American discrimination. In May 1964, Ellington was photographed showing support for Senator Hubert H. Humphrey (D-MN) for his efforts to pass the Civil Rights bill despite the "verbal 'stall-in' staged by Dixiecrats."

Further signaling his changed image in the black community, two separate *Pittsburgh Courier* editorials from the same month revisited Ellington's 1951 statement of "we ain't ready yet." They did not criticize it, they found it prescient. The most extensive comment came from columnist P. L. Prattis, one of the leading critics during the 1951 controversy:

> The time was, not too long ago, that any Negro who turned to his own people and complained "we ain't ready yet," would have been condemned as an "Uncle Tom." Such a Negro would have been deemed to have no pride in his own people. He would have been regarded as "white folks" colored man.
>
> Duke Ellington let some such thought emanate from his lips some years back, in St. Louis. Negroes forgot all about the Duke's genius and what it had meant in raising them in the esteem of others. They jumped down the Duke's throat. What right did he have to express [himself] on social matters, anyhow? He was only a musician.
>
> Well, no one gets conked any longer when he says we ain't ready yet. The long lines of unemployed Negroes prove the fact . . . Were we ready for integration? Senator Richard Russell, Georgia, says no. You don't want to take his word for it, but you really don't know how to argue back. The best answer is that some of us were, and some of us were not.

A week before the opening of *My People*, a columnist in the *St. Louis Argus*, another black newspaper, agreed: "It seems that ever since Duke Ellington uttered that infamous remark about us not being ready . . . all of us at one time or another have echoed the remark." Even Jackie Robinson, the baseball star and business executive, lectured in 1964 to the NAACP in Florida on the subject of "Is the Negro Ready [for Integration]?" He spoke, accurately as it turned out, about how the fight for equality would not be over when new laws were passed and that African Americans still had to be pre-pared to agitate for their rights.[25] Now that the end of Jim Crow and segre-gation were in sight from a legislative standpoint, black leaders and writ-ers were wondering how African Americans would handle their (hopefully) improved status.

But Ellington's embrace of King and increased involvement in speaking out on civil rights issues did not mean that he completely turned his back on his earlier viewpoints. Mercer recalled that his father viewed Dr. King as his "main man . . . He felt that whatever Martin represented, was something worthwhile going after. He adored Martin. He felt he was one of the few real people who involved themselves in what matters count." Yet, in a pri-vate 1964 interview with Carter Harman, Ellington expressed a displeasure with the March on Washington based largely on the ideas he had expressed during the 1951 "we ain't ready" controversy. "You got 20 million Negroes, every Negro give one day's pay, how much money you got?" asked Elling-ton. "$100 million," replied Harman. Ellington continued:

> Thank you. Then you're going somewhere. All this bullshit. They had the big-gest parade in the world, and all these people, everybody who went to Wash-ington that day, instead of spending 50 or 100 dollars, all they had to do was give $5. They'd have a million dollars. It's just very simple, simple arithmetic. Everybody gets involved in all this high-powered bullshit . . . They get their pictures in the papers and all that. It's great. They get on television. But fuck it, the cause stands still . . . I told them once, I told them a helluva long time ago—they told me I didn't know what I was doing and I should go play my music . . . I told them in 1951. How much would $100 million be worth to-day? . . . It pays all your expenses and you still got your principal. The only people who did good out of the goddamn parade was the people who owned businesses in Washington, the hotels and all that, they had a fucking ball, put all the fucking money in their pockets. To begin with, let's take, for instance, the propaganda. It was . . . the biggest demonstration in the world, but any-thing they do after that is anti-climactic, it's too big to follow. What else can they do? How can you do your best number and follow it? This is simple dra-matics, this is a kind of thing you think of in a high school play. You don't have to be a mastermind to figure that out.

"I'll give up the band and direct the whole fucking thing [civil rights move-ment]," Ellington told Harman after his monologue. "Passive resistance is wonderful, if you own the ground you're resisting on, like India and Gan-dhi," he further argued. "This [in the United States] is something else . . . can't do anything without money."[26] Ellington's point of view deserves serious consideration. Long-requested and long-needed laws were passed in the mid-1960s, mainly due to the bravery and political skill of many civil rights organizations and the risks street protesters assumed, but financial and personal security and equality were still far from the reach of most black Americans during the rest of Ellington's lifetime and beyond. Ellington may have represented a point of view from an earlier time, but it had relevance to the civil rights era.

The civil rights movement brought enormous changes that blacks had agitated for since emancipation, especially the Civil Rights Act of 1964 and the Voting Rights Act of 1965. Yet these legislative victories were quickly followed by the "long hot summers" of 1964–68, which brought some of the worst riots in American history, which occurred in black communities, particularly ghettoes, across the country and claimed hundreds of lives and hundreds of millions of dollars in property damage. Historians have since blamed the incidents on a "revolution of rising expectations." The 1964 and 1965 acts were monumental, but they only changed the laws on the books, not the reality on the streets. In 1966, a third of black American males still lived in poverty, and those who worked earned an income that, on average, represented only 55 percent of what whites earned. The legislation did not magically erase discrimination from the workplace or the housing industry—or from the hearts of many whites. Shortly after the 1965 Watts Riots in south Los Angeles, which ran for six days and left thirty-four dead, Dr. King realized the shortcomings of the legislation he had worked so hard to get passed. He told one of his most trusted aides that "I worked to get these people the right to eat hamburgers, and now I've got to do something . . . to help them get the money to buy [them]." After the Watts Riots, he told the press that "the main issue is economic."

After 1965, the racial situation became even more heated in the United States, with calls for black separatism and "black power" emanating from the formerly biracial Student Nonviolent Coordinating Committee (SNCC) and others, and calls for lethal violence against racists emanating from the Black Panthers. Before 1965, the *Billboard* Top 100 singles chart had become unprecedentedly integrated by black artists, which led Dr. King to tell a convention of black DJs in late 1967 that "you have paved the way for social and political change by creating a powerful, cultural bridge between black and white. School integration is much easier now that they share a common music, a common language, and enjoy the same dances." But, as Brian Ward has documented, King was overly optimistic. Segregation between the races actually became more common after 1965, on the *Billboard* sales charts and in the streets. During the same period, protests against the Vietnam War increased. Yet, at the end of the decade, after demonstrations that drew hundreds of thousands of people, the war seemed no closer to ending, just as the miseries of the black ghetto seemed intractable. For the younger generation of blacks and whites "the result was frustration," according to historian Terry Anderson. "Realizing that they were having little or no impact on national policy, they began moving from protest to resistance." Black identity was shifting: this more aggressive attitude of demanding respect, of willingness to break the laws to register complaint was about as far as could be imagined from the culture of "commanding respect" that Ellington had learned in turn-of-the-century black Washington, D.C.[27]

A politically aggressive mood had pervaded the jazz world since at least the early 1960s, long before the long hot summers and calls for black separatism. Famous jazz artists of the bebop generation such as Art Blakey, John Coltrane, Charles Mingus, Max Roach, and Sonny Rollins referred directly to civil rights themes of protest and freedom within the titles of their pieces and sometimes in their lyrics. Ellington's *My People* show fit within that milieu. Dizzy Gillespie played numerous benefits for civil rights organizations and even ran for president in 1964. Jazz writer Nat Hentoff said Gillespie's candidacy was mostly "for kicks," but also noted that he called at least one press conference where he spoke seriously on civil rights and discrimination issues. "The concept of a jazzman making this kind of statement—let alone attracting a sizable press representation to hear it—would have seemed utterly fanciful thirty years ago," Hentoff noted in early 1965. The same would have held true ten years previously as well.

Perhaps the biggest difference in the new jazz generation lay in its onstage attitude. Hentoff cited artists such as Coltrane, Miles Davis, and Thelonius Monk, who refrained from making "speeches on prejudice in their music, but their jazz speaks from a position of strength in their self-images as creators who do not have to—and will not—grin for the white man" and "will not suffer [their] dignity to be chipped—either by a cop or by a drunken member of the audience." Yet Ellington had laid the foundation for this supposedly new aesthetic decades before in his insistence on "commanding respect" for his music and race, even as he also developed a reputation for grinning at his audience. And Ellington had penned songs and suites with a racial emphasis since the 1920s. The performers of Ellington's generation believed in entertaining the audience as well as providing great music, while the younger performers tended to let the music do the talking, weren't afraid of showing anger or other disturbing emotions or themes onstage, and shied away from show business traditions of the past. But they also knew and talked about how closely they were linked with the innovations, musical and racial, that Ellington brought to the jazz world. One of the most famous proponents of "free jazz" during the 1960s, Cecil Taylor, a trained musician with a background in classical music, known for banging his piano with his arms and elbows, described Ellington as "the only prophet I recognize." "The problem is to utilize the energies of the European composers . . . and blend this with the traditional music of the American Negro, and to create a new energy," he told the *Saturday Review* in 1963. "That's what I did. And was it unique? No. Historically not. Ellington did it."[28]

Many themes Ellington had propagated over the decades, especially those of black entrepreneurship and stressing the value of black culture, were embraced by black artists of the period. During the 1950s and 1960s, Ray Charles and Sam Cooke founded their own publishing companies and record labels, taking more control of their careers and using their success to help younger black artists, just as Ellington had created Tempo Music and Mercer Records in the 1940s and early 1950s, respectively. Berry Gordy's Motown Records label unabashedly set their sights on and succeeded in bringing a huge white crossover audience during the 1960s—an Irving Mills–like strategy with black entrepreneurs reaping the profits from over $100 million in sales during the decade. Even the Art Ensemble of Chicago, the Association for the Advancement of Creative Musicians, and the Black Arts Movement, formed in the mid-1960s, owed something to the Ellington legacy in their celebration and financial support of an eclectic, often dissonant array of African American music and art, though Ellington's earlier music wouldn't readily fit within their avant-garde explorations of the "New Thing" in jazz. But perhaps the *Far East Suite* (1966) and *Afro-Eurasian Eclipse* (1971) would.[29]

During this period of rising racial conflict, journalists more frequently called on Ellington for his opinion on the situation. He did a much better job answering these questions and his critics in the black community during this period than in the 1950s. Jazz journalist Ralph J. Gleason watched Ellington react at a 1965 press conference. "What do you think of what happened at Watts?" a TV reporter asked him. Ellington said he wasn't there and therefore did not know. More questions on the subject followed, until the reporter asked, "Can we take it you are putting down the civil rights movement?" Gleason reported that "Ellington looked at him with the cold stare of a man who knows he's been talking to a man who doesn't know but thinks he does." Ellington quietly replied: "I started my own civil rights movement in the Thirties. I went down South without federal troops."

Ellington also frequently mentioned the musical works he wrote that illustrated black history and life, and that, as he said in 1965, his "work in this direction preceded courts and night sticks." In an interview from the early 1970s, he went into more detail:

> "Black Beauty" was written in 1928. "Black and Tan Fantasy" was in 1927, "Creole Love Call" in 1927, and it's always been black something. All the way up.
>
> "Jump for Joy," which we did in 1941, was the first social significant review . . . We've always been pioneers in everything we did. We pioneered the movie theaters for bands. We pioneered the social movement with the history of the Negro in America, with *Black, Brown and Beige* [in 1943] and every year after that in Carnegie Hall.[30]

Ellington also referred the doubters of his fealty to the cause to the hundreds of benefits he had attended and played for civil rights and other African American–affiliated organizations since the 1930s. Such benefits continued during the 1960s, including shows by Ellington and his orchestra on behalf of the NAACP, CORE, SNCC, the Urban League, the United Negro College Fund, the African American Institute, the children of Dr. Martin Luther King, Jr., Mustevec (an organization of African American youth jazz musicians), Yale black scholarships, the Interracial Council, and many others. Ellington also performed at benefits for numerous organizations not affiliated with blacks. "We've done more benefits for civil-rights groups than anybody, and I don't think there's been any doubt how we felt concerning prejudice," Ellington commented in 1965. "But still the best way for me to be effective is through music." Ellington proved skillful in using his own history and work to establish his civil rights bona fides without sacrificing his view of how the struggle should be waged. He supported the cause with action, money, and commanding respect, while resisting adoption of the more militant methods of the period. When a Dallas reporter asked Ellington to "assess" whether his music had "helped [in] any way in race relations," Ellington replied: "There would be no way to take a census of this. You try to make your contributions, try to do it with dignity, and to command respect. This is our life. Our responsibility [is] not only to our people, but to America and to our fellow man."[31]

Not all blacks agreed with Ellington's civil rights approach in the late 1960s. At a 1969 Ellington symposium at the University of California, Berkeley, the editor of *Soul Illustrated* magazine reported that "several young people and his mother . . . figure that Ellington doesn't possess enough 'soul' to compete with currently popular performers," but that, if alive, Charlie

Parker would. On the same program, Charles Mingus "tersely" reminded the audience that Parker was an Ellington fan. A North Carolina reviewer in the same year felt that Ellington's manner and image were too reminiscent of the age of Jim Crow: "Duke is a fine musician but I cannot stand to watch him perform. Ellington is straight out of the 1930s—Stepnfetchit and Mr. Bojangles! He epitomizes plastic—his mannerisms, gestures, greased down hair, and the repetitious 'we all really love you' were just too much. The fact that the band was clad in what purported to be African dress [dashikis] made it even worse." Commitment to the cause in the 1960s, especially for the younger generation of activists, was signified by marching and speeches and by political or cultural rebellion—Ellington would never measure up on that account in the 1960s, and the younger generation could not recall or was not made aware of strides he made in the 1930s and 1940s.[32]

When Ellington spoke of racial issues in the United States, he tended to stress the positive while not denying the negative. Perhaps part of this attitude emanated from the people he met during his international tours on behalf of the State Department, where "the big question when they meet an American negro [sic] is always the race problem," according to Ellington in 1966. "Some one came up and asked me if it was true that a negro had been beaten up in Alabama a few days back. 'It's true,' I said, 'but where else in the world could that happen and you'd know about it the next day way over here?' We have all the problems of a *free* country." Undoubtedly, a lot of his views on the subject emanated from his upbringing. In Berkeley in 1969 for a celebration of his seventieth birthday and the first anniversary of the integration of the Berkeley school system, Ellington made comments to high school students that one of Ellington's elders in Washington, D.C., at the turn of the century could have made:

> Asked about the importance of black studies programs, Ellington replied: "The major thing is to command respect, not to beg for it."
>
> "Whatever you decide to do in life," he added, "be sure to acquire all the skills and perform them well. That way you'll be able to execute them better than your opposition if and when your opportunity comes."
>
> What about integration, queried one black youth. "Education is essential for survival," the Duke counseled, "Without survival, you can't do anything. The United States has got to get together on education."

Rather than downplaying the concept of integration, which Ellington practiced in every facet of his life, he was telling students to worry about themselves, their character, and abilities first, not to allow racial issues to impede them mentally or physically. In a private interview from 1964, Ellington expressed concern that black children were no longer being instructed to "command respect . . . this has not been taught. This has not been organized. And seen to." It was one of the major faults he found in the civil rights movement, because he believed the lack of this behavior trait damaged the image of black Americans: "For Christ's sake, every time somebody [black] does something good, ten [black] assholes go out and do something bad. So what? You're fucked." Ellington did not see the sense in the rising interest in the black community during this period for separatism. He felt that judging or excluding people based on color on any basis represented prejudice. When asked about black separatism in 1969, Ellington replied with lyrics he wrote for *My People*: "What color is virtue? What color is love? What color is God?"[33]

While he deflected a question about black studies programs before high school students in Berkeley in 1969, Ellington endorsed the concept five months earlier.[34] In May 1969, Ellington came to San Francisco State University, invited by its acting president S. I. Hayakawa, who had been embroiled in a long-running controversy because of the lack of a black studies program on the campus. A months-long strike by the Black Student Union had caused tension and produced extensive negative press coverage, and Hayakawa hoped that a free concert by Ellington, "his friend of 15 years," paid for out of Hayakawa's contingency fund, would serve as "some kind of happy event that everyone could enjoy after months of disturbance and misery." The omens for that kind of outcome were not promising. Before the show, Ellington received a telegram from Ecumenical House, a religious organization near campus that had served as a center of the protests. They claimed he was being used as a "political pawn to defeat aspirations of the entire minority community in San Francisco. You are being asked in the traditional manner to be an instant Negro, whose purpose is to be a decoy, so as to confuse and obscure the real issues." Protesters paraded around the auditorium during the show, one holding a sign that read "Hayakawa Smells— He's the Racist, Not Duke."

The overall reception for Ellington was mixed, but he was certainly no one's pawn or decoy. Before the show, Hayakawa sent a replying telegram to the Ecumenical House students insisting that the implication that Ellington "could be duped into being made 'a tool of a racist scheme' is an insult to his intelligence and character." The university's gym was standing room only for the performance, with some students placed onstage. According to a nationally syndicated newspaper article, "the 2,600 students greeted Duke's orchestrated jazz as enthusiastically as though it were a combination rock band concert and a psychedelic light show." Ellington was cheered when he announced that "This concert is totally dedicated to those of us who are determinedly dedicated to developing the Black Studies program." Later on in the show, Ellington and Hayakawa danced impromptu onstage with a coed, resulting in a picture that made many newspapers the next day. When Ellington called Hayakawa "our choreographer" after that, the audience "strongly booed." At a reception Ellington attended after the show, "a BSU member, smarting from Ellington's even mentioning Hayakawa, put the Duke down in plain terms."

United Press International's syndicated story reported that Ellington and his music "seemed able to heal wounds with ease," and probably for most students attending the show, this was true, but the situation proved more complicated that that. The more aggressive BSU and Ecumenical House students were more interested in embarrassing Hayakawa than welcoming Ellington as an ally of their cause, as someone who had fought a similar fight to theirs for many decades, making a case for the centrality of African Americans to American history. Ellington was also more effective in this struggle than they were, and much more successful at getting all Americans to share his point of view without having to resort to confusing and offensive epithets like "instant Negro" and "political pawn."

The students probably had no idea that it made a lot of sense for Ellington to support a black studies program. In the 1960s, black history still rarely had a place in the curriculum American school children grew up with, a circumstance that concerned Ellington, and one to which he often drew attention. Ellington spoke privately in 1964 about how, with the abolition of Jim Crow because of federal legislation, valuable parts of the black community would be lost, especially black businesses that previously were forced to cater to the black community because of segregation: "A lot of people down South have tremendous investments in business, Negroes, but integration is going to completely ruin them. But they're fighting for it anyway, making a tremendous sacrifice . . . his business that he has run and financed, and put his entire life into, [such as] a Negro hotel—he's going to . . . lose everything." In addition to the losses of black entrepreneurs, the possibility existed that there would be less opportunity for black children in segregated black schools to be taught their own history. Black studies departments sought to give college students the kind of instruction in African American and African history and culture that Ellington received in his youth and that was difficult to obtain elsewhere during the 1960s, and it is no surprise that Ellington supported such programs.

Langston Hughes, born three years after Ellington, encountered similar conflicts with the younger, more politically confrontational generation of black activists at the end of his life. In 1965, an underground mimeographed magazine accused Hughes of lacking courage and likened him to a dinosaur for questioning the black "ultra-nationalism" present in some of the work of LeRoi Jones [nee Amiri Baraka]. "Although he had always been proud to be a 'race man,' the central tenet of [Hughes's] pride in belonging to the race was that blackness was a normal aspect of world humanity. He claimed very little more," wrote biographer Arnold Rampersad in a statement that could easily have applied to Ellington as well.

Hughes felt disturbed by the trends toward black separatism and nationalism. At one emotional reading in the mid-1960s, he reminded his audience about the many whites who had died down South in the fight for civil rights. Ellington harbored similar convictions about integration. "There is so much organized resistance built up against integration," he said in 1965. "It's frightening to hear some [black] people talk. They sound like the [people] who killed those six million Jews." He felt that such anti-integration separatist efforts were "financed by the enemies of the United States." Ellington also went against the current fashion by insisting on the significant contributions of white musicians/composers George Gershwin and Paul Whiteman. "I don't go along with that race nonsense," Ellington said in 1966, about those who would only acknowledge black antecedents in the history of jazz. Hughes insisted that "the problem was not one of blacks and whites . . . but 'people of good will' against the rest." Hughes and Ellington stood for lasting accomplishment and the respect that would accrue to their race for it; earning respect rather than demanding it, working hard and creating an internationally accessible and lasting vision of African American life over the long run.[35]

On at least one occasion, in 1967, Ellington had his beliefs on civil rights activism questioned by members of his own orchestra. According to Norman Granz:

> There was a big discussion between Mercer and some of the guys in the band and Duke. At that time, they were having a lot of the [civil rights] marches, particularly outside of Chicago, in Cicero, which . . . was one of the most vicious racist towns you could imagine . . . and I think it was Mercer, or somebody else in the band said, "Duke, are you gonna march, or is the band gonna march?" And Duke said, "Hell no, I'm not going to march." Then I think it may have been Mercer that said, "Well, why not, pop? I mean it's something you can make a statement on." And he said, "I make my statements with my music." I suppose one could say that's not the way to go, you've got to utilize

your name . . . the sight of you walking in the streets protesting what's happening . . . might be more important than the subtlety of your music. On the other hand, you could defend Duke's position and say it's not gonna make that much difference for me to put myself out whereas I can make a positive statement with my music . . . it became an issue for a while, in the bandroom, just with the cats changing clothes, and the subject came up. Because you know the bands talk a lot about those problems on the road, it takes up a lot of time in conversation.[36]

In racial matters, just as in musical matters, Ellington existed in a milieu of his own. As chapter 13 will show, his singular path on the race issue alienated older conservative African Americans during his First Sacred Concert during the mid-1960s, as well as the younger, more militant blacks depicted in this chapter. Despite such misgivings, Ellington was named one of the "100 Most Influential Black Americans" in 1971 by *Ebony* magazine, alongside such civil rights stalwarts as Dr. Ralph Abernathy, Julian Bond, and Angela Davis.[37]

Throughout his career, Ellington conquered prejudice in the musical realm, constantly demonstrating that the fight for equality was waged on more battlefronts than marches, speeches, and protests. He acted as an influence that showed something beyond the black anger so prevalent, as well as justified, in the 1960s, someone who had preached black beauty since the 1920s and now found millions adopting the same outlook.

12

1963 STATE DEPARTMENT TOUR

We seek to influence people's thinking through the various means of communication ... our individual country programs are not scattershot efforts but carefully designed to gain support for established U.S. foreign policy objectives relating to the particular country ...

We emphasize the ways in which U.S. policies harmonize with those of other peoples and governments, and underline those aspects of American life and culture which facilitate sympathetic understanding of our policies. We endeavor to unmask and counter hostile attempts on the part of communists and others to distort or frustrate American objectives and policies ...

And above all, it is what we do—not what we say—that has the greatest impact overseas ...

Our arsenal of persuasion must be as ready as our nuclear arsenal, and used as never before. EDWARD R. MURROW, director of the United States Information Agency, 28 March 1963

So long as the racial situation remains unsolved in the U.S., sending jazz musicians abroad puts them in an untenable situation when the people overseas ask questions. DIZZY GILLESPIE, November 1963[1]

In the fall of 1963, after years of urging from the press, the United States government sent Duke Ellington and his orchestra on a three-month State Department goodwill tour. *The Far East Suite* (1966), the band's best album of the 1960s, arose from the continental and colorful sights and sounds Ellington and co-composer Billy Strayhorn absorbed during the trip. But, despite the title of the album, the band actually toured in the Near and Middle East for the most part, visiting (in order) Syria, Jordan, Afghanistan, India, Ceylon (now Sri Lanka), Pakistan (including what is known today as Bangladesh), Iran, Iraq, and Lebanon. Shows in Turkey, Cypress, the United Arab Republic, Greece, Egypt, and Yugoslavia were cancelled after the assassination of President Kennedy.

The government could not have picked a more appropriate ambassador and spokesman than Ellington during this period of heightened civil rights activism and violence in the midst of some of the more tense moments of the cold war. Ellington had always couched his verbal and musical statements for equality within a love of country. Throughout his career, the struggle for civil rights represented to him an opportunity to fulfill the great democratic promises embedded in America's founding documents; he generally did not view the struggle as an example of fundamental problems within the United States. His views fit in perfectly with the conservative political and foreign policy consensus that reigned in the cold war administrations of both Eisenhower and Kennedy.

Yet, Ellington was no propaganda-spouting mouthpiece for the American government. He had his own ideas to communicate as well, ideas expressed for decades that would now receive an unprecedented international airing. As seen in publicity for the 1963 state tour and in international press clippings distributed by the government in the years preceding and following the tour, Ellington was portrayed abroad as a symbol of the best in American culture. The United States government depicted jazz as high culture. Times were changing.[2]

With the placing of Ellington on a state tour, music served again as an instrument signifying change in the portrayal and treatment of blacks in America and around the world and as evidence of what blacks could achieve in the United States. For years, Ellington had represented black achievement and artistry like no one else in the jazz and black communities. Starting in the 1960s, the U.S. government appropriated that image to sell a positive vision of American character and respectability to the world. Once again, Ellington was seen as existing in a realm beyond entertainment, as signifying something important about America and the world. In this period, his influence moved beyond the U.S. and Western Europe and would continue to do so for the rest of his career. The 1963 state tour's expansion of Ellington's international audience and appeal initiated a series of lucrative private and state-sponsored tours for Ellington in Africa, Asia, South America, the Soviet Union, and other far-flung areas in years to come. Such shows brought higher guarantees than usual, partly because of the tours' rarity and expense, and provided a major financial boost to the orchestra during the last decade of Ellington's career.

The 1963 tour also signified the growing importance of jazz in the cold war. In the years immediately following World War II, the State Department steered clear of the music in its cultural efforts, but a new perspective had taken shape since the mid-1950s, and not just within government circles. As cold war cultural historian Reinhold Wagnleitner has documented, the popularity of jazz among foreign audiences rose exponentially in this period, and the State Department slowly realized that "jazz didn't need propaganda to succeed, the propaganda needed jazz." Critic Gilbert Seldes, host of the 1958 NBC-TV series *The Subject Is Jazz*, talked about the popularity of jazz around the world, including unexpected places like Germany, Pakistan, and the Communist satellite countries. "The communists have tried to create a communized version of jazz but they won't succeed because there's something rebellious in the very essence of jazz," Seldes commented on air. "We know this because in Hungary during the revolution, shards of jazz were whistled as passwords between the revolutionaries." The musical and political power of jazz around the world would not have surprised the globe-trotting Ellington; he heard such stories from fans for years. "In Germany, we had occasion to drink beer with people who had been put in the concentration camp during the war for listening to our records," he told Voice of America jazz radio host Willis Conover in 1956, when asked for stories of "unusual or happy occasions" in the countries he had visited over the years.[3]

The Ellington State Department tour also signaled the U.S. government's increasing involvement and identification with the civil rights movement. In many ways, cold war and civil rights events left them little choice. A barrage of Soviet propaganda ridiculed the irony of America's civil rights abuses and violence within a country where "all men are created equal." Slowly, over the course of the 1950s and 1960s, the cold war helped create a situation in which the United States government could no longer afford to ignore American racism. Before 1963, American presidents tended to act on these issues only when their hands were forced, as in Eisenhower's initially reluctant, eventually forceful reaction to the Little Rock school integration incident in 1957.[4] The 1963 March on Washington and the violent Birmingham response to peaceful black protesters galvanized an increase in American support across racial lines for equal rights for blacks.

The 1963 Ellington state tour demonstrated that the aligning of the U.S. government with blacks such as Ellington played well overseas, burnishing the image of the United States and aiding cold war objectives of keeping communism at bay in the developing countries that the Ellington orchestra visited. Biographies of Ellington in local papers on the tour often resided alongside notices of official American support of the civil rights movement, particularly Kennedy's repudiation of the Birmingham church bombing that killed four black schoolgirls and his post–March on Washington meet-and-greet with black leaders. In the countries Ellington visited, extensive polling showed that black artistry along with evidence of civil rights progress resonated with the young people who the United States feared were most likely to be attracted to communism. Such tempting international dividends, closely observed by the State, probably helped spur President Johnson's aggressive campaign to secure the passage of the Twenty-Fourth Amendment, which abolished the poll tax, and the 1965 Civil Rights Act, which outlawed Jim Crow segregation. The United States needed to live up to the ideals of the country's founding documents, and civil rights protesters made the continuance of discrimination in America a huge political liability around the world. With his eloquence, patriotism, and fame, Ellington well represented both American opportunity and culture.

State Department–sponsored cultural tours by American performers emerged from World War II and the ensuing cold war. The Soviets initiated the trend of using touring artists as "cold war troops" to promote the spread of communism, which led to President Eisenhower's efforts to fund an American response to such tactics in 1954. The issue of American race relations was an especially volatile weapon in this propaganda war, and had been for some time. The Nazis and the Japanese used propaganda concerning lynching in America in order to discredit the ideals of democracy for which the United States claimed to fight. After the war, Soviet foreign minister Vyacheslav Molotov needled President Truman's secretary of state James Byrnes about the exclusion of blacks from voting in Byrnes's home state of South Carolina whenever the subject of "Soviet high-handedness and ruthlessness in Eastern Europe" was broached. The Soviets publicized disturbing facts about American race relations to newly decolonized postwar developing nations that they hoped would join the communist bloc.

The lack of civil rights for blacks marked a major vulnerability for the United States, but cultural tours addressed more issues than race. They sold the American way of life, the constitutional freedoms Americans enjoyed, and they spotlighted American culture as a way to develop bonds between countries and build a positive image of American character and an alluring vision of modernity. The tours also seemed built on the idea that the appreciation of American culture would engender a personal respect as valuable and perhaps more lasting than the respect accorded American military and technological prowess. John Paine, an ASCAP officer, referred to American music in a 1946 speech as the United States' "most potent propaganda device" and called for its increased exposure around the world to increase esteem and commerce for Americans. The United States Information Service (USIS), an international propaganda wing of the State Department, heeded Paine's advice. Several documents from the period show that senior officials made sure that USIS libraries in foreign countries featured American music, but in this period most of it was American orchestral music, though some jazz and blues were noted in the files as well.[5]

In 1954, in response to Soviet cultural efforts, President Eisenhower and Congress assembled and approved the President's Special Program for Cultural Presentations (CP) to organize and supervise State Department–sponsored tours of American artists, authors, academics, theater productions, religious leaders, and athletes. The program received an annual allotment of $2.25 million, which stayed relatively steady until 1962. In the first eight years of the program, 206 American cultural "projects" visited 113 countries. From the 1940s to the early 1960s, some felt that the State Department tours should help build markets for American cultural products overseas, but CP programs were mandated to serve U.S. foreign policy designs first, concentrating on countries with little opportunity to see and hear American artists, not more developed countries in Western Europe. Earlier musical genres like rock and roll, blues, and country music were almost uniformly passed over for the allegedly more highbrow genres of classical, jazz, and folk. The overall goal was to sell America and democracy, not to criticize the Soviets. The Soviets' propaganda was more "mallet-like," while the American efforts were usually more subtle. Sometimes, as in the case of the extremely successful Voice of America radio network, many in targeted countries did not even realize the stations represented propaganda.[6]

Seeking to counter the racist image of the United States, the State Department increasingly turned to black performers and artists—but not without some ambivalence. Artists and other figures were picked to display the status and opportunities available to blacks in America. Tours featuring performances by American athletes, usually including black athletes, proved very popular. But the most visible presence by blacks on State Department tours was in the musical realm, in the classical and jazz fields. William Warfield, an accomplished bass-baritone vocalist, was the first, touring as a vocal soloist with the Philadelphia Symphonic Orchestra in the summer of 1955, and in later tours, as a solo artist with piano accompaniment. In widely disparate countries, Warfield, with his mastery of both classical and black spiritual repertoires, supplied the kinds of results the State Department hoped for. A 1956 embassy dispatch from Addis Ababa in Ethiopia noted the "excellent psychological results" accruing from Warfield's visit. In Penang, Malaya, traditionally seen by American performers as a "showman's grave," Warfield received an enthusiastic response in 1958, "allowing local people to see for themselves what a highly talented and personable American Negro had made of his opportunities . . . American stock in the community has risen appreciably," according to the local American Public Affairs Officer.[7]

Several 1950s tours by two other black, classically oriented vocalists, Marian Anderson and Camilla Williams, received similar glowing notices in reports filed by American embassies. Anderson, whose 1957–58 Asian tour happened to occur just after the Little Rock school integration incident, received especially significant extramusical notices in the Philippines press. They wrote that "she looms much larger than Little Rock" and "makes up for Faubus." She also was viewed in a category beyond that of her race, extolled as an example of character triumphing over prejudice and proof that "America is not all jukebox" and shallow materialism. America sent so many blacks abroad on state-sponsored tours that, in at least two instances, friction resulted. In 1956, the white minority colonial government of the Central African Federation (most of which is now called Zimbabwe) complained that the American practice of using only black performers on tours in the area "is not helping race relations in this country." In early 1959, after receiving three straight African American performers, "the Cairo public was beginning to wonder whether the United States had white artists or whether Egypt was not considered important enough to be the recipient of either name or non-name non-negro [*sic*] artists."[8]

The tours by blacks in the 1950s that received the most attention stateside, however, were by jazz artists Dizzy Gillespie and Louis Armstrong. Gillespie's tour received mixed notices from local governments and U.S. embassies, functioning as a test run for future state jazz tours. In areas with an existing audience for jazz, as in Eastern European countries such as Yugoslavia, where the Voice of America and local radio stations regularly broadcast jazz, Gillespie did well, drawing crowds and enhancing American prestige.

But in countries without a jazz presence, the State Department found that more involved preparation was usually needed, or else financial and public relations disasters could occur, as happened in Greece and Peru.[9]

Despite mostly positive notices from American embassies and the press, dozens if not hundreds of stateside constituents seemed offended by the notion of the U.S. government paying the salaries of jazz musicians and demanded explanations from their elected representatives and the State Department. Many seemed offended by the expense, reported incorrectly in one news story as $133,000. The 1956 Gillespie state tours of Europe and South America actually cost the government $84,381, after ticket revenues. As the State Department pointed out in numerous replies to congressional representatives and citizens, all artists, particularly famous ones, took significant cuts in their usual salary (in Armstrong and Gillespie's case, approximately a third) to perform for their country on exhausting schedules that included diplomatic as well as musical duties.[10]

In 1956 and 1957, Louis Armstrong began making major international trips in Africa and South America that some at the time and even his biographer Laurence Bergreen viewed as State Department–sponsored, but were actually independent, though the State Department kept tabs on them and occasionally threw receptions on behalf of Armstrong and foreign dignitaries. Armstrong was probably the most famous black person in the world, certainly the most famous black American, and his appearances drew the kinds of massive crowds and international press coverage usually accorded a famous politician. Armstrong's initial show in Ghana, held outdoors on 24 May 1956, drew one hundred thousand, and skittish local police feared a riot if Armstrong played jazz that was too frenetic. Several days later, he performed for Prime Minister Kwame Nkrumah, who within a few months would lead his country to independence. Bergreen reported that Armstrong responded with a particularly passionate show, centered on "(What Did I Do to Be So) Black and Blue."[11]

Just before Armstrong's next major international (non–state sponsored) tour to South America in 1957, the Little Rock school integration incident occurred, and the usually ebullient Armstrong, seeing black children treated roughly by white adults on television, including an incident of a man spitting in the face of a black girl, reacted angrily. "The way they are treating my people down South, the government can go to hell," he told a reporter in North Dakota. "It's getting so bad a colored man hasn't got any country." He called President Eisenhower "two-faced" and claimed he displayed "no guts" because he had so far refused to send in federal troops to quell the situation. Armstrong knew that, in his role as "Ambassador Satch," the foreign audiences he would soon face would ask him about the American race question, and he felt a need to speak in the face of such disturbing events. "The people over there ask me what's wrong with my country," he commented. "What am I supposed to say?" When Eisenhower commissioned the National Guard to escort the students into Little Rock High School, Armstrong immediately cheered the action in a personal telegram: "If you decide to walk into the schools with the little colored kids, take me along, Daddy. God Bless you." Armstrong's comments, particularly the initial angry ones, were reprinted widely in the United States, and criticized. Bergreen argued that the comments risked career "suicide" in America. A torrent of letters arrived at the State Department, twenty-eight of which are preserved in their files. All of them question Armstrong's suitability as a representative of the U.S. government, and many make racist and even anti-Semitic comments.[12]

Armstrong's quotes displayed the vulnerability of the United States on these issues and the risks and opportunities involved in sending black jazz musicians to tour on behalf of the United States. Artists like Armstrong and Gillespie represented more than mere entertainers. If the government wished to dull the racist image of the United States using these internationally renowned blacks, their work had to be seconded by racial peace or improvement. Men like Armstrong and Gillespie would not automatically assume a blindly positive view of American race relations unless they felt such a stand was justified by American actions back home. Perhaps the State Department should have realized that even Armstrong attacking presidential policy represented a powerful statement about freedom in a democratic society that by itself undercut images of African American subservience.

Armstrong's sharp words, despite his tour successes in Africa and South America, may have kept the Republican State Department from sponsoring any more black jazz tours until 1960. Tours featuring jazz bands led by Woody Herman and Dave Brubeck ably represented the United States from 1957 to 1959, and embassies expressed relief that such tours did not elicit discussion about American race relations. In signaling their enthusiasm for securing a Brubeck appearance, the Prague embassy noted that "For US purposes white jazz group [as the Brubeck quartet was] preferable, as this sidesteps [Soviet communist] regime propaganda linking jazz to oppression negroes [sic] in America."[13]

While no major black jazz artists went out on state tours from 1957 to 1959, a production of the Gershwins' folk opera *Porgy and Bess* featuring an all-black cast did tour the Soviet Union under government auspices, which inspired anger among the black press and, apparently, Ellington as well. In 1964, he still seemed annoyed about it in a private interview:

When they got ready to send somebody to represent America in Russia . . .
they sent *Porgy and Bess*, which is the image of the Negro that they want
in Russia . . . Those people in those alleys, waking up, dusting those carpets
out the window, and beatin' their brooms in time, and all that bullshit . . .
Well, this is it. You want to know about America? You gonna make a cultural exchange? We send you *Porgy and Bess*. This is the complete image of
our Negro.[14]

After Armstrong's first state-sponsored tour of Africa in 1960, the Cultural Presentations program went quiet, presenting no high-profile jazz acts
for a year while undergoing reevaluation by the incoming Kennedy administration. In memos from the fall of 1961, including one requested by the president, State Department personnel decided that the primary target audiences for CP tours in fiscal year 1963 (the year of the Ellington tour) should
be "youth (meaning first of all university students), labor, and intellectuals."
The idea was that enthusiasm fostered in these demographics would, in the
long run, reach a broader portion of foreign populations.[15]

In late May 1962, the State Department sponsored a series of concerts in the
Soviet Union by Benny Goodman, the most high-profile and controversial
state tour by a jazz artist since Gillespie's in 1956. The controversy erupted
when the choice was announced in the spring of 1962. Because this tour
represented the first live appearance of American jazz in the Soviet Union,
America's primary adversary in the cold war, many observers, particularly in
the black press, were sensitive. The *Amsterdam News* summed up the "reaction in Negro circles." "Why should Benny Goodman be our jazz representative, they ask, when Duke Ellington, Count Basie, and all the other great
Negro musicians are still around? After all jazz is a Negro-born art form,"
they noted. "Is this another instance of disenfranchisement of the Negro?"
    Others in the black and jazz press wondered why the State Department
picked a retired bandleader for this important assignment rather than an
active, more adventurous one. Max Roach, the politically outspoken black
drummer, told *Jet* that Goodman "is not a representative of jazz music in
this country." Gillespie followed suit, commenting that "nobody is playing
Benny Goodman's music today." Miles Davis "growled" that "Duke Ellington should be the man to lead the first jazz mission to the Soviet Union."
No one disputed Goodman's status as a major jazz figure, both musically
and in terms of his efforts in successfully promoting integrated bands during the 1930s, but it was also true that he had not made a significant musical

contribution in two decades. The band he assembled for the Soviet tour, in the words of the *New York Times*, contained "top-flight jazz men" (including Zoot Sims and Phil Woods) but no "advanced experimenters." Goodman made it a point to include blacks on the tour. His twelve-piece band included the excellent composer, arranger, and saxophonist Oliver Nelson and a black vocalist, the Ellington veteran Joya Sherrill. Offers to Ellington and Quincy Jones were tendered and refused. According to the *New York Times*, Goodman offered Ellington a "guest star" pianist segment during two weeks of the six-week tour, dedicated to "whatever Duke saw fit." Ellington's supposed reply made the cover of *Jet*, along with a photo collage that paired Goodman and Ellington face to face: "Man, I know you're kidding. Aren't you?" He also told the *Times* that his band's relentless touring schedule made such an arrangement impossible.[16]

The selection of Goodman for the 1962 Soviet tour had been in the works for years. Ellington assured the *New York Times* that it "had absolutely nothing to do with race," and he was probably right. Goodman had offered his services to his country for a Soviet tour since at least the late summer of 1955, when he wrote letters to the American ambassador to the Soviet Union and the officer in charge of U.S.S.R. affairs at the State Department. "In thinking about ways in which to aid in that worthy goal of our country, it occurred to me that I might be able to make a small contribution in the musical area," Goodman wrote. He noted his own efforts to promote jazz and democracy on Voice of America radio broadcasts that reached the Soviet bloc, the interracial make-up of his current ensemble, and his ability and willingness to perform with a Russian classical ensemble during the tour as a means of fostering cultural exchange.[17]

The Soviets probably wielded more influence over the 1962 selection of Goodman than the State Department. George Avakian, recording executive and producer, spoke with Madame Ekaterina Furtseva, head of the Soviet Ministry of Culture, while trying to set up a separate jazz event in the Soviet Union during the early 1960s. She asked for Avakian's recommendations on American jazz performers for a State Department tour of the Soviet Union. Avakian mentioned three artists that he had produced in the past. First, he forwarded Armstrong. "Too popular," Furtseva quickly replied. His next suggestion was Ellington, which she rejected as "too intellectual." Avakian argued that Ellington represented "our classical jazz artist" and that this would help Russians relate to him and his work. "Our people wouldn't like him," she stated. Next, Avakian mentioned Goodman, who Furtseva liked best, particularly after he mentioned that Goodman's family emigrated from Russia and that his wife was Georgian. Avakian diplomatically did not mention that Goodman's Jewish family fled Russia to avoid pogroms.

"The State Department could not dictate to the Soviet government," Avakian said decades later. "It was either Benny or nobody. I don't think they would have invited anybody else" from the jazz world. Avakian understood why Armstrong met with such resistance from Soviet officials. "Armstrong would have caused riots in the streets," he argued, just as he had in other, less policed areas of the world during international tours. Frank Siscoe, the State Department's director of Soviet and Eastern European cultural exchanges, told *Jet* that Soviet officials expressed the fear that "their youth would get too excited if they saw the more established jazz groups [such as Ellington and Armstrong] in person and it would look like they [the youth] had completely accepted Western ideas," an outcome unacceptable to the Soviets. A dispatch from the American embassy in Moscow reported similar concerns from Soviet officials, who "seem pleased at the prospect of having Goodman, but claim to fear he may arouse the baser instincts among the 'rowdier' elements of Soviet society." A State Department source told the *New York Times* that Ellington's name never emerged in negotiations, but Armstrong and Goodman did, with the Soviets stating their preference for the latter. As scholar Penny Von Eschen has noted, a successful Soviet tour by Ellington or another black jazz performer would also have contradicted the Soviets' assertions of American racism. Goodman's more "conservative" approach and his ability to perform classical music won over Soviet officials, who also previously declined Armstrong's offer of a privately sponsored Soviet tour in 1961.

Goodman expressed frustration over the reaction to his selection in the black and jazz press. "It's a shocking thing to find, nowadays, that race hate has crept into the arts and music," he said in a somewhat naïve statement. "This used to be one place that it did not exist and should not exist." Columnists from the black newspapers *Amsterdam News* and *Columbus Sentinel* ultimately blessed the Goodman Soviet tour, citing his historic contributions. Siscoe explained the politics of the overall diplomatic situation to *Jet*, which never openly endorsed the Goodman tour: "I know Goodman is regarded as a pale reflection of true jazz, but we have to get our foot in the door first." [18]

But Goodman reportedly disappointed younger Soviet jazz fans who saw him as too "mild" and "old-fashioned" compared to the more challenging forms of jazz being broadcast by Willis Conover on his popular *Music USA* program on the Voice of America. VOA and Radio Free Europe's most effective programs were probably those dedicated to jazz, clearly an effective diplomatic weapon in the early 1960s. In 1962, the *New York Times* lauded Conover's trademark "extended biographies in sound—10 hours with Duke Ellington, for instance . . . aural profiles of unusual quality and lucidity." The music of Ellington and the best American jazz performers on the airwaves proved more effective in spreading ideals of freedom and interest in the American way of life than any propaganda could. To quote the *Times*:

> foreigners are enjoying the finest sampling of a contemporary American form free of any semblance of raucous rock 'n' roll, untimely interruptions, or sense of haste. It is civilized and sensible radio, an export that does the country proud in broadcasting.
>
> In their unpublicized way Mr. Conover and the current enlightened Voice leadership may be proving a point much larger than the significance of the popularity of jazz. The quiet, unadorned and understated presentation of our cultural attributes may give a far more accurate picture of ourselves than calculated advertising campaigns.[19]

Terrence F. Catherman, the cultural attaché assigned to the tour, issued a decidedly mixed report on Goodman's overall performance in the Soviet Union, probably the most devastating report on a jazz performer in State Department files. The single-spaced, nineteen-page dispatch portrayed Goodman as difficult and petulant, ready to call off rehearsals, performances, and receptions, and ruffle diplomatic feathers if his standards were not immediately met. Most audiences are described as giving the Goodman band a "polite" or "mild" reception, and large sections of empty seats are mentioned in spots, although exceptions existed to this, especially in Leningrad. The attaché mentioned in his report, perhaps pointedly, that "Take the 'A' Train," the Ellington orchestra theme penned by Billy Strayhorn, served as the theme song for *Music USA*.[20]

As Goodman's tour kicked off in the USSR, Ellington was the master of ceremonies and main musical attraction throughout the four-day People to People First International Jazz festival in Washington, D.C., which "implicitly recognized the importance of jazz in American culture." The Ellington orchestra appeared three times during the weekend, including one night in Constitution Hall with the National Symphony Orchestra, where the combined ensembles played Ellington's *Night Creature*. Among the many events, seven new jazz works including a jazz ballet were commissioned and premiered. The program, far more ambitious and wide ranging than the usual festival lineup, featured a jazz liturgical service, a children's jazz concert, and a gospel vocal showcase, alongside appearances by leading jazz acts such as Julian "Cannonball" Adderly, Lionel Hampton, Thelonius Monk, and Sonny Rollins. The festival benefited the People to People committee, of which President Kennedy was honorary chairman and ex-President Eisenhower was executive chairman. In a preview of the festival in the *Washington Post*, Jouett Shouse, the event's chairwoman, noted that "the reason for the festival is to demonstrate that the President's Music Committee [which she also chaired] realizes the importance of jazz, recognizing that jazz reaches people even in the remotest parts of the world." To further demonstrate the international cold war scope of the event, there was a performance by the Warsaw Wreckers, a group from Poland that learned about jazz from Conover's VOA broadcasts and was "believed to be the first Iron Curtain jazz group to ever play in the West." [21]

Yet, despite the work done by jazz on behalf of the United States, despite Kennedy's honorary chairmanship of the event, and despite the fact that the night before the festival Soviet Premier Nikita S. Khrushchev viewed Benny Goodman's concert in Moscow, Kennedy and his administration almost totally ignored the festival. Neither Kennedy nor his wife nor secretary of state Dean Rusk attended the concerts. When the press noticed, a White House press spokesperson meekly insisted, "They do like jazz." News stories recalled the warm White House reception given classical performers like Pablo Casals.

On the first day of the festival, Ellington was awarded the keys to his home city and driven slowly down Pennsylvania Avenue behind an elderly marching brass band. The group stopped in front of the White House, and it appeared they were expecting a brief presidential appearance. "For the Duke it was a momentous occasion—he had finally arrived in the nation's capital from which he had to emigrate forty years ago in order to launch a career that years later resulted in a command performance before the King and Queen of England at Buckingham Palace," George T. Simon reported. "Yesterday he at last stood with honor in front of the White House." "President Serenaded," rang a headline in the *New York Times*. But it was not true. Ellington and the men stood outside in the hot sun with no recognition from the White House. The D.C. police had broken up the impromptu parade that trailed his car, and made fans walk instead on the sidewalk. It was reported elsewhere that Kennedy was working and did not hear the band. Perhaps he was too busy dealing with the fallout from the minor stock-market crash earlier that week or still reeling from the birthday wishes Marilyn Monroe bestowed upon him recently. Probably his fear of alienating Southern voters kept him from taking advantage of a photo opportunity with a group of black men. Press secretary Pierre Salinger remained in the press room, marking the occasion of jazz outside the White House with a wisecrack that the remarks he was making had "better wait until the saints come marching in." Newspapers across the country carried a syndicated UPI story quoting various figures "chiding" Kennedy for "ignoring" the festival. Shouse, the festival chairman, upbeat in previous stories, cited the absence of "cooperation" from the White House, especially the lack of a response concerning the invitation to meet with the brass-band parade. "It's a shame he couldn't go two blocks to hear the concert although Khrushchev went to hear Benny Goodman," she told the press. Clearly, Kennedy did not understand the potential for jazz and black musicians as a diplomatic weapon.

Ellington, as usual, appeared outwardly unperturbed and thanked the city for the honor. "This is the time when hometown boys seem to be getting recognition. There was John Glenn in New Concord and Scott Carpenter in Boulder," he said, referring to newly returned and celebrated astronauts. "But we've flown higher than any of them have. After all, when you get on the interval of a twenty-second chord, that's when you're looking down at the 'orbiteers'!"[22] Was resentment hidden in that quote? People close to Ellington claimed that he avoided and disliked visiting Washington during his last years. His sister Ruth felt that the main reason for this rested in a local cemetery's disinterring of their parents in the early 1960s, after the land was sold. The Ellington family was told that they had to dig up Daisy and James's bodies or lose them. After that, her brother "had a completely different feeling about Washington. It was as if Washington had disinherited him." Mercer Ellington and Phoebe Jacobs also recalled Ellington's agitation on the subject. Perhaps the potentially embarrassing situation and lack of recognition at the White House on a day when his city was supposed to be honoring him also contributed to his latter-day feelings concerning his hometown. Five months later, Paul Winter became the first performer to play a jazz concert at the White House.[23]

On 17 December 1962, the Kennedy administration released their reappraisal of the CP program; it received a glowing report. They laid down new guidelines for State Department tours, and the Ellington 1963 tour was the first major jazz tour to follow these dictates. Initially, in the mid-1950s, the CP program mounted many "competitive displays of cultural accomplishment" by the United States at fairs and expositions, sometimes purposely in opposition to similar displays by communist countries. The 1962 report termed such displays and attitudes "wasteful and inappropriate" and directed future CP activities to use culture as a way to demonstrate

American character and "the development of a flourishing national culture," not to harp on obvious political points. State Department tours needed to focus on long-term, not immediate, goals. They needed to especially target youth of foreign countries, giving them a positive view of the United States before negative stereotypes took root in their minds, yet the actual presentations should remain apolitical. The report justified the paying of "high salaries to outstanding artists . . . on the basis of extraordinary artistic talent and their value to the program" and called for an increase in the CP budget, which had not risen in eight years while the Soviets continually increased their spending on cultural tours. Lastly, in a decision that particularly affected the Ellington tour, the report called for more offstage appearances by performers so that foreigners could interact and trade stories and skills with American artists in a relaxed setting.[24]

On 21 May 1963, the State Department announced their CP touring lineup for the 1963–64 season, the first time they had done so in such a public manner. The Ellington orchestra was the only big-name or jazz act on the schedule, with most of the tours occupied by amateur and collegiate performing groups, "mostly longhair" (classical and dance-oriented ensembles), according to *Variety*. The Ellington orchestra's contract with the government paid Duke Ellington, Inc., $175,355 for fourteen weeks' work (almost $1.2 million in today's dollars), along with all travel and insurance expenses. The pay was about what they would have earned in a comparable time on the road, without the need for paying travel expenses. Promoter George Wein doubled the asking price that Ellington's usual agent, Joe Glaser, first secured. Wein accomplished this "by talking about the needs that Mr. Ellington had," Wein recalled. "When [Ellington] left [the country], he had to support, keep the office going . . . Glaser was willing to just sell him, collect the commission, and never care." The contract stipulated an easier week for the orchestra than usual in terms of number of shows, although the travel was often grueling on small, noisy, and hot airplanes and buses. The orchestra had to appear at "up to" four performances per week, with none on travel days. Usually Ellington made his expensive, debt-incurring orchestra work every day of the year, even during foreign tours. Their cooperation in "off-stage" personal appearances was also contractually mandated, though left up to the discretion of negotiations between each embassy and Ellington and his advisors. Some of these appearances were embassy parties, but the most significant "off-stage" activities were the lecture-demonstrations during which Ellington orchestra members met with musicians and students of other countries, the first time this was officially done on a State Department tour. This latter activity received much complimentary attention internationally and stateside.[25]

In its official report on the tour, the State Department commented that it chose Ellington due to his "universal appeal . . . to both the young and old audiences, his background on festivals of jazz with students, as well as his knowledge and ability to discourse on jazz as an art form [which] ably suited area requirements."[26] The countries Ellington visited were in particular need of these skills. In Iran, an August 1963 State Department survey of students at Tehran University showed that they favored USSR radio 26 percent of the time, compared to a figure of 14 percent for VOA, and that Americans surpassed the Russians in the estimation of most students except in the area of culture. In Iraq, the State Department was working hard to reestablish cultural relations after a twenty-month ban on them instituted by the Iraqi government from 1958 to 1960—a boycott that even closed down USIS libraries. The 1963 Country Plan for Iraq formulated by the United States Information Agency (USIA) named "personal contacts in all areas related to communications media" as top priority in order to shore up America's image in a country where the government was notably cool towards the United States and where most mentions of the United States in the media were negative.

According to 1961–63 polls of university students in India, student opinion of the United States topped that of the Soviet Union for the first time since the polling began six years previously, following the United States' boost in military aid to India in the wake of a Chinese border attack in October 1962. The embassy wished to encourage this trend. But Indians tended to be either unfamiliar or hostile to American culture (with the exception of Hollywood movies), especially jazz music and American literature. "On the whole Indian students don't like jazz," concluded an August 1962 report. The June 1963 USIA Country Plan for Syria specifically used the example of the Ellington tour to make clear a point only hinted at in other embassy reports. Sending "top quality US cultural presentations" such as Ellington to Syria served "to reflect the fact that the Syrian cultural level is such as to foster appreciation of the best of other cultures." One of the United States' four major "psychological objectives" for Syria in this period was to "convince Syrians of US respect and Arab traditions and contemporary achievements."[27] The refined image Ellington embodied helped carry off this key goal of the State Department in the Near East and Middle East countries he visited. Ellington's long-honed reputation as a serious artist as well as entertainer was being put to use by the U.S. government.

All countries on the Ellington itinerary offered substantial coverage of the American racial situation, which the State Department hoped to influence with the Ellington tour. With the assassination of Medgar Evers and the racial violence in Birmingham, 1963 represented a disturbing year for the issue of civil rights in America. The State Department commissioned extensive international polling to gauge the effect and damage of such events on the image of the United States. In June and July 1963, they examined public opinion as expressed through polls and the press in the countries Ellington planned to visit in the fall. Most featured balanced media coverage of U.S. civil rights events, but angry, negative commentary was not uncommon, and it worried the State Department. Pakistan gave particularly critical coverage to Kennedy's civil rights policies, as did Arab nationalist and communist newspapers in Lebanon. The *Times of Ceylon* and *Times of India* objected to official American policy in numerous articles and "had little praise for Kennedy, saying that his actions were belated, and that a large share of the blame for racial strife must go to the administration." An August 1963 poll in Delhi, India, showed that opinion of the United States was dropping from the high level achieved earlier in the year, mostly due to reaction over violence in Birmingham, a situation that eight of ten college students recognized. Two major national Turkish papers also "condemned racial strife" and administration reaction to it. A front-page June headline from *Maraket* in Istanbul proclaimed that "Human Rights Are Still Crushed," while *Gumhuriyet* argued that "America had taken part in a . . . war to smash the Nazi racism . . . but hers is still standing." A press survey issued just as Ellington arrived in Jordan for the second stop of the tour showed that newspapers in Pakistan and the Jordanian section of Jerusalem linked the oppression of black Americans with what they viewed as American-supported oppression against the South Vietnamese and the Palestinians.[28]

In light of this news coverage, the choice of Ellington as the first world-famous black American celebrity to head a State Department tour in nearly three years was no coincidence. Ellington, even without uttering a word about race relations, provided a counterweight to images of police dogs biting black children on television; he offered living proof that other opportunities and situations existed for black Americans. As State Department literature accompanying the tour intimated, his career hinted at another side to the nation's racial situation. Press releases often spotlighted Ellington's longer works inspired by African American history, his contact with classical figures (such as Leopold Stokowski and Arturo Toscanini), and his recent concerts with the La Scala Orchestra in Milan and the Hamburg Symphony.[29]

The State Department used Ellington's reputation to balance recent incidents of civil rights violence and present an image of American democracy and progress on such issues to an international audience. The pages of State Department–funded newspapers in Arabic and Sinhalese (the language spoken in Ceylon) distributed during the Ellington tour reveal this tactic. The Arabic *News Review*, with Abraham Lincoln, "the great emancipator," on the cover, featured an article on the impending Ellington tour positioned opposite a large picture of two black American lawyers, one of them Thurgood Marshall, clasping hands with an Arab American lawyer in front of the Supreme Court. An article by deputy national security advisor Walt Rostow concerning American efforts to help "developing countries" is paired with a story on the "peaceful" March on Washington that included a detailed list of "What the Civil Rights Marchers Wanted." On a lighter but no less pointed note, the *News Review* also sported a feature detailing the increasing popularity of Arabic cooking (especially "shish kebab") in the United States.

In the Sinhalese *American News*, similar juxtapositions existed. In the 27 September issue, three pages on Ellington are surrounded by a report of Kennedy's recent UN speech calling for a nuclear test ban and a roundup on civil rights activity, including the national mourning following the deaths in Birmingham, the March on Washington, and Kennedy's calls for "peaceful progress" on civil rights. Another article trumpeted how the "United States Government Does Not Favor One Religion or Another," a key issue in Ceylon. The 11 October issue devoted yet more space to Ellington, the history of jazz, and the civil rights movement, including a two-page photo spread of the March on Washington with a large picture of Kennedy meeting that day with black leaders. The 25 October edition featured four pages on Ellington's activities in Ceylon sandwiched between stories on Kennedy's support of the UN and an international science program. U.S. officials linked American progress on racial issues, as seen in their coverage of Ellington and Kennedy, with overall American efforts to create a more peaceful, democratic, and tolerant world.[30]

Hugh Parry, a USIA official, gave a speech in February 1964 suggesting the importance of images like Kennedy's Oval Office welcome of civil rights leaders and majestic figures like Ellington. "When the man on the street reacts to America's stands on a specific issue, he does not simply weight the rights and wrongs of the particular issue, or even consider it purely in terms of national and individual self-interest," he argued. "His reaction often stems from emotion, from a gut-feeling based on pre-conceptions about the United States." According to Parry, the USIA needed to change negative preconceptions by stressing positive images, personalities, and facts about the United States, not pointed counterargument. This approach would lessen damage from negative news about the United States in the future, producing a more balanced reaction to such news and helping the State Department more easily manage any detriment to foreign opinion caused by an isolated incident. Parry mentioned how people around the world heard and read about Little Rock abuses but knew relatively little about the progress made in American race relations. Similarly, a July 1963 policy update on civil rights issues sent to all embassies by USIA director Edward R. Murrow blamed some of the "genuine misunderstanding" on racial issues to "deliberate distortion by our enemies who are fostering and exploiting an impression of pervasive injustice and intolerance in the United States."[31]

In addition to American propaganda in the newspapers of the countries that Ellington visited, more culturally oriented approaches were used as well, such as USIS library exhibits focusing on American life. A 1963 State Department–constructed exhibit focusing on Ellington proved to be one of the top draws in USIS libraries, drawing tens of thousands of observers in Iran, Iraq, Syria, and Hyderabad, India. In Beirut and Calcutta, the exhibit was not as popular compared to others, yet in the latter area it still drew tens of thousands of spectators during 1963. The exhibit on Ellington, along with other exhibits focusing on American jazz, formed a mainstay in USIS libraries around the world during the 1960s.[32]

Duke Ellington, Inc., received capsule historic and political descriptions, as well as security warnings, for each country before the tour. They also received a single-spaced, six-page document listing "Suggestions on Methods of Answering the Critic of the United States Abroad." It stressed finding "common ground" with a foreign critic, being calm and reasonable, answering with "yes, but," and avoiding arguing. In a section entitled "Try to Get the Discussion out of an Exclusively American Context," the State Department suggested pointing out that problems of racial prejudice are "rather universal problems of human beings the world over," a somewhat impolitic recommendation in countries that had recently shed a colonial past, as was the case with several nations on the Ellington tour. The document also suggested that the visiting musicians size up "the questioner and come to some conclusions as to whether he is genuinely and honestly seeking information and enlightenment or whether he is a professional needler." At least one band member, Buster Cooper, recalled receiving no instructions from the government, so he spoke his mind freely about the American race situation to foreigners he met on the tour. It seems likely that Ellington did not pass on State Department documents concerning the tour to his orchestra.[33]

*

The State Department and international press reports judged the 1963 Ellington state tour an overwhelming success. The orchestra "played to capacity or near capacity audiences" during its forty-three performances, with shows in Bombay and Bangalore attracting thousands outside the sold-out venues. Their two shows in New Delhi, one exclusively for students, sold out all 2,180 seats in a little more than twenty-four hours. All six of the orchestra's shows sold out in three cities in Pakistan, with a combined attendance of 8,800 persons. Both shows in Baghdad sold out, despite the bombing of the Iraqi presidential palace during the band's stay. In Kabul, Afghanistan, site of particularly tense cold war relations, "Ellington attracted the largest paying audience ever for such an event, approximately 4,000," including an unprecedented mix of Afghans, Americans, and "Soviet citizens who turned out in large numbers." The band's "readiness to talk to students and other young people was favorably remarked." During the tour, the thirty-three official offstage activities garnered even more positive notice. "The effectiveness of . . . off-stage functions was considered outstanding and according to one field mission 'possibly more valuable than the concerts themselves,'" according to a State Department synopsis. Onstage and offstage, the Ellington orchestra performed before seventy-five thousand people during the tour.[34]

The lecture-demonstrations proved particularly popular and memorable—for audiences and the embassies. The groups invited for such occasions usually included students, musicians, and members of various local cultural organizations. Ellington began most lecture-demonstrations alone onstage with an informal twenty-minute talk. "My subject was the American idiom that is promoted under the banner of jazz, and I would explain to the people that jazz, to me, meant having fun through freedom of expression," he recalled in a 1964 article he penned about the tour. "Before I got to the members of the band, their instruments, and what they were famous for, I spoke about some of the great musicians who preceded us, like Sidney Bechet and Louis Armstrong." Thomas W. Simons, Jr., the State Department escort officer for the tour, indicated in his report that he had hoped for something more academic and inclusive from the lecture-demonstrations, but Ellington was no traditional educator. In the musical portions of the lecture-demonstrations, Ellington often called for material the band had not performed in years with no guide for them but their memories, causing the band to "play beautifully" and with spontaneity onstage but to walk offstage "cussin' like dogs" out of earshot of the crowd.

Simons reported that Ellington's approach to these events, however grating on the band, made the lecture-demonstrations "musically the most enjoyable events of the tour." In Karachi, Pakistan, nine hundred "enthusiastic" university students were "enthralled," and "many were of the opinion that the orchestra was at peak form due to the informality of the occasion." A crowd of three thousand, mostly students, were "wildly enthusiastic" at the Bombay lecture-demonstration. When Ellington musicians were paired with musicians of the host country, each side explained attributes of their music and instruments. Ellington, along with the band, spent many pleasant afternoons being serenaded and informed by musicians of other countries and pronounced himself "inspired." In Ceylon, Ellington drummer Sam Woodyard marveled at the timbral varieties demonstrated by a Sinhalese drum orchestra. "Could I get a record of this?" he asked, and he received one. "This is something I'd like to try my hand at sometime." After the drum orchestra performed a few traditional harvesting songs, they finished with "Take the 'A' Train"—"in Sinhala style!" according to the local paper. Although Ellington and Strayhorn wrote very little during the tour, the sounds they heard provided the basis for their *Far East Suite*, a group of works performed live by the orchestra frequently in the years after the tour. Ellington explained the creative process he sought for the project at a Bombay press conference:

> With this much beauty in India—the music, the scenery, the colors, the people—there is bound to be some effect on my music, but I cannot tell now exactly what it will be . . . I have nothing definite in mind. I prefer to absorb everything, to drink it all in, and then to have it come back to me naturally. I want it to be an external process; I want it to be reflection and not refraction. Of course, we have had the fascinating experience of hearing Indian music, of seeing your instruments, of touching them, but I can't say to what extent I will use the ideas I have picked up here.[35]

Press conferences were not among the most pleasant experiences for Ellington on the tour, but he handled them brilliantly. In India, especially, he found plenty of the "professional needlers" the State Department warned him about. "Those Indian press cats, at a press conference, I'm totally aware of the fact that out in that part of the world they're going to throw in a couple of communist boys to upset me . . . they always get back to that race situation in America," he recalled a year later. Ellington and the band found that, after jazz, civil rights represented the most asked about subject among foreign fans and journalists.

Nothing seemed able to place Ellington in an untenable situation, even openly procommunist and anti-American figures seeking to goad him. He told a press conference in Lahore, Pakistan, that American artists had been "the most fearless of all" in opposing racial prejudice and that civil rights in America was a "big issue," but that concern should also be placed on the issue of "world domination." Always a strong defender of his country, he seemed angered, but not thrown off balance, by inferred attacks on America. In 1964, Ellington paraphrased his reply to a question during a press conference on the tour from "a communist . . . sympathizer" who asked "why, if the United States government is so great, why didn't they subsidize their artists":

> Why? I don't know why they don't, but I know damn well I sure wouldn't want to be subsidized, by anybody's government, the United States or any- body else. Because to lose the thrill of the chase and the competition that goes with this free enterprise, I mean, you lose a hell of a lot more than money. Because if somebody's gonna subsidize me, then they're gonna tell me how much I'm gonna have to spend, cause I can't spend any more than they're gonna give me, you know? And if my drive and so forth is greater than an- other guy's, then I'm entitled to earn more and spend more. On the other hand, if I was subsidized, I mean what the hell, I would just lay around and get fat, uninspired, you know, work up to a quota, make a showing, and fob the rest of the time off . . . I work, work, and work, and if I don't, then there's a guy across the street who will, and so he gets that pheasant that's down the street in the grocery store, you know, just brought in, that *I* want for dinner . . . I had a bitch of a battle over that one [the question of government subsidization], 2 or 3 pretty rough ones, but I was in fairly good shape [chuckles].[36]

Ellington received ecstatic press attention abroad, generating sto- ries that dovetailed well with State Department goals for the tour. "Duke Ellington—that charming American face—is preaching love and visiting people in the name of humanity . . . On a lush carpet of music, Ellington is extending his hands to greet other peoples on behalf of the United States, and indeed on behalf of humanity as well," *Al Manar*, a Jordanian newspa- per, wrote on 16 September. "In the name of love, the Negro can surmount the white's prejudice and obliterate it. And with a smile of love, the Ne- gro can transcend the inequity of his white brother, and erect a bridge of security and peace through which humanity can pass." The State Depart- ment calculated that Ellington generated more than a thousand column inches of news coverage in India, reaching an "aggregate circulation of over 2 1/2 million." In Hyderabad, India, the *Deccan Chronicle* published a multi- article feature that profiled each of the orchestra members and focused on the Ellington compositions that documented African American history. The State Department issued multipage press releases rounding up highly complimentary quotes concerning Ellington and his music in Ceylon, Iran, and Pakistan.[37]

Despite extensive preparation by the State Department, however, problems occurred behind the scenes, most of which were unpublicized. After the first month, the band generally refused to attend receptions and embassy parties. They were tired of the road, tired of meeting the well-off people who tended to congregate at such occasions, and they felt that such people only wished to talk with Ellington anyway. The band members also became distressed "that large parts of their audience were splendidly dressed and were so familiar . . . with Ellington music as to be nostalgic about it," according to Simons, the escort officer. Trumpeter Herbie Jones encountered fans in India, Pakistan, and Turkey who brought prized old recordings of the band to shows and knew more about the history of the band than most American fans did.

The band originally thought they would play for "the people" on the tour, spreading American jazz and their expertise to average citizens with no previous exposure to the music. Many of them became frustrated that their audiences consisted mostly of the elite. While some shows were free or inexpensively priced, particularly those aimed at students, most charged admission to offset government outlays and alleviate political resistance to the program back home. As Simons indicated, in order to reach a more plebian audience, they needed to tour little villages, a task not only economically unfeasible but also more taxing to the men, who already complained of living and traveling conditions in the bigger cities they visited. Simons "point[ed] out that societies in that part of the world are less fluid and more highly stratified than American society, that a small upper class exercises a determining influence on society and culture to a much greater extent than is true in our country, that the 'people', the lower classes, do not in fact 'count' as much as they do with us, and that we were trying to reach those who did count." Despite these explanations, Simons wrote, "band members continued to feel that they would rather play for the 'people', for the men in the street whom they saw clustered around tea-shop radios." Hearing a rumor that the Soviets presented Russian folk dancing free in the middle of the Calcutta Maidan for tens of thousands of spectators only exacerbated their feelings on the subject. Jimmy Hamilton often "played sick," as many other band veterans did, to avoid the parties and receptions.[38] Ellington made no documented comments on this subject.

The State Department was troubled by the Ellington orchestra's late-night "extracurricular" carousing, which the escort officer had not experienced with symphony orchestra tours. "Jazz musicians live at night and sleep the day through," Simons warned future escort officers. "It is unwise for the Department to expect anything else." Wherever and whenever "nightclubs, the company of other musicians, the company of unmarried women" beckoned, the musicians actively sought such "habitual distractions." Probably the most dangerous and humorous incident of this nature occurred in Iraq, where a coup attempt took place as the band arrived in Baghdad, and gunfire could be heard in the streets. Despite being warned of "street violence and ordered to keep to the hotel," two band members, including one of the more famous veterans of the orchestra, ventured out to a nightclub. Simons considered using "main force" to prevent them, but "all Marines were at the Embassy." When they returned, the band members said their time was "wonderful": "two men and twenty girls, shaking like leaves" in the club and, in their words, "all these cats with sub-machine guns sitting around outside."

The diaries of Naomi Huber, the department's advance person for the tour, show that one of her main concerns was keeping track of political violence in countries visited (Israeli-Palestinian skirmishes occurred near where the band stayed in Jordan) and scouting venues where cigarettes and whisky could be procured, in hopes of keeping the band happy and in their hotel. Buying alcohol proved a more difficult task in Muslim countries. She noted that the band comprised "night people" and that her interest was in keeping them "alive and interested for the rest of the tour." The tour officials worried about negative press publicity concerning these nighttime adventures, which they felt could reflect badly on the United States, especially in the more conservative countries. "The image we seek to project of ourselves varies from country to country, but is in general one of a people who are honest, good-willed, informal, hard-working and chaste," Simons wrote, though no other State documents indicated a need for chastity. "Every member of the group had the first four characteristics in abundance; rather fewer possessed the last." In Colombo, Ceylon, where the local press had a reputation of "shady character" and leanings toward communism, allegations emerged in print of vague and unsavory "nocturnal doings" between the band and the U.S. ambassador that were "mean and baseless," according to Simons. Buster Cooper recalled a headline in that city that read "Harlem Negro Boys Wreck Hotel," which was also untrue. "The Department can consider the [fictional] incident[s] a tiny wart on an image of great success during a twelve-week tour," Simons concluded.[39]

Another problem concerned longtime Ellington trumpeter, violinist, and vocalist Ray Nance. He arrived in Idlewild, CA, for the flight to the Middle East in a "not precisely normal" condition that Simons seemed to hint may have been caused by drug use. Nance had battled drugs for years and had been arrested in Las Vegas while with the band in 1961. On the tour, Nance refused to attend anything but stage performances and spoke often in a "loud" and "startling" voice. Onstage in Damascus, the tour's first stop, during a solo he defiantly crossed his legs and displayed the bottoms of his feet, a Muslim taboo. "The Ambassador . . . was sitting on a front seat, he almost have a heart attack," trombonist Buster Cooper recalled. "He said, 'Duke, please get him out of here, right now.'" At first, Ellington, Al Celley, and the band defended Nance and asked Simons to leave him alone and expect less of him offstage, but further problems changed their attitude. In Amman, Nance "shocked and insulted" the ambassador by making a loud scene at customs, refusing to stand for the national anthems at the concert, and wandering around the stage during the performance, which "perplexed" the audience and "detracted from but could not spoil the excellent impression made by a fine performance." After a "violent [and private] exchange" between Nance and Ellington, and at the insistence of State Department officials and the ambassador, Nance was sent home. The State Department told columnist Dorothy Kilgallen that a doctor examining Nance was "unable to diagnose a drug influence and felt it would be most unfair to say so." Instead, he was sent home on 15 September for behavior that broke the terms of his contract. A native Indian citizen named Patrick Blake took over the trumpeter's chair on short notice and acquitted himself admirably. When Herbie Jones arrived from America two weeks later as an official replacement for Nance, Blake cried, seeing that his realized dream of playing with the Ellington band was coming to an end.[40]

Despite various troubles with the band, which included stage tardiness on all occasions but two, Ellington uniformly received complimentary remarks in State Department documents for his diplomatic manner and activities on- and offstage. Two matters related to him, however, caused great concern among department officials. Almost everyone in the band experienced "intestinal discomfort" during the first two weeks of the trip, but Ellington contracted "a very significant illness . . . some organism close to typhoid," according to his close friend and personal physician Dr. Arthur Logan, and was hospitalized for five days, followed by a week of convalescence at the residence of Chester Bowles, the newly installed U.S. ambassador to India. Band member and close friend Harry Carney maintained that Ellington went to the hospital on doctor's orders because Ellington would not rest unless drastic action was taken. In Logan's opinion, a "tinned American ham" from Bowles's wife and three quality steaks (the staple of Ellington's usual main daily meal) from a State Department official were instrumental in helping Ellington regain his health. Simons believed that Ellington's weakened state may have been due to the fact that "he has been a great steak-eater all his life, and in the absence of steaks, especially in India, he could not and/or would not enjoy most of the food set before him." The issue of steaks for Ellington would resurface during his 1971 state-sponsored Soviet Union tour. Logan also observed that "the squalor and poverty of India was . . . very depressing to Ellington" and may have contributed to his condition. Ellington rejoined the band in Bombay, but seemed weaker than usual for two weeks, causing Bowles to order his offstage activities cut to one hour per day. Sweltering heat and a schedule of performing, meeting, and greeting much more strenuous than that of the orchestra was also noted. In Ellington's absence, the longest serving member of the orchestra, Harry Carney, took the helm, and Strayhorn filled in on piano.[41]

State Department officials were also agitated by the unannounced arrival in New Delhi of Fernanda de Castro Monte, a "very cultured" woman of intriguing character and mysterious multinational background. She was Ellington's romantic companion throughout much of the 1960s and frequently accompanied him on foreign tours, helping him translate (she knew five languages) and keeping him company. Monte had booked air tickets for the tour without telling State personnel and, immediately upon meeting the band in the airport, "whisked Ellington off to the hotel." Naomi Huber described her as "a striking blonde of about fifty, uses heavy make-up, incl. long eye-lashes, and her daytime attire is tight capri-pants and top—white, pale blue, red and black." The Delhi embassy and other posts, especially in Pakistan, expressed concern, fearing that her presence as an unmarried, tightly attired woman who drew significant attention would cause controversy and headlines in Muslim countries. In a conference with Ellington, Strayhorn, and Celley, Huber strongly suggested that Monte, known to the band as "The Countess," stay in the background, personally and in terms of her wardrobe. "I doubt if these three said anything to her about her dress," Huber wrote, but Huber made the point in person to her later, seemingly to no avail. Huber also refused Celley's request to arrange Monte's visas in each country, informing him that the State Department "could not touch" her Argentinean passport. Since Monte did not register her presence in India properly, Indian customs officials delayed her departure, made her sign a document that listed her activities in the country, and made her swear "that she didn't want to give trouble to anyone." Ellington expressed that she was a comfort to him and that he wanted her along for the tour. The State Department reluctantly acquiesced, although Simons, in his report, recommended that if Ellington was hired again, his contract should forbid her presence or that of anyone not expressly on the State Department manifest.

Though Simons was harsh with Monte in his written report, he also noted her beneficial effects upon Ellington, particularly in the difficult weeks as he regained his health. "She nursed him fondly, and devoted to the satisfaction of his every need and whim an attention and patience little short of heroic," he observed. "In the escort's opinion, she had the hardest job of anyone connected with the tour. Most important of all, there was a deep and abiding affection between them: their relationship could not under any reasonable definition of the word be described as tawdry." "There may have been an exaggerated concern in New Delhi—[but] I think not!" Huber wrote. "We do have an investment and a reputation to protect!"

State Department officials were correct in assuming the press's prurient interest in the couple. In Ankara, another area where the print media had a "shady" reputation, a press representative acting on behalf of a "barrage of hungry press photographers" tackled Celley as he and a State Department official walked in front of Ellington and Monte to prevent their picture being taken. An assistant Cultural Affairs officer swatted the cameras away, but one photograph of "half the incident" ended up in the next morning's paper. Any damage from the photo was washed away by Kennedy's assassination that day.[42]

State Department and embassy dispatch reports mostly ignored these problems and focused on how successfully State Department objectives were achieved. In Syria, officials were concerned earlier in the year about the lack of an American presence at the annual Damascus International Fair and asked the State Department for "an outstanding cultural and/or athletic presentation" such as "a 'big name' jazz orchestra," the Harlem Globetrotters, or *Holiday on Ice.* The Ellington orchestra, helped by an elaborate two-month marketing campaign, fulfilled all expectations. "The orchestra's two performances . . . constituted the only performances by a Western country in the context of the Fair's cultural program and marked the first American use of the Fair Theatre," the post reported. "Not only did Mr. Ellington's performance save the Fair's cultural program from East Bloc domination, but they also added a genuinely American flavor to the Fair in a year when the United States did not participate with a pavilion." American newspapers widely reproduced this story and quote in 1965. At the time of the tour, a nationally syndicated story in dozens of newspapers talked about Ellington's reception at his first concert on the tour. Cheers of "ash al Duke" (Arabic for "long live Duke") echoed as the first big band jazz heard live in Syria began.[43]

An extensive poll undertaken at all thirteen Ellington shows in India demonstrated the band's success in helping the State Department reach targeted audiences. Twenty-seven percent of the 20,600 audience members at concerts responded to a four-question survey. The poll results and observers at the shows indicated that at least half the audience at Ellington shows consisted of the target audience of youth, especially students, and the intellectual and cultural elite. Attracting audiences that had never previously attended a U.S. State Department cultural event also figured as a priority; approximately 45 percent of the Indian audiences were attending their first U.S. state-sponsored cultural event. Only 10 percent had been to three or more such events in the past, allaying the post's fears that the tours always attracted the same people. While the poll indicated that most attending were jazz fans, 28 percent did not "especially enjoy" jazz before the show, which pointed to the desired new audience. The poll also found that 86 percent of the audience members were Indians. The overwhelming majority of the audience found the Ellington shows "very enjoyable" (69 percent) or "rather enjoyable" (25 percent), with 6 percent not finding the performances enjoyable at all, figures that surpassed those posted by Dave Brubeck in 1958, the last jazz tour in India. Fifty percent of the "professed non-enjoyers of jazz" found the show "very enjoyable," a fact suggesting success in the goal of building respect and appreciation of American culture. "They loved Duke. Duke has a knack for feeling out the audience," Harry Carney recalled, noting that Ellington would change the program based on their reaction on the tour. "People really responded to the remarks he made, they really gobbled him up out there." Logan remembered that Ellington tended to do a very commercial program with concertos scheduled for each instrumentalist in the band so that audiences unfamiliar with jazz could learn about its foundations. A majority of poll respondents picked "Skin Deep," with its lengthy Sam Woodyard drum solo, as their favorite song of the program. But Ellington's ability to draw 49 percent of his crowds from targeted audiences, including 40 percent who were under twenty-five years of age, merited special notice in the year-end embassy report: "With jazz, at least, we are reaching youth rather than the older generation." Folk singer Tim Prentice and accordionist Lloyd LaVaux brought in larger percentages of students than Ellington to their shows in India during fiscal year 1964, but each attracted only half the audience overall and much less media coverage.[44]

In Colombo, Ellington's appearances were viewed as "an amazingly successful visit" involving "Ceylonese in all fields," a valuable counterpoint to a year of news events that reflected badly on the United States. These events included the suspension of American aid after the government nationalized American oil holdings, explosive coverage of civil rights struggles, and Vietnamese Buddhist concerns, which became a "strongly and burningly insistent" issue in light of escalating American military involvement.

The embassy report from Karachi, Pakistan, the next stop on the tour, recorded that "no other American visitor except Mrs. Jacqueline Kennedy received such a popular ovation from the press in recent years" and that coverage increased with each performance. Two single-spaced pages of newspaper raves in the report demonstrated Ellington's extramusical significance within the country during a period in which "anti-American sentiments . . . were on a very high pitch." The *Karachi Morning News* complimented "Ellington's vivid brilliance" and called it a "spell of happiness and harmony in the middle of this year's harvest of suspicion, fear and disillusionment . . . Americans were clever enough to score success by shifting emphasis to cultural when political climate was not favorable." *Dawn*, Pakistan's largest daily newspaper in English, "usually restrained in its appreciation of American sponsored programs," called Ellington an "Ambassador of Goodwill" and equated Ellington's boosting of the prestige of American music with a commensurate rise in the image of the United States. His tour was "one of the indications that the creative vitality of the arts on the western side of the Atlantic is outliving the long period of obeisance to the proud Old World capitals." The embassy's report also noted that Ellington's Karachi appearances "helped the post in promoting and fortifying contacts with such groups as artists, writers, newspapermen, and government officials."[45]

In Iran and Iraq, two Middle East countries with little previous experience with jazz, the Ellington orchestra worked their charm in similar ways. In Isfahan and Abadan, Iran, the majority of the audiences had never heard a Western orchestra, and students made up a substantial portion of the audience. Much marketing was needed to attract an audience since, as the embassy noted, "Persians have a long music tradition, but theirs is simply too diverse from jazz to allow for . . . an immediate reception." The embassy seemed to get the job done well enough. Television Iran carried a live Ellington broadcast for far longer than the originally scheduled half hour, and a spokesman for the station characterized response as "phenomenal." "In Isfahan, the applause was so long that the police had to interrupt," and surprised radio stations received requests for jazz records, according to the embassy report. Perhaps this overflow of appreciation for jazz in a place where it had previously hardly existed accounted for the titling of the song "Isfahan" on *The Far East Suite*, the last jazz standard Ellington and Strayhorn ever wrote.

In Iraq, sponsors wanted to cancel one of two Baghdad concerts because they doubted that enough interest existed, but both shows sold out, despite a simultaneous coup attempt which brought a citywide curfew, military skirmishes near the U.S. embassy, and a cessation of telephone service. It was the fourth coup attempt of 1963 in Iraq (two of the four were successful). The November 1963 coup displaced the more repressive wing of the Ba'ath party's Iraqi regime (which included the young Saddam Hussein), a government in power for just seven months but already making inroads in establishing a repressive one-party state. In the midst of the uncertainty and violence, Ellington's standing-room-only concerts turned people away nightly and represented the "one cultural event that had the power to suspend the curfew," State Department historian Jewell Fenzi, along with Carl L. Nelson, wrote four decades later. Iraq's television station originally scheduled a short period of the Ellington concert for broadcast, but later cleared all of its programs after 7:30 PM so that the concert could be televised in its entirety. Seven months before, after the successful March 1963 coup, the body of the previous government's leader, Abd al-Karim Qasim, was immediately and proudly displayed live on the same station by the Ba'ath forces who assassinated him.

In the American press, Ellington made light of happening to live at the epicenter of a violent political coup, calling Baghdad a "swinging town" and threatening to write a new composition called "Baghdad bump or boom or bounce or something like that." Yet Ellington and numerous band members said they witnessed holes being blown into the side of the Iraqi presidential palace by Iraqi air force jets, and tanks guarding radio stations and government buildings. Dr. Logan recalled "concerts in Baghdad between shootings" and "lots of people . . . killed in the streets." The State Department had the band leave Iraq earlier than scheduled. Political tensions between Iraq and Iran, the band's previous tour stop, forced the band to stop in Kuwait because Iraq did not accept flights arriving directly from Iran. A year later, band member Russell Procope was asked if Ellington felt nervous on the trip. "I suppose he was, and he was not alone," replied Procope.[46]

In their last full tour stop in Lebanon, the Ellington orchestra's four-night engagement reached four thousand, "primarily Lebanese students," along with an estimated fifty thousand viewers for the televised last performance.[47]

The assassination of President Kennedy on 22 November found the Ellington orchestra in Ankara, Turkey, before they had played a show in the city.[48] "We had just gone to the hotel and ordered some food when a representative of the embassy came to give us the terrible news," Ellington recalled. "We didn't know what to do. The food we had ordered lay there and got cold." The band, stunned and saddened, waited a couple days in their hotel, without performing, to see if the tour would continue. The State Department decided to halt the tour. In a telegram dated 25 November addressed to the embassies in the countries still ahead on the Ellington itinerary, assistant secretary of state Lucius D. Battle explained the reasons for the cessation. "In light [of the] reference cables from Cairo and Nicosia, it [is] evident that Department's or Embassy's presentation of jazz orchestra per se could be interpreted by prospective audiences as disrespect to late President Kennedy and thereby offend local traditions," wrote Battle. "This of course would create the opposite effect intended by sending Ellington group on tour." He also thanked Ellington for his "understanding attitude." In some press accounts, Ellington agreed with the judgment of the department, both for emotional reasons and for reasons of not offending Muslim traditions. "I wouldn't even have known how to walk on to the stage" after the assassination, Ellington told the *New York Herald-Tribune.* "It just wouldn't have been right to continue." He also spoke about the forty-day mourning period observed by most Muslims, a majority religion in most of the countries remaining on the tour.

But another side of Ellington's feelings on the subject emerged as well. Immediately after the horrible news from Dallas, the Ankara embassy asked Ellington about his feelings on continuing the tour. He expressed the desire "to play wherever we're wanted." The post's dispatch reported that "it was the Duke's feeling that jazz expresses the spectrum of human emotions and that, in this case, his orchestra's performances under the 'circumstances would signify tribute rather than disrespect.'" A few days later, back in New York, he revealed to the *New York Post* his offer to the State Department to play Kennedy memorial concerts instead of his usual show, but they refused because, in his opinion, they did not view jazz as a music capable of expressing such emotions: "they thought jazz concerts might be considered in bad taste . . . I'm always fighting against the shady associations people have given it." Perhaps his remarks were inspired by the fact that no other state tours were cancelled—the Joffrey Ballet, Los Angeles Chamber Orchestra, Dorian Quintet, and Jose Limon Dance Troupe continued their sojourns through Western Europe, Africa, and the Soviet Union. Ellington told the *Post* that it would have meant a "complete turnabout," but he gladly would have stayed up all night writing new memorial music for Kennedy, "a lot of slow, sad music." He had done a similar program on the radio in 1945 when President Franklin Roosevelt passed away. "Of course, I'd have cut out the theatrical stuff and there couldn't have been any swinging," he continued. "But it would have had a beat. Religious music, you know, does have a beat. And I'd have eliminated the glib sense of humor from my annotations."

After the months of proclamations emanating from the State Department concerning the artistry and national importance of Ellington and jazz music, it seemed ironic that Ellington's request to play Kennedy memorial shows was refused. The State Department, and perhaps the world in general, had still not gotten past the hoary decades-old definition of jazz as an evanescent and vaguely immoral music associated with dancing, drinking, sexuality, and unschooled spontaneity. The kind of influence that Ellington had forwarded and represented for years still was not fully accepted. As patriotic and ambitious a man as Ellington was, it was a bittersweet way to end a tour that demonstrated how far the influence of black American music, particularly jazz, had progressed around the world since he began performing and composing, yet how limited its respect still remained as an art form that could encompass the full scope of human emotion.

Coincident with Kennedy's death, a five-man film crew arrived in Ankara to film the last month of the tour for the *Twentieth Century* CBS-TV series, which represented another loss for Ellington at the time. "Ellington was mad as hell that he didn't get some . . . valuable publicity from the trip," reported Dr. Logan. Long-form national television coverage was scarce for the band in these years. "That TV show would have been the biggest thing that could have happened to us," Ellington lamented to a Toronto newspaper months later. Yet this did not represent the dominant emotion Ellington felt in the situation: a member of the Duke Ellington Society recalled speaking to Ellington upon his return and how Ellington spent "ten minutes" talking about the death of Kennedy and what it meant to him.[49]

Ellington felt good to be back in New York City, and he spoke with many journalists. "I feel wonderful, all I needed was to get away from the various types of insects we'd been encountering—and to wrap myself around a good solid steak at [his favorite restaurant] the Hickory House," he told Leonard Feather. To columnist Atra Baer, he expressed disappointment that the cancellation of the tour kept him and the band from representing the United States before communist audiences behind the iron curtain in Yugoslavia, but he hoped that the State Department would ask them to travel to that part of the world sometime soon. He especially wanted to tour the Soviet Union on behalf of his country.[50] The State Department was very happy with Ellington's efforts, and, despite the dispiriting conclusion to the 1963 tour, Ellington would represent his country many times in the next decade. He did more tours with the State Department than any major jazz figure during the period, heading to Africa, Asia, and South America on their behalf. And, in 1971, he fulfilled his dream of playing behind the iron curtain in the Soviet Union for his country.

13

SACRED CONCERTS

FIGURE 11. The Duke Ellington Orchestra performs the First Sacred Concert at Great St. Mary's, the University Church of Cambridge, United Kingdom, 20 February 1967, one of dozens of Sacred Concerts they played around the world during the 1960s and 1970s. Johnny Hodges, probably the most famous instrumentalist to ever play in the orchestra, is soloing in this picture. Photograph by Val Wilmer.

Prelude

In the mid-1960s, as Ellington's Sacred Concerts premiered, some in the press speculated that Ellington's religious faith represented an eleventh-hour conversion, an attempt to atone for a life of supposed indiscretions. Ellington biographer James Lincoln Collier argued that the Sacred Concerts were Ellington's bid to be viewed in the same light as the great pre-twentieth-century classical composers, many of whom wrote religious oratorios and masses. Misperceptions like these emerged because, as with some of his deeper and angrier feelings about black history and civil rights, Ellington generally kept his religious thinking private and separate from his role as an entertainer. Before 1965, he did not view them as topics for public discussion. But as the Sacred Concerts garnered international acclaim and controversy, and religious institutions of many denominations clamored to present them, it inspired him to open up on the subject increasingly in his last years. Ellington's relationship with God was unconventional in that he adhered to no denomination and did not live a "moral" life according to usual religious dictates. But many sources indicate a sincere longtime faith revealed to family and friends over the decades.

Herb Jeffries saw Ellington's deeply religious side many times, long before the 1960s. Jeffries, who had worked as a staff songwriter for Irving Mills, knew Ellington well enough to chat with him backstage at a show in Detroit before his longer successful association with the band as a vocalist in the late 1930s and early 1940s. Ellington questioned him, perhaps feeling him out for the job he eventually landed. "How you doin'?" Ellington asked him.

> And I said, "Oh I'm doing pretty good. I just can't seem to, I don' know, everything I do seems to go wrong. Everything I've tried . . . my music, everything is not going right. Everything goes wrong. I've tried everything." He says, "You've tried everything?" I says, "Yeah." He says, "Have you tried God?"
>
> We all write . . . about him, and these guys go out and they do their research . . . I've read just about all the books on him, including his own. Somehow they miss talking about his philosophy of religion, or his belief in God, let's put it that way. He was a man who was free, very free, about using the word God. I heard it many times from him, you know . . . No, I don't recall him . . . saying, "Hey today is Sunday, we must all go to church." I don't recall him ever doing a sermon for the orchestra. I don't know that it would've done much good [laughs]. I saw within him this in-depth of a kind of a

religion, not so much organized religion . . . [but] a respect for the church, a love of the Bible . . . Those things are important and we should know about that. Because it tends to tell you what motivates the man. A great love of the Bible. And he read it. And I saw him reading it. Many times. Captured my interest as to why this great man [read the Bible so much]. What is in that book, you know? Hey, I was born and raised a Christian. But like many Christians, you know, sure, I had the Bible around. Yeah. I think many, many of them have it around because it's impressive and not only that, I think a lot of people might as well drive a ten penny nail through it and put it up over the front of their door like they would a horseshoe, because I think a lot of people have it around for good luck. But Ellington didn't. These are things that people don't know about.

He had a great ministry. It was hidden in his music. I think a lot of the things that he read from the Bible that he did practice in his music and that people felt it . . . I still haven't come down from it . . .

Ellington was an evangelist, as far as I'm concerned. 'Cause he was practicing his ministry moving about here and there, making people happy.[1]

✳

After at least two years of planning, Duke Ellington and his orchestra performed a Sacred Concert in San Francisco's stately Grace Cathedral on 16 September 1965. By late 1973, he had created three separate Sacred Concerts, performed over a hundred times to sold-out audiences in churches and secular venues around the world. He called them his "most important" work, though as Janna Tull Steed pointed out in her short history of the spiritual side of Ellington's life, he did not refer to them as his best work. They certainly were not his best work, though strident denunciations of them by latter-day observers such as James Lincoln Collier miss their beauty and sincerity, as well as their historical, musical, and personal context.[2] They were significant events, heavily covered and discussed in the mainstream and religious media. Once again, Ellington was using his music to bring issues of personal and historical importance to center stage in American society, transforming American culture.

The Sacred Concerts represented another chapter of Ellington's continuing interpretation of the complicated history of blacks and religion in America, an area he had explored previously in *Symphony in Black* (1935), *Black, Brown and Beige* (1943), and *My People* (1963), among other pieces. Throughout religious history, music has served as a force of change and renewal, a means to draw people into church and elicit intense emotional response through song. The Sacred Concerts were used by Ellington and the churches that welcomed him in the same manner, and, especially because of Ellington's reputation in the secular world, they represented another way in which he broke and blurred boundaries and categories in American life.

The idea of a "jazz" orchestra in churches (although Ellington never allowed that word in ads or programs) elicited serious resistance in many quarters at first, especially in the black community. But Ellington's presentations, highly differentiated from the band's usual approach, eventually won over critics, and the Sacred Concerts became the most profitable and publicized ventures of the last decade of his career. They represented another important step in Ellington's efforts to divorce jazz and African American music from an unsavory or limited reputation and depict black music as it was defined in the Washington, D.C., school system of his boyhood—as a rich and exalted tradition capable of expressing and encompassing any human emotion. Ellington's Sacred Concerts, like the Great Awakenings of the eighteenth and nineteenth centuries and the Social Gospel embrace of popular culture at the turn of the twentieth century, were a concerted attempt to make American religion more soulful and inclusive at a time when religious spokespeople of all denominations noted with alarm a significant decrease in their congregations. News reports that mentioned the presence of youth at Ellington's Sacred Concerts held in churches and temples inspired other religious venues to follow suit. With the viability of the Judeo-Christian tradition questioned as never before in American society during the 1960s, especially by younger Americans and blacks, Ellington provided a personal testament before multiracial, multigenerational audiences about the benefits faith had worked in his life.

The Sacred Concerts also proved beneficial for Ellington in terms of earnings and publicity. Ellington's booking and management representatives found themselves unexpectedly bombarded by requests from religious institutions for performances of the Sacred programs. The Sacred Concerts earned close to twice the money of a regular Ellington concert, though more benefits were held in the Sacred Concert format than usual, with Ellington several times donating his and the band's services. These shows attracted an audience united by a belief, or at least an interest, in God—and in America, the most religious industrialized country in the world, this represented a sizeable audience. It was an audience that reached beyond the radio formats that had typically excluded Ellington for decades. The controversies over whether jazz belonged in a religious setting and the relative novelty of the event brought an avalanche of press coverage. Because of the Sacred Concerts, along with the furor over the perceived snub of Ellington by a Pulitzer Prize jury, 1965 saw the greatest American media presence for Ellington since his 1943 Carnegie Hall debut. Press reports painted Ellington at age sixty-six as an unpredictable personality and artist, still drawing headlines and controversy, still restless for new challenges and viewing his work as unfinished. He also became somewhat of a religious spokesperson for the first time, though he made clear he spoke only from a personal point of view.

But more than anything else, the Sacred Concerts represented Ellington's personal statement, prayer, and journey that he wanted to share with audiences. Within the concerts, Ellington stressed the priorities of love, freedom, family, and an interdenominational, nonjudgmental belief in God. The Sacred Concerts brought together blacks and whites, Jews and Christians, young and old, and they voiced appreciation for the benefits of living in the United States under a system of freedom and democracy. Yet these universal themes were grounded in an African American musical vision that drew from blues, jazz, and gospel. The concerts were a vivid reminder that, culturally and religiously, blacks and whites were closer together than often recognized. Ellington had made this same point to his secular audience in *Black, Brown and Beige*; now he directed it to the religious community. As Dr. Martin Luther King often did, Ellington used religion to unite the races and various other groups during the divisive tensions of the civil rights, black separatist, and black power movements, and the 1965–68 riots. As during other tumultuous times in American history, religion helped define ideals to bind people together in a more loving world. Despite resistance, the Sacred Concerts eventually became a successful endeavor to heal divisions, old and new, and to evoke eternal verities to sanctify the possibility of unity within the nation's changed, and in some ways more embittered, racial world.

The swelling of public interest in the nexus between jazz and religion during the 1960s probably influenced Ellington to publicly testify about his own beliefs, a facet of his character previously known only to intimates. "I think his relationship toward God was very sincere and had nothing to do with public opinion," his son Mercer told the Smithsonian in 1991. "He didn't give a damn what they thought of him, he was worried about what God thought of him." Numerous sources paint Ellington as man serious about God, though not a churchgoer. He did not claim a denomination and lived a life full of nonmarital sexual liaisons. Yet Ellington called himself "deeply religious" in 1958, and he wore a gold cross under his shirt, though he almost never spoke about Jesus Christ directly, either in conversation or in the lyrics for his sacred compositions. He carried a Bible throughout his career, read a little of it daily, and knew where certain passages were located when he needed to make a point about them. "It taught me to look at a man's insides instead of the cut of his suit," he said in the late 1950s. When his mother died in 1935 and he went into "personal crisis," he read the Bible three times over, which might explain the lack of new works by Ellington in the three months after her passing. "I'm certain religion gives you strength," Ellington told a British newspaper in 1958. "It makes you feel that if you are God's son you are strong and don't have to worry." He prayed twice daily, "regularly and devoutly and privately," upon waking and before retiring, and he told interviewers that he feared sitting in a house full of people who did not believe in some sort of God, "afraid the house would fall down." "I respect every man's religion," Ellington told writer Henry Kane in 1959. "As long as he believes in God, I'm with him; if he doesn't, well, I just keep as far away from him as I can." When Stanley Dance admitted to Ellington that he did not know the reference Ellington was making to the book of Solomon in his composition "Apes and Peacocks," Ellington insisted his friend reread the Old and New Testaments. When Ellington trumpeter John Saunders left the band shortly before the Sacred Concerts to attend a Catholic seminary for older men seeking to become priests, Ellington happily blessed Saunders's decision. "We're on the same team," he told Saunders.[3]

Perhaps the most important evidence concerning Ellington's religious feelings is found not in his daily life and interactions, but in his work.[4] While Ellington made few public comments concerning religion before the mid-1960s, his feelings were manifest, if unstated, within his compositions. "Whenever one has the occasion to compose music, one runs into the spiritual aspect of man and his world," Ellington told the *Detroit News* in 1969. "It's inevitable." In a 1956 private interview, he expressed hesitation over using the lyrics he wrote for "Come Sunday" in a potential new production of *Black, Brown and Beige*. "I've written words to it, but I don't know if the words are adequate. Well, I'm that way about God you know," he said. "I don't know whether the words are good enough, know what I mean?" Helen Oakley Dance, an Ellington friend and record producer, was present in the studio when Ellington quickly wrote and recorded "Solitude" in 1934. "It was a rather serious piece of music, and I said right away 'It's church music' . . . which it was, in essence," she recalled years later. "And all through Duke's life, he did things that you might consider, the source of it, the root of it, is church music."

The examples that scholar Mark Tucker cited of Ellington songs inspired by the emotional, tear-inducing hymns his mother played for him provides a good start for a search of the spiritual side of Ellington's oeuvre before the

Sacred Concerts. Those songs included some of the most simultaneously painful and beautiful compositions in the Ellington repertoire: "Mood Indigo" (1930), "In a Sentimental Mood" (1935), "Melancholia" (1953), and "The Single Petal of a Rose" (1959). These are each searching, gorgeous, and personal pieces that evoke otherworldliness. Perhaps the premiere composition in this category, and one of Ellington's best, was "Reminiscing In Tempo," the thirteen-minute elegy to his mother written after her death in 1935. In working out his grief and perhaps coming to a personal resolution, Ellington constructed an ambient and drifting piece that, with its insistent yet relaxed midtempo groove and pleasant melody edged with dissonance, bequeaths a meditative feel. Sequestered in hotels on tour, Ellington spent much time alone. Perhaps religion comforted him in the midst of this solitude. In the opening paragraph of his program essay for the First Sacred Concert, Ellington commented on "everyone's aloneness . . . Everyone is so alone—the basic, essential state of mankind." That sentiment had surfaced repeatedly in his music over the decades and contributed to many of its most affecting moments, but he had never before said it aloud. Ellington's close friends all commented on his resistance to total openness; his music may represent the place where he let his guard down the most. As witty and fluent as he was with language, it seemed easier for Ellington to communicate personal sentiments through music rather than words.

But not all of Ellington's spiritually influenced music assumed a melancholic and dramatic stance. Ellington was also an avid celebrant and connoisseur of God-given beauty within his writing and personal life, both the natural and geographic wonders that inspired *The Queen's Suite* and the contours of the more intimate areas of the female, which were said to be the subject of his instrumental "Warm Valley" (1940). During the period of the Sacred Concerts, Ellington came up with an expression that turned into something of a mantra, repeated to the press and used as a title for a composition in the Third Sacred Concert: "Every man prays in his own language, and there is no language that God does not understand." Most in the press viewed the statement as internationalist. But Ellington was primarily speaking about praying through the language of music. Father Norman O'Connor, a Catholic priest famous for his TV show, newspaper column, and regular appearances as an MC at the Newport Jazz Festival, spoke often about how "the intensity in religion was similar to the intensity of creative jazz" and advocated the use of jazz as a form of prayer. From all indications, Ellington, a friend of O'Connor's, felt the same way.

According to Ellington, the concept of the Sacred Concerts had germinated within him for decades. In a 1971 article, he traced his first religious feelings to his parents, both the music played for him by his mother Daisy and his family's unorthodox tradition of attending church. "Every Sunday we first went to my father's church, Methodist. Then my mother took us to her church, Baptist," he recalled. "Their respect for each other was a lesson in itself. You don't forget that kind of teaching." Ellington's nonjudgmental attitude concerning religious denominations probably emerged from that "teaching." He also intimated in the same article that the original idea for the Sacred Concerts was connected to the death of his parents in the mid-1930s, when "the bottom just dropped out" of his life, and he turned to the Bible and the religious teachings of his parents. Jazz journalist Leonard Feather speculated that the idea for the concerts may have developed out of Ellington's 1945 radio tribute to the recently deceased President Franklin Delano Roosevelt, which exclusively featured somber and spiritual themes. George Avakian, Ellington's producer at Columbia Records during much of the 1950s, recalled Ellington and band copyist Tom Whalley discussing plans for a project focusing on religious music sometime during the 1956–57 period.[5]

The Christian church has long held a significant place in the history of black Americans as one of the chief contributors to African American community, public expression, and antiracism efforts. The black church represented a central organizing force for schools, banks, insurance companies, literacy, political activities, and cultural endeavors in black neighborhoods, as well as a key outlet for emotional support and release. A disproportionate number of black American leaders and artists received initial training for their public lives through the church. Music was especially significant within the black church, and African Americans synthesized parts of their African heritage and the English hymns of the eighteenth century into what are now called black spirituals, a musical form that enhanced African American identity outside ecclesiastical authority.[6]

According to historian and sociologist E. Franklin Frazier, attempts during the eighteenth century to convert blacks to Christianity began the process of breaking down the isolation of the segregated black and white worlds. From the first Great Awakening in the 1730s, when the charismatic itinerant preacher George Whitefield challenged colonists North and South to reconsider their view of blacks and reach out to them as equals, Christianity led some white religious leaders to welcome black American slaves into their churches. By the late eighteenth century, most Quakers, and many Methodists, Presbyterians, and Baptists, both North and South, embraced slaves in Christian fellowship. Some challenged slavery as an institution.[7]

Yet such tendencies did not go unchallenged, or indeed unreversed. After 1800, in Virginia, partly inspired by Gabriel Prosser's ultimately unsuccessful plans for a thousand-strong slave revolt, powerful interests wielded pressure on Methodist and Baptist leaders to change their racial course. Southern ministers ceased attacking slavery and became the institution's chief defenders. The eviction of blacks from white churches, however, led to the establishment of the first black churches, the first public institutions in the North that African Americans controlled in the United States, and the establishment of their own styles of worship.[8]

Black churches were especially successful in cities like Baltimore and Philadelphia, where large populations of free blacks actively sought independence from white churches during this "first black freedom movement," as historian Gayraud S. Wilmore termed it. Such churches, expressing outrage at racist and slave practices, became core institutions for the black community for generations. Wilmore argued that for African Americans, attending church represented a "necessity," not a social custom or convention, as it was for most whites. It signified "the one impregnable corner of the world where consolation, solidarity and mutual aid could be found and from which the master and the bossman—at least in the North—could be barred." The most famous and longest lasting of these independent black churches was the African Methodist Episcopal (AME) Zion church, established in 1818 from a "Christian club" called the Free African Society, which was founded in the 1780s. Establishing educational and social service facilities in the black community and developing strong black leaders such as Frederick Douglass, Sojourner Truth, and Harriet Tubman, the AME earned a reputation as "the freedom church." Black churches also were important in serving as the birthplaces of slave rebellions. The black church could house the most educated and respectable sides of black American character as well as, before the Civil War, the more aggressive sides.[9]

With the rise of black colleges during Reconstruction and the Gilded Age, the character of the black church changed. A divide opened during these years between university-trained black preachers, who stressed respectability and calm reasoning, and their rural folk counterparts, with their reliance on shouting and physical performance to inspire parishioners. Both sides contained valid points and served important needs. Educated clergy promoted blacks as intelligent and refined community leaders worthy of comparison to any whites. Folk clergy, including the Holiness churches, which began in the South during the 1890s, and the Pentecostals, who emerged in Los Angeles a decade later, may have contributed to the image of blacks as unable to control their emotions, but they fulfilled the need for a refuge and emotional release during the worsening of racial oppression.[10]

After World War I, in the midst of the Great Migration from the rural South to the urban North, black Americans became the "most secularized" section of American society. Particularly in urban and ghetto areas, a growing number of blacks either ignored or attacked Christian institutions, characterizing them as irrelevant, materialist, and linked too closely with a white society that discriminated against them. The writers of the Harlem Renaissance provided visceral evidence of this point of view. Claude McKay's *Home to Harlem* (1928), the first bestselling novel by a black Renaissance writer, featured characters routinely unleashing blasphemous curses that implied an inherent futility and racism associated with Christianity. "I'm gonna cut your throat just so sure as God is white" and "God is white and has no . . . time for niggers" are but two examples. As Lawrence Levine found in his study of sacred traditions among black slaves, African Americans were never "uncritical recipients of white Christianity." [11]

The precarious position popular music had in American religious institutions represented another historical circumstance that impacted Ellington's Sacred Concerts. Music critic Alan Rich, responding to criticisms of the Sacred Concerts, argued that the tension concerning popular music in a religious setting was older than America itself:

> The process of cross-feeding between the sacred and the secular in the arts, most notably in music, has been a source of continued vitality in all forms of religious observance . . .
>
> From time to time the church has tried to stamp out popular influences and keep its liturgy "pure." It has never worked for very long. A papal bull in 1322 threatened excommunication to church composers practicing "modern" techniques. In the 16th century the Council of Trent toyed with the idea of reinstating Gregorian chant as the only permissible church music. In both cases the overwhelming power of public taste forced the authorities to abandon their stand . . .
>
> Instead the official liturgical composers of the day filled their masses with vocal lines taken from the popular songs of the day.

When American congregations dwindled, popular music and culture were frequently used to bring crowds back to church during the first and second Great Awakenings. At other times, popular music was forced out of religious use, as seen in the rise in the 1860s of the American Sunday School Union, which sought to reform hymnody by excising popular-music influences. Some of the more respectable black churches in the decades around the turn of the century retired the simply arranged black spirituals from their services for much the same reason, often replacing them with classier and more musically sophisticated arrangements of the same songs by college-trained black composers such as R. Nathaniel Dett. But the pendulum swung back. Starting in the 1870s, urban Congregationalist preacher and religious entrepreneur Dwight Moody and his musical companion Ira Sankey applied assertive Gilded Age–era marketing to religion to gain worldwide fame, convert hundreds of thousands of people, and sell over fifty million of their hymnals. Sankey specialized in a roughhewn style, employing a melodeon (a small, wheezy, accordion-like instrument) and singing in an untrained manner. His philosophy eschewed fancy arrangements and argued that "if you have that which reaches the heart, it will fill the church every time," and it did, as Ellington's Sacred Concerts would decades later.

Gospel music served a similar function in the black church. Its first recordings and songbooks surfaced at the end of the nineteenth century, but by the 1920s, with the rise of an African American market for recordings, the often raw, blues-inflected gospel music was a hit commercially and in some churches. But not among those who sought a more respectable image for black religion and criticized the "religious frenzy and escapism" that gospel music supposedly aroused. By the 1950s, however, traditional gospel music became acceptable to most black churches and became an even bigger market, as well as an influence on early rock and roll.[12]

By the mid-1960s, black and white churches publicly worried over the lack of younger members in their congregations. The problem seemed particularly acute in the black community, where both clergy and church membership declined during the 1960s. In 1964, seeing this trend and wishing to reverse it, E. Franklin Frazier wrote a book entitled *The Negro Church in America,* which argued that the integration of blacks into American life was undermining traditional black life and rituals. If the church lost its place as the center of black life in America, then blacks would lose their heritage, he predicted. C. Eric Lincoln, writing a decade later, found that the civil rights turmoil of the 1960s brought an "agonized death" to the older vision of the black church. For many, especially younger people, black Christianity seemed too rooted in a history of slavery and oppression, and the categories of "Negro" and "Christian" seemed "irreconcilable." The more aggressive political stance made by younger and more activist-minded blacks during those years set aside anything that hinted at meekness and suffering. Beginning in the mid-1960s and continuing on into the 1970s, a new "black theology" emerged that specifically "addressed blacks" and devised ways of making Christianity more relevant to their situation. C. Eric

Lincoln viewed these as positive circumstances, since, in his opinion, only religion had the ability to address the new issues in black life while keeping a sense of tradition and history.[13]

Ellington might have agreed with Lincoln's arguments. With the Sacred Concerts, he too rejected Frazier's notion that the church represented the irreplaceable center of black life in modern America. Ellington's vision of religion in the Sacred Concerts represented a kind of universalism during a period when black separatism was rising in popularity. The Sacred Concerts encompassed all races and Judeo-Christian denominations, as well as Victorian and modern elements, grounded in an African American musical sensibility and history. The plea to God heard in "Come Sunday" to "see my people through" underlined the theme of "freedom," which tied black struggles to universal American ideals. While "black theology" challenged European Christian precedents, Ellington had long struggled against European "standards" that had relegated American and African American music to the margins of artistic respect.

With his Sacred Concerts, Ellington brought his vision of black culture and history into areas it had not previously penetrated. He intimated that black religion and culture were not nearly as fragile as Frazier feared. If anything, Ellington's vision coalesced smoothly with Dr. King's integrationist approach of using religion as a force that could unite the races behind a policy of reform. King regularly used the Bible to criticize blacks who withheld their talents from the civil rights struggle while also praising "merciful" white strangers who stepped up to help the cause. He criticized the segregation of U.S. churches. "All humanity is tied together," King stated in May 1964.[14] The phrase could serve as a central theme for the content and venues of the Sacred Concerts.

The growth of the black Muslim movement during the 1960s also accounted for the disaffection with and desertion from Christianity among younger blacks. With their philosophy of racial solidarity, exclusively black membership, concern for the underprivileged, and an "eye for an eye" philosophy on racial violence, the black Muslims had "an inevitable appeal to Blacks who have difficulty with American Christianity because of its racism, and with the Black Christian Church because of its posture of accommodation." The autobiography of the most famous and outspoken Muslim leader of the 1960s, Malcolm X, was filled with excerpts from his speeches that eloquently excoriated Christianity as a religion for blacks. He called it "the white man's religion ... and his interpretations of it have been the greatest single ideological weapon for enslaving millions of non-white human beings" around the world. He argued that the "turn-the-other-cheek" ethos was used to make black Americans docile when they possessed every historical right to react violently against their longtime white oppressors. The promotion of black capitalism as a way of advancing black power and equality formed another major facet of their ideology, a concept that Ellington had forwarded for years in a different context. As a teenager during the Swing Era, Malcolm X, then known as Malcolm Little, shined shoes for Ellington and Ellington orchestra members before shows at Boston's Roseland Ballroom. They never met in the 1960s; as much as Ellington advocated blacks building up their own businesses and accruing capital to secure their rights and improve their status, he did not agree with the confrontational tactics and language of separatists like the black Muslims.[15]

In the white church community, authorities tried to reach out in various ways during the 1960s, often through the media, to enhance their declining congregations and make their services and literature more relevant to modern audiences. Pope John Paul XXIII's Vatican II reforms paralleled efforts in other Christian denominations. Protestant and Catholic scholars published more accessible translations of the Bible, Catholic mass was allowed in languages besides Latin, prominent religious figures hosted television and radio shows and wrote newspaper columns, and theologians Reinhold Neibuhr and Paul Tillich were viewed as media celebrities of a sort. Tillich's "theology of culture" argued that artistic activity represented a revealing conduit between God and his subjects. In a May 1964 address at the Museum of Modern Art in New York City, he offered his theories as to why churches often backed away from the use of art in worship. "The arts open up a dimension of reality which is otherwise hidden . . . Without breaking our natural adherence to the familiar, the power of our art cannot grasp us," he argued. "Therefore, new ways of disclosing the world have always aroused the resistance of those who wanted to stay securely with the familiar."

By the time of the First Sacred Concert, a growing constituency in the American religious leadership was calling for modern popular culture, especially jazz, to assume a larger role in church life because of the emotions it inspired as well as the audiences it brought. In an article published in *Saturday Review* five months before the First Sacred Concert, Father O'Connor rued "that [anonymous] character in history who staked out a claim for religious music as something clear and distinct from secular music." He called for church music featuring rhythms that resembled "the strident, jerky world we live in" and lyrics with "a reality that the popular audience understands," citing Woody Guthrie and Leadbelly as examples. What he most wanted to hear were composers who were not afraid to traverse beyond strict and staid church musical forms, who brought the "depth" associated with American artists such as Louis Armstrong, Bob Dylan, George Gershwin, Charles Mingus, and Ellington to the pulpit. Like his friend Ellington, O'Connor felt that the ability to inspire the worship of God, not denominational or even Christian concerns, was what mattered most in a piece of religious music. "The music that has the strength and understanding of the popular forms will be automatically the music with strong liturgical effectiveness," O'Connor wrote. The church needed to communicate, like the best popular and jazz music did—to reach people's profoundest emotions.[16] In the 1960s, as the ideas and music of the counterculture were disseminated and lived out by many young people, churches were worried that they were losing their impact on society.

In at least one intriguing instance, the church reached out to jazz musicians themselves. Rev. Dr. John G. Gensel, pastor of the Advent Lutheran Church on upper Broadway in New York City, made the jazz constituency a central component of his ministerial work beginning in the early 1960s. "One night between sets, one of the musicians" asked to talk with him, Gensel said in 1965. "I realized there was an open field here . . . I began to think a lot about this whole jazz world, and I realized there was a lot of pastor work that could be done . . . that there was a need, and wherever there's a need, there's a need for the Church of JC to do something about it." Gensel found fame within jazz circles for hitting the jazz clubs several times a week, making it a point to stop in at the rattier as well as ritzier venues. Soon, many of the musicians, including Charles Mingus and Max Roach, began bringing their problems to him and showing up at his church, both to perform and to worship. Ellington admired Gensel's commitment to jazz and its players, famous and obscure, and felt particularly impressed by Gensel's lack of hesitation in assuming the appropriateness of jazz as a means of worship. "Pastor Gensel often went without, denying the needs of his own family, and even using money earned by his beautiful wife as a schoolteacher in order to pay the rent, or doctor's bills, or to buy food for some of the less fortunate night people," Ellington recalled in his autobiography. Ellington's sister Ruth regularly attended Gensel's services, and she and her brother donated one of Ellington's pianos, on which many of his famous compositions were written, to his church in the early 1960s. He officiated at the last rites of John Coltrane and Billy Strayhorn, among other jazzmen. Gensel's jazz mission continued until the end of his life in the 1970s, despite "many scathing letters" sent to him accusing him of "serving Satan" and "corrupting religion." His defense against them was grounded in the New Testament and the changing cultural conditions that he and other religious leaders faced in the 1960s:

> Our Savior Himself did not hesitate to mingle with all types of persons. He preached and taught outside of the Temple. Today, it is especially important that religion should not be confined within the walls of churches and synagogues. If people will not come to priests, the ministers, or the rabbis . . . [they] should go to the people wherever they are.[17]

Ellington's Second Sacred Concert, first performed in 1968, featured an instrumental tribute to Gensel, "The Shepherd (Who Watches over the Night Flock)."

Ellington was not the first to compose jazz for a religious setting, but his participation and commitment brought the trend widespread international attention and proved the major influence in prodding churches of all denominations and races to become more inclusive in their musical selections. Other churches experimented with popular and jazz music in the years before Ellington's First Sacred Concert. Such experiments, however, especially concerning jazz, almost never occurred in black churches, which generally stood against such cultural mixing before the mid-1960s. The Reverend Daniel Lyman Rideout, writing in the *Baltimore Afro-American* in 1960, responded to reports that jazz, a genre he associated with "orgiastic frenzy" and "the world," was played at religious services in England and at a Methodist Youth Convocation. "We do not condemn jazz music to itself, and we give credit to those who would make something of it in a high artistic form," he stated. "But I insist it has no more place in a service of Christian worship than an animal trainer would have no place, putting his monkey on the pulpit and having him do tricks in that holy place while the congregation was singing." In a poll taken during the 1960s, only one-fifth of over two thousand black preachers surveyed across the country approved of jazz or blues being used in worship services; just 6.5 percent of rural preachers in the same survey approved of it, and over 90 percent of them expressed strict disapproval of the idea.[18]

The movement to include jazz, folk, and popular music as part of church repertory started slowly in the late 1950s.[19] Anglican priest Geoffrey Beaumont wrote a "Twentieth-Century Folk Mass" in 1957, which was issued stateside. Beaumont said he was responding to requests from soldiers he served with in World War II who wanted hymns and masses that they could readily understand and sing. He put traditional hymn lyrics to the music of popular tunes, something attempted more commonly in the 1500s. Episcopalian Father Ian Douglas Mitchell in Chicago followed not long after with an "American Folk Song Mass" that adapted a Joan Baez–like folk feel. In 1960, a "new jazz score for a Methodist morning service" aired on the NBC-TV network, and Edgar Summerlin, a music professor in Texas, "wrote a jazz requiem to assuage his grief over his small daughter's fatal illness, and later composed several jazz liturgies." In the same period, a rash of jazz "gospel" songs by such artists as Cannonball Adderly, Art Blakey, and Ramsey Lewis sought to bring some of the atmosphere of the church into the jazz club.

In February 1962, a jazz quintet organized by an Episcopal priest performed at the National Council of Churches conference on religious education, and the United Lutheran Church sponsored a three-day contemporary jazz workshop in, as Nat Hentoff put it, "the secular cavern of the Village Gate [Club] in New York." Later in the year, Don Ellis's *Frontiers in Worship: Experiment in Jazz* was performed at the Church of Religious Science in Los Angeles, a panel on jazz and religion headed by Father O'Connor was featured at the Newport Jazz Festival, and a jazz liturgical service formed part of the lineup for the People to People international jazz festival in Washington, D.C.

The most significant of the many events during 1962 that linked religion and jazz was the premiere of Mary Lou Williams's *St. Martin de Porres, Black Christ of the Andes,* a jazz hymn dedicated to a recently canonized black saint. Williams was then and is still now considered to be the leading female jazz composer, and she did arrangements for the Ellington orchestra during the 1940s. She left the business in 1954 to embark on a long period of prayer and meditation, eventually converting to Catholicism. *St. Martin de Porres* toured the country in subsequent years along with other original religiously inspired pieces by Williams, sometimes accompanied by a ballet troupe. "The ability to play good jazz is a gift from God," she asserted in 1966. "This music is based on the spirituals—it's our only original American art form—and should be played everywhere, including church. Those who say it shouldn't be played in church do not understand they are blocking the manifestation of God's will."

The Washington, D.C., black cultural scene in which Ellington grew up similarly mixed secular and sacred music. Using oral history evidence, scholar Ted Gioia argued in 1997 that religious influences may have held more sway over the initial development of jazz in New Orleans than the gin joints and brothels commonly credited with incubating the music. Famed black bandleader and composer James Reese Europe included religious music alongside the protojazz he performed with his Clef Club Orchestra during the 1910s.[20] The historical relationship between jazz and religion was closer than many realized in the 1960s, and besides giving voice to their personal religious convictions with their sacred compositions, Ellington and Williams were also calling attention to the inaccuracy of the stereotypes concerning jazz's heritage.

Ellington's spiritual theme "Come Sunday" was featured as part of a May 1963 Washington, D.C., Presbyterian service that mixed Christian themes with prayers aimed toward the "Unsung Heroes of Yesterday's Auction Block," "for Claimants of Dignity in Birmingham, Albany, Greensboro," and "Our Nation, for Freedom, for Black, Brown, Beige, and White." The mixture of jazz, history, and civil rights, along with more traditional religious selections, made this a rare event for a black church of the time, and it was partially organized by Ellington's friend and "number two son" Maurice Lawrence. During this same period, composer and saxophonist John Coltrane created a series of bestselling jazz compositions and albums, such as "Alabama" and *A Love Supreme,* that tied together civil rights and gospel influences. None of his works were performed in churches at the time, but they were part of jazz's increasing exploration of the divine, and many jazz and rock artists followed Coltrane's example. Later in 1963, Tom Vaughn, a student at Yale Divinity School, created a jazz liturgy with drummer Charlie Smith entitled "A Musical Offering to God" and performed it in Yale's Marquand Chapel. In 1965, RCA Records recorded the piece, and Vaughn got a spot on NBC's *Tonight Show* to promote it. In the year before the premiere of Ellington's Sacred Concert, numerous jazz liturgical pieces appeared, some by well-known figures in the jazz world such as Vince Guaraldi, Paul Horn, Lalo Schifrin, and Randy Weston. In November 1965, in San Francisco, a Jewish cantata by classical and jazz composer David Amram and Langston Hughes entitled "Let Us Remember" premiered. The work, commissioned a year earlier, was "ecumenical" and peaceful in spirit, combining Old Testament imagery with more modern images of bigotry against Jewish and black Americans in hopes of creating a spirit of brotherhood.

The formal origin for the Sacred Concerts began in the late 1950s. The Reverend C. Julian Bartlett and the Reverend John S. Yaryan, canon of Grace Cathedral in San Francisco, impressed by the religious passion of Ellington and Mahalia Jackson's 1958 recording of "Come Sunday" and Ellington's casting of "The 23rd Psalm," asked him to present "a concert of sacred music" at their church. Ellington initially felt reticence at the prospect, simultaneously honored and awed by the request:

> When you get that kind of invitation, you're not in show business. You think to yourself, *It has to be kind of right. You have to go out there and make a noise that tells the truth.*
>
> I had to stop and figure out my eligibility. I prayed.

It took years and many letters to finally convince him. In December 1962 and January 1963, Bartlett and Yaryan each wrote Ellington, asking about his requirements for a "concert of sacred music." "I am confident that such an event would be a signal one in our time," concluded Bartlett. A February 1964 letter from Yaryan expressed wishes that Ellington perform the Sacred Concert, or whatever he felt appropriate, during the year of celebrations for the dedication of the new, gigantic Grace Cathedral, situated on Nob Hill in San Francisco, commanding beautiful views of the city and bay. They were happy to host him and his orchestra for a week or a single performance or somewhere in between, whatever he preferred. Other notables who scheduled appearances at Grace during that year included President Lyndon B. Johnson, Dr. King, Tillich, the archbishop of Canterbury, and members of the British royal family. Yaryan gave Ellington total latitude for the content of his performance, making it clear that he did not have to limit his presentation to "service music." He even suggested that, instead of composing new work or an exclusively religious project, the band could reprise *My People* at Grace. Finally, during a fall 1964 week-long stand at a nearby club in Redwood City, CA, Ellington invited the Grace Cathedral clergy to a show and committed to the Sacred Concert. He had already begun planning the program, and, according to Bartlett, "he was just so eager to have this done. He had never done anything like this in his life." Ellington described his decision-making process to *Africa* magazine in 1966: "At first I was taken aback. God . . . religion . . . it's a personal thing with me, not to be mixed with a theatrical performance. But I thought about it . . . and wanted to give my best to God."[21]

In the weeks preceding and following it, the initial First Sacred Concert enjoyed wide national press coverage. The word "jazz" purposely did not appear in the publicity; the music Ellington performed was termed "contemporary sacred music." Ellington made it clear that it did not represent a usual performance for him. "No, we're not going to have a jam session," he told reporters. "This is my greatest opportunity to say something." Months after agreeing to the concert, Ellington still found himself worrying over his eligibility and making sure in his mind that he approached the Sacred Concerts in a proper manner:

> It took quite a lot of doing—getting ready for it. First there had to be the bolstering of your own eligibility. For it is different than anything else. Far different from the theatre. In the theatre, in one sense, you play games, play upon people, to their eyes, to their ears. But here you must only worship. The commitment has to be complete. It has to be total.[22]

No Ellington hits were included in the hour-long program, only a special selection of music for the occasion, some new, most of it not. It began with the alternately brooding and placid new twenty-minute composition "In the Beginning God," named after the first six syllables of the book of Genesis. Particularly in its first eight-minute section, it's an evocative and stirring piece of writing and performance, perhaps the best original work Ellington penned for the Sacred Concerts. With its clarion calls of trumpet, low rumbles of baritone sax and vocal, and ringing and pounding drum solo, it seemed designed to suggest the majesty and power of the subject matter and to take advantage of the acoustics of cathedrals. Ellington instructed drummer Louis Bellson to "simulate the sounds of trees . . . and then the sound of thunder" during his solo. The spoken litany of items in the piece that did not exist before God created the world represented another instance of Ellington making fun of American materialism during his career, this time stressing the primacy of religion and God: "no poverty, no Cadillacs, no sand traps, no mudflats, no pedestrians, no carriage trade, no bodyguards, no credit cards, no conference calls, no TV commercials, no headaches and no aspirin." A reviewer commented that "what this section succeeded in invoking was the realization that there is no essential difference between spiritual emptiness and meaningless physical acquisition, that true fulfillment is a matter of the spirit, and this can neither be spent or hoarded."[23] The calling out of the books of the Old and New Testaments in the middle of "In the Beginning God" seems somewhat trite in retrospect, if in context with the event and the venue. Another new piece was Ellington's tambourine-shaking gospel revival setting of "The Lord's Prayer."

The rest of the First Sacred Concert program recycled material from previous Ellington projects. The bulk of it emanated from *My People*. All of its spiritual and gospel themes were featured, including the infectious "Ain't but the One," a rousing Ellington composition that deserves more notice. His tribute to his parents, "My Mother, My Father, and Love," was given the honor of the last composition performed, symbolizing Daisy and James's centrality in Ellington's religious life. The concert also featured the introspective nine-minute solo piano piece "New World A-Comin'" (1943), based on the 1943 Roi Ottley book that forecast optimistic times for black Americans. It probably serves as another example of the many spiritually inspired Ellington pieces written before the Sacred Concerts. "Come Sunday" was offered in three different versions, including one that cast it within its original setting, the gorgeous extended spiritual section from *Black, Brown and Beige* that suggested the importance of religion to American slaves. A sprightly version of the theme entitled "David Danced (Before the Lord with All His Might)" featured tap dancing accompaniment.

Altogether, the selections of the First Sacred Concert made for an entertaining and soulful program, radiating love, commitment, tribute, and respect for God, Ellington's heritage, and his family. Its grounding in black history and musical sources made many observers in the press, and almost certainly in the audience, think about the issues of civil rights and how they related to Christianity. It featured biblical references but mostly consisted of a personal viewpoint. With the exception of a couple of the gospel songs, it did not preach; it did not demand any specific behavior or creed and mentioned Jesus only once, in passing. It was a singularly Ellingtonian blend of influences that blurred categories and redefined genres and attitudes: the sacred and the secular; the sensual and the moral; the popular and the serious; reverent Sunday morning and swinging Saturday night. Its sincerity and ability to touch people is palpable. No wonder, then, that in this period of growing alarm over declining religious participation, over sixty venues around the world, mostly churches, brought the Ellington Sacred Concerts to their communities during the next three years.[24]

Despite the genial tone of the First Sacred Concert, it raised resistance from parishioners, the press, and even some close Ellington associates before and after its premiere. Along with requests from far and near for tickets, letters critical of the Sacred Concerts arrived at Grace Cathedral in the months preceding the program. Janna Tull Steed reported that "someone clipped a copy of the *Time* article [about the Sacred Concert] and wrote across it 'Everything about this concert is disgusting,'" and sent it. Ellington personally heard comments of disbelief:

> In discussing it, they say, "*You?!*" in a tone like that, "You gonna write a *mass?*" They don't say it, but it sort of sounds like eligibility. "You, you gonna write a mass? You're a man of the world and all that sort of thing." Well, you

know, it isn't a matter of writing or performing it that inspires the serious side of it, the sincerity. I don't think it's a matter of eligibility, of what I am eligible to write. It's a matter of whether God will accept it.

Joya Sherrill, a vocalist for the Ellington band off and on since the mid-1940s and a Jehovah's Witness, rejected his invitation to sing at the First Sacred Concert and the whole concept behind it. He asked her because of her serious interest in religion and the Bible. In 1989, she told the Smithsonian:

> It was quite an honor, he said "You are the one that must do this," not because of my religious thing, but because he was saying, vocally I was the one to do it . . . It was really a difficult thing, I'd never refused him anything before . . . But I just did not go along with religious jazz concerts; I just don't put the 2 things together . . . "But this is for the church," he said, "people will come and hear it, it's a way of getting a message." I said "But Duke, it's not a message, you're playing music. The people love your music . . . it's not a question of getting people into the church, people should learn something about God . . . when they finish your concert, they're not going to know anything more about God." He said, "Joya, anything that gets people in the church is good." I said, "Well, if you want to get people into the church, what you do is have the concert, you can have prostitution upstairs and gambling downstairs," and I said "There will not be a seat empty." That's getting them into the church, but for *what* are they in the church, you know what I'm saying? . . . So then he was telling me . . . what he was going to pay me, and I said "That's another thing. Even if I would do this, you couldn't pay me one penny for this, because I don't believe that anything connected with religion or God should be financial." . . . It was kind of a difficult thing for me. He said "I don't even understand why you feel that way."

For Sherrill and other observers, especially in the black community, religion could not be as easily melded with the secular world as Ellington wished. In this view, a religious concert by definition needed to be evangelical, based on scripture, dedicated to using doctrine to achieve goals of education and conversion. But Ellington was going into the church as an artist, not a preacher. He sought to reach people emotionally, putting personal feelings into music, as he had for decades. His religious view was individual, not doctrinal. Such a stance threatened many, as welcoming an atmosphere as the Sacred Concerts represented. Ellington knew that spiritual feelings reached people in more environments than just churches and synagogues. Sherrill and others were not willing to consider an alternate, non-institutional path that mixed the sacred and secular in challenging ways. As Sherrill discussed:

> Sure, you're going to feel good when you leave, but you feel good after you've had a drink, you know what I'm saying? It's not a question of what makes you feel good, my feeling was, and I still say, those people who left that concert, did not say "Now I'm gonna be better to my fellow man, now I'm going to stop doing this, that or the other." They didn't say that. *Nobody* said that. They said, "Man, was that great. Oh, that was inspiring." What does "inspiring" *mean*? A beautiful woman walking down the street can be inspiring. So the point is, I didn't feel good about in participating in [the Sacred Concert] because it becomes a farce. Why do it in the church? The purpose of doing it in the church is to say that it's religious. And it isn't religious.[25]

But Ellington did have something valuable and religious to contribute, even if based on his feelings and background and not strictly on the Bible and traditional teachings. It was a personal message, accessible, based on love in a number of contexts. It resembled the embracing and tolerant Sermon on the Mount more than the doctrinal and moral messages of the Apostle Paul.

Bartlett attempted to defuse potential criticism of the concert in the weeks before its premiere. "I know that there will be those who will be critical . . . but we are trying to get away from the idea that the church is a place where one always has to be quiet," he told the *San Francisco Examiner.* "There is a wrong idea that anything enjoyable or entertaining is sinful and profane . . . sometimes the prayer of music and the prayer of the dance can be more powerful than any words." Bartlett told them that Ellington was not trying to "improve on traditional spiritual music," yet he planned to make a "serious Christian statement" and "a good chunk of entertainment as well." Gensel, the "Jazz Priest," also defended Ellington's approach. A month after the Sacred Concert, he stated: "we have been pontificating . . . too much and too long . . . we find many people are bypassing the church, that they think . . . is not very relevant and pertinent to their life. So many people think the church is primarily a place of judgment, it's kind of a monitor that will slap your fingers if you say anything wrong, or do anything wrong . . . cracking your knuckles, you know." Gensel strongly argued that this was not how the Christian or Jewish religions should operate.

Bartlett was walking an ecclesiastical tightrope, trying not to alienate his core constituency while updating and challenging traditions in the manner of his superior, the controversial Episcopal bishop of California, James A. Pike. Through his actions and words, Pike was determined to make Christianity more relevant to modern Americans, especially in the liberal city of San Francisco and the large number of California churches he supervised. "The most formidable roadblock to understanding and acceptance of Christianity has been erected by the church itself in its refusal to abandon concepts, words, images, and myths developed in past centuries when men were operating under different world-views and differing philosophical structures," Pike wrote in 1965. To that end, he recommended jettisoning the idea of the Trinity as well as the notion that Mary was a virgin, which led to fourteen Arizona clergymen filing heresy charges against him (which were dropped a few days before the Sacred Concerts) and publicity and outrage in various quarters. His installation of portraits of Albert Einstein, John Glenn, and Thurgood Marshall in the clerestory windows at Grace Cathedral marked another example of his efforts to update Christianity. Ellington's Sacred Concerts fit Pike's strategies perfectly, and Bartlett and Yaryan no doubt knew that this creative and headline-producing way of worshipping God would make their boss happy.[26]

The initial San Francisco Sacred Concert was an unequivocal success.[27] Laudatory wire-service reviews appeared in newspapers across the country, and the event graced the cover of *Down Beat*. Some of the headlines included: "Ellington to New Peak," "3,000 in Church Get Ellington's Message," and "Cathedral Echoes to Jazzman's Hymns." It sold out the house of three thousand patrons at prices of up to $25 (about $165 in today's dollars) per seat. Ellington worked for the lowest possible union scale, declining to collect his usual fee, and the band performed on a simple wooden platform mounted on the pulpit. He also turned down most media requests from newspapers and radio and television stations, insisting that the concert not descend into a media event with banks of lights and dozens of cameras. The local public television station did tape the proceedings.

As hoped, a different and more diverse audience than usual filled the pews: "a wild mixture of jazz musicians up from the Monterey [Jazz] Festival, a few bearded hipsters, matrons, students, and the great well-dressed mass of Ellington lovers." At first, the audience felt unsure about the etiquette of applause in church. But, following Episcopal Bishop Pike's lead of unrestrained clapping after each number, "even the ones [in the audience] inhibited by the huge house of worship stood in spontaneous ovations." At the close of the final selection, "the cathedral was silent for a moment, with just the clanging of a [San Francisco] cable car going by outside."

Before the show, Ellington experienced trepidation concerning "David

Danced," the tap dancing number performed by Bunny Briggs. "Bishop Pike was very enthusiastic about this, but I was a bit nervous about him dancing around the sanctuary," Ellington recalled later. "I was afraid . . . the altar is so sacred, but it was beautiful! When a man feels what he enjoys in life is only because of the grace of God, he rejoices, sings, and sometimes dances. And so it was with David [in the Old Testament], in spite of his wife's prudishness." Briggs also felt "very nervous" about the propriety of tap dancing in church. "This was the first time I'd danced in a church . . . on the altar," he recalled in 1967. "I was saying to myself: 'I hope God will understand this.' As it started, all the fear left me . . . Duke was always calm." Overall, "David Danced" illustrated the scripture passage quite aptly.

For this show, criticism of Ellington playing music in church was almost nonexistent; in other locales, resistance emerged more frequently during the first couple years of Sacred Concerts. At a press conference before the Grace Cathedral Concert, though, a reporter asked Ellington "how he reconciled his vocation and his beliefs. How could he, as a religious man, play in dark, dingy places where depravity and drunkenness reign?" Ellington replied in a "hardly audible" and "humble voice": "Isn't that exactly what Christ did—went into the places where people were, bringing light into darkness?" It represented a mild preview of the backlash to come.

On 19 November 1965, Dr. Bryant M. Kirkland, minister of the Fifth Avenue Presbyterian Church in New York City announced the next Sacred Concert, to be held at his church on 26 December. As in San Francisco, the press release announcing the Sacred Concert featured some preemptive spin control on the potential controversies surrounding the use of popular music in a religious setting. "Modern music catches the melancholy of contemporary life and the paradox of communication; built-in answers keep some from hearing their brother's cry of loneliness," Kirkland wrote, somewhat paraphrasing comments Ellington made in his program notes for the Grace Cathedral concert. "When communication takes place in honesty and courage without fear or bitterness the miracle of understanding transpires." He pointed out that the Fifth Avenue church, established in 1808, founded by men who lived their boyhood during the American Revolution, was one of the first in New York City to introduce organ music during the nineteenth century, a practice once viewed as an "abomination." In the program, at the show, and in press interviews, Kirkland also quoted Psalm 150 in order to justify Ellington's musical contributions to the church. Three years later, for the Second Sacred Concert, Ellington built a composition around the psalm:

Praise ye the Lord! Praise God in his sanctuary; praise Him in His mighty firmament!...

Praise Him with the trumpet blast; praise Him with lyre and harp!...

Praise Him with clashing cymbals; praise Him with loud clanging cymbals!

Let everything that has breath praise the LORD! Praise ye the LORD!

According to Gensel, the chairman of the concert committee, which featured representatives from the Greek Orthodox, Methodist, and Lutheran faiths, the show was "a non-profit event" with most tickets priced at $2 and 165 "patron" seats at $15 and $25 each. All 1,800 tickets sold out weeks before the concert, and Pinkerton guards turned away the overflow crowd at the church. Ellington offered his services and those of his orchestra "at cost," with any extra income earmarked toward Gensel's Jazz Ministry.[28] The CBS-TV network filmed the concert for later national broadcast.

Ellington requested that Kirkland remove the word "jazz" from his essay in the program (it appeared twice in Kirkland's original draft), reflecting his long-held desire not to be confined to one category. "I don't like to place my music in pigeonholes, and I don't like the word jazz," he told the *Pittsburgh Courier* for a story on the Sacred Concerts. "It has too many meanings, some of them bad, for too many people. This concert is a very personal statement, so let the theme of the concert speak for itself." Ellington's sacred music, like his other works, was too diverse to be corralled under one category anyway. Gensel's attitude on the Sacred Concert seemed shaped by Ellington's famous stance on categories and intimated that the blurring of such boundaries could enhance the vitality of the church and Christianity. He said that the increasing use of jazz in religious services resulted from a desire to move beyond sacred and secular musical distinctions: "there is a feeling that everything is a part of God's world, and that the old, arbitrary separation no longer makes sense."[29] By claiming that his work existed in a realm beyond category, Ellington gained for himself and others the creative freedom to explore any genre, including those beyond the categories black artists were usually consigned to before Ellington arrived on the scene. The Sacred Concerts inspired churches to adopt similar philosophies, creating excitement and headlines that underlined the continuing relevance of the centuries-old beliefs they represented in a changing world. It is easy to imagine the attraction between Ellington and religious leaders like Bartlett, Gensel, Kirkland, and Pike: each emphasized a modern, emotional, daily relationship with God and a desire to instill that vision within new generations. Each ignored social and religious mores that, in their view, unnecessarily kept Christianity from reaching a wider audience.

The Fifth Avenue Sacred Concert and the CBS-TV special that resulted from it inspired more comment across the country than the initial concert at Grace Cathedral. Most reviews within New York were positive, as were syndicated wire-service reports, two of which mentioned "the smartly gowned, fur-clad socialites" in attendance. A reviewer in a Haddonfield, New Jersey, newspaper called it "one of the most moving confessions of faith I've ever heard." Alan Rich, in the *New York Herald-Tribune,* delivered the most positive verdict among the major New York critics and the view that best captured Ellington's intentions:

> In a sense, there was nothing truly liturgical about his music. In another sense, it was totally liturgical. His music, at its best, is a powerful distillation of emotion and emotional gesture; it speaks, whether through a singer, a piano, a solo saxophone, or a set of drums, of tremendously personal things. As such it is never removed from the purest meaning of prayer.

Ebony viewed Ellington's achievement in a historical context, as the continuation of efforts he started long before: "A type of music once disdained as being fit for only bars and bordellos was being performed in a sacred concert by the man who had helped earn for it the greatest respect."[30] Ellington was again redefining the parameters of American and African American culture, dispelling older cultural prejudices, and demonstrating the versatility of both traditions.

Three essays in the religious press shared an initial skepticism about the Sacred Concert but found that, in the end, Ellington's unorthodox approach won them over. "To many of us [evangelists], 'jazz' is a dirty word— the absolute antithesis of what the church should stand for," wrote the correspondent for *Eternity.* The Sacred Concert, however, helped demonstrate that "Time is the great sanctifier, and jazz has clearly emerged as an art of its own." But this commentator also felt that the concert was "missing . . . sound biblical and theological theoretical orientation . . . it is obvious that [Ellington's] doctrinal understanding is muddled." Joe Brieg, writing in *Ave Maria,* said that while some may judge Ellington's religious work a "wild" or "radical . . . experiment," he viewed it as part of "the great central historical truth of our time—the gradual ending of the great divorce between religion and the world," an event that, in its repercussions of "experimentation" and "diversity," coalesced perfectly with Pope Pius XII's calls for "the consecration of the world." Marnie Mellblom, the correspondent from the *Lutheran* felt "squeamish and uneasy" as "Ellington stepped into the chancel, dressed in a white suit, baby blue shirt, white tie and bright blue suede shoes. Was this all right, inside a church? Could this possibly be a religious experience?" The overture from *Black, Brown and Beige* marked the turning point for her, "a stirring statement of Ellington's belief that since all men are God's people, God cannot be separated from social problems." Mellblom also wrote about the feelings of "JOY" and "REVERENCE" the presentation raised in her. By the end of the program, she answered her own question of whether the concert represented a religious experience: "Oh yes!" While maintaining that she would not want "jazz concerts every Sunday," she concluded that "when men like Duke Ellington proclaim their faith through their talent, God alone knows where this might lead."[31]

Despite the positive notices from some surprising quarters, the Fifth Avenue Presbyterian Church show and the television show drawn from it also inspired the first serious critical resistance to Ellington's Sacred Concerts. Jack Wyrtzen, a Christian radio and television host in New Jersey, publicly criticized the Protestant Council of New York for reaching "a new low, presenting such cheap jazz. How much further is the Protestant Council going to contribute to the apostasy that will one day become the world church under the anti-Christ?" The *Tampa Sentinel,* a black newspaper, vehemently argued in an editorial that "a jazz orchestra, even one as good as Duke's, does not belong in a house of worship." The paper especially disapproved of the applause and the dancing. An advertising man interviewed in Tulsa for a local paper characterized Ellington's Sacred Concert as a "cheap publicity stunt" that degraded the church with its "sensationalism." "The church's image today is rather shabby and this kind of publicity doesn't help . . . a jazz festival in church makes it the laughing stock of the world," he added. "How can the church command the respect of the people if it does everything the world does?" A minister with a newspaper column in Altus, Oklahoma, lumped Ellington's church performances with screenings of controversial commercial films for church discussion and the use of "the watusi" and "the frug" for contemporary worship services for children. To him, all of this served as evidence that "strange things are happening on the religious scene." An editorial in another Oklahoma newspaper called it "a shock," but decided that no harm had occurred and "there is a chance that others might be brought into the fold."

A Baltimore Sunday school teacher argued against Ellington's comments, which were supported by her local paper, that "every man prays in his own language," insisting that "true worship and prayer is not accomplished through the medium of jazz, but through the teaching of God's word." Such modern viewpoints represented a "tragic" message for "our young people," in her opinion. A *Des Moines Register* reader railed against the positive spin of the wire-service story the paper ran about the Sacred Concert, claiming that it did not intend to "promote worship" but to "prove that some church leaders are daringly 'liberal'" and "to have fun shocking a few old fuddy-duddies." Reverend William Vanden Berg's weekly Iowa newspaper column argued that spreading the "words of Jesus" represented the only "reason for the Church being in existence." For him, Ellington's Sacred Concert and a recent suburban evangelical meeting featuring rock and roll music called "Revival-a-Go-Go" were distractions that reflected "this sin-sick world" rather than "the responsibility of presenting Jesus Christ in all his glory." Berg's angry comments demonstrated that Ellington's Sacred Concerts aroused some of the same tensions that bitterly divided the country on issues such as the Vietnam War, the counterculture, family values, and the changing status of African Americans during the 1960s:

> This crazy world of swivel-hips; sickening, long, stringy haircuts on boys and girls; dumb bell demonstrators, and big mouths with empty heads don't need more of what they already have. They need the power of a new affection—the love of Christ in their hearts and if the Church doesn't give them this, who in all the world will?[32]

While most of the criticism of the Sacred Concerts emanated from a conservative viewpoint, some on the left also chimed in. The *Village Voice*'s "Jazz Journal" columnist, Michael Zwerin, seeing the well-off people gathered at the Fifth Avenue church, felt "confronted by the fact that this kind of power structure is really big business." He continued on in a half-humorous, half-serious rant of paranoia, wondering if Ellington and his drummer Louis Bellson were the Messiah and, at the end of the article, drowning his confusion and alienation in a "double Dewars on the rocks." Underneath the light and perhaps mocking tone, however, some issues behind the concert genuinely troubled him. They were not the same issues that concerned the more conservative crowd, but they were still built on a kind of uneasiness:

> Gensel . . . was chairman of the committee. I know him, and he is a straight cat. Nevertheless, I mistrust the sudden interest of the church in selling God to jazz musicians and in selling jazz to their flocks. It's like they just discovered this barbaric, primitive country with a pagan population and are moving in

with the missionaries. Maybe they try to sell too hard . . . The presence of the cameras and the bright lights didn't exactly help. If they are really interested in my welfare why did they sacrifice it to the gods of publicity, that night?[33]

For the most part, Ellington ignored the criticism on all sides. In one of the press interviews for his next Sacred Concert, at Coventry Cathedral in England in February 1966, he did respond to those who questioned his approach. "This is very personal work, and reflects me. It is a form of worship . . . Some say it is too modern. I don't agree," he told a British newspaper. "After all, we don't live in the fifteenth-century, and when I was approached about the concert, I realized they didn't want that sort of music either. If you're going to confine religion to the fifteenth-century atmosphere this means you can rule out discussing it on the telephone or over TV."[34] The Coventry concert was filmed for the ABC-TV network, giving the Sacred Concert more national exposure.

If he had wished, Ellington could have told those who disliked the presence of jazz in church that, especially in African American culture, the lines between the sacred and secular in music were thin, and had been for a long time. Jazz had serious roots in Christianity. Albert Murray, in his treatise on the blues, made the same case for the blues and argued that the music shared much in its intent and effect with the black church, even if the two institutions were at odds at times. The music of the black church, especially the mood of loneliness, death, and reckoning expressed in the lyrics and music of the spirituals, served as a key influence on the blues as well as jazz. "Hence," Murray argued, black blues (and jazz) performers often treated the "the dance hall as temple." The "merriment" that the blues musicians could summon often offended and was "condemned" by "down-home church elders," but the two groups actually shared much in common. Within his Sacred Concerts, Ellington brought these two sides of black culture together again, and it disturbed some Americans. Within the three Sacred Concerts Ellington assembled and wrote between 1965 and 1973, he stressed the same "rituals of propitiation" that Murray viewed as key to the religious presentations of the black church: prayer, sacrifice, forgiveness, and thanksgiving.[35] He also was bringing, as he had many times before in his career, black culture and history to venues where it rarely existed before.

One of the reasons that Ellington could afford to dismiss the often passionate outcry against the Sacred Concerts was because they "triggered an avalanche of calls" from churches who wished to stage similar shows in their communities. "Why we get more calls for bookings from churches now than we're getting from dance halls," Ruth Ellington "chuckled" to *Jet*. The Sacred Concerts were changing the minds of more people than just religious leaders. "I thought it was wrong [at first]," Ella Fitzgerald told the *Washington Post*. "I felt like jazz and religion didn't mix." But then, in the months after the initial Sacred Concerts, Fitzgerald starting singing some traditional hymns in addition to her usual blend of bebop and ballads.[36]

The financial underpinnings of the Sacred Concerts were handled carefully, partly because they were so much more expensive to produce than the usual Ellington show. In October 1965, the Ellington orchestra received an average guarantee of a little over $1,750 per night, according to surviving booking contracts. The contracts for Sacred Concerts during 1966, with one exception, all guaranteed the band between $3,000 and $4,000 per show. Starting in the fall of 1968, as Cress Courtney assumed duties as Ellington's manager, a policy mandated a $5,000 guarantee for a Sacred Concert during a period when, according to the October 1968 booking contracts, non-Sacred Concerts brought in a guarantee of slightly more than $3,100 per night. In 1970, Courtney said that he had "sat down with the accountant," figured out exactly what a Sacred Concert cost (including robe rentals and rehearsals for the choirs in each town), and charged only that. "We're not going to make anything to speak of," he stated, something Ellington maintained as well. Judging from business documents at the Smithsonian, it appears that Courtney, Ruth Ellington, and lawyer Benjamin Starr seemed more involved with Sacred Concert contracts than other contracts for the band. Courtney felt that he "had to control them, and I don't allow anybody to arrange [them] except myself . . . for the very simple reason that I don't want anyone to be able to say that Ellington is proselytizing or commercializing on religion, so I make a standard price and that is it, and I don't care if you're a very wealthy diocese or little church on the south side of Chicago." In fact, Courtney said, some churches called to ask why Ellington chose a certain church in their town for a Sacred Concert "when we can offer you so much more money." Courtney's reply: "No one's going to give us more money."[37]

The musical structure of the Sacred Concerts insured additional publishing income for Ellington. Changes to ASCAP policy enacted in 1960 and 1962 mandated that extended "concert and symphony performances" of compositions received "twice the credit" of regular-length works and that "religious works" of four minutes' duration or more received "triple credit" when performed as part of a religious program. As he had many times before, Ellington made artistic decisions that also yielded economic benefits, although no one anticipated the international success and interest such concerts would inspire during the initial planning. But Ellington made it clear that money was a secondary or even less important issue in the Sacred Concerts. He publicly proclaimed that he would not allow any church to lose money on an event and told the *National Catholic Reporter* that he had personally invested $8,000 in one Sacred Concert held at a small church. "I consider myself a very lucky man to be able to do what I love to do best. This is my way of expressing thanks to God," Ellington said in 1966. "Some people go to church and leave a couple dollars. This is my chance to feel I am on the team, even if I only make batboy."[38]

The Sacred Concerts also brought massive media coverage to Ellington and his music. It allowed critics and audiences to view and judge Ellington, his work, and his legacy afresh, apart from critical clichés that had gathered around him during his lengthy career. It pushed the press, from glossy national magazines to small newspapers in Middle America, to write about Ellington in the 1960s instead of the supposed glory days of the 1930s and 1940s. The coverage accorded the Sacred Concerts portrayed Ellington as a trailblazing, unpredictable, and controversial artistic figure, even in his mid-60s, a man whose achievements and manner were associated in the white and black press once again with images of black history and the continuing struggle of black Americans for equality. His public airing of his religious views probably also helped attract new fans, especially in the United States, a country where religion has always resided at the center of culture and where the overwhelming majority believed in God.

Churches also used Sacred Concerts for their own purposes: for promotion, recruitment, and fundraising, just as they had used popular music during previous periods in American history. Many of the churches also used their hosting of the Sacred Concerts to demonstrate their viability, diversity, and versatility during a period when religious institutions were frequently questioned. "The church is in trouble and we've got to come up with some new answers . . . [we need to] adopt innovating trends, not sit Sunday after Sunday doing the same things by rote," said James McKeaver, explaining why his Princeton church sponsored a Sacred Concert in 1966.

Hosting a Sacred Concert served as notice that a certain church or synagogue had not gone stale, that it could engage with modern ways of exploring and expressing religious belief. In a February 1966 interview, professor Robert Baker, dean of Union Seminary's School of Sacred Music in New York, criticized the church for its unwillingness to use contemporary sources for church music. He reluctantly credited Ellington for shaking up the system and hoped the Sacred Concerts would inspire reform. Earlier churchmen, such as Martin Luther, did not hesitate "to adopt secular practices which they found valid and musically exciting." Jazz in church, he argued, "has about as much chance of righting things as has a skin poultice for deep-seated cancer. But the important thing is that the illness is finally being recognized." A Jewish synagogue in Lawrence, New York, citing Ellington's example, joined their cantor and choir with local jazz musicians for a fifteen-minute "jazz-oriented worship" portion of a Sabbath service in February 1966. But the Sacred Concerts were not a panacea for all the problems, especially recruiting, that churches and synagogues faced in the 1960s. As Bishop Pike told a conference in England five months after Ellington's appearance at Grace Cathedral, "The 'beat' services draw large crowds, but these crowds rarely return."[39]

Throughout 1966, Ellington staged the Sacred Concert across the country, in varying communities and religious and secular venues, the audiences making up a diverse mosaic of American life in the mid-1960s. On 10 March 1966, the Brooklyn First AME Zion Church became the first black church (of four that year) to host a Sacred Concert. With a reputation in the black community as a "freedom church," it was fitting that this occurred within an AME church. The pastor, in his essay from the program, took the occasion to expound upon the links between black history and music. "Negro church music has always served as a bridge linking the sacred and the secular. When all other avenues of expression and communications were closed to him, the Negro sent his plea for freedom around the world on the wings of song," wrote the Reverend Ruben L. Speaks. "Christ never attempted to compartmentalize or segmatize life; rather, He sought to spiritualize the whole of life. There is no rhythm, tune, or melody that is not acceptable to God." At the Sacred Concert held at the Washington Street AME Zion Church in Newburgh, New York, later that year, "all proceeds" went toward the building of a new church-sponsored community center.[40]

The demand for the Sacred Concerts went beyond the confines of churches. The first one held in a secular venue occurred in August 1966, at a fair called the St. John Terrell's Music Circus in Lambertville, New Jersey. "You don't *have* to play sacred music only in church," Ellington told the *New York Times* the day before the show. "Man, you can pray anywhere you want to pray." Since the September 1965 premiere in San Francisco, he had also played excerpts from the Sacred Concert on the road at regular gigs.[41]

In Phoenix, Arizona, Trinity Cathedral hosted two performances of the Sacred Concert in November 1966. Senator Barry Goldwater, one of the architects of the modern conservative movement and the Republican nominee for president in 1964, was in the audience, as was part of a group of "prominent Phoenicians who helped underwrite the cost of the concerts" so that "over 100 young people from Phoenix's impoverished southside" could attend. While some of the typically older crowd, including "elderly women with mink stoles approved audibly . . . not everyone was pleased." Some left after intermission, some asked for their money back, and others "protested earlier when they heard that jazz music and tap dancing were planned for the sanctuary." But the primary impressions of the concert, as reported by the *Phoenix Gazette* and *Episcopalian* magazine, were of patrons exclaiming that they would attend church more often if similar presentations were offered and of the uncommon number of young people in church, including "scores of teen-agers [which] had to be turned away."[42]

Temple Emanuel in Beverly Hills, California, became the first Jewish synagogue to host a Sacred Concert, a few days after the Phoenix performances. The show bestowed an indisputable aura of multidenominational identity upon the Sacred Concerts. *Hep* magazine, a monthly aimed at black audiences, later wrote that "much discussion has been made of this concert, some were for it, and some were against it." H. Robert Udkoff, a local businessman, temple member, and longtime Ellington friend helped set up the conditions leading to the concert. When Ellington returned from an Asian tour in 1964, Udkoff picked him up at five in the morning and delivered him to a bar mitzvah Udkoff was attending at Emanuel. Ellington, fascinated by the ritual, engaged afterward in a long conversation with Rabbi Sanford Shapero, who pronounced Ellington "a superb audience for Jewish lore" and noticed Ellington's own serious religious commitment. Two years later, the concert was held as a benefit for religious educational scholarships, with tickets ranging from $10 to $100. "The ecumenical Ellington receives no fee, on faith," reported the *Los Angeles Times,* and no booking contract exists for the show in the Smithsonian's archives. The concert program reflected the upper-class atmosphere of the evening: it is the fanciest Sacred program in the Ellington files, gold-embossed, as were the invitations. By welcoming a Christian to perform a religious concert in his temple, Shapero probably knew that he could be courting controversy. He called the Sacred Concert "a gift to God and a contribution to human brotherhood" and outlined what he viewed as the value of Ellington's presence and message:

"Duke" is to me the outstanding example of the universal man. He loves all, has malice towards none. His code book of behavior contains no categories of human beings, nor classifications as to race, caste, or faith . . .

We welcome this man to our altar. We thank him for his tribute to God Almighty. We welcome his prayers and his devotions expressed to the Ellington "liturgy." Surely God will rejoice in having an offering so sincerely and beautifully presented—and yet, so unlike all others.

No negative feedback was reported at the Temple Emanuel Sacred Concert. Leonard Feather, in the *Los Angeles Times,* wrote that Ellington played to a "joyously mixed crowd of Jews and Gentiles, whites and Negroes. Some came as regular Ellington camp followers, others perhaps out of curiosity, as if to watch a tennis match played underwater; by the time the evening was over, a spirit compounded of reverence and respect had been instilled in the congregation of the overflowing synagogue." Tony Watkins, a former Ellington band boy recently graduated to band vocalist, sang "Come Sunday" that night in Hebrew. The evening featured an integration of audiences and forces that rarely united in American society, particularly in this period, with black separatism on the rise and the formerly strong links between blacks and Jews, which proved so important years earlier in the civil rights movement, fraying.[43]

The strongest resistance to any Sacred Concert came in Ellington's hometown of Washington, D.C., in December 1966.[44] The Interdenominational Church Ushers Alliance sponsored the performance at Constitution Hall, but the Baptist Ministers Conference (BMC), a mostly black group which represented the leaders of about 150 local churches, passed a resolution "against endorsing the Ellington performance" by a vote of 100–2. It was a charged situation: many of the ushers worked under the leaders who voted against the concert, and the Washington papers quoted some of the ushers anonymously accusing BMC leaders of telling their congregations to boycott the concert, a potential financial disaster for the nonprofessional promoters. One source accused the BMC of trying to sabotage the concert, whose proceeds benefited multiracial children's charities, because it was arranged without their consent or help. Similar procedures were followed in the ushers' presentations of Mahalia Jackson in the same venue in past years with no repercussions, but the hiring of Ellington to perform a Sacred Concert was another matter. BMC leaders willing to go on record claimed that the reasons for their disapproval of the Sacred Concert rested solely and personally on Ellington. The Reverend John D. Bussey of the Bethesda Baptist Church told the *Washington Post* that he drew up the resolution against the Sacred Concert because Ellington's life "is opposed to what the church stands for . . . [his] nightclub playing and the fact the music is just considered worldly." When a person becomes a Christian, he asserted, "they stop their worldly ways." Another local minister told the Washington press that

"Duke Ellington represents the type of service that we as Baptist ministers didn't feel represented the Christian impact." One of the few clergymen supporting the concert and taking issue with the BMC was Rev. E. Franklin Jackson of the John Wesley AME Zion Church. Jackson delivered the invocation for the Sacred Concert and felt that "Ellington's music is wonderful for the church, but perhaps I am prejudiced since Duke grew up in my church playing the piano for Sunday school here."

Ellington commented immediately, his remarks picked up by wire services and printed around the country. "Doesn't God accept sinners anymore?" he asked. "I'm just a messenger boy trying to carry the message . . . If I was a dishwasher or a waiter in a nightclub, does that mean I couldn't join their church?" Others joined in his defense. "The Duke is a religious man, he's spent his life doing nothing but good. Everybody loves him," Joe Morgen, Ellington's longtime press agent and unabashed partisan, told the press. "He's 67 and he's upset. This is his hometown, and these are ministers criticizing him." Drew Pearson, the national columnist who usually concentrated on political and foreign policy issues, weighed in as well, comparing the intolerance shown Ellington to that faced by Marian Anderson in her attempt to play at Constitution Hall in 1939. Roy Meachum, a local radio news commentator on WTOP-AM, felt "baffled" by BMC actions. "Having spent some time reading the Bible I seem to recall that Christ accepted some precious oil from Mary Magdalene, despite the fact that his friends objected to the way she earned the money to pay for the gift," Meachum commented on the air. "Hopefully Mr. Ellington's evening will be filled with [an] audience so that the groups can have the money to get on with the work of suffering little children to come unto them." The *Washington Post* published two letters to the editor. One felt that the biblical verse "Judge not lest ye be judged" needed to be applied to the Baptist ministers; the other said when she heard the news about the BMC vote she felt "compelled" to round up a group of friends to immediately buy tickets to the event. "This narrow-minded, joyless, anti-life attitude, under the guise of Christianity can only serve as another little-needed setback to organized religion," wrote Jean T. Faught of Bethesda.

A few days later, when Ellington arrived in town to face his "unwelcoming committee," as the *Washington Post* put it, he had more to say. "I don't have debates with people elected to represent the church," he said at a press conference. He openly wondered if "the people making this criticism have ever heard [the Sacred Concert] before." An editorial in the *Washington D.C. Capitol Spotlight* wrote later that many of the preachers, who were referred to as the "We Ain't Ready Club," had not heard any of the music.

The name referenced Ellington's controversial (and probably misreported) 1951 comment of "we ain't ready," which originally inflamed comment in black newspapers, now ironically applied to what the paper viewed as narrow-minded religious leaders who resisted the Sacred Concerts. Ellington ended his remarks on an outwardly conciliatory note with a hard edge: "What it takes to make music sacred is a matter of sincerity; worship is a matter of profound intent," he commented. "I tried to invite everybody. It's very easy to misunderstand."

On 5 December, Ellington presented his Sacred Concert at Constitution Hall "with no apologies to his ministerial critics," according to the *Washington Daily News,* which judged the performance a "musical success." But the reviewer felt that the hundreds of empty seats in the hall probably prevented a financial success. A month later, the fifty-two-year-old Bussey had no regrets concerning his instigation of the BMC resolution, and, if anything, came down even harder on Ellington. "We think the man himself is incapable of writing sacred music," he declared to the *Washington Post.* "His life does not commend itself to the sacred." He also expressed his dislike for excessive emotionalism in religious worship and gospel music, which he viewed as an "anachronism in the new day of the educated Negro." Jumping, clapping, and screaming in church, he argued, took people's minds too far from the Christian message that should be central in any religious service. But he could not name one offensive gospel song by Ellington or anyone else.

Bussey was mistaken in several ways. The Sacred Concerts featured none of the emotionalism of black religion that characterized the rise of Pentecostal and Holiness churches during the same period. Ellington's approach was calm and reasoning, full of warmth and love. Sometimes the music swung, but more often it was reflective and devotional; people stayed in their seats and did not sing along or jump in the aisles.

The whole episode illustrated the changes that had occurred in black Washington society since Ellington had left the city for Harlem as a young man. From the 1870s until at least World War II, Washington represented the cream of black American society, an area where blacks enjoyed unprecedented respectability, professional careers in public and private fields, and the best black school system in the country, dedicated to instilling black culture and history. As a boy, Ellington was the model of the "educated Negro" that Washington, D.C., schools hoped to produce—eloquent in history, art, and music, an internationally recognized spokesman on behalf of the race. But by the mid-1960s, the culture of black Washington had changed. These black church leaders still hung onto the old images of black respectability, but their field of vision had drastically narrowed outside of that concept and seemed out of touch with the modern environment. They had not grown with the times, and they lashed out at Ellington when their goals and methods were actually more alike than different. Ellington still followed the vision of inclusiveness that his old hometown inculcated in him in earlier decades, using art to fashion powerful and personal messages about God and black America that resonated worldwide, while they were still subscribing in some ways to a quasi-Victorian sensibility. The Sacred Concert at Constitution Hall marked yet another event that contributed to the estrangement Ellington felt from his hometown during the 1960s.

By the end of 1966, many in the press noted a "current of change . . . coursing through Christianity around the country," a new willingness to experiment with modes of worship and presentation. The *Wall Street Journal* rounded up some of the events in the past year that signaled this transition: more services translated into idiomatic English; more youth input in the planning of services; more pastoral comment on controversial topics such as social ills, civil rights, and the Vietnam War; and a new flexibility on musical genres used in services, of which the Sacred Concerts were cited as a prime example. The Vatican issued an edict banning "jazz masses" in January 1967 and called the guitar a "profane" instrument, but many in the American Catholic Church protested, including Father O'Connor, who contributed liner notes to an album called *The Jazz Mass* released that same month on Columbia Records. The "jazz mass" rule, while occasionally broken by a few American Catholic churches, was not rescinded for years, and Ellington did not perform a Sacred Concert in a Catholic venue until 1973.

As the 1960s progressed, the trend of more diverse and personal approaches to liturgical music grew deeper and stronger. A February 1969 *New York Times* article by Issachar Miron, chairman of the music faculty at the Jewish Teachers Seminary, stated that "never in the history of religion has there been such a radical transformation in sacred music as in recent years." Miron listed dozens of examples drawn from the widest perspective of Christian and Jewish denominations to prove his point, citing the use of rock, jazz, folk, and more adventurous modern classical music by composers such as Krzysztof Penderecki and Oliver Messianen. A decade before Ellington's Sacred Concerts, this development could not have been imagined. Ellington did not initiate this trend, but of all the attempts to forge new and more passionate models of religious music, his example earned the most media and clerical notoriety, opening up wide discussion and possibilities for churches and composers. The Sacred Concerts broke a barrier that reverberated in the halls of American religion for a long time afterward.[45]

As composers from more fields than ever were writing for the church, Ellington premiered his Second Sacred Concert on 19 January 1968 at the Cathedral Church of St. John the Divine in New York City. In contrast to the First Sacred Concert, it was an all-new assemblage of Ellington works composed over the course of more than a year. "I'm working on another sacred concert now that should be better than this one," he said in late 1966. "I'm simply making a statement from my naïve point of view after reading the Bible four or five times. I want it to be strong." Three days before the event, in a *New York Times* interview he shared with the Reverend Horace W. B. Donegan of St. John the Divine, Ellington made it clear that his two and a half years on the road with the First Sacred Concert had only strengthened his resolve to present religious music with his orchestra. "Since then, I've been getting very close to some of these wonderful people who have dedicated their lives to this—bishops, priests, rabbis, preachers," he remarked. "They have somewhat accepted me and I feel very honored to be considered part of the team now."

While religious leaders usually indicated a desire to attract youth as a main reason for their widening of liturgical music, Ellington felt particularly well equipped to lure adults back to the fold. In discussing this subject, he referred back to the education he received as a teen in Frank Holliday's Washington, D.C., pool parlor, trading banter with a colorful parade of black musicians, lawyers, pool sharks, and gamblers, as well as renowned figures such as Dr. Charles Drew. Much of Ellington's skill at communication and argument was honed there, and he was prepared to put that to use in the cause of God:

If you had an argument in a pool hall last week, win, lose, or draw, if you come back with the same argument next week you're dead because that cat's ready for you. I've got my arguments stacked up for 10 more concerts for people who say they don't believe.

Our song is to people. Not to people such as missionaries encountered in the wilderness who don't talk the language and don't understand what you mean. Our song is to people who were raised in the church and are used to the influence of the church. Then one day they went out in the street and encountered people who say "That ain't hip—that's square." We hope some may hear our message.

Bishop Donegan, like other religious leaders, wished to demonstrate the flexibility and continuing viability of the Christian faith and his church. "We're interested in having the gospel communicated," he said, after executing a few piano runs with Ellington at his side. "It's my conviction that a cathedral should be a place where creative people can express themselves, as well as where those who appreciate creative people can gather."[46]

Somewhere between 5,000 and 7,500 people, stretching out over a tenth of a mile, jammed the long and cavernous cathedral (the second largest in the world) on 19 January to hear 155 minutes of brand-new religious music. The concert's proceeds benefited Exodus House, a local facility designed to help drug addicts through withdrawal. Though not reported by the press, one of Ellington's nephews had recently undergone treatment at the facility. CBS-TV filmed the event, WRVR-FM broadcast the show live on the radio, and the New York press provided extensive coverage before and after the concert. Wire services carried the story across the country, as seen by the dozens of clippings in the Smithsonian's Ellington Scrapbooks.

Reviews were almost uniformly warm and effusive. "The Duke appeared on the stage and a new song rose to the Lord. And it sent the multitude," according to the *Daily News,* which also reported some scattered dancing in the aisles during the closing number, "Praise God and Dance." John S. Wilson, usually tough on Ellington's newest and more extended pieces, rhapsodized in the *New York Times* that "this new work glowed with Mr. Ellington's artistry as a direct, highly communicative melodist." He also cited the "wry humor" in Ellington's lyrics. The *Standard Times,* a Massachusetts paper, remarked that "Ellington brought show business to religion to lure the wandering flock back to church" and noted the many bowed heads during Ellington's piano solo on "Meditation," one of the most memorable and frequently performed pieces of Ellington's last years.[47]

Live performance reviews at its premiere and over the next five years indicated that the Second Sacred Concert proved successful at reaching and captivating its intended audience. But, artistically speaking, it is not one of Ellington's more successful works, and much of it sounds mediocre in recorded form. In previous decades, his richer and more complicated extended works, such as *Black, Brown and Beige* (1943) and *Suite Thursday* (1960), received poor reviews when premiered live, but glowing reassessments when critics were presented with recordings that allowed them repeated listenings to absorb the work. The Second Sacred Concert works in almost opposite fashion. Many of the melodies used are limited in their range, almost in a monotone (such as "Supreme Being," "It's Freedom," "Something about Believing"), which allowed the lyrics to come through clearly in a live situation and provided an easy chart for the various choirs to perform. But because of this quality, these songs are not as emotionally and musically compelling as those usually featured in Ellington compositions, with their glides up and down the scale, a quality that sometimes proved difficult for vocalists. "The Shepherd (Who Watches over the Night Flock)" and "The Biggest and Busiest Intersection" were examples of average or worse Ellington jazz (despite a soulful performance by Cootie Williams on the former), with no great melody holding them together. Ellington was still capable of creating memorable albums of material that measured up to the best of his past work, as seen in stellar 1970s releases such as *The Afro-Eurasian Eclipse* and *The River,* but this did not mark one of those occasions. It was a different kind of writing than usual for Ellington: the commitment to communicating a strong message about his faith was more of a priority than communicating on a strictly musical level. Despite these problems, however, significant musical and lyrical themes are developed in the Second Sacred Concert that bear examination.

One interesting theme lies in the childlike imagery that runs through the concert's lyrics. Some, including Whitney Balliett in the *New Yorker* and Collier in his later Ellington biography, accused Ellington of writing childish and even immature words for these compositions. Sometimes the rhymes and imagery are embarrassingly simple and corny. But perhaps Ellington assumed this poetic stance because, as he said in many interviews, religion for him was always tied to his parents and his childhood. In some ways, Ellington's approach suggests the way early memories often come back sharply to the aging. The first vocal number, "Supreme Being," featured a children's choir performing a slightly annoying monotone melody that described God's creation of the world in terms a child might employ, naming many of God's creatures and making fun of "that cute little old snake" that bit Eve. In "Almighty God," one of the highlights of the concert, a simple and beautiful melding of jazz and spiritual melody, the last line describes Ellington's vision of heaven. He talks about angels "up above" who are "waiting to dress, caress, and bless us all in perpetuity." It sounds very much as if he viewed heaven as a place where he hoped to resume his relationship with his mother, who had always assured him of his "blessed" existence.[48]

However, the main conceptual theme of the Second Sacred Concert, repeated by Ellington many times during concerts and in interviews, is freedom.[49] "We talk about freedom—many freedoms, all of which boil down to the freedom to be whatever you are," he told the *Washington Post.* The freedoms mentioned included religious freedom, the freedom to belong to any denomination and believe in God. Artistic and musical freedom probably was in Ellington's mind as well, as it often was during his career. "Freedom is sweet, on the beat," according to Ellington's lyrics. In the First Sacred Concert, his freedom to play respectfully dedicated music in church was questioned. The Second Sacred Concert itself was a study in musical freedom, with wildly varying transitions within compositions and influences from jazz, gospel, the black spirituals, classical, choral music, Latin music, show tunes, and more. "T.G.T.T.," with its difficult melodic intervals executed perfectly by Swedish soprano Alice Babs, illustrated this concept particularly well. "'T.G.T.T.' means 'Too Good to Title,' because it violates conformity in the same way, we like to think, that Jesus Christ did," Ellington wrote in the program. "The phrases never end on the note you think they will." Ellington also violated conformity and expressed personal freedom by dressing in dazzling colors for the performances. At St. John the Divine, he donned a blindingly white suit with pink shirt and long pink bowtie, and the tradition continued for the next five years, with bright blues and deep purples often employed onstage for Sacred Concerts.

The freedom found in his country formed another strand of the concert's themes. In the conclusion of the essay he wrote for the Second Sacred Concert program, which also accompanied the album release, he elaborated on this subject. "It has been said that what we do is deliver lyrical sermons, fire-and-brimstone sermonettes, and reminders of the fact that we live in the promised land of milk and honey, where we have prime beef and 80% butterfat ice cream," Ellington wrote, name-checking his two favorite foods. "I am sure that we appreciate the blessings we enjoy in this country, but it wouldn't hurt if everyone expressed his appreciation more often."

Freedom, of course, also functioned as a key word in American history, especially associated with the civil rights struggle of the 1960s, when "Freedom Ride" and "Freedom Summer" became common phrases. As historian Eric Foner has demonstrated, freedom has always represented a contested, not fixed, concept in the United States, particularly for black Americans. In the twentieth century, the word became particularly linked to the idea of equality, a connection embraced by civil rights activists. The concerts underlined this concept, as vocalist Alice Babs made clear:

> I hear this number ["It's Freedom"] and I could cry . . . It's hard to believe how such things can be. They want freedom *now*. They can't wait longer. So much talk . . . When I sing "Freedom," I feel I have to change also. *We* have to change. We need to free ourselves of the thoughts we harbor about other races. When I first heard "It's Freedom," I was happy. I told myself this would be performed all over the world. It says something the world has a need to

hear. Duke has written: "Freedom is not just a word, Freedom is something we have to have."

In such ways, the First and Second Sacred Concerts linked Judeo-Christian ideals with concepts of racial equality. Just as preachers did in the nineteenth-century black church, the concerts stressed the ideal of humanity united by a higher relationship with God, with other perceived differences painted as antithetical to and beneath that brotherhood and sisterhood. Like Dr. King, Ellington implicitly argued that the civil rights movement reflected a love of freedom, country, and God. This philosophy portrayed black freedom as intrinsically American and Christian. Blacks wished to live the patriotic and religious life other Americans enjoyed, argued Ellington and King in their separate ways, and the teachings of the Bible, the Old and New Testaments, confirmed and blessed this idea.

Perhaps most importantly for Ellington, freedom stood for a way of treating people with love and respect. In the Second Sacred Concert, he called this a "moral freedom." In May 1967, his "writing and arranging companion" and perhaps his best friend, Billy Strayhorn, passed away after a long bout with cancer. To Ellington, who frequently remarked privately and publicly how much he had learned from and leaned on his younger friend, Strayhorn epitomized this kind of "moral" freedom and respect. In the middle of "It's Freedom," as the band bowed out and a female choral group repeated the word "freedom" slowly in a style that resembled Gregorian chant, Ellington listed the "four major moral freedoms" Strayhorn lived by:

> Freedom from hate unconditionally; freedom from self-pity; freedom from fear of possibly doing something that might benefit someone else more than it would him; and, freedom from the kind of pride that could make a man feel that he was better than his brother.

On the CBS-TV special filmed at the St. John the Divine, Ellington had tears in his eyes as he listed Strayhorn's freedoms. They were very different from the famous "Four Freedoms" (freedom of speech and worship; freedom from want and fear) that President Franklin Roosevelt promised the world in his 1941 State of the Union address at the dawn of World War II. Yet, like Strayhorn and Ellington, Roosevelt meant for his freedoms to be enjoyed by "men of every creed and race, wherever they live" and linked them to a respect and love for God.

By applying the historically and racially loaded word of "freedom" in this moral, personal, and nonracial manner, Ellington was also signaling that he would not allow the problems and prejudices associated with race to rule his world or control his art. When asked about race issues in interviews about the Second Sacred Concert, he almost always replied with the title of a song from *My People:* "What color is virtue, what color is love?" As always, he favored stressing positive actions and images of achievement, grace, and idealism—not complaint or bitterness. Ellington's tribute to Strayhorn's "four major moral freedoms" also may have represented his subtle response to critics of the First Sacred Concert who intimated that Ellington's personal life and his career spent in nightclubs disqualified him from making religious statements. For Ellington and Strayhorn, morality was tied to issues of brotherhood and generosity, a love of oneself and others; it went far beyond niggling issues of sexual activities between mutually consenting adults and Saturday-night carousing.

14

FIGHTING NOSTALGIA

FIGURE 12. Duke Ellington energetically fighting nostalgia during the mid-1960s. Library of Congress Prints and Photographs Division.

Prelude

It's a beautiful sight, an image that should be better known: Duke Ellington onstage under a white spotlight in the late 1960s or early 1970s, around seventy years old, dressed in a mod, royal blue suit and a thick white string tie, with the unorthodox rounded collar of a baby blue shirt laying on his lapels and a ponytail hanging a little below his neck. He's dancing animatedly to the sound of his band, swaying side to side, swinging his hips, lifting his feet, slicing the air in front of him as he snaps his fingers, loudly egging on tenor saxophonist Harold Ashby as he solos during a performance of *The Afro-Eurasian Eclipse,* one of Ellington's newest multimovement suites. Ellington stands less than a yard from Ashby, looking directly at him, pointing at him, gesturing upwards, exhorting Ashby to take his solo higher. For a second, Ellington even plays some air saxophone. Ellington looks exalted, supremely happy, it's not just show business. He's loving it. It looks like the kind of musical moment that made the constant traveling and economic worries of keeping afloat his large orchestra worthwhile.

This scene is captured in the documentary *A Duke Named Ellington.* The performances from the 1960s and 1970s in this film, as well as many others preserved at the Library of Congress's Motion Picture Division, demonstrate that Ellington and the orchestra could be as exciting and swinging onstage and just as capable of producing jaw-dropping musical beauty as they ever were.[1] Alone among contemporaries, they produced a modern sound that reflected the times they lived in, buoyed by the foundation of new material by Ellington and Billy Strayhorn, most of it sounding nothing like the band's 1930s and 1940s output and bearing titles that reflected the band's new international status and travels, such as *The Far East Suite* and *The Afro Eurasian Eclipse*—no wonder that the fans who grew up listening to Ellington during the Swing Era and went on to write Ellington biographies tended to dismiss this period. But much of the music from this era has aged well, despite its initial lukewarm commercial reception. And, onstage, Ellington never wished to alienate the fans who followed the band in previous generations, providing them with plenty of the old hits.

Too often, talk about Ellington centers on the Cotton Club or Swing Era years, but, in many ways, the 1960s and early 1970s represented another golden age for Ellington. He prevailed, doing his music his own way, despite the wholesale changes in the music marketplace during the 1950s and 1960s. In 1964, Dr. Arthur Logan commented on the difference of Ellington's approach compared to much of the culture of his time:

I think we live unhappily in a society in which mediocrity is our God. I think if you look at . . . what is available through the mass media of television and radio—we dare not have anything provocative said on network radio, we mustn't have any controversial plays, discussions, music, I think we have to conform. I think this is . . . a major characteristic of American society in this part of the twentieth-century. And I think Ellington is not, has not been and never will be a conformist. Ellington, like you, like I, I think he wants acceptance . . . But maybe you, maybe I, are willing to compromise with the accepted norm of our society in order to get acceptance. And I think Ellington is very different in this, this is what sets him apart from the rest of us. While he wants acceptance, he will insist that the acceptance he gets will be on his level. On his level, rather than the level of mediocrity that characterizes our society.[2]

To use a term popular in the 1960s, Ellington was a nonconformist, and had carried that status for decades. To keep his career, his writing, and his orchestra moving forward, he spent a lot of time during his last years actively fighting nostalgia. He assumed a nonconformist bearing that fit in with the 1960s: he grew his hair longer, dressed colorfully (sometimes even psychedelically), his new pieces focused on different musical and programmatic themes than older pieces in his catalog, and he refused to indulge in the institution of marriage even after his long-estranged wife Edna died in 1966, preferring instead to have long- and short-term relationships with various women in different cities around the world. He continued to live in the present tense, asking reporters to not write about his past achievements and regularly premiering new works to his audiences, often just hours after rendering them.

Through these kinds of actions, Ellington also established a new image for a senior citizen in American popular music, without slavishly following current fads or losing his dignity. Popular music had traditionally operated as a young person's game, with most hit singles and the artists and songwriters who made them popular enjoying an ephemeral status. Ellington's generational peers in show business, such as Louis Armstrong and Bing Crosby, were important innovators in their day and still enjoyed tremendous popularity in the 1960s, probably more so than Ellington. But they were largely performing the same kind of material as they had since the 1930s, while Ellington had moved on, always trying to add to and refine his legacy. Artistically and economically, Ellington's traveled a much tougher road, but his personality and muse was so restless and individual that one cannot imagine him taking any other kind of path. In our era, artists like Bob Dylan and

Wayne Shorter have continued to create challenging new works and present vital live performances into their sixties, but Ellington acted as a trailblazer in this regard.

✣

Jazz continued its trajectory, begun in the mid-1940s, of being less tied to the pop music, commercial mainstream and drifting away from the center of American life. Leonard Feather reported in 1964 that nightclub and concert attendance for jazz acts was "deteriorating." The circulation of *Down Beat,* the premiere jazz magazine, devolved from eighty-two thousand readers in 1966 to sixty-seven thousand readers in 1967. The bobby-soxers of the Swing Era were no longer the central jazz audience. According to Dan Morgenstern, the editor of *Down Beat,* a 1966 demographic study showed that the majority of his readers were "17–24, relatively few are over 45. We lose a lot of people when they get married and settle down." The baby boomers, the offspring of those settled down swingers, were now teenagers and young adults and their tastes tended toward the rock and soul music dominating radio playlists. Unsurprisingly, Morgenstern began covering rock artists in the magazine in 1967, and the Beatles had a place in the top ten of the *Down Beat* readers' Record of the Year poll that year. A subscriber in North Carolina who appeared to be a Swing Era veteran voiced his displeasure at the editorial changes: "I promise Mr. Morgenstern an 'open mind,' even though I plan to cancel my subscription." At roughly the same time, *Jazz* magazine changed its masthead to *Jazz and Pop.*

The experimental, decidedly noncommercial approaches of artists supported by the Art Ensemble of Chicago, the Association for the Advancement of Creative Musicians, and the Black Arts Movement, as well as more famous artists such as John Coltrane, Cecil Taylor, and Archie Shepp, were exciting, and much of their work is more popular today than when originally released, but they did little to stem the slide in the overall popularity of jazz in the United States. By the end of the 1960s, rock music became common at the formerly all-jazz Newport and Monterey festivals. In 1968, for the first time, rock music enjoyed more coverage than jazz in *Playboy*'s influential year-end music survey. Two years later, in 1970, jazz was not mentioned in the *Playboy* survey until the sixth page of an essay reviewing the musical events of 1969. By 1972, jazz had less than 10 percent of the $1 billion-per-year record business.[3]

But Ellington shared a strong connection with the aesthetic, though not the sound, of the rock music that ruled the market. In the mid-1960s, Bob Dylan, by putting protest and poetry into the jukeboxes of America, led the trend of rock performers being viewed as serious artists. This influence spread across the Atlantic—after exposure to Dylan, the Beatles went from sentiments like "I Want to Hold Your Hand" to more existential and emotionally complex statements such as "I'm a Loser" and "You've Got to Hide Your Love Away." Dylan's "electric" albums as well as the Beatles' releases from the mid-1960s onward were viewed (and still are) as objects worthy of concentrated attention, not as disposable pop music. Ellington wrought a similar transformation during the 1930s by making a case for the seriousness of jazz and African American music, which, like rock before the arrival of Dylan, previously had a reputation as sexual, ephemeral party music for teens, blighted for some by its association with black American culture.

Just as Ellington's approach to music redefined the genres he worked in and inspired the rise of new magazines such as *Down Beat* to provide a more critical perspective on 1930s popular music, the arrival of Dylan and the Beatles similarly stirred the birth of *Rolling Stone* and *Creem,* magazines that gradually began to replace the fawning, teen-oriented coverage that previously ruled rock-music journalism. Ellington and Dylan, in separate eras, inspired critics to review popular music in a sophisticated fashion previously reserved for reviews of literary works. Through their stellar compositions, as well as their focus in dealing with issues and personalities of American history in their music and interviews, they each made a compelling case to a skeptical public about the lasting quality of American music.

Some observers also saw the connections between Ellington and the best rock music. "Of course, you can't talk about the Beatles without mentioning the transcendent Duke Ellington," enthused the *New Yorker*'s Talk of the Town column upon the release of *Sgt. Pepper's Lonely Hearts Club Band* in 1967. "Just as he has never fit into the jazz scheme of things, the Beatles don't fit into the rock-n-roll scheme. They are off by themselves doing their own thing, just as Ellington always has been . . . like Ellington, they are working in that special territory where entertainment slips over into art." Leonard Feather, perhaps the most famous jazz critic of the period, recognized the "intricate" contributions of Dylan and the Beatles, but worried that the publicity they generated might obscure the contributions of the older generation of songsmiths: Ellington, Strayhorn, the Gershwins, and Cole Porter. Alan Rich, in the *New York World Journal Tribune,* compared the multigenre "depth and invention" witnessed in recent Ellington performances with his jazz orchestra and the New York Philharmonic with the "grown-up rock" of the Beatles. Rich concluded that "it seems very much as if these dour critics (myself included now and then) who deplore the dearth of contemporary creativity in concert halls, may be overlooking the very area where much of it is taking place." Not all rock critics viewed classical or jazz comparisons as a positive trend: Richard Goldstein, writing in the *New York Times* in 1968 about a Dylan album, noted that rock had "evolved into a full-fledged art form," but also worried that such respectability could "endanger . . . [its] raw vitality." As Nat Hentoff pointed out, Ellington heard similar plaints in the 1930s when he started composing longer suites of varying tempos in addition to short pieces aimed at the dance floor.[4]

While some observers outlined the links between Ellington and the new rock scene, others cast him as a saviorlike deliverance from the music. A 1969 Memphis reviewer proclaimed that "in this tawdry musical age of sham, fraud, and incompetence, where what is bizarre, hirsute and loud is glorified, Ellington's band is a welcome antidote." A report on the 1969 Charlotte Jazz Festival compared the youthful vitality of Ellington and his orchestra with the "ragged, unkempt, longhaired Mothers of Invention," Frank Zappa's far younger counterculture rock group. A columnist in Indianapolis commented on how the "thoughtful popular music" of Ellington and Arthur Fiedler's Boston Pops (appearing in a joint concert) not only out-classed the "mindless and tormentingly noisy rock and rhythm output of recent years" but also made a more convincing statement on civil rights than others had: "Ellington, well over 20 years ago, was writing music of protest against racial injustice. In his debonair way (he didn't lose his cool), the Duke conveyed some ideas better than more recent, more strident protesters."[5]

However, most observers, if they discerned a connection between Ellington and the rock world, noted how well he fit into the countercultural spirit of the times. In 1968, the *New York Times* reported that Ellington and his orchestra "developed an initial polite curiosity into enthusiastic cheers" while being only the second large jazz band to play at the rock-dominated Fillmore West. In reviewing a 1967 Boston show, a *Christian Science Monitor* reporter gushed that:

> The flower children have no monopoly on love-ins. They happen whenever and wherever Duke Ellington and his band get on a stand and blow for people . . . the place was so full of love you could cut it with a knife . . . A lock or two of [Ellington's] wavy hair curled slightly over his collar. But the faithful didn't panic. They knew he hadn't sold out to the Mothers of Invention.

In a 1967 interview, Herb Jeffries, an Ellington vocalist during the 1940s, remarked that "the greatest hippie I ever knew was Duke Ellington. He was a nonconformist, dressing the way he wanted to dress, and playing the kind of music he wanted to play." With his rich history, and his refusal to stagnate as a composer while simultaneously performing his old hits, Ellington had resonance with every side of the various generation gaps of the 1960s.[6]

At the same time that jazz was experiencing commercial decline, a simultaneous rise in support and respect for the music within academic and high-culture circles occurred, starting in the mid-1960s. The 1920s vision of jazz as an immoral influence had faded, if not entirely vanished, from the scene. The hoary myth of jazz musicians possessing only primitive innate talent was gone, replaced by the realization that many jazz performers were among the most significant artists America had produced during the twentieth century. Ellington, of course, had placed himself at the center of these efforts to break down such prejudices for decades. Consequently, he received more awards, honors, and honorary degrees than any other jazz figure during his last decade.

But, ironically, what seemed to trigger increased adulation and respect for Ellington and jazz was the rejection of Ellington for a special Pulitzer Prize in 1965.[7] Initial news reports focused on the "snubbing" and "rejection" of Ellington and the resigning of two of the Pulitzer music judges in protest. Judging from the volume of clippings in the Ellington Scrapbooks at the Smithsonian, the Pulitzer controversy represented the largest burst of publicity concerning Ellington since he debuted at Carnegie in 1943.

However, initial media reports missed the complete story. For the music awards, a jury of three nationally known critics made recommendations to the Pulitzer advisory board, which then made its recommendations to the Columbia University trustees who awarded the prizes and who had only rejected the board's choices once before. In 1965, for the second year in a row, the music jury found no composer that deserved the award, but it unanimously recommended Ellington for a special citation, not a formal Pulitzer Prize, honoring his contributions to American music for four decades. The idea was rejected by the board.

Many press reports stressed the injustice of the decision. "If you think there is any connection between this disgraceful action and the fact that Ellington is generally classified as a jazz musician . . . and that his skin is black, you got it, baby," wrote nationally syndicated jazz columnist and Ellington partisan Ralph J. Gleason. The African American leftwing newspaper *Liberator* also saw racism in this situation: "Should we really be concerned about recognition from a society that oppresses us, exploits us; and which will even use its 'acceptance' of us as another instrument of enslavement?" A syndicated *National Review* editorial in a Minneapolis paper asked: "Does the advisory board not consider jazz to be music? Ellington to be a composer?" The *Philadelphia Afro-American,* while arguing that the consideration of Ellington for a special Pulitzer citation represented "an important breakthrough for the recognition of pop and jazz music," also noted that Ellington was not alone in being ignored by the Pulitzer board. Ellington's peers, including Irving Berlin, Cole Porter, the Gershwins, and Rodgers and Hammerstein, "who have written the music that America sings," also boasted no Pulitzers on their mantels at home.

There was good reason for this. According to the rules, the Pulitzer Prize in music recognized "distinguished musical composition in the larger forms of chamber, orchestral or choral music, or for an operatic work (including ballet)" published by an American in the preceding year. It was an award specifically geared toward classical composers, the rules written decades before American or African American popular music was viewed as serious or lasting. Winthrop Sargeant, one of the music critics who quit the jury in protest, said that they did not recommend Ellington for the prize because they felt his work did not qualify under the current rules, "but we felt a special citation ... appropriate because Ellington, though outside the symphonic field, has created a great deal of music in the past 40 years that is better than a great deal of symphonic music in that it has reached an audience and can be regarded as outstanding in every sense of the word." The Pulitzer advisory board disagreed, and one member who refused to be named told *Newsweek:* "The jury was a craven goddam jury. They expressed contempt for contemporary composition and then threw in a special recommendation." Every board member interviewed by *Newsweek* "spoke against giving special citations" and thought they should be avoided, yet twenty special citations had been awarded by the Columbia trustees since 1938. One board member told *Newsweek,* without attribution, that they "dilute the prizes."

There may well have been racism or prejudice involved—no African American or performer of popular music of any color had ever won a Pulitzer or special citation before. Is this why the anonymous Pulitzer board member maintained that such citations would "dilute" the prizes? But, then again, Ellington was in good company: the list of people ignored by the Pulitzer Prize committee before Ellington included Saul Bellow, Theodore Dreiser, Ralph Ellison, F. Scott Fitzgerald, Arnold Schoenberg, Igor Stravinsky, Edgar Varese, and Thomas Wolfe. Ernest Hemingway and William Faulkner received the nod in the mid-1950s, many years after their best work. The history of the Pulitzer seemed to indicate that trailblazers who challenged or overturned previous literary and musical traditions had trouble gaining recognition from a relatively conservative, exceedingly private and elite system of judgment. An investigative article from 1967 found that a majority of Pulitzer board members usually did not hear or read the submissions of literary and musical works from their juries, and that they generally "have spent only the better part of a single day in joint and good-natured [secret] deliberation" before passing on jury recommendations to the Columbia trustees.[8]

Ellington's official reaction to the supposed snub, carried in dozens of news stories across the country, was typically diplomatic, yet pointed. "I've absolutely no disappointment. I feel very lucky to have been mentioned at all for such an honor," he said, and then added one of his most famous quotes: "Fate is being kind to me. Fate doesn't want me to be too famous too young." To Nat Hentoff, a trusted jazz journalist, he let down his guard a bit more:

> I never give any thought to prizes. I work and I write. And that's it. My reward is hearing what I've done, and unlike most composers, I can hear it immediately . . . And secondly, I'm hardly surprised that my kind of music is still without, let us say, official honor at home. Most Americans still take it for granted that European music—classical music, if you will—is the only really respectable kind. I remember, for example, that when Franklin Roosevelt died, practically no American music was played on the air in tribute of him. We were given a dispensation, I must admit. We did one radio program dedicated to him. But, by and large, then as now, jazz was like the kind of man you wouldn't want your daughter to associate with.

A. H. Lawrence has claimed, without attribution, that Ellington privately was angry that the incident leaked to the papers and became a national cause célèbre. It was, after all, publicity for an award he did not win, and in a 1968 interview he seemed to admit some personal anguish concerning the situation. When asked if his aversion to traditional categories cost him the Pulitzer citation, Ellington replied: "No [laughing modestly]. I don't know . . . It was just some wonderful people who wanted to honor me, and I took it very seriously when the coordinating committee threw it out." But the savvy show-business veteran also understood the benefits of the controversy. In a 1967 interview, Ellington maintained that his career upswing of the past two years was due to the hubbub around the Pulitzer, and he was probably right.[9]

In any case, numerous other organizations, especially universities and the U.S. government, more than made up for the lack of Pulitzer recognition for Ellington in the following years. It became obvious to many that Ellington's contributions needed to be valued more fully by his own country, and these various institutions also realized the status that according such respect to Ellington would bring to them. Between 1966 and 1971, Ellington received twelve honorary doctorates. Previously he had received two, from Wilberforce College (1949) and Milton College (1964), but the universities giving Ellington degrees after 1965 were among the most prestigious in the country, including Yale, Brown, Howard, Washington University, the University of Wisconsin, and the Berklee School of Music.[10]

Ellington also began speaking more on college campuses. In April 1966, the University of Cincinnati asked him to deliver one of the Corbett Music Lectures, an honor bestowed on Igor Stravinsky the year before. Ellington "gave a treatise on the subject of category" and how he "refuses to recognize" them. He also spent the time discussing the history of American music, particularly as played by black Americans, and providing musical examples on piano. "The blues is the great harmonic pattern of America and it's going around the world," he maintained. "I consider the Beatles an offshoot of this." He knew something about the Beatles; he and the orchestra had recently recorded a couple of their songs, with arrangements by Strayhorn, for the *Ellington '66* album. Later in 1966, the University of California extension program held classes and symposiums on "The Negro and the Arts" at four of their campuses. A panel discussion featuring Ellington, along with Leonard Feather, Quincy Jones, and Ellington veteran Barney Bigard was held at each campus. An Ellington orchestra concert followed each symposium, and attendance was high. Much of the talk centered on dispelling the myths of jazz as a "primitive" musical form. Jones insisted many prejudices still existed: "Only recently, a house conductor in Las Vegas came up and asked me whether Count Basie's band could read [music]. There's a terrible misunderstanding in a remark like that." A similar panel discussion and course, focusing purely on Ellington and featuring Ellington and others, took place at UC Berkeley in 1969.[11]

Jazz in general represented a growing field of scholarly inquiry during 1966, with concert series, workshops, and symposia being held at Columbia, Hunter, New York University, San Francisco State, the University of Chicago, and Wayne State. According to *Playboy*'s yearly summary of the jazz world, "the most ambitious undertaking of all was . . . [at Stanford]—the first full-scale program of and about jazz at an American university, encompassing concerts, lectures, and exhibits." Perhaps most importantly, 1966 saw the initiation of the Institute for Jazz Studies at Rutgers University in Newark, New Jersey, which today is one of the most extensive and important jazz archives in the world.[12]

But until the mid-1960s, jazz performers found little support for their homegrown American music at the White House, despite the music's fervent recognition amongst foreign governments. "Louis Armstrong gets mobbed on arrival at airports and is carried triumphantly into African towns; here he might easily have trouble finding a cab," wrote jazz columnist George T. Simon in 1961. "And Duke Ellington, by special request of the King and Queen of England, plays a concert in Buckingham Palace; his band, and any other jazz band, for that matter, have yet to blow inside the walls of the White House." Ellington led the way in changing this situation.

Acceptance of Ellington and jazz from the top level of government increased during Lyndon Johnson's presidential terms. As *Down Beat* proclaimed in a 1964 headline, "Jazz [was] on the Upswing at the White House," and Ellington visited and performed there more during the Johnson years than at any other time and more than any jazz figure previously. Johnson does not seem to have been a jazz aficionado, but he invited many jazz figures to the White House, and Willis Conover, the famous jazz radio host for the Voice of America, recalled Johnson being "genuinely thrilled with the fact that Duke Ellington was coming on the stage" during a White House reception for the president of Thailand. Efforts by Johnson, or perhaps by his aides, to display more jazz seemed part of his efforts to demonstrate the importance of culture within his ambitious Great Society domestic program and to build support for the creation of the National Endowment for the Arts and the National Endowment for the Humanities during his term. At a White House reception in 1966 for the National Council of the Arts, a Johnson-created organization whose panel of famous cultural figures (Charlton Heston, Sidney Poitier, Isaac Stern, and many more) helped choose federal grants for the arts, Johnson said he wished to "distribute the fruits of that [American artistic] talent to all Americans, rich and poor." This sentiment resembled similar pronouncements he made concerning his War on Poverty, his efforts to set up institutions to fund public television and radio, and other Great Society hallmarks. At the same event, Johnson also pointed out that "not long ago our country was scorned for its 'dime store culture'" and that Americans had only relatively recently begun to appreciate their own literature, painting, music and drama—a situation Ellington had worked to reverse for decades.[13]

The premiere arts event during the Johnson administration was the unprecedented twelve-hour White House Festival of the Arts on 14 June 1965. It featured some of the best American artists from the fields of painting, sculpture, music, ballet, drama, literature, and poetry. To cite but a few examples: Saul Bellow and John Hersey read from their novels; a temporary sculpture garden on the south lawn featured work from Alexander Calder; the Joffrey Ballet and Gene Kelly danced; scenes from Arthur Miller and Tennessee Williams plays were staged; excerpts from films directed by Alfred Hitchcock, Elia Kazan, and George Stevens were screened; paintings by Edward Hopper, Jasper Johns, and Jackson Pollock were displayed in an East Wing corridor; and the Ellington orchestra closed the show, playing their own material as well as previously unheard Cole Porter compositions, with John Steinbeck and John Updike loitering near the bandstand "calling out requests." According to the *Boston Globe,* Ellington found performing on the White House grounds "an especially emotional experience" because it made him think of his father who used to work there as a butler during the early 1920s. One can imagine Ellington's thoughts on this occasion—the boy whose father once served food at the White House was now closing a show there honoring the finest artists in America. It served as a marker of how far he had traveled. It could not have been an accident that he concluded his set that night with selections from *Black, Brown and Beige.*

Unfortunately, good intentions and a stellar lineup could not stop the daylong affair from becoming "an unmitigated disaster" politically. Eleven days before, poet Robert Lowell wired the President and rescinded his original acceptance of the invitation to the festival, explaining that he could not "enjoy public celebration [with the president] without making subtle commitments." In the weeks before the event, Johnson had ordered continuous bombing of North Vietnam, and throughout the year, he greatly increased the American troop commitment, which had inspired resistance and criticism, especially in artistic and intellectual circles. Lowell felt his appearance at the White House would indicate support of these policies. Writer and academic Mark Van Doren, who introduced the readings by writers, and Hersey expressed sympathy with Lowell's viewpoint at the festival. A few of the artists, such as Mark Rothko and Larry Rivers, signed a telegram backing Lowell's stance while still showing up at the White House. This questioning of Johnson's policies, even though it came from an extreme minority of those invited, overshadowed media coverage and caused him to largely steer clear of the artistic crowd, abandoning his original plans to spend more time mingling with them.[14]

Other presidentially related events featuring Ellington during the Johnson administration fared better. In the spring of 1964, Ellington played piano at a White House reception for two thousand, including the president and the First Lady, along with other ASCAP-represented songwriters (including Harold Arlen and Jule Styne) for ASCAP's fiftieth anniversary. In

1966, Ellington was awarded the President's Gold Medal "for his unofficial ambassadorial duties around the world." Ellington, along with Supreme Court nominee Thurgood Marshall, attended the swearing-in of Clifford Alexander, Jr., the first chairman of the Equal Employment Opportunity Commission (EEOC), in 1967. Johnson told the assembled crowd, which included many black Americans, that the EEOC "exists because millions of Americans are still barred from full participation in the American dream" solely because they are the "wrong color." Though media reports did not acknowledge it, Alexander was the son-in-law of Dr. Logan. During the last months of the administration in 1968, Ellington, along with Marian Anderson, was named to a six-year appointment on the National Council of the Arts. After a meeting and dinner at the White House, Ellington performed with a couple marines as his rhythm section, and Isaac Stern and Supreme Court justice Abe Fortas did a violin duet. The next morning, Ellington and Anderson accompanied Lady Bird Johnson, the First Lady, on a trip to New Orleans' French Quarter and a slum area.[15]

During the Johnson administration, the Ellington orchestra made their second State Department–sponsored foreign tour, a ten-day stint heading the American delegation of cultural representatives at the First World Festival of Negro Arts in Dakar, Senegal, in April 1966.[16] It was a part of the administration's efforts to ensure that Johnson was "identified with African aspirations," according to historian Penny Von Eschen. While the festival was mostly termed a success, it also represented an occasion where cold war and civil rights tensions surfaced repeatedly and threatened to dominate media coverage. The Americans assembled the largest of forty-three international delegations, with anywhere from 75 to 130 (reports varied) artists and educators attending, including Alvin Ailey and his dance company, Marian Anderson, Langston Hughes, and University of Chicago sociology professor Dr. St. Clair Drake. African countries were also well represented. Ellington proudly wrote in his autobiography that "never before or since has the Black Artist been so magnificently represented and displayed."

The festival was the brainchild of Senegal's President Leopold Senghor, who had held the office since Senegal's independence exactly six years earlier. He enjoyed equal fame as an award-winning poet. As Newsweek pointed out when his poems were translated from French into English in 1964, "When a head of state so much as writes his own speeches, it is news, but when he writes a distinguished volume of poems, it is epochal. How often has it happened since King David?"

Senghor also claimed notoriety as the intellectual architect of the concept of "negritude," which he hoped the festival would embody. Many definitions of the term circulated at the festival and in news accounts. According to the *New York Times,* Senghor viewed negritude as "embracing the artistic intuitiveness that he believes all black men share, whether they live in Cuba or Brazil, Uganda or Alabama . . . the Negro's creative roots are African, and negritude sums up the black African's special sense of symbol, sense of image, sense of rhythm." Langston Hughes remarked that in his Harlem neighborhood, they called it "soul." But others at the festival felt the concept of negritude had little use and offered more heat than light. Some saw it as racist, divisive, and promoting "some form of esthetic black nationalism." In answering these charges, Senghor insisted that negritude "welcomes the complementary values of Europe and the white man." African American choreographer Katherine Dunham, who advised Senghor on the festival program, called the term "meaningless. I see no reason for putting any particular label in front of what we are doing that requires an elaborate explanation." Some wondered, in an observation tainted with reverse racism, how the champion of negritude could be married to a white French woman. Ellington, who many times throughout his life described his life's work as "Negro music," made no comment concerning this controversy. In the 1960s, Ellington tended to describe his output more often as "American music," but one still suspects he would have sided with Senghor. In the "Dakar Journal" he included in his autobiography, Ellington described jazz as "a most unusual tree" whose "roots are permanently married to, and firmly ensconced in, the rich black earth of beautiful Black Africa."

Other controversies surfaced. An attempt at private funding of the American delegation failed miserably. The *Washington Post* reported that "despite direct appeals to heads of American corporations doing business in Africa, foundations, and prominent Negro businessmen, the committee was unable to raise more than $100,000, including a $40,000 grant from the Rockefeller foundation, falling far short of its ambitious goal of $600,000." In the end, the U.S. government stepped in to supply $250,000, and the Arthur Miller dance company had to be replaced by the smaller Ailey group. Additional government funds were still not sufficient to honor previous financial commitments made to African American painters and sculptors. Ten of sixteen of them withdrew their works from the festival because the government would not pay each artist a $1,000 honorarium. One of the artists, Romare Bearden, told the *New York Times* that American dancers and musicians were getting paid, and he saw no reason why "the full weight of sacrifice was placed solely on the visual arts."

Many observers blamed these problems on racial issues. Hoyt W. Fuller, in *Negro Digest,* pointed to the fact that the chairman of the American committee was white and had contacts in the mostly white worlds of finance, government, and mass media, but knew little about and very few people in African American circles, and coverage in the black press accordingly suffered. The chairman had little or no knowledge of contemporary black pop and had never heard of Motown Records recording artists the Supremes, who had scored eight American top-twenty hits in the two years preceding the festival. A Motown representative said the label would have contributed money and artists to the festival if they had known about it. Fuller criticized the booking of several acts, including an African American "classical" pianist and soprano. "There is nothing particularly 'Negro' about a pianist playing Bach preludes and a soprano singing Verdi arias," he argued. He also rued that one of the best performances by a black American, the passionate gospel performer Marion Williams, took place at a Christian cathedral where the audience was mostly white and elite, since more than 90 percent of Senegalese were Muslims.

In addition to these controversies, Harry Belafonte refused to attend because of Senghor's acceptance of brutality in Rhodesia, an accusation that garnered wide press coverage and probably embarrassed Senghor. "Half of Senegal seemed to have assumed that Harry Belafonte should have been present," reported Fuller. Africans also wondered why the United States did not send in "the most exciting" young artists and intellectuals, such as James Baldwin, Ray Charles, Miles Davis, and LeRoi Jones (Amiri Baraka). Accusations of stingy reimbursement of artists by Senegal also plagued the festival and caused South African international singing star Miriam Makeba to cancel her appearance. Ticket sales were routinely mishandled, with shows labeled as sold out sometimes taking place in half-empty venues. The First World Festival of Negro Arts was planned as a biennial event, but these kinds of conflicts and logistical problems seemed to doom future stagings, and none occurred.[17]

The cold war also made its presence felt in Dakar. With the United States sending numerous artists and garnering headlines for it around the world, "the Russians were bound to react," according to the *New York Times.* The Soviet ambassador "told Senegal's Foreign Ministry [that the Russians had Caucasian] painters who had painted African settings, poets who had visited Africa and written poems with African themes, and musicians and composers who had been inspired by Africa's traditional music and dance. Naturally, such artists should be included in the program." Senghor disagreed, but "gratefully" accepted a Soviet offer of a cruise ship to help house the overflow of festival-goers. Guests on the Soviet ship viewed "an exhibit extolling Russian-Negro brotherhood" while imbibing their drinks and were reminded repeatedly that "there is no prejudice" in the Soviet Union and that "the Russians never engaged in the slave trade," unlike the United States. The *Chicago Daily News* wrote that in order to counter the "smash performance" of Duke Ellington at the festival, "the U.S.S.R. matched [it] with a flamboyant reading by their rebel poet Yevgeny Yetushenko," who had recently received a Beatles-like reception in Australia. Not for the first or last time, cold war brinksmanship invaded the artistic world.[18]

For Ellington, whose music had been described as "jungle music" four decades before at the Cotton Club, the Dakar festival marked his first visit to Africa, and the controversies surrounding the festival did not seem to touch or engage him. In anticipation of the trip, he composed a new piece, "La Plus Belle Africaine." From all reports, he was utterly charmed by Senegal, and Africans loved him right back. "I've been playing and writing African music for thirty-five years," Ellington told *Africa* magazine. "And when I got to Africa, I knew it and *they* knew it." "Duke Ellington conquered," reported the *New York Times*. "His smash performances clearly established the United States as the festival favorite." The State Department used that quote in their report of the festival, which also noted that the Ellington orchestra's four public performances drew an estimated audience of twelve thousand. "We get the usual diplomatic applause from the diplomatic corps down front, but the [nonelite] cats in the bleachers really dig it. You can see them rocking back and forth back there while we play," wrote Ellington in his "Dakar Journal." "When we are finished, they shout approval and dash for backstage, where they hug and embrace us, some with tears in their eyes. It is acceptance at the highest level, and it gives us a once-in-a-lifetime feeling of having truly broken through to our brothers."

On 8 April 1966, Ellington and Senghor met for a half hour, along with seven other American dignitaries. Senghor told Ellington that "I knew that you would be a success, but it turned out to be even greater than I had anticipated." According to a State Department cable, Senghor then "reminisced about the early thirties, during student days in Paris, when Duke's music had inspired him and other early devotees of negritude." In his poem "Nde'sse' or Blues," Senghor wrote: "Just play me your 'Solitude,' Duke, and I will cry myself to sleep." Another diplomatic and personal highlight for Ellington was a private performance at the residence of the U.S. ambassador to Senegal, Mercer Cook, the son of Ellington's musical mentor, Will Marion Cook, and the man after whom Ellington had named his own son.[19]

Ellington seemed particularly moved by the history he felt and heard around him while in Dakar:

> Every night, on the balcony of the ninth floor of the Engar Hotel, I sit and listen to the sea singing her songs of the historic past on the island from which the slaves were shipped. Farther in the distance, I can hear the tribes that have gathered on another island to rehearse for their show next day. And then sometimes I wondered whether it was really a rehearsal, or was it a soul brothers' ceremonial gathering with all of its mystical authenticity. Anyway, I wish I could have seen or recorded it. Too much, baby! Full distance.

Ellington, who thought and communicated so much about black history during his lifetime, obviously felt that, in some manner, he had traveled "full distance" from his ancestors' homeland to his return to the continent. The island of Goree, two miles off the Dakar coast, operated centuries before as a staging area where many slaves began their torturous journey from West Africa to North America. Ellington was treading upon the African ground where the first scene of his *Black, Brown and Beige* scenario took place. His 1943 scenario commenced with the words:

> A message is shot through the jungle by drums.
> BOOM! BOOM! BOOM! BOOM!
> Like a tom-tom in steady precision.
> Like the slapping of bare black feet across the desert wastes.
> Like hunger pains.
> Like lash after lash as they crash and they curl and they cut. DEEP! . . .
> Like the crush of the weight of a hob-nailed boot stomping on bare black feet.
> Like exploding a shell in a gun.
> This BOOMing is echoing in the brain. Nerves of a black brood . . . in tempo.
> BOOM! BOOM! BOOM! BOOM![20]

Perhaps such images ran through Ellington's mind as the sounds of African musicians and dancers wafted across the water into his luxurious hotel room.

Ellington's increased association with the White House continued during the Nixon administration, at least in the first months of it. Ellington's band, along with Lionel Hampton's and Guy Lombardo's, played at a packed inaugural ball at the Smithsonian Institution Museum of History and Technology. Though Nixon characterized himself mainly as a fan of classical music, he later told the *Salt Lake Tribune* that "I dig [Ellington]. He's my generation." Still, he fumbled with one of Ellington's most famous titles at the ball: "Our theme is 'Bring us together.' Duke Ellington says, 'It don't mean a thing if you don't have that thing—er—swing.'"[21]

The White House appearance that brought Ellington the most honor and publicity occurred on Ellington's seventieth birthday on 29 April 1969, when Nixon gave Ellington the Presidential Medal of Freedom, the nation's highest civilian honor. News reports indicated that this represented the first time that a black American, a jazz musician, had been honored with a dinner at the White House. In the Smithsonian's collection of Ellington clipping scrapbooks from the 1930s to the 1970s, no other occasion elicited so much newspaper coverage during Ellington's life. The only other American composer to have previously received this honor was Irving Berlin on his eightieth birthday in the Johnson White House. As a black newspaper in Oklahoma wrote, "This is a rare tribute paid any individual regardless of color and certainly an affair which would have been unheard of or socially unacceptable just a few short years ago."[22]

The White House had never hosted a similar night. An all-star cast of American music masters joined Ellington, including Harold Arlen, Dave Brubeck, Cab Calloway, Dizzy Gillespie, Benny Goodman, Earl Hines, Mahalia Jackson, and Richard Rodgers, among many others. Guests were predominantly jazz-related figures and Ellington's relatives, rather than the government officials that usually gathered at such events, and "were drawn about equally from black and white Americans," according to *U.S. News and World Report*. *Time* added that "never before had a White House dinner been so dominated by Negroes." Nixon played "Happy Birthday" on the piano for Ellington "in the key of G" after warning the audience: "I'm going to play—don't anybody leave." Vice president Spiro Agnew also got into the spirit of the evening, playing the Ellington classics "In a Sentimental Mood" and "Sophisticated Lady" in a "surprisingly light, sophisticated style." The president and his family retired to their chambers at 12:30 AM, but a jam session in the East Room continued until two in the morning. Later, First Lady Pat Nixon confided to friends that "we sat upstairs and listened!"

When the president, First Lady, Ellington, and his sister Ruth first entered the East Room, the guests stood in tribute. As Nixon presented the award, he said: "I was looking at this name on here and it says 'Edward Kennedy.'" Nixon quickly paused at this mention of one of his political nemeses in the Democratic Party, looked at his audience, then finished: "Ellington." The room burst into laughter. On a more serious note, Nixon seemingly ad-libbed an accurate depiction of how Ellington saw himself and the concept of freedom symbolized by the medal awarded him that night: "When we think of freedom, we think of many things, but Duke Ellington is one who has carried the message of freedom to all the nations of the world, through music, through understanding, understanding that reaches over all national boundaries, and over all boundaries of prejudice and over all boundaries of language." Nixon then proclaimed that "in the royalty of American music, no man swings more or stands higher than the Duke." Ellington thanked the president and, using the royal "we," mentioned how he and his orchestra repeatedly referred to the concept of "freedom" in his Second Scared Concert. Quietly and slowly, in a voice full of understated emotion, Ellington then recited the four freedoms that he said Billy Strayhorn "lived by and enjoyed." Later in the evening, while giving a toast, Ellington told his assembled audience that "there is no place I would rather be tonight, except in my mother's arms." At the moment in his life when the world focused most intensely on him, during the most reported and honored incident of his career, he hardly mentioned himself, but took care to mention Strayhorn and Daisy Ellington, two people that seemed to touch Ellington and guide his life like no others had.

On this night, Ellington did not mention his father, who had worked at the White House, and, like the great majority of blacks until the 1960s, could not enter the mansion from the front door as Ellington had that evening. He did not mention how no president ever took it upon himself to pass an antilynching law, even when such crimes were claiming hundreds of black lives per year during the decades surrounding the turn of the century. He did not mention President Woodrow Wilson, who, with his insistence on strict segregation, tried to destroy the somewhat increased status and opportunities blacks enjoyed in Washington, D.C., compared to the rest of the country. He did not mention being rebuffed at the White House door by presidents Hoover and Kennedy. As always, Ellington radiated a positive outlook. His lifelong credo of commanding respect and his fervent belief that black and popular music could represent serious and lasting art had at last been recognized by the highest authorities in his country. But to a man as historically attuned as Ellington, other, darker thoughts must have crossed his mind as well, if only fleetingly, amidst the momentousness of this presidential honor.

In some ways, his White House birthday celebration was just another gig. The morning after, Ellington flew to rejoin his band for a show that night in Oklahoma City, followed the next night by a date in McAlester, Oklahoma. In McAlester, someone remarked to him: "The White House on Tuesday and McAlester on Thursday." Ellington replied that "you see, we're going up in the world and playing better and better places each time." A few days later, at a Sacred Concert in Saginaw, Michigan, Ellington commented to the press that "you can never compare any audience you're enjoying at the moment with one from the past." Then he added, smiling: "But this was better than the White House." Less than two weeks after the White House gig that was splashed across the pages of newspapers around the world, Ellington was again refusing to live in the past, refusing to place previous glories on the same level as his present endeavors. He was still fighting nostalgia, even as most news stories prominently mentioned that he had just turned seventy. "Who's 70?" he twice asked a *Christian Science Monitor* reporter. "That's an awful weight to put on an up-and-coming man like me. Let's not talk about it. It's exhausting."[23]

The White House show also resembled a normal gig in that it carried an ironic reminder of Ellington's constant financial problems of the 1960s. On the day he received the nation's highest civilian honor from the president, Ellington also received a letter from ASCAP informing him that the IRS was about to start diverting thousands of dollars of his royalties to the U.S. Treasury. The government was bestowing honor with one hand while taking away funds he needed to support his band and organization with the other—and there seemed to be no end to such financial difficulties in the near or long term.[24]

As with any widely promoted White House event, politics entered the picture. Editorial columnists, especially in black newspapers, accused Nixon of staging an event with Ellington to obscure his general antipathy toward progress on civil rights. "Do not fall into the mistaken notion that a party given by the Nixons attended by blacks and whites together has solved anything in this country or abroad nor does it necessarily portend better days," wrote the *Washington D.C. Afro-American*. "Keep your eyes on the ball. Listen to Nixon's words as carefully as we have listened to Duke's music." In particular, the black press felt that programs initiated under the Johnson administration to help the poor and blacks were being thrust aside and that the unprecedented high positions achieved by blacks in the previous administration would not be duplicated in Nixon's. The chief evidence of this was Republican senator Everett Dirksen's public declaration that he could persuade Nixon to fire Clifford Alexander, Jr., the head of the EEOC under Johnson, for being too harsh in dealing with employers that discriminated against blacks. His prediction proved true. The *New York Times* reported that Ellington had submitted Alexander's name on his list of invitees, but he had not come or was nixed by the White House. An editorial in the *Louisville Defender* noted that while Ellington was welcomed to the

White House, the Reverend Ralph Abernathy, Dr. King's successor at the SCLC, had to settle for a "disappointing and fruitless" meeting with Nixon, Agnew, and selected cabinet members concerning "the problems of poor black Americans." Abernathy's requests for individual meetings with these officials to work one-on-one on specific problems were rejected.[25]

Historians in recent years have uncovered evidence that confirms these columnists' suspicions about Nixon's policies on racial issues and strongly suggests that Nixon was a racist. "Private scorn on racial matters, leavened by necessary public gestures, was an ambiguity that had a long history with Nixon," commented Anthony Summers in a book largely critical of Nixon. Despite a couple incidents in his early life where Nixon "raised his voice" against racial prejudice, numerous racial slurs can be found on tapes made of conversations during his presidency as well as more telling quotes that delineate private views concerning civil rights in his administration: "With blacks you can usually settle for an incompetent because there are just not enough competent ones. And so you put incompetents in and get along with them, because the symbolism is vitally important. You have to show you care." According to historian Kenneth O'Reilly, Daniel Patrick Moynihan, Nixon's assistant for urban affairs, proposed a policy of "benign neglect" concerning black Americans, especially since neither he nor Nixon foresaw picking up votes from them. When Nixon asked his aide Leonard Garment for more "proposals for the *inclusion* of various minorities in our political planning," Nixon rejected all of his suggestions, save "an occasional dinner with black editors and publishers, breakfast with Sammy Davis, Jr. at Camp David," and the Ellington event. Despite the fact that Ellington richly deserved the honor Nixon bestowed upon him, it is also likely he was being used by the administration to shed a better light on their efforts, or lack of efforts, on behalf of black Americans.[26]

The Nixon administration viewed the night as a unique and important public relations opportunity. For the first time ever, motion picture cameras were allowed to document a postdinner White House ceremony and the entertainment that followed. The United States Information Agency subsequently assembled a film, *Duke Ellington at the White House,* and distributed it to American embassies and libraries around the world. Many of the themes emphasized in USIA-sponsored publicity surrounding Ellington's 1963 state-sponsored tour were repeated. During a time of increasing black separatism and violent protests, the *White House* film shows close interaction between blacks and whites at the highest level, from Ellington kissing Nixon four times on the cheek (Nixon seemed a bit shocked by Ellington's typically continental greeting) to shots of racially mixed couples dancing to jazz music performed by both black and white musicians. *Duke Elling-ton at the White House* proved very popular. In embassies and USIA librar-ies around the globe, it significantly outdrew another USIA film commis-sioned by the White House in 1969 entitled *The Silent Majority,* which argued, as the Nixon administration often did, that a "silent majority" of Americans frequently ignored by the media supported his approach and goals for the Vietnam War. The film sought to counter negative publicity concerning Nixon's policies after a quarter million people in Washington, D.C., protested them in November 1969, just a few days after Nixon called for "national unity" on the war.[27]

At least one prominent Democrat, Johnson's White House social secre-tary Bess Abell, expressed disappointment when she heard that Ellington agreed to be hosted by the Nixons. "My God, I thought he was ours!" she exclaimed. As reporter Betty Beale explained, "President and Mrs. John-son had him there so often either as a guest or as a musician that Mrs. Abell took it for granted that he was strictly an LBJ man or at least a Democrat." Beale predicted that the Nixons' celebration of Ellington would "outdo the Johnsons." But Ellington refused to take political sides in his public life. "I'm not in politics, I'm in the realm of art," he told columnist Earl Wilson three months after the White House fete. "As long as I stay in the realm of art, I'm welcome in the White House no matter who's living there." Beale argued that the reasons behind Ellington's popularity with both parties at the White House were "obvious." In this period of rising black nationalism and militance, "he is a distinguished and very popular member of his race who doesn't publicly declaim against the country that has given him honor and riches."[28]

In truth, according to friends and relatives, Ellington in his later years be-came more politically conservative and may have identified more with Nixon's stances on selected issues, rather than the Democratic Party.[29] El-lington's son Mercer along with Ellington's close friend H. Robert Ud-koff recalled how, from the 1950s forward, Ellington had become notice-ably more "paranoid" and spoke repeatedly in private about the communist threat and other conspiracies. In a 1980 interview, Mercer Ellington said his father disliked communism "because he was so religious, and anything that downed religion had to be wrong . . . Aside from that, he liked the idea of one day becoming rich." Ellington's strong beliefs on freedom of expression, repeatedly enunciated around the world, also probably entered the equa-tion. According to Udkoff, Ellington believed communists had infiltrated the civil rights movement, to its detriment. "While he believed that communists worked ceaselessly to overthrow the power of the United States, he also held that capitalists worked exclusively for personal gain, something he considered true of unions as well," according to Mercer Ellington. "The impact of their machinations on the society he lived in truly disturbed him." Udkoff recalled that Ellington:

> was very conservative in his politics, which many people may not know. He could've been at the time a John Bircher. As a matter of fact, it was during the Watts riots, he was opening at Disneyland, and my wife and I and my daughter picked him up at the airport and drove him to Disneyland. My daughter was a student at Berkeley at that time and she was quite radical. She was involved in the Free Speech Movement. When we're watching [the riots] on television . . . Ellington said "Those communists! They're causing all this trouble, all these communists!' And Julie says, "It is not, these people are rioting because blah, blah, blah." And they got into a violent argument, and you would've thought the roles were reversed . . . that she was the black and he was the white. He respected her opinion, he'd known her since she was a baby. I didn't say a word, I let them do it, and they went to it pretty good. And he said something like: "How would you know? You're not a Negro." And she said, "Well, you never lived as a Negro either. What would you know about how a Negro lives?"

In a 1969 interview, Ellington also inveighed against prayer being banned in public schools, a signature issue among American conservatives of the period. He called it a "dangerous" development that had produced "a lot of brainwashed kids." "When they take prayer out of schools, what kind of country is this?" he asked. In 1972, Ellington accepted an honorary chairmanship of the Portland, Oregon, chapter of the Right to Life Committee, a national antiabortion group.

Ellington also "at one time" mentioned his belief in a "faggot mafia," according to Udkoff, and maintained that "the homosexuals controlled the theaters and Broadway, and they only allowed you to get in if you were one of them." Mercer Ellington and Stanley Dance corroborated that Ellington mentioned this as well, although this contradicts Mercer Ellington's later statements on Duke Ellington and homosexuals in an interview he did for David Hajdu's biography of Billy Strayhorn. It also contradicts Duke Ellington's multidecade history of public respect for and close personal friendship with Strayhorn and his lover Aaron Bridgers, among other homosexuals. Perhaps Ellington's musings on this matter were linked with his inability to produce a hit Broadway show, the one area of show business he failed to conquer, despite many attempts.

Ellington possessed an interesting and strange set of sometimes contradictory strands in his political make-up, especially for someone of his generation during the 1960s. Though a nonconformist in his dress, sexual habits, and approach to music, he surely did not belong in the counterculture, and he rejected some of its key tenets. While forward thinking in many respects, some of Ellington's actions and character also echoed the socially conservative aesthetic of his black, middle-class upbringing in Washington, as well as the modern conservative movement that began in the mid-1960s. Yet he also firmly supported civil rights organizations, and especially Dr. King. In the 1930s and 1940s, Ellington supported the Democratic Party, allowing his name and image to be used in a campaign ad for President Franklin D. Roosevelt. But like others, including former FDR supporters Ronald Reagan and Frank Sinatra, his beliefs changed in the postwar era. As in other areas of his life and like the music he most respected, Ellington in his politics and lifestyle steadfastly remained "beyond category," impossible to pin down.

Ellington had fought nostalgia since at least the mid-1950s, but he became more aggressive and outspoken about it in the 1960s. He realized that he resided in a new era and that, in order to stay in business and not succumb to existing purely as a nostalgia act, he needed to evolve. This did not represent a commercial calculation. If anything, changing the band's sound in the 1960s made it more likely to lose fans than gain them. But Ellington's muse and his pride constantly goaded him to push his own envelope, surpass past achievements, and tickle his own musical fancy. By his own admission, he immediately jotted down any "crispy, crunchy, fresh ideas" for new music at whatever time of the day the notion hit him. This was a man who had difficulty sitting still in almost any way. In 1964, when a reporter asked, "Why did you change?" Ellington answered:

> I think if you love music, you want to bathe yourself in it. If you love money you can adjust yourself to playing a commercial type of music. You can do that and have people say "There's Old Duke, isn't he cute." People are always coming up to me and saying "Why don't you play the music that you did in the 1930s?" I couldn't do that. If you love music and want to take a chance, you can allow your mind to indulge in a little adventure.

Ellington also embarked upon this path to satisfy the audience that seemed closest to his heart since the 1930s: the listeners. "We could've gone on for 50 years just playing the old things and saying, 'This is our noise, baby,'" he told *Time* magazine in 1967. "But it's a form of condescension, the worst of all artistic offenses." Ellington constantly reminded and chided the media that he was an artist as well as an entertainer, and in his band's 1965 press manual, he was referred to as "a man who moves with the times."[30]

The strategy seemed to work; many journalists caught on and wrote about the Ellington difference in the 1960s. "One song will irritate you, but pleasantly, with the discordant sounds of an avant-garde piano rubbing against the wailing moans of an alto sax, and the next number will be a well-known tune played simply and melodically—sounding as if came off an old phonograph record from someone's attic," wrote a reviewer for a small Pennsylvania paper in 1966. "And the most exciting moments in an Ellington concert are when the avant-garde is contrasted with the Harlem 1920s in the same number." A year later, Leonard Feather wrote that his music of the 1960s entered "into areas that would have seemed improbable, even impregnable, to the Ellington student of a decade or two ago." A 1971 *Variety* review stated that "any Ellington concert is worth hearing, if only for those superb ensemble renditions of newer Ellingtonia." New creations from Ellington's hotel-room workshops around the world ensured that a visit to an Ellington show would be, at least for a few numbers, an unpredictable musical adventure. The old marketing strategy developed with Irving Mills—that of separating himself from the pack by stressing his status as a serious composer—was still paying dividends and bringing in audiences and critics four decades after it debuted.[31]

Ellington constructed a new image for a senior citizen in American popular music. He resisted being typecast, realizing the limitations that followed from that status:

> People become identified with things. Some critics in some schools of thought, they say that jazz is free, freedom of expression, and all that sort of thing. But actually they are very biased in their thinking because they think a personality should be confined to his principal mark of identification . . . they feel that Louis Armstrong should always have his handkerchief and Cab Calloway should always sing "hidey-ho." And the minute they do anything new, they're out of character. They think that no one grows up, that everyone stays a child. And that's jazz, that's the way they think about jazz.[32]

Ellington sought to bypass such nostalgic confinement. It was supremely important to him that he retained the ability to surprise his listeners, to enter any musical genre he wished, or invent new ones.

It was not just his composing that had a surprisingly vital edge during the 1960s and early 1970s, but also his performing, according to many films and press reviews. "Duke is 65 now. There's a wrinkle here or there," wrote an Atlantic City reviewer. "As he moved lithely around the dressing room . . . while the band was shooting off its first fireworks you were glad to see his movements still rhythmic and fluid. The old tiger is still a kid with a long future ahead of him." In 1966, Ellington told a reviewer "I'm the oldest man in the band" then proceeded to "play up a storm" during "a vigorous 3 1/2-hour one-night stand" in Buffalo, New York.[33]

Ellington's insistence on forging ahead artistically ensured that he, Strayhorn, and the orchestra consistently scored top rankings in the critics and fans polls of international jazz magazines during the 1960s and early 1970s. In these arenas, Ellington usually competed against new jazz and pop artists of the day like Miles Davis and the Beatles, not against his Swing Era peers. From 1960 to 1965, Ellington was named best big band, arranger, and composer the majority of the time in *Down Beat*'s yearly poll of international critics. In 1967, *Jazz* magazine named Ellington the year's best "Jazzman" and also awarded him best composition and best arrangement; the year before, he was the number-two Jazzman, losing to John Coltrane. *Melody Maker*'s readers and critics both agreed on Ellington's status as the top composer and big band in 1967, with critics also naming him musician of the year (Ornette Coleman had the honor the year before). In *Down Beat*'s 1969 readers' poll, Ellington scored the number-one rank as arranger, big band, composer (Lennon and McCartney were number two in the latter category), and number-three Jazzman of the year (Miles Davis held the top spot). In 1972, *Down Beat*'s international critics' poll again voted Ellington as the top big band, composer, and arranger. And these represent just a few of many examples of Ellington's performance in jazz-magazine polls during this period. Ellington also received several Grammys during the period for new compositions during nationally televised ceremonies. Such consistent laudatory publicity must have spurred sales of records and show tickets, especially among the jazz cognoscenti. It also demonstrated Ellington's continuing relevance beyond the nostalgia market.

Ellington relentlessly promoted himself in the present tense during the last decade of his life, steering journalists away from reminiscing over the band's past and trying to keep their stories focused on current and future activities. When an interviewer obviously knew nothing of Ellington's recent work during an interview in the late 1960s, he took the writer to task: "You're not familiar with our music. You don't know what we're doing." When the interviewer countered that he had heard a record of the First Sacred Concert a year and a half previously, this did not meet the standard of the "up and coming" Ellington. "That was made three, no, five years ago," he dismissively countered. "My competitors in the band business are not playing across the street. My competitors are the Duke Ellingtons of the 1940s and 1930s," Ellington told columnist Art Buchwald in 1961. "Everybody wants me to play the way I always did. Macy's been in business 50 years, but they're not selling the same stuff they did in 1920." In some press interviews, Ellington put an ever finer point on it. "Let's not get into that," he told a reporter who wanted to talk about Ellington's forty years as a bandleader. "I have the most expensive payroll for a band. I have a product to sell. I can't sell the past." In a 1970 Canadian newspaper article, when asked to talk about the past and the future, Ellington replied: "Oh my God, what a hell of a depressing idea! To talk about the past. It bugs the hell out of me when reporters expect a recital of 'And then I wrote . . . Mood Indigo . . . Sophisticated Lady . . . and all the rest of that jazz.'"[34]

Ellington also took steps to ensure that his image and style were not mired in the past. His clothing changed with the times, and he sported electric colors and psychedelic patterns during the last decade of his life. Though he still wore suits and never attempted to look like a member of the counterculture, they assuredly were not the suits most men of his generation wore. He often wore his hair in a short ponytail extending about an inch below his collar in the back, and he wore an earring. In a reversal of the usual generation gap, his son Mercer "couldn't stand" the way his father looked and felt "mortified" by it, according to his daughter Mercedes. Longtime Ellington vocalist Joya Sherrill offered to snip off the offending ponytail, but Ellington firmly replied, "I want it." "I couldn't believe it," she said over a decade later. Mercedes Ellington felt that her grandfather attired himself the way he did during this period

> because that was what he wanted to do. Cuffs and I mean really turned up pants . . . his shirts—it was just really unique. I mean, nobody else dressed like that. Nobody wrote like that. Nobody talked like that . . . he really found himself, I think. Something about maybe being alone. Talk about somebody who knows what they're all about. He really knew what he was about. As a person.

According to longtime Ellington associate Phoebe Jacobs, Ellington's sense of artistic creation extended to his clothes, particularly in the 1960s:

> Nobody groomed him into this. He didn't have any managers around telling him "wear your hair this way." When he got bored with formal jackets in the 1950s, he said to me, "I want you to go to an upholstery shop, and bring me some slipcover fabrics." "What are you doing?" "Well, I decided I want to make some formal jackets that will be interesting." Maybe he saw it in Europe, I don't know, but he made himself certain styles that eventually other

people copied. He had me go to Capezio's to make him velvet moccasins because his toes were hurting when he put his foot on the [piano] pedal . . . It was the first time Capezio ever made a pair of shoes for a man . . . [Ellington] was bored with stiff shirts. So we had a silk shirt made, and he got what we used to call pussy tails. He had little silk things made that he could make [into] a bowtie, a very soft tie. He was an artist, he painted. He was a multifaceted human being.[35]

Ellington also strenuously resisted being reminded of his past by his closest friends and associates. A group of them, including Ellington's two best friends Arthur Logan and Billy Strayhorn and Columbia record producer Irving Townsend, conspired to surprise Ellington on his birthday in 1962 with bound-leather scrapbooks of Ellington's entire oeuvre. They incorporated the project as a nonprofit organization called the Ellington Manuscripts, received donations from fifty people to fund it, and hired band member and band librarian John Saunders for nine months to work on it fulltime. Strayhorn also worked on the manuscripts. More than six hundred Ellington pieces were compiled into twenty-six volumes. Dr. Logan explained the impetus behind the project: "We thought this was a worthwhile thing because we think of Ellington as a creator in the mainstream of music, not a jazz musician or a writer of jazz but a writer of fine music which is the music of the 20th century and we think that as Bach's music is known today . . . is it important that Ellington's music be known" and documented.

Ellington was not pleased by the gift. "He kept refusing to accept it," according to Marian Logan, Dr. Logan's wife. "He gave us all four kisses, as he always did and said, 'That's lovely,' [but] . . . he didn't want to see it . . . he was very superstitious about life and insurances . . . [anything that could] remind you of the fact that you could possibly die . . . he thought that having all the music catalogued and copied meant that his life was over, and he wasn't ready for that." The Logans recognized this problem and subsequently added three or four blank volumes for the music he had yet to write, but Ellington still would not look at the volumes and eventually had them stored in a warehouse, where he never saw them again. "He doesn't care about this sort of thing, you know—collecting his stuff," Strayhorn observed. He had predicted Ellington's reaction to Saunders. "He was not very happy . . . at the idea of the thing," Dr. Logan commented two years later. "We did it despite him." Over a decade later, Townsend still seemed to feel resentment at Ellington's reaction to their work and expense: "the son of a bitch didn't even bother to take it home."[36]

Ellington sometimes would even go so far as to deny his past, in a humorous fashion. In 1966, when a backstage admirer told Ellington she used to dance to his music at the Cotton Club in the early 1930s, he answered: "No, no, you're thinking of Louis Armstrong—Louis and Lionel Hampton. They're the daddies of jazz. I'm just a young sprout." When a "middle-aged matron" reminisced with Ellington in 1968 about how he played at her college prom, he good-naturedly corrected her: "Oh no, that was my uncle from whom I inherited the title."[37]

In the last years of his life, Ellington went on a personal campaign against age discrimination in the press. Most articles on Ellington featured his age prominently, sometimes in the headline. "That's probably the best known fact about me . . . my age," he lamented in 1971. An advanced age, Ellington felt, provided another reason for people to dismiss him without experiencing his current contributions. He felt that a person's age had little to do with their vitality or potential. "What does age matter?" he asked an Australian reporter in 1970. "Some people are older at 20 than I am." At another stop on the same Australian tour, a band member, probably manager/trumpeter Mercer Ellington, issued a "dire warning" to the press before Ellington arrived to interact with them: "don't no-one ask him about how old he is, or how he gets around at his age." Earlier the same week, according to the *Sydney Morning Herald*, "Ellington had been close to blows with the Melbourne Press for dragging out the talk about his age—70—and how he managed to keep so much on the go. He had had enough." Ellington's frustration was understandable, yet the touring and composing regimen at his age was astonishing, and one can see why reporters dwelled on the story.[38]

Another query from the press that brought endless irritation during the last decade of his life concerned the issue of his retirement. Ellington had no use for the idea. In 1963, he called rumors of his retirement "the columns of my enemies" and claimed he couldn't even think about taking a holiday. "I don't know what I'd do [during a holiday], except sleep maybe," he told a reporter the same year, adding a personal and telling comment: "What else is there to do if you don't do music? Without music, you're nothing." "People ask 'when are you going to retire,'" Ellington said in 1967. "Retire to what? Stagnation?" As always, his composing seemed to drive his actions: "I have an unlimited accumulation of plans that are impossible," he said in 1964. It was true; even on his deathbed, he furiously composed and edited new work. This personality trait ran in the family, according to his sister Ruth, who observed that "he's something like our father . . . [who] said 'I'd rather wear out than rust out.'" Besides, Ellington loved his life and worked like a stevedore in his last years to keep it as he wanted: "What's there to retire to? My band and I travel all over the world, see the sights and people. You can't beat that . . . I visited a friend who'd retired. His wife saw him sitting there, doing nothing, and told him: 'Take out the garbage.' That's not for me." As he expressed in his 1955 play, *Man with Four Sides*, the idea of being a retired homebody, of living a soulless suburban life in the American nuclear-family tradition, seemed to either bore or frighten him, or perhaps both. It was another of the links he shared with the counterculture of the 1960s.

Ellington cherished being on the road, each day promising potential surprises of the musical, geographical, and female variety. He especially appreciated the moments when he was out of reach of everyone, and in control of his destiny. "If you have the right kind of temperament, traveling can get to you like whisky and cigarettes," he told Nat Hentoff in 1964. "Getting into a car or train is like being released. You know there'll be no business problems to talk about while you're moving."[39]

Since at least the early 1960s, and especially in this period, many observers of the pop music scene urged Ellington to abandon his punishing road schedule, live on his royalties, or, better yet, secure a grant that would allow him to spend his days doing nothing but composing. Ellington laughed when Stanley Dance mentioned this idea in 1972: "It'd be wonderful, wouldn't it? Just to sit there. I could see the green growing around, you know, the stagnation. The greatest form, the most ornamental stagnation. They'd say, 'This cat is not only black, he's green.'" If he ever gave up the life of a rolling stone, he feared he would gather moss, especially in terms of his composing. An anonymous Ellington band member interviewed in 1965 seemed to encapsulate the effect of the stage on Ellington and counseled against any curtailing of his schedule or accepting a government grant:

I hope he never does [that]. He'd age overnight. He's found the way to stay young. Watch him some night. Those bags under his eyes are huge, and he looks beat and lonely. But then we begin to play, he strides out on the stand, people in the audience turn their faces to him and the cat is a new man.

Pulitzer Prize? Who could give a musician anything to top what Duke has?

Ellington argued that the ability to perform his music nightly and meet various people from all over the world inspired his writing—it didn't deter him. In 1964, Ellington said he wouldn't retire from the road to write because "my music talks about the new people I keep meeting, the places I've seen, and the places I've seen change." In 1972, he provided more detail:

The people? Oh listen, man, I go a lot of places. Idaho. The state of Idaho probably has got more mountains than anywhere else in the world and there's no way of going anyplace without going over half a dozen mountains. And there's a guy out there who's a sign painter. He's not rich or anything or important. He's got his wife and their two boys and they get in that truck and they drive 2 or 300 hundred miles over those mountains and come and hear us in Boise or whatever. These are the people. These are the people who do it. They give you something that you need, whatever it is, I don't know. I don't dare to analyze it, because, I mean, it's a beautiful flower, and once you analyze a flower, you have no more flower.[40]

Ellington's relentlessly peripatetic schedule functioned as another contributing factor in his campaign against nostalgia. Those who followed Ellington closely were frequently shocked by his level of activity and travel. Leonard Feather described a week for Ellington in May 1966 in which he slept only three hours a night as he filled a commission from Frank Sinatra to score his movie *Assault on a Queen,* while playing consecutive nights in Wichita, Little Rock, and San Francisco. The day after that last show, Ellington recorded the score in Los Angeles while simultaneously playing with the band at Disneyland for three nights straight. The morning after the last show at Disneyland, Ellington and the orchestra took off for a two-week tour of Japan. On the day they flew back into Los Angeles, they played a gig that night. But recording and touring duties formed only part of Ellington's marathon life, as Feather again reported in 1967. Ellington's social life also proved prodigious:

"I'm sorry, Duke, I'd really like to come along, but I just can't keep up with your pace."

This was the excuse offered by a young man when he reluctantly turned down an invitation from Duke Ellington. The time was 3:00 a.m., the place a Los Angeles apartment. Ellington had gone to bed the previous morning at 7:00 a.m., after traveling, socializing and telephoning throughout the night. Following a few hours' sleep, he had spent the afternoon with business associates, consumed a vast dinner, hastened to a panel-discussion in which he took part at a college, proceeded immediately to a concert with his orchestra, and thence to a party where he was the most ebullient, enthusiastic and wide-awake of all the guests. The young man who addressed him was apologizing because he felt incapable of following a suggestion by Ellington, who wanted to take everyone over to his hotel suite, where they would find a piano, sandwiches, drinks, coffee and continued lively conversation. (The party continued, chez Ellington, until a little after 6:00 a.m.)[41]

This pattern of activity lasted well into the early 1970s. Following a European tour in the summer of 1970, new band member Fred Stone felt he had to take a rest and couldn't perform at the residency at New York City's Rainbow Grill that commenced a day after the band returned from playing twelve countries in thirty-five days, sometimes playing two shows a night. The band had six days off during the tour, but Ellington worked on at least two of those days. Ellington "never seems tired," marveled Stone at his seventy-one-year-old boss. "The band will be dropping from exhaustion and he wants to play encores. Sometimes they get up, walk out one by one, and Duke is left alone with the rhythm section." In 1971, the band finished a date at Caesars Palace in Las Vegas at 5 AM and, without sleep, immediately set out for a date the same night in Houston. "Some of the band was late arriving, so the Duke, with no introduction or fanfare, played a little dinner music on the piano," according to a Houston columnist. "The packed house loved it. The band slowly gathered and proceeded to play some of the prettiest dance music . . . patrons had ever heard."[42]

In addition to the activities listed above, the early hours of daylight were Ellington's favorite time to write during this period. If an idea entered his consciousness after finally going to bed, he would immediately figure it out on the electric piano he carried with him all over the world and commit it to paper before returning to sleep. In 1969, choreographer Alvin Ailey spent a week with Ellington while they collaborated on *The River*. After playing two shows a night, every night, and receiving guests before, after, and between those shows until 5:00 AM, Ellington began to compose. Ailey had the hotel room next to Ellington's: "I would hear him. I could hear the piano between 5:00 in the morning and 10:00 . . . working away." Sometimes Ellington would call him during those hours and ask him to come by and hear something new for the ballet. "And I'd jump and get myself together. Act like I was, you know, ready," recalled Ailey. He was in supreme physical condition but still experienced difficulty keeping up with Ellington. Ellington never saw a formal performance of Ailey's choreography of *The River*, one of the most significant pieces of Ellington's later career—he was too busy traveling with the orchestra. In his twilight years, Ellington could not afford to waste any time.[43]

Ellington stepped up his already hectic writing regimen after Billy Strayhorn died from cancer on 31 May 1967. Ellington, by all reports, was devastated by the death of Strayhorn, the man he referred to as his "favorite human being" as well as "my right arm, my left arm, all the eyes in the back of my head, my brainwaves in his head, and his in mine." During the last weeks, Ellington did not visit, unable to bear seeing his friend in the last throes of cancer, but spoke with him daily on the phone, sent numerous packages to him, and paid for several pianists in Paris to record sessions especially for Strayhorn, which were played at his bedside. According to Marian Logan, when the news of Strayhorn's death came, Ellington cried for hours, and when asked by her husband Dr. Logan if he was going to be all right, Ellington replied: "Fuck no, I'm not going to be all right. Nothing is all right now." Ellington chose not to attend Strayhorn's viewing or the private service for him and stayed instead with the band in Reno. Though he flew to New York City for the public funeral and wrote a eulogy for Strayhorn, he might have missed the funeral if Dr. Logan had not goaded the upset Ellington out of bed that morning. In his autobiography, Ellington wrote that "Many people are indebted to Billy Strayhorn, and I more than anybody." In the weeks after Strayhorn's death, Ellington slept far more than usual, produced less music, and Dr. Logan pronounced Ellington depressed. "It was a big blow to the old man," remembered Mercer Ellington. In terms of his work and personal life, things would now become more difficult for Ellington, but he rose to the challenge. "When Strayhorn passed, [Ellington] was in the midst of various projects, and realizing he did not have Strayhorn at his side, he found that in order to cover the same ground that he had been covering . . . he had to work harder," according to Mercer. "If anything, Strayhorn's passing stimulated Ellington's ability to write more music than he'd ever had to do before."[44]

With Strayhorn's death, a schism developed between the Ellington organization and the Strayhorn family almost immediately. Strayhorn's nephew Gregory Morris, the family member closest to Billy aside from his mother Lillian, was the executor of his uncle's estate. Morris recalled that a few days after his uncle's death, someone from Duke Ellington, Inc., came to Strayhorn's apartment and started "pulling [folders of Strayhorn's sheet music] off the shelves and throwing it on the floor" with the ultimate goal of taking it to Ellington's offices. Morris did not recognize the person, felt affronted, and said "whatever's here is going to stay here and it's not going anywhere unless I say so." When told that the material belonged to Ellington, Morris insisted that it resided in Strayhorn's apartment, "so nobody's going to take it. I control everything here and that's the way it's going to be." Ellington later contacted Morris "and wanted to work out something. Well, my family thought there was a gold mine in the music and they didn't want to give it up. So I was fighting with my family, I was negotiating with the Ellingtons . . . we never did get it resolved." Long-term accounting problems, especially with tax returns, kept Morris from settling the estate for more than a decade.[45]

In many ways, the ensuing decades-long legal battles between the Strayhorn and Ellington families represented a struggle for Strayhorn's soul and legacy, as well as the money Strayhorn's work would continue to earn for decades. Ruth Ellington explained her position on Strayhorn's manuscripts years later: "I was simply looking after Edward's business interests in my capacity as president of Tempo Music. Billy worked for Edward. Therefore, his work was rightly Edward's." But more than that seemed to be going on beneath the surface. From the limited records available, it seems that, while Ellington and Tempo Music were generous while Strayhorn lived and one Strayhorn family source claimed that Strayhorn died a multimillionaire, royalty checks were not going out to the Strayhorn family after Strayhorn's death. Judging from Yale's oral interviews of the Strayhorn family, they did not seem to know Strayhorn well. None of them seemed familiar with his music, none of them mentioned the way he lived his life as an openly gay man. Morris said that no unreleased music existed among the sheet music found in Strayhorn's apartment, but subsequent research by Walter van de Leur has shown this to be wrong. With the exception of Morris, Strayhorn only visited his relatives during the holiday season in his last years, and sometimes not even then. Could the Ellingtons, who had virtually adopted him into their family for three decades, have felt that he belonged more to their family than his own? Could Strayhorn have felt that way? Did Strayhorn's relatives disapprove of the way he lived his life? If Duke Ellington, Inc., and Tempo Music denied Strayhorn's royalties to his appointed heirs, this was illegal or worse. But the Ellingtons appeared to feel they earned more propriety over Strayhorn, both personally and in terms of his work, than Strayhorn's own family. In the controversy over the sheet music in Strayhorn's apartment, Morris recalled Ruth Ellington telling him, "That music was Billy's. It belongs to us." Morris felt that what she was really saying was: "in other words, 'Billy belonged to us.' We [the Strayhorn family] had a real problem with that point of view."[46]

In June 1969, Ellington bought Strayhorn's 10 percent share of Tempo Music from the Strayhorn family for $100,000. It is apparent from business records that Ellington wanted the deal to include all the sheet music found in Strayhorn's apartment, but the Strayhorn estate would not relent. When Ellington insisted that his lawyer Benjamin Starr get tougher on this point, Starr removed himself from the negotiations in January 1969, because he disagreed with how Ellington wanted the matter handled. Starr felt that Ellington's request was impossible, because the estate had possession of the manuscripts, Strayhorn had never submitted them to Tempo, and Strayhorn had, over the years, as Ellington knew, given songs of his to other publishers, since Ellington never insisted on signing Strayhorn as an exclusive songwriter with Tempo. Starr mentioned twice in his letters "the unbelievable meeting at [Ruth's] home" in September 1968 when they discussed the situation and Ellington apparently became very angry, one of the few times in Ellington's life that such a reaction was noted. The matter seemed to have gone beyond business considerations for Ellington—it was personal, and Starr saw no way of ethically giving Ellington what he wanted in the buyout. Once again, Ellington was willing to be generous with Strayhorn, but apparently not Strayhorn's family.[47]

For the rest of his life, Ellington acknowledged the influence of Strayhorn from the bandstand almost every night. Strayhorn songs did not disappear from the band's repertoire. Ellington closed dozens, if not hundreds, of shows in his last years with an emotional solo piano version of Strayhorn's "Lotus Blossom" in tribute to Strayhorn. In the late summer and fall of 1967, Ellington and the orchestra recorded . . . *And His Mother Called Him Bill,* a collection of Strayhorn pieces in honor of the composer. His best-known pieces were not recorded for this session ("'A' Train," "Chelsea Bridge"). Instead, the tracks seemed more like Ellington's personal favorites, some obscure, many of them swinging, and all of them filled with Strayhorn's pungent gift of melody. Few of the songs reflect the sadness and tragedy surrounding Strayhorn's demise, except for one of Strayhorn's last compositions, the haunting "Blood Count," seemingly inspired by his time in the hospital, and one of his most memorable pieces. On a 1970 French television special taped in Paris, Ellington paused between songs to talk about Strayhorn:

> Strayhorn loved Paris, and it was one of his favorite places. And of course I love Strayhorn because Strayhorn and I got so close that when I did my 1st Sacred Concert he was sick in the hospital and I was in California, he was in New York. I called him, I says "Strays, I'm doing the theme [from] the first 4 words of the Bible, 'In The Beginning God,' and I'd like for you to do either an interlude, an introduction or something" to keep him busy . . . And his theme had six syllables or six tones, and mine had six syllables, six tones, naturally, 'In The Beginning God.' And there were only two notes that were different [he plays the six notes] . . . His started in the same place and ended in the same place, and only two of the notes in between were different. So it was a very, very close thing. Billy Strayhorn. He wrote "Lotus Blossom" and he always said that I played it better than he. He was a very gracious man, you know.

Then Ellington, alone at the piano, played the song. As the sustain faded at the close of his performance, Ellington cleared his throat and said softly: "I'm sure Aaron Bridgers plays it better than I do." For those who knew the relationships of the players, this marked a touching moment. Bridgers was a close romantic and musical partner of Strayhorn's over the years, and they had spent many happy months together in Paris, as well as in other locales. Ellington knew him well, and Bridgers had done arranging work for Ellington. With his televised comment, Ellington was acknowledging and honoring Bridgers's relationship with Strayhorn, Bridgers's loss, and Strayhorn's sexual identity. It would be difficult to imagine Ellington making a similar statement, however veiled, in the United States.[48]

Ellington's antinostalgia campaign principally focused on encouraging the public and critics to notice his newest compositions and not just his golden oldies. Much of the work during Ellington's last decade merited the attention, and some of it ranked among the best he ever released. During the 1960s, he redefined the sound and scope of a big band; he was writing the future of the big band sound almost without any competition. Mercer Ellington felt that the Ellington studio sessions of the period were "more purposeful, a little more absolute. Because he was aware of the fact that he didn't have much more time, and he didn't have the luxury of experimenting and playing around and letting everything work itself out. He was now on the schedule of life and he had to work hard at making sure that [he could finish as much as he could]." Clark Terry, an important Ellington band member in the 1950s, noticed that Ellington studio sessions seemed more planned and organized and less off the cuff in the 1960s than in previous years. With all the commissions he accepted, Ellington "felt he had too much to do to lollygag," Terry recalled. Terry also recalled hearing Ellington say that his band in the 1960s was his best band, especially because "the newer guys" all read music proficiently, while some band members in past decades did not, "so, as a result, he reached a point where he knew that he could write anything or bring anything in to do written by Strayhorn . . . and that band would play it."[49]

Besides his Sacred Concerts and the new influences they brought to the table, international themes dominated his last major works, inspired by his numerous tours around the world. As Ellington's view of the world expanded through travel, so did his musical palette. Preeminent among these works is the *Far East Suite* (1966), an album of pieces by Ellington and Strayhorn inspired by sights and sounds gleaned from the band's 1963 State Department tour, as good as anything Ellington ever released. In a 1964 article about the tour, Ellington discussed how he wanted to make the *Far East Suite* "a reflection" of "the adventure" he experienced, not an attempt to duplicate the music heard in the countries they toured.[50] In the same spirit, Strayhorn took the melody of "Bluebird of Delhi (Mynah)" from the song of a bird outside his window in New Delhi. While many of Ellington and Strayhorn's major works were prepared with a strict deadline or a festival premiere in mind, *Far East Suite* may have benefited from the fact that they were able to take their time, allowing the themes to marinate for three years and experimenting with the pieces onstage before committing the music to tape. With its highly attuned sense of jazz exoticism, musical adventurousness, and understated tips of the hat to India, Iran, and Japan, the *Far East Suite* probably ranked as the most satisfying in the long line of distinguished Ellington/Strayhorn collaborations. It also marked the last of their major collaborations. As a historical and musical document, it fit in perfectly with the cosmopolitan, jetsetting world of the international jazz scene of the 1960s, just as "Black and Tan Fantasie" captured jazz's early days of Harlem sophistication forty years earlier.

Ellington's *Latin American Suite* (1968) also had its origins in international touring and the sounds of foreign instruments, and is very enjoyable. It continued Ellington's long-term experimentation with Latin music accents, with its tango rhythms, warm dissonance, and a generous supply of the icy treble piano stabs that Ellington employed frequently in his later works. Though some of the suite was written in the weeks before the band's 1968 Latin American tour (a scheduled premiere in Mexico City necessitated this), Ellington also revised it in light of his experiences south of the border before recording it. Perhaps some of the sunny feeling that pervades most of the record comes from the rabid reception Ellington and the band received throughout South and Central America. Ellington orchestra tenor saxophonist Paul Gonsalves claimed the band never had a better reception outside the United States, with crowds demanding nine encores regularly instead of the band's usual complement of two. He also recalled a woman in Chile crying when she met Harry Carney, the longest-serving member of Ellington's orchestra, whom she'd been waiting twenty years to meet. She became so emotional that nearby police grew "suspicious" and questioned if he had beaten or hassled her. "Of all the cities he conquered . . . I remember particularly Buenos Aires when [Ellington] went there for the first time," recalled Stanley Dance. "He had played his final concert and sat in the car outside the theater before going to the airport. People clutched at him through the open windows, people who were crying, people thrust gifts on which they hadn't even written their names. It was one of the few times I saw him moved to tears." To cap the tour, the Ellington orchestra acted as the United States' cultural representatives (along with classical pianist Van Cliburn) at the 1968 Olympic Games in Mexico City, where they premiered the unfinished suite.[51]

The early 1970s saw three worthy editions to the Ellington canon that should be much better known. The *New Orleans Suite* is a soulful musical portrait of the city that provided the catalyst of so much American music, encompassing blues and gospel in addition to jazz and featuring instruments new to the Ellington palette: organ, flugelhorn, and flute. The New Orleans musical style had been central to the Ellington sound since the mid-1920s, when bassist Wellman Braud and clarinetist Barney Bigard had joined the band. But the sound of the *New Orleans Suite* is not nostalgic; it is 1970s jazz informed by the rich musical history of New Orleans. Ellington's programmatic portraits on this album, the last in a long series that began in 1928 with his tribute to Florence Mills, were a particular highlight, spotlighting Louis Armstrong, Sidney Bechet, Braud, Mahalia Jackson, and in perhaps the best track on the album, the Mississippi River. Once again, Ellington was offering a black history lesson through music.

The Afro-Eurasian Eclipse was another of Ellington's internationally inspired pieces, an aural trip around the world influenced by Marshall McLuhan's theory, as interpreted by Ellington, that "the whole world is going Oriental and that no one will be able to retain his or her identity, not even the Orientals. And of course we travel around the world a lot and in the last 5 or 6 years, we too have noticed this thing to be true." In his autobiography, he added detail to this picture: "I had seen saris on the Cote d'Azur, British musicians playing the sitar, and everywhere a trend toward the exotic. Youngsters . . . were dressing in oriental styles . . . The beards, the long hair, and the fact that many Americans have taken to Eastern religions were all consistent with McLuhan's statement."[52]

Afro-Eurasian Eclipse features an especially percussive sound and various instrument combinations that suggest the music of several foreign lands the band visited. "Didjeridoo" features Harry Carney on baritone saxophone imitating the low-toned Australian instrument. "Afrique" gives tribute to the polyrhythms of African music. Several tracks (particularly "Chinoiserie" and "Gong") feature melodies with an Asian tint to them, without resorting to the stereotypes attending jazz records with Asian-referencing titles in the 1920s. The influences of 1960s soul and even rock, particularly in the drum sound, could be heard in such titles as "Tang," "True," and "Acht O'Clock Rock," as well as on previous tracks on the *Far East Suite* ("Blue Pepper"), *New Orleans Suite* ("Portrait of Mahalia Jackson"), and the surprisingly hip and danceable 1968 track "Cool and Groovy," which should have been released as a single.

The River was a delightful forty-three-minute piece that traced the course of flowing water in thirteen short movements from "The Spring" to "The Giggling Rapids" to "The Lake" over "The Falls" into "The Whirlpool" and eventually reaching "Her Majesty the Sea." It was commissioned by the American Ballet Theatre and choreographed by Alvin Ailey. Like most of Ellington's best extended pieces, it's an evocative journey in song. Its unjust obscurity is partly explained by the fact that it was not released until thirteen years after Ellington's death. In addition to the five suites mentioned here, Ellington also composed other suites during his last years, perhaps of lesser quality but with excellent portions, as well as numerous memorable miniatures, some released and most not (such as "Elos" from 1968)—in all, too many to mention without resorting to a laundry list of titles.

At the same time as Ellington was fighting nostalgia and fighting to move forward on several fronts, he also had to provide a lot of nostalgia. While he had long cultivated an audience that allowed him to present fresh new material onstage, they also wanted the hits, and Ellington gladly delivered. "The idea . . . is to try to play things that will have the best overall sense of communication with these people, with everybody," Elllington told a BBC interviewer. "You've got an audience to play for, and I respect everybody in it." When a club owner in Las Vegas worried about the crowd reception for a "jazz" band, Ellington said he replied: "Look sweetie, [there's] nobody in your place we don't touch with something." Some members of the band complained about the repetitive nature of the Ellington set list night to night, but as bassist John Lamb explained, "we have so many requests for the same tune, we have to repeat." As Ellington remarked in 1964, "if I were to play just for the guys in the band and the hippies, I often wouldn't get invited back. After all, those people who aren't so hip have paid their money and they like to feel part of what's going on." In the same article, Nat Hentoff compared Ellington's approach to live repertoire with "the new generation of jazzmen [who] scorn showmanship and will make concessions to no one, but they keep listening to and learning from Ellington."

Many band members and associates report that Ellington possessed an innate knowledge of what an audience wanted, a preternatural ability to satisfy different audiences in the same venue and keep a good balance between old and new material.[53] Ellington described the process in 1964:

> When you play for one audience, you play something that they understand. Like we play in a nightclub, and the audience changes in the middle of the night, and your music changes with the audience, that is, *our* music does. Because we're influenced in one of many different ways. Sometimes by requests, sometimes you can just tell by the response to one number just what character of music this particular audience will respond to. We keep them pretty well pegged... you play one place where, say, they will want smooth music... So you play another club and you find they want to jump. But in that same club where they want to jump, there is still another audience. When the music changes, the dance floor changes. You can see them move on. And very early in the night, you learn the percentages . . . Audiences are wonderful, great. I think that's what's got me hung on this thing. Well, I mean, because, what the hell, you wouldn't make any less money if you didn't do anything but make records, you know. You don't actually make any money playing personal appearances. I don't, I know. It's a very expensive thing. The only thing I get out of it is constantly having this communication with audiences, going from place to place, noting the contrasts, the relief from going to a bad piano to a good one.

Perhaps the reason that Ellington anticipated the desires of audiences so well is that he viewed himself principally as a listener. He felt he was part of the audience for his own music. During a public television interview in the early 1960s, Ellington's views on this subject seemed to surprise Ralph J. Gleason:

ELLINGTON: You and I, I always feel, are in the same category. I feel that I'm on the same level with you because you have proven that you are a great listener. I know the only thing I do in music is listen, not the only thing maybe, but the big thing I do in music is listen.

GLEASON [SOUNDING SHOCKED]: How do you mean the big thing you do in music is listen?

ELLINGTON: Well, that's it, listening is the most important thing in music.

GLEASON: Of course it is to the listener, but there must be sounds to be produced to listen to.

ELLINGTON: Oh no, because before you can play anything, or before you can write it, you gotta hear it. If you can't hear it, then it's a mechanical thing.

GLEASON: Then the composer is a listener primarily.

ELLINGTON: Well, I should say so in music, yeah. It has to do with the ear. Some of the prettiest things on paper come off drab.

In the same interview, Ellington stated: "I never concern myself about the size of an audience, I only want to know whether they're listening or not." While Ellington skillfully and gladly sought to satisfy all audiences who came to see him, he most worried about satisfying "the listeners," especially those who had followed his career closely for decades.

Perhaps Ellington's true feelings about his audience could be discerned in the phrase that he told every audience he faced numerous times during the last quarter century of his career: "Love you madly." While some observers viewed the phrase as a perfunctory or even insincere part of Ellington's stage manner, he insisted on the sincerity of it in a 1966 interview:

> I'm all hung up on this thing of actually encountering the people and seeing them have a reaction to the music. "Love you madly" . . . is a thing I started saying to audiences a long time ago. It gets a giggle every now and then, but it's true, I love those people madly . . . For me, there's no substitute for this. You go up there and you play and they react and you can taste it . . . Oh, maybe 30 years ago I used to think "I play for myself," "I express me," and any artist has to please himself first, but the whole thing isn't complete until someone else, the listener, is involved. When someone else happens to like what you're doing, too, this brings on a state of agreement that is the closest thing there is to sex, because people do not indulge themselves together unless they agree that this is the time. This is the thing.

The decision to perform the same old favorites also had a financial dimension. The constant exposure of Ellington evergreens increased the money Ellington made as a songwriter in ASCAP public performance royalties. Mercer Ellington explained that the medley of hits the band performed every night starting in the 1950s was designed to ensure maximum income while allowing maximum time for the more challenging and newer Ellington pieces. Aaron Bell, a bassist for the Ellington orchestra during the 1960s, put it this way: "Duke is not making too much money . . . off the band in profits . . . so he figures 'I can't get the money on the gate, I'll get it through ASCAP.'"

Yet some musicians, such as Bell, trumpeter Cat Anderson, and drummer Louis Bellson felt that the same hit song represented "a different experience every time," especially with new sidemen. Bellson said he needed to watch Ellington carefully each night to pick up on nuances Ellington added to the songs. Yet, several Ellington band members from the 1950s and 1960s also rued that out of the six-inch-thick sheaf of material in their band books, they almost never played half the songs. The Ellington cognoscenti also expressed frustration about this, although never during a show. John Saunders, who doubled as a music copyist for the band as well as a trombonist, recalled that some longtime Ellington fans would give him their cherished copies of rare Ellington 78-rpm records in the hope that Saunders would duplicate their arrangements, place them in the band book, and have Ellington play them live.

Many companies and industries had an interest in pushing Ellington as a nostalgia artist in the 1960s and 1970s. Rafts of Ellington reissues emerged from record company vaults during the period, taking valuable attention away from Ellington's newest works in newspapers, record stores, on the radio, and in year-end magazine award polls. Though this must have represented a frustrating situation for Ellington at times, it did boost his royalty checks, which helped support the current orchestra. In 1965, when Ellington received extensive media coverage because of the Pulitzer controversy and the First Sacred Concert, Irving Mills took advantage of the moment by circulating a slickly produced circular that promoted the Ellington songs Mills owned to performers, orchestras, and TV and film music supervisors. "There is a gold mine of Ellington music in the Mills catalog," went one blurb. "Remember 'Reminiscing In Tempo'? It was the Duke's first big success in a longer composition." No note was made of Mills's initial resistance to this landmark work from 1935.[54]

American television and radio also tended to focus on the nostalgic and more conservative forms of jazz. In the late 1960s and early 1970s, Ralph J. Gleason and George Wein both complained in the press that plenty of airtime and support existed for the experimental wings of rock and R&B on radio, while jazz was usually represented by older swing bands and an ubiquitous 4/4 beat. Gleason felt that such programming strategies were denying the jazz community a chance to catch on with the younger baby boomers that were catalyzing the music and radio businesses of the 1960s. Wein went further, calling the situation "disgraceful," having just returned from a successful 1971 European jazz tour and seeing the media attention that jazz commanded across the Atlantic. He reported that broadcasting companies in England, France, and Germany "picked up the freight" for touring American jazz bands that performed on their stations and often presented American jazz without commercials as a sign of respect. "It's ironic that in this country, where jazz originated, it's practically impossible to find a broadcaster or a sponsor who is willing to underwrite a series or a special devoted to this native type of music," Wein complained. Gleason and Wein were not "moldy figs" wishing to spark a return to the Swing Era, when big band jazz ruled the American music scene; they were both involved with and supporters of some of the most innovative young jazzers of the 1960s. The African American magazine *Jet* went even further in their analysis of the situation, siding with a 1971 suit against the FCC charging that white-owned commercial radio stations had shown "patterns of bias" for years against playing black artists, particularly in the jazz field. They also decried the lack of station ownership by blacks, noting that most black stations had weaker signals, could only broadcast from sunrise to sunset, and were located on the far end of the dial, while whites predominantly owned the more powerful stations that broadcasted continually.[55]

In many ways, television represented an even worse situation in the 1960s and 1970s for jazz musicians, particularly Ellington.[56] The 1950s trend of Ellington usually being relegated to playing medleys of old hits on American television, forced to appeal to the lowest common denominator while being paid well for it mostly held, even into the 1970s. Some of the more major examples of this include major network primetime specials starring Barbara McNair (1967) and Lou Rawls (1971), as well as appearances on a short-lived 1970 CBS-TV series called *Happy Days* that sought to recreate the aura of the Swing Era. On the McNair and Rawls shows, the music was vapid, commercialized, and almost painful at times, consisting only of old hits in truncated versions, and Ellington did not speak. Ellington also made regular appearances throughout the era on talk shows hosted by Dick Cavett, Mike Douglas, and Merv Griffin, as well as NBC's long-running morning show *Today*. In a review of a 1964 appearance on the latter show, a Long Island jazz critic noted the "rather desultory manner" in which Ellington played, yet again, a medley of his hits, even though he had a new album to promote. He added: "One could almost hear the producer telling Ellington—'Look, baby, none of that far out stuff . . . the jaspers in Elephant's Breath, Wis. won't dig it. And by the way, you guys got any funny hats?' . . . TV has struck again and jazz takes another fall."

In a panel discussion on the state of jazz in 1964, some major jazz figures bemoaned the waste of the potential for jazz on television. "TV, of all media, is ideally suited to . . . jazz because you can hear and see it while being created," argued Dizzy Gillespie. "I think the big mistake [of TV shows featuring jazz] has been their lack of spontaneity." Stan Kenton countered that "If you're talking about the major networks, I'd say there's no place on television for jazz at all, because television has to appeal to the masses, and . . . jazz is a minority music, it appeals to a minority, and that minority is not large enough to support any part of commercial television." In his characteristically blunt way, Charles Mingus summed up his view of the situation: "Let's face it. Television is Jim Crow." Mostly he was correct. During the 1960s and before in the United States, black faces were rarely seen on network television unless they were part of news events, Bill Cosby, or older nonthreatening musicians like Ellington or Louis Armstrong. Certainly exceptions existed to this unstated but clear policy—the Ed Sullivan show in particular sought to present top young black talent—but such exceptions were rare.

What particularly chagrined American jazz enthusiasts and musicians was the high artistic quality and respect of European and Canadian jazz TV broadcasts. Often, these non-American jazz programs focused solely on the music and performers, with no show business or variety trappings. *The Duke,* a 1965 Canadian program, featured extended takes of Duke being interviewed while also playing the piano, intercut with complete band performances of new material from *My People* and the *Far East Suite,* music never heard on American television. *Indigo Musikaliska,* a 1964 Danish special, obviously gave Ellington free reign with his repertoire, so he responded with an eclectic set of new material from the unreleased *Afro-Bossa* album; little known gems from *Beggars Holiday, Paris Blues,* and *Such Sweet Thunder;* as well as some familiar hit material. It was a sophisticated multisided portrayal of the Ellington palette adorned with generous shots of individual orchestra members in action. Similarly staged broadcasts from the BBC (1963) and French television (1970) can be viewed at the Library of Congress's Motion Picture Division.

Though most of Ellington's American TV appearances were vapid and unchallenging, a few realized the potential for greatness in the presentation of jazz on TV. Ellington's best TV moments, unsurprisingly, tended to be on independent or public stations. In 1964, the independent Metromedia network presented *Duke Ellington—A Portrait in Music,* an hour-long show that featured, in a rare moment for American television, an unexpurgated performance of Ellington's thirteen-minute "Harlem." In 1967, Ralph J. Gleason produced two Emmy-nominated documentaries on Ellington for public television: a film that captured the first performance of Ellington's First Sacred Concert, and *Love You Madly,* an insightful, behind-the-scenes look at Ellington at work, with some beautiful black-and-white photography. Earlier in the 1960s, Gleason hosted and produced *Jazz Casual,* a public television series focusing on one jazz musician or group for a half hour and featuring nothing but music and informed conversation. Ellington and Strayhorn appeared on the show together in 1960, as had younger artists like John Coltrane.

Major TV networks also managed some respectable hour-long primetime Ellington-themed programs, including CBS-TV's *The Twentieth Century: Duke Ellington Swings through Japan* (1964), NBC-TV's *The Bell Telephone Hour: On the Road with Duke Ellington* (1967), and CBS-TV's airing of Ellington's Second Sacred Concert in 1968. *A Contemporary Memorial* represented the highlight of Ellington's American major-network TV appearances in this period. The show aired on 8 June 1968, the day of Senator Robert F. Kennedy's funeral, and featured Ellington with a trio including Johnny Hodges providing movingly mournful music and exchanging a few words about the solemn occasion with his friend Father Norman J. O'Connor. Ellington was again assuaging the loss of a nation, as he had after President Franklin Roosevelt's death, and as he was not allowed to do on the 1963 State Department tour when President John F. Kennedy was assassinated. It's a broadcast that deserves a public release.

Over the course of the 1960s and 1970s, Ellington gained the reputation of someone who could, within his audiences, unite groups that usually remained separate in American society, especially during this period: young and old, black and white, rural and urban. A 1968 Rochester, New York, editorial commented on the scene at an Ellington show:

> That great and good man of music, Duke Ellington, worked his magic, from the hottest rock to the nostalgic "Mood Indigo."
>
> What a scene! Whites and blacks mingled in a tribute that extinguished barriers of color and race; they stood shoulder to shoulder; they smiled at each other; some brought lightweight folding chairs; red-headed white kids played tag with spic and span black children around the pillars at one end of the plaza; white and black teenyboppers argued the merits of sax and clarinet. The magic of the Duke and his music made one people of them, one admiring people.

"A sophisticated mixture of beautiful women of all hues" from the "chic" set, with their dates, attended a 1965 Urban League tribute to Ellington in New York City, an occasion a local black paper called a "'Swinger'—Both Socially and Musically." Twenty-two thousand "Fans of all ages, races, and economic strata snapped their fingers at the Duke's command" in Washington, D.C., in 1966, according to the *Washington Post*. "Executives up front in Palm Beach suits contrasted with shirtless beer drinkers stretched out on the grass." An identical description of an Ellington audience appeared two months later in a Northern California newspaper. A 1969 picture montage in a Florida newspaper depicted well-dressed black and white locals backstage at a concert.[57]

Ellington also made clear how much he enjoyed performing in the more rural sections of the United States and occasionally attempted to dispel some of the prejudices against them. "Iowa is a good state," Ellington said in 1969. "Most people think of it as a state where they grow corn. It is a cultural plateau. I've played 'Tattooed Bride' [an extended and dissonant Ellington piece] for audiences there. Indiana, too. Things don't have to be on the hit parade [for them to enjoy it there]." He spoke on numerous occasions about his fans in Idaho. "We go where the people want to hear music," Ellington stated. "I had just as soon play in Pocatello as the biggest show business place in the world—as long as the people are interested."[58]

Throughout the 1960s, newspapers stressed Ellington's multigenerational appeal in an attempt to elicit interest and sell tickets. He was constantly viewed as a figure capable of bridging the generation gap. In 1961, a Wisconsin newspaper claimed that Ellington's upcoming show "has evoked a great deal of interest from adults and young people"; five months later, an article in a Columbus, Ohio, paper used similar language, demonstrating that this line of argument probably emanated from the office of Duke Ellington, Inc. Ellington himself told an Idaho paper in 1962 that "the band does not arrange its music for any certain age group." "All I'm interested in is communication," he explained the same year. "We want everybody to come to the party." Economically, he needed everybody to come to the party, especially when the band performed at least three hundred shows a year; the big band market was so sparse that he needed to appeal to several different kinds of audiences in many different locales in order to survive.[59]

The trend of diverse Ellington audiences continued. In 1964, articles from local papers in Oregon and New Jersey trumpeted Ellington's ability to attract "all ages and types," while an Erie, Pennsylvania, paper proved it in a photo montage from a show. A 1965 San Diego Ellington audience consisted mostly of "old-timers," while mostly teens gave Ellington "spontaneous bursts of applause to the Ellington music that apparently knows no age limit" at a 1967 Seattle high school show. At a 1967 New York City stand, a *Billboard* reviewer found that "the miniskirted and the more staid—all dug the Duke's rhythms." In 1972, a Minneapolis audience included "everybody from the liniment set to the teenyboppers," while a Sacramento paper reported that Ellington appealed to both the "the nostalgic" and "now people" and that "3 generations [were] impressed." Ellington found delight in the fact that his older fans brought their children along and got them hooked on the Ellington experience. "I'm getting to be like an inheritance, people leave me to their children," he bragged in 1967.

Perhaps during this period of yawning generation gaps in music tastes in the 1960s and 1970s, young people enjoyed Ellington not only because his music changed with the times but also because he did not cast disdainful judgment upon their music. During the band's 1967 Seattle stand, Ellington talked to a reporter about "'the kids' who are getting better with their pop songs," and he usually complimented the Beatles during the numerous instances journalists dropped their name, hoping for an incendiary comment. One enterprising Northern California promoter tried to lure the younger generation to an Ellington show by arguing that Ellington and jazz in general "gave rise to Rock and other forms that have entranced young people." Ellington tried not to cast aspersions at the new happenings on the scene (perhaps he recalled the resistance encountered when he changed the music scene decades previously), and it is likely that young people recognized and appreciated his lack of rigidity and the youthful spirit of musical adventure in his personality. Ellington was restlessly moving, just as they were.[60]

Ellington's propensity for uniting disparate people through force of music and personality inspired a flight of fancy in the *Washington D.C. Afro-American*. European correspondent Ollie Stewart argued that Ellington should be employed to help the cause of world peace during a time of various severe conflicts. On 31 July 1970, the Ellington orchestra played an unprecedented show at Saint Ludovic Bridge at the French-Italian border near Menton, France. For several hours, the border post between the two countries was closed completely as the band played, the first time this had occurred for a concert. The event inspired Stewart to wax rhapsodic about Ellington's diplomatic powers:

> A pity that Duke Ellington isn't invited to perform on the Israeli-Jordan border, or along that Suez Canal, so that peace could be enhanced.
>
> Come to think of it, the same thing would be marvelous along the demilitarized zone between the two [Vietnams]. And it just might be possible [that] foreign armies would pack up and go home.[61]

By the early 1970s, Ellington had successfully presented himself and his music as a vital force during the previous decade, one with cross-generational and cross-racial appeal that probably no one else could claim. His fight against nostalgia, while not entirely victorious, had allowed him to remain a vital creative force in American culture and American history, a constant presence in the jazz and popular-music press, even in rock-oriented magazines. For the remainder of his life, Ellington increasingly and more aggressively brought his vision of American identity, black identity, music, and freedom to the world with an increased schedule of State Department tours.

15

1970s STATE TOURS

Some excerpts from U.S. embassy reports on the Ellington orchestra's thirteen-country State Department–sponsored 1971 Latin American tour:

In the midst of a seeming Russian cultural offensive in Costa Rica and during the tremendous public furor over the establishment of a Russian embassy here, the triumphal appearance of Duke Ellington in San José served as a fine counterpoint.   SAN JOSÉ, Costa Rica

One is accustomed to a great performance from Duke Ellington, but his November concert in Lima may well have been, as one music critic wrote, "the leading artistic event of Lima in 1971"—a year that had the Siberian and Armenian ballets, the Frankfurt Orchestra and Choir, and a good number of excellent chamber music groups.   LIMA, Peru

Following the December 2 concert the Post offered a late reception at the home of the Cultural Affairs Officer. The Duke and almost his entire company attended. In all about 125 persons were present, including Caracas' leading jazz practitioners, jazz aficionados, media representatives, some cultural figures and just plain enthusiasts . . . The Duke was the epitome of cordiality, freely mixing among the guests and, before the evening (morning) was over sitting down at the Steinway to provide a special treat by playing through many of the old favorites.   CARACAS, Venezuela

The impact of Duke Ellington's performances in Nicaragua cannot be overstated. While many in Nicaragua have only a limited exposure to jazz . . . all were impressed by the artistry of the performance and touched by the magnetism of "the Duke." Nicaraguans seem to understand a little bit better what U.S. culture is all about . . . [ellipses in the original] that we're something "alive and now." As one Nicaraguan intellectual remarked after the concert . . . "This marks the beginning of a cultural revolution in Nicaragua." That is doubtful, but Duke Ellington has made his mark here and it's a credit to us all.   MANAGUA, Nicaragua[1]

During the 1970s, the State Department greatly increased Ellington and the orchestra's diplomatic appearances around the world, probably inspired by the immense amount of positive international publicity resulting from Ellington's appearance at the Nixon White House in April 1969. Ellington could be counted on to represent the United States with grace and the consistent support of the idea of "freedom." With the foundation of years of exposure courtesy of Voice of America's jazz broadcasts, Ellington found not just acceptance in Communist and satellite countries, but often rabid enthusiasm that belied official government disdain or censorship of American jazz.

In early 1970, a two-day State Department–sponsored stand by Ellington and the orchestra in Burma ended an eight-year "shut-out" of the United States "in the field of cultural presentations and educational exchange programs," during which time Soviet bloc countries had booked numerous cultural tours.[2] With Burma's proximity to China and its transition in 1962 to a military authoritarian socialist/Marxist government that called itself the Revolutionary Government of the Union of Burma (RGUB), the United States had a great interest in promoting engagement. The Ellington shows almost didn't happen when, in late 1969, Burma's Revolutionary Council felt preoccupied by student unrest and postponed their final decision on approving the concerts until 13 January. This meant the embassy had less than three weeks to assemble logistics for Ellington's arrival on 31 January 1970 at Burma's Mingaladon Airport.

Personally and musically, Ellington found an overwhelming response, both from Burmese audiences and the American diplomatic community. Both shows were filled to capacity with the kinds of audiences the State Department yearned to reach: "high government officials (both civilian and military), rectors, faculty members and university students, press representatives, and music lovers among the intelligensia." On the second night, the seated capacity of 2,045 was exceeded by two hundred to three hundred students on a standing-room-only basis. In a country where students were challenging the authoritarian regime, the U.S. embassy viewed this as an important achievement. For each show, the regime insisted on assigning most of the seats, leaving five hundred for the embassy to distribute. Since most of the government's tickets went to the kinds of Burmese the State Department wanted to reach, they lodged no protest over the arrangement, and some of the U.S. embassy's tickets were distributed to diplomats from Communist satellite countries such as Hungary and Bulgaria. The demand for the thousand nongovernment tickets proved intense, but the Burmese government refused the U.S. embassy's request for an open-air Ellington stadium "public concert" to meet demand. "At this time, the students are restive and the RGUB discourages the congregation of large groups," according to the U.S. embassy's report. The military presence surrounding the show was probably the most intense the band had experienced since their shows in Iraq during a presidential coup in 1963. The backstage area was cordoned off for security purposes, and armed guards were stationed. A different audience reaction than usual greeted the Ellingtonians, according to the embassy's report:

> On the first night, the clapping was desultory and one could see that the orchestra was startled by what they considered a cool response. We explained that Burmese audiences generally do not clap. However, the Secretary of the Minister of Culture was happily patting his foot as he listened—which corresponds to wild enthusiasm in Burma. The second night's performance received much stronger applause, perhaps because there were more students present or perhaps, the Burmese had gotten the message. In any case, the comments from the audience for both performances were enthusiastic.

Ellington's shows in Burma generated loads of positive publicity, some of it independent and some engineered by U.S. influence. For the first time, materials from the United States Information Service were aired on Radio Burma, including "USIS-produced tapes of Ellington music" and two fifteen-minute programs about Ellington "based on USIS written material and using USIS-produced tapes" in Burmese and English. The Ministry of Culture hosted a luncheon for the Ellington orchestra. The *Guardian* newspaper in Burma called the Ellington performances "a welcome goodwill gesture by the United States of America. The very fact that our select audience was entertained by the man who was conferred with the highest honor by the US President [Nixon], should be proof enough of the goodwill the US Government seeks to show to Burma." Nixon's 1969 fete for Ellington was paying diplomatic dividends, and secretary of state William P. Rogers made sure Nixon knew this by sending him a memorandum on the concerts compiled from embassy reports. It concluded with the embassy's contention that Ellington's success represented "a significant breakthrough." In addition, following the Burma shows, Ellington "lost a packet" of money by agreeing to cancel a commercial appearance in Hong Kong in favor of two shows in Vientiane, Laos, at the urging of the State Department. In 1971, Ellington volunteered to perform in Vietnam, underlining his belief that the Vietnam War represented a war fought for the sake of freedom and against Communism, even though most Americans did not support the war at this juncture. No American cultural presentations occurred in Vietnam until the Martha Graham Dance Company performed in Saigon under State Department auspices in 1974.

The real impact of Ellington's first shows in Burma revealed itself when he returned two years later in 1972. Count Basie had visited the country in the interim, and there existed no doubt that Burma's Ministry of Culture would gladly accept an encore of the Ellington tour. Ellington and the orchestra again performed two shows at the same theater in Rangoon, but for the first time in the history of the RGUB, Burmese officials, after some resistance, allowed an American act to perform in Mandalay, Burma's cultural center. Extensive effort by the U.S. embassy and the lucky circumstance of the chairman of security in Mandalay being a jazz buff allowed Ellington and the orchestra to perform at a twenty-thousand-capacity, open-air theater where the regime usually held their own official entertainments, a venue where no foreign act had previously performed. According to the embassy's report, "these negotiations . . . resulted in the establishment of a number of high-level contacts which will be invaluable for future programming."

Once again, in the Burmese style, the audience hardly clapped for the band, but showed their affection after the Mandalay concert when "it [became] necessary to force a path through the thousands of fans who were waiting to shake hands with [Ellington] and shout congratulations and good wishes." In each year since 1970 Burmese interest in American cultural presentations had increased, and the embassy reported that Burmese citizens regularly asked about which cultural attraction the Americans were bringing next. For a country with a military regime, no records or television, and limited motion picture and radio capability, this was viewed as a major achievement by the embassy. A 1972 *Washington Post* article documented how Burma "appears to be relaxing, a tiny bit, the rigid, rigorous and parochial practices of the past decade which have made Burma a loner in world affairs, and stagnant in material progress at home." Besides the allowing of a partial "free market" for farmer's goods and slowing the nationalization of industry, the article also mentioned the Ellington orchestra's presence as evidence: "They were a smash hit." Ellington and his music were again opening doors previously sealed. Yet, as Ellington and the State Department worked hard to open doors by scheduling increased American cultural tours to Southeast Asia in the early 1970s, the Nixon administration simultaneously damaged the image of the United States by ratcheting up the level of secret bombings in Cambodia, Laos, and elsewhere in the area during the same period.

A few months after his initial Burma visit in 1970, Ellington went on another brief state visit to Yugoslavia, a country where Ellington witnessed firsthand the large influence of American jazz through the Voice of America.[3] Yugoslavians had waited impatiently for Ellington for years; a scheduled appearance on his 1963 state tour was cancelled after the Kennedy assassination. The U.S. embassy in Belgrade calculated that "844 column inches of press space were devoted" to the Ellington orchestra's three performances over two days, which "in recent years was only surpassed by the coverage accorded to American space efforts." The Belgrade Radio/TV jazz orchestra welcomed Ellington at the airport, along with "press, radio and TV correspondents, a delegation of Embassy officers as well as local fans." A photo in the State Department files shows Ellington on the tarmac surrounded by journalists wielding movie and still cameras and microphones. When the orchestra was delayed entry into the country because they arrived without visas, Ellington "smilingly took over from [jazz orchestra] leader Vojislav Simic the direction of the pleased Belgrade musicians who performed with such vigor that all activity in the airport terminal including announcements of plane arrivals and departures was forced to a halt."

Ellington played two concerts on his first night in Belgrade, and "despite his obvious fatigue the Duke was prevailed to give two interviews during the short one hour pause between performances." The second performance of the evening aired live on national TV and radio and featured the European premiere of Ellington's forty-minute *New Orleans Suite,* an event difficult to imagine happening on a major American TV network. Both performances featured Ellington telling the audiences "I love you madly" in Serbo-Croatian. The Dubrovnik Summer Festival hosted the band's third appearance in Yugoslavia, the first time a jazz band performed at this "traditionally classical program." Before the Dubrovnik show, Ellington spent two hours with the Yugoslavian and Hungarian press. The most telling moment of his time with the media, according to the embassy's report, happened when:

a question [was] asked by Mr. Nikita PETRAK, the music editor of Zagreb Radio/TV, who inquired whether Ellington knew Willis Conover of VOA. When the Duke responded that he knew Conover personally, Petrak commented that Willis Conover is fondly considered to be the principal tutor and friend of a whole generation of Yugoslav jazz buffs. Petrak went on to say that not only have he and thousands of Yugoslav youth learned and kept abreast of the best in popular music through Mr. Conover's program but for over 15 years he has also been their inspiration and teacher in English. Petrak's spoken (American) English is letter perfect and one can, in fact, easily detect the tonal qualities of Conover's voice.

A handwritten note on the embassy's report stored in State Department files reported that the embassy's account of Ellington's Yugoslavia trip had been "read to Conover's office," possibly for inclusion on his *Music USA* VOA radio show.

The moment served as an example of how much VOA and American jazz had contributed to the cold war struggle against communism. As historian Reinhold Wagnleitner has argued, *Music USA* represented the "most effective propaganda coup" in VOA's history, a show that inspired 1,400 fan clubs in ninety countries. The show's popularity loomed especially large in Eastern Europe.[4] Thanks to VOA, Yugoslavia, a Soviet satellite country led by the Communist dictator Marshal Tito, had thousands, probably tens of thousands, fans of American jazz, a forbidden currency in the Soviet Union. Conover never spoke of foreign policy on *Music USA,* and young Yugoslavians' support of jazz was not directly tied to a support of American policy. But like internationally touring American musicians such as Ellington and Armstrong, Conover's show balanced the worldwide image of overwhelming and sometimes ill-used American power with examples of American creativity, soul, and grace. Culture did not represent the most important weapon in the eventual American cold war victory, but it played a powerful role. Through the promotion and display of American music and genius, American ideas of political and artistic freedom seeped into authoritarian, Communist, and socialist-led countries, and an interest in American life was nurtured.

The Ellington orchestra's visit to the Soviet Union (USSR) during September and October 1971 marked their most important and publicized State Department tour ever. It occurred during the efforts of President Nixon (a key supporter of Senator Joseph McCarthy's over-the–top anti-Communist efforts of the 1950s) to establish détente at the height of the cold war between the United States and the Soviet Union and China. The announcement of the tour made the front page of the *New York Times,* and the *Washington D.C. Star* linked the Soviets' acceptance of Ellington (who they ruled out for a tour in 1962) to Soviet counterstrategy in response to Nixon's recent friendly overtures, including the announcement of a visit to

Communist China. Before the tour began, Nixon also announced an upcoming trip to the Soviet Union. The *Chicago Tribune*'s Moscow correspondent reported that Ellington's arrival was being "seen as a big shot in the arm for the [cultural] exchange program . . . [which] serve[s] as one barometer of the overall state of Soviet-American relations. The current situation, on that standard, has not been good." A six-month American freeze after the Soviet-led invasion of Czechoslovakia in 1968, a cancellation of a 1970 Bolshoi Ballet American tour because of Jewish Defense League protests, and a currently unfulfilled exchange contract between the U.S. and USSR were cited as evidence for this observation.

Other jazz figures preceded Ellington to the USSR, including Benny Goodman (1962), Earl Hines (1966), and Charles Lloyd (1967), but Ellington was the most famous single American cultural figure to tour the country yet. The *Fresno Bee* voiced "one misgiving" about the tour. They characterized Goodman as a "notably taciturn fellow whose stage talk, if any, was brief." Ellington, on the other hand, "has a penchant for wry, elaborate, ornamental, mock-pretentious, multi-syllabic patter between numbers." They warned the Russians to "start prepping their most facile and sophisticated interpreter." Ellington, as usual, experienced no trouble communicating: his Soviet audience, prepared for his appearance by years of VOA jazz broadcasts and expensive illegal bootleg recordings, gave him a reception of Beatlemania proportions wherever he went.[5]

It took several months to nail down logistics for the tour. Originally, either Ella Fitzgerald or Sarah Vaughan was penciled in to accompany Ellington and the orchestra, but the idea was quickly dropped. In early negotiations during January 1971, Cress Courtney, Ellington's personal manager, told State Department personnel that Ellington initially felt hesitant to tour the Soviet Union "because he's such an anti-communist." When Alla A. Butrova, head of the Western European and American section of the USSR Ministry of Culture, voiced skepticism about bringing Ellington to her country, the State Department's director of cultural presentations in Europe noted that "Duke Ellington was held in particularly high esteem by the President."[6] Once again, Ellington's birthday appearance at the White House lent additional status to his presence.

The State Department, mindful of the tensions between Ellington and the Associated Booking Agency (ABC) during the 1963 state tour, wondered if they should draw up a contract with them or with Ellington directly. Ellington, ABC, and the State Department eventually agreed upon a rate of $19,000 per week (almost $100,000 in today's dollars), for four 140-minute concerts and one guaranteed nontravel, nonperforming day per week. The

State Department also paid $10,856 in pretour expenses. Two extra shows booked during the tour in Moscow earned the band another $18,000. Altogether, the Ellington orchestra played twenty-two sold-out shows in five locales over thirty-three days for a combined audience of 126,000— more shows per week than the original contract called for. ABC informed the State Department that, on his last European tour, Ellington earned $26,500 per week, which they felt showed "he is sincere in his desire to serve." With the added shows, the orchestra actually pulled in a little more than $25,000 per week. Actually, they would have made that much if the Internal Revenue Service did not insist on taking the contract's final payment of $16,000 to help defray over $100,000 in back taxes they claimed Duke Ellington, Inc., owed them. It seemed particularly crass to garnish Ellington's wages when he was working on behalf of his country.

Perhaps Ellington's "desire to serve" was best demonstrated by the fact that he and the orchestra consistently played much longer shows than contracted for, of anywhere between 180 and 210 minutes, some of the longest concerts the band ever performed. The USSR state-run promoter Goskontsert paid most tour expenses, including airfare and hotels, as well as fees of $1,000 per show to the United States and $2,000 to the Soviet Union. Such conditions did not keep Goskonsert from making "a great deal of money out of the tour," according to the tour's State Department escort officer Joseph A. Presel. The State Department's share of money from the concerts came to $73,111, including the fees from Goskontsert, reducing the net cost of the Ellington tour for the U.S. government to just $58,812—an absolute bargain considering the wealth of positive international publicity garnered.[7]

Before the tour, minor complications surfaced. On 2 August 1971, a Soviet delegation attended the opening for a four-week Ellington stand at New York City's Rainbow Grill. According to a local paper, they recognized Ellington's biggest hits, but, perhaps because of Nixon's upcoming trip to Communist China, "they showed no emotion when the Duke introduced his 'Afro-Eurasian Eclipse' by quoting Marshall McLuhan's recent conclusion that 'the whole world is going Oriental.'" Something else bothered the delegation even more. Soon thereafter, Vladimir Golovin, Goskontsert's deputy director, contacted the State Department to object to "the body gyrations of [Ellington] vocalist Tony Watkins." The department informed Courtney that "Mr. Golovin has no objections to Watkins performing as long as his body movements are controlled . . . [his] major concern is that if the body gyrations are not markedly reduced, Soviet audiences will respond unfavorably and the Soviet press will be critical, thus jeopardizing the success of the whole tour."[8]

Another complication surrounding the tour was that during the summer of 1971, Ellington made certain personal dietary requests. In the last years of his life, he drank six to seven glasses of Coca Cola per day, with several spoonfuls of sugar and fresh lime or lemon juice added, and he felt it necessary to continue this energy-enhancing regimen on his Soviet tour. Coca Cola had not yet arrived in the Soviet Union, but the U.S. embassy in Moscow offered to supply fifteen cases of it for his exclusive use (not the orchestra's). They warned him that the embassy commissary frequently ran out of sugar, and that limes were impossible to procure in the USSR, but lemons were commonly available. Ellington would have to reimburse the embassy's expenses for these items "upon arrival," since such beverage requests stretched "diplomatic customs regulations." Ellington also demanded a daily steak on tour, the central item in his main daily meal. Golovin worried that steak might not be available in all five of the cities the band performed in, and the U.S. embassy informed Ellington that "steak in the Soviet Union does not taste like steak in the United States. And that is one thing the Embassy cannot provide the Duke. Cokes and lemon, yes; American steak, no." The steak issue would return to haunt the State Department during the tour.[9]

For their initial descent into the Soviet Union, every member of the Duke Ellington orchestra flew first class for the first time, on Ellington's orders. Ellington had Courtney communicate to the State Department his insistence that he "does not want to arrive in Moscow in a segregated group." "He said he didn't want any distinction between himself in first-class and the band in a different class," recalled band aide Robert L. Jones. "They were all first-class . . . it was the only time he ever mentioned something like that, and he himself flew first-class all the time and nobody cares. Actually, to the guys, he was first-class, that was their kind of attitude." The gesture demonstrated that, for Ellington, this represented a different State Department tour than previous trips. He had long communicated his antipathy towards communism. While he was magnanimous as usual to Soviet fans and engaged in no political grandstanding on the tour, he wanted his performances and presence to embody the differences between what he viewed as the freedom and democracy of his home country and the current situation in the Soviet Union. As he had many times throughout his career, Ellington communicated by example, rather than more confrontational methods.[10]

In his tour report, escort officer Joseph A. Presel touched upon some of the reasons why the Ellington orchestra proved so popular and why Soviet leaders had been resistant to and threatened by jazz for decades:

The US could send performing seals and get away with it, so great is the desire of the Soviet population to experience things American. The Ellington orchestra operated within the atmosphere that those considerations create. It had two other attributes, though, that set it still further apart from other, similar ventures. First, it was jazz, and second it was historic. Those who govern the Soviet Union have always had an ambivalent attitude towards jazz, one that mostly treated it as a phenomenon, and an undesirable one at that, of the bourgeois world, rather than as an expression of the oppressed working class in capitalist society. It has always been hard for jazz to be performed in the USSR.

Life magazine noted that Stalin banned the music during most of his reign, though a couple of American jazz bands, including one featuring Sidney Bechet, performed in the Soviet Union during the mid-1920s.[11] The principal reason the power of jazz loomed threateningly to the leadership of a Communist country went beyond the ideological and political explanations offered by Presel: the music promoted avid freedom of expression, not just musical, but also sexual, racial, and social. It radiated individual, unpredictable, unquantifiable creativity, on the bandstand and on the dance floor. Its foundation lay partly in the religious roots of the spiritual and of gospel music. These were all forbidden properties in a totalitarian state. These qualities also marked the reasons jazz was so threatening to many whites and blacks in the United States during the first decades of the twentieth century, as Ellington well knew from experience.

Upon arrival in Moscow, the orchestra was greeted by Alexei Batushev, a physicist and the head of the Moscow Jazz Club, who gave Ellington a bear hug, and "40 other diehard jazz fans eager for a glimpse of one of their long-time favorites of the American music world." One of those fans yelled at Ellington: "We've been waiting for you for centuries!" Ellington told the assembled fans and press at the airport that "These are guys who've been listening to what we've been doing for a long time, so you feel like it's all the same family, the same tribe." Though almost no Western recordings were officially available in the Soviet Union, VOA had made Soviet audiences familiar with the Ellington repertoire. One fan at the Moscow airport said he had taped five hundred Ellington songs over a twenty-year period. A relatively small number of fans gathered for Ellington's initial arrival, but the Soviet press, controlled by the cautious government, had provided "almost no publicity" of the Ellington tour yet. The jazz grapevine in the Soviet Union, however, had spread the word and "tickets to the concerts [were] already much sought by Russians with foreign friends and tastes." In Leningrad, the tour's first official stop, as Ellington recalled in his autobiography, "we are met by a big band that marches across the airfield toward us playing Dixieland jazz, with trombones sliding, clarinets smearing off, and all the musicians blowing in the traditional manner."[12]

Audience reaction to Ellington started ecstatically and stayed that way. Leningrad audiences packed a 4,200-seat venue for five nights straight. Tickets were priced at five rubles ($5.50—almost $30 in today's dollars) for orchestra seats, and about $4 for balcony seats, with black-market prices reaching $50 or more per ticket, since demand greatly exceeded quantity. Every night, hundreds surrounded the venue hoping to scalp tickets. This ticket situation stayed constant during Ellington's run in the Soviet Union. In Kiev, tickets proved so hard to procure that members of the local police band wore their uniforms in order to sneak into a show. An "American official" initially expressed alarm about the heightened police presence until one of them explained the situation. The audience, "predominantly a young crowd and, by Soviet standards, quite fashionably dressed [with] a few midiskirts, turtleneck sweaters, wide ties, and bright colors sprinkled through[out]," demanded forty-five to sixty minutes of encores nightly and stood and applauded for ten minutes or more after the band finally left the stage. Even Communist party officials were witnessed smiling and clapping along. This kind of behavior became common on the tour but reached a height on the last night in Leningrad, when Ellington and the band played an hour and a half of encores. Circumstances like these formed the main reason why Ellington played at least three and sometimes close to four hours per show.

When asked by United Press International if the Leningrad audience "was one of the more enthusiastic" he'd ever seen, Ellington replied, "Absolutely. Only more so." Trumpeter Harold (Money) Jackson, who later in the tour sang and played "Hello Dolly" when USSR fans asked for something by Louis Armstrong, agreed with his boss: "It's great to play for Soviet audiences. They go wild." Ellington also found himself impressed by the fact that "an awful lot of young people" were requesting his autograph. Although Ellington performed esoteric material on the tour, such as "Fife," "Happy Reunion," "La Belle Plus Africaine," and the full version of *Harlem* (dedicated on the first night to the U.S. ambassador), Soviet audiences were most excited about the band's old hits, and to the orchestra's chagrin, the repertoire changed little from night to night. Russian crowds also appreciated tenor saxophonist Paul Gonsalves's improvisations on Russian songs entitled "Moscow Nights" and "Dark Eyes." Escort officer Presel felt that Ellington should have showcased more of his newer, more challenging pieces in order to inspire Russian jazz composers, as he felt Alvin Ailey did in the recent tour of his ballet company. After Presel pointed this out, Ellington included "more modern pieces." Ellington nightly closed the Russian shows with his solo piano version of Billy Strayhorn's "Lotus Blossom." Just as in his mentioning of Strayhorn at the 1969 White House birthday party, Ellington seemed to want to ensure that his late friend and musical partner retained a key presence during the most momentous events of his career.[13]

The State Department seemed particularly excited about afterhours jam sessions, some official and some not, between Soviet musicians and the Ellington orchestra.[14] On the afternoon of 16 September, an official jam session sponsored by the Leningrad Union of Composers occurred at the Dom Druzhby (the "Friendship House" of the Institute of Soviet-American Relations). This represented the kind of "generally stiff and structured 'warm meetings' which the Soviet officialdom has become so adept at staging over the years," according to the embassy's report.

But, as a State Department telegram noted in detail, "a more important informal session" transpired that same night after Ellington's show at the Kamerton ("Tuning Fork") Jazz Club. Unlike the other session, permission for this show was sought through U.S. embassy, not Soviet, channels. When Presel brought up the idea to road manager Mercer Ellington, he "enthusiastically" agreed to it. The event was held in "strict secrecy" with supposedly only club members attending, and Ellington's musicians were only told the location ten minutes before their arrival. Despite such measures, 150 people packed the club, including "several prominent Soviet jazz musicians . . . the head of the Leningrad Composers Union . . . Life and AP photographers . . . and watch dogs from the Dom Druzhby and Gostkontsert." They saw an impromptu seventeen-piece jazz band, almost evenly composed of Soviet jazzers and Ellington band members, perform. Presel found the show "remarkable because . . . the Ellington band members and Soviet jazz musicians [were joined] as equals, because of the sophistication of the Soviet musicians and the depth of their knowledge of jazz . . . and because the [Ellington] band found it fun." Over a hundred people waited outside, watching the proceedings for hours through sidewalk-level windows. When Ellington arrived, he was promptly "caught in [the] press of [the] enthusiastic crowd, and left almost immediately. Kamerton members said later they were 'mortified' by the incident and hoped Duke was not offended." The next day, U.S. embassy officials were informed that the club "would be made inactive for at least a year" for scheduling the jam session sans official permission. The man who headed the Dixieland band that greeted the Ellingtonians at the airport "is also scheduled for at least an oral dressing down for not requesting prior permission." The main organizer of the Kamerton jam session, Vladimir Khavkin, "twenty-six, Jewish . . . [with] a full beard and rather wild bushy hair," was assigned the task of submitting himself to Soviet officials because he was the organization's "expendable man." "The police all know me, because I am a suspicious person," he told State Department officials. "I have friends in Europe, America, and Israel and have therefore been photographed, bugged, and taken in for questioning many times." Such was the price of dissent in the USSR; these incidents during the Ellington tour demonstrated that Soviet government officials were prepared to allow only so much freedom without sanction.

State Department files document an additional official session at the Dom Druzhby in Moscow near the end of the tour. A big band composed of both American and Soviet musicians, including electric guitar and flugelhorn, offered several impromptu numbers. Ellington performed a new song on piano, announcing it by saying: "I have composed a new song for you called 'My Love.'" He later joined the group on balalaika, a present from the Soviet musicians.

Soviet authorities tended to discourage, or at least insist on closely scrutinizing, any contacts between Soviet and American citizens, especially musicians. When Mercer Ellington planned to accept an invitation for him and other Ellington band members to witness a rehearsal of the Minsk Philharmonic, a Goskonsert representative told him "that they had checked with the appropriate parties and that Mercer was mistaken." According to the embassy report, the representative claimed that Mercer had been "led . . . down the garden path. Mercer, a man of the world if ever there was one, somewhat heatedly let Goskonsert know in no uncertain terms that if anyone was trying to fool anyone else, it was Goskonsert, not the Minsk musician" who invited the band. Mercer, his father, and other band members ended up viewing and enjoying the rehearsal. As B. H. Klosson of the U.S. embassy recalled, guards, police, or Goskonsert interpreters and employees were ubiquitous at Ellington shows, particularly at theater doors after performances, to keep social and musical fraternization between Soviets and Americans to a minimum. "In Minsk, the lobby of the stage entrance was almost wall-to-wall with 'goons,'" Klosson reported. While Goskonsert officials assured U.S. officials that security personnel were just "simple employees of the theater," embassy employees and some Russian civilians present felt that some of the "goons" were KGB officers. However, as Klosson noted, such attempts at intimidation and isolation did not curtail Ellington and the band's efforts to establish contacts with Soviets "in every city" they visited. Ellington "talked and met and jammed with Soviets." More importantly, the State Department encouraged such activity, which served as a counterpoint to the Ellington orchestra's extensive 1963 state tour through the Middle and Near East, when the band complained that they only encountered elites. In the Soviet case, and in the band's subsequent dates in Eastern Europe, "it was the Communist elite that that U.S. officials were hoping to bypass" in order to reach the "man in the street," according to historian Penny Von Eschen.[15]

Presel found that "the Soviets were scared of Ellington, both personally and because . . . of his relationship with the President, and because of the Duke's importance in the United States." He felt that the announcement of Nixon's upcoming visit to the USSR exacerbated this fear and the accompanying desire to do nothing to offend Ellington in his travels. Presel also felt that such circumstances ensured a smoother tour for the Ellingtonians, resulting in far fewer inconveniences, such as the lost luggage, stolen costumes, last-minute scheduling, and bad pianos that plagued Earl Hines's 1966 Soviet tour. But Presel kept the true identity of the object of the Soviets' fear a secret: "I saw no need to enlighten the Soviets who accompanied us as to Ellington's true nature: that he is a very thoughtful 72-year-old gentleman who wants basically to be left alone to compose and play music and have someone—me in this case—to whom he could bitch for an hour or so every few days." Presel also remarked that "Ellington was very happy to get mad at the Soviets when I asked him to; it was very effective." Ellington seemed to have no trouble occasionally venting frustration at the Soviets for his own reasons as well, without government intervention.[16]

Tensions of a different kind arose from the introduction of the issues of race on the tour. Many articles in the Soviet press dwelled on the subject of Ellington as a black composer, as if to stress his status as an oppressed minority and cast aspersions on American treatment of minorities while praising one of them. "The interviewers were by no means knowledgeable about jazz and were much more interested in getting Ellington to admit that he was a black composer than they were in his musical accomplishments," recalled Presel. At such times, Ellington pointed out the fact that he had received the Presidential Medal of Freedom, America's highest civilian honor, "and that he was an 'American' composer. He was uninterested, he said, in people's color and assumed they were indifferent to his. The Soviet journalists normally found this a baffling line of thought." The embassy reported what occurred when the Ukrainian Composers Union in Kiev explored the same tack with Ellington present:

It was a fascinating mixture of proclamations of brotherhood and slinging of words. Here was a self-styled rugged individualist of the American music world meeting with composers who had made their careers rocking no boats in the sea of socialist realism. Sparks were inevitable, and when one of the Ukrainians suggested that the Duke as a "successful Negro musician and composer" really represented the product of his environment, Ellington flared. Every man must play his own music, he said, and if he tries to imitate others he is a failure. He, Ellington, had succeeded by creating his own distinct music, and he owed his success to no one and nothing but his own hard work and creativity. And furthermore, to say that there is such a thing as Negro jazz is simply ignorant. There is only jazz, and every musician plays it in his own style, if he is genuine, regardless of skin color. Neatly mousetrapped, the Ukrainians all nodded in pious acknowledgement of the truth in this, and the meeting ended soon after with words of brotherhood and an exchange of gifts.[17]

Ellington's difference of opinion with these observers represented a declaration of the musical and racial freedom he had fought for and won in the United States, a freedom that clearly did not exist in the Soviet Union. It also signified his broad rejection of any kind of categorization. As was true on his previous State Department–sponsored tours, especially in 1963 and 1966, Ellington was not about to allow others, particularly Communists, use his race to bash his country and its way of life or call into question why he had achieved so much success.

The Soviet press gave the Ellington tour unprecedented coverage. While the Soviet media often interviewed foreign artists, "published results are generally woefully small," according to the embassy's report. "If an article does result, it is generally well after the performing arts group has left town—the Soviets don't believe in free advertising for foreign groups." This established model didn't apply on the Ellington tour. The embassy counted nine "favorable" reviews printed while Ellington remained in the country, with some of them classified as "raves." Most impressive was a large spread across a third of the page entitled "Orchestra of Virtuosos" in *Pravda,* the largest circulation newspaper in the Soviet Union. Jacob Beam, the U.S. ambassador to the Soviet Union, wrote in a telegram to secretary of state William P. Rogers that this marked the first time "*Pravda* has even acknowledged the existence in the country of a U.S. performing arts group." Lavish compliments were offered by the review, as well as this comment about Ellington's *Harlem,* a perennial feature on the tour: "full of melancholy, sadness and the rebelliousness of the Negro ghetto." This article was followed by a piece called "Duke Ellington: I Love You!" in *Sovetskaya Rossiya*, one of Russia's most conservative papers. "This, from the organ of the Party Central Committee, was heady stuff indeed!" exulted the embassy's report.[18]

North American press reaction also proved voluminous and telling. Aside from syndicated reviews of the concerts, the Ellington tour also inspired many pieces on editorial pages that linked him to the hopes and anxieties of the cold war. A Canadian paper noted the "delirious reaction" to Ellington in the Soviet Union and viewed it as "a further reminder that not all Russians are cast in the same mould as the bureaucratic and diplomatic zealots who speak and act for them." The editorial page of the *Topeka (KS) State Journal* commented that "the international language of music—especially lighthearted jazz—is a good way to take minds off sober world problems. We might even dare hope it is a 'disarming' exchange of pleasantries." In an editorial called "'Da' for the Duke," the *Hartford (CT) Times* remarked that "it is the good fortune of the United States that it has other things to export besides computers, office machines and automobiles . . . we can safely say the Duke is one of our superior exports." A *Schenectady Gazette* editorial on "Duke Power" pointed out how many of the concerts were sold out early, "attesting to the popularity of American jazz in a country whose officialdom frowns on it."[19]

To the chagrin of Ellington, the State Department, and the Soviets, the story that dominated American media coverage of the tour centered on the steak controversy.[20] "Duke Can't Cut It on Russian Steaks," ran a typical headline in the 20 September edition of the *Los Angeles Times*. The article claimed Ellington "was unable to eat Russian steak and was losing five pounds a day" and that the tour was in possible jeopardy.

The truth proved less dramatic, but underreported. As the U.S. embassy and Goskonsert warned, Soviet steaks were far from Ellington's usual standard. Just a few days into the tour, he requested steaks from Reuben's, one of his favorite restaurants in New York, shipped at his own expense. Pan Am Airlines flew them from New York to Moscow gratis. Russian customs officials held up and ruined the first shipment for lack of an international certificate of origin. A second batch caught up with Ellington in Minsk, the second stop on the tour. While State Department personnel noticed that the steaks helped the "Ellington morale," they also reported that his health was never in "jeopardy." When Dr. Logan, Ellington's personal physician and close friend, visited the tour in Rostov, he found that Ellington had actually gained five pounds. Even before the steak controversy, Ellington had voiced his enjoyment of Russian food on the tour, especially borscht and caviar. But steak represented his staple food, and he missed it, though he also told the Associated Press that "there is nothing like a cheeseburger." "While admiring Duke's patriotism and taste," Secretary of State Rogers, in a priority telegram, let the U.S. embassy in Moscow know that the international publicity resulting from such remarks inspired McDonalds and Gallagher Steak Houses to contact the State Department with offers to ship cheeseburgers and steak to Ellington, supposedly in hopes of gaining publicity. Rogers instructed the embassy to ask Ellington to avoid making food-related comments. Later, Ellington's friend H. Robert Udkoff visited the tour and, to Ellington's delight, taught Russian chefs how to make American cheeseburgers.

The State Department attempted to find out who leaked the incorrect information about Ellington's health. The news stories referenced "U.S. officials," but the department determined that it must have been one of the American "hangers-on" in Ellington's entourage. While the State Department, including the secretary of state, were clearly unhappy about the publicity over the steak controversy, it is also true that a memo written by the director of cultural presentations before the story was leaked to the American press explored the possibilities of exploiting Ellington's culinary displeasure:

> Jokingly, if we wanted to embarrass the Soviets a little it would have been tempting to suggest to Reuben's that they advertise Reuben's steaks going to Duke Ellington in Russia. It was not suggested. But Reuben's is the eatery of a lot of New York columnists, and Reuben's would not be concerned about foreign relations or diplomatic delicacies—only Reuben's delicacies. Headline: Duke Only Likes American Steaks.

Ellington, in keeping with his communist conspiracy beliefs and fears, blamed the rumors on "someone in Washington working for the opposition." He also believed that his rooms were bugged and photographically surveillanced while in the Soviet Union. Musician/arranger Aaron Bridgers recalled Ellington telling him that he bowed out of politeness to potential eavesdroppers whenever entering his Soviet hotel rooms.[21]

Luckily, the press either did not pick up on or chose not to report on various alcoholic and sexual shenanigans engaged in by band members. In a handwritten note composed during the tour, Presel reported that "I circle on the black edge of catastrophe all the time but we've avoided it so far . . . both alcoholic and sexual frustrations appear to be overcome sufficiently often that none of the band has gone round the bend . . . in fact morale is better than I feared." In his more formal tour report, Presel marveled at the band's "remarkable ingenuity in contriving to supply themselves with both [sexual and alcoholic] commodities despite all of the difficult conditions that obtain in the USSR. I am in awe of the band's abilities in these areas." The band particularly objected to the "ubiquitous little old ladies" that handled room keys on each floor of their hotels, thereby making it difficult to sneak guests into their rooms. An English businessman living in the band's Moscow hotel complained to the *Washington Post* of "a lot of parties" late at night. Somehow the tour avoided scandal, sometimes by a small margin, according to Presel. One of his favorite memories in this regard featured a Goskonsert official objecting to two local girls riding the band's bus in Leningrad. The official objected "bitterly" to their presence and said: "I don't mind people who aren't in the band on the bus, but why do they have to pick the two people who are well known as local prostitutes? It's very uncultured!"[22]

Living conditions for Ellington and the band were actually quite rough much of the time in the Soviet Union. They frequently complained of being cold in their hotel rooms. Udkoff remembered Ellington composing in the bathroom with a hot shower constantly running so the steam would keep him warm while he finished a commission for a post-USSR concert piece in Jacksonville, Florida. As usual on Soviet tours, everyday staples in America like soap, hair conditioner, pens, film, and razors were difficult to procure. Aside from the steak controversy, food often presented problems for the band. Presel felt the problems may have been purposeful. Not only did food usually arrive "cold, delayed and unattractive," but often the senior Goskonsert representative failed to guarantee "that restaurants stayed open late enough to ensure that the group got a hot meal after the show." While he could never prove it, Presel believed that the head Goskonsert contact "was spending less than the budgeted [five rubles] per day per man and was pocketing the difference. It would not surprise me either to be told that he had a good sideline going in selling Ellington buttons and records and the jazz brochures," which were supplied by the State Department for Soviet fans. The band's hotels generally had no room service. Food problems were not made easier for the State Department by the fact that no one had told them until arrival that the Ellington orchestra had two vegetarians and two diabetics controlling their insulin through diet. These four band members endured a particularly difficult culinary experience during the tour. A *Washington Post* reporter concluded that "Ellington and his men seem to have survived the Soviet Union rather than thrived." When he went to see the band at breakfast in Moscow one morning "he found that almost half the men had gone to the American embassy to see the doctor there."[23]

Ticket problems also surfaced in Moscow, the tour's last stop.[24] The

State Department discovered that only eight hundred of the 4,400 seats for the band's four shows went on sale to the public. The majority of seats were assigned to "middle and lower level party functionaries" by orders of the Fourth Department of the Party Central Committee. Music editors at Soviet newspapers received no tickets and the Moscow Composers Union only got two. Such were the perils of Goskonsert's direct connection to the Soviet government. As a result, long, all-night lines of Muscovites gathered at the Teatr Estrady hoping to score tickets, and the militia was called out to break up the lines. The State Department felt this approach emanated from the Soviets' long-term unwillingness to permit "good exposure for American performing arts groups" in Moscow, "the seat of government." The Soviet government wanted to control the audience and perhaps dampen enthusiasm at the shows for Ellington. With many members of the international press present in Moscow, they did not wish to provide a ready platform that demonstrated how hugely popular an American artist could be in the Soviet Union.

Ultimately, because of the "general scandal" and uproar over the lack of Moscow tickets, Goskonsert "made a late and unprecedented request" to the American embassy for extra Ellington shows in Moscow. The U.S. cultural affairs officer in Moscow agreed, but stipulated that the shows take place in a much larger venue than the Estrady, such as the Lushniki Sports Palace, which seated nearly ten thousand and had never hosted an American act. Golovin, deputy director of Goskonsert, replied: "Impossible." He told the embassy that the Sports Palace was currently laying down ice for future hockey matches. The embassy responded: "Melt the ice." Golovin again claimed this was "impossible," but, as the State Department crowed in the official tour report, "Goskonsert blinked" and "the ice melted."

Presel, in his tour report, wrote about what he viewed as the significance of the Sports Palace shows:

> Despite the total lack of advertisement, the hall was sold out for both concerts. While it meant much more work for the band, it was worth a great deal to experience the Soviets coming to us to ask us to perform more, to expose still larger numbers to Ellington's art. It made up for a lot of no-saying that is a constant feature of Soviet officialdom on these tours. Obviously they had so badly miscalculated the pressure for tickets that they had to give in. It was extremely good for our morale.

But not for the band's morale. They registered their "intense disgust" at the arrangement, which took away days they would have had off. Even Ellington had to be "worked on" by Presel and Mercer Ellington before he acceded. The $9,000 fee per show, one of the band's biggest ever paydays, must have helped convince him, especially after the IRS had garnished $16,000 of the band's salary. Another extra show in Moscow occurred when the Protestant chaplain of the U.S. embassy asked Ellington to perform a Sacred Concert before a private audience of about two hundred international diplomats at Spaso House. The choir consisted of hastily assembled embassy employees and their families, rehearsed by Tony Watkins, the band vocalist whose body movements had so upset Soviet officials in New York City.

Most involved viewed Ellington's Soviet tour as an unprecedented success. Within a month following it, he had received letters of thanks and congratulation from both President Nixon ("a job well done") and his Democratic rival in the 1968 election, Senator Hubert H. Humphrey ("America is even more in your debt"). Ellington's influence in the Soviet Union outlasted his presence. After he left, a leading radio and TV figure in the Soviet Union devoted two of his programs to American jazz, particularly Ellington, a rare and probably unprecedented occurrence in the Soviet media. Eight months after the Ellington tour, the Soviet Union welcomed the Jones-Lewis orchestra, "the first . . . strictly contemporary, innovative [American] jazz" group allowed to tour the country.

Ellington told many interviewers that his time in the Soviet Union had inspired his writing. "Anybody who writes music, plays music, has a sincere interest in music wants to come to Russia, particularly the people who write music I'm sure, they all want to come here to see if breathing the same air that those great composers breathed might help them a little bit," he told an interviewer for Radio Moscow during the tour. "This is really the plateau of music." During the broadcast, he mentioned Tchaikovsky, Rimsky-Korsakov, Shostakovich, and Rachmaninoff. During shows in 1972, he played a piece called "Moscow Metro."[25]

Ellington's multilayered vision of freedom and the various struggles that he, the band, and State Department officials encountered during the tour had provided a sharp contrast to the domineering presence of the Soviet government. The tour helped expose the limits of what the closed society of the Soviet government could shield from their own people. Ellington had made a strong impact, the strongest that any American artist had yet made in the Soviet Union. In a 1972 interview with the *New York Times,* Ellington reminisced about meeting audience members who had traveled to see the band from as far as Mongolia and the Baltics, and how he had brought back "three truckloads" of presents from Soviet citizens. "The concerts ran [for] hours but not a person moved out of a chair the whole time," he told them. "How often in a lifetime do you get 24 audiences like that?"[26]

In the month after their last Moscow concert, the Ellington orchestra toured seventeen European countries, including the Soviet satellite states of Poland (where Dizzy Gillespie guested with the band), Yugoslavia, and Hungary, under the billing of "American Jazz Week in Eastern Europe." Two days after their last European date in Barcelona, the band began a twenty-four-day Latin American tour with a show in Rio de Janeiro on 16 November 1971. Once again, the seventy-two-year-old Ellington embarked upon a schedule that would have exhausted most people but seemed renewing for him.

Ellington's 1971 Latin American tour operated as a cooperative venture between private promoter Alejandro Szterenfeld and the State Department, with both parties contributing to the payment of the Ellington orchestra. This reflected "sweeping changes" in the cultural presentations programs enacted in 1970. In an effort to cut costs, State Department managers insisted on "greater private-sector involvement and more commercial pick-ups" for the tours. For the government's money, each American embassy along the tour's path received a dozen show tickets and a guarantee of fifty to a hundred inexpensive tickets reserved for students, the department's favored target audience. All concert programs were contracted to list Ellington appearing "with the cooperation of the United States Department of State" or "under the patronage of his excellency the American Ambassador." Under the terms of the initial contract, State Department sponsorship was noted in advance in five cities: Bogata, Colombia; Lima, Peru; Montevideo, Uruguay; Santiago, Chile; and Quito, Ecuador. In these cities, net proceeds were split between local sponsors and the State Department. For the other seven cities on the tour (in Argentina, Brazil, Mexico, and Venezuela), advance publicity carried no mention of State Department involvement, and they would not financially benefit from the shows. Foreign policy historian Penny Von Eschen noted that State Department sponsorship went unadvertised mainly in countries with a recent history of difficult relations with the United States, and surmised that this was done because "the raging critiques of the American war in Vietnam, on top of resentment of the ubiquitous American imperial presence, would make State Department association a liability" in those countries. Years later, Mercer Ellington commented that "he and other band members had concerns about being used by the State Department" on this tour. After the initial contracts were signed, shows were added in Costa Rica, Nicaragua, Panama, and Puerto Rico, for a total of thirteen countries in twenty-four days. In typical Ellingtonian fashion, the band endured back-to-back dates in Monterrey, Mexico, and Chicago over the nights of 10 and 11 December 1971, followed by consecutive shows in Muncie, Indiana, and New York City.[27]

The State Department paid less for the Latin American tour and seemed to get less in return. Not that they minded. Unlike the Soviet shows, most of the Latin American dates did not sell out. But the embassy reports tended to share a valedictory tone: young people were usually well represented, Ellington's press conference skills and patience led to uniformly good publicity, Ellington and the band regularly attended embassy-sponsored after-show parties targeting elites and students, many of the countries' television and radio stations broadcasted USIS programs featuring Ellington, and press reviews of Ellington shows proved universally positive. Though not mentioned in State Department cable traffic, the tour passed through some of the darker regions of American foreign policy during the Nixon administration. President Anastasio Somoza, one of the most brutal and repressive of the dictators supported worldwide by the United States, attended Ellington's show in Managua, Nicaragua. The Ellington orchestra also visited Chile, where, two years later, elected socialist leader Salvador Allende was overthrown and killed in a coup that the CIA, and quite possibly Nixon, had a hand in.[28]

By the time Ellington returned from an extensive Asian tour in February 1972, he had visited over forty countries during the preceding five months, many under State Department auspices, leaving behind hundreds of thousands of satisfied ticket holders and dozens of adulatory State Department embassy reports. He had earned acceptance from both major American political parties as an important, though unofficial, American diplomat. The letters from American citizens and representatives during the 1950s and 1960s protesting the idea of the U.S. government sponsoring jazz musicians abroad formed a distant and nonrecurring memory.[29] No one questioned anymore the idea of jazz as a worthy ambassador of the United States, even when the State Department began sponsoring shows by more controversial maverick musicians such as Ornette Coleman and Charles Mingus during the 1970s. If anything, State Department officials hoped that Coleman and Mingus's Eastern European audiences would pick up on the sense of rebellion these performers radiated. While Ellington would continue to tour relentlessly as long as he was physically able, including a couple additional short State Department tours, the last two years of his life yielded fewer distinguished compositions and performances than usual. Though still quite active, Ellington was finally beginning to lose energy.

16

FINAL DAYS

Prelude

During 17–21 July 1972, the University of Wisconsin hosted an unprecedented five-day Duke Ellington Festival, the first time a major university had devoted so much time to an event honoring a figure in popular music.[1] It followed the university's awarding of an honorary Doctor of Music degree to Ellington the year before. The festival featured Ellington and the orchestra performing five concerts, including a Sacred Concert, and various musicians' workshops led by Ellington band members. Ellington taught two master classes, and students came from as far as Switzerland, Brazil, and Uganda to attend the event.

Though honors were bestowed upon him at an increasing pace in his last years and his publicity constantly touted him as "the world's most honored musician," Ellington seemed uncomfortable being honored in Madison, as a documentary film demonstrates. He acted in a self-deprecating manner during one of his master classes, insisting that he usually only took bows for the rest of the band. Despite the fact that it was an Ellington conference, Ellington only wanted to talk about the general history of jazz, allowing two younger pianist fans of his, Richard "Two-Ton" Baker and Brooks Kerr, to demonstrate on piano the trajectory of the music. When the crowd encouraged him to play some of the stride piano music he used to play in his early gigs as a professional musician in Washington, D.C., he tried to play "What You Gonna Do When the Bed Breaks Down," the first song he ever wrote. After a few bars, he stopped and said, "That's no good, I have no left hand" and walked away from the piano, allowing Kerr to play the song in its entirety.

While he seemed to appreciate everyone's intent in honoring him, he had always harbored strong feelings against any attempts to sum up his career while he was still alive and creating. His sister Ruth affirmed that Ellington did not want books written about him. "He doesn't wish to have too many roses thrown at him. This is rather my own personal thought, but I think he has a sort of superstition about finales, and a book is rather like a finale . . . if one writes a book about him, it is saying he is finished . . . and so, you see, he would be against testimonials, books, and all things that had a final connotation," she said in 1960. In the 1940s, Ellington told his first biographer, Barry Ulanov, that biographies were for dead people. The British music journalist Derek Jewell spent more than a decade during the 1960s and 1970s convincing Ellington to cooperate with him on a book. Ellington consistently told him it was a great idea and that they should start it "next year," but it never happened, and Jewell finally realized that Ellington was putting him off in a firm but gentle manner:

> He didn't want biographies written, actually . . . he hated the very idea of biographies . . . he said . . . something like, "Biographies are tombstones. Who wants one?" And lots of things in his life, he didn't do because he thought that that would encourage death, as it were. He died without a proper will. He didn't take out proper insurance and so forth. Because he was intensely superstitious . . . And he used to believe, or appeared to believe, that if you did certain things to prepare for death, that very act hurried death along.[2]

Ellington finally participated musically in the 1972 program at Wisconsin. While sitting in a metal folding chair on the far side of the stage, he sang the old song "I'm Afraid of Loving You Too Much," accompanied by Baker on piano. Ellington almost never sang in public during his career, and he turned in a charming, surprising, and touching performance. Then, after the two younger musicians finished, Ellington sat down at the piano. He refused to play anything definite and ignored requests shouted at him, but he deigned to "experiment" at the keyboard. He then produced, apparently off the top of his head, a beguiling, moody piece, far removed from the speedy showoff piano music of the 1910s and 1920s that the other two pianists performed. With this move, Ellington seemed to make a statement. He was willing to sit at the side of the stage and smile at the audience and the pianists and clap while they revived the music of his youth. He was willing to outline his version of the history of American jazz from Africa to New York City, without mentioning his own role in that story. He would even sing along a little. But he was not, for the most part, going to join them in such historic pursuits, not even at the age of seventy-three. He was going forward, he still had plenty to do, creating and improvising something memorable in the moment, summoning his muse and finding her there, beautiful, once again.

✳

In the spring of 1972, Ellington's longtime close friend and personal physician Dr. Arthur Logan determined that Ellington was seriously ill with lung cancer from his decades of smoking. According to Logan's wife Marian, the two of them agreed to keep the news strictly to themselves. To the end of his days, this remained a subject upon which Ellington would make no public comment. But, in retrospect, his family realized that the information weighed on him, particularly at the funeral for Florence Hartgrave, his mother's sister, in 1972. During his life, he had "worshipped" her, paid

her living and medical expenses, and visited her immediately whenever he·
returned from long trips away. Hartgrave's daughter Bernice Wiggins and
granddaughter Juanita Middleton recalled the scene:

WIGGINS: And the strangest thing—at the cemetery when we were burying
  mother, before lowering her into the ground and something that had never
  been done in our family, he requested the casket to be opened and he knelt
  down and he kissed her. And we never had that before.
MIDDLETON: And then, you see, he was very sick himself which we didn't
  know ... He was very sentimental. So maybe he said to Aunt Florence in his
  way, "Take this kiss to my mother," you know what I mean?[3]

Hartgrave represented the last close link to Ellington's beloved mother and
her bevy of sisters who had nurtured him during his charmed childhood in
Washington, D.C.

But perhaps in his own way Ellington also made a comment on his impending demise by finally finishing the autobiography he had contracted to write
for Doubleday for a $50,000 advance in the late 1960s, despite his distaste
for books about himself.[4] Stanley Dance, hired by Doubleday to help Ellington finish the book, and Mercer Ellington felt that Ellington originally
agreed to write the book mainly for the advance. Doubleday had offered
him a $10,000 advance for years, but when Nelson Doubleday's excitement
over watching the band perform one night inspired him to offer quintu-
ple that amount, Ellington exclaimed: "Sold!" RCA producer and executive
Brad McCuen claimed in a 1989 oral interview that Ellington told him that,
in another example of his lackadaisical and generous way with finances, his
sister Ruth spent the advance in eight days, and asked for more. Ellington
named the eventual book *Music Is My Mistress*.

The book endured a long gestation. Ellington mostly pushed it aside for
years until Doubleday started pressuring him in the early 1970s. Stanley
Dance recalled the book being due, nothing typed up, the money "long
gone," and Ellington "irritated" over having to deliver it. It seems that most
of the work in producing the book occurred during 1972. For years, Ellington had occasionally jotted down ideas and prose "on hotel stationery, nap-
kins, old sheets of manuscript," "on the backs of envelopes . . . he wrote on
anything that came to hand, all over Europe, all over the world, these little scribbled notes," according to Stanley and Helen Dance. Many of these
scraps are preserved in the Smithsonian's files.

During the final stages of assembling the book, Irving Mills called Stanley
Dance "repeatedly," "terrified" at what Ellington might write about him in

Mistress. "I think [Mills] was afraid Duke was going to tell the truth" about him, according to Stanley Dance. But Mills had no cause for worry: Ellington had Dance ask Mills to meet them in Las Vegas to help him recall the early years of his career. "Now, I come in, and I brought along all the sketches of the early days, of what happened, so he could get all the information . . . reminders of a lot of the things that happened, from the very first day that he came into my office, and how he got the first recording dates," Mills recalled. "And he started to read the papers, and he said 'Oh yeah. Oh, yeah. Oh yeah!' Well, this 'oh, yeah' was tingling in my ears for three days." In his book, Ellington made no reference to the outsized, probably unethical portion of his career proceeds that Mills took during the 1920s and 1930s, nor the songwriting royalties Mills still received for music that he in all likelihood did not write. Instead, Ellington put the most positive spin possible on Mills's contributions, complimenting Mills's music business savvy and praising him for preserving "the dignity of my name." All the same, however, it was probably telling that over a hundred of Ellington's friends and associates from the 1920s to the 1970s earned their own short chapters in *Mistress,* while Mills, such a pivotal figure in Ellington's career, had no chapter reserved for him. Mills was not satisfied with Ellington's generous treatment, complaining in a 1981 interview that his years with Ellington "still weren't written up right" in the book.

While Stanley Dance helped Ellington complete *Mistress* in its last stages, others also aided the process. Louise Michelle, who booked jazz artists for the Barclay agency in Europe, helped Ellington with *Mistress* in Europe and the United States before Stanley Dance signed on. She transcribed some of Ellington's handwritten notes, and recalled that

> the best part of it all, he would read it out loud and I would transcribe it directly into the typewriter. So we had a lot of good times doing that because the book was very funny. Now, when the book came out it wasn't exactly the way we got it originally . . . He was very sly, very witty, he was a very special person. And some of the things that he had [written]—I never saw them in the book . . . I don't know where they went . . . We worked on it very hard together day and night on this book . . . [but] Many of us who read the book and who were around Duke a lot, we looked at the book and said, "It should have been better" . . . Because there's not a hell of a lot of him in there.

Betty McGettigan, one of Ellington's romantic companions during the last six years of his life, said she helped Ellington "a lot" on *Mistress,* including proofing the galleys. "If you note the questions in the back [of the book in an extended self-interview called "The Mirrored Self"], most of those are my questions and I was trying to draw him out," she recalled. "But he avoided the real answers most of the time."

Mercer Ellington felt strongly that his father did not view *Mistress* as a biography. "It's not a biography. It's a way to get $50,000," Mercer said, laughing, in 1990. "He didn't want to do a biography . . . A biography is your life from beginning to end. OK now, if he does a biography, that means his life is over. He was superstitious, you know, highly superstitious." So, instead of a traditional autobiography, Ellington turned in a book that mostly reflected his public diplomatic persona rather than any inner dialogue or insight. As John Edward Hasse has written, Ellington

> offered anecdotal, generous remembrances of over a hundred people, some breezy historical narrative, and, predictably, limited self-revelation. He took an almost uniformly positive tone—the literary equivalent of his conceit "We love you madly"—and there's hardly a negative word in the book: little about the gangsters at the Cotton Club, nothing about Jim Crow, the feud with the NAACP, drinking, drugs, disputes, or other unpleasantness within the band. Key women in his life . . . are absent as well. It was another protective veil for the ultimately private man who spent his life before the public.

Some of his remarks about family and friends could double as banal Hallmark card prose, such as this excerpt: "Mercer [Ellington] has a beautiful wife, like all his forefathers. All their wives were beautiful. He has two beautiful daughters, too." The same tone applied to everyone described in the book. "You would have never gotten Duke Ellington to write a revealing book about his life . . . and so he tried to be polite about everybody," McGettigan said. Saying "bad things about people . . . would be bad manners to begin with and what would it accomplish anyway." Did Stanley Dance, a man notoriously protective of Ellington's image, toss out the "funny," "sly," and more personal sections of the book that Louise Michelle described working on with Ellington? Or did Ellington himself have a change of heart and decide to reveal less? As Mercer Ellington put it, perhaps Ellington reverted to previous habits: "He talks about everybody but himself [in the book], it's an old trick of his!" After they had finished the book, Ellington told Stanley Dance: "We've written the good book. Now we're going to write the bad book." "It would be much more interesting," Dance reflected in 1977. Despite its occasional Ellingtonian wit and anecdotes, *Music Is My Mistress* mainly serves as a reminder that the only place where Ellington ever emotionally laid it on the line in public was in his music. McGettigan recalled Ellington telling a PBS-TV producer that "I wish I hadn't written that book."

*

A few months after the Ellington Festival in Madison, Ellington and his orchestra formed the "centerpiece" of another unprecedented academic event.[5] Yale music professor and bassist Willie Ruff assembled and hosted what he called the "Conservatory without Walls": three days of concerts, jam sessions, and workshops in two concert halls at Yale University in October 1972. Ruff intended the name of the event as a "description and celebration of the Afro-American legacy," according to the *New York Times*. He pointed out an anomaly that Ellington had discussed and rued for decades: "We have no school of Afro-American music, yet we have the golden age of that music alive and among us." In 1972, American conservatories were beginning to feature jazz and other forms of African American music in their instruction, but overall classical remained the sine qua non even though jazz represented the most famous and honored form of homegrown American music. As Ellington told Ruff, he and others during the Jim Crow era almost always learned their craft from those who went before them, not from formal instruction. Ellington appreciated how the phrase "Conservatory without Walls" hinted at this situation: "I can't beat that title, man. Print it!" he told Ruff in the planning stages.

To honor these masters of the jazz form largely unacknowledged by the academic world, Ruff invited forty of the most significant black American musicians to Yale to receive "Ellington medals," which, as Yale president Kingsman Brewster, Jr., told them at the ceremony, were "a symbol of our appreciation of the great art to which you have contributed." Marian Anderson, a recipient herself, accompanied Ruff to the August press conference that announced the "Conservatory without Walls." One of the greatest ever gatherings of jazz greats convened at the actual event: Eubie Blake, Ray Brown, Benny Carter, Harry Edison, Dizzy Gillespie, Charles Mingus, Max Roach, Noble Sissle, Mary Lou Williams, and many more. Classical artists Anderson, Roland Hayes, Paul Robeson (who was ill and could not attend), and William Warfield were also part of the festivities. Ellington insisted that the oldest among the group, especially Hayes, Noble, Sissle, and his mentor Willie "The Lion" Smith, occupy "center-stage." "One never knows about time, baby," he told Ruff. "Tomorrow is, too often, too late. We should honor the greats among us while they can still smell the flowers." From all reports, the subsequent all-star workshops and jam sessions radiated love and respect, especially since Ruff invited promising young musicians to interact with the veterans.

But apparently not everyone in the New Haven area felt pleased about dozens of black jazz greats visiting and being honored on the Yale campus.

During a performance by an all-star sextet led by Gillespie, a bomb threat was called in, and police asked everyone to evacuate the building while they searched it. Gillespie continued playing outside for the crowd, but according to Ruff most people's attention focused on someone else:

> The music was silenced. But not for long. One who hadn't deserted the hall was Charles Mingus. There he was onstage with his bass, talking on the microphone as the police captain tried to get him out of the hall.
>
> From the door I heard him say to the cops, "You all just get Duke, Eubie, Noble Sissle, and all of my musical forebears out of here. I'm staying. I'm not moving, do you understand? . . . I've got to die sometime, and it ain't never gonna get better than right now. Racism planted that bomb, but racism ain't strong enough to kill this music; if I'm going to die, I'm ready. But I'm going out playing 'Sophisticated Lady.'"
>
> The bass version Mingus played of the song was so great I hated to miss it . . . Ellington, standing among the waiting crowd out on the street, smiled as he listened through the open doors. Mingus was getting hotter, and the police captain's pleas for him to leave the stage couldn't have fallen upon deafer ears . . .
>
> Mingus' indomitable spirit rained on the old devil's hellfire and completely defused the ugly trick.
>
> "False alarm," declared the police captain after about twenty minutes, and the musicians returned to the stage, hell-bent on raising the roof—with music.

Many beautiful moments transpired during those three days of jazz fellowship, but in the long run, the event proved disappointing in important ways. The *New Haven Register* termed it a "financial flop." The "Conservatory without Walls" hoped to raise $1 million for a financial principal to permanently fund the study of African American music at Yale. But, in an article published a week after the event, the *Register* reported only $40,000 collected initially—before subtracting the musicians' food and lodging expenses. Ruff, who had spent time encouraging local businessmen to pay for $100 seats for inner-city children, had hoped the "Conservatory" weekend would net more than $200,000. Even more discouraging was the failure to secure filming of the event, which would have brought in far more money. Ruff initially thought TV networks would jump at the chance to present the stellar group of jazz talent, but such artists "lacked audience appeal," according to the major networks, and no deal materialized. The *Register* laid the blame on resistance from the New York musical unions and record companies, who worried about underpayment and overexposure of their artists.

"Our publicists were shocked, but not Ellington," recalled Ruff. Ellington had fought against the devaluation of African American culture for decades and had his own perspective. "We learn from our experiences, don't we, Willie?" Ellington asked Ruff. "We're honoring all those beautiful musicians *because* they have become great *even* in their invisibility. Maybe fate is trying to tell us something about invisible. Why spoil a good thing, man?" Max Roach, the famous drummer and a professor at the University of Massachusetts, exhibited less diplomacy. He claimed the event represented "racism in all its incandescent splendor . . . Yale isn't doing a thing for us—it's just giving us the opportunity to work our tails off onstage." He asked why, if Yale was so intent on creating an African American music program, they relied on external sources to fund it. As seen with the similarly lukewarm American fundraising reception for the 1966 Dakar festival, funding for the study and appreciation of African American culture still represented an uphill and perhaps impossible struggle in 1972.

During the year before his death in May 1974, Ellington, struggling with cancer, became more irritable. According to his son Mercer, Ellington's whole manner changed, as often happens with people suffering from terminal cancer. "As the days went on, the smile turned into a grimace, there wasn't any sincerity at all, it was just like he was onstage and the people would just more or less have to accept him on those grounds or they would just disappear from the scene," Mercer recalled in 1991. "I think he got pretty cynical there toward the end." The *New York Times* noticed that "Ellington is getting a bit stiff-legged. His body bends forward from the hips when he walks, and around his right wrist he wears one of those copper bracelets that are supposed to ward off arthritis."[6]

This new attitude especially surfaced in Ellington's relations with the press. Once verbally spry and generous with his time with them, the last two years of his life saw him become more distrustful and dismissive. He hated the trivia and the same old tired questions most reporters tended to ask. He particularly resented reporters who came to him unprepared, who expected Ellington to do their homework for them. While digging into a dinner from McDonalds in Binghamton, New York, he forbid reporters from interviewing him while he was eating (something that did not stop him in years past) and at the outset refused to answer any question about his personal life or events more than two years old. As was true for two decades, Ellington also resented questions that tried to provoke him into making controversial statements about race issues, and at least twice referenced the hubbub over his 1951 "we ain't ready" comment as an example of why he preferred to remain silent about such issues among journalists. "I don't like interviews," he told a South Carolina paper in 1972. "I got thrown out of a race because of one once." "I don't understand this craze to know how everything works," Ellington "grumpily" told the *New York Times*. "People want to know how I do it, or they say they want to get behind the scenes. Why should the audience *ever* be behind the scenes? All it does is pull the petals off the creative flower." A Canadian reporter found that Ellington resented his questions and "flew into a rage":

> Why are you askin' me such questions? Who cares where I get my men, or what I do in my spare time, or if flying makes me nervous? You're diggin' into my spit, man, that's what you're doin'. You know why? Cause you figure I'm stupid, don't you? Well, I'm not, ya hear . . . nobody cares about that stuff. What is the point of siftin' through the dirt? . . . Why don't you ask me what happened in Russia? How 10,000 people sat listening to Duke Ellington and nobody moved for four hours. Four hours, man!

Ellington also resisted having his picture taken in his last years, especially with a flash, and doused a photographer with one of his sugar-supplemented Cokes for using a flash during a show, and doused others offstage. "There was no more syrup or veneer," wrote Mercer Ellington in his autobiography. "He didn't placate *anyone* in the press anymore. And I think he was right."[7]

Ellington's malaise was probably largely due to his losing battle with cancer, but his financial situation also continued to worsen and the increasing pressure probably impacted his behavior as well. The IRS continued to hound Ellington with bills and every so often garnished his concerts. In the three years after his death in 1974, partial paperwork in the Ellington files from the IRS indicates that his estate owed them approximately $175,000 for his 1964–66 returns; $200,000 to $250,000 for unpaid personal income, payroll, and New York City taxes for the period 1971–74; $37,000 in penalties for the 1967–73 period; and $300,000 for the 1969–73 period. At the time of his death, then, they claimed he owed them between $600,000 and $700,000, or roughly $2.75 million in today's dollars.[8]

In his last years, Ellington found he could no longer live in the manner he wished, and had trouble supporting his family in the way he wanted. The IRS actually tried to stop him from supporting them, insisting that money paid to certain family members during the 1960s constituted not salary but gifts, which entailed a higher taxation rate. "During those last horrible days financially . . . he had so many problems with taxes, also meeting expenses for rent and the number of people in the family that he supported, they kept him to a point where basically he had [few possessions]," recalled Mercer Ellington. "As far as luxury is concerned, he didn't own any building, he didn't have his automobile, he didn't have lavish jewelry, he had some things that people would present to him and all that. But there was no basic [financial] status of [what] Ellington . . . represented." In some ways, Ellington had no one to blame but himself. According to his sister Ruth, who became increasingly involved in the financial dealings of Duke Ellington, Inc., during the last decade of his life, he refused to think of money, sent all bills to her, and usually carried no ready cash except for three $1,000 bills in his pocket in case he ran into trouble. Yet, at the same time, his ASCAP royalties alone came to almost $100,000 a year during 1973, almost $500,000 in today's dollars. He lived beyond his means, and purposely so, in order to support his music, family, and friends—and he, or rather his heirs, paid the financial price in the end.[9]

Others believed that Ellington's family took financial advantage of him during his last years. Betty McGettigan told Yale oral history and music professor Vivian Perlis that she felt they used "his name and his money through the years without being very good to him." She recalled that Ellington could not stay at Hilton hotels because of unpaid bills, a constant problem in his last years. She felt that members of his family were living "very nicely" on his money, while Ellington's lifestyle deteriorated on the road. Mercer Ellington suspected that "once in a while, there were hidden presents to various people . . . set up for Ruth, or one of Ruth's sons, and I would think the business would intentionally be kept secret." Evidence in the Ellington files suggests some of the same conclusions. After Ellington's death, Ruth Ellington and her son Stephen James assured E. Lisk Wyckoff, Jr., the Ellington estate lawyer, that the 1973 Cadillac James drove was no longer registered to and insured by Duke Ellington, Inc. A few weeks later, Wyckoff discovered that the car was indeed registered to and insured by Duke Ellington, Inc., and that James incurred numerous unpaid outstanding parking tickets on it. Also, Wyckoff found that $500 was transferred every month from Ellington's checking account to his sister Ruth's checking account for at least the last eighteen months of his life in addition to her salary as the president of Tempo Music, with the money going unreported to the IRS or anyone else. But these kinds of activities could very well have represented more examples of Ellington wishing to provide for his closest family while not caring about rules set down by his accountants or the IRS and with little regard for consequences that emerged after his demise.[10]

Ellington spent most of his writing time during the early morning hours of 1973 working on his Third Sacred Concert, which premiered in October at Westminster Abbey in London.[11] Throughout his career, he was infamous for writing and revising important works at the last minute, but the preparations for this premiere were particularly grueling, especially for a seventy-four-year-old composer secretly dealing with life-threatening cancer. He stayed up for two nights straight before the premiere trying to finish the Third Sacred Concert, and even then he was writing music up to ten minutes before showtime and during the intermission. Ellington became so exhausted that he skipped a postshow reception and dinner at 10 Downing Street with the British prime minister and Princess Margaret, and, for the first time in his life, he used a wheelchair the next morning to make the flight to the band's next show in Sweden.

The Third Sacred Concert itself represented a mixed artistic effort. Ellington's still-facile piano playing dominated much of the piece. On the released recording, the performances sometimes feel a little unsure, probably due to the chaotic circumstances of the premiere, and a few minor flubs are noticeable. Ellington edited out some sections of it, including entire songs, before approving the final recorded presentation. Most of it seems dull and unremarkable and sometimes conservatively reverential, as if he was deferring to the traditional music one usually heard in churches rather than trying to expand their offerings with an unorthodox yet respectful approach, as he did in the first two Sacred Concerts. "Ain't Nobody Nowhere Nothing without God," for example, was a standard jazz gospel swinger, but Ellington used a better one in the First Sacred Concert ("Ain't but the One"), and the new track's lyrics seemed close in concept to "In the Beginning God."

But in its best material, the Third Sacred Concert may allow a window into Ellington's personal feelings of the period. While the central theme for the Second Sacred Concert was freedom, Ellington said that the third focused on the theme of love. "The Lord's Prayer/My Love" and "Is God a Three-Letter Word for Love?" are beautiful and contemplative pieces and feel like a very personal sort of musical worship. Their melodies, sung by Alice Babs, rise high on the scale, as if Ellington was reaching out through them to God, or as if he knew that God was near for him. The restrained yet passionate long baritone saxophone solo on "My Love" by Harry Carney continues the mood. These two pieces, like many of Ellington's best, conjure a bittersweet atmosphere: they're beautiful and they hurt, simultaneously. Albert Murray's observation that death forms a central theme of the Sacred Concerts applies most appropriately in these compositions. It's hard to imagine that the pain heard in these two compositions was not related to the exhaustion and the cancer Ellington experienced and fought during the fall of 1973. A recitative portion of "Three-Letter Word" quotes the Reverend

Gerald Pocock: "the best of all treasures we have is today," a maxim Ellington lived to the fullest. The melodies of "The Lord's Prayer/My Love" and "Is God a Three-Letter Word for Love" are not melodies one can imagine Ellington producing in decades past and seem to represent a different, higher purpose than usual. They were probably his last great original pieces.

Following the premiere of the Third Sacred Concert, Ellington left immediately for his last dates outside the United States: a five-and-a-half-week tour of Europe with a week in Africa comprising Ellington's last State Department–sponsored shows.[12] During the band's three-day stay in Addis Ababa, Ethiopia, Ellington was honored by His Imperial Majesty Haile Selassie I, the aged Conquering Lion of the tribe of Judah, as Commander of the Imperial Order of Ethiopia, and each band member received a gold medallion. According to State Department documents, Ellington and the band were "visibly moved" by the honor and, as usual, met and jammed with local musicians. Once again, the State Department noted a particularly enthusiastic reception from younger audiences, who knew little of his music beforehand but "metaphorically tore the place apart with their enthusiasm and cheers" during a reduced-price student matinee performance. At the command performance, where demand for tickets from African diplomats and government officials across the continent forced the embassy to increase the number of "table seating accommodations" at the last minute, Ellington "was suffering from extreme pain from arthritis," yet still made it to a postshow reception featuring the Ethiopian prime minister and other officials, even though the embassy excused him from attending because of his affliction.

The U.S. embassy seemed especially happy that the Ellington presence coincided with a meeting in Addis Ababa of the Organization of African Unity's Council of Ministers, who spent much of their agenda castigating the United States for its "open military collusion" with Israel, South Africa's apartheid regime, and other allies during the recent Yom Kippur War. To one embassy employee, Ellington's fervid reception demonstrated that Ethiopians "are capable of feeling good about the U.S. in some respects even while they feel less good about others." After leaving Ethiopia, the Ellington orchestra spent two and a half days in Zambia. Both African countries featured USIS- and USIA-supplied Ellington programs on their national radio and TV stations, a rare occurrence in Africa.

On Ellington's last day in Zambia, his close friend and personal physician Dr. Arthur Logan fell to his death from the Henry Hudson Parkway in

Harlem. Differing accounts suggest a mugging, an accident, and a suicide. Whatever happened, the news devastated Ellington, particularly since Mercer and Ruth Ellington kept the news from him for more than three days, despite pleas from Dr. Logan's widow Marian to tell Ellington since she felt he should "have the right to make his own decision about coming" to the funeral. Mercer and Ruth were worried about how Ellington's reaction would affect a command performance before Queen Elizabeth that week in London. Immediately upon finally being told in Dublin, Ellington called Marian Logan at 9:20 AM—the funeral was starting at noon in New York City. "I don't know what I'm going to do," he told her, sounding "very confused." "I won't be able to get back and I can't do anything." "Then he went on to say that he would never make it; he would never survive six months without Arthur," Logan recalled. "And . . . he didn't." Mercer Ellington witnessed his father's reaction:

> So as Pop cried for Arthur Logan he cried for himself, all through the night. He felt there was no one left in the world to take care of him. What would happen to him? It was as though he were in a wilderness. The words he kept repeating after I told him were: "Why did he have to die?" For the next two or three days he unashamedly went through moments of mental hysteria . . . It was the first real breakdown I ever saw him get into, and it made what happened subsequently so much more difficult [since Ellington no longer had the advice of the doctor he trusted most].

In 1978, Marian Logan said she felt that Mercer and Ruth had done Ellington a "cruel injustice" by not allowing him to decide for himself whether to leave the European tour and attend Dr. Logan's funeral. Less than a week later, on 4 December 1973, Ellington flew back to the United States, never to leave his home country again.[13]

After undergoing surgery to remove his thyroid gland at the end of 1973, Ellington slowed down his touring schedule in 1974, but not by much.[14] By this time, it was common knowledge among the family, though not among the band members, that Ellington's illness was in an advanced stage. "The doctors gave him a choice," Mercer Ellington recalled. "And he said 'I'd rather stay out there working and do something constructive than sit in a hospital room and look out the window.'" Ellington knew that when he finally needed to return to the hospital, he would never be resuming his normal life again. So, according to scholar Klaus Stratemann's best estimates, Ellington played fourteen dates in January, ten in February, and fifteen in March before he left the road for the last time, after playing two shows in one night at the Sturgis-Young Auditorium in Sturgis, Michigan, on 22 March. "People said it was cruel to push him like that, to have him do two shows, but the second show was actually better than the first because he seemed to summon up more energy," wrote Mercer Ellington in his autobiography. A tape from one of his last gigs, in Sarasota, Florida, on 8 March, documented Ellington still playing some sharp piano, performing newer material such as the *Toga Brava Suite,* and telling stories about the new pieces. It seemed like audiences were getting their moneys' worth. After the Sturgis gig, Ellington returned to New York City where he rested at home for two days then checked in to the Harkness Pavilion at the Columbia Presbyterian Medical Center, which Frank Sinatra had recommended to him.

All reports agree that Ellington did his best to have as good a time as possible in the hospital, chatting with family and friends and working on new material including an opera entitled *Queenie Pie* and a ballet piece called *Three Black Kings* (a tribute to the black king of the Magi, King Solomon, and Martin Luther King, Jr.). As usual, he made it a point to never acquiesce to negativity. Pastor John Gensel, the jazz priest Ellington had immortalized in a piece from the Second Sacred Concert, visited Ellington numerous times in his last weeks and noted that he never spoke of death even though "he knew that his situation was very critical. It seemed as though he felt that he was just going to go on forever, you know, and that he was interested in life and not in dying." For the first time in decades, Irving Mills and Ellington spoke frequently on the phone during the last weeks, sometimes for extended periods, which Mercer Ellington interpreted as forgiveness by Ellington toward Mills's past actions. His granddaughter Mercedes Ellington recalled those final weeks:

I know he must have been depressed at points or had bad moments I never knew. I know my father [Mercer] probably knows. But I never saw that side even in the hospital. When I was with him in the hospital, I'd bring him pads and pencils and he'd love to talk about his great affairs, you know, the women in his life . . . I mean, a man's dying in a hospital. This is what he's talking about. He's not talking about anything.

Ellington revealed his innermost feelings to few, if anyone, during his lifetime. With Logan and Strayhorn gone, it was unlikely that he would change his ways in his last days, and he did not.

Though he could not leave his hospital room, the world marked Ellington's seventy-fifth birthday on 29 April with various events. Stanford University presented a three-day symposium examining Ellington's "contributions to music." Ellington's orchestra appeared at a concert of his Sacred Music at St. Peter's Church in New York City, just a couple miles from the hospital. The State Department took full advantage of the promotional possibilities. The Voice of America paid tribute to Ellington "on every news, discussion, educational, cultural and music—classical and pop as well as jazz—program" on Ellington's birthday. Willis Conover, host of the *Jazz USA* program assembled fifty radio programs featuring exclusively Ellington music that aired throughout 1974. United States Information Agency films about Ellington were shown in 189 posts in 108 countries around the world. Sixteen different USIA magazines published in twenty-five languages featured Ellington articles and photographs. Photo exhibits and live concerts by local musicians were scheduled to take place at the U.S. embassies of the more than fifty countries that Ellington and the orchestra had visited on behalf of the State Department. Clearly, the federal government wished to keep the genial, groundbreaking, and freedom-cherishing image that Ellington represented fresh in the minds of the citizens of the countries he toured over the decade for the State Department. "Maybe the political scientists will never find the cure for intolerance," Sinatra wrote for the occasion of Ellington's birthday. "Until they do, I challenge anyone to come up with a more effective prescription than Duke Ellington's music, and Duke Ellington's performance as a human being."

Despite urgings from family and business associates, Ellington did not leave a will. Betty McGettigan insisted that his lack of action in this regard did not have to do with any superstitious feeling that talking about death would bring it on faster:

> He didn't much care what happened after he left here. He figured that he did a good job and if people couldn't get along on what he left them, that's just tough. And I think that was his attitude . . . I think also his personal life and activities and accounts probably got so out of hand and got so complicated that . . . at his age, in his 70s, that it was just probably an impossible task to unravel it and straighten it out. So, I mean, he couldn't be bothered by that. He was busy writing music . . . "If people can't do it after I'm gone," he said, "they'll just have to get along without it."

Ellington's grandson Edward held a similar perspective, though he did feel that Ellington thought it was "bad luck" to draw up a will. "He knew that everybody would be running all around trying to figure out which way to get the most of whatever," he remarked in 1978. "And that wasn't going to be his deal and while he was alive he just didn't want to deal with that." Ellington had achieved his business goals in life, composed with his big band by his side as long as he could last, supported his family, friends, and band members for decades and supported them well. His royalties would continue to support them and their descendants for decades.

Norman Granz, Irving Mills, and Betty McGettigan all claim to be the last one to see Ellington alive. Mills's claim is implausible, probably yet another exaggeration of the important role he played in Ellington's life. Granz's claim is similarly fanciful. McGettigan's account is more believable. Since the family disliked her, she tended to arrive at the hospital in the wee hours of the morning, when Ellington, the lifelong "night creature," felt more awake. She claimed that the nurses and family expected Ellington to be up during the day even though this had not been his schedule throughout his life. She prepared food for him at the nurses' station late at night when Ellington became hungry, since he tended not to eat during the day when hospital meals were served. The family heard of her visits in early May and banned all nighttime visits for Ellington, but McGettigan says a nurse who felt she was helping ease Ellington let her in on the last night of Ellington's life, during which they spoke briefly and she watched him die in his sleep while she held his hand on 24 May 1974.

Ellington's funeral, held three days later, seemed more like a service for a head of state rather than a civilian or celebrity.[15] Fifteen thousand guests packed St. John the Divine Cathedral Church in New York City, where Ellington had previously premiered his Second Sacred Concert, and another twenty-five thousand to thirty thousand people milled outside. Funeral director John Joyce arranged the security in the same manner as for a president, with a police escort through traffic lights. Fifty police officers were staged in and around the church, and the church's security lieutenant told Joyce that at least two hundred federal agents were present. The service reflected Ellington's life, character, and values appropriately. It was ecumenical, like the Sacred Concerts, featuring readings from Catholic, Lutheran, and Methodist clergy, including Gensel. Joe Williams performed a perfect choice for the occasion: "My Mother, My Father (Heritage)," Ellington's loving tribute to the influence of his family, from the show *My People*. Ella Fitzgerald, Ellington's frequent musical partner over the years, contributed heartbreaking versions of "Solitude" and "Just a Closer Walk with Thee" in a quieter and more throaty voice than usual. It is a performance that should be more widely heard. Stanley Dance delivered the eulogy and made it the most insightful of the many pieces he had written over the years about his friend. Some brief excerpts:

> He was loved throughout the world, by all levels of society.
> He worked hard, did not spare himself, and virtually died in harness.
> Very tolerant.
> Child-like, but not childish.
> It is Memorial Day, when those who died for the free world are very properly remembered. Duke Ellington never lost faith in his country and he served it well. His music will go on serving it for years to come.

The pragmatic realities and hurdles Ellington faced over his lifetime, the racial and cultural hierarchies he challenged and altered, were in the far distance. Some have argued that his work was all that remained or mattered after he finally succumbed to lung cancer. And, surely, the influence and power of his best work has only increased since his death. But his personal journey communicated just as much about his America and his world as his music. He helped transform his nation's historical, racial and cultural landscape as he contributed to creating its musical heritage.

NOTES

Abbreviations

Introduction

1. Duke Ellington interview, CHIC 1964 #7, tape 1, AC/NMAH/SI. When the tapes are listened to chronologically, one can hear Ellington's steadily declining enthusiasm for working with Harman. Harman was an accomplished writer, but he did not display much insight on matters concerning American music, and seemed to not have done his research on Ellington's career before embarking on the conversations, which sometimes seems to irk Ellington. The failure of the Harman project may have had even more to do with Ellington's preference of viewing his life as an unfinished, still developing story. Producer, promoter, and jazz entrepreneur Norman Granz bought the film rights to Ellington's life in the mid-1960s, and established a sound financial deal in which Ellington owned half the rights, the orchestra would supply the music, and Granz even got Sidney Poitier interested in playing the lead role. Granz eventually gave up the rights, angry at Ellington's unwillingness to devote even three days off from the band to helping him develop the project, let alone the two to three months that Granz thought the project needed (interview with Norman Granz, conducted by Patricia Willard, 23 and 24 August 1989, SIEOHP, tape 4, AC/NMAH/SI).

The movie that Strayhorn and Harman are talking about is *The Story of Louis Pasteur* (United Artists, 1936).

2. This idea of a "culture hero" is taken from the definition provided in the introduction to Wyn Wachorst, *Thomas A. Edison: An American Myth* (Cambridge, MA, 1981).

3. Langston Hughes, "The Negro Artist and the Racial Mountain," *Nation* (23 June 1926); Robert Hemenway, introduction to *Dust Tracks on a Road*, by Zora Neale Hurston (Urbana, IL, 1942; reprint 1984), xvii; Roberta S. Maguire, ed., *Conversations with Albert Murray* (Jackson, MS, 1997), 130; Albert Murray, *The Blue Devils of Nada: A Contemporary Approach to Aesthetic Statement* (New York, 1996), 26; Arnold Rampersad, *The Life of Langston Hughes*, vol. 2, *1941–1967: I Dream a World* (New York, 1988), 265.

Chapter One

1. Ruth Ellington interview, conducted by the author, 26 January 1996.

2. David Levering Lewis, *District of Columbia: A Bicentennial History* (New York, 1976), 44–46, 58, 66; Jacqueline M. Moore, *Leading the Race: The Transformation of the Black Elite in the Nation's Capital, 1880–1920* (Charlottesville, VA, 1999), 9, 21; Kenneth O' Reilly, *Nixon's Piano: Presidents and Racial Politics From Washington to Clinton* (New York, 1995), 82–86; Mark Tucker, *Ellington: The Early Years* (Urbana, IL, 1990), 3–7. For an account of the more disturbing and abusive side of the black experience in Washington, D.C., consult James Borchert, *Alley Life in Washington: Family, Community, Religion and Folklife in the City, 1850–1970* (Urbana, IL, 1980).

3. Angel Kwolek-Folland, *Engendering Business: Men and Women in the Corporate Office, 1870–1930* (Baltimore, 1994), 8–13; Roi Ottley, *New World A-Coming* (Cambridge, MA, 1943), 176; Arnold Rampersad, *The Life of Langston Hughes*, vol. 1, *1902–1941: I, Too, Sing America* (New York, 1986), 101–3.

4. Kwolek-Folland, *Engendering Business;* Willard B. Gatewood, *Aristocrats of Color: The Black Elite, 1880–1920* (Bloomington, IN, 1990), 335–39; D. L. Lewis, *District of Columbia:* 71–72; Moore, *Leading the Race,* 3–14, 51–52, 171–89.

For documentation of other black elite communities of this period, consult: Glenda Gilmore, *Gender and Jim Crow* (Chapel Hill, 1996); Evelyn Brooks Higginbotham, *Righteous Discontent: The Women's Movement in Black Baptist Churches, 1880–1920* (Cambridge, MA, 1993); Stephanie J. Shaw, *What a Woman Ought to Be and Do: Black Professional Women Workers during the Jim Crow Era* (Chicago, 1996). The aforementioned Gatewood book also views the black elite in various sections of the United States.

For examinations of nineteenth-century white American middle-class history, goals, and behavior, consult: Mary Ryan, *Cradle of the Middle Class: The Family in Oneida County, New York, 1790–1865* (Cambridge, 1981); Richard L. Bushman, *The Refinement of America: Persons, Houses, Cities* (New York, 1992).

5. Duke Ellington interview, CHIC 1964 #2, AC/NMAH/SI; Moore, *Leading the Race,* 6, 70–76, 91–110, 132–37, 193–97; *Duke Ellington's Washington* (Hedrick Smith Productions, aired on PBS, 7 February 2000).

6. Tucker, *Ellington,* 3–7; Edward Kennedy Ellington, *Music Is My Mistress* (New York, 1973), 17, 457; SIEOHP: interview with Mercer Ellington, 18 September 1990, conducted by Dr. Marcia M. Greenlee, tape 3, AC/NMAH/SI. Albert Murray, "Storiella Americana as She Is Swyung: Duke Ellington, the Culture of Washington, D.C., and the Blues as Representative Antidote," *Conjunctions* (Winter 1980): 209–14.

7. This section on the Ellington family home is drawn from the following sources: *Duke Ellington's Washington* (PBS); E. K. Ellington, *Music Is My Mistress,* 12, 20; Duke Ellington interview, CHIC 1956 #2, 1964 #7, AC/NMAH/SI; SIEOHP: interview with Mercer Ellington, 18 September 1990, conducted by Dr. Marcia M. Greenlee, tape 1, AC/NMAH/SI; Mercer Ellington interview, conducted by Harriet Milnes, 19 June 1983, OHAM/YSC, #521E, F, pg. 25–28; SIEOHP: interview with Ruth Ellington, 18 August 1989, conducted by Dr. Marcia M. Greenlee, tape 1, AC/NMAH/SI; Ruth Ellington interview, 26 January 1996; Ruth Ellington, interviewed by the Duke Ellington Society, 1960, SC Audio C-451, side 1, SCBC; Leonard Feather, *From Satchmo to Miles* (London, 1974), 52; Marc Fisher, "D.C. Proved a Cradle for Young Duke and His Gift," *Washington Post* (11 April 1999); John Edward Hasse, *Beyond Category: The Life and Genius of Duke Ellington* (New York, 1993), 21–27; Moore, *Leading the Race,* 33–47; Tucker, *Ellington,* 16–25; Bernice Wiggins and Juanita Middleton interview, conducted by

Mark Tucker, 6 September 1983, OHAM/YUSC, #551A, B, C, D; *Springfield Union,* "Duke Ellington's Unruffled Music Comes Naturally" (7 July 1958).

8. Duke Ellington interview, 29 April 1969 (listed on the box as 5 May 1962), VOA Music Library Collection, LOC, RWB 3057 A2; Duke Ellington interview, *Bell Telephone Hour: On the Road with Duke Ellington* (NBC, 13 October 1967), LOC/MPD.

9. Duke Ellington interview from *Conversation in Music* (Canadian Broadcasting Company, 1964), LOC/MPD; Ruth Ellington interview, 1960; Wiggins and Middleton interview, 6 September 1983.

10. E. K. Ellington, *Music Is My Mistress,* 17–24; Sonny Greer interview, JOHP, January 1979, IJS/RU; James Lincoln Collier, *Duke Ellington,* (New York, 1987), 21.

11. Phoebe Jacobs interviews, conducted by the author, 27 January 1996, 13 November 1999.

12. David Krasner, "'The Pageant Is the Thing': Black Nationalism and *The Star of Ethiopia,*" in *Performing America: Cultural Nationalism in American Theater,* ed. Jeffrey D. Mason and J. Ellen Gainor (Ann Arbor: University of Michigan Press, 1999), 106–22; Tucker, *Ellington,* 9–14, 61–62; E. K. Ellington, *Music Is My Mistress,* 98–104; Murray, "Storiella Americana," 213; Richard O. Boyer, "The Hot Bach," in *The Duke Ellington Reader,* ed. Mark Tucker (New York, 1993), 238–40.

13. E. K. Ellington, *Music Is My Mistress,* 47; Leroi Jones [Amiri Baraka], *Blues People: Negro Music in White America* (New York, 1963), 28–29; Thomas L. Morgan and William Barlow, *From Cakewalks to Concert Halls: An Illustrated History of African-American Popular Music from 1895 to 1930* (Washington, D.C., 1992), 91; Robert Palmer, *Deep Blues* (New York, 1981), chap. 1. For an example of an African griot narrative that imparts lessons of history and proper behavior, consult: Djibril Tamsir Niane, ed., *Sundiata: An Epic of Old Mali* (Essex, 1965; reprint 1986).

14. Duke Ellington interview, CHIC 1964 #6, AC/NMAH/SI; E. K. Ellington, *Music Is My Mistress,* 24–28; "A Conversation with the Duke," BBC Radio 1, 1972, interview by Stanley Dance, JVC/LOC, RYJ 3072; SIEOHP: interview with Helen Oakley Dance, 26 and 27 September 1989, conducted by Patricia Willard, tape 4, AC/NMAH/SI; Wiggins and Middleton interview, 6 September 1983.

Ellington's contemporary in classical music, Aaron Copland, also eschewed college, creating his own ad hoc conservatory-like education, a decision that "presumably fostered his growing individuality and daring"; Howard Pollock, *Aaron Copland: The Life and Work of an Uncommon Man* (New York, 1999), 34.

15. E. K. Ellington, *Music Is My Mistress,* 23–24; Mark Tucker, "Ellington in D.C." (lecture, Ellington 1999 international conference, Washington, D.C., 30 April 1999); Tucker, *Ellington,* 8–12, 22–26.

16. E. K. Ellington, *Music Is My Mistress,* 30, 33, 66, 72; Gunther Schuller, *Early Jazz: Its Origins and Musical Development* (New York, 1968), 319–25; Tucker, *Ellington,* 17, 32–33, 44, 49–50, 53–59.

17. Neil Leonard, *Jazz and the White Americans: The Acceptance of a New Art Form* (Chicago, 1962; reprint 1972), 10–11; Lawrence W. Levine, *Black Culture and Black Consciousness* (New York, 1977), 195–96; William H. Moiles, Jr., "Jazz Music Today Good as Ever, Ellington Says," *Worchester Daily Telegram* (5 January 1948); Morgan and Barlow, *From Cakewalks to Concert Halls,* 26, 33, 49; Harry Smith, ed., *Anthology of American Folk Music* (Folkways 1952; 1997 reissue); Harry Smith, ed., *Harry Smith's Anthology of American Folk Music,* vol. 4 (Revenant, 2000); Eileen Southern, *The Music of Black Americans: A History* (New York, 1971), 310–16.

18. Nathan O. Hatch, *The Democratization of American Christianity* (New Haven, 1989), 1–16, 102–13; Rhys Isaac, "Evangelical Revolt: The Nature of the Baptist Challenge to the Tradi-

tional Order in Virginia, 1765–1775," in *Colonial America,* ed. Stanley Katz, John Murrin, and Douglas Greenberg (New York, 1993), 640–56; Levine, *Black Culture,* 23, 37–38, 50–51, 137; Philip D. Morgan, "Slave Life in Piedmont, Virginia, 1720–1800," in *Colonial Chesapeake Society,* ed. Lois Carr, Philip D. Morgan, and Jean Russo (Chapel Hill, 1988), 474–80.

19. Ellington 29 April 1969 VOA interview; Tucker, *Ellington,* 49–63; Hasse, *Beyond Category,* 48–49; *Springfield Union,* "Duke Ellington's Unruffled Music."

20. D. L. Lewis, *District of Columbia,* 74–75; Moore, *Leading the Race,* 214.

21. E. K. Ellington, *Music Is My Mistress,* 35, 36, 50; Stanley Dance, *The World of Duke Ellington* (New York, 1970; 1981 reprint), 56–57; Otto Hardwicke, interviewed by the Duke Ellington Society, 1961, SC Audio C-475, side 1, SCBC.

22. James Weldon Johnson, *Black Manhattan* (New York, 1930), 78–81; Jay Krush, liner notes, *Hail to the Chief: American Political Marches, Songs and Dirges of the 1800s* (Sony Classical, 1996); Southern, *Music of Black Americans,* 111–14.

23. Johnson, *Black Manhattan,* 89–94; Jones/Baraka, *Blues People,* 81–86; Morgan and Barlow, *From Cakewalks to Concert Halls,* 15–19, 64; Thomas L. Riis, *Just before Jazz: Black Musical Theater in New York, 1890–1915* (Washington, D.C., 1989), 4–7, 50–53; Russell Sanjek, *American Popular Music and Its Business: The First Four Hundred Years,* vol. 2, *From 1790–1909* (New York, 1988), 171–73; William F. Stowe and David Grimsted, "White-Black Humor," *Journal of Ethnic Studies* 3 (Summer 1975); Robert C. Toll, *Blacking Up: The Minstrel Show in Nineteenth-Century America* (New York, 1974).

24. Riis, *Just before Jazz,* 5; Sanjek, *American Popular Music* 2: chap. 9; Southern, *Music of Black Americans,* 106–9, 200–12.

25. Morgan and Barlow, *From Cakewalks to Concert Halls,* 41–42, 62–63; Albert Murray, *The Blue Devils of Nada: A Contemporary American Approach to Aesthetic Statement* (New York, 1996), 92; Murray, "Storiella Americana," 216; Riis, *Just before Jazz,* 26–28, 40–43, 79–81, 164–66; Hollie I. West, "A Talk with Duke Ellington, Age 70," *New York Post* (29 April 1969); A. H. Lawrence, *Duke Ellington and his World: A Biography* (New York, 2001), 52.

26. Ann Charters, *Nobody: The Story of Bert Williams* (New York, 1983), 6, 9, 64, 112, 131–34, 138; Mabel Rowland, ed., *Bert Williams: Son of Laughter* (New York, 1927), 30, 95, 112, 212; Sanjek, *American Popular Music* 2:289.

27. Edward A. Berlin, *King of Ragtime: Scott Joplin and His Era* (New York, 1994), 28–29, 57–72, 87, 94; Sanjek, *American Popular Music* 2:411–12.

28. Maurice Banks interview, conducted by Mark Tucker, 29 September 1983, OHAM, YUSC, #582A, B, p. 10; Reid Badger, *A Life in Ragtime: A Biography of James Reese Europe* (New York, 1995), 3–9, 31–40, 54–72, 78–97, 115–24; Johnson, *Black Manhattan,* 120–24; Morgan and Barlow, *From Cakewalks to Concert Halls,* 69–73; Southern, *Music of Black Americans,* 344–50.

29. Nathan Huggins, *Harlem Renaissance* (New York, 1971), 236; David Levering Lewis, introduction to *The Portable Harlem Renaissance Reader* (New York, 1994), xvii–xx.

30. Langston Hughes, Zora Neale Hurston, and Claude McKay faced long periods, while they crafted their greatest works, of having no residence of their own, borrowing money from (usually white) friends, having to do hack or domestic work, experiencing near-starvation, and seriously endangering their health because of lack of livelihood: Wayne Cooper, *Claude McKay: Rebel Sojourner in the Harlem Renaissance* (New York, 1981), 96, 103, 197, 223, 231, 301–2, 363; Rampersad, *Life of Langston Hughes,* 1:285, 299, 308.

31. Randolph Bourne, "Trans-National America," in *War and the Intellectuals: Essays, 1915–1919,* ed. Randolph Bourne (New York, 1964), chap. 8; Huggins, *Harlem Renaissance,* 21, 28; Alain Locke, introduction, from Alain Locke, ed., *The New Negro* (New York, 1925), 4–6, 11, 15.

32. For more on the predominantly black live audiences for black music in the 1920s, consult: Palmer, *Deep Blues,* 55–60, 105–7; Burton W. Peretti, *Jazz in American Culture* (Chicago, 1997), 45.

33. See: Richard J. Powell and David A. Bailey, eds., *Rhapsodies in Black: Art of the Harlem Renaissance* (Berkeley, 1997); *Voices from the Harlem Renaissance* (Rhino Records, 2000).

34. Samuel A. Floyd, Jr., "Music in the Harlem Renaissance: An Overview," and Paul Burgett, "Vindication as a Thematic Principle in the Writings of Alain Locke on the Music of Black Americans," both in *Black Music in the Harlem Renaissance: A Collection of Essays,* ed. Samuel A. Floyd, Jr. (New York, 1981), 4–18, 29–39. Examples of other Harlem Renaissance intellectuals forwarding Locke's ideas about music: Albert C. Barnes, "Negro Art and America," and Joel A. Rogers, "Jazz at Home," both in Locke, *New Negro,* 19–24, 217–223.

35. Cab Calloway and Bryant Rollins, *Of Minnie the Moocher and Me* (New York, 1976), 105; Ted Gioia, *The History of Jazz* (New York, 1997), 95.

36. Leonard, *Jazz and the White Americans,* 30–49; "British Critic Excoriates Jazz: Newman, in Stinging Invective, Calls It an Industry without Art, 'Dead from Neck Up,'" *New York Times* (12 September 1926); Chadwick Hansen, "Social Influences on Jazz Style: Chicago, 1920–1930," *American Quarterly* (Winter 1960): 496–500.

37. Daphne Duval Harrison, *Black Pearls: Blues Queens of the 1920s* (New Brunswick, 1988), 44–47; Leonard, *Jazz and the White Americans,* 12–13; Levine, *Black Culture,* 221–32; Morgan and Barlow, *From Cakewalks to Concert Halls,* 92–103; Southern, *Music of Black Americans,* 374–77.

38. Harrison, *Black Pearls,* 47–61; Leonard, *Jazz and the White Americans,* 92–104; Morgan and Barlow, *From Cakewalks to Concert Halls,* 101; Paul Mills interview, conducted by the author, 9 February 1996; Albert Murray, *Stomping the Blues* (New York, 1976), 50; Russell Sanjek, *American Popular Music and Its Business: The First Four Hundred Years,* vol 3., *From 1900 to 1984* (New York, 1988), 87, 100; Klaus Stratemann, *Duke Ellington: Day by Day and Film by Film* (Copenhagen, 1992), 35–36.

39. Levine, *Black Culture,* 221–32; Morgan and Barlow, *From Cakewalks to Concert Halls,* 100–101; Paul Oliver, *Songsters and Saints: Vocal Tradition on Race Records* (Cambridge, 1984), 122–27; Sanjek, *American Popular Music* 3:64; Southern, *Music of Black Americans,* 399–400.

40. Gioia *History of Jazz,* 124; Morgan and Barlow, *From Cakewalks to Concert Halls,* 111–13; Al Rose, *Eubie Blake* (New York, 1979), 69–83.

41. This section on Ellington's early career in New York City is based on the following sources: Duke Ellington interview, *Friday with Galloway* (NBC broadcast, 29 April 1955), NBC Radio Collection, LOC, RGA 0838 A1–B1; Duke Ellington interview from *A Duke Named Ellington* (1988), LOC/MPD; "A Conversation with The Duke," BBC Radio 1, 1972, interview by Stanley Dance, JVC/LOC, RYJ 3072; Sonny Greer, interviewed by the Duke Ellington Society, 1961, SC Audio C-475, side 1, SCLC; Lawrence, *Ellington and His World,* 62; Louis Metcalf, interviewed by the Duke Ellington Society, 1962, SC Audio C-467, side 1, SCBC; Tucker, *Ellington,* 85, 124–35, 145–46, 161–62, 168–70, 220, 253, 260–61; Tom Whaley interview, JOHP, conducted by Milt Hinton, reel 1, pg. 30–31, IJS/RU.

42. 1926 Gennett advertisement, from Franz Hoffman, ed., *Jazz Advertised,* vol. 4, *Out of the Chicago Defender, 1910–1934* (privately published, 1981), 136. IJS/RU.

43. Langston Hughes, "The Negro Artist and the Racial Mountain," *Nation* (23 June 1926); Rampersad, *Life of Langston Hughes,* vol.1, chaps. 1 and 2.

44. Duke Ellington, "Ellington on the Air in Vancouver," and Roger Pryor Dodge, "Bubber," both in *The Duke Ellington Reader,* ed. Mark Tucker (New York, 1993), 338–39, 455–56.

Chapter Two

1. Barry Ulanov, *Duke Ellington* (New York, 1946), 56; Michael Schudson, *Advertising, the Uneasy Persuasion: Its Dubious Impact on American Society* (New York, 1984), 206.

2. Except as indicated, all pre-1929 information about Irving Mills and the depiction of the early Mills/Ellington relationship comes from the following sources: Milton Berle with Haskel Frankel, *An Autobiography* (New York, 1974), 190; Hoagy Carmichael with Stephen Longstreet, *Sometimes I Wonder* (New York, 1999; orig. 1965), 221; Helen Oakley Dance, liner notes for Duke Ellington, *The Duke's Men: Small Groups,* vol. 1 (Columbia/Legacy, 1991); Edward Kennedy Ellington, *Music Is My Mistress* (New York, 1973), 77, 87; Mercer Ellington with Stanley Dance, *Duke Ellington in Person* (New York, 1975), 33; Duke Ellington interview, CHIC 1964 #8, AC/NMAH/SI; Ross Firestone, *Swing, Swing, Swing: The Life and Times of Benny Goodman* (New York, 1993), 52, 85; Abel Green, "Mills Music's 40-Year Success Story; From 5G & 3 Songs To $5,000,000 Empire," *Variety* (28 October 1959); John Edward Hasse, *Beyond Category: The Life and Genius of Duke Ellington* (New York, 1993), 88–92; Paul Mills interview, conducted by the author, 9 February 1996; Stephen Kemp, "New Talent His Specialty: Irving Mills Discovers and Develops Unknown Personalities," *Metronome* (April 1930); G. E. Lambert, *Duke Ellington* (New York, 1959), 7; A. H. Lawrence, *Duke Ellington and His World* (New York, 2001), 32; Irving Mills interview, conducted by Stephen Lesser, 9 April 1975, New York Pubic Library, Humanities—Jewish Division, box 54, #2; Irving Mills interview, conducted by Irene Kahn Atkins, 23 April 1981, #567A–E, OHAM/YUSC; Irving Mills interview, *Reminiscing In Tempo* (Robert Levi Films, 1992), LOC/MPD; Irving Mills, as told to Charles Emge, "I Split with Duke When Music Began Sidetracking," *Downbeat* (5 November 1952); "Irving Mills Dies at 91; Jazz Music Publisher," *New York Times* (23 April 1985); Richard M. Sudhalter, *Stardust Melody: The Life and Music of Hoagy Carmichael* (New York, 2002), 97, 133, 139, 375, 379–80; Mark Tucker, *Ellington: The Early Years* (Urbana, IL, 1991), 94, 198–99; Ulanov, *Duke Ellington,* 57–59.

The version of "St Louis Blues" that Ellington references is probably the version described by Louis Metcalf in chapter 1.

3. David W. Stowe, *Swing Changes: Big Band Jazz in New Deal America* (Cambridge, MA, 1994): 102–4. During the Swing Era, the Music Corporation of America (MCA) and the William Morris Agency (WMA) employed many of the marketing concepts and economic strategies that Mills developed, but they were not involved as intimately on an artistic level as Mills. Prominent agents of the 1940s like Willard Alexander of MCA and William Morris, Jr., were rarely if ever seen in a recording studio, consulting with songwriters to find hit songs, or promoting their artists as important American composers. They also, unlike Mills, mostly steered clear of black talent, or at least accepted segregation and poor pay for their black entertainers.

4. The following brief summary of how developments in the mass media of the 1920s changed the production and marketing of American music is garnered from: Melissa Axelrod, "In Search of the Lost Rhythm with R. Crumb," *Pulse* (November 1999): 59–61; Robert Crumb, liner notes, *That's What I Call Sweet Music: American Dance Orchestras of the 1920s* (EMI British import recording, 1999); Nicholas Dawidoff, *In the Country of Country: People and Places in Country Music* (New York, 1997), 4–19, 53–60; Philip K. Eberly, *Music in the Air: America's Changing Taste in Pop Music 1920–1980* (New York, 1982), 34, 61; Philip Furia, "Irving Berlin: Troubadour of Tin Pan Alley," in *Inventing Times Square: Commerce and Culture at the Crossroads of the World,* ed. William R. Taylor (Baltimore, 1991), 191–211; Daphne Duval Harrison, *Black Pearls: Blues Queens of the 1920s* (New Brunswick, 1988), chap. 2; Neil Leonard, *Jazz and the White Americans: The Acceptance of a New Art Form* (Chicago, 1962; reprint 1972), 16–22; Greil Marcus and Jeff Place, liner notes, *Anthology of American Folk Music* (Smithsonian Folk-

ways, 1997); Robert Palmer, *Deep Blues* (New York, 1981), chap. 3; Russell Sanjek, *American Popular Music and Its Business*, vol. 3, *1900–1984* (New York, 1988), chaps. 3–8; Joel Whitburn, *Pop Memories 1890–1954* (Menomonee Falls, WI, 1986), 7–16.

5. For a musical snapshot of the fascinating, sometimes strange, geographically and ethnically diverse American musical scene that existed before the more formulaic American popular music marketplace of the 1930s and beyond, consult these compilations: *American Pop: An Audio History—From Minstrel to Mojo: On Record, 1893–1946* (West Hill Audio Archives, 1998); *Anthology of American Folk Music* (Smithsonian Folkways, 1997).

6. Juliet E. K. Walker, *The History of Black Business in America: Capitalism, Race, Entrepreneurship* (New York City, 1998), 213.

7. This material on anti-Semitism and black/Jewish artistic and business relationships is based on the following sources: Hasia R. Diner, *In the Almost Promised Land: American Jews and Blacks, 1915–1935* (Westport, CT, 1977), xv–xvii, 3, 28, 35–36, 90–105, 114; Ann Douglas, *Terrible Honesty: Mongrel Manhattan in the 1920s* (New York, 1995), 354–64, 371, 375–76; Lewis A. Erenberg, *Steppin' Out: New York Nightlife and the Transformation of American Culture, 1890–1930* (Westport, CT, 1981), 74, 187–92, 240; Nelson George, *The Death of Rhythm and Blues* (New York, 1988), chap. 2; Kenneth Aaron Kanter, *The Jews on Tin Pan Alley: The Jewish Contribution to American Popular Music, 1830–1940* (New York, 1982), 13–16, 26, 37–39; David Levering Lewis, "Parallels and Divergences: Assimilationist Strategies of Afro-American and Jewish Elites from 1910 to the Early 1930s," *Journal of American History* (December 1984).

On the Jewish "moguls" in the film industry, consult: Neal Gabler, *An Empire of Their Own: How the Jews Invented Hollywood* (New York, 1988); Robert Sklar, *Movie-Made America: A Cultural History of American Movies* (New York, 1994), 39–47.

8. Certificate of incorporation of Duke Ellington, Inc., 23 December 1929, MC-468, box 61, BECAHC/SCD/UAL.

Mercer Ellington interview, conducted by Dan Caine, 22 July 1979, OHAM/YUSC, #521D, pg. 1–2; John Hammond interview, conducted by the Duke Ellington Society, 1965, SC Audio C-482, SCBC; H. Robert Udkoff interview, conducted by the author, 28 September 1995; Hasse, *Beyond Category*, 90; Tucker, *Ellington*, 198; Ulanov, *Duke Ellington*, 58.

9. Helen Oakley Dance interview, conducted by Patricia Willard, 26 and 27 September 1989, SIEOHP, tapes 1 and 2, AC/NMAH/SI; Sonny Greer interview, January 1979, JOHP, IJS/RU, cassette 1, p. 62; John Hammond interview, conducted by Paul Kolderie, 3 April 1978, OHAM/YUSC, pg. 17; Dan Morgenstern (with Michael Cuscuna and Charlie Lourie), "Milt Gabler Interview," in *Reading Jazz: A Gathering of Autobiography, Reportage, and Criticism from 1919 to Now*, ed. Robert Gottlieb (New York, 1996), 216; Hasse, *Beyond Category*, 90; P. Mills interview, 9 February 1996; Tucker, *Ellington*, 198; M. Ellington, *Duke Ellington*; Stuart Nicholson, *Reminiscing In Tempo: A Portrait of Duke Ellington* (Boston, 1999), 208; *Observer*, "The Observer Profile: Duke Ellington" (5 October 1958). Clipping from DES 3:15, NMAH/SI.

10. Helen Oakley Dance interview, 26 and 27 September 1989, tape 4; Mercer Ellington interview, 22 July 1979, pg. 3; Greer interview, January 1979, cassette 1, pp. 62–63; P. Mills interview, 9 February 1996; I. Mills and Emge, "I Split with Duke"; John Hammond, with Irving Townsend, *John Hammond on Record* (New York, 1977; reprint 1981), 138–39; I. Mills, 9 April 1975, tape 1, pg. 21.

11. Numerous examples of these press books and publicity manuals are cited later in this chapter; P. Mills interview, 9 February 1996; Udkoff interview, 28 September 1995.

12. Roland Marchand, *Creating the Corporate Soul: The Rise of Public Relations and Corporate Imagery in American Big Business* (Berkeley, 1998), 166–67, 258–70.

13. Interviews with Ellington business associates from the 1940s forward stressed that, while Ellington did not design ads or contracts, he did want to see and approve them, especially the

more significant ones. Additionally, he made sure that all were filed so that he could examine them at will (although he almost never did): Ruth Ellington interview, conducted by the author, 26 January 1996; Claire Gordon interview, conducted by the author, 15 November 1995; Patricia Willard interview, conducted by the author, 30 October 1995.

14. Erenberg, *Steppin' Out,* 254; Jeff Kisseloff, *You Must Remember This: An Oral History of Manhattan from the 1890s to World War II* (Baltimore, 1989), 309–12; Graham Lock, *Blutopia: Visions of the Future and Revisions of the Past in the Work of Sun Ra, Duke Ellington, and Anthony Braxton* (Durham, 1999), 88–89.

15. Barney Bigard interview, July 1976, conducted by Patricia Willard, JOHP, reel 5, pg. 24, IJS.RU; James Lincoln Collier, *Duke Ellington,* (New York, 1987), 92–94; Greer interview, January 1979, cassette 1, p. 33; Jim Haskins, *The Cotton Club* (New York, 1977), 57; Langston Hughes, "When Harlem Was in Vogue," in *The Langston Hughes Reader* (New York, 1958), 78–79; Marshall Stearns, *The Story of Jazz* (New York, 1970), 184–86.

16. Haskins, *Cotton Club,* 107–9; Kisseloff, *You Must Remember This.*

17. Duke Ellington interview, CHIC 1964 #3, AC/NMAH/SI.

18. Duke Ellington interview, CHIC 1964 #7, AC/NMAH/SI; Lawrence, *Duke Ellington and His World,* 116, 118.

19. Duke Ellington interview, *Reminiscing In Tempo* (Robert Levi films, 1992), LOC/MPD; Ted Gioia, *The History of Jazz* (New York, 1997), 127–28; Dave Peyton, "The Musical Bunch," *Chicago Defender* (27 August 1927), from the Duke Ellington clipping file, SCBC [this article features extensive quotes from an August 1927 article about Ellington in the *New York Tribune*].

20. Greer interview, January 1979, cassette 1, p. 62; Eberly, *Music in the Air,* 43–49. Ken Steiner's recent research shows that Ellington and his bands of the period made numerous radio appearances on local New York stations, often broadcasting after midnight, during the 1923–25 period: Ken Steiner, *Wild Throng Dances Madly in Cellar Club,* given out to attendees at the May 2008 Duke Ellington International Conference in London.

21. Uncited source, "Columbia Broadcasting Stars" (1930); "Back Stage in Dukedom," *Duke Ellington News* (a flyer advertising an upcoming Chicago show) (19 August 31); Terry Pettus, "Ellington Big Hit at Music Box," uncited Tacoma, WA, source (probably dates late May, 1934); "Ellington Takes Lead in Popularity Contest: First Returns Show Hot Players Favored for Individual Honors," *Orchestra World* (April 1931); "Radio Personalities: Famous Stars of the Ether Help You Sell Sheet Music," uncited source and date (probably fall of 1931); "Village Boys Crash Radio: Most of the Leaders of Smart Dance Bands Come from Small Towns," *Detroit News* (20 September 1931); Radio Speeds Band Leaders on to Riches: Big-Time Fame Rewards Obscure Musicians Who Strike Fancy of Listening Fans," *New Haven Register* (20 September 1931). Clippings found in DES, series 8, subseries 2, vols. 1 and 2, NMAH/SI. The article by Terry Pettus is from vol. 6.

22. For Ellington's Cotton Club–era releases, including all tracks cited in this discussion, consult: Duke Ellington and His Orchestra, *Early Ellington: 1927–1934* (RCA/Bluebird, 1989).

23. Nathan Huggins, *Harlem Renaissance* (London, 1971), 85–92; David Levering Lewis, *When Harlem Was in Vogue* (New York, 1981), 162–164; Sanjek, *American Popular Music,* 124.

24. Uncited author (most likely the work of Ned Williams), "Advertising Manual: Duke Ellington and His Famous Orchestra" (c. 1931), 8, 12, 16. Courtesy of Steven Lasker.

25. "Advertising Manual," 1. Sonny Greer (Greer interview, January 1979, cassette 1, p. 80) suggested that Sophie Tucker, a white vocalist who often covered black music, coined the nickname of "aristocrat of jazz" for Ellington.

26. Mercer Ellington interview, conducted by the Duke Ellington Society, 1962, SC Audio C-462, SCBC; John McDonough, "Reminiscing In Tempo: Guitarist Freddie Guy's Ellington Memories," *Downbeat* (17 April 1959); Juan Tizol interview, 15 November 1978, conducted by

Patricia Willard, JOHP, reel 1, pg. 26, IJS/RU; Stratemann, *Duke Ellington: Day by Day and Film by Film* (Copenhagen, 1992), 2; Hasse, *Beyond Category,* 94. Greer, in his oral history interview, maintained that Mills booked the Chevalier gig, but the other two sources base their findings on some solid research. For Chevalier's interest in Ellington, see Daniel Ringold and Philippe Guiboust, *Maurice Chevalier: Le Sourire de Paris* (TF1 Editions, 1995), translation of portion about Ellington by Bernard Dupuis, from *DEMS [Duke Ellington Music Society] Bulletin* 02/3 December 2002–March 2003, 17/1. Courtesy of Sjef Hoefsmit.

27. Schudson, *Advertising,* 18–19.

28. Advertisement for "Creole Rhapsody," *Variety* (2 June 1931): 34.

29. The ads, in order of their appearance in the text: "Solitude," *Melody News* (a publication primarily dedicated to Mills artists and songs) (1 January 1935): 8; "Five Star Genius," *Melody News* (1 October 1934): 5; "In A Sentimental Mood," *Metronome* (September 1936): 13; Mills Music advertisement, *Melody News* (1 March 1935): 10–11; "Reminiscing In Tempo" promotional handout (probably a co-production of Brunswick [Ellington's record company] and Mills Music—both of their imprimaturs are on the document) (c. Autumn 1935): 1–4 (part of the folder "Duke Ellington 1924–40 File") IJS/RU.

30. Schudson, *Advertising,* 204–5.

31. Schudson, *Advertising,* 51, 96.

32. I. Mills and Emge, "I Split with Duke."

33. Tucker, *Ellington,* 89–90; E. K. Ellington, *Music Is My Mistress,* 70; M. Ellington, *Duke Ellington In Person,* 66; Greer interview, January 1979, cassette 1, p. 76, cassette 4, p. 21; I. Mills interview, 23 April 1981, pg. 14, 32, 33; P. Mills interview, 9 February 1996.

34. Robert and Evelyn Udkoff interview, conducted by Dr. Marcia M. Greenlee, 11 March 1991, SIEOHP, tape 1, AC/NMAH/SI; Bret Primack, "Ellington Is Forever: A Centennial Salute," *Jazz Times* (March 1999): 39; Ulanov, *Duke Ellington,* 74; uncited author, "Orpheum: Duke Ellington" (unattributed 1933 review); uncited author, "Duke Ellington Is Greeted with Enthusiasm Here: His Opening Performance Superior to That of Cab Calloway" (unattributed 1933 review). Clippings from DES, series 8, subseries 2, vol. 6, NMAH/SI.

Irving Mills says he helped devise some of the different lighting schemes for the band presentation: I. Mills interview, 23 April 1981, pg. 30.

35. Cab Calloway, as anthologized in Gottlieb, *Reading Jazz,* 119; Phoebe Jacobs interview, conducted by the author, 27 January 1996.

36. E. K. Ellington, *Music Is My Mistress,* 54; Lawrence Otis Graham, *Our Kind of People: Inside America's Black Upper-Class* (New York, 1999), 85–90; Jacqueline Moore, *Leading the Race: The Transformation of the Black Elite in the Nation's Capital, 1880–1920* (Charlottesville, 1999), 9–12, 192–93; Primack, "Ellington Is Forever," 38. Italics are Ellington's.

37. Calloway and Rollins, *Of Minnie the Moocher,* 106, 120; Stratemann, *Duke Ellington,* 45, 52, 69, 288; Ulanov, *Duke Ellington,* 180, 191; Nat D. Williams, "Duke's Band Breaks Precedent at Orpheum," *Commercial Appeal* (2 December 1937); "Music: Jazzmen off Beat," *Time* (23 December 1940); Hy Gardner, "Coast to Coast," *New York Herald Tribune* (7 November 1956); "Things Theatrical: Ellington vs. Petrillo," *Washington D.C. Tribune* (11 February 1936). Further examples in Stratemann, *Duke Ellington,* 150, 261, 267, 268, 288, 362.

38. Sanjek, *American Popular Music,* 66–69, 78–79, 121–22, 128–29; Steven Lasker interview, conducted by the author, 25 September 1995; P. Mills interview, 9 February 1996; Leonard, *Jazz and the White Americans,* 96.

There is an excellent collection of record bulletins, ranging from the 1920s to the 1950s, at the Institute for Jazz Studies, Rutgers University, Newark, New Jersey.

39. Sanjek, *American Popular Music,* 66; Lawrence, *Duke Ellington and His World,* 94–96. See also Dan Morgenstern, liner notes for *Early Ellington: 1927–1934* (RCA Bluebird, 1989).

40. Greer interview, January 1979, cassette 2, pp. 23–24; Hammond, *John Hammond on Record,* 133; Lawrence, *Duke Ellington and His World,;* Louis Metcalf, interviewed by the Duke Ellington Society, 1962, SC Audio C-467, side 1, SCBC; I. Mills interview, 23 April 1981, pg. 12; P. Mills interview, 9 February 1996; I. Mills and Emge, "I Split with Duke"; Udkoff interview, 28 September 1975.

41. Whitburn, *Pop Memories,* 648–51. While there were no bestselling record charts as we know them today during the period, Whitburn's research combines knowledge gleaned from sheet-music sales, royalty documents, and post-1929 primitively compiled charts that appeared in *Variety* and *Billboard.* A problem in tracking Ellington's bestsellers is that from 1927 to 1931 his orchestra often recorded the same songs under different nom de plumes (such as the Harlem Footwarmers and the Jungle Band) for several different labels, possibly diluting the sales for the individual recordings that Whitburn cites.

The situation of most 1930s hit singles emanating from films followed the major Hollywood studios' purchasing of most of the top New York City–based publishing companies in the 1920s and '30s: Sanjek, *American Popular Music,* 54–55, 72–75.

42. Sanjek, *American Popular Music,* 24, 28, 92; William Howland Kenney, *Recorded Music in American Life: The Phonograph and Popular Memory* (New York, 1999), chap. 3; Leonard, *Jazz and the White Americans,* 19.

43. D, Ellington interview, *Reminiscing In Tempo* (Robert Levi films, 1992); Eliot Tiegal, "Duke and Irving Mills: They Helped Each Other Grow in the Early Years," *Billboard* (10 February 1973); P. Mills interview, 9 February 1996; "Reminiscing In Tempo" (promotional handout); Collier, *Duke Ellington,* 110–11; Hammond, *John Hammond on Record,* 139; Leonard, *Jazz and the White Americans,* 121.

44. Hayes Alvis interview, conducted by the Duke Ellington Society, 1965, SC Audio C-478, SCBC; Bigard interview, July 1976, reel 5, pg. 8; Barney Bigard, *With Louis and the Duke: The Autobiography of A Jazz Clarinetist* (New York, 1985), 47–49; memorandum, John Hammond to Walter Dean, "Ellington Royalties," 9 November 1965, John Hammond Collection, YUSC; Hammond DES interview.

In the memorandum, John Hammond said that, based on contracts in the Columbia Records files, Ellington did make 5–10 percent royalties on records released in all countries but the U.S. and Canada starting in late 1935. William Mittler, Ellington's accountant from the 1930s to the mid-1960s, felt that Mills had negotiated an artist royalty for Ellington starting in 1935 in the U.S. and Canada, and that Mills took a whopping 50 percent commission from it. Hammond could not find documentation of this, but also acknowledged that "side deals" might not have been formally documented or preserved in the Columbia files. .

45. Schudson, *Advertising,* 18–19.

46. The Ivie Anderson recordings in this discussion can all found on: *Ivie Anderson with Duke Ellington and His Famous Orchestra* (Jazz Archives, France, 1991). Many of the Anderson recordings were hits in the 1930s: Whitburn, *Pop Memories.*

47. I. Mills interview, 23 April 1981, pg. 14; P. Mills interview, 9 February 1996. Ellington did become more involved in the writing of lyrics in the 1940s and afterward.

Band trombonist Lawrence Brown also recalled that the band recorded many songs without titles that were later named by the Mills office: Lawrence Brown interview, conducted by Patricia Willard, July 1976, JOHP, IJS/RU, reel 3, pg. 17–18.

48. P. Mills interview, 9 February 1996; Gerald Marks interview, conducted by the author, 27 January 1996; Sanjek, *American Popular Music,* 324, 398; Wilma Cockerell interview, conducted by the author, 22 January 1996.

49. Laurence Bergreen, *Louis Armstrong: An Extravagant Life* (New York, 1997), 293; P. Mills interview, 9 February 1996; I. Mills interview, 9April 1975, tape 1, pg. 34.

50. Some examples of these as culled from the Smithsonian Institution's Sam DeVincent Sheet Music Collection, housed at the Archives Center at the Museum of American History (collection 300, series 3, box 126, folders AA and Z): *Duke Ellington's Piano Solos* (Mills Music, c.1937); *Duke Ellington's Song Folio* (Mills Music, c.1940); *Duke Ellington's Streamlined Piano Solos* (Mills Music, c.1938); *Bird of Paradise: A Modern Composition for Piano* (Robbins Music Corporation, 1935—some of Ellington's 1930s works were licensed to Robbins during the 1930s; after he left the Mills organization and before he started his own publishing company, Tempo Music, Ellington's compositions in the 1940s for a brief time were published by Robbins); *Boy Meets Horn: Piano Transcription* (American Academy of Music, c.1938). There are more examples on file there, including many single pieces of Ellington's music from the Mills period.

51. Examples in which Ellington was cross-promoted in his sheet music with exclusively or at least 90 percent white songwriters or artists: *Duke Ellington's Piano Solos* (Mills Music, c.1937); *Duke Ellington's Song Folio* (Mills Music, c.1940); *Bird of Paradise* (Robbins Music Corporation, 1935); *Boy Meets Horn* (American Academy of Music, c.1938); *Caravan* (Exclusive Publications, c.1938); *Mood Indigo* (Mills Music, c.1931); *Solitude* (Millsons, c.1935); *Sophisticated Lady* (Mills Music, c.1934).

There are many examples in the cited folders that demonstrate this trend continuing in the 1940s and 1950s.

Examples from the 1930s of Ellington cross-promoted in his sheet music with black songwriters/artists: *Mood Indigo* (Mills Music, 1938); *Skrontch* (Mills Music, 1938); *Swingtime in Honolulu* (Mills Music, 1938); these first three examples feature only ads for Ellington. *I Let a Song Go out of My Heart* (Mills Music, c.1938) features a Fats Waller ad for a group of songs entitled *Swingtime in Scotland,* as well as his song *Ain't Misbehavin'* in a book called *Mills Radio Song Faves.* Ads for *Duke Ellington's Streamlined Piano Solos* (Mills Music, c.1938) feature James P. Johnson and Fats Waller.

All individual songs mentioned in this footnote were either written or co-written by Duke Ellington.

All cited sheet music is housed at the Smithsonian Institution's Sam DeVincent Sheet Music Collection (collection 300, box 126, series 3, folders AA and Z).

52. E. K. Ellington, *Music Is My Mistress,* 103; Edward Jablonski, *Gershwin: A Biography* (New York, 1987), 62–63; Peretti, *Jazz in American Culture,* 34–43.

53. "Duke Ellington's 'Creole Rhapsody,'" *Oklahoma Eagle* (15 August 1931). The same article and photo also appear in: *(Paducah, KY) Lighthouse* (14 August 1931); *Tampa Bulletin* (14 August 1931); *Chattanooga Reader* (14 August 1931). The fact that this article and photo appeared in numerous Southern newspapers is significant as well. Clippings from DES, series 8, subseries 2, vol. 1, AC/NMAH/SI.

54. Jablonski, *Gershwin,* x, 51, 57–60, 75, 136, 176.

55. Peretti, *Jazz in American Culture.*

56. D. Ellington interview, *Reminiscing In Tempo* (Robert Levi films, 1992); Lambert, *Duke Ellington,* 14.

In today's music business, Hammond's dual position as critic and recording executive would be viewed as an unethical conflict of interest. But, in the mid-1930s, jazz criticism was in its infancy, with *Downbeat* magazine, the first dedicated to the jazz scene, created less than a year before the release of "Reminiscing In Tempo."

57. Marks interview, 27 January 1996; P. Mills interview, 9 February 1996; I. Mills and Emge, "I Split with Duke"; Brooks Kerr interview, conducted by the author, 25 January 1996; Hammond, *John Hammond on Record,* 133, 137; Jacobs interview, 27 January 1996.

The large amount of financially and artistically successful danceable Ellington orchestra recordings of the 1930s and '40s make Hammond's grousings seem almost humorous.

58. P. Mills interview, 9 February 1996; Helen Oakley Dance interview, 26 and 27 September 1989; Collier, *Duke Ellington,* 138, 141, 144, 183; Hammond, *John Hammond on Record,* 89, 138; Lasker interview, 27 September 1995; Marks interview, 27 January 1996; "Desperation Salaries: 80 'Name Acts,' $2K or More," *Variety* (8 March 1932); E. K. Ellington, *Music Is My Mistress,* 89.

59. Stratemann, *Duke Ellington,* 26.

60. Ruth Ellington interview, CHIC 1964 #8, AC/NMAH/SI; Mercer Ellington interview, 22 July 1979.

61. P. Mills interview, 9 February 1996; Allen Keiler, *Marian Anderson: A Singer's Journey* (New York, 2000): Chapters 5 and 9.

62. Ned E. Williams, as featured in Best Contest Letters of the Week column, *Pittsburgh Courier* (31 October 1931). In his letter, Williams never acknowledged his role in managing and promoting Ellington. Today, such nondisclosure would be viewed as unethical.

63. "Negro Race Produces Another Leader," *Savannah Journal* (23 May 1931). Other syndicated appearances of the same article: *Night Club News* (20 May 1931), *Tampa Bulletin* (c. May 1931).

"Duke's Home Town Pays Him Fine Tribute as He Returns with Band: 'Rhythm King' to Be Guest of President Hoover at the White House," *Pittsburgh Courier* (c. October 1931); "Duke Ellington News" promotional circular (19 August 1931); "Duke Ellington: A Work of Art," *Chicago Whip* (29 January 1932); "Duke Ellington Getting Famous," *San Antonio Register* (15 January 1932); Floyd G. Snelson, ed., "Noble, Fletcher, on Heels of Leader as Votes Leap Ahead," *Pittsburgh Courier* (12 September 1931).

Clippings from DES, series 8, subseries 2, vols. 1 and 2, NMAH/SI.

64. Ruth Ellington interview, conducted by Dr. Marcia M. Greenlee, 18 August 1989, SIEOHP, tape 2, AC/NMAH/SI; I. Mills interview, 23 April 1981, pg. 7, 18; advertisement for 12 October 1931 Scottsboro/NAACP benefit in Washington, D.C.; "Duke Ellington Raises $425 in Washington Benefit: Branch Launches 'Spend Where You Can Get Work' Program," *Topeka Plain Dealer* (30 October 1931); Stratemann, *Duke Ellington,* 45 (7 December 1930 NAACP benefit); "Stage Stars Aid Scottsboro Boys: Performers Entertain 400 at Les Seize Benefit Given in Town Hall," *Amsterdam News* (31 May 1933); uncited author, "6,000 at NAACP Ball," source obscured (11 February 1939). Clippings from DES, series 8, subseries 2, vols. 2, 5, and 8, NMAH/SI.

It should be noted that proceeds of benefits were collected using different systems. For some performances, all door proceeds went towards the cause; at other times the performers took a small fee or covered their expenses before the balance was donated to charity. At the benefit covered in the 31 May 1933 clipping in this footnote, audience donations were sought on a voluntary basis.

65. Ruth Ellington Smithsonian interview, 1964; Ruth Ellington interview in Lawrence, *Duke Ellington and His World,* 187.

66. Lawrence, *Duke Ellington and His World,* 180; Stratemann, *Duke Ellington,* 50.

67. "Duke Ellington Sponsors Benefit," *New York Graphic* (9 May 1932); "Harlem Benefit Show for Pullman Porters," *New York Post* (19 May 1933); "The Duke Entertains Shut-Ins" (photo caption of concert featuring Ellington orchestra, Adelaide Hall, and Bill "Bojangles" Robinson at Harlem Hospital, *Pittsburgh Courier* (4 July 1934); Stratemann, *Duke Ellington,* 132 (November and December 1935 benefit for Harlem's Needy organization).

Clippings from DES, series 8, subseries 2, vols. 2 and 5, NMAH/SI.

68. "Duke Ellington Fund Benefit Dance Offers Bargain Entertaining: Receipts from Coronado Event to Go to Community Budget," *St. Louis Daily Globe-Democrat* (5 December 1931);

"Duke Ellington News," *St. Louis Daily Globe-Democrat* (circular); "Ellington at 8 This Morning!" *San Francisco Examiner* (19 February 1932); uncited author, "Duke Ellington and Band in Welcoming Broadcast: Roosevelt Therapy Pool Dedication Program Will Be on Air from Cleveland; James Roosevelt to Speak," unidentified Cleveland clipping (c. January 1934). Clippings from DES, series 8, subseries 2, vols. 2 and 6, NMAH/SI.

69. "So Many Benefits, Can't Grab Enough Change to Make 'Em," *Variety* (14 March 1933).

70. Hollie I. West, "A Talk with Duke Ellington, Age 70," *New York Post* (29 April 1969).

71. Walter Winchell, On Broadway column, *New York City Mirror* (16 May 1933).

72. Max Lasser, "Famous Leader Building $25,000," *Syndicate Broadcaster* (February 1932). Article and accompanying information about Investors Syndicate and its magazine courtesy of Pamela Feltus.

73. Walker, *History of Black Business in America,* chap. 7.

74. "Who Will Be the 'Bojangles,' Waters or Mills of Tomorrow?: Promising Performces [*sic*] Mentioned," *Pittsburgh Courier* (3 October 1931); Sime, "Mills Blue Rhythm Band" review, *Variety* (6 October 1931). The headline in the *Courier* referred to Florence Mills, not Irving Mills.

75. *Zits* (23 April 1932); uncited author, "New Duke Ellington Discovered by Mills," unidentified clipping, probably from *Variety* (c. February 1932); advertisement for Mills Blue Rhythm Boys, *Variety* (2 June 1931); uncited author, "Ellington Makes Way for Others," unidentified, undated fragment (c. Fall 1931); "New Ellington Unit" picture and caption, *Chicago Defender* (27 June 1931) from Hoffman, *Jazz Advertised,* 4:274. The 1933 film short, entitled *The World at Large,* can found on *Duke Ellington Hits on Film, 1933 to 1969* (Big Band Series videocassette, made in Canada, no year listed for publication). Clippings from DES, series 8, subseries 2, vols. 1 and 2, NMAH/SI.

76. Tom Kelly, Radio News column, *Yonkers Daily Record* (24 May 1933); Tom Kelly, Radio News column, *Yonkers Daily Record* (5 July 1933); Nick Kenny, "Editor Gives Radio Fans Lowdown: Clarke's Work on WINS Attracts Lots of Attention," *New York City Mirror* (23 July 1933); uncited author, column item concerning publication of songs from the New Cotton Club on Parade by Mills-owned Exclusive Publications, *Orchestra World* (December 1933); Stratemann, *Duke Ellington,* 62, 65. Clippings from DES, series 8, subseries 2, vols. 4 and 5, NMAH/SI.

77. "Irving Mills Connoisseur of Dapper Stage Beauties," *San Antonio Register* (15 January 1932). This article was also found syndicated verbatim in the following newspapers, with all articles carrying the date of 16 January 1932: *(Augusta, GA) Echo, Pittsburgh Courier, Oklahoma Eagle.*

Harlem Speaks featured a band headed by "Buba" (usually known as Bubber) Miley, one of the central musicians in Ellington's band during the Cotton Club years, and the co-composer of such important works as "Black and Tan Fantasie."

"'Harlem Scandals' to Go on RKO Tour," *Negro World* (19 December 1931); "Irvin [*sic*] Mills New Show Now Playing Warner Circuit," *Chicago Whip* (16 January 1932); Ted Yates, "Harlem Scandals Yeah Man! Yates Rates Show Aces," *Inter-state Tattler* (14 January 1932); Ned E. Williams, Musical Jottings column, *Echo* (19 December 1931). In the last article, there was no notice given to readers that Williams worked for the Mills organization as the chief publicity writer at this time. Clippings from DES, series 8, subseries 2, vol. 4, NMAH/SI.

78. Stratemann, *Duke Ellington,* 154; Isadora Smith, "Duke Is Honored by ASCAP: Receives Award for His 1938 Composition, 'I Let a Song Go out of My Heart,'" source of clipping obscured (February 1939). Clipping from DES, subseries 2, vol. 8, NMAH/SI.

Chapter Three

1. Barry Ulanov, *Duke Ellington* (New York, 1946), 188–89; John Edward Hasse, *Beyond Category: The Life and Genius of Duke Ellington* (New York, 1993), 403.

2. Gordon S. Wood, *The Radicalism of the American Revolution* (New York, 1991), introduction, chap. 15.

3. Klaus Stratemann, *Duke Ellington, Day by Day and Film by Film* (Copenhagen, 1992), 47–49.

4. Hollie I. West, "A Talk with Duke Ellington, Age 70," *New York Post* (29 April 1969).

5. Laurence Bergreen, *As Thousands Cheer: The Life of Irving Berlin* (New York, 1990), 200–202; Philip Furia, "Irving Berlin, Troubadour of Tin Pan Alley," in *Inventing Times Square: Commerce and Culture at the Crossroads of the World,* ed. William R. Taylor (Baltimore, 1991): 200–203.

6. Archie Bell, "Duke Ellington's Orchestra Draws Big Crowds: RKO Palace Enjoys Phenomenal Business; Leader of Cotton Club Syncopators Traces Jazz to Africa," *Cleveland News* (8 July 1931).

7. "Colored Band Wins over Publix Circuit," *Motion Picture Herald* (8 August 1931); "Duke Ellington to Begin Six Months' Tour of Motion Picture Theatres," *Oklahoma Eagle* (3 October 1931); "Vaude Gives Bands Break," *Billboard* (9 February 1932).

8. Joe Schoenfeld, "Paramount, New York," *Billboard* (23 April 1932); Bige, "Paramount, N.Y.," *Variety* (19 April 1932). Clippings from DES, series 8, subseries 2, vol. 2, NMAH/SI.

9. Gilbert Chase, "The Man Who Made Jazz Hot: Duke Ellington and His Band a Big Success—in Paris—Farewell Concert Tomorrow," uncited source (c. 1933); William S. Cunningham, "Duke and Ivie Click," *Columbus Citizen* (29 December 1932). Clippings from DES, series 8, subseries 2, vols. 3 and 5, NMAH/SI.

10. Grover Sales, "Duke Was the King: A Friend and Scholar Shares Memories of Ellington," *San Francisco Examiner and Chronicle* (21 February 1999). Courtesy of Dennis and Patti Mulqueeney.

11. James Lincoln Collier, *Duke Ellington* (New York, 1987), 100; "Hot Jazz: The Duke," *Phonograph Monthly Review* (January 1931); Rob Reel, "Ellington Band, Corking Film on Bang-Up Bill," *Chicago American* (18 February 1931); uncited article, *Cleveland Press* (10 October 1931). Clippings from DES, series 8, subseries 2, vol. 1, NMAH/SI. The last citation is from vol. 2.

12. Louis Reid column, *New York City American* (3 June 1933); Gilbert Swan, Jazz in the Classroom column, *Poughkeepsie Eagle News* (4 Nov 1932). Also found syndicated in: *Danville (IL) News* (6 November 1932), *Oklahoma City News* (9 November 1932), *Jackson (MS) Ledger* (22 November 1932). The Ellington NYU appearance also appeared in: William Gaines, About New York column, *Brockton (MA) Times* (7 November 1932); Walter Winchell, On Broadway column, *San Francisco Call* (11 November 1932).

Uncited gossip columns about a possible Carnegie show from *New York City Sun* (4 March 1933), *Norwalk Sentinel* (27 March 1933), unidentified March 1933 column by Aircaster.

Clippings from DES, series 8, subseries 2, vol. 5, NMAH/SI.

13. Mark Hellinger, Broadway Episodes column, *Daily Mirror* (21 February 1931); Ellington advertisement, *Variety* (4 March 1931): 72; "Duke Ellington Packs Palace; Special Show: Midnight Program Given to Care for Crowds; Standout All Night," *Peoria Journal Transcript* (29 March 1931); "Gets over $5,000 per Week," *Pittsburgh Courier* (3 October 1931); Ellington advertisement celebrating Oriental engagements, *Variety* (1 December 1931): 56; "Duke Ellington Fund Benefit Dance Offers Bargain Entertaining: Receipts from Hotel Coronado Event to Go to Community Budget," *St. Louis Daily Globe Democrat* (5 December 1931).

For some stands, as in their multiple-week engagement in San Francisco in 1932, the Ellington orchestra received $5,000 per week, not including extra payments based on gross sales participation: "Ellington at 8 This Morning!" *San Francisco Examiner* (19 February 1932).

Clippings from DES, series 8, subseries 2, vols. 1 and 2, NMAH/SI. Additional source for this note: Stratemann, *Duke Ellington,* 47–50.

14. Langston Hughes, *The Big Sea* (New York, 1940), 334.

15. The majority of films discussed in the following pages can be viewed at AC/NMAH/SI, Ernie Smith Film Collection, collection 491.

16. James Weldon Johnson, *Black Manhattan* (New York, 1930), 229–30; Laurence Bergreen, *Louis Armstrong: An Extravagant Life* (New York, 1997), 381–85; Phoebe Jacobs interview, conducted by the author, 27 January 1996.

17. Bergreen, *Louis Armstrong.*

18. Stratemann, *Duke Ellington,* 5–14. For more on the personality and views of Bessie Smith, see: Chris Albertson, *Bessie* (New York, 1972); Angela Yvonne Davis, *Blues Legacies and Black Feminism: Gertrude "Ma" Rainey, Bessie Smith, and Billie Holiday* (New York, 1998).

19. Stratemann, *Duke Ellington.*

20. Thomas Cripps, *Slow Fade to Black: The Negro in American Film, 1900–1942* (New York, 1977), 269; Stratemann, *Duke Ellington,* 29–42.

21. Stratemann, *Duke Ellington,* 59–64.

22. The factual information concerning these two films is from Stratemann, *Duke Ellington,* 73–101.

23. Stratemann, *Duke Ellington,* 121–24.

24. All films discussed in this section are part of the Ernie Smith Film Collection, AC/NMAH/SI.

25. Harry Carney interview, conducted by the Duke Ellington Society, 1960, SC Audio C-455, side 2, SCBC; Helen Oakley Dance interview, conducted by Patricia Willard, 26 and 27 September 1989, SIEOHP, tape 1, AC/NMAH/SI; Stanley Dance interview, conducted by Dr. Marcia M. Greenlee, 28 August 1990, SIEOHP, tape 1, AC/NMAH/SI; Duke Ellington interview, England 1933, from *Souvenir of Duke Ellington's First Visit to England* (Black Jack LP 3004), LOC/RSD; John Hammond interview, conducted by Paul Kolderie, 3 April 1978, OHAM/YUSC, pg. 27; Len W. Hunt, "Ellington's English Reception: Duke Scores Triumph with People, But Critics Puzzled by His Ultra-Modern Music," *Metronome* (August 1933); Max Jones interview, conducted by Patricia Willard, 15 October 1989, SIEOHP, tape 1, AC/NMAH/SI; Allen Keiler, *Marian Anderson: A Singer's Journey* (New York, 2000), chap. 4; Cootie Williams interview, conducted by Helen Oakley Dance, May 1976, JOHP, pg. 115, IJS/RU.

26. Duke Ellington, "A Royal View of Jazz," *Jazz* (Spring 1959); Spike Hughes, "Duke Ellington: A Personal Note by 'Spike' Hughes," *Melody Maker* (Spring 1933). Clippings from DES, series 8, subseries 2, vol. 8. For further Ellington and Tizol reactions to 1933 English tour, see Stuart Nicholson, *Reminiscing In Tempo: A Portrait of Duke Ellington* (Boston, 1999), 134.

27. Neil Leonard, *Jazz and the White Americans: The Acceptance of a New Art Form* (Chicago, 1962; reprint 1972), 141; Hasse, *Beyond Category,* 174–77; Mercer Ellington with Stanley Dance, *Duke Ellington In Person* (New York, 1975), 59–61; Edward Kennedy Ellington, *Music Is My Mistress* (New York, 1973), 84.

A few examples of this trend of quoting classical critics/composers concerning the artistic significance and quality of Ellington's compositions gleaned from contemporary Ellington orchestra press manuals: "Irving Mills Presents Duke Ellington and His Famous Orchestra" (from the Duke Ellington Ephemera Collection at the Smithsonian Ellington Archives [SEA], circa 1933), 2; "Duke Ellington and His Famous Orchestra" (from the Duke Ellington Oral History Project at SEA, listed as "Press Manual—WMA, Inc., circa 1941"), 2; "Duke Ellington and His Orchestra Press Manual," collection 301, series 11, box 1, folder 6 (circa 1946), 34–35. The

press release that features Ellington accolades by Lambert, Percy Grainger, and Leopold Stokowski, among others, is reproduced verbatim in similar press manuals from the years 1949,
1953, and 1955: collection 301, series 11, box 1, folders 11, 14, and 15.

28. Max Jones interview, 15 October 1989, tapes 1 and 2, ibid.; Constant Lambert, "The Spirit
of Jazz," in *Music Ho! A Study of Music in Decline* (London, 1934; reprint 1985), 186; Hasse, *Beyond Category,* 171–73; Mike's Report column, "The Duke Disappoints: But Only in His Choice
of Programme," *Melody Maker* (5 July 1933); Mike's Report column, "Results of 'Mike's' Competition: Readers' Views on the Ellington Concert," *Melody Maker* (15 July 1933); John Hammond, U.S.A. Letter column, *Melody Maker* (29 July 1933); Mike's Report column, "'Mike's'
Report on the Second Ellington 'M. M.' Concert," *Melody Maker* (22 July 1933). For Ellington
show advertisements in England, consult DES, series 8, subseries 2, vol. 3, NMAH/SI. Sonny
Greer interview, conducted by Stanley Crouch, January 1979, JOHP, IJS/RU.

29. "The Art of Duke Ellington: Some Reflections," *Wood Green Sentinel* (27 July 1933); Reviews section, *Sound Wave* (July 1933); Censeur, Record Notes column, *Dancing Times* (Summer 1933); Playfellow, "On Duke Ellington: Is Modern Jazz Going High-Brow?" *Huddersfield
Examiner* (22 July 1933). Clippings from DES, series 8, subseries 2, vol. 3, NMAH/SI.

30. Plays and Pictures column, *New Statesman* (22 July 1933).

31. Sonny Greer in *Reading Jazz: A Gathering of Autobiography, Reportage, and Criticism from
1919 to Now,* ed. Robert Gottlieb (New York, 1996), 54; Spike Hughes, "The Technical Lesson
of Ellington," parts 1–4, *Melody Maker* (19 and 26 August, 2 and 9 September 1933); The Rambler's Diary column, *Tune Times* (September 1933); Jones interview, 15 October 1989; Sid Phillips, The Saxophone Team column, *Rhythm* (August 1933); Peter Rush, "The Music of Duke Ellington: Some Impressions and Criticisms," *Tune Times* (September 1933).

32. "Hot Record Circles Are Increasing, and Now There Are Six 'M. M.' Affiliations," *Melody
Maker* (2 September 1933); "For Those Who Know Their Ellington," *Melody Maker* (26 November 1933); Collie Knox column, "The B.B.C. Is Spoofing You," *Daily Mail* (8 November 1933).

33. Rex, "Will This Never Cease? The Armstrong-Ellington-Calloway Controversy Shows
No Sign of Abating," *Melody Maker* (18 November 1933); The Rambler's Diary column, *Tune
Times* (December 1933); Sir Anthony Jenkinson, "Oxford Wants Hot Music!" *Melody Maker*
(18 November 1933); Russell Woodward, "Duke and the Snobs: A Reader Airs His Views on
What Ellington Should and Should Not Do," *Melody Maker* (16 December 1933). The immediately preceding notes also contain numerous examples of the Ellington phenomenon continuing in the music press long after the band's last performance in England on 22 July 1933.

34. "Duke Ellington's Trip Abroad Answers European Plea for the Best in Jazz," *Kansas City
Call* (23 June 1933).

35. Bergreen, *Louis Armstrong,* 349–68; "No Dough—No Duke," *Orchestra World* (March
1933). Mills did cancel, for lack of a sufficient financial guarantee, a week of dates in Paris and
three additional dates in the Netherlands: Stratemann, *Duke Ellington,* 66.

36. "The Armstrong War," *Rhythm* (September 1932); uncited and undated article from
Glasgow newspaper; *Scotland Sun-Mail,* "Trumpeter, What Are You Sounding Now? (No-
body Seems to Know)" (14 August 1932); Paul Whiteman, "What I Think of Louis Armstrong,"
Rhythm (probably September 1932); Dan S. Ingman, "England's Welcome to Louis Armstrong,"
Melody Maker (c. August 1932); "Further Armstrong Surprises: Three Bands in Five Weeks,"
Melody Maker (c. September 1933). All of these clippings are from scrapbook 6 (1932 London
Tour), housed at the Louis Armstrong House and Archives, Queens College, CUNY. The clippings in the scrapbook, probably compiled by avid amateur historian Armstrong himself, do
not always properly cite the date and source of the articles, as indicated by the above incomplete information.

37. Stanley Dance interview, 28 August 1990; Jones interview, 15 October 1989: Ulanov, *Duke Ellington,* 151.

38. "Black Folk of the Bright Lights: Negroes Invade Our Theaters," *Pearson's Weekly* (5 August 1933); Russell Woodward, "Duke and the Snobs"; Mathison Brooks, Gramophone Notes column, *Daily Herald* (26 July 1933); "Old Songs Are Best," *Sound Wave* (July 1933); Ralph Hill, "Currente Calamo," *Music Lover* (2 September 1933); Jones interview, 15 October 1989. For more on British criticism of the 1933 tour, consult Ulanov, *Duke Ellington,* 138–39.

39. The Busker, Fermata column, *Melody Maker* (12 August 1933); Olympian, "This Is the Age of Rhythm: In Defense of Jazz," *Portsmouth Evening News* (18 November 1933).

40. John A. Kouwenhoven, *Made in America: The Arts in Modern Civilization* (New York, 1948; 1975 reprint), 269; Lawrence W. Levine, *The Opening of the American Mind: Canons, Culture, and History* (Boston, 1996), chap. 4.

41. Leonard Bernstein, "Positively Yes! Says Leonard Bernstein," in *Reading Jazz: A Gathering of Autobiography, Reportage, and Criticism from 1919 to Now,* ed. Robert Gottlieb (New York, 1996), 780; J. Peter Burkholder, *Charles Ives: The Ideas behind the Music* (New Haven, 1985), 1–4, 12–17, 43–56, 95–109; Rosalie Sandra Perry, *Charles Ives and the American Mind* (Kent, OH, 1974), introduction, chaps. 1–3; Paul E. Bierley, *John Philip Sousa: American Phenomenon* (Englewood Cliffs, NY, 1973), 7–31, 119, 124; Joseph Horowitz, *Understanding Toscanini: How He Became an American Culture God and Helped Create a New Audience for Old Music* (Minneapolis, 1988), 136–37; Leonard, *Jazz and the White Americans,* 16–22.

42. Constance Rourke, *American Humor* (New York, 1931), 161.

43. "Newman Resumes Attack on 'Jazz'; British Critic Declares Our Tunes Are the 'Last Word in Musical Insanity,'" *New York Times* (26 December 1927); Paul Whiteman, "In Defense of Jazz and Its Makers; An American Exponent of the 'New Art' Calls It the Folk Music of the Machine Age," *New York Times* (13 March 1927). In the former, British critic Ernest Newman observes that "our American friends are laudably anxious to have music of their own like other nations. Jazz being the one form that is indisputably American, it is natural that Americans should feel for it the admiring affection of a young mother for her very own first baby, regardless of the doubts cast by detached outsiders upon its looks." In the latter, American jazz and popular composer/bandleader Paul Whiteman argues against Newman by writing that "It is an American flavor, an American spirit. It is the only art Europe has ever accepted from America . . . we simply claim that jazz music mirrors in new idioms a spirit and flavor distinctly American. German music, French music, Italian music, alas, English music, above all Russian music, have their own characteristic idioms."

44. W. E. B. DuBois, "My Evolving Program for Negro Freedom," in *What the Negro Wants,* ed. Rayford W. Logan (Chapel Hill, 1944), 41; W. E. B. DuBois, *The Souls of Black Folk* (Boston, 1997; reprint of 1903 original), chap. 14.

45. W. E. B. DuBois "Criteria of Negro Art," in *The Portable Harlem Renaissance Reader,* ed. David Levering Lewis (New York, 1994), 102. The original article appeared in the October 1926 issue of the *Crisis.*

46. Bill Wiseman, Radio Programs column, *Omaha News* (15 July 1933); Arthur Johnson, Dial Twists column, *Boston Transcript* (19 August 1933); *Chicago Tribune,* uncited article concerning *London Times* review of Ellington (30 July 1933); "Ellington Goes over Big," *Norwalk (CT) Sentinel* (10 July 1933); "Famous Band Still Abroad" (photo caption, *Kansas City and Topeka Plaindealer,* 21 July 1933). Ellington's BBD interview is from Ulanov, *Duke Ellington,* 136.

A sample of American newspaper reprints of the S. R. Nelson column from the *Era:* Ben Washer, "In Broadway's Wings: A Busman's Holiday," *New York City Telegraph* (30 June 1933); "Duke Ellington in London Moves Critic to Tears: Writer Asks What Wagner Would Have

Thought of 'Tiger Rag,'" *Denver News* (2 July 1933); "Duke," *Buffalo (NY) Times* (edited reprint of the article) (23 July 1933).

A sample of American newspaper notices concerning Ellington and the BBC: The Listener, As I Hear It column, *Albany News* (8 July 1933); "Ramblings," *Norwalk (CT) Sentinel* (8 July 1933).

All clippings in this footnote, and many more concerning American coverage of the 1933 European tour, are from DES, series 8, subseries 2, vol. 5, NMAH/SI.

47. George F. Frazier, ed., Radio—Music column, *Playhouse* (19 August 1933); "Duke's A 'Pioneer,'" *Cleveland News* (13 July 1933).

48. "Ellington to Show Piano Art at Appearance Here," *Youngstown (OH) Vindicator* (11 September 1933); "Versatile," *Columbus Journal* (photo caption, 12 September 1933); H. E. Cherrington, "Duke Ellington Edifies the Dale; DeMille Picture for Loew's Ohio," *Columbus Dispatch* (14 September 1933); "Duke Ellington Airs Mystery of Dance Music at Idora," *Youngstown Vindicator* (10 September 1933); "Ellington to Be at Casino: Hot Symphonist Will Appear in Memphis on Tuesday with Orchestra," *Memphis Scimitar* (2 August 1934); J. R., Jr., "Higher Development of Jazz Expounded by Duke Ellington," unidentified clipping from Dallas Ellington tour (September 1933); Louis Reed, The Loud Speaker column, *New York City American* (5 May 1934). Clippings from DES, series 8, subseries 2, vols. 5 and 6, NMAH/SI.

49. Carl Shaefer, "He's Expert with the 'Blues': Chief Exponent of Negro Music Here for Film Engagements," *Hollywood News* (21 February 1934).

50. Ralph Holmes, "Duke Ellington's Great Jazz Band Vies with Fred Stritt," unidentified clipping from Detroit newspaper (Fall 1933); uncited author, "Harlemesque Harmonies Share Program with Jungle Thrills," unidentified clipping from Seattle appearance (May 1934); Lloyd S. Thompson, "Ellington's Band Scores by Hit on Stage at Orpheum," *San Francisco Examiner* (21 April 1934). Clippings from DES, series 8, subseries 2, vols. 5 and 6, NMAH/SI.

51. Edward E. Gloss, "Duke's Blue Melodies, Hot-Footed Steppers Please Palace Crowds," *Akron Beacon Journal* (c. Fall 1933); Robert and Evelyn Udkoff interview, conducted by Dr. Marcia M. Greenlee, 11 March 1991, tape 1, SIEOHP, AC/NMAH/SI.

The Ellington set lists changed nightly: Everhardt Armstrong, "Duke's Melodies Have Primitive Rhythmic Urge," *Seattle Post-Intelligencer* (21 May 1934).

Clippings from DES, series 8, subseries 2, vol. 6, NMAH/SI.

52. Don Heckman, "Honoring a Legend: UCLA, Where Duke Ellington and His Band Once Gave a Historic Concert, Is the Site for the Celebration," *Los Angeles Times* (29 April 1999). Courtesy of Joyce L. Cohen.

53. Otto Hardwick interview in A. H. Lawrence, *Duke Ellington and His World* (New York, 2001), 182.

54. Ulanov, *Duke Ellington,* 52, 152.

55. Generally, blacks were only seated in the balconies of theaters, with a special, less expensive show exclusively for a black audience sandwiched in during one night (often at midnight) of the band's week engagement at a theater: uncited author, "Duke Ellington to Invade Dallas: World's Famous Band at Majestic Sept. 30; Band and 20 Entertainers to Open Week's Engagement; Play Big All-Negro Dance Oct. 5th," unidentified Dallas newspaper (September 1933); uncited author, "Ellington Band to Play at Ice Palace Dances," unidentified Dallas newspaper (Fall 1933); uncited author, "Midnight Ellington Show for Negroes," unidentified Oklahoma City newspaper (Fall 1933); uncited author, "Duke Ellington's Band Exceptional: Negro Musicians Open Three-Day Engagement at the Pulaski," unidentified Little Rock newspaper (Fall 1933).

In Waco, advertisements declared 3,000 seats each would be saved for "whites" and "colored," and predicted that "All of Central Texas Will Be Represented at This Joy Jamboree": advertisement, "Mastodonic Colored Dance and Joy Jamboree," unidentified Waco newspaper (October 1933).

The policy of separate shows for each race in the South continued throughout the decade, as seen, for example, in engagements in Knoxville in November 1937 and New Orleans in October 1938: Stratemann, *Duke Ellington,* 150, 156.

Clippings from DES, series 8, subseries 2, vol. 6, NMAH/SI. Details on segregated shows during the fall of 1933 in Memphis and Kansas City can also be found in the same volume.

56. Whitney Balliett, "Sunshine Always Opens Out," in Gottlieb, *Reading Jazz,* 410–11; Bergreen, *Louis Armstrong,* 346–47; Ann Charters, *Nobody: The Story of Bert Williams* (New York, 1983), 25–26.

57. "A Rare Entertainer," photo caption, *Oklahoma Eagle* (27 February 1932).

58. Duke Ellington interview, CHIC 1956 #5, AC/NMAH/SI; Greer interview, January 1979.

59. Duke Ellington interview for Canadian Television, c. 1965. Audiotape courtesy of Michael James; I. Mills interview, conducted by Irene Kahn Atkins, 23 April 1981, OHAM/YUSC, pg. 17; Nicholson, *Reminiscing In Tempo,* 162–63.

60. Uncited author, "Ellington Composing: Musician at Work in Apartment Here," unidentified Dallas clipping (September 1933); J. R., Jr., "Higher Development."

Other references to European tour praise during the 1933 Southern tour: uncited author, "Duke Ellington to Be at Majestic," unidentified Dallas clipping (September 1933); Johnnie Mae E. Newton, "Duke Ellington," unidentified Houston clipping (October 1933); "Duke Ellington to Play in City: Famous Negro Orchestra Booked for Majestic October 21," *Houston Post* (24 September 1933); uncited author, "Ellington Blues Experts Playing in Waco Tonight: One of the Nation's Best Dance Orchestras Engaged at Waco Theatre and Shrine Temple," unidentified Waco clipping (October 1933).

Clippings from DES, series 8, subseries 2, vol. 6, AC/NMAH/SI.

61. Uncited author, "Call It Music or Not—It's Duke; 'Dusky Maestro' Holds Forth at Paramount," unidentified Amarillo clipping (October 1933); Larry Gibbard, Headline Hunting column, unidentified Dallas clipping (September 1933); Omar LaGrange, "Texas Town Still Raves over Duke Ellington: Amarillo People Wild about Famed Musical Aggregation—Have Use of White Theater for Midnight Performance When Duke Uses His Influence on Last Night," unidentified African American newspaper (Fall 1933); "Negro Bands Successful in Dallas," *Variety* (3 October 1933); Ulanov, *Duke Ellington,* 154.

Clippings, except for the last, from DES, series 8, subseries 2, vol. 6, NMAH/SI.

62. Ralph Ellison, *Going to the Territory* (New York, 1986), 220; Burton W. Peretti, *Jazz in American Culture* (Chicago, 1997), 68.

63. Poster for 5 October 1933 Ellington "Colored Only" performance at the Ice Palace, Oak Cliff, TX (near Dallas). Clippings from DES, series 8, subseries 2, vol. 6, NMAH/SI.

64. Newton, "Duke Ellington"; Stratemann, *Duke Ellington,* 129; Ellison, *Going to the Territory,* 221–22; LaGrange, "Texas Town Still Raves."

65. Roger Pryor Dodge, "Harpsichords and Jazz Trumpets," in Gottlieb, *Reading Jazz,* 761–62.

66. Lewis Erenberg, *Swinging the Dream: Big Band Jazz and the Rebirth of American Culture* (Chicago, 1998), 137–41; Bernard Gendron, "Moldy Figs and Modernists: Jazz at War (1942–1946)," in *Jazz among the Discourses,* ed. Krin Gabbard (Durham, 1995), 34, 47; Joseph McLaren, *Edward Kennedy (Duke) Ellington and Langston Hughes: Perspectives on Their Contributions to American Culture, 1920–1966* (Brown University, PhD diss., 1980), 72; Peretti, *Jazz in American Culture,* 78–79; David W. Stowe, *Swing Changes: Big Band Jazz in New Deal America* (Cambridge, 1994), 75, 76, 93.

The books McLaren cites include: Constant Lambert's *Music Ho!* (1934), Alan Locke's *The Negro and His Music* (1936), Hughes Panassie's *Hot Jazz* (1936), Winthrop Sargeant's *Jazz: Hot and Hybrid* (1939), and many more.

67. Copland did not achieve financial security until after World War II and did not become a household name until the early 1950s. While he was known in composers' circles as early as the mid-1920s, he did not receive significant public attention until the premieres of *Billy The Kid* (1939) and *Appalachian Spring* (1944): Howard Pollack, *Aaron Copland: The Life and Work of an Uncommon Man* (New York, 1999), 90–93, 158, 320–23, 388–405.

Though Ives had composed most of his works at the turn of the century, and some as late as the 1910s, they were not "dusted off" and given national premieres and attention until the late 1930s: Burkholder, *Charles Ives,* chap. 1.

68. Howard Pollack, *Aaron Copland: The Life and Work of an Uncommon Man* (New York, 1999), 116; Ulanov, *Duke Ellington.*

69. Gerald Early, *One Nation under a Groove: Motown and American Culture* (Hopewell, NJ, 1995), 5; Gendron, "Moldy Figs and Modernists," 33; Leroi Jones [Amiri Baraka], *Blues People: Negro Music in White America* (New York, 1963), 190.

70. Art Blakey argued that Ellington and Armstrong were not given enough credit "for what they did": Art Blakey, in Gottlieb, *Reading Jazz,* 210.

Miles Davis readily admitted that his pioneering *Birth of the Cool* recordings that brought him to prominence at the start of the 1950s were inspired by the sophisticated arrangements of Ellington and his writing partner, Billy Strayhorn: Miles Davis, with Quincy Troupe, *Miles: The Autobiography* (New York, 1989), 119. Davis's musical aesthetic, with its aversion to categorization, willingness to experiment in numerous genres, and embrace of both the commercial and the avant-garde obviously resembled Ellington's lifetime modus operandi.

Charles Mingus, at a 1972 Ellington tribute concert and seminar at Yale, proclaimed the decisive influence of Ellington on his iconoclastic artistic ways: Willie Ruff, in Gottlieb, *Reading Jazz,* 277.

Ralph Ellison also argued that bebop musicians adapted their views concerning jazz as an art from the "high artistic achievement" exhibited by Ellington and his peers Armstrong, Count Basie, and Coleman Hawkins in the 1920s and '30s: Ralph Ellison, *Shadow and Act* (New York, 1964), 252.

Chapter Four

1. Adam Clayton Powell, Jr., "My Grandfather's Branded, Our Musicians Are Slaves, Owned Body and Soul, Work for Massa Mills," Soap Box column, *Amsterdam News* (21 November 1936); John Hammond interview, conducted by the Duke Ellington Society, 1965, SC Audio C-482, SCBC; Edward Kennedy Ellington, *Music Is My Mistress* (New York, 1973), 89.

Powell did not have access to financial records of the Mills organization; he seemingly based his account on interviews with musicians and others in the music business. Some of his remarks resemble those of John Hammond, who worked briefly in the Mills organization and whose opinions on the Ellington/Mills financial relationship are included in this chapter and earlier ones. There exists no record of Ellington being a vice president of the Mills organization, though, as shown previously, he was a major stockholder (but arguably not "major" enough) in Duke Ellington, Inc., and he probably also owned some of Cab Calloway, Inc., as well. Also, no record exists of Ellington owing Mills money after they broke off their relationship in 1939 or of Ellington owing Mills large sums during the period of their business relationship. It is true that Ellington's lawyer and accountant during this period also worked for Mills. At the beginning of Powell's op-ed article, the *Amsterdam News* included a disclaimer: "the publishers do not necessarily subscribe to the opinions expressed in this column."

2. Klaus Stratemann, *Duke Ellington, Day by Day and Film by Film* (Copenhagen, 1992), 69, 119; "Brunswick-Columbia Sign Ellington and Calloway," *New York City Radio Merchant* (August 1934).

3. Photo captions underneath pictures of Mills and Ellington, *Zits* (11 Jan 1930); "Cotton Club Boys Feted," *Inside Facts* (August 1930); Walter Winchell, "Duke Ellington's Score in 'Blackbirds of 1930,'" unidentified clipping (c. August 1930); "Irving Mills in Hollywood," *Metronome* (September 1930); "Irving Mills Returns from Coast," *Metronome* (October 1930); Bob Landry, "Disc Reviews," *Variety* (25 February 1931).

Roger Doulens, On the Air column, *Norwalk Sentinel* (27 July 1933); short blurb on Ellington and Mills's return from Europe by uncited gossip-column author, *New York City Film Daily* (4 August 1933); "Ellington's Stay Prolonged," *New York City Radio World* (29 July 1933); John Rosenfeld, Jr., "Reviewing the Reviews: From Dance Musician to Jazzist," *Dallas News* (10 September 1933).

Clippings from DES, series 8, subseries 2, vols. 1 and 5, NMAH/SI.

4. Stratemann, *Duke Ellington,* 53; Nat Presser, Press-ing It Out column, *New York City East Side News* (23 June 1934).

5. Such traditions apparently began early in the history of Mills Music. A 1923 article on the firm in a newspaper called the *Clipper* contended that Irving and Jack Mills assigned song credits "liberally": A. H. Lawrence, *Duke Ellington and His World: A Biography* (New York, 2001), 31–32.

Steven Lasker interview, conducted by the author, 25 September 1995; Herb Jeffries interview, conducted by Patricia Willard, 22 and 23 September 1989, SIEOHP, tape 3, AC/NMAH/SI.

Maria Cole interview, conducted by Vivian Perlis, 5 July 1980, #545, OHAM/YUSC, pg. 28; Daniel Mark Epstein, *Nat King Cole* (Boston, 1999), 100–104.

Ellington, in three different instances during the Carter Harman interviews, talks about the composing of the music and lyrics for "Mood Indigo" and "I Let a Song Go out of My Heart," mentioning co-writers such as Henry Nemo, but never Mills's contribution, except to say that Mills felt "Mood Indigo" was not a commercial enough title and that he insisted Ellington name it "Dreamy Blues." When Ellington played the instrumental on the radio from the Cotton Club, he called it "Mood Indigo" and the numerous requests from listeners settled the question, according to Ellington: Duke Ellington interviews, CHIC 1964 #1, tape 1; 1964 #6, tape 2; 1964 #8, tape 2, AC/NMAH/SI.

6. Helen Oakley Dance interview, conducted by Patricia Willard, 26 and 27 September 1989, SIEOHP, tape 2, AC/NMAH/SI; Frank Driggs interview, conducted by Paul Kolderie, 13 December 1977, #504A, OHAM/YUSC, pg. 7, 22; Mercer Ellington with Stanley Dance, *Duke Ellington In Person* (New York, 1975), 33–34; Irving Gordon interview, conducted by the author, 7 March 1996; Brooks Kerr interview, conducted by the author, 25 January 1996; Lasker interview, 25 September 1995; Gerald Marks interview, conducted by the author, 27 January 1996; Willie "The Lion" Smith interview, conducted by the Duke Ellington Society, 1964, SC Audio C-476, SCBC.

7. Helen Oakley Dance interview, 26 and 27 September 1989, tape 1.

8. Maurice Lawrence interview, conducted by the author, 1 May 1999.

9. Arnold Rampersad, *Jackie Robinson: A Biography* (New York, 1997), 122–32.

10. Mary L. Dudziak, "Josephine Baker, Racial Protest, and the Cold War," *Journal of American History* (September 1994): 543, 546. Courtesy of Richard Lentz.

11. Robin D. G. Kelley, *Race Rebels: Culture, Politics, and the Black Working Class* (New York, 1994), 4; Lawrence interview, 1 May 1999.

12. David W. Stowe, *Swing Changes: Big Band Jazz in New Deal America* (Cambridge, 1994), 124; Ted Gioia, *The History of Jazz* (New York, 1997), 136–37; Duke Ellington, "The Most Essential Instrument," in *The Duke Ellington Reader,* ed. Mark Tucker (New York, 1993), 370; Rampersad, *Jackie Robinson,* 122–32; Laurence Bergreen, *Louis Armstrong: An Extravagant Life* (New York, 1997), 373–78; Arnold Rampersad, *The Life of Langston Hughes,* vol. 1, *1902–1941: I, Too, Sing America* (New York, 1986), 110–14.

13. James Lincoln Collier, *Duke Ellington,* (New York, 1987), 138, 141, 144, 183; Helen Oakley Dance, liner notes for Duke Ellington, *The Duke's Men: Small Groups,* vol. 1 (Columbia/Legacy, 1991); E. K. Ellington, *Music Is My Mistress* (New York, 1973), 89; John Hammond, with Irving Townsend, *John Hammond on Record* (New York, 1977; reprint 1981): 89, 138; Lasker interview, 25 September 1995; Marks interview, 27 January 1996; Paul Mills interview, conducted by the author, 9 February 1996; Juliet E. K. Walker, *The History of Black Business in America: Capitalism, Race, Entrepreneurship* (New York, 1998), xviii–xxii, 182, 238; Robert E. Weems, Jr., *Black Business in the Black Metropolis: The Chicago Metropolitan Assurance Company, 1925–1985* (Bloomington, IN, 1996), xii–xiii; "Desperation Salaries: 80 'Name Acts,' $2K or More," *Variety* (8 March 1932).

14. This discussion on the issue of writing credits within the band is based on the following sources: Barney Bigard interview, conducted by Patricia Willard, July 1976, JOHP, reel 2, pg. 12–17, reel 3, pg. 29–30, reel 5, pg. 5–6, 33, IJS/RU; Lawrence Brown interview, conducted by Patricia Willard, July 1976, JOHP, reel 4, pg. 32–40, reel 6, pg. 15–16, IJS/RU; Bill Coss, "Ellington & Strayhorn, Inc.," *Downbeat* (7 June 1962); Helen Oakley Dance interview, conducted by Mark Tucker, 9 January 1987, #594A, B, OHAM/YUSC, pg. 12, 14, 15; Sonny Greer interview, conducted by the Duke Ellington Society, 1961, SC Audio C-475, SCBC; Louis Metcalf interview, conducted by Jeremy Orgel, 1979, #538A, B, OHAM/YUSC, pg. 12; H. A. Overstreet, "Touching Tomorrow's Frontiers Is Duke Ellington's Music," *Metronome* (October 1933); Juan Tizol interview, conducted by Patricia Willard, 15 November 1978, JOHP, reel 1, pg. 41–46, reel 2, pg. 2, 37, reel 4, pg. 23, reel 5, pg. 4–7, 21–22, IJS/RU; Clark Terry interview, in *Duke Ellington: Reminiscing In Tempo* (Robert Levi Films, 1992), LOC/MPD; Cootie Williams interview, conducted by Helen Oakley Dance, May 1976, JOHP, pg. 130–34, IJS/RU.

Bigard also claimed to write or co-write "Saturday Night Function" and "Rockin' in Rhythm." Brown claimed authorship or coauthorship of "Goin' Up" and "Golden Cress."

15. Stuart Nicholson, in his compilation of Ellington-related quotes and clippings, averred that money problems, spearheaded by Ellington's underwriting of medical treatment for his parents and two band members, necessitated his leaving Mills: "The harsh truth was that Ellington had been guilty of letting business matters drift following the deaths of his parents [in the mid-1930s] and was all but broke." Supposedly, Mills refused to help Ellington in this matter and instead negotiated Ellington's more lucrative management deal at the William Morris Agency in 1939. In a book laden with citations, Nicholson does not footnote any of the sources for the allegations quoted above, and no further corroboration from other sources was found: Stuart Nicholson, *Reminiscing In Tempo: A Portrait of Duke Ellington* (Boston, 1999), 212–13.

A front-page article in *Down Beat* detailing the Ellington/Mills split reported that, immediately upon leaving Mills, Ellington would get a prestigious set of show dates with the William Morris Agency that he could not have secured previously with Mills, which makes Nicholson's allegation that Mills secured the William Morris deal seem unlikely: "Ellington and Mills in Split," *Down Beat* (May 1939).

16. "Ellington and Mills in Split," *Down Beat* (May 1939).

17. "Irving Mills to Head New Phono Co.," *Metronome* (September 1936); "Mills, CRA Set Booking Deal," *Variety* (13 January 1937); "Irving Mills Seeks Own Label," *Variety* (13 January 1937); "165 Sides Waxed as Mills Starts; 75 Every Month," *Variety* (24 March 1937); Helen Oakley Dance interview, 26 and 27 September 1989, tape 2.

The Ellington small band sessions on Mills's Master and Variety labels can be found on: Duke Ellington, *The Duke's Men: Small Groups,* vol. 1 (Columbia/Legacy, 1991); Duke Ellington, *The Duke's Men: Small Groups,* vol. 2 (Columbia/Legacy, 1993).

18. P. Mills interview, 9 February 1996; Barry Ulanov, *Duke Ellington* (New York, 1946); Lawrence interview, 1 May 1999; H. Robert Udkoff interview, conducted by the author, 28 September 1995; Mercer Ellington interview, conducted by Dr. Marcia M. Greenlee, September 1990, SIEOHP, tape 3, AC/NMAH/SI; Mercer Ellington interview in Lawrence, *Duke Ellington and His World,* 302; Brad McCuen interview, conducted by Patricia Willard, 2 and 3 August 1989, SIEOHP, tape 1, AC/NMAH/SI.

Lawrence also confirmed, without prompting, Udkoff's story about Ellington's mother's casket, although he did not hear the story from Ellington himself.

19. Irving Mills interview, conducted by Irene Kahn Atkins, 23 April 1981, #567A–E, pg. 12, OHAM/YUSC; Irving Mills, as told to Charles Emge, "I Split with Duke When Music Began Sidetracking," *Downbeat* (5 November 1952); Kerr interview, 25 January 1996.

20. All the recordings mentioned in this discussion can be found in: Duke Ellington, *Braggin' in Brass: The Immortal 1938 Year* (Portrait Masters/CBS, 1989).

21. This unattributed anecdote is from: Lawrence, *Duke Ellington and His World,* 268–69.

22. Abel Green, "Mills Music's 40-Year Success Story; From 5G & 3 Songs to $5,000,000 Empire," *Variety* (28 October 1959); *Down Beat,* "Mills Music Publishing Complex Sold For $5,000,000" (8 October 1964). One of the very few hit songs Mills introduced after Ellington left his company was Nat King Cole's "Straighten up and Fly Right" (1943), the origin of which is discussed in this chapter.

Chapter Five

1. George Avakian interview, conducted by the author, 16 April 2001.

2. Duke Ellington, "Duke Says Swing Is Stagnant," *Down Beat* (February 1939); Paul Eduard Miller, "'Roots of Hot White Jazz Are Negroid': Five Varieties of Music Left Their Mark on Original Ragtime Swing," *Down Beat* (April 1937).

3. Peter Bellamy, "Duke Ellington Says 'Swing Has No Future,'" *Cleveland News* (8 October 1938); Ellington, "Duke Says Swing Is Stagnant"; Duke Ellington, "Duke Becomes a Critic," *Down Beat* (July 1939).

4. Lewis A. Erenberg, *Swingin' the Dream: Big Band Jazz and the Rebirth of American Culture* (Chicago, 1998), 15; Gama Gilbert, "Higher Soars the Swing Fever: The Business of Jam, Jive and Jitter Seems to Suit the Temper of the Times, Drowning Out the Moralists," *New York Times Magazine* (14 August 1938); Irving Kolodin, "The Dance Band Business: A Study in Black and White," *Harpers* (June 1941); Frank Rose, *The Agency* (New York, 1995), 1–7, 76–79; Russell Sanjek, *American Popular Music and Its Business,* vol. 3, *1900–1984* (New York, 1988), chaps. 5, 9, and 10. David W. Stowe, *Swing Changes: Big Band Jazz in New Deal America* (Cambridge, MA, 1994): 99, 107–11; "The Booking of Bands: Who Does It and What They're Like and Why," *Metronome* (October 1945).

5. ,Erenberg, *Swingin' the Dream,* xiii, 64; 13–14; Blanche Wiesen Cook, *Eleanor Roosevelt,* vol. 2, *The Defining Years: 1933–1938* (Penguin Books, 1999), chaps. 9 and 10; Kenneth O'Reilly, *Nixon's Piano: Presidents and Racial Politics from Washington to Clinton* (New York, 1995), 109–20.

6. R. L. Larkin, "Are Colored Bands Doomed as Big Money Makers? . . . 'Negro Leaders Could Make More Money Running a Rib Joint,'" *Down Beat* (1 December 1940).

7. Erenberg, *Swingin' the Dream,* 26, 154–65; Kolodin, "The Dance Band Business," 173; Ralph J. Gleason, *Celebrating the Duke and Louis, Bessie, Billie, Bird, Carmen, Miles, Dizzy, and Other Heroes* (Boston, 1975; reprint 1995), 13–14; Stowe, *Swing Changes,* 124–30; Brad McCuen

interview, conducted by Patricia Willard, 2 and 3 August 1989, SIEOHP, tape 6, AC/NMAH/ SI.; "Why?" *Metronome* (March 1943); "Song Writers Feel Blow as ASCAP Continues Old Policy," *Chicago Defender* (14 February 1942); Otis Ferguson, "Mood Indigo," *New Republic* (April 1941), from the Duke Ellington file, 1941–44, IJS/RUN.

8. Helen Oakley Dance interview, conducted by Patricia Willard, 26 and 27 September 1989, SIEOHP, tape 2, AC/NMAH/SI; Albert Joseph Celley interview, conducted by Patricia Willard, 12 July 1989, SIEOHP, tape 1, AC/NMAH/SI.

9. Burton W. Perretti, *Jazz in American Culture* (Chicago, 1997), 82.

10. John Hammond, "'From Spirituals to Swing,'" *New York Times* (18 December 1938).

Ellington responded to Hammond five months later with perhaps the only personal attack he ever issued publicly, albeit in his own graceful, but subtly cutting fashion:

> The swing critic who has perhaps stirred up the greatest resentment, while at the same time was earning the deepest gratitude of others, has been John Henry Hammond, Jr., son of a prominent New York family and possessed of wealth in his own right. To properly judge the "modus operandi" of Hammond, it is necessary to devote some thought to the man himself. He appears to be an ardent propagandist and champion of the "lost cause." He apparently has consistently identified himself with the interests of the minorities, the Negro peoples, to a lesser degree, the Jew, and to the underdog, in the form of the Communist party.
>
> Perhaps due to the "fever of battle," Hammond's judgment may have become slightly warped, and his enthusiasm and prejudices a little bit unwieldy to control.

Duke Ellington, "'Situation between the Critics and Musicians Is Laughable'—Ellington," *Down Beat* (April 1939).

The two men had been good friends before the mid-1930s, Hammond even giving Ellington a portable phonograph and some "good records" to help Ellington deal with the long hours of his ocean voyage to England for the band's first tour there in 1933. Both Ellington and Hammond were seen as champions of African American music at that point in time, but their friendship seriously deteriorated because of the controversies listed above: Duke Ellington interview, CHIC 1964 #5, tape 2, AC/NMAH/SI.

11. Erenberg, *Swingin' the Dream*, xiv, 59, 82; Stowe, *Swing Changes,* 40–42.

12. Rose, *The Agency,* 1–7, 76–79; "Willard Alexander Quits MCA; Has No Future Plans," *Variety* (29 March 1939); "Wm. Morris Plans Mature: Alexander to Head Band Dept.," *Variety* (12 April 1939).

13. Harold Jovien interview, conducted by the author, 21 March 1996; Paul Mills interview, conducted by the author, 9 February 1996; H. Robert Udkoff interview, conducted by the author, 28 September 1995; Brooks Kerr interview, conducted by the author, 25 January 1996; Herb Jeffries interview, conducted by the author, 26 September 1995; Ruth Ellington interview, conducted by the author, 26 January 1996.

The 10 percent figure for the William Morris commission comes from the three-year contract signed with the company on 2 June 1941, which can be found in: collection 386, box 6, AC/NMAH/SI.

14. Rocky Clark, "'Spotlight Bands' Recruit Negro Bands after Column Complaint," The Listening Post column, *Bridgeport Post* (n.d.—c. November 1942); Isadora Smith, "Another First for 'Duke': Duke Ellington Returning to Broadway—Will Be First Race Musical Unit to Play Dave Wolper's 'Hurricane,'" *Variety* (date obscured—c. March 1943); Stratemann, *Duke Ellington: Day by Day and Film by Film* (Copenhagen, 1992), 158–71, 198–200, 238–42; uncited author, "Duke Ellington on Coca-Cola Program," source obscured, probably *Variety* (c. November 1942); uncited author, "'Million Dollar Band' Breaks Down for Duke," source obscured (c. April 1943); Mercer Ellington interview, conducted by Dr. Marcia M. Greenlee,

September 1990, SIEOHP, tape 7, AC/NMAH/SI. Clippings from DES, subseries 2, vol. 8, AC/NMAH/SI.

15. Lauren Sklaroff, "Variety for the Servicemen: The Jubilee Radio Show, Race, and Military Morale during World War II" (paper presented at the Organization of American Historians, Washington, D.C., April 2002).

16. Ramona Lewis, "'Cabin' Picture Called Insult," *Amsterdam News* (12 June 1943); Donald Bogle, *Toms, Coons, Mulattoes, Mammies and Bucks: An Interpretive History of Blacks in American Films* (New York, 1973), 130; Laurence Bergreen, *Louis Armstrong: An Extravagant Life* (New York, 1997), 416–18; Krin Gabbard, *Jammin' at the Margins: Jazz and the American Cinema* (Chicago, 1996), 178; Stratemann, *Duke Ellington,* 179–89, 201–26.

17. Stratemann, *Duke Ellington,* 45, 52, 69, 165, 288; Hy Gardner, "Coast to Coast," *New York Herald Tribune* (7 November 1956). Further examples can be found in Stratemann, *Duke Ellington,* 150, 261, 267, 268, 288, 362.

18. Stratemann, *Duke Ellington,* 163, 167; uncited author, "Duke Hits 7,000 in Atlanta," obscured source, probably *Variety* (c. August 1940). Clipping from DES, subseries 2, vol. 8, AC/NMAH/SI.

19. Wilma Cockerell interview, conducted by the author, 22 January 1996; Jovien interview, 21 March 1996; Henrietta Livingston interview, conducted by the author, 4 March 1996. P. Mills interview, 9 February 1996.

20. "Ellington to Victor: Back on 75-Cent Pancakes through Transfer," *Variety* (21 February 1940); Stratemann, *Duke Ellington,* 161. In advertisements, the Victor artists and songs were always featured first in ads, over artists and songs on the lower-priced Bluebird label: RCA Victor ads #9595, 9696, 9757, 9758, 9859, from DES, subseries 2, vol. 11, AC/NMAH/SI. See also A.H. Lawrence, *Duke Ellington and His World: A Biography* (New York, 2001), 290.

21. Jeffries interview, 26 September 1995; Jovien interview, 21 March 1996.

22. Cockerell interview, 22 January 1996; C. Gordon interview, conducted by the author, 15 November 1995; Jeffries interview, 26 September 1995; Jovien interview, 21 March 1996; Udkoff interview, 28 September 1995.

23. For samples of these RCA Victor publications that feature Ellington, and their circulation claims, consult the RCA Victor advertising campaign preserved in DES, subseries 2, vol. 11, AC/NMAH/SI.

24. Unless otherwise noted, the 1940–41 recordings discussed in this section can be found on: Duke Ellington, *The Blanton-Webster Band* (RCA/Bluebird, 1986).

In this section, I have mainly avoided discussing the compositions from this period that have attracted the most discussion among Ellington's latterday musical appraisers and biographers, such as "Koko," "Concerto for Cootie," and "Harlem Air Shaft." For essays concerning the importance of these compositions, consult: Andre Hodeir, "Why Did Ellington 'Remake' His Masterpiece?" in *The Duke Ellington Reader,* ed. Mark Tucker (New York, 1993), 276–88; Ken Rattenbury, *Duke Ellington: Jazz Composer* (New Haven, 1990), chaps. 6 and 8; Mark Tucker, liner notes, *Blanton-Webster Band.*

25. ASCAP ban: John Edward Hasse, *Beyond Category: The Life and Genius of Duke Ellington* (New York, 1993), 241; Tucker, *Blanton-Webster Band.*

Authorship of songs: Annie Kuebler and Scott Schwartz were archivists for years during the 1990s at the Smithsonian Institution Archives Center and helped process the Ellington sheet music collection. Both of them felt that Mercer's songs were written in his father's (very recognizable) handwriting, and that Mercer Ellington probably did not write the songs attributed to him. Also: Mercer Ellington interview, conducted by Dick Buckley, WBEZ Chicago, March 1980, #521B, C, OHAM/YUSC; Billy Strayhorn interview, conducted by the Duke Ellington Society, SC Audio C-457, side 2, SCBC.

26. Richard O. Boyer, "The Hot Bach," in *The Duke Ellington Reader,* ed. Mark Tucker (New York, 1993), 235.

27. The personal information concerning Strayhorn's initial months in New York City with Ellington and his family are drawn from: Bill Coss, "Ellington & Strayhorn, Inc.," *Downbeat* (7 June 1962); David Hajdu, *Lush Life: A Biography of Billy Strayhorn* (New York, 1996), 57–62; Walter van de Leur, *Something to Live For: The Music of Billy Strayhorn* (New York, 2002), 30–35.

28. Edward Kennedy Ellington, *Music Is My Mistress* (New York, 1973), 152–53; Hajdu, *Lush Life,* 87; Tucker, *Blanton-Webster Band;* van de Leur, *Something to Live For.*

Will Friedwald has argued that Axel Stordahl's picturesque and dramatic string arrangements for Frank Sinatra in the 1940s deserve equal credit with Strayhorn's arrangements for bringing a more sophisticated underpinning to vocal hit records. Stordahl's arrangements are superb and underrated (as is much of Sinatra's 1940s output for Columbia, most of it arranged by Stordahl), but his best work arrived after Sinatra moved to Columbia in 1943, years after Strayhorn arranged and brought to the top of the charts such hits as "Flamingo" and "Take the 'A' Train." Also, many Strayhorn arrangements boast an adventurous, much less predictable sensibility not present in Stordahl's work: Will Friedwald, *Sinatra! The Song Is You: A Singer's Art* (New York, 1995), 141–42. Most of Stordahl's best arrangements for Sinatra can be found on: Frank Sinatra, *The Voice: The Columbia Years 1943–1952* (Columbia, 1986, 6 discs).

The notes on Strayhorn's salary come from: collection 301, box 55, folders 2–46, AC/NMAH/SI. The Smithsonian's Ellington collection does not contain accounting records from the 1940s, which would have recorded Strayhorn's publishing income. As noted in chapter 14, Strayhorn, at the time of his death in 1967, owned 10 percent of the shares in Tempo Music. If this was true from the inception of the corporation in December 1940, Strayhorn probably earned money from this arrangement as well.

29. Cockerell interview, 22 January 1996; Jovien interview, 21 March 1996; Livingston interview, 4 March 1996; P. Mills interview, 9 February 1996.

30. Duke Ellington interview, CHIC 1964 #4, tape 3, AC/NMAH/SI.

31. Fred Johnson, "Duke Ellington and Crew Lift Mercury," *San Francisco Call/Bulletin* (21 May 1942); Eugene Stinson, "Music Views: Duke Ellington," *Chicago News* (11 September 1940); Will Davidson, untitled review, *Chicago Tribune* (15 September 1940); Frank E. Bolden, Orchestra Whirl column, *Pittsburgh Courier* (21 February 1942); Mauri Orodenker, "Earle, Philadelphia: Reviewed Friday Afternoon, March 13," *Billboard* (21 March 1942). The first article was taken from reel 1 of DES, NMAH/SI. The next two were found in this file of the Duke Ellington Oral History Project at AC/NMAH/SI: Press Manual—William Morris Agency, Incorporated (c.1941). The last two are from DES, subseries 2, vol. 10, NMAH/SI.

32. Sources for the information on Tempo Music, unless otherwise noted: E. K. Ellington, *Music Is My Mistress,* 46; R. Ellington interview, 26 January 1996; C. Gordon interview, 15 November 1995; Hasse, *Beyond Category,* 260, 276–78; Michael James interview, conducted by the author, 11 November 1999.

The information concerning the ownership of Tempo Music stock comes from the following sources: tax protest submitted on behalf of Duke and Edna Ellington, 20 July 1964, collection 301, series 3, box 125, folder 9, AC/NMAH/SI; Stephen Burn to Benjamin Starr, "Re: Estate of William Strayhorn and Tempo Music, Inc.," 2 January 1969, collection 301, series 3E, box 103, folder 23, AC/NMAH/SI. For more on the financial reasoning behind the incorporation of Tempo, consult chapter 11.

33. Laurence Bergreen, *As Thousands Cheer: The Life of Irving Berlin* (New York, 1990), 115.

The famous and pioneering gospel and blues artist-songwriter Thomas A. Dorsey (sometimes known as Georgia Tom) established his own gospel publishing company in 1932, although his recording career was nearly over by that time: Robert E. Weems, Jr., *Desegregating the Dollar: African-American Consumerism in the Twentieth Century* (New York, 1998), 48–50; Robert M. W. Dixon, John Godrich, and Howard W. Rye, *Blues and Gospel Records, 1890–1943* (New York, 1997), 222–25.

34. Angel Kwolek-Folland, *Engendering Business: Men and Women in the Corporate Office, 1870–1930* (Baltimore, 1994), 163, 183.

35. Juliet E. K. Walker, *The History of Black Business in America: Capitalism, Race, Entrepreneurship* (New York City, 1998), 227; Robert E. Weems, Jr., *Black Business in the Black Metropolis: The Chicago Metropolitan Assurance Company, 1925–1985* (Bloomington, IN, 1996), 19, 66–71, 96; Weems, Jr., *Desegregating the Dollar,* 58.

Kathy Peiss documented how female African American beauty and fashion entrepreneurs harbored similar business motives of promoting personal dignity and collective African American advancement through their products, although skin whitener products did become controversial in this regard: Kathy Peiss, *Hope in a Jar: The Making of America's Beauty Culture* (New York, 1998).

36. Duke Ellington interview, CHIC 1964 #3, AC/NMAH/SI; Mercer Ellington Smithsonian interview, tape 3; Udkoff interview, 28 September 1995; Weems, Jr., *Desegregating the Dollar,* 54–60; Walker, *History of Black Business in America,* 183–85.

37. Edgar T. Rouzeau, "The Duke's Kid Sister Has Revolutionary Ideas about Art of Teaching Like Brother Had about Music" (source and date obscured—c. 1936), DES, subseries 2, vol. 8, NMAH/SI.

38. Sources for the material on *Jump for Joy:* Gilbert Allen, "'Jump for Joy' Search for New Form," *California Eagle* (21 August 1941); Almena Davis, "Opus Gets Once-Over," *Pittsburgh Courier* (date obscured—c. 24 July 1941); Almena Davis, "'Jump for Joy' Closes in L.A.," *Pittsburgh Courier* (date obscured—c. September 1941); Duke Ellington interview, Carter Harman Collection, 1964 #7; E. K. Ellington, *Music Is My Mistress,* 175–80; "An edited talk between Duke Ellington and Henry Whiston," *Jazz Journal* (February 1967); Duke Ellington interview, conducted by Stanley Dance, BBC Radio 1, 1972, RYJ 3072, JVC/LOC; Mercer Ellington Smithsonian interview, tape 3; John Franceschina, *Duke Ellington's Music for the Theatre* (Jefferson, NC, 2001), 28–45; Norman Granz interview, conducted by Patricia Willard, 23 and 24 August 1989, SIEOHP, tape 1, AC/NMAH/SI; Hasse, *Beyond Category,* 246–48; Emery Holmes II, "When the A-Train Hit L.A.," *Los Angeles Times* (25 April 1999); Herb Jeffries interview, conducted by Patricia Willard, 22 and 23 September 1989, SIEOHP, AC/NMAH/SI; Kerr interview, 25 January 1996; John Kinloch, "'Jump for Joy' Is Sensational Eve in Theater—Kinloch: Wit and Sparkle, Exile of Uncle Thomas, Satire Surprise of Duke Ellington's Hit," *California Eagle* (17 July 1941); Herbert Klein, "'The Duke' Grooms a Lulu for Broadway," *PM's Weekly* (10 August 1941); Lawrence, *Ellington and His World,* 305–6; Billy Rowe, "Duke Ellington's Opus and La Belle Helene Appear Set," *Variety* (date obscured—c. summer 1941); Patricia Willard, liner notes for *Jump for Joy* (Smithsonian Collection of Recordings R037, 1988); *Jump for Joy* (original concert program), collection 301, series 2, box 10, AC/NMAH/SI; "Stars Become Fans at Ellington Show," *Variety* (date obscured—c. July 1941); "Jump with Joy," *Variety* (16 July 1941); "Ellington Revue $9,500 in L.A.; 'Tree' Good 9G," *Variety* (23 July 1941); "'Cabin' Strong $11,500, Ellington 10G in L.A.," *Variety* (29 July 1941); "Hellz' Big $24,000 in L.A.; 'Jump' $6,500," *Variety* (13 August 1941); "Hellz' 24G Shames L.A. Crix; 'Jump' Skids," *Variety* (20 August 1941). The Davis and Rowe clippings, along with the story on "Stars Become Fans," found in DES, subseries 2, vol. 8, AC/NMAH/SI. The *California Eagle* clippings found in Duke Ellington file, 1941–44, IJS/RU. The Klein article, which includes the quote from the *Inter Church Tribune,* is from Duke Ellington clipping file, SCBC.

39. Later in the interview, Jeffries said Duke was "angry," something he had seen only one other time in their thirty-nine-year friendship.

40. "'Jump for Joy' Run Closes Saturday," *California Eagle* (25 September 1941), Duke Ellington file, 1941–44, IJS/RU; "May Use Duke Ellington's Band in Picture, 'Life of Old Satchmo,'" *Chicago Defender* (21 February 1942); "'Jump for Joy' All-Negro Revue to Be Revived," *Chicago Tribune* (15 Mar 1942). Last two clippings from DES, subseries 2, vol. 10, AC/NMAH/SI.

41. Duke Ellington, "We, Too, Sing 'America,'" in Tucker, *Duke Ellington Reader,* 147; Stratemann, *Duke Ellington,* 242, 255, 258; "Duke Ellington Buys Victory Loan Bond: Famous Band Leader Thinks Classical Music Influencing Swing," *Toronto Daily Star* (25 February 1942); "Leaders Help Sell Bonds via Bach Recording Plan," *Down Beat* (1 March 1942); "Boys Sell $5,000 in Bonds to Duke, Fraternal Bodies," *Baltimore Afro-American* (21 March 1942); "Ellington Band Plays for Cadets," *Orange (CA) News* (21 April 1942); "Ellington and Draper in Anti-Fascist Benefit," *PM* (10 May 1944). Clippings from DES, subseries 2, vol. 10, AC/NMAH/SI, except last clipping from Duke Ellington clipping file, SCBC.

Discrimination by the USO: Eric Porter, *What Is This Thing Called Jazz? African American Musicians as Artists, Critics and Activists* (Berkeley, 2002), 85.

42. Duke Ellington to Goddard Leiberson, 18 January 1944, Goddard Leiberson papers, OHAM/YUSC; Erenberg, *Swingin' the Dream,* 133–35; Stuart Nicholson, *Reminiscing In Tempo: A Portrait of Duke Ellington* (Boston, 1999), 231, 242, 258–60; Arnold Rampersad, *The Life of Langston Hughes,* vol. 2, *1941–1967: I Dream a World* (New York, 1988), 92–95, 168, 208; "This Trio Was There Too," picture caption, *Pittsburgh Courier* (c. April 1944). Clipping from DES, subseries 2, vol. 8, AC/NMAH/SI.

43. "Captain Hugh Mulzac and Dr. Frank Boas Head Lists for 1942: Duke Ellington, Dr. Carver, William Hastie, Wendell Willkie, Channing Tobias, Alain Locke Also Named," *Kansas City Call* (12 February 1943); Claire Gordon, "Me 'n' Duke" (presentation at the Ellington 1999 International Conference, 30 April 1999); Lawrence, *Ellington and His World,* 266. Clipping from DES, subseries 2, vol. 10, AC/NMAH/SI.

44. Herb Jeffries Smithsonian interview, tape 5; Max Jones interview, conducted by Patricia Willard, 15 October 1989, SIEOHP, tape 3, AC/NMAH/SI; Robert and Evelyn Udkoff interview, conducted by Dr. Marcia M. Greenlee, 11 March 1991, SEOHP, tape 3, AC/NMAH/SI.

45. John Reilly, "Afterword," in *Native Son,* by Richard Wright (New York, 1940; reprint 1989), 395–96.

Chapter Six

1. James Baldwin, "Many Thousands Gone," in *Notes of a Native Son,* ed. James Baldwin (New York, 1955), 18–19; Richard O. Boyer, "The Hot Bach," in *The Duke Ellington Reader,* ed. Mark Tucker (New York, 1993), 238.

2. Janet Mabie, "Mood in Indigo," in Tucker, *Duke Ellington Reader,* 43; Florence Zunser, "'Opera Must Die,' Says Galli-Curci! Long Live the Blues!" in Tucker, *Duke Ellington Reader,* 45; John Del Valle, "Duke Ellington Here: Composes African Saga," *San Francisco Call-Bulletin* (February 1932); uncited author, "Ellington Composing: Musician at Work in Apartment Here" (date and source obscured—c. June 1933); Arthur Johnson, Dial Twists column, *Boston Transcript* (19 August 1933); Jack Reel, "Ellington and His Band Get Big Ovation" (source obscured—probably from Omaha, c. late 1933 or 1934); "Jungle to Harlem: Ellington Writes Music Tracing History of His Race," *Columbus (OH) Citizen* (21 August 1934). Clippings found in the Duke Ellington Scrapbooks, series 8, subseries 2, vols. 2, 5, and 6.

David Krasner, "'The Pageant Is the Thing: Black Nationalism and *The Star of Ethiopia,*" in

Performing America: Cultural Nationalism in American Theater, ed. Jeffrey D. Mason and J. Ellen Gainor (Ann Arbor, 1999), 106–22; Mark Tucker, "The Genesis of *Black, Brown and Beige,*" *Black Music Research Journal* (Fall 1993): 70–72. Krasner article courtesy of David Grimsted.

3. "Little Red Cottage in a Painting by Ellington," *Stockholms Tidningen* (17 April 1939); "Negro Opera by 'Duke' Awaits Premiere: Ellington in Town after Musical Night on Train; Jazz and Classical Music Can Be United," *(Stockholm) Aftonbladet* (16 April 1939). Translation of the clippings from Swedish from DES 9:45, NMAH/SI. Alfred Frankenstein, "'Hot Is Something about a Tree,' Says the Duke," *San Francisco Chronicle* (9 November 1941); Belle Ayer, "Duke Ellington Is Versatile Entertainer," Film Fanfare column, *Rock Island (IL) Argus* (28 March 1942). Clippings from DES, subseries 2, vol. 10, NMAH/SI.

4. Alexander DeConde, *Ethnicity, Race, and American Foreign Policy: A History* (Boston, 1992), 130–44; Kenneth O'Reilly, *Nixon's Piano: Presidents and Racial Politics from Washington to Clinton* (New York, 1995), 124–45. DeConde especially focuses on how the Soviets picked up on and amplified this line of criticism of American racism (initially used as a policy weapon during World War II by the Nazis and Japanese) during the cold war.

5. A flurry of news stories prematurely announced an Ellington Carnegie date in the late winter of 1933, reporting that "arrangements are under way" and that "Duke Ellington plans to hire New York's Carnegie Hall to show 'em something about American music": "Duke to Carnegie," *New York City News* (23 February 1933); Aircaster, " . . . For Beer," (uncited fragment—c. March 1933); uncited column, *New York City Sun* (4 March 1933); uncited column, *Norwalk (CT) Sentinel* (27 March 1933). Clippings from DES, series 8, subseries 2, vol. 5, NMAH/SI.

Potential 1937 Ellington Carnegie concert: Edmund Anderson interview, conducted by Valerie Archer, 15 October 1980, #550A, pg. 13–15, OHAM/YUSC; Ross Firestone, *Swing, Swing, Swing: The Life and Times of Benny Goodman* (New York, 1993), 213.

The Ellington orchestra had also been scheduled to play Carnegie in the spring of 1939 and the fall of 1942, the dates cancelled by, respectively, their 1939 European tour and their participation in the film of *Cabin in the Sky:* Klaus Stratemann, *Duke Ellington, Day by Day and Film by Film* (Copenhagen, 1992), 239.

6. Sources for the initiation of the January 1943 Carnegie concert: Duke Ellington interview, CHIC 1964 #8, AC/NMAH/SI; Leonard Feather, liner notes, *The Duke Ellington Carnegie Hall Concerts: January 1943* (Prestige 2PCD-34004-2); Michael James interview, conducted by the author, 11 November 1999.

7. Stratemann, *Duke Ellington,* 198–200, 237–38.

8. Ted Gioia, *The History of Jazz* (New York, 1997), 189. See chapter 5 for more on the Petrillo ban.

9. Duke Ellington interview, CHIC 1964 #8, tape 2, AC/NMAH/SI. Ellington's memory was surprisingly good: the tour itinerary he cites for December 1942 is correct in all details except for the dates of the Hartford engagement, which are 11–13 December 1942, not 19 December, as Ellington remembered: Stratemann, *Duke Ellington,* 238. Also, Mark Tucker's research concluded that Ellington had remembered the wrong movie playing as he composed *Black, Brown and Beige.* Tucker claimed it was *Secrets of the Underworld* or *Secrets of the Underground:* Tucker, "Genesis," 80.

10. John Edward Hasse, *Beyond Category: The Life and Genius of Duke Ellington* (New York, 1993), 260–61; Stratemann, *Duke Ellington;* William Morris Agency advertisement, *Variety* (20 January 1943), 45; "The Duke Steps Out: Carnegie Hall Opens Its Doors to a Great Negro Musician," *Look* (12 January 1943); uncited author, "Duke's Concert Draws Press," uncited source (c. January 1943). Last clipping from DES, subseries 2, vol. 8, NMAH/SI.

11. Advertisement, "Ellington's Music Is Never Dated!" (c. December 1942): DES, subseries 2, vol. 10, NMAH/SI.

12. Joseph Horowitz, *Understanding Toscanini: How He Became an American Culture-God and Helped Create a New Audience for Old Music* (Minneapolis, 1988), 268–69.

The following ads are from collection 301, series 2, box 10, AC/NMAH/SI: advertisement, "Duke Ellington: Genius of Jazz" (c. January 1943), folder 6; advertisement, "Hear Duke Ellington, Genius of Jazz, on Victor Records" (c. January 1943), folder 10; advertisement, "'Black, Brown and Beige' by Duke Ellington, a New RCA Victor 'Showpiece'" (c. 1945), folder 21.

Leonard G. Feather, "Duke Ellington at Carnegie Hall," *RCA Record Bulletin* (c. January 1943); "Ellington Classics," *Victor Record News* (c. January 1943). These RCA Victor marketing materials and many others used in the 1943 publicity campaigns can be found in DES, subseries 2, vol. 11, NMAH/SI.

13. Harold H. Kassarjian, "The Negro and American Advertising, 1946–1965," in *The Black Consumer: Dimensions of Behavior and Strategy,* ed. George Joyce and Norman A. P. Govoni (New York, 1971), 326–34. The magazines Kassarjian surveyed include: *Esquire, Fortune, Good Housekeeping, Harpers, Life, Mademoiselle, Newsweek, New Yorker, Popular Mechanics, Sports Illustrated,* and *Vogue.*

14. Helen M. Oakley, "Ellington to Offer 'Tone Parallel': Black, Brown and Beige Are Three Movements of New Concert Piece," *Down Beat* (15 January 1943); Howard Taubman, "The 'Duke' Invades Carnegie Hall," *New York Times Magazine* (17 January 1943). *Harlem's People's Voice* quote is from Maurice Zolotow, "The Duke Is Hot," *Saturday Evening Post* (7 August 1943). "Barzillai Lew" can be heard on the following broadcast: Duke Ellington Orchestra at the Hurricane, 14 July 1943, RWC 9054, JVC/LOC.

15. Duke Ellington, *A Duke Ellington Panorama,* RCA Victor, P-138; RCA Victor press release, "Victor's 'Panorama' Album Traces Ellington's Career" (c. January 1943). Latter item found in DES, subseries 2, vol. 11, NMAH/SI.

16. Grena Bennett, "'Lost' Verdi Score Played by Toscanini," *New York Journal-American* (25 January 1943); Irving Kolodin, "Ellington Band Gives a Concert," *New York Sun* (24 January 1943); Daniel Richman, "Ellington Set for Carnegie: Duke Writing New Music for Jan. Concert," *New York Post* (2[?] November 1942); uncited author, "Duke—The Great—Ellington," uncited African American newspaper (c. January 1943). Clippings from DES, subseries 2, vols. 8 and 10, NMAH/SI.

Ruth Ellington said that several organizations were contacted before Russian War Relief agreed to be the beneficiary of Ellington's debut Carnegie Hall concert. Was this because the organizations did not wish to be associated with an African American composer's debut at Carnegie Hall, or because they felt uncomfortable with the black history subject matter of the main piece premiered that evening? She did not provide additional details: Ruth Ellington interview, conducted by the Duke Ellington Society, 1960, SC Audio C-451, side 1, SCBC.

17. John Briggs, "The Low-Down on Duke's Concert: Our Jive Arm, Longhair Dept. Have It Out in Print," *New York Post* (25 January 1943); Dolores Calvin, "Duke Ellington's Concert Leaves His Fans Gasping for More—Swing," uncited source (c. January 1943); Alfred A. Duckett, "Ellington Scores in Carnegie Hall Debut: Jitterbugs and Millionaires to Hear Classical Concert," *Washington Afro-American* (30 January 1943); Abel Green, "Ellington, at B.O. and Musically, Niftily in Groove at Carnegie Hall Concert," *Variety* (27 January 1943); Elsa Maxwell, Music of the People syndicated column, *Salt Lake City Telegram* (5 March 1943); "Duke Ellington Artistry Sets Critics, Celebrities Agog as Duke Makes Jazz History in Staid Carnegie Hall, New York," *Pittsburgh Courier* (30 January 1943); uncited author, "Duke's Concert Sold Out 12 Days Ahead," uncited source (c. January 1943). Clippings from DES, subseries 2, vols. 8 and 10, NMAH/SI.

18. Most of the 23 January 1943 Carnegie concert can be heard on the following release: *The Duke Ellington Carnegie Hall Concerts: January 1943* (Prestige 2PCD-34004–2). The defini-

tion of "hit singles" is taken from the sales charts compiled in the 1980s by Joel Whitburn, *Pop Memories 1890–1954: The History of American Popular Music* (Menonomee Falls, WI), 148–49. An exception to this statement would be "Koko," a commercially minor hit single for the band in 1940. "Don't Get Around Much Anymore," performed at the first Carnegie concert, would not become a hit single until later in the year.

19. Juan Tizol interview, conducted by Patricia Willard, 15 November 1978, reel 1, pg. 33–34, JOHP, IJS/RU. See also Taubman, "'Duke' Invades Carnegie Hall."

20. This section, except as indicated, is drawn from: Duke Ellington, "Black, Brown and Beige," undated and unpublished narrative sketch (c. late 1942 / early 1943), collection 415, series 6, folder 7, AC/NMAH/SI.

The "Black, Brown and Beige" scenario went through numerous drafts, some or all of which are filed at the Smithsonian: collection 301, series 4, box 3, AC/NMAH/SI. © 2004 Estate of Mercer K. Ellington, cannot be reproduced without permission from the estate.

In a 1956 private interview, Ellington remarked that he also completed a "stage presentation" script of *Black, Brown and Beige* in 1955, with "songs and narration and all that." That document could not be found at the Smithsonian, and Ellington indicated that it represented a different treatment than the 1942–43 scenario: Duke Ellington interview, CHIC 1956 #1, tape 1, AC/NMAH/SI.

21. Boyer, "Hot Bach"; Zolotow, "Duke Is Hot."

22. Wilson Jeremiah Moses, *Afrotopia: The Roots of Afro-American Popular History* (Cambridge, 1998), 22–25, 86–90, 187–88. Two examples of the pamphlets published by Joel A. Rogers: J. A. Rogers, *Worlds Greatest Men and Women of African Descent* (New York, 1935); J. A. Rogers, *100 Amazing Facts about the Negro with Complete Proof: A Short Cut to the World History of the Negro* (New York, c. 1920s/1930s; reprint 1957).

23. Ellington's comments on the Songhay and Sudan section quoted earlier in the text are also much the same, though not directly quoted from, W. E. B. DuBois, *The Negro* (New York, 1915), 55–56, 110, 114–17. Ellington's references to the smelting of iron, the notion of slavery strengthening the character and resilience of blacks, historians' general ignorance of African and African American history, and the inclusion of Toussaint L'ouverture and slave-revolt leaders as an essential part of black American history is echoed in DuBois' 1910s pageant *The Star of Ethiopia*: Krasner, "Pageant Is the Thing."

24. Duke Ellington, script notes, "Boola," 2–4: collection 301, series 4, box 3, folder 8, AC/NMAH/SI. © 2004 Estate of Mercer K. Ellington, cannot be reproduced without permission from the estate.

Though these notes were named "Boola" (though there is no title on the actual notes), they are obviously a rough draft for the *Black, Brown and Beige* scenario. "Boola" was the original name for the project. Ellington indicated in the 1956 Carter Harman interview that the scenario was written before the music: Ellington interview, CHIC 1956 #1, tape 1, AC/NMAH/SI.

25. Recent historical scholarship has shown that Africans arriving in the colonies during the seventeenth century were not automatically relegated to slave status, as Ellington assumed in his scenario. Much depended on which area of the country the slaves lived: Lois Carr and Lorena S. Walsh, "Economic Diversification and Labor Organization in the Chesapeake, 1650–1820," in *Work and Labor in Early America,* ed. Stephen Innes (Chapel Hill, 1988), 144–61, 176–83; Carl S. Degler, "Slavery and the Genesis of American Race Prejudice," in *Interpreting Colonial America: Selective Readings,* ed. James Kirby Martin (New York, 1978), 128–33; Ira Berlin, *Many Thousands Gone: The First Two Generations of Slavery in North America* (Cambridge, MA, 1998), 64, 77–79.

26. John William Riley, "Ellington's New Tone Poem Features Concert Tomorrow," uncited source (22 January 1943). Clipping from DES, subseries 2, vol. 10, AC/NMAH/SI.

27. John W. Blassingame, *The Slave Community: Plantation Life in the Antebellum South* (New York, 1972), 19–29, 96–103, 104–7, 210; W. E. B. DuBois, *The Souls of Black Folk* (New York, 1903), chap. 14; Stanley Elkins, *Slavery* (Chicago, 1959); Eugene Genovese, *Roll Jordan Roll: The World the Slaves Made* (New York, 1972), xv–xvii, 4–21, 30–33, 91–107, 127–39, 583; Ulrich B. Phillips, *Life and Labor in the Old South* (Boston, 1929), chaps. 1 and 9; Kenneth M. Stampp, *The Peculiar Institution* (New York, 1956), 3–15, 97–102.

28. Gilbert Chase, *America's Music: From the Pilgrims to the Present* (Urbana, IL, 1987), 38, 56–69; Ken Emerson, *Doo-Dah: Stephen Foster and the Rise of American Culture* (New York, 1997), 67–70; Russell Sanjek, *American Popular Music and Its Business: From the Beginning to 1790* (New York, 1988), 408–22; Eileen Southern, *The Music of Black Americans: A History* (New York, 1971), 39–53, 84–97.

In 1956, Ellington told interviewer Carter Harman that the black spiritual "came from singing counter-melodies to the hymns being sung in church. They [African Americans] were on the outside of the church." Harman asked, "Is that a historical fact?" "That's right," answered Ellington: CHIC 1956 #1, tape 1, AC/NMAH/SI.

29. Ellington, script notes, "Boola," 8.

Eugene Genovese, among others, has further delineated how slave owners, particularly in the first half of the nineteenth century, viewed slavery as a moral and Christian duty since African Americans and slaves, in their view, were childlike, immature beings who did not have the skills or wisdom to take care of themselves. This paternalistic system, according to Genovese, "grew out of the necessity to discipline and morally justify a system of exploitation": Genovese, *Roll, Jordan, Roll,* 4–7, 76–96.

30. Nathan O. Hatch, *The Democratization of American Christianity* (New Haven, 1989), 1–16, 102–13; Rhys Isaac, "Evangelical Revolt: The Nature of the Baptist Challenge to the Traditional Order in Virginia, 1765–1775," in *Colonial America,* ed. Stanley Katz, John Murrin, and Douglas Greenberg (New York, 1993), 640–56; Lawrence W. Levine, *Black Culture and Black Consciousness: Afro-American Folk Thought from Slavery to Freedom* (Oxford, 1977), 23, 37–38, 50–51, 137; Leon Litwack, *Trouble in Mind: Black Southerners in the Age of Jim Crow* (New York, 1998), 352–64, 380–403; Philip D. Morgan, "Slave Life in Piedmont, Virginia, 1720–1800," in *Colonial Chesapeake Society,* ed. Lois Carr, Philip D. Morgan, and Jean Russo (Chapel Hill, 1988), 474–80.

31. Ellington, script notes, "Boola," 19.

32. These verses are quoted in order from Proverbs 11:1–3 (King James Version). Other verses in the book of Proverbs (especially 4–10, 17, 18, 28) express similar sentiments that could be applied to the unfairness and eventual comeuppance of slaveholders. Numerous accounts of Ellington through the decades cite his habit of carrying a Bible with him and reading it frequently.

33. Litwack, *Trouble in Mind,* 413.

34. An event also described in DuBois, *Negro,* 175–76.

35. Ellington, script notes, "Boola," 23.

36. Brian Priestley and Alan Cohen, "Black, Brown and Beige," in Tucker, *Duke Ellington Reader* (New York, 1993), 197.

37. Eric Foner, *The Story of American Freedom* (New York, 1998), 89.

38. Ellington, script notes, "Boola," 24–25.

39. Ellington, script notes, "Boola," 26.

40. Robert Palmer, *Deep Blues* (New York, 1981), 39. See also: W. C. Handy, *Father of the Blues: An Autobiography* (New York, 1941), 72–81; Litwack, *Trouble in Mind,* chap. 8; Levine, *Black Culture,* chap. 4.

41. The comments were later restored in an edition published long after her demise: Zora

Neale Hurston, *Dust Tracks on a Road: An Autobiography* (Chicago, 1984), 338–342. Stratemann, *Duke Ellington,* 243. There is some undated evidence in the Smithsonian files indicating that Ellington tried to set the scenario to music: see John Franceschina, *Duke Ellington's Music in the Theatre* (Jefferson, NC, 2002), 171.

42. W. E. B. DuBois, "Criteria of Negro Art" (1926), quoted in Krasner, "Pageant Is the Thing," 110.

43. Michael James interview, conducted by the author, 11 November 1999.

44. Duke Ellington interview, conducted by Stanley Dance, BBC Radio 1, 1972, RYJ 3072, JVC/LOC. This interview probably took place in 1971, but was originally broadcast in 1972.

45. Duckett, "Ellington Scores." One critic wrote that "many of the merely curious straggled out" during *Black, Brown and Beige:* Douglas Watt, "The Duke Has Hot Concert at Carnegie," *New York Daily News* (25 January 1943).

46. Robert Bagar, "Duke Ellington Marks 20th Year as Musician," *New York Telegram* (25 January 1943); Kolodin, "Ellington Band Gives a Concert"; Henry Simon, "The Duke Shows Carnegie How," *PM* (25 January 1943). Clippings from DES, subseries 2, vol. 10, AC/NMAH/SI.

47. Paul Bowles, "Duke Ellington in Recital for Russian Relief: Jazz Musician and Orchestra Heard at Carnegie Hall in Anniversary Concert," *New York Herald-Tribune* (25 January 1943); Dolores Calvin, "Duke Ellington's Concert Leaves His Fans Gasping For More—Swing," obscured source (25 January 1943); Green, "Ellington, at B.O. and Musically, Niftily in Groove"; Briggs, "The Low-Down on Duke's Concernt; Richman, "Ellington Set for Carnegie." Clippings from DES, subseries 2, vol. 10, AC/NMAH/SI.

48. Bowles, "Duke Ellington in Recital"; John Hammond, "Is the Duke Deserting Jazz?" in Tucker, *Duke Ellington Reader,* 173 (originally published May 1943); Bob Thiele, "The Case of Jazz Music," in Tucker, *Duke Ellington Reader,* 177 (originally published July 1943).

49. Gioia, *History of Jazz,* 10–14; Palmer, *Deep Blues,* 27–33.

50. Bagar, "Duke Ellington Marks 20th Year"; Bowles, "Duke Ellington in Recital"; Kolodin, "Ellington Band Gives a Concert"; Watt, "Duke Has Hot Concert at Carnegie."

51. Lillian Cutlp, "Ellington Says Jazz Will Last," *Washington DC Herald* (28 January 1934); Carl Shaefer, "He's Expert with the 'Blues': Chief Exponent of Negro Music Here for Film Engagements," *Hollywood News* (21 February 1934); Fred M. White, "Negro Music as Individual Unit Aim of Duke Ellington: Tunes, Like People of Race, Must Pass Quickly from Joy to Gloom and Back Again, Orchestra Leader Says," *Oregonian* (c. May 1934). Clippings from DES, series 8, subseries 2, vols. 5 and 6, AC/NMAH/SI.

52. Ayer, "Duke Ellington Is Versatile Entertainer"; Riley, "Ellington's New Tone Poem."

53. Priestley and Cohen, "Black, Brown and Beige," 197–98, 202.

54. Arnold Rampersad, *The Life of Langston Hughes,* vol.1, *1902–1941: I, Too, Sing America* (New York, 1986), 326, 358–61.

55. Leonard Feather, "Leonard Feather Rebuts Hammond," in Tucker, *Duke Ellington Reader,* 173–75; Mike Levin, "Duke Fuses Classical and Jazz! Stuff Is There, Says Mix, Needing Development to Attain New Art Form," *Down Beat* (15 February 1943); Maxwell, "Music of the People"; Nina Naguid, "Ellington in a Class by Himself," *Chicago Musical Leader* (February 1943); Billy Rowe, Billy Rowe's Notebook column, *Variety* (27 January 1943). Clippings from DES, subseries 2, vols. 8 and 10, AC/NMAH/SI.

56. David S. Reynolds, *Walt Whitman's America: A Cultural Biography* (New York, 1995), 179–92.

57. Duke Ellington Orchestra at Carnegie Hall, 11 December 1943, RYJ 3447, JVC/LOC; Ruth Ellington interview, 1960; Brooks Kerr interview, conducted by the author, 25 January 1996; H. Robert Udkoff interview, conducted by the author, 28 September 1995. For the performance and publishing history of *Black, Brown and Beige* in the Ellington orchestra after Jan-

uary 1943, consult Andrew Homzy, "*Black, Brown and Beige* in Ellington's Repertoire," *Black Music Research Journal* (Fall 1943): 87–109. For more on how and why Ellington turned away from more ambitious forms of composing after the initial reception of *Black, Brown and Beige,* see Walter van de Leur, *Something to Live For: The Music of Billy Strayhorn* (New York, 2002), 91–92.

58. Stratemann, *Duke Ellington,* 241.

59. Ray Lanning, Night Club Notes column, *Cincinnati Enquirer* (22 October 1944); *Minneapolis Tribune,* "Duke Ellington" (8 October 1944). Ellington's recordings of four excerpts from *Black, Brown and Beige* had not been released when these writers came to their conclusions. Praise for *Black, Brown and Beige* continued for decades, as seen in the various Duke Ellington Scrapbooks, almost always portrayed in preshow publicity as a major musical and career milestone.

Music critic and Ellington confidant Leonard Feather felt that one reason the full *Black, Brown and Beige* did not get recorded was because "the A&R man at Victor," probably Eli Oberstein, "did not have the fondest feeling for Ellington." For more on their contentious relationship, see chapter 8: Leonard Feather interview, conducted by the Duke Ellington Society, 1964, SC Audio C-474, SCBC.

60. Green, "Ellington, at B.O. and Musically, Niftily in Groove."

61. Concert program, "A Concert of the Music of Duke Ellington, Presented by the *Melody Maker*" (c. 1933): collection 386, box 2, AC/NMAH/SI; concert program, "Duke Ellington and His Orchestra, Presented by the Musical Organizations Board" (21 January 1937): collection 301, series 2, box 10, folder 1, AC/NMAH/SI.

62. Examples of national publicity for subsequent Ellington Carnegie performances: "Ellington to Do 3rd Carnegie Hall Concert," *Los Angeles Tribune* (5 June 1944); Walter Winchell, syndicated column, *Aberdeen Journal* (20 November 1944) (the column reports that "New Yorkers are talking about Duke Ellington's Carnegie Hall concert, December 19, with few tickets left"); Jack O'Brian, "Ellington Dons Top Hat: Duke at Carnegie," Associated Press syndicated column, *Milwaukee Journal* (20 December 1944).

William Morris Agency "SRO" poster handout: collection 301, series 11, box 1, folder 3, AC/NMAH/SI. The "SRO" poster also features many positive press stories surrounding the January 1943 concert. Most of these stories were drawn from preshow publicity prompted by the celebrations of "National Ellington Week," not reviews of the concert.

63. "Wham Coin for Jazz 'Longhairs': Concert Payoff on the Upbeat," *Variety* (1 October 1947).

64. This estimation is based on the following accounting report: Frendel, Brown & Co., "Duke Ellington Inc. Statements at December 31, 1944," collection 301, series 3, box 112, folder 9, AC/NMAH/SI. Because of the rounding off of the figures given for the amount of money paid the Ellington orchestra in this document, these figures almost certainly only represent the guarantee promised the band, not the bonuses received when attendance or receipts grew above a predetermined point. Such bonus payments were customarily made in cash, and not recorded, to avoid tax liability.

65. "Ellington on Negro Music," *Variety* (9 December 1942).

66. Roi Ottley, *New World A-Comin': Inside Black America* (Cambridge, MA, 1943), chaps. 1–3, 17, 21, 23; Roi Ottley and William J. Weatherly, eds., *The Negro in New York: An Informal Social History, 1626–1940* (New York, 1940; 1967 reprint). The 1972 solo performance of *New World A-Comin'* can be found on: Duke Ellington, *Live at the Whitney* (Impulse IMPD-173).

67. Rayford W. Logan, "The Negro Wants First-Class Citizenship," and W. E. B. DuBois, "My Evolving Program for Negro Freedom," in *What The Negro Wants,* ed. Rayford W. Logan (Chapel Hill, 1944; reprint 1969), 13, 29–79, 88, 113–30, 209.

68. Stratemann, *Duke Ellington,* 241–42. Some of the *Pastel Period* broadcasts can be heard at the Library of Congress: 6 June 1943 (RWC 9056), 27 June and 11 July 1943 (RWC 9054), JVC/LOC. The quote on listening is from All Star Jamboree & War Drive Program, 1 May 1943, NBC Radio Collection, RWB 612–613 B3-B3, LOC. Another example of the listening angle being promoted: Duke Ellington A-Train Show, 1943, OWI Radio Collection, LWO5833 GR35 7A2, LOC.

69. Densmore Donaldson, Calling All Turns column on Ellington Harvard appearance, *Elizabeth (NJ) Union County Home News* (18 March 1943); Isadora Smith, "Another First for 'Duke': Duke Ellington Returning to Broadway—Will Be First Race Musical Unit to Play Dave Wolper's 'Hurricane,'" *Variety* (c. March 1943); Stratemann, *Duke Ellington,* 241–43, 253–56; Whitburn, *Pop Memories,* 148–49; John S. Wilson, "Ellington Ends 5-Year Absence: Band's Engagement at Basin Street East Called Rare Event," *New York Times* (9 December 1961); *Pittsburgh Courier,* "Harvard Profs Discuss New Ellington Opus" (20 March 1943). The last clipping was reproduced widely, and many versions of it exist in the Duke Ellington Scrapbooks. Clippings from DES, subseries 2, vols. 8 and 10, AC/NMAH/SI, except for the 1961 article.

Ellington interview: CHIC 1964 #3, tape 2, AC/NMAH/SI; CHIC 1964: #8, tape 2, AC/NMAH/SI.

70. Duke Ellington, "Certainly It's Music!" *Listen* (October 1944), in Tucker, *Duke Ellington Reader,* 246–47; Herb Jeffries interview, conducted by the author, 26 September 1995.

Chapter Seven

1. Ernest Bornemann, "Diary—68 Hours without Sleep: The Duke in Paris—Part II," *Down Beat* (8 September 1948); Max Jones interview, conducted by Patricia Willard, 15 October 1989, SIEOHP, tape 3, AC/NMAH/SI; Max Jones interview, conducted by Valerie Archer, 24 March 1981, #557A, B, OHAM/YUSC; Klaus Stratemann, *Duke Ellington: Day by Day and Film by Film* (Copenhagen, 1992), 292–93.

2. Stratemann, *Duke Ellington,* 256–64; A. H. Lawrence, *Duke Ellington and His World: A Biography* (New York, 2001), 326.

3. Set lists and recordings of *Your Saturday Date with the Duke* were provided by Jack Towers, who engineered and produced a reissue of the treasury broadcasts on the Storyville label. He remembers hearing the broadcasts while on duty in the Philippines during the late stages of the war.

4. Rob Bamberger, liner notes, Duke Ellington and His Orchestra, *The Treasury Shows: Volume 1* (D.E.T.S., 2000); John Edward Hasse, *Beyond Category: The Life and Genius of Duke Ellington* (New York, 1993), 151, 181–82; Stratemann, *Duke Ellington,* 262; *PM,* "These Famous Stars Say: 'Hollywood Is for Roosevelt'" (2 October 1944); advertisement from Independent Voters' Committee of the Arts and Sciences, *New York Times* (3 November 1944).

A publicized meeting between Ellington and Hoover in 1931 never took place, even though pictures of Ellington outside the White House surfaced accompanying newspaper stories that claimed the meeting happened. According to Hasse, the meeting was "stopped because the man who set it up . . . had a police record. Perhaps too proud for himself and his race to admit to being rebuffed, or perhaps wanting to make a statement, Ellington posed for photographers on White House grounds, without anyone from the presidential staff. The African American press accused Hoover of being afraid to be photographed with black visitors."

5. Alexander DeConde, *Ethnicity, Race, and American Foreign Policy: A History* (Boston, 1992), 130–44; Manning Marable, *Race, Reform and Rebellion: The Second Reconstruction in Black America, 1945–1990* (Jackson, 1991), 15–26; Harvard Sitkoff, *The Struggle for Black Equality, 1954–1992* (New York, 1993), 11–16.

6. Marable, *Race, Reform and Rebellion;* Sitkoff, *Struggle for Black Equality,* 11–16.

7. Albert Joseph Celley interview, conducted by Patricia Willard, 12 July 1989, SIEOHP, tape 1, AC/NMAH/SI; Norman Granz interview, conducted by Patricia Willard, 23 and 24 August 1989, SIEOHP, tape 1, AC/NMAH/SI; Joya Sherrill interview, conducted by Dr. Marcia M. Greenlee, 15 August 1989, tape 2, AC/NMAH/SI. For more stories of discrimination and violence on the road for the Ellington orchestra, consult: Al Hibbler interview, conducted by Martha Oneppo, 1 December 1980, #553, pg. 5, OHAM/YUSC; *Ebony,* "Problem in Vivid Music" (c. 1946–47), Duke Ellington clipping file, 1945–47, IJS/RU.

For more on black jazz musicians' struggles with Jim Crow during this period, including how the film industry followed similar prejudices and how discrimination affected performances, consult Roy Eldridge, as told to James Goodrich, "Jim Crow Is Killing Jazz," *Negro Digest* (October 1950).

8. Shirley Courtney interview, conducted by Dr. Marcia M. Greenlee, 3 February 1992, SIEOHP, tape 1, AC/NMAH/SI; Jimmy Hamilton interview, conducted by Dr. Marcia M. Greenlee, 26 March 1991, SIEOHP, tape 4, AC/NMAH/SI; Richard O. Boyer, "The Hot Bach," in *The Duke Ellington Reader,* ed. Mark Tucker (New York, 1993), 232; Celley interview, 12 July 1989; Sherill interview, 15 August 1989.

9. Duke Ellington interview, CHIC 1964 #3, tape 2, AC/NMAH/SI; Lawrence, *Duke Ellington and His World,* 325–26. The example of Ellington pressuring club owner Dave Wolper to admit blacks while his orchestra played a prestigious six-month residency at the Hurricane Club in Times Square during 1945 is detailed in the previous chapter.

10. Celley interview, 12 July 1989; Hamilton interview, 26 March 1991.

11. Celley interview, 12 July 1989; Granz interview, 23 and 24 August 1989; Boyer, "The Hot Bach," 218.

12. Celley interview, 12 July 1989; Granz interview, 23 and 24 August 1989; Robert L. Jones interview, conducted by Dr. Marcia M. Greenlee, 30 and 31 January 1992, SIEOHP, tape 2, AC/NMAH/SI; Boyer, "The Hot Bach," 234–35.

13. This section on the economic and artistic changes of the postwar music industry is based on the following sources, except where indicated: Celley interview, 12 July 1989, tape 2; Jim Dawson, "Boogie Down on Central: Los Angeles' Rhythm and Blues Revolution," liner notes for *Central Avenue Sounds: Jazz in Los Angeles (1921–1956)* (Rhino Records, Los Angeles, 1999), 58–65; Scott DeVeaux, *The Birth of Bebop: A Social and Musical History* (Berkeley, 1997), 15–16, 24, 170–71, 202–5, 252–53, 303–4, 382, 389, 433–34; Stephen B. Elworth, "Jazz in Crisis, 1948–1958: Ideology and Representation," in *Jazz among the Discourses,* ed. Krin Gabbard (Durham, 1995), 63–68; Nelson George, *The Death of Rhythm and Blues* (New York, 1988), 19–29; Hasse, *Beyond Category,* 290–97; Michael Levin, "Music Biz Just Ain't Nowhere! Leaders, Men and Buyers All Hit Sour Notes," *Down Beat* (18 November 1946); Burton W. Peretti, *Jazz and American Culture* (Chicago, 1997), 126–30; Russell Sanjek, *American Popular Music and Its Business,* vol. 3, *1900–1984* (New York, 1988), 325; David W. Stowe, *Swing Changes: Big Band Jazz in New Deal America* (Cambridge, MA, 1994), 180–84; Stratemann, *Duke Ellington,* 304, 324; Brian Ward, *Just My Soul Responding: Rhythm and Blues, Black Consciousness, and Race Relations* (Berkeley, 1998), 19–36; "Dance Band Biz Needs Stimulus," *Down Beat* (6 October 1948); Doc, "Will Funny Hats Be Savior?" *Down Beat* (1 December 1948); "Biz May Be 'Off' but Not This Much," *Down Beat* (1 December 1948).

14. Some examples, culled from Stratemann, *Duke Ellington,* 265, 267, 268, 286–88, 292, 294, 303: two *Down Beat*–sponsored shows at Chicago's Civic Opera House on 20 January 1946 brought in six thousand people—a $10,000 take for Ellington—and turned away three thousand people; Ellington's "largest one-nighter take to date," $10,000, was earned at the Water-

gate in Washington, D.C., on 6 June 1946, a show that also had to turn away three thousand patrons and was the first by any black band in an open-air summer concert in the very segregated national capital; a 7 August 1946 show at the Shrine Auditorium in Los Angeles elicited "the largest" gross "for such a concert west of Chicago"; the band's two-day November 1946 Carnegie stand sold out a week in advance; multiweek engagements at the Paramount in New York City did very well in the spring of 1947, 1948, and 1949; the band did record business on the West Coast during tours of fall 1947 and winter 1949.

15. Joel Whitburn, *Top Pop Records, 1940–1955* (Menomonee Falls, WI, 1973), 3, 21, 77–79.

16. Ted Gioia, *The History of Jazz* (New York, 1997), 256–58; "Down Beat Predicts: Dolores Hawkins Will Score with 'Rocks in My Bed,'" *Down Beat* (18 April 1952); Michael James interview, conducted by the author, 11 and 12 November 1999; Albert Murray interview, conducted by the author, 18 April 2001; "Who Killed Bop?" photo editorial, *Ebony* (April 1950).

17. Stuart Nicholson, *Reminiscing In Tempo: A Portrait of Duke Ellington* (Boston, 1999), 279–81; "Duke Gets Hot," *Newsweek* (11 September 1950), from Duke Ellington clipping file, SCBC; Duke Ellington material from Columbia sessions tapes, September 1956, RGA 8452, LOC.

18. Don Freeman, "TD Wrong; TV Won't Hurt Bands, Says Pastor," *Down Beat* (7 September 1951); "Hey, TV, We're Still Waiting," *Down Beat* (2 November 1951); Al Portch, "Video Means the Rebirth of Band Biz, Says Calloway," *Down Beat* (16 November 1951); Charles Emge, "H'wd Leads TV Bands Parade," *Down Beat* (18 April 1952); "Band Business Begins to Boom: Optimistic Biz Looks to TV, Hefty Grosses," *Down Beat* (21 May 1952).

19. Ben Gross, Televiewing column, (obscured) *News* (10 August 1950). Clipping from DES, reel 2. Ben Gross, "'The Duke' Has Composed 3,000 Numbers & Grossed $20,000,000 from Music," Looking and Listening column, *New York Daily News* (22 October 1950), from Duke Ellington clipping file, SCBC. For a complete listing of Ellington's TV appearances, see Stratemann, *Duke Ellington,* 677–84.

20. "Duke Ellington, Peeved at RCA Victor, Asks for Release from Disk Contract," *Variety* (19 December 1945); "RCA Still Won't Release the Duke," *Variety* (27 March 1946); Lawrence, *Duke Ellington and His World,* 334; Bill Gottlieb, "'I'm Not Slipping'—Duke Ellington: 'My Current Ork Just as Good and Perhaps More Flexible,' He Says," *Down Beat* (17 June 1946). Italics are from the original source.

21. Helen Oakley Dance interview, conducted by Patricia Willard, 26 and 27 September 1989, SIEOHP, tape 4, AC/NMAH/SI; Brad McCuen interview, conducted by Patricia Willard, 2 and 3 August 1989, SIEOHP, tape 2, AC/NMAH/SI.

22. The songwriting and recording information are taken from the liner notes of Duke Ellington, *Black, Brown and Beige* (RCA/Bluebird, 1988). The chart information is drawn from Whitburn, *Top Pop Records,* 149.

23. "Trade Buzz on Ellington Switch to Musicraft," *Down Beat* (6 May 1946); "Duke Ellington Sealed to Musicraft 100G Deal while Still with RCA," *Variety* (22 May 1946); "Ellington Quits Musicraft; Talks Col., Decca Deal," *Variety* (18 June 1947); Bill Gottlieb, "Indies Losing Out in Wax Race: Big 4 Controls Industry, 300 Indies May Soon Be Holding Collective Bag," *Down Beat* (7 May 1947); Stratemann, *Duke Ellington,* 286.

24. "Oberstein Buys Musicraft Sides," *Down Beat* (14 January 1953).

25. Frank Rose, *The Agency* (New York, 1995), 90; "William Morris Ork Dept. Snafu," *Down Beat* (28 January 1946); "Only Ellington, Spivak Left on WM Band Roster; AFM Backs Thornhill," *Variety* (2 February 1949); Stratemann, *Duke Ellington,* 304.

26. Documents from collection 301, series 11, box 1, AC/NMAH/SI: "Advertising Manual" (Mills Artists, Inc., c. 1933–38), folder 2; "Advertising Manual" (William Morris Agency, Inc., c. 1946), folder 12; "Duke Ellington and His Orchestra Press Manual" (William Morris Agency,

Inc., c. 1949), folder 11; "Duke Ellington and His World Famous Orchestra" (Associated Booking Corporation, c. 1953), folder 14; "Duke Ellington and His Famous Orchestra" (Associated Booking Corporation, c. 1955), folder 15.

Chapter Eight

1. Sources for this section on *Beggar's Holiday:* Daniel C. Caine, "A Crooked Thing: A Chronicle of 'Beggar's Holiday,'" *New Renaissance* (Fall 1986); Duke Ellington interview, CHIC 1964 #8, AC/NMAH/SI; Mercer Ellington interviews, conducted by Dr. Marcia M. Greenlee, 18 September 1990, 5 and 7 May 1991, SIEOHP, tapes 3 and 6, AC/NMAH/SI; John Franceschina, *Duke Ellington's Music for the Theatre* (Jefferson, NC, 2002), chap. 4; David Hajdu, *Lush Life: A Biography of Billy Strayhorn* (New York, 1996), 100–105; John Edward Hasse, *Beyond Category: The Life and Genius of Duke Ellington* (New York, 1993), 292–93; Luther Henderson interview, conducted by Valerie Archer, 7 July 1981, #561 A, B, pg. 7, OHAM/YUSC; A. H. Lawrence, *Duke Ellington and His World* (New York, 2001), 330–31; Mike Levin, "Beggars' Show Opulent Affair but Misses Hit," *Down Beat* (15 Jan 1947); Arnold Rampersad, *The Life of Langston Hughes,* vol. 2, *1941–1967: I Dream a World* (New York, 1988), chap. 5; Klaus Stratemann, *Duke Ellington: Day by Day and Film by Film* (Copenhagen, 1992), 280–84; Walter van de Leur, *Something to Live For: The Music of Billy Strayhorn* (New York, 2002), 91; Perry Watkins interview, conducted by the Duke Ellington Society, 1966, SC Audio C-483, SCBC; Douglas Watt, "'Holiday' End Seen Mar. 29 or Sooner; Millenium on B'Way," *New York Daily News* (7 March 1947).

2. The songs from *Beggar's Holiday* are found on the following disc: Duke Ellington and His Orchestra, *1947* (Classics, 1999). The 1959 version of "Brown Penny" is featured on Duke Ellington, *Blues in Orbit* (Columbia, 1990).

3. Norman Granz interview, conducted by Patricia Willard, 23 and 24 August 1989, SIEOHP, tape 1, AC/NMAH/SI; Michael James interview, conducted by the author, 11 and 12 November 1999; Richard O. Boyer, "The Hot Bach," in *The Duke Ellington Reader,* ed. Mark Tucker (New York, 1993), 232–35.

4. The articles and letters cited in this discussion, in chronological order: Bill Gottlieb, "'I'm Not Slipping'—Duke Ellington: 'My Current Ork Just as Good and Perhaps More Flexible,' He Says," *Down Beat* (17 June 1946); Michael Levin, "Ellington Fails to Top Himself: Mix Finds Concert Good, Not Great," *Down Beat* (16 December 1946); Ted Hallock, "Duke's Chicago Date Lacks Flair," *Down Beat* (28 January 1948); Marshall W. Stearns and Patricia A. Samson, "Critic Rapped; Crowds Pleased," *Down Beat* (25 February 1948); Mike Levin, "Reputation Shredded, Duke Should Disband, Mix Claims" and Diggin' the Discs with Mix column, *Down Beat* (17 June 1949); Charlie Barnet, "Storm Rages over Duke Story: You Made a Bad Error, Mix—Barnet," *Down Beat* (15 July 1949); John S. Wilson, "NYC Radio Forum Calls Mix Insincere, Irrelevant," *Down Beat* (15 July 1949); Chords and Discords letters column, *Down Beat* (15 July 1949); Pat Harris, "I Like Way Band Sounds—Duke," *Down Beat* (12 August 1949); Charles Allen, Chords and Discords letters column, *Down Beat* (15 July 1949).

5. Stratemann, *Duke Ellington,* 287; Lawrence, *Duke Ellington,* 335.

6. Russell Sanjek, *American Popular Music and Its Business,* vol. 3, *1900–1984* (New York, 1988), 231–38, 246, 314–15; Levin, "Reputation Shredded"; "Dance Band Biz Needs Stimulus," *Down Beat* (6 October 1948); Ralph J. Gleason, "Let Us Now Give Thanks for the Huge Flood of LPs," Swingin' the Golden Gate column, *Down Beat* (14 January 1953); Alexander C. Magoun, "Shaping the Sound of Music: The Evolution of the Phonograph Record, 1877–1950" (University of Maryland, PhD diss., 2000).

7. Mike Levin, Diggin' the Discs with Mix column, *Down Beat* (12 February 1947); George

Hoefer, "'Play It 'til 1953—Geo. after Which LPs Get It," The Hot Box column, *Down Beat* (28 July 1948); Paul Eduard Miller, "Nix Disc Packages; More Single Sales!" *Down Beat* (28 July 1948); J. E. G., "'Round, 'Round We Go on RPMs," *Down Beat* (11 March 1949); "Columbia on New LP Kick," *Down Beat* (20 May 1949); Sanjek, *American Popular Music.*

8. George Avakian interviews, conducted by the author, 11 November 1999, 16 April 2001, 24 November 2001.

9. Avakian interviews, 11 November 1999, 16 April 2001, 24 November 2001; Charles Allen letter, "Duke's Dud Sells," Chords and Dischords column, *Down Beat* (12 August 1949).

10. Avakian interviews, 11 November 1999, 16 April 2001, 24 November 2001; "Columbia Issues Old Ellingtonia," *Down Beat* (4 June 1947); Levin, "Diggin' the Discs"; Mike Levin, "Mix Names Best Discs of Year," *Down Beat* (30 December 1949).

11. Joseph Horowitz, *Understanding Toscanini: How He Became an American Culture God and Helped Create a New Audience for Old Music* (Minneapolis, 1988), 270–74, 399–400; Will Leonard, "Sales of Classics on Way Up; LPs Credited," *Down Beat* (3 June 1953).

12. Avakian interviews, 11 November 1999, 16 April 2001, 24 November 2001; Horowitz, *Understanding Toscanini,* 6–7, 311–13; Dwight Macdonald, "Midcult and Masscult," *Partisan Review* (Spring 1960).

13. Granz interview, 23 and 24 August 1989, tapes 1 and 3; Robert and Evelyn Udkoff interview, conducted by Dr. Marcia M. Greenlee, 11 March 1991, SIEOHP, tape 3, AC/NMAH/SI.

14. Uncited author, "Composing Still Thrill to Ellington," uncited source (looks like the *New York Post,* c. 1948), from DES; Boyer, "Hot Bach," 229; Mercer Ellington interview, 18 September 1990, tape 1.

15. This section on Ellington's 1947–53 tenure at Columbia is based on the following sources: Avakian interviews, 11 November 1999, 16 April 2001, 24 November 2001; George Avakian, "Our Trick, Your Treat, Says Columbia of LPs," *Down Beat* (3 June 1953); Ruth Ellington interview, conducted by Dr. Marcia M. Greenlee, 18 August 1989, SIEOHP, tape 1, AC/NMAH/SI; Will Friedwald, *Sinatra! The Song Is You: A Singer's Art* (New York, 1995), 159, 186, 302; Mark Tucker, liner notes, *Duke Ellington: The Reprise Studio Recordings* (Mosaic, 1999); "Duke Switches Record Labels," *Down Beat* (6 May 1953); "LP Boon to Music World, as Seen after 5 Years," *Down Beat* (23 September 1953).

16. "Col Opening Purse Strings in Pop Field: Loading up on Names," *Billboard* (26 August 1950); "Music Record Programming Guide," *Billboard* (15 September 1951); "Youth Movement Sweeps Records," *Billboard* (29 September 1951); "Columbia Pop Albums Jump By 40%," *Billboard* (21 March 1953); "Major Record Firms Show Gain in Incomes for 1952," *Billboard* (28 March 1953); Avakian, "Our Trick."

17. "Music World to Salute Ellington on Silver Jubilee," *Down Beat* (24 September 1952); Hal Webman, "Editorial: 'Beat' Congratulates a Genius—Edward Kennedy Ellington," *Down Beat* (5 November 1952).

Mills, of course, had enormous financial interest in promoting Ellington nostalgia. Of the seventeen compositions named in a poll of music celebrities and critics as Ellington's best in the issue, eight were published by Mills: Hal Webman, "Stars, Sidemen and Scribes Salute Duke and His Discs," *Down Beat* (5 November 1952).

18. Frank Sinatra signed with Capitol and began recording for them at roughly the same time. Dave Dexter, Jr., *Playback: A Newsman/Record Producer's Hits and Misses from the Thirties to the Seventies* (New York, 1976), 138; Patricia Willard interview, conducted by the author, 30 October 1995.

19. This section on Mercer Records is drawn from the following sources: Mercer Records, Inc., correspondence, June 1951, collection 301, series 3, box 107, folder 13, AC/NMAH/SI; Mercer Records, Inc., recording release announcements, June 1951, collection 301, series 3,

box 108, folder 33, AC/NMAH/SI; Mercer Records, Inc., press releases, 1951, collection 301, series 3, box 108, folder 10, AC/NMAH/SI; Mercer Records, Inc., statements and invoices to distributors, 1951–52, collection 301, series 3, box 109, folder 14, AC/NMAH/SI; Mercer Records, Inc., statements of royalties paid, 1950–53, collection 301, series 3, box 109, folder 15, AC/NMAH/SI. Also: Mercer Ellington with Stanley Dance, *Duke Ellington in Person* (Boston, 1978), 103–4; David Hajdu, *Lush Life: A Biography of Billy Strayhorn* (New York, 1996), 122–23; Ted A. Steele, "Mercer Ellington Does Good Miami Biz with Unusual Sounding Unit," *Down Beat* (7 October 1949); Stratemann, *Duke Ellington,* 323–24. Most of the Mercer masters were burned in a fire. No new significant artists were introduced via Mercer Records.

20. "Ellington's Tempo Music Reactivated," *Billboard* (12 August 1950); Albert Joseph Celley interview, conducted by Patricia Willard, 12 July 1989, SIEOHP, tape 4, AC/NMAH/SI. There are no tax records for Ellington and the orchestra housed at the Smithsonian during the period that Mercer Records was in operation (1950–52). My comments on tax issues surrounding Mercer Records and Tempo Music are based on what is known about Ellington's patterns concerning income taxes in the 1960s. For Ellington's tax problems in the 1960s, consult chapters 10, 13, and 14.

21. "NAACP Plans to Boycott Duke Ellington," *Richmond Times-Dispatch* (21 January 1951); "Ellington Concert Off: Cancels Richmond Program—Best Seats Given to Negroes," *New York Times* (29 January 1951); "Duke Ellington Cries 'Shame' at NAACP Action Here," *Richmond News-Leader* (24 January 1951); "Self-Defeating Zeal," *Newport News Press* (28 January 1951); "Top Talent Bears Brunt of Virginia Segregation Law," *Variety* (31 January 1951); P. L. Prattis, "The Time Has Come When Negro Artists Must Take a Stand against Jim Crow," The Horizon column, *Pittsburgh Courier* (24 February 1951); Joseph V. Baker, "Concert Segregation NAACP Issue," *Philadelphia Inquirer* (25 February 1951); "Duke Flays NAACP for Halting Richmond Concert," *Down Beat* (9 March 1951).

The Ellington quote about "old people living all their lives in filth and dirt" comes from the *Down Beat* article, which intimated that Ellington was speaking about the members of the Richmond NAACP in that instance. This is most likely a misprint or mistake.

22. Kenneth O' Reilly, *Nixon's Piano: Presidents and Racial Politics from Washington to Clinton* (New York, 1995), 147–62; Brian Ward, *Just My Soul Responding: Rhythm and Blues, Black Consciousness, and Race Relations* (Berkeley, 1998), 26.

23. Granz interview, 23 August 1989, tape 1; David W. Stowe, *Swing Changes: Big Band Jazz in New Deal America* (Cambridge, 1994), 237; Eunice Truckenbrodt, "Granz and the Jazz Philarmonic," *Crisis* (May 1947).

24. Allan Keiler, *Marian Anderson: A Singer's Journey* (New York, 2000), 235–38, 255–58, 265; Baker, "Concert Segregation"; Prattis, "Time Has Come."

25. The account of the "We Ain't Ready" newspaper story and the reaction to it is drawn from the following sources in chronological order: Otis N. Thompson, "Duke Calls Fight for Rights 'Silly': Bandleader Waxes Hot, Assails Efforts against Segregation," *Baltimore Afro-American* (24 November 1951); "Who Is Not Ready Yet?: An Editorial," *Baltimore Afro-American* (1 December 1951); James L. Hicks, "'Some of My Best Friends Are Show People, but . . .':Duke Benefit for NAACP Netted $1,500, Not 13Gs," *Baltimore Afro-American* (1 December 1951); "Maestro Says 'We Ain't Ready Yet': Duke Ellington's Views on Jim Crow Shock Nation," *Baltimore Afro-American* (1 December 1951); Josephus Simpson, Joe's Diary column, *Baltimore Afro-American* (8 December 1951); Al Moses, "Credit Duke's Rise to 'Fight for Rights': 'Silly' Talk a Disservice," *Baltimore Afro-American* (8 December 1951); Duke Ellington, "Duke Ellington Says He Didn't Say It: The Duke Says . . . ," *Baltimore Afro-American* (15 December 1951); Otis N. Thompson, Jr., "Reporter Insists That He Did: Reporter Says . . . ," *Baltimore Afro-American* (15 December 1951); "Thompson Is Ace Reporter: War Vet, Honor Grad Native of Batlimore [*sic*],"

Baltimore Afro-American (15 December 1951); What Our Readers Say letters column, *Baltimore Afro-American* (15, 22, and 29 December 1951).

26. Harvard Sitkoff, *The Struggle for Black Equality, 1954–1992* (New York, 1993), 17–21; Taylor Branch, *Parting the Waters: America in the King Years, 1954–1963* (New York, 1988); Taylor Branch, *Pillar of Fire: America in the King Years, 1963–1965* (New York, 1998).

27. The exceptions to this rule, according to Stratemann, *Duke Ellington,* 310–61: Lexington, KY (5 June 1952); El Paso, TX (21 March 1953); St. Louis, MO (17 May 1953); three dates in Texas in April 1954, which included two U.S. armed services bases.

28. Clark Terry interview, conducted by Dr. Marcia M. Greenlee, 10 October 1990, SIEOHP, tapes 3 and 4, AC/NMAH/SI.

29. Duke Ellington interviews, CHIC 1956 #1, 1964 #4, AC/NMAH/SI. The Thunderbird asked that the band members not gamble, and it segregated the audiences, but by the 1960s both those caveats were abandoned. ·

30. Gene Santoro, *Myself When I Am Real: The Life and Music of Charles Mingus* (New York, 2000), 5, 95, 140, 175, 181.

31. The expenses: $6,997.72 for "expenses incurred and paid by Ellington's office, including rental of hall and payment of musicians (exclusive of Mr. Ellington)"; $887.87 in additional expenses incurred by the Ellington office, which the NAACP paid; $2,353.58 in federal admission taxes, plus the money used to promote the show: What Our Readers Say letters column, *Baltimore Afro-American,* 15 December 1951.

32. Terry interview, 10 October 1990; Mercer Ellington interview, 18 September 1990, 5 and 7 May 199, tape 3; Stratemann, *Duke Ellington,* 330–63.

33. Frank Schiffman Apollo Theater Collection, collection 540, series 3: booking cards, box 3, AC/NMAH/SI; Nelson George, *The Death of Rhythm & Blues* (New York, 1988), 40–46; Rampersad, *Life of Langston Hughes,* 2:199–207.

34. This section on Billy Strayhorn is based on the following sources: Robert Conaway interview, conducted by Harriett Milnes, 24 August 1984, #591A, pg. 7, OHAM/YUSC; Duke Ellington and Marion Logan interviews, *Duke Ellington: Reminiscing In Tempo,* (Robert Levi Films, 1992), LOC/MPD; Milt Grayson interview, conducted by Harriett Mlilnes, 11 July 1983, #573A,B, pg. 7–8, OHAM/YUSC; Hajdu, *Lush Life,* 109; Gregory Morris interview, conducted by Harriett Mlilnes, 23 August 1984, #590A-E, pg. 7–8, OHAM/YUSC; Russell Procope interview, conducted by Chris Albertson, 6 March 1979, JOHP, reel 4, pgs. 15–17, IJS/RU; Walter van de Leur, *Something to Live For: The Music of Billy Strayhorn* (New York, 2002), 27, 61, 88, 94–98, 102, 105, 110–11, 115, 130, 146, 162.

35. Information and quote concerning the two Capitol sessions is from two episodes of "Friday with [Dave] Galloway" featuring Duke Ellington, 21 January and 29 April 1955, NBC Radio Collection, RGA 0925 A1-B2 and RGA 0837 A1-B1, respectively, LOC.

36. "The Critics' Choice: The World's Top Jazz Critics Name the Musicians Who Excite Them," *Down Beat* (24 August 1955); "Here Are Your Final, Complete Tabulations of 1955 'Down Beat' Annual Music Poll," *Down Beat* (28 December 1955).

37. Avakian interviews, 11 November 1999, 16 April 2001, 24 November 2001; Duke Ellington interview, CHIC 1964 #8, AC/NMAH/SI; Jimmy Hamilton interview, conducted by Dr. Marcia M. Greenlee, 26 March 1991, SIEOHP, AC/NMAH/SI; Hasse, *Beyond Category,* 316–17; Terry interview, 10 October 1990. John Saunders felt the same way about the Aquacade as his fellow band member Jimmy Hamilton: John Saunders interview, conducted by Anthony Coleman, 19 October 1978, #532A, B, pg. 14, OHAM/YUSC.

38. Duke Ellington, script, *Man with Four Sides* (c. 1955), collection 301, series 4, box 1, folder 9, AC/NMAH/SI; Duke Ellington, prospectus, *Man with Four Sides* (c. 1955), collection 301, series 4, box 6, unmarked folder, AC/NMAH/SI. Another Ellington script, entitled *Lane,* has

a similar plot and exists in at least two different drafts. The Smithsonian dates it earlier than *Four Sides,* but there are no markings on the script to confirm that. The version co-written with Lorella Val-Mery seems like a revised version of *Four Sides,* more streamlined and cinematic, yet missing some of the earthiness of the Ellington original: Duke Ellington and Lorella Val-Mery, scripts, *Lane,* collection 301, series 4, boxes 2 and 6, folder 3 and unmarked folder, AC/NMAH/SI. John Franceschina (see below) thought the *Lane* script dated back to the 1940s.

Probably hoping to snare investors, Ellington read excerpts from *Man with Four Sides* to accompaniment by members of his band on the NBC *Monitor* radio show, hosted by Dave Garroway, in late August 1955: Stratemann, *Duke Ellington,* 361.

For more on the songs of *Man with Four Sides* and the attempts to secure financing for a Broadway run, see John Franceschina, *Duke Ellington's Music for the Theatre* (Jefferson, NC, 2002), 87–93; Robert Sylvester, "Real Rich Cat," Dream Street column, *New York Daily News* (15 September 1955), from Duke Ellington clipping file, SCBC. This last article describes Ellington performing songs from the play for rich potential backers with the names of Armour, DuPont, etc.

Chapter Nine

1. Alfred T. Robbins, "'It's a Stimulus': Music Is Life for Ellington," *New York Journal-American* (18 June 1962); Stanley Dance, "Festival: Preparation and Aftermath, the Story of 'Suite Thursday,'" *Metronome* (July 1961).

Composing while performing live: Quentin Jackson interview, conducted by Milt Hinton, June 1976, JOHP, reel 5, pg. 65, IJS/RU; Maurice Lawrence interview, conducted by the author, 1 May 1999; John Saunders interview, conducted by the Duke Ellington Society, 1962, SC Audio C-465, SCBC. Lawrence recalled a night in 1961 when Ellington went backstage to rewrite part of an arrangement during a lengthy Paul Gonsalves solo, and how Ellington, while jotting down his idea for a different song, kept track of how many choruses Gonsalves played so that he knew when he had to return to the stage. Lawrence: "He knew exactly where Paul was . . . it shows his mind going in more than one direction at the same time. When he came back out with that affable smile to the audience, he laid down the changes he made right down on [trombonist] Lawrence Brown's [music] stand."

2. The quotes about Ellington's composing, in order: Charles Greuenberg, "The Duke Calls 'Jazz' the Wrong Word for It," *New York Post* (28 August 1961); Duke Ellington interview, CHIC 1956 #1, tape 1, AC/NMAH/SI. Ralph J. Gleason, "Ellington Talks about 'Paris Blues,'" Rhythm Section syndicated column, *Milwaukee Journal* (25 Mar 1961); Robbins, "'It's a Stimulus'"; Jeremy Hornsby, "Duke Ellington: Music Is Like a Meal, You Add Spice," *San Francisco Examiner* (31 May 1964); James Greenwood, "The Duke Who's Been Chasing a Melody for 40 Years," *Daily Mail* (13 February 1965); Max Jones, "Jazz Scene: Duke Suites in a Hotel Suite," *Melody Maker* (date obscured—c. February 1967); Burt Korall, "Views of the Duke," *(Philadelphia) Daily Bulletin* (May 1967); Allen Hughes, "Dr. Ellington Sounds Like Same Old Duke," *New York Times* (3 August 1967). Clippings from DES, rolls 3, 4, 7, 9, and 10, vols. 15, 24, 35, 37, 46, 47, and 49, NMAH/SI.

3. Duke Ellington interview, CHIC 1964 #8, tape 2, AC/NMAH/SI; Klaus Stratemann, *Duke Ellington: Day by Day and Film by Film* (Copenhagen, 1992), 362; Whitney Baillett, "Celebration for the Duke," *Saturday Review* (12 May 1956).

The March 1956 Ellington orchestra recordings can be found on: Duke Ellington, *The Private Collection,* vol. 1, *Studio Sessions: Chicago, 1956* (Saja, 1988).

4. Walter van de Leur, *Something to Live For: The Music of Billy Strayhorn* (New York, 2002), 115, 130–31.

5. Lillian Ross, "You Dig It, Sir?" in *Reading Jazz: A Gathering of Autobiography, Reportage, and Criticism from 1919 to Now,* ed. Robert Gottlieb (New York, 1996), 686–700; 1955 Newport Jazz Festival program, featuring Duke Ellington, "The Future of Jazz," collection 301, series 2B, box 11, folder 15, AC/NMAH/SI; John S. Wilson, "Jazz: Fusion at Newport; Traditional and Modern Styles Mixed during Second Day of Festival," *New York Times* (7 July 1956); Robert S. Taylor, "The Memory Will Linger On: Fantastic Popularity of Jazz Mounting Daily at Newport," *Boston Herald* (8 July 1956); "Here's Your Program to . . . The American Jazz Festival at Newport," *Down Beat* (11 July 1956). Clippings from DES, 3:16, NMAH/SI.

6. Laurence Bergreen, *Louis Armstrong: An Extravagant Life* (New York, 1997), 455–56; David O. Ives, "Hometown, U.S.A: Social Newport Clings to Its 'Cottages' but Subdivisions Threaten," *Wall Street Journal* (25 July 1956); Taylor, "Memory Will Linger On"; Leonard L. Levinson, "Third Newport Jazz Fete Swinging in the Rain; '400' Likes Blast 'n' Beat," *Variety* (11 July 1956); Langston Hughes, "Jazz Boys Whale in an Old Whaling Town" syndicated column, *New York Age-Defender* (21 July 1956); Arnold Rampersad, *The Life of Langston Hughes,* vol. 2, *1941–1967: I Dream a World* (New York, 1988), 253–54. Clippings from DES, 3:16, NMAH/SI.

7. George Avakian interviews, conducted by the author, 11 November 1999, 16 April 2001; George Wein interview, conducted by Dr. Marcia M. Greenlee, 9 May 1991, SIEOHP, tape 1, AC/NMAH/SI.

8. Avakian interviews, 11 November 1999, 16 April 2001; John Edward Hasse, *Beyond Category: The Life and Genius of Duke Ellington* (New York, 1993), 319–22; Nat Hentoff, "The Duke," *Down Beat* (7 January 1957); Phil Schaap, liner notes for Duke Ellington, *Ellington at Newport 1956 (Complete)* (Columbia/Legacy, 1999).

9. Avakian interviews, 11 November 1999, 16 April 2001; Schaap, *Ellington at Newport 1956;* Michael James interview, conducted by the author, 11 and 12 November 1999.

A controversy has ensued over the 1999 re-release of the *Ellington at Newport* album. Schaap, a Sony executive who oversaw the production of the undoctored tapes of the Newport 1956 performance, argued that Avakian unilaterally insisted on re-recording most of the Newport concert for release, over the objections of Ellington and the orchestra. He further reported that Columbia brought in producer Irving Townsend to replace Avakian and "salvage" the project, a contention mainly backed by a statement from Michael James, Ellington's nephew and occasional musical confidante. In my interview with James, he insisted he never made any such statement about Avakian and Townsend to Schaap. Avakian received producer credit on the original album.

Schaap also cited band member Russell Procope as recalling that Ellington told the band to pack up and walk out of the studio while Avakian was attempting to have the band artificially recreate the conditions for Gonsalves's historic solo. Schaap quoted Gonsalves as remembering that Ellington insisted on using the original recording of "Diminuendo," but did not recall a walkout—no Ellington band members interviewed by the Smithsonian or myself related a similar confrontation. Furthermore, from the evidence presented in this book about the Avakian/ Ellington relationship, it is hard to imagine Avakian setting the dictatorial tone that Schaap implied. To quote Avakian: "Can you imagine that I, a lifelong Ellington fan, who first met my idol at the age of seventeen, and never imagined that I would become his record producer . . . can you imagine that I would ever ask Duke Ellington to do something he didn't want to do? I wouldn't even dream of it. It would be an insult to a great man. I can't imagine anybody doing it, and if they did, that would be the last time they had anything to do with Duke Ellington." According to Avakian, he and Ellington discussed beforehand booking a studio on the day after the Newport concert because they anticipated that overdubs might be required to clean up a less-than-perfect performance of the new suite. Avakian said the decision was mutual between Ellington and himself and that Ellington indicated to Avakian just after walking offstage that night that overdubs were necessary. The Newport 1956 album was the last time Avakian produced Ellington, but they seemed to have a good relationship afterwards, with Ellington several times publicly giving Avakian credit as the man who revived his career.

An unexpected problem also needed to be addressed during the following day's visit to the studio: Gonsalves blew his solo into the Voice of America's microphone, not Columbia's. VOA recordings, by law, could not be used commercially, so Avakian needed to employ studio effects to elicit more of the famous Gonsalves solo out of the Columbia recordings.

10. Carter Harman, "Mood Indigo and Beyond," *Time* (20 August 1956); Wein interview, 9 May 1991; Clark Terry interview, conducted by Dr. Marcia M. Greenlee, 10 October 1990, SIEOHP, tape 2, AC/NMAH/SI.

11. Harman, "Mood Indigo and Beyond"; James interviews, 11 and 12 November 1999; Wein interview, 9 May 1991. The portions of the concert described can be heard on: Duke Ellington, *Ellington at Newport 1956 (Complete)* (Columbia/Legacy, 1999).

12. Jim Dawson, "Boogie Down on Central: Los Angeles' Rhythm and Blues Revolution," liner notes for *Central Avenue Sounds: Jazz in Los Angeles (1921–1956)* (Rhino, 1999); Peter A. Grendysa, liner notes for Ruth Brown, *Rockin' in Rhythm: The Best of Ruth Brown* (Rhino, 1996); David Halberstam, *The Fifties* (New York, 1993), chap. 31; Rampersad, *Life of Langston Hughes;* Russell Sanjek, *American Popular Music and Its Business,* vol. 3, *1900–1984* (New York, 1988), 324–45; Brian Ward, *Just My Soul Responding: Rhythm and Blues, Race Consciousness, and Race Relations* (Berkeley, 1998), chaps. 1 and 3.

13. Dawson, "Boogie Down on Central." For more concerning the societal reaction to jazz in the 1920s and 1930s, consult chapters 1 and 2.

14. Halbertsam, *The Fifties* (New York 1994), chap. 31; Sanjek, *American Popular Music and Its Business,* 324–325; Ward, *Just My Soul Responding,* chaps. 1 and 3.

15. Duke Ellington, "Boogie, Shake, Rattle, Rock 'n' Roll, Duke Ellington Tells All about 'Em: Foundation Folk Music, Blues Themes Masters Listed," *Detroit Times* (9 July 1955). The original typed manuscript for the article, with Ellington's handwriting on it and several passages edited out of the final article, can be found in: collection 301, series 10, box 1, folder 31, AC/NMAH/SI.

For Mercer Records' 1956 activities, consult: Mercer Records, Inc., correspondence 1956, collection 301, series 3, box 107, folders 31 and 32, AC/NMAH/SI. For more on Mercer Records history between 1951 and 1953, consult chapter 8.

"'Waltz Sexier Than Rock 'n' Roll' Says Duke Ellington," *Baltimore Afro-American* (1 December 1956); Thornton Hagert, liner notes, *Come and Trip It: Instrumental Dance Music 1780s–1920s* (New World Records, 1978).

For the multiracial, multiethnic, multigenerational, multigenre origins of rock and roll music, consult: Robert Palmer, *Rock and Roll: An Unruly History* (New York, 1995), chap. 1; Jeff Place, Greil Marcus, liner notes, *Anthology of American Folk Music* (Smithsonian/Folkways Recordings, 1997); Ward, *Just My Soul Responding.* The *Anthology* liner notes and recordings also serve as an excellent source for tracing how the roots of American folk music of the 1920s, 1930s, and before influenced generations of rock and folk artists around the world during the second half of the twentieth century.

16. Duke Ellington, *Music Is My Mistress* (New York, 1973), 507–9; Harman, "Mood Indigo and Beyond."

The uncited 1956 clippings promoting the film *Rock and Roll Riot* can be found in DES 3:16, NMAH/SI. The film *Rock and Roll Revue,* not *Riot,* is available at the LOC/MPD.

17. Frank Brookhouser, Man about Town column, *Philadelphia Bulletin* (11 December 1956); Patricia Willard interview, conducted by the author, 30 October 1995. Clipping from DES 3:16, NMAH/SI.

18. Julian Crawchick, "'Hot' or 'Cool,' Music Has Duke's Label," *Cleveland Press* (29 November 1956); Bill Ladd, "Is Duke a Musician—a Playwright—or Both?" Bill Ladd's Almanac column, *Louisville Courier Journal* (2 May 1957). Clippings from DES 3:16, NMAH/SI.

19. The ad featuring Bernstein, Copland, and Walter can be found in: collection 301, series 11, box 1, folder 18, AC/NMAH/SI. Other Columbia ads of the period can be found in the same folder as above, and also: Newport 1957 program, collection 301, series 2B, box 11, folder 23, AC/NMAH/SI; *Jazz 1958: The Metronome Yearbook* and *Jazz 1959: The Metronome Yearbook,* both found in DES 3:17, NMAH/SI; "The Most Jazz" advertisement, from the Saugatuck Jazz program (13 August 1960), collection 301, series 2B, box 11, folder 32, AC/NMAH/SI; "Jazz Sounds the Greatest" advertisement, from The First International Jazz Festival program (Spring 1962), collection 301, series 2B, folder 35, AC/NMAH/SI.

20. Duke Ellington interview, CHIC 1956 #1, tape 1, AC/NMAH/SI.

21. The sources for this discussion of *A Drum Is a Woman:* The Theater Guild, *Duke Ellington's 'A Drum Is a Woman'"* (New York: CBS-TV, The United States Steel Hour, 8 May 1957; viewed at the Museum of Television and Radio, New York City); Duke Ellington interview, CHIC 1964 #6, tape 1, AC/NMAH/SI; William Ewald, "Duke Ellington Puts New Story of Jazz on TV," *Three Rivers (MI) Commercial* (1 May 1957); Leonard Feather, "Two Thumps on 'A Drum': Thumps Up," *Down Beat* (27 June 1957); Anthony LaCamera, "Ellington Explains Show Title," *Boston American* (3 May 1957); Ladd, "Is Duke a Musician"; Anne W. Langman, Television column, *Nation* (4 May 1957); Will Lorin, *Duke Ellington's 'A Drum Is a Woman'* (revised script based on the original conception by Duke Ellington), collection 301, series 4, box 4, AC/NMAH/SI; Stratemann, *Duke Ellington,* 375–76; "'Crazy Little Story,'" *Newsweek* (6 May 1957); "Fellow Artists Laud Duke's 'Drum' Effort," *Baltimore Afro-American* (25 May 1957)—this article also appeared in the *St. Louis Argus,* another black newspaper, the day before; "Duke Turns a Drum into a Woman," *Hue* (June 1957). Clippings from DES, 3:16, NMAH/SI.

22. For Ellington's television career in the first half of the 1950s, consult chapter 8 and Ben Gross, Televiewing column, (obscured) *News* (10 August 1950). Clipping from DES, reel 2, NMAH/SI. For a complete listing of Ellington's TV appearances, see Stratemann, *Duke Ellington,* 677–84.

Daniel Mark Epstein, *Nat King Cole* (Boston, 1999), 263–91. Many of the *Nat King Cole Show* programs can be viewed at the Museum of Television and Radio, New York City.

23. To take 1959 as an example, the Ellington orchestra was paid $8,500 for another edition of the *Timex All-Star Jazz Show* (7 January 1959; CBS-TV), and at least $10,000 (the number is inexact because of union fees not listed on the contract) to appear on the Grammy Awards telecast (13 November 1959; CBS-TV). During this period, the band made about $1,500 per show in guaranteed salary, with certain percentages allotting extra money for particularly well-attended shows. The 1958 and 1959 booking contracts for shows and TV appearances can be found in collection 301, series 3A, boxes 1 and 2, AC/NMAH/SI. Another example of high fees for Ellington appearances on national television: $7,500 for *The Garry Moore Show* on 8 May 1962 (Oscar Cohen to William Mittler, 12 and 13 December 1961, collection 301, series 3A, box 13, folder 1, AC/NMAH/SI).

For Ellington's insistence on certain fees for national TV appearances: Joe Glaser to Bill Mittler, 5 November 1958, collection 301, series 3A, box 10, folder 12, AC/NMAH/SI. Telegrams from TV producer Henry Jaffe and Glaser attached to this letter also deal with this issue.

Standard Oil 75th Anniversary (New York: 13 October 1957); *Timex All-Star Jazz Festival* (New York and Chicago: 30 December 1957). Programs from the mid-1960s evince a similar aesthetic during the appearances of Ellington: *The Ed Sullivan Show* (24 May 1964; CBS-TV); *The Ed Sullivan Show* (24 October 1965; CBS-TV); *The Strollin' '20s* (21 February 1966; CBS-TV). An exception to this general rule of banal and abbreviated Ellington television segments, and probably the premiere Ellington television appearance of his career in terms of musical performance and emotional impact, occurred during a tribute to Senator Robert F. Kennedy a few days after Kennedy's assassination: *A Contemporary Portrait (Robert F. Kennedy Tribute)* (9 June 1968; CBS-TV). All of these programs are housed at the Museum of Television and Radio, New York City.

24. Ted Hudson, "Duke Ellington's Literary Sources," *American Music* (Spring 1991); Helen McNamara, "Stratford Thunder: The Duke Meets the Bard in Jazz," *Toronto Telegram* (16 August 1957); Stanley Dance interview, conducted by Dr. Marcia M. Greenlee, 28 August 1990, SIEOHP, tape 6, AC/NMAH/SI. Clipping from DES 3:15, NMAH/SI.

25. Leonard Feather, review of *Such Sweet Thunder, Down Beat* (17 October 1957); Eugene Lees, "Ellington Suite Proves He's Re-Arrived," On the Record column, *Louisville Times* (22 October 1957); John S. Wilson, "Jazz: Ellington; 'Duke' Bounces Back with Provocative Work," *New York Times* (13 October 1957). Other very favorable reviews: Robert R. Metz, On the Records column, *Savannah Morning News* (10 November 1957); "Duke Does It: 'Such Sweet Thunder' Is Disc Classic," *Columbus Citizen* (17 November 1957).

26. Ruth Ellington interview, conducted by the Duke Ellington Society, 1960, SC Audio C-451, SCBC; Murray Kempton, "Command Performance," *New York Post* (23 August 1960), from the Duke Ellington clipping file, SCBC. Information on the Duke Ellington Society gleaned from the collection of Duke Ellington Jazz Society newsletters in the Duke Ellington clipping file, IJS/RU, especially the December 1958, March/April 1959, and February/March 1960 issues.

27. Eddie Lambert, *Duke Ellington: A Listener's Guide* (Lanham, MD, 1999), 196.

28. Duke Ellington interview, "Program PM" (WBZ Boston, c. late 1957), RWC 9195, JVC/LOC; Nat Hentoff, *Black, Brown and Beige* review, *Hi Fi & Music Review* (November 1958); Ralph J. Gleason, "Duke Turned off the Light to Get Sound He Wanted," Jazz Session syndicated column, *Des Moines Register* (23 August 1958). Clipping from DES 3:15, NMAH/SI; Ray Nance interview, conducted by the Duke Ellington Society, 1975, SC Audio C-471, side 2, SCBC.

29. The sources for this discussion on *The Queen's Suite:* Stanley Dance, liner notes, Duke Ellington and His Orchestra, *The Ellington Suites* (Pablo, 1990); Ellington, *Music Is My Mistress,* 196, 447; John London, "Now—Royal Jazz by 'The Duke,'" *Melody Maker* (c. Fall 1958). Clipping from DES 3:15, NMAH/SI.

30. The sources for this discussion on *Anatomy of a Murder:* Ralph J. Gleason, "Duke Scores for Film," Rhythm Section syndicated column, *Pittsburgh Sun-Telegraph* (25 July 1959); Max Harrison, "Ellington's Music for *Anatomy of a Murder,*" in *The Duke Ellington Reader,* ed. Mark Tucker, 313–15; Jeff Millar, "Duke Wows His Fans at TSU Concert," *Houston Chronicle* (5 October 1966); Jack Moffitt, "'Anatomy of a Murder' Surefire Entertainment: Preminger Prod'n Sock, Well-Acted, Tops the Novel," *Hollywood Reporter* (1 July 1959); Vernon Scott, It's Happening in Hollywood . . . syndicated column, *Milton (PA) Standard* (13 June 1959), found in collection 301, series 9, box 2, folder 2, AC/NMAH/SI; Stratemann, *Duke Ellington,* 403–12; "Anatomy of a Murder" review, *Film Daily* (1 July 1959); "Anatomy of a Murder: Socko Hit for Otto Preminger," *Box Office Digest* (15 July 1959); "Anatomy of Hollywood," *Ebony* (September 1959); "Bobby Darin Tops Grammy Awards," *Los Angeles Examiner* (30 November 1959), found in collection 301, series 9, box 4, folder 13, AC/NMAH/SI . Unless otherwise indicated, clippings from DES, rolls 3, 4, and 9, vols. 18, 22, and 44, NMAH/SI.

31. Jack Guinn, "The Duke Shows Jazz Can Be Music," *Denver Post* (23 October 1960). Clipping found in the Duke Ellington Scrapbooks, roll 4, vol. 23, National Museum of American History, Smithsonian Institution. The midnight to dawn recording regimen for *Blues In Orbit* is described in: Stanley Dance, liner notes, Duke Ellington, *Blues In Orbit* (Columbia, 1988).

32. The sources for this discussion of *Suite Thursday:* Dance, "Festival"; Ellington, *Music Is*

My Mistress, 196; Ralph J. Gleason, *Celebrating the Duke and Louis, Bessie, Billie, Bird, Carmen, Miles, Dizzy and Other Heroes* (New York, 1975; reprint 1995), 192; Dick Hadlock, "Special Report: Monterey Jazz Festival," *Metronome* (December 1960); John S. Wilson, "Duke Ellington Still the Pioneer," *New York Times* (2 April 1961); "Sweetness and Fruit," *Time* (10 October 1960). Clippings from DES 4:23, NMAH/SI.

As one can notice in the quotes used, Strayhorn's contribution to *Suite Thursday* was often ignored by the press.

For more on Ellington's unproduced *Man with Four Sides* play, consult chapter 9.

33. Frank Driggs interview, conducted by Paul Kolderie, 13 December 1977, #504A, pg. 26–38, OHAM/YUSC; Jerry Valburn interview, conducted by Mark Tucker, 9 October 1986 and 19 March 1987, #592A–F, pg. 24, OHAM/YUSC.

34. United Artists Records, Inc., contract, 13 September 1962, collection 301, series 3H, box 129, folder 55; ABC-Paramount Records, Inc., royalty statement, 30 June 1965, collection 301, series 3I, box 138, folder 5, AC/NMAH/SI.

35. "Duke and the Clan: Free Loaders Mill as Frank Signs Ellington," *Billboard* (8 December 1962); "Doubling Up of Act and A&R Man Accented Anew with Ellington, Cooke Deals," *Variety* (5 December 1962); "Duke to Head New Jazz Wing of Sinatra's Record Company," *Jet* (13 December 1962); Ralph J. Gleason, "Jazz Leaders Are Turning Directors," *San Francisco Chronicle* (16 December 1962); "Reprise Settled in New Hollywood Building," *Cash Box* (16 February 1963); Stuart Nicholson, *Reminiscing In Tempo: A Portrait of Duke Ellington* (Boston, 1999), 338. Clippings from DES 5:27, NMAH/SI.

36. "Jazz Picks of the Week," *Cash Box* (20 April 1963); "Jazz: Afro-Bossa," *New Haven Register* (21 April 1963); Bill Espalon, "Jazz Records: Something Better than Bossa Nova," *San Francisco News-Call Bulletin* (18 May 1963); uncited author, *Afro-Bossa* review (23 May 1963). Clippings from DES 5:27, NMAH/SI.

37. "Warner Bros.-Reprise Merger," *Jet* (21 November 1963); Ralph J. Gleason, "Duke's Latest Gem," On the Town column, *San Francisco Chronicle* (28 January 1964). Clippings from DES 7:34, NMAH/SI.

Chapter Ten

1. Duke Ellington interview, CHIC 1964 #4, tape 3, AC/NMAH/SI.

2. The $100,000 figure is derived from the following sources and calculations: Ellington's 1964 ASCAP distributions are $32,226.89. Six months of royalties from the various Mills Music companies are $5,889.42, according to their 1 August 1964 statement; the full twelve months would be roughly $12,000, though the other six months' statement of Mills-era royalties is not in the Smithsonian files. The quarterly royalty statements from Robbins Music and other miscellaneous publishing companies add up to about $3,250 per quarter, based on the 24 August 1964 statement from the American Guild of Authors & Composers, which would add up to roughly $13,000 per year. Royalties for 1964 from Tempo Music, Ellington's publishing company, cannot be found in the files, but are probably roughly equivalent to the Robbins and Mills figures of $12,000 per year. Foreign royalties for 1964 are not extant, but the 1965 foreign royalties added up to more than $27,000. Total 1964 royalties for Ellington, then, are roughly calculated at $104,000. These royalty statements are found in collection 301, series 3, box 123, folder 5, AC/NMAH/SI.

3. Duke Ellington, Inc., five-year summary of income and expense, collection 301, series 3, box 121, folder 13, AC/NMAH/SI.

4. Joe Sullivan, "Duke in Business: Ellington Sighs at Jazz Band Payroll," *Newark News* (4 September 1959). Clipping from DES 4:22, NMAH/SI.

5. Duke Ellington, Inc., statements at 31 December 1956, collection 301, series 3, box 112, folder 9; Duke Ellington, Inc., statements of operations for the years ended 31 December 1958, 31 December 1959, 31 December 1960, collection 301, series 3, box 121, folder 6. The losses for the years 1953–55 are garnered from the Duke Ellington, Inc., 1958 federal income tax return in the last mentioned folder, AC/NMAH/SI.

6. "At March 28 Concert: Ellington to Play With Symphony," *Detroit Free Press* (7 February 1963); Francis Raffetto, "Dallas after Dark: Plenty of Duke's Themes Planned for $1 Concert," *Dallas Morning News* (14 November 1965). Clippings from DES: 5:27, 8:40, NMAH/SI.

7. Duke Ellington interview, conducted by Thomas R. Rees, c. 1967, collection 301, series 4, box 1, folder 4; Duke Ellington interview, CHIC 1964 #4, tape 3, AC/NMAH/SI.

8. Albert Joseph Celley interview, conducted by Patricia Willard, 12 July 1989, SIEOHP, tape 3, AC/NMAH/SI; *Albert J. Celley v. Duke Ellington, Inc.,* examination before trial, court transcript, 8 March 1966, collection 301, series 3, box 113, folder 6, pg. 41, AC/NMAH/SI; Duke Ellington interview, CHIC 1964 #4, tape 3, side B; Herb Jeffries interview, conducted by Patricia Willard, 22 and 23 September 1989, SIEOHP, tape 3, AC/NMAH/SI; Clark Terry interview, conducted by Dr. Marcia M. Greenlee, 10 October 1990, SIEOHP, tape 4, AC/NMAH/SI.

9. George Wein interview, conducted by Dr. Marcia M. Greenlee, 9 May 1991, SIEOHP, tape 1, AC/NMAH/SI.

10. Terry, Smithsonian interview, 10 October 1990; Duke Ellington interview, CHIC 1956 #1, tape 1, AC/NMAH/SI; Robert and Evelyn Udkoff interview, conducted by Dr. Marcia M. Greenlee, 11 March 1991, SIEOHP, tape 2, AC/NMAH/SI; Wein, Smithsonian interview, 9 May 1991. Another example of Ellington's spending on trips was the $759 he spent on jewelry during the band's 1963 State Department tour of the Middle East. The receipt is found in collection 301, series 3A, box 56, folder 8, AC/NMAH/SI.

11. This section on Ellington's support of his family, except where indicated, is based on the following sources: Stanley Dance interview, conducted by Dr. Marcia M. Greenlee, 28 August 1990, SIEOHP, tape 5, AC/NMAH/SI; Mercer Ellington interviews, conducted by Dr. Marcia M. Greenlee, 18 September 1990, 5 and 7 May 1991, SIEOHP, tapes 2, 4, and 6, AC/NMAH/SI; Ruth Ellington interview, conducted by the author, 26 January 1996; R. and E. Udkoff interview, 11 March 1991; Phoebe Jacobs interviews, conducted by the author, 27 January 1996, 13 November 1999. For more on Ruth Ellington's ownership and presidency of Tempo Music, consult chapter 6.

Information about the exemptions for the Ellington cousins and aunt drawn from: Duke and Edna Ellington 1040 U.S. individual income tax return, 1965, collection 301, series 3, box 121, folder 13. Protest of Duke Ellington and estate of Edna Ellington (Mercer Ellington, administrator) [for the tax years 1964–66], 1 December 1971, collection 301, series 3, box 112, folder 8. AC/NMAH/SI.

12. Juliet E. K. Walker, *History of Black Business in America: Capitalism, Race, Entrepreneurship* (New York, 1998), xviii–xxii, 182, 227, 238; Robert E. Weems, Jr., *Black Business in the Black Metropolis: The Chicago Metropolitan Assurance Company, 1925–1985* (Bloomington, IN, 1996), xii–xiii, 19, 66–71, 96; Robert E. Weems, Jr., *Desegregating the Dollar: African-American Consumerism in the Twentieth Century* (New York, 1998), 58.

13. Mercedes Ellington interview, conducted by Valerie Archer, 30 June 1980, #547A, B, pg. 32, OHAM/YUSC; Irving Townsend, "Ellington in Private," *Atlantic* (May 1975): 80–83.

14. Celley interview, tape 4, 12 July 1989; Frank Driggs interview, conducted by Paul Kolderie, 13 December 1977, #504A, pg. 1, OHAM/YUSC; Michael James interview, conducted by the author, 11 November 1999; Jacobs interviews, 27 January 1996, 13 November 1999 [last quote]; S. Dance interview, 28 August 1990; tape 5; Mercer Ellington interview, 18 September 1990, 5 and 7 May 1991, tapes 2 and 4; R. and E. Udkoff interview, 11 March 1991; Bernice

Wiggins and Juanita Middleton interview, conducted by Martha Oneppo, 20 October 1980, #551A, OHAM/YUSC; Bernice Wiggins and Juanita Middleton interview, conducted by Mark Tucker, 6 September 1983, #551C, D, OHAM/YUSC. Driggs recalled that Greer experienced financial difficulties after Ellington died because Duke Ellington, Inc., stopped paying him.

15. Duke Ellington, Inc., 1960–64 ledgers, collection 301, series 3B, box 66, AC/NMAH/SI. *Celley v. Duke Ellington, Inc.,* 115–18. Wein interview, 9 May 1991.

16. Duke Ellington, Inc., 1960–61, 1962–64, 1965, 1968 ledgers, collection 301, series 3B, box 66, AC/NMAH/SI.

Incidences of Ellington assigning medical and publicity costs to his ABC account: Joe Glaser to Bill Mittler, 20 April 1960, collection 301, series 3A, box 11, folder 4; Joe Glaser to Bill Mittler, 3 April 1964, collection 301, series 3A, box 14, folder 4. The "number's man" letter: Joe Glaser to Bill Mittler, 28 April 1959, collection 301, series 3A, box 10, folder 17. AC/NMAH/SI.

Advances from the ABC account in the amount of $8,500 in 1960: David Gold to Bill Mittler, 10 June 1960, collection 301, series 3A, box 11, folder 6; David Gold to Bill Mittler, 19 October 1960, collection 301, series 3A, box 11, folder 10; David Gold to Bill Mittler, 7 December 1960, collection 301, series 3A, box 11, folder 12. AC/NMAH/SI.

R. and E. Udkoff interview, 11 March 1991; Wein interview, 9 May 1991.

17. As shown earlier in this chapter, the statements of operations and the booking contracts for the 1956–60 period show that Duke Ellington, Inc., earned between $350,000 and $400,000 per year in income and royalties, while receiving about $1,500 to $2,000 per performance. In the statement of operations for 1944, the only year with such information available during the 1940s, the income from services and royalties is $404,969.67, and the guaranteed salary that the band received every night is strikingly similar to what the band earned ten to fifteen years later. Duke Ellington, Inc., statements at 31 December 1956, collection 301, series 3, box 112, folder 9; Duke Ellington, Inc., statements of operations for the years ended 31 December 1958, 31 December 1959, 31 December 1960, collection 301, series 3, box 121, folder 6; Duke Ellington, Inc., statements at 31 December 1944, collection 301, series 3, box 112, folder 9. AC/NMAH/SI.

18. Will Friedwald, *Sinatra! The Song Is You* (New York, 1995), 224–28; Ralph J. Gleason, *Celebrating the Duke and Louis, Bessie, Billie, Bird, Carmen, Miles, Dizzy and Other Heroes* (New York, 1975; reprint 1995), 113; Burton W. Peretti, *Jazz in American Culture* (Chicago, 1997), 114–21.

19. Jacobs interviews, 27 January 1996, 13 November 1999; Wein interview, 9 May 1991. Another example of Ellington's lack of box-office draw in this period is seen in a letter to Associated Booking Corporation sent by the owner of a Bridgeport, CT, jazz club, in which he compares the business done by Lionel Hampton and Count Basie with that of Ellington. The club owner ended up rejecting ABC's offer for Ellington: Joseph R. Barry to Bob Bundy, 17 April 1958, collection 301, series 3A, box 10, folder 5, AC/NMAH/SI.

20. Celley interview, tape 3, 12 July 1989; S. Dance interview, 28 August 1990, tape 3; Norman Granz interview, conducted by Patricia Willard, 23 and 24 August 1989, SIEOHP, tape 3, AC/NMAH/SI; M. James interview, 11 November 1999; Terry interview, tape 1, 10 October 1990.

21. Uncited authors, "History of the Year," in *Jazz 1958: The Metronome Year Book* (c. January 1959). Clipping found in DES 3:17, NMAH/SI.

22. "Duke at Shorewood," *Milwaukee Sentinel* (17 January 1960). Clipping from DES 4:22, NMAH/SI. George Wein, "Duke Ellington Still Capable of Exploiting Own Genius," The Jazz Beat column, *Boston Herald* (27 October 1957).

Instances of newer numbers mixed with the old: Forrest Saunders, "Music: Duke Ellington, Foster Auditorium," *Ithaca Journal* (6 December 1957) (three *Thunder* tracks, one from *Drum,* and "Clarinet Melodrama"); Paul M. Bruun, Moon over Miami column, *Miami Sun* (5 January 1958) (three *Thunder* tracks and "Newport Up"); Virginia Roberts, "Duke Ellington Pleases Crowds at the Peacock," *California Eagle* (6 February 1958) ("highlight" of show was tracks from *Thunder* and *Drum,* also "Clarinet"); Don DeMicheal, "The Festival at Evansville [IN]," *Down Beat* (3 August 1961) (*Suite Thursday,* pieces from *Queen's Suite* and *Drum*).

Even in a show aimed toward an older and nostalgic audience that gathered in Stockton, CA, the band did two newer numbers ("One More Twist" and "Look at Me") along with two older numbers associated with other big bands that the Ellington orchestra rarely performed ("Tenderly" and "Stompin' at the Savoy"): Helen Flynn, "Duke Ellington Thrills Older Music Lovers," *Stockton (CA) Record* (25 October 1962). Clipping from DES 5:27, NMAH/SI.

23. This discussion on the background of Joe Glaser, Associated Booking Corporation, and their relationships with Louis Armstrong and Ellington is based on the following sources: George Avakian interviews, conducted by the author, 11 November 1999, 16 April 2001; Laurence Bergreen, *Louis Armstrong: An Extravagant Life* (New York, 1997), 373–81, 476, 489–91; Oscar Cohen interview, conducted by Dr. Marcia M. Greenlee, 17 June 1992, SIEOHP, tape 1, AC/NMAH/SI; M. Ellington interview, 18 September 1990, 5 and 7 May 1991; M. James interview, 11 November 1999; Wein interview, 9 May 1991.

24. Concerning "sit-down dates": Joe Glaser to Duke Ellington, 26 February 1958, collec-tion 301, series 3A, box 10, folder 3; Bob Phillips to Duke Ellington, 22 Mar 1960, collection 301, series 3A, box 11, folder 3. AC/NMAH/SI.

Concerning the delay of contracts, for reasons of brevity, only letters from 1958 are listed: Paul Bannister to William Mittler, 7 January 1958, 24 January 1958, 20 November 1958; Bob Bundy to William Mittler, 29 January 1958, 21 February 1958, 27 February 1958; Joe Glaser to Duke Ellington, 22 July 1958. Collection 301, series 3A, box 10, folders 2, 3, 8, and 11. The letters quoted in the paragraph: Joe Glaser to Bill Mittler, 20 February 1961, collection 301, series 3A, box 11, folder12; Bob Bundy to William Mittler, 17 October 1961, collection 301, series 3A, box 12, folder 5. AC/NMAH/SI.

M. Ellington interview, 18 September 1990, 5 and 7 May 1991, tape 8; M. James interview, 11 November 1999.

25. Wein interview, 9 May 1991; Ada Cirillo, memorandum to file, 29 November 1963, MC468, 61–6, BECAHC/SCD/UAL.

Joe Glaser to Duke Ellington, 6 December 1963, collection 301, series 3A, box 14, folder 9; Duke Ellington to Joe Glaser (never sent), c. December 1963, collection 301, series 3A, box 14, folder 9; Joe Glaser to David Braun, 111 December 1963, collection 301, series 3A, box 13, folder 13. AC/NMAH/SI.

26. Brad McCuen interview, conducted by Patricia Willard, 2 and 3 August 1989, SIEOHP, tape 4, AC/NMAH/SI.

27. This section on Al Celley is based on the following sources: *Celley v. Duke Ellington, Inc.,* 24–29, 59–117, 136–37; Celley interview, 12 July 1989; M. James interview, 11 November 1999; Juan Tizol interview, conducted by Patricia Willard, 15 November 1978, JOHP, reel 4, pgs. 43–44, IJS/RU; R. and E. Udkoff interview, 11 March 1991.

Steven A. Burn to Dave Auerbach, 1 August 1966, collection 301, series 3, box 113, folder 6; Stephen F. Huff, on behalf of Pryor, Braun, Cashman & Sherman, to Ruth Ellington, re: *Celley v. Duke Ellington, Inc.,* 17 October 1968, collection 301, series 3G, box 115, folder 21. AC/NMAH/SI.

Jeff Millar, "Duke Wows His Fans at TSU Concert," *Houston Chronicle* (5 October 1966). Clipping from DES 9:44, NMAH/SI.

28. This section on William Mittler, except as indicated, is drawn from the following sources: William Mittler to Duke Ellington, 18 May 1965, box 134, folder 21; Ruth Ellington to Wil-

liam Mittler, 16 July 1965, box 134, folder 21; Max W. Frendel to Ruth Ellington, 28 July 1965, box 134, folder 21; Ruth Ellington to Max W. Frendel, 9 September 1965, box 134, folder 21; Steven A. Burn to Dave Auerbach, 25 April 1966, box 135, folder 3; Steven A. Burn to Dave Auerbach, 18 October 1966, box 135, folder 3. All of these letters are found in collection 301, series 3I, AC/NMAH/SI.

Max W. Frendel and William H. Mittler v. Duke Ellington, Inc., and Duke Ellington, examination before trial, court transcript, 20 December 1966, collection 301, series 3I, box 135, folder 3; *Max W. Frendel and William H. Mittler v. Duke Ellington, Inc., and Duke Ellington,* examination before trial, court transcript, 8 August 1967, collection 301, series 3, box 112, folder 15. Both of these documents can be found in AC/NMAH/SI.

Mercer Ellington interview, 18 September 1990, 5 and 7 May 1991, tape 7; M. James interview, 11 November 1999.

29. Lawrence Brown interview, conducted by Patricia Willard, July 1976, JOHP, reel 10, pgs. 8–9; Tizol interview, 15 November 1978, reel 4, pgs. 33–34. Both housed at IJS/RU.

Lawrence Epstein to Ruth Ellington, 24 July 1969, collection 301, series 3G, box 115, folder 9, AC/NMAH/SI.

30. Benjamin Starr to Bob Phillips, 6 November 1965, box 115, folder 8; Benjamin Starr to Cress Courtney, 1 March 1968, box 15, folder 3; Benjamin Starr to Ruth Ellington, 16 May 1969, box 15, folder 17; Benjamin Starr to Ruth Ellington, 26 May 1969, box 15, folder 17; Zenith endorsement contract, 12 June 1970, box 15, folder 22. All of these letters are from collection 301, series 3A, AC/NMAH/SI.

Celebrity endorsement deals in this period were far less lucrative than they are today. For the deal with Zenith, Ellington made $7,500 plus residuals and a top-of-the-line stereo system and television set.

31. Steven Burn and Harold Thau, agenda for meeting of 24 April 1967, collection 301, series 3G, box 115, folder 16, AC/NMAH/SI.

32. This section on Cress Courtney is based on the following sources: Cress Courtney interview, conducted by the Duke Ellington Society, 1970, SC Audio C-499, SCBC; Shirley Courtney interview, conducted by Dr. Marcia M. Greenlee, 3 February 1992, AC/NMAH/SI; Mercer Ellington interview, conducted by Dick Buckley, March 1980, #521B,C, pg. 3–4, OHAM/YUSC; H. Robert Udkoff interview, conducted by the author, 28 September 1995; Wein interview, 9 May 1991; George Wein, with Nate Chinen, *Myself Among Others* (Cambridge, MA, 2003), 173.

33. Maxwell T. Cohen to director of Internal Revenue Service, 4 November 1963, series 3I, box 135, folder 2; tax examination of 1964, series 3, box 125, folder 9; tax protest of Duke and Edna Ellington, by Steven A. Burn, 20 July 1964, series 3, box 125, folder 9; tax petition of Duke and Edna Ellington, c. 1966, series 3I, box 135, folder 1. All four documents from collection 301, AC/NMAH/SI.

As further tax documents from collection 301, series 3, box 112, folder 5 document, similar fights over the nature of the taxation of Tempo Music continued for the rest of the 1960s and 1970s. According to a 1971 schedule of unpaid taxes, Ellington still owed the IRS over $30,000 on 1957 and 1960 taxes and almost $67,000 overall for similar reasons: collection 301, series 3, box 118, folder 9.

In a 1970 agreement reached between the IRS and Duke Ellington, Ellington was assigned 50 percent of the royalty income of Tempo Music beginning in 1962. In this same document, dated less than a month after Ellington's death, the IRS claims they are owed over $175,000 just for the years 1964–66 alone: notice of deficiency, 20 June 1974, collection 301, series 3, box 114, folder 1, AC/NMAH/SI.

Ruth Ellington interview, 26 January 1996.

34. 1040 U.S. individual tax returns, 1965–67, Duke and Edna Ellington, series 3, box 121, folder 13; tax protest on behalf of Duke Ellington and estate of Edna Ellington for tax years 1965–67, 1 December 1971, series 3, box 112, folder 8. Both documents from collection 301, AC/NMAH/SI.

Notice of deficiency, 20 June 1974.

Wiggins and Middleton interviews, 20 October 1980, 6 September 1983.

35. Shirley Courtney interview, 3 February 1992,; Stuart Nicholson, *Reminiscing In Tempo: A Portrait of Duke Ellington* (Boston, 1999), 387.

The Carneys and Ellis: Steven A. Burn to Ruth Ellington, 29 January 1969, folder 7; Steven A. Burn to Ruth Ellington, 10 April 1969, folder 9; Larry Epstein to Ruth Ellington, 28 May 1969, folder 14. All three letters from collection 301, series 3G, box 115, AC/NMAH/SI.

Letters to the SCLC, NAACP, and seven other organizations: collection 301, series 3H, box 129, folder 59, AC/NMAH/SI.

Juan and Rosebud Tizol interview, conducted by Brad Dechter, 30 July 1980, #562 A, B, pg. 31, OHAM/YUSC.

When Carney joined the Ellington band in the mid-1920s, he was underage, and his parents had to sign papers to allow him to tour with them. Ellington was appointed "as a sort of guardian to me," Carney said, and Ellington had to ask permission of Carney's mother. Perhaps this history and Ellington's promises influenced Ellington still taking care of and looking out for Carney four decades later: Harry Carney interview, conducted by the Duke Ellington Society, 1960, SC Audio C-455, SCBC.

36. S. Dance interview, 28 August 1990; Jacobs interviews, 27 January 1996, 13 November 1999; James interview, 11 November 1999.

ASCAP royalties to the IRS: George Hoffman to Steven A. Burn, 29 April 1969, collection 301, series 3E, box 103, folder 38, AC/NMAH/SI.

37. Allen Holbert, "Big Band Is Big Kick for Ellington," *Minneapolis Tribune* (4 September 1966). Clipping from DES 9:44, NMAH/SI. Britt Woodman interview, conducted by Brad Dechter, 8 August 1978, #530A, B, pg. 34, OHAM/YUSC.

Chapter Eleven

1. Maurice Lawrence interview, conducted by the author, 1 May 1999; Carter Harman, "The Duke Clicks in Squaresville," *Life* (27 August 1965). Clipping from DES 3:15, NMAH/SI.

2. "The Spingarn Medal," *California Eagle* (9 July 1959), also in *Little Rock State Press* (17 July 1959); "Duke Longtime NAACP Backer," *Chicago Defender* (8 September 1959); "Ellington and the Spingarn," *Los Angeles Tribune* (11 September 1959). Clippings from DES 3, 4:18, 22, NMAH/SI. The Little Rock clipping is from collection 301, series 9, box 3, folder 1, AC/NMAH/SI.

3. "Duke Ellington Deserves the Spingarn Medal," *Detroit Chronicle* (11 July 1959); untitled fragment, *Pittsburgh Courier* (29 August 1959). Clippings from DES 3, 4:18, 22, NMAH/SI.

4. "Duke Says Jazz Means Fredom [*sic*], Peace," *Louisville Defender* (17 September 1959); the same story was syndicated as "Ellington Awarded Spingarn Medal by Benny Goodman," *Tulsa Eagle* (17 September 1959). Clippings from DES 3, 4:18, 22, NMAH/SI.

5. Nat Hentoff, *Listen to the Stories: Nat Hentoff on Jazz and Country Music* (New York, 1995), 11; Brian Ward, *Just My Soul Responding: Rhythm and Blues, Race Consciousness, and Race Relations* (Berkeley, 1998), 269, 270, 290–336, 448; Don George, *Sweet Man: The Real Duke Ellington* (New York, 1981), 112–13; Donald Freeman, "'Asphalt Jungle' Theme by Duke Ellington," *Springfield (IL) State Journal* (25 February 1961). Clipping from DES 4:23, NMAH/SI.

6. Duke Ellington interview, CHIC 1964 #7, side B, AC/NMAH/SI.

7. Helen Oakley Dance interview, conducted by Patricia Willard, 26 and 27 September 1989, SIEOHP, tape 4, AC/NMAH/SI. For the history of Ellington's 1951 "we ain't ready" comment and the furor that followed it, consult chapter 8.

8. You Said It! column, *Amsterdam News* (2 April 1960). Clipping from DES 3:19, NMAH/SI.

9. Duke Ellington, "The Race for Space" (c. late 1957), as anthologized in *The Duke Ellington Reader*, ed. Mark Tucker (New York, 1993), 293–96.

For more on the State Department's propaganda efforts concerning American race relations during the 1950s and 1960s, consult chapter 12.

10. Stanley Dance interview, conducted by Dr. Marcia M. Greenlee, 28 August 1990, SIEOHP, AC/NMAH/SI; Mercer Ellington interviews, conducted by Dr. Marcia M. Greenlee, 18 September 1990, 5 and 7 May 1991, SIEOHP, AC/NMAH/SI; Robert and Evelyn Udkoff interview, conducted by Dr. Marcia M. Greenlee, 11 March 1991, SIEOHP, AC/NMAH/SI; Phoebe Jacobs interviews, conducted by the author, 27 January 1996, 13 November 1999; "Sammy Davis Miffed over His Critics," *St. Louis Argus* (9 November 1956); Nat Hentoff, "The Murderous Modes of Jazz," *Esquire* (September 1960). Clippings from DES 3:16, 19, NMAH/SI.

11. Ward, *Just My Soul Responding*.

12. The sources for this section on the February 1960 Baltimore sit-in: Ruth Fegley interview, conducted by the author, 5 November 2001; Wally Orlinsky interview, conducted by the author, 6 December 2001.

"Duke Ellington Joins in as Bias Protests Grow," *Newsday* (23 February 1960); "Restaurant Refuses to Serve Duke Ellington," *New Brunswick Home News* (23 February 1960); "Food Denied to Ellington: Balto. Restaurant Closes after Refusing Service to Negro Musician," *Wilmington (DE) Journal* (23 February 1960); "Duke Ellington Refused Service at Restaurant," *Baltimore Sun* (23 February 1960); "Café Denies Service to Duke Ellington," *Richmond Afro-American* (27 February 1960); "Duke Can't Eat: Baltimore Café Turns out Lights," *Philadelphia Afro-American* (27 February 1960); "Across the Board," *Amsterdam News* (27 February 1960). The described photo of the scene is from *Baltimore Afro-American* (5 March 1960). Clippings from DES 4:22, AC/NMAH/SI. There are many more clippings about the incident in the scrapbooks, in addition to the articles cited. Most of them are syndicated repeats of cited articles. The cities in which articles ran about the incident include: Jamaica, NY; Harrisburg, PA; Lexington, NC; Cleveland, OH; Des Moines, IA; Detroit, MI; Washington, DC; Minneapolis, MN; New Haven, CT; Richmond, VA; St. Louis, MO; and Los Angeles, CA.

13. Harvard Sitkoff, *The Struggle for Black Equality, 1954–1992* (New York, 1993), 58–60, chap. 3.

14. "Fire Damages Restaurant," *Baltimore Sun* (25 February 1960); "No Arson Found at Restaurant," *Baltimore Sun* (26 February 1960); Orlinsky interview, 6 December 2001.

15. Instances of Duke Ellington, Inc., rejecting contracts that lacked the antisegregation clause: William Mittler to Bob Bundy, 13 March 1962, collection 301, series 3A, box 13, folder 3; William Mittler to Oscar Cohen, 29 October 1962, collection 301, series 3A, box 13, folder 10. Numerous examples of this occur in the 1964 booking correspondence as well: see collection 301, series 3A, box 14, folders 6 and 12. The decision to not play the private Missouri jazz club is discussed in the following letter: William Mittler to Paul Bannister, 23 October 1962, collection 301, series 3A, box 13, folder 10. Correspondence concerning the Ellington orchestra's playing two segregated private clubs in 1964: Ann Brock to Bob Bundy, 31 March 1964, collection 301, series 3A, box 14, folder 4; Tony Papa to William Mittler, 27 August 1964, collection 301, series 3A, box 14, folder 9. AC/NMAH/SI.

16. "Duke Ellington Won't Play in LR Because of Segregated Seating," *Hot Springs (AK) New Era* (1 September 1961); "Bits of News in Arkansas," *West Memphis (AK) Times* (1 September

1961); Gene Wilburn, "In Music Hall Tonight: Ellington Concert Will Be Integrated," *Houston Press* (7 September 1961); "Ellington's Stand Here Open to All," *Tucson Citizen* (8 September 1961); "Duke Will Not Play to Jim-Crow Texas House," *Baltimore Afro-American* (16 September 1961); Dorothy Kilgallen, "'Kicks and Co.' Have a Kick Coming," The Voice of Broadway column, *New York Journal-American* (21 September 1961); "Either Jim Crow or Ellington," *California Eagle* (21 September 1961); Ralph J. Gleason, "Managers Are Joining the Fight against Segregated Audiences," *San Francisco Chronicle* (12 November 1961); Klaus Stratemann, *Duke Ellington: Day by Day and Film by Film* (Copenhagen, 1992), 444. Clippings found in the Duke Ellington Scrapbooks, roll 4, vol. 24, National Museum of American History, Smithsonian Institution. The *California Eagle* and Gleason clippings are from collection 301, series 9, box 7, folders 43 and 50, AC/NMAH/SI.

17. "Ellington Says Rights Activity Should Be Handled by Experts," *Milwaukee Journal* (24 March 1966); "Baltimore," *Down Beat* (9 February 1967). Clippings from DES 8, 9:42, 46, NMAH/SI.

18. Bill Berry interview, conducted by Yale American Studies course, 2 December 1977, #510A, pg. 20–21, OHAM/YUSC; Stuart Nicholson, *Reminiscing In Tempo: A Portrait of Duke Ellington* (Boston, 1999), 332–33; Ole Nosey, "Those South Africans Again," Everybody Goes When the Wagon Comes column, *Chicago Defender* (24 September 1962); Stratemann, *Duke Ellington*, 447–58. Clipping from DES 5:27, NMAH/SI.

19. "Chicago to Support Negro Exposition," *Houston Informer* (22 June 1963); "Duke to Present 'My People' Show," *Pittsburgh Courier* (27 July 1963); Joya Sherrill interview, conducted by Dr. Marcia M. Greenlee, 15 August 1989, SIEOHP, tape 3, AC/NMAH/SI; M. Ellington interview, 18 September 1990, 5 and 7 May 1991, tape 5, . Clippings found in collection 301, series 9, box 9, folder 33, AC/NMAH/SI.

20. "Ellington Plays Down Social Protest in His Musical for Chi's Negro Expo," *Variety* (7 July 1963); Bob Hunter, "Duke's Centennial Show Sure Fire Hit," *Chicago Defender* (19 August 1963). Clippings from DES 6:30, NMAH/SI.

21. Duke Ellington interview snippets from Nicholson, *Reminiscing In Tempo*, 345, 347, 348; Duke Ellington, *My People* script, collection 301, series 4, box 8, folder 7, AC/NMAH/SI; David Krasner, "'The Pageant Is the Thing: Black Nationalism and *The Star of Ethiopia*," in *Performing America: Cultural Nationalism in American Theater*, ed. Jeffrey D. Mason and J. Ellen Gainor (Ann Arbor, 1999), 106–22; "Ellington Deplores Race Fights," *Rochester Times-Union* (11 May 1963); Dan Morgenstern, "*Jazz* Goes to Newport '63," *Jazz* (August 1963). Clippings from DES 5, 6:29, 30, NMAH/SI. For other Ellington references to *The Star of Ethiopia,* consult chapters 1 and 6.

22. Marion Logan interview, conducted by Sonia Rosario, 27 February 1978, #524, pg. 15–17, OHAM/YUSC; Marion Logan interview, *Duke Ellington: Reminiscing In Tempo,* (Robert Levi Films, 1992), LOC/MPD; "Racial Attitudes Are Encouraging, Dr. King Says Here," *Chicago Sun-Times* (22 August 1963). Clipping from DES 6:30, NMAH/SI.

23. Duke Ellington interview, *The Duke: Conversation in Music* (Canadian Broadcasting Company, 1964), LOC/MPD; Ellington, *My People* script; Don DeMicheal, review of *My People, Down Beat* (26 September 1963); Perry Watkins interview, conducted by the Duke Ellington Society, 1966, SC Audio C-483, SCBC. Clipping from DES 6:30, NMAH/SI.

24. Nicholson, *Reminiscing In Tempo*; Stratemann, *Duke Ellington*, 473–74; M. Ellington interview, 18 September 1990, 5 and 7 May 1991, tape 3.

25. Buddy Lonesome, "A Grave Responsibility," Hell Box column, *St. Louis Argus* (9 August 1963), from collection 301, series 9, box 9, folder 40, AC/NMAH/SI; Whitelaw McBride, People in the News column, *Pittsburgh Courier* (23 May 1964), clipping found in collection 301, series 9, box 11, folder 7, AC/NMAH/SI; Arnold Rampersad, *Jackie Robinson: A Biogra-*

phy (New York, 1997), 389–90; "Courier Editorials: The Job's on Your Foot," *Pittsburgh Courier* (2 May 1964); P. L. Prattis, "Are We—Are You—Ready?" Horizon column, *Pittsburgh Courier* (23 May 1964). Clipping from DES 7:34, NMAH/SI. For Prattis's 1951 comments, consult chapter 9.

26. M. Ellington interview, 18 September 1990, 5 and 7 May 1991, tape 3; Duke Ellington interview, CHIC 1964 #3, tape 1.

27. Terry H. Anderson, *The Movement and the Sixties: Protest in America from Greensboro to Wounded Knee* (New York, 1995), 133, 182; David J. Garrow, *Bearing the Cross: Martin Luther King, Jr., and the Southern Christian Leadership Conference* (New York, 1986), 439–40; Ward, *Just My Soul Responding*, 124–30, 174–76, 205, 232, chaps. 9 and 10.

28. Joe Goldberg, "Cecil Taylor and the New Tradition," *Saturday Review* (9 February 1963); Nat Hentoff, "Music as Protest: Jazz and Race," *Commonweal* (8 January 1965); Burton W. Peretti, *Jazz in American Culture* (Chicago, 1997), 136–46; Lorenzo Thomas, Music and the Black Arts Movement," in *Jazz among the Discourses*, ed. Krin Gabbard (Durham, 1995), 260. Clippings from DES 5, 7:27, 37, NMAH/SI.

29. Gerald Early, *One Nation under a Groove: Motown and American Culture* (Hopewell, NJ, 1995), 28–33, 123; Nelson George, *The Death of Rhythm and Blues* (New York, 1988), 80–81, 86–89; Ted Gioia, *The History of Jazz* (New York, 1997), 354–57; Peretti, 141–45; Thomas, "Ascension," 256–65.

30. George B. Clay, "Duke Ellington Spins a Magic Musical Thread around a Capacity Summer-Ithaca Audience," *Ithaca Journal* (23 July 1965); C. Gerald Fraser, "Duke Ellington Celebrates 73rd Birthday as a Star and Guest," *New York Times* (c. late April 1972); Ralph J. Gleason, "The Duke Explains a Sacred Concert," On the Town column, *San Francisco Chronicle* (30 August 1965). Clippings from DES 7, 8: 38, 39, NMAH/SI. The Fraser article is from the Ellington vertical file at IJS/RU.

31. List of articles about Ellington appearances at benefits for civil rights or black-affiliated organizations: "Duke Ellington at CORE Concert," *Malverne (NY) Herald* (3 June 1965); "Freedom Ball Will Benefit United N.C. F.," *Philadelphia Tribune* (3 July 1965) (this was also a benefit for the Association for the Study of Negro Life and History); "Artists' Tribute to Farmer," *Amsterdam News* (12 March 1966) (CORE Tribute to James Farmer); "Ellington Honored for Civil Rights Contributions," *Jet* (7 December 1967) (Ellington appeared at a luncheon for the benefit of the National Committee for Rural Schools, which aided "people in the South who were left jobless because of their participation in voter education drives"); John L. Cavnar, "Fair Housing Ball: Duke Ellington Stars in Morris," *Newark (NJ) Evening News* (5 March 1966) (an organization looking for "new housing opportunities for Negroes"); John Cross, "At Jackie Robinson's Sunday: Jazz Greats Thrill 2,500 Crowd," *Stamford (CT) Advocate* (1 July 1968) ($30,000 was raised to support the late Dr. King's children); Ernest Ostro, "Is the Black Musician Making It?" *New York Manhattan Tribune* (20 September 1969) (about Ellington's "quiet" contributions to Mustevic); Robert Shelton, "Duke Ellington Enlivens Benefit: Joined by Dinizulu in a Show Aiding African [American] Institute," *New York Times* (10 December 1966). Clippings from DES, rolls 7, 8, 9, and 10, vols. 38, 42, 44, 51, and 53, NMAH/SI. Last clipping from the Schomburg Center's clippings file on Ellington. Also, a 4 April 1968 fundraiser at Carnegie Hall for the Tougaloo College Library Fund: Stratemann, *Duke Ellington*, 564.

After a request from an activist audience member, Ellington asked a Philadelphia audience in March 1965 to contribute funds to help protesters fly to the SNCC-sponsored civil rights march from Montgomery to Selma, AL. The audience coughed up $1,000: Barry Cunningham, "A Career of Protest," Closeup column, *New York Post* (22 December 1967).

Ellington's FBI file claimed that Ellington would make an appearance with SNCC leader James Forman "on a programme sponsored by the United Ministers on Texas Southern University campus in October, 1966. Forman was to speak on the theme, 'Black Power: A New Religion?'" No other evidence can be found for such an occasion, and an article from the Ellington Scrapbooks about the band's TSU gig on 4 October doesn't mention an Ellington SNCC appearance: Jeff Millar, "Duke Wows His Fans at TSU Concert," *Houston Chronicle* (5 October 1966). FBI file from: Nicholson, *Reminiscing In Tempo*, 374.

On 11 May 1969, Ellington performed at a Soul Food Dinner benefit at the Waldorf Astoria for the Free Southern Theatre, an organization that "brought theatre to poor, black communities": Stratemann, *Duke Ellington*, 591.

Ellington and his orchestra also made many appearances at benefits for organizations not affiliated with blacks: "Ellington Band to Play for Benefit," *Detroit Free Press* (for St. Leonard's House for released prisoners) (5 July 1965); "Duke Ellington Concert for Stamford Museum," *New York Times* (7 July 1965); "Dollars for Scholars Ball Features Duke Ellington" (no citation or date; c. 1965); "Duke Ellington to Play at Hospital Charity Ball," *Mt. Pleasant (MI) Times-News* (4 April 1966); "Jazzman Ellington in CAM Benefit," *Chicago Garfieldian* (6 April 1966). Clippings from DES, rolls 3, 7, and 8, vols. 15, 38, and 42, NMAH/SI. Also, a 20 June 1967 benefit for the USO in Palm Springs and an 11 June 1968 benefit for mentally disabled children: Stratemann, *Duke Ellington*, 550, 568.

This footnote covers examples, and not all examples, of this trend from 1965 to 1969—plenty of other evidence exists for similar Ellington activities in other periods of the 1960s and 1970s and other periods of Ellington's career. Further benefits for Ellington's Sacred Concerts are listed in chapter 12.

Ellington quotes: Nat Hentoff, "This Cat Needs No Pulitzer Prize," *New York Times Magazine* (12 September 1965); Francis Raffetto, "Plenty of Duke's Tunes Planned for $1 Concert," Dallas after Dark column, *Dallas Morning News* (14 November 1965). Clippings from DES 8:40, NMAH/SI.

32. Jack Fletcher, "Oppressive Heat and Music at Charlotte Jazz Festival," *Durham (NC) Anvil* (5 July 1969). Jack Hadlock, "The Ultimate Ellington Tribute," *Down Beat* (27 November 1969). Clippings from DES 12:61, 62, NMAH/SI.

33. Duke Ellington interview, CHIC 1964 #2, tape 1, AC/NMAH/SI.

Harry T. Cook II, "Jazzman Blends the Sacred, Secular: Duke Ellington Gets Religion into His Music," *Detroit News* (5 July 1969); Sister Mary Felice, W.S., "An Interview with the Duke," *Africa* (Summer 1966), collection 301, series 10, box 4, folder 2, AC/NMAH/SI; Noel Lieberman, "'Lucky' Duke Idol of Berkeley Kids," *Oakland Tribune* (17 October 1969). First and last clippings from DES 12:61, 62, NMAH/SI.

34. This section on Ellington's 5 May 1969 performance at San Francisco State University is based on the following sources: "Ellington 'Turns On' S. F. State Students," *Los Angeles Times* (6 May 1969); "The 'Duke' Brings Jazz to SF State," *Richmond (CA) Independent* (6 May 1969); "Duke's Music Cools Tempers at SF State," *Watsonville (CA) Register Pajaronian* (6 May 1969); "The Duke's Music Crosses Generations," *Raleigh (NC) Times* (6 May 1969); "Duke's Jazz Wows Crowd at SF State," *Chico Enterprise-Record* (6 May 1969); photo of Ellington, Hayakawa, and coed dancing together, *Detroit News* (6 May 1969) (and many other papers); Ralph J. Gleason, "Behind the Scenes at the Duke's Show," On the Town column, *San Francisco Chronicle* (7 May 1969). Clippings from DES 12:59, NMAH/SI.

Ellington interview, CHIC 1964 #2.

35. Arnold Rampersad, *The Life of Langston Hughes*, vol. 2, *I Dream a World* (New York, 1988), 358, 383, 387–88, 398, 411; Leonard Feather, "'Jazz' Just a Legend? Maybe, Says Ellington," *Rochester (NY) Democrat and Chronicle* (18 December 1966); Bill Lorentz, "Ellington Pleases All Fans with Varied Jazz Pieces," *Waukesha (WI) Freeman* (29 May 1965). Clippings from DES 7, 9:38, 45, NMAH/SI.

36. Norman Granz interview, conducted by Patricia Willard, 23 and 24 August 1989, SIEOHP, tape 1, AC/NMAH/SI.

37. "The 100 Most Influential Black Americans," *Ebony* (April 1971). Clipping from DES 14:69, NMAH/SI.

Chapter Twelve

1. Edward R. Murrow, "Statement before the Subcommittee on International Organizations and Movements of the Committee on Foreign Affairs, House of Representatives," United States Information Agency Press Release (28 March 1963), found in collection 301, series 2A, box 2, folder 17, AC/NAMH/SI; Ralph J. Gleason, Gleason on Jazz column, *Huntington (WV) Herald-Advertiser* (17 November 1963). Clipping from DES 6:32, NMAH/SI.

2. Nan Robertson, "Arts Hold Sway at White House: Mrs. Johnson Greets 400 at Cultural Festival," *New York Times* (15 June 1965); Howard Taubman, "White House Salutes Culture in America: Dissent of Artists on Foreign Policy Stirs 400 at All-Day Fete," *New York Times* (15 June 1965). These front-page clippings from DES 7:38, NMAH/SI.

3. Duke Ellington interview, conducted by Willis Conover for *Music USA*, 17 August 1956, VOA Music Collection, RWB 3069 A1, LOC; Gilbert Seldes monologue, *The Subject Is Jazz* (NBC-TV, 26 March 1958), LOC/MPD; Reinhold Wagnleitner, *Coca-Colonization and the Cold War: The Cultural Mission of the United States in Austria after the Second World War* (Chapel Hill, 1994), 197–214.

4. For presidential policies on race after World War II and before the 1963 Ellington State Department tour, consult: Kenneth O' Reilly, *Nixon's Piano: Presidents and Racial Politics from Washington to Clinton* (New York, 1995), chaps. 4 and 5.

5. Alexander DeConde, *Ethnicity, Race, and American Foreign Policy: A History* (Boston, 1992), introduction, chap. 1, 128–30; Robert Heger, "African-Americans as Cultural Ambassadors: The Unofficial Visits of the U.S. Department of State, 1945–1963," courtesy of Robert Heger, NA2/CP; Don DeMicheal, "Jazz in Government," *Down Beat* (17 January 1963), clipping from DES5:27, NMAH/SI; O'Reilly, *Nixon's Piano*, 125, 134, 146–47; Penny M. Von Eschen, "Who's the Real Ambassador? Exploding Cold War Racial Ideology," *Cold War Constructions: The Political Culture of United States Imperialism, 1945–1966*, ed. Christian G. Appy (Amherst, 2000).

John Paine speech, c. 1946, American Music Programs Overseas, Department of State Decimal File 811.42700(M)/4-1046; Luther H. Evans, Librarian of Congress to Richard H. Heindel, Chief, Division of Libraries and Institutions, Department of State, 16 August 1946, American Music Programs Overseas, Department of State Decimal File 811.42700(M)/8-1646; State Department Memo to Certain Diplomatic and Consular Officers: Orchestral Music Sent to Date (February 1, 1947) to the Department's European Depositories of American Orchestral Music, 11 February 1947, American Music Programs Overseas, Department of State Decimal File 811.42700(M)/2-1147. All of these documents located in NA2/CP. Other letters from the same period (currently stored in the same decimal file, in box 4741) deal with similar American musical holdings in USIS libraries in France, Vienna, China, and Norway, among other countries.

6. DeMicheal, "Jazz in Government"; Heger, "African-Americans as Cultural Ambassadors"; President's Special International Program Eighth Semi-Annual Report, 1 January–30 June 1960, p.3, USIA, Agency Library, Archives Collection, U.S. State Department, Washington, D.C.; Paul Specht, music producer, to Hon. Wm. Benton, Assistant Secretary of State, 27 November 1945, American Music Programs Overseas, Department of State Decimal File 811.42700(M)/11-2745, NA2/CP; Memo to All AF [African], FE [Far East], and NEA [Near

East/Asia] Posts: President's Special International Program for Cultural Presentations—Plans for FY 1961 and 1962, 24 August 1960, Department of State 1960–63 Central Decimal File 032/8-2460, NA2/CP.

Wagnleitner, *Coca-Colonization*, chap. 2.

Country and rock and roll acts not used on state tours: William B. Macomber, Assistant Secretary, to Senator Estes Kefauver (regarding a complaint on a lack of country acts from Kenneth F. Nelson of the Country Music Association), 20 February 1961, Department of State 1960–63 Central Decimal File 032/2-861, box 25, NA2/CP. A meeting of the American National Theater and Academy, the group that vetted all acts for the State Department, vetoed the offer of Fats Domino for a state tour because "this is mainly rock and roll": Music Advisory Panel Meeting, International Cultural Exchange of ANTA, 15 Mar 61, MC-468, box 100, folder 7, BECAHC/SCD/UAL.

7. Heger, "African-Americans as Cultural Ambassadors"; Elisse Wright, "Black Ambassadors and American Foreign Policy in the Early Cold War Years, 1958–68" (paper presented at the Conference of the Society for Historians of American Foreign Relations, Georgetown University, 19–22 June 1997).

Reports on William Warfield tours: Joseph Simonson, Addis Ababa Public Affairs Officer, "Educational Exchange: President's Special International Program: Visit of William Warfield, Baritone," 10 October 1956, Department of State Central Decimal File 1955–59, 032-Warfield, William/9-1856; John C. Donnell, Penang Public Affairs Officer, "Educational Exchange: Visit of William Warfield to Penang," 20 March 1958, Department of State Central Decimal File 1955–59, 032-Warfield, William/3-2058; Paul D. Bethel, Habana [*sic*] Public Affairs Officer, "President's Special Fund: Visit of William Warfield to Cuba," 24 July 1959, Department of State Central Decimal File 1955–59, 032-Warfield, William/7-2459. All documents located at NA2/CP.

8. Reports on the Marian Anderson and Camilla Williams tours are in the Department of State Central Decimal File 1955–59, 032, National Archives at College Park, MD. The quotes about Anderson are from Richard S. Barnsley, Acting Chief Public Affairs Officer, "Educational Exchange: President's Fund: Visit to Manila of Marian Anderson," 6 December 1957, Department of State Decimal File 1955–59, 032-Anderson, Marian/12-657, National Archives at College Park, MD. More press clips for the Anderson 1957–58 tour are located in President's Special International Program Third Semi-Annual Report, 1 July 1957–31 December 1957, p.13, USIA, Agency Library, Archives Collection, U.S. State Department, Washington, D.C.

The complaints are noted in the following dispatches: Loyd V. Steere, American Consul General, Salisbury, "Visit of William Warfield to the Central African Foundation," 12 October 1956, Department of State Central Decimal File 1955–59, 032-Warfield, William/10-1256; Joseph A. Kitchin, Cairo Acting Public Affairs Officer, "Cultural Presentations: President's Program: Camilla Williams," 30 January 1959, Department of State Central Decimal File 1955–59, 032-Williams, Camilla/1-3059. Both documents located at NA2/CP.

9. Reports on the 1956 Dizzy Gillespie tours are in the Department of State Central Decimal File 1955–59, 032, at the NA2/CP. The quotes are from Joseph C. Kolarek, Country Public Affairs Officer, "Educational Exchange: Visit of President's Fund: ANTA-sponsored Jazz Musician Dizzy Gillespie and Band to Yugoslavia," 1 August 1956, Department of State Central Decimal File 1955–59, 032-Gillespie, Dizzy/8-156, NA2/CP.

10. Dozens of examples of letters from congressional representatives, constituents, and State Department replies reside in the Department of State Central Decimal File 1955–59, 032, box 103, at the NA2/CP.

11. Laurence Bergreen, *Louis Armstrong: An Extravagant Life* (New York, 1997), 459–63.

12. Bergreen, *Louis Armstrong*, 470–73. The twenty-eight letters in reaction to Armstrong's

comments about Little Rock are filed in the Department of State Central Decimal File 1955–59, 032, NA2/CP. The anti-Semitic quote is from: Charles E. Larson, President, 54th District Republican Assembly, Los Angeles, to the U.S. State Department, Washington, D.C., 23 September 1957, Department of State Central Decimal File 1955–59, 032-Armstrong, Louis/9-2357, NA2/CP.

A State Department letter answering Larson indicated that "Armstrong's public relations representative approached the Department and expressed an interest in obtaining Government sponsorship for tours to several areas of the world, including the Soviet Union" in June 1956 and was refused: John P. Meagher, Chief, Public Services Division, to Charles E. Larson, 17 October 1957, Department of State Central Decimal File 1955–59, 032-Armstrong, Louis/9-2357, NA2/CP.

13. The files concerning the 1958 Dave Brubeck Jazz Quartet State Department tours are located in the Department of State Central Decimal File 1955–59, 032, box 96, NA2/CP. The quotes are from: Incoming Telegram, from Johnson/Prague to Secretary of State, 7 November 1957, Department of State Central Decimal File 1955–59, 032 Brubeck, Dave Jazz Quartet/11-757; Outgoing Telegram, Department of State, 31 December 1957, Department of State Central Decimal File 1955–59, 032 Brubeck, Dave Jazz Quartet/12-3157; Frank J. Lewand, Warsaw Cultural Attaché, "Report on Dave Brubeck Jazz Quartet Concerts in Poland," 24 March 1958, Department of State Central Decimal File 1955–59, 032 Brubeck, Dave Jazz Quartet/3-2458; Barrett Parker, Kabul Acting Public Affairs Officer, "Visit of the Dave Brubeck Ensemble to Kabul," 7 May 1958, Department of State Central Decimal File 1955–59, 032 Brubeck, Dave Jazz Quartet/5-758. All documents located at NA2/CP.

The files concerning the 1958 Woody Herman State Department tour are located in the Department of State Central Decimal File 1955–59, 032, NA2/CP.

During 1957–59, the jazz groups Jack Teagarden Sextet, Wilbur DeParis Band, and Glenn Miller Orchestra (headed by Ray McKinley; Miller died in action during World War II) also toured on behalf of the State Department, though they received far less notice in the press and in State Department files, mostly because of their second-tier or less status in the jazz world at the time. For a complete list of all State Department tours by jazz artists during the 1956–66 period, consult: Jazz and Folk Units Which Have Toured under the Cultural Presentations Program (c.1966), MC-468, box 100, folder 26, BECAHC/SCD/UAL.

14. Duke Ellington interview, CHIC 1964 #7, tape 3, AC/NMAH/SI.

15. Lucius D. Battle, Executive Secretary of State, "Memorandum for Mr. McGeorge Bundy, the White House; Subject: Report to the President on International Cultural Presentations Program," 30 November 1961, Department of State Central Decimal File 1960–63 511.00/11-3061, NA2/CP; United States Government Memo from OCE R. Gordon Arneson to CU Alfred V. Boerner, 18 December 61, MC-468, box 47, folder 21, BECAHC/SCD/UAL.

16. Milton Bracker, "Goodman Signs 12 for Russian Tour: Band Will Include at Least Four More Musicians," *New York Times* (10 April 1962); Dave Hepburn, In the Wings column, *Amsterdam News* (7 April 1962); Lucius Lee, As I See It! column, *Columbus (OH) Sentinel* (26 April 1962); Larry Still, "How U.S. Ignored Jazz Founders for Soviet Tour: Selection of Goodman Fires Shot Heard around Jazz World," *Jet* (12 April 1962); "Musicians Agree the 'Duke' Should Head Tour: Ellington Spurns Bid to Go as an 'Added Attraction,'" *Philadelphia Tribune* (7 April 1962); "Benny Goodman Shocked at Negro Reaction to Tour," *Amsterdam News* (21 April 1962). Clippings from DES 5:25, 26, NMAH/SI.

17. Bracker, "Goodman Signs 12." Benny Goodman to Ambassador Charles Bohlen, Moscow, 19 August 1955, Department of State Central Decimal File 1955–59, 032 Goodman, Benny/8-1965; Benny Goodman to Mr. Walter J. Stoessel, Jr., Officer in Charge of U.S.S.R. Affairs, Department of State, 12 September 1955, Department of State Central Decimal File 1955–59,

032 Goodman, Benny/9-1255; Carl W. McCardle, Assistant Secretary, State Department, to Benny Goodman, [obscured] October 1957, Department of State Central Decimal File 1955–59, 032 Goodman, Benny/9-1955. All documents located at NA2/CP.

18. George Avakian interview, conducted by the author, 16 April 2001; Bracker, "Goodman Signs 12"; DeMicheal, "Jazz in Government"; Benny Goodman, as told to Leslie Leber, "Why I'm Taking Jazz to Russia," *This Week* (27 May 1962); Lee, "As I See It!"; Still, "How U.S. Ignored Jazz Founders"; "Benny Goodman Shocked," *Amsterdam News*,. Avakian produced and recorded a live album of Goodman concert performances from Russia.

Eugene S. Staples, Counselor for Cultural Affairs, American Embassy, Moscow, 26 March 1962, "Preparations for Benny Goodman Tour of the Soviet Union," Department of State Central Decimal File 1960–63, 032 Goodman, Benny Band/3-2662, NA2/CP.

Penny M. Von Eschen, *Satchmo Blows Up the World: Jazz Ambassadors Play the Cold War* (Cambridge, MA, 2004), 102–3, 111.

19. "Free Radio Getting through to 'Kids,'" *Levelland (TX) Daily Sun News* (9 November 1961); Jack Gould, "Jazz on a 'Global Scale': Willis Conover Heard in Eighty Foreign Countries over Radio Broadcasts by 'Voice of America' Network," *New York Times* (21 October 1962). Clippings found in collection 301, series 9, boxes 7 and 8, folders 45 and 49, respectively, AC/NMAH/SI.

20. Terrence P. Catherman, Cultural Attaché, Moscow, "Benny Goodman and His Band in the Soviet Union," 10 July 1962, Department of State Central Decimal File 1960–63, 032 Goodman, Benny Band/7-1062, NA2/CP.

The Soviets spurned major jazz acts for the next three years, allowing Earl Hines to tour in 1966. The full account of Ellington's 1971 Soviet tour appears in chapter 15.

21. Tony Gieske, "Ambitious Festival Ready for Take-Off," *Washington Post* (27 May 1962); Ralph J. Gleason, "Duke's Doings at D.C. Festival," *New York Journal-American* (21 April 1962); George T. Simon, "Youth Jumping 'All Over' Poland," The Jazz Beat column, *New York Herald-Tribune* (1 July 1962); Milton Viorst, "Cold War Foes Get Hot Together—Jazz Does It," *Washington Post* (2 June 1962); John S. Wilson, "A Jazz Festival Opens Thursday: First International Event to Take Place in the Capital," *New York Times* (27 May 1962). Clippings from DES 5:26, NMAH/SI.

22. Michael Kraft, "Kennedy Is Chided for Ignoring Jazz Festival," *Fresno Bee* (1 June 1962); George T. Simon, "Jazz in Washington," *New York Herald-Tribune* (1 June 1962); George T. Simon, "Jazz Blows Door Open to Diplomatic Domain," *New York Herald-Tribune* (2 June 1962); John S. Wilson, "A Jazz Festival Opens in Capital; First International Event Is Begun with Parade That Includes Brass Band; President Serenaded; New Orleans Group Stops at White House—Ellington Given Keys to the City," *New York Times* (1 June 1962). Clippings from DES 5:26, NMAH/SI. Numerous syndicated copies of the Kraft story are on the same roll of microfilm, including stories from the *Cocoa (FL) Tribune* and the *Middletown (CT) Press*. Simon's quote about the king and queen is not entirely correct, though Ellington did have an audience with Prince George and the Prince of Wales on his 1933 European tour and with the Queen during his 1958 European tour. For more on these events, consult chapters 4 and 10. For more on Ellington's disappointing lack of engagement with presidents Hoover and Roosevelt, consult chapter 7.

Paul Winter: Nat Hentoff, "The 1963 Playboy All-Stars: A Look at the Current Jazz Scene and the Winners of the Seventh Annual Playboy Poll," *Playboy* (February 1963). From DES 5:27, NMAH/SI.

23. Mercer Ellington interview, conducted by Dr. Marcia M. Greenlee, 18 September 1990, 5 and 7 May 1991, SIEOHP, tape 2, AC/NMAH/SI; Ruth Ellington interview, conducted by Dr. Marcia M. Greenlee, 18 August 1989, SIEOHP, tape 1, AC/NMAH/SI; Phoebe Jacobs interviews, conducted by the author, 27 January 1996 and 13 November 1999.

24. Roy E. Larsen, Chairman of the Executive Committee, Time, Inc., Vice Chairman, Advisory Committee, and Glenn G. Wolfe, Foreign Service Officer, "Report of Survey Cultural Presentations Program for the U.S. Advisory Commission on International Educational & Cultural Affairs," 17 December 1962, Department of State Central Decimal File 1960–63, 032/1-1463, NA2/CP.

25. Contract between the Government of the United States of America and Duke Ellington, Incorporated, 17 June 1963, collection 301, series 3I, box 133, folder 8, AC/NMAH/SI. The Ellington orchestra was making, on average, somewhere between $1,500 and $2,000 per show in 1963, or about $10,500 to $14,000 per week (the State Department contract paid them a little more than $12,500 per week). For exact figures, consult: Duke Ellington booking contracts, collection 301, series 3A, boxes 3 and 4, AC/NMAH/SI.

"Exchange Lineup Mostly Longhair," *Variety* (22 May 1963); Ralph J. Gleason, "Overseas Tour for the Duke," *San Francisco Chronicle* (7 June 1963). Clippings from DES 5:29, NMAH/SI.

Norman Granz interview, conducted by Patricia Willard, 23 and 24 August 1989, SIEOHP, tape 3, AC/NMAH/SI; George Wein interview, conducted by Dr. Marcia M. Greenlee, 9 May 1991, SIEOHP, tape 1, AC/NMAH/SI; George Wein with Nate Chinen, *Myself Among Others* (Cambridge, MA, 2003), 165–66.

26. The Duke Ellington Orchestra 6 September 6–28 November 1963: Synopsis (c. December 1963), MC-468, box 61, folder 5, BECAHC/SCD/UAL. This document lists every on- and offstage performance by the orchestra during the 1963 state tour.

27. Teheran University Student Survey: Attitudes and Aspirations, August 1963, Records Group 306, Records of USIA, Office of Research, Country Project Files 1951–64, Iran 1957–63; Foreign Service Despatch from USIS Baghdad to USIA Washington: Country Assessment Report, 5 April 1960, Records Group 59, Entry 5118, General Records of Department of State, Bureau of Cultural Affairs, Planning and Development Staff Country Files 1955–64, Folder t10e9; Field Message from USIS Baghdad to USIA Washington: Country Plan for Iraq, 30 January 1961, Records Group 59, Entry 5118, General Records of Department of State, Bureau of Cultural Affairs, Planning and Development Staff Country Files 1955–64, Folder t10e9; Country Plan for Iraq, United States Information Agency, Records Group 306, Records of USIA, Exhibits Division, Records Concerning Exhibits in Foreign Countries, 1955–67, Iraq File; Lorraine D. Hyde, "A Preliminary Study of Indian University Student's Knowledge and Image of the U.S.A.," July 1961, Records Group 306, Records of USIA, Research Reports, 1953–86, Folder IN-7-61; "Highlights of Discussion with 'Project India' Students," 30 August 1962, Records Group 306, Records of USIA, Research Reports 1953–86, Field Research Reports 1953–86, Project file #IRS.IND.123; Bert T. King, "Impact of Chinese Border Attack upon Delhi Opinions of the U.S., Britain, and the Soviet Union," 29 March 1963, Records Group 306, Records of the USIA, Office of Research, Country Project Files 1951–64, India 1962–63, Project file # IN6204; Country Plan and Revised Section V (Program Activities) of the Country Plan for Syria, 6 June 1963, Records Group 306, Entry 1039, Records of USIA, Exhibits Division, Records Concerning Exhibits in Foreign Countries 1955–67, Syria Folder. All of these documents located at NA2/CP.

28. "Briefing Note: Except in Pakistan, U.S. Race Issue Given Balanced Press Play in Near East, South Asia," 21 June 1963, Records Group 306, Report M-176-63, Records of USIA, Office of Research, Current Briefs 1963–66, M Series Reports, June 1963 Folder; "Briefing Note: Near East and South Asian Press Exhibits Mixed Reactions to Integration Struggle," 3 July 1963, Records Group 306, Report M-191-63, Records of USIA, Office of Research, Current Briefs 1963–1966, M Series Reports, July 1963 Folder; "Delhi Reactions to Race Relations in the U.S.," August 1963, Records Group 59, Entry 5118, General Records of the Department of State, Bu-

reau of Cultural Affairs, Planning and Redevelopment Staff, Country Files 1955–64, File t1oq; "Briefing Note: "Near East, South Asian Comment Links U.S. Race Question with Viet-Nam and Palestine," 12 September 1963, Records Group 306, Report M-303-63, Records of USIA, Office of Research, Current Briefs 1963–66, M Series Reports, September 1963 Folder. All of these documents located at NA2/CP. The M Series reports cited above contain dozens of surveys of foreign populations concerning impressions of American race relations during the 1960s.

29. U.S. Information Service Press-Radio Background Kit: "Duke Ellington—A Biographical Sketch," c. October 1963; U.S. Information Service Press-Radio Background Kit: "Duke Ellington—'Musician's Musician,' to Perform in Pakistan," c. October 1963. Both of these press releases are located in collection 301, series 11, box 1, folder 28, AC/NMAH/SI.

30. *News Review* (in English and Arabic translations), c. September 1963; *American News* (in Sinhalese with English translations of the subjects of each story), 27 September, 11 October, 25 October 1963. Clippings from DES 6:31 and 33 (*News Review*), NMAH/SI.

31. John Pauker, IOP, United States Information Agency, "News Policy Note No. 28–63: Civil Rights and Race Relations," Records Group 84, Records of the Foreign Service Posts of the Department of State, Iraq, Baghdad, General Records 1962–63, Program 1963 Folder; Hugh J. Parry, "America's Human Rights Image Abroad," 26 February 1964, Records Group 306, Records of USIA, Office of Research, Special Reports, 1964–82. Both documents located at NA2/CP.

32. The 1963 Statistical Reports on the USIS Exhibits Programs are located in: Records Group 306, Records of USIA Exhibits Division, Records Concerning Exhibits in Foreign Countries 1955–67, and are listed by country at NA2/CP.

33. "Suggestions on Methods of Answering the Critic of the United States Abroad," collection 301, series 2A, box 2, folder 10, AC/NMAH/SI; Buster Cooper interview, conducted by Patricia Willard, 29 September 1989, SIEOHP, tape 1, AC/NMAH/SI.

34. Ellington Orchestra 6 September–28 November 1963: Synopsis, BECAHC/SCD/UAL; USIS Press Release: "Duke Ellington and Orchestra Arrive in New Delhi," 21 September 1963; "Admirers Mob Ellington: U.S. Jazz Maestro," *Times of India* (10 October 1963); Ralph J. Gleason, "The Duke's Impact in the Near East," *San Francisco Chronicle* (4 April 1965). Clipping and press release from DES 6:31, NMAH/SI. The 1965 clipping is from DES 7:37.

35. "The Maestro," *Hindustan Times* (23 September 1963); USIS Press Release: "Duke Ellington and Orchestra in Bombay," 9 October 1963; USIS Press Release: "Duke Ellington Honoured at Press Guild Reception in Bombay," 9 October 1963; USIS Press Release: "Students Cheer Ellington Orchestra Lecture-Demonstration," 14 October 1963; Tarantelle, "'Jam Session' . . . with the Duke," My Week column, *Ceylon Daily Mirror* (26 October 1963); Duke Ellington, "Orientations: Adventures in the Far East," *Music Journal* (March 1964). Clippings from DES 6:31, NMAH/SI. The Ellington-authored article is in DES 7:34.

Thomas W. Simons, Jr., Report on the 1963 Duke Ellington State Department Tour, c. December 1963, MC-468, box 61, folder 5; William B. King, Counselor of Embassy for Public Affairs, Karachi, "Educational and Cultural Exchange: Cultural Presentations: Duke Ellington Orchestra," 27 May 1964, MC-468, box 61, folder 6. Both from BECAHC/SCD/UAL. The Simons report is missing a cover page, but since the document was obviously written by someone who followed the tour closely, and since there were only two State Department personnel who were with the tour at all times, and the other's (Naomi Huber's) report is clearly marked and documented, I have deduced that this document must be by Simons.

36. USIS Information Service Press-Radio Background Kit: Duke Ellington Presents: Jazz, The Duke Ellington Orchestra on Records," c. October 1963; "U.S. Artists That Fight against Segregation: Duke Ellington's Press Interview," *Pakistan Times* (30 October 1963); Gleason,

"Gleason On Jazz"; "Jazz Seemed Off Key, Ellington Tour Ended," *New York Herald-Tribune* (29 November 1963). Clippings from DES 6:31, 32, NMAH/SI.

Duke Ellington interview, CHIC 1964 #8, tape 1, AC/NMAH/SI.

37. Ellington Orchestra 6 September 6–28 November 1963: Synopsis, BECAHC/SCD/UAL; "Duke Ellington Orchestra: A 'Deccan Chronicle' Feature," *Deccan Chronicle* (28 September 1963); Unidentified State Department Press Release: "Ellington Wins Colombo Jazz Fans at Monsoon-Drenched Opening," 24 October 1963; United States Information Service News, "Capacity Audiences Cheer Ellington Band in Iran, Pakistan," 7 November 1963. Clippings and press releases from DES 6:31, NMAH/SI.

38. Simons, Report on the 1963 Duke Ellington State Department Tour; Jimmy Hamilton interview, conducted by Dr. Marcia M. Greenlee, SIEOHP, 26 March 1991, tape 4, AC/NAMH/SI; Herbie Jones interview, conducted by Patricia Willard, 15 December 1989, SIEOHP, tape 1, AC/NMAH/SI; Brian Bate, "With Duke on Tour," *Down Beat* (27 February 1964). Clipping from DES 7:34, NMAH/SI. More comments from band members on interacting only with the elite on the 1963 State Tour: Lawrence Brown, Harry Carney, Russell Procope interview, conducted by the Duke Ellington Society, 1964, SC Audio C-498, SCBC.

39. Simons, Report on the 1963 Duke Ellington State Department Tour; Cooper interview, 29 September 1989; Jones interview, 15 December 1989; Naomi Huber to Charles Wolfe, 5 October 1963, collection 429, box 1, folder 5, AC/NMAH/SI; Naomi Huber, Diary 1963, collection 429, box 1, folder 6, AC/NMAH/SI.

40. Thomas W. Simons, Jr., to Glenn Wolfe, Office of Cultural Presentations, 17 September 1963, MC-468, box 61, folder 5, BECAHC/SCD/UAL; Cooper interview, 29 September 1989; Jones interview, 15 December 1989; Dorothy Kilgallen, "Liz Ready to Deal Romantic Ace," The Voice of Broadway column, *New York Journal-American* (9 October 1963). Clipping from DES 6:32, NMAH/SI.

41. Brown, Carney, Procope 1964, SCBC interview; Dr. Arthur Logan interview, conducted by the Duke Ellington Society, 1964, SC Audio C-452, SCBC; Simons, Report on the 1963 Duke Ellington State Department Tour; Telegram from Ambassador Chester Bowles, 5 October 1963, collection 429, box 1, folder 5, AC/NMAH/SI; Klaus Stratemann, *Duke Ellington: Day by Day and Film by Film* (Copenhagen, 1992), 475.

42. Simons, Report on the 1963 Duke Ellington State Department Tour; Thomas W. Simons, Jr., "Part II: The Role of an Escort Officer," MC-468, box 61, folder 5, BECAHC/SCD/UAL; Naomi Huber to Glenn Wolfe, c. 5 October 1963, collection 429, box 1, folder 5, AC/NMAH/SI; John Edward Hasse, *Beyond Category: The Life and Genius of Duke Ellington* (New York, 1993), 370.

While she never sang in public with the Ellington orchestra, a document in the collections at the Smithsonian seems to indicate that Fernanda de Castro Monte may have recorded a session with Ellington or Strayhorn accompanying her on piano on 27 November 1962, the night before Ellington signed to Reprise Records. If so, the tape has not been released and does not seem to be listed in Ellington discographies: recording session documentation: Duke Ellington (client), Fernanda Montel (title of product), 27 November 1962, collection 704, series 3A, box 1, folder 15, AC/NMAH/SI.

43. Ridgway B. Knight, "Educational and Cultural Exchange: Cultural Presentations for Damascus International Fair, 1963," 14 February 1963, Records Group 59, Entry 5118, General Records of the Department of State, Bureau of Cultural Affairs, Country Files 1955–64, File t10h9, National Archives at College Park, MD; Ellington Orchestra 6 September–28 November 1963: Synopsis, BECAHC/SCD/UAL. "Damascus Jumps to 'Ash Al Duke,'" *Omaha World-Herald* (10 September 1963). This clipping and dozens more like it found in DES 6:30, NMAH/SI.

Instances of the embassy dispatch being used in the American press: Gleason, "Duke's Impact"; "America's 'Big Beat' Shaking—and Shaping—the World!" *Every Week* (20 October 1965). Clippings from DES 7, 8:37, 40, respectively, NMAH/SI. Additional press clippings of Gleason's nationally syndicated column can be found in collection 301, series 9, box 13, folder 15, AC/NMAH/SI.

44. "Reactions to Duke Ellington Concerts and Cultural Presentations in India," Prepared by Research Section of United States Information Service, New Delhi, India, February 1964, Records Group 306, Records of USIA, Research Reports 1953–86, Field Research Reports 1953–86, Folder IN-1-64; uncited author, "Educational and Cultural Exchange: Annual Report on the Educational and Exchange Program for FY64—July 1, 1963 to June '64,13 October 1964, MC-468, box 318, folder 1, BECAHC/SCD/UAL; Ellington Orchestra 6 September 6–28 November 1963: Synopsis, BECAHC/SCD/UAL; William B. King, "Educational and Cultural Exchange." Brown, Carney, Procope 1964 SCBC interview; Logan 1964 SCBC interview.

45. Field Message from USIS Colombo to USIS Washington: "USIS Monthly Reports," 20 December 1963, Records Group 59, Entry 5118, General Records of Department of State, Bureau of Cultural Affairs, Planning and Development Staff Country Files 1955–64, Folder t10h9, NA2/CP.

46. Ellington Orchestra 6 September 6–28 November 1963: Synopsis, BECAHC/SCD/UAL; USIS Press Release: "Capacity Audiences Cheer Ellington Band in Iran, Pakistan" (7 November 1963); "[Ellington] Says Baghdad Swinging . . . Bullets, Jazz!" *Gary (IN) Post-Tribune* (15 November 1963). Clipping and press release from DES 6:31, 32, NMAH/SI. Dozens of syndicated clippings about Ellington in the midst of the Iraqi coup are preserved in volume 32. More eyewitness accounts from the band and their entourage: Brown, Carney, Procope, 1964 SCBC interview; Logan, 1964 SCBC interview.

The historical information about the 1963 Iraqi coup is drawn from: Douglas A. Boyd, "Radio and Television in Iraq: The Electronic Media in a Transitionary Arab World Country," *Middle Eastern Studies* (October 1982); Jewell Fenzi and Carl L. Nelson, "The Duke in Baghdad," *Foreign Service Journal* (August 1991); Phoebe Ann Marr, "The Iraqi Revolution: A Case Study of Army Rule," *Orbis* (Fall 1970); Marion Farouk-Sluglett and Peter Sluglett, *Iraq since 1958: From Revolution to Dictatorship* (London, 1987), 68–92.

According to Ellington scholar Sjef Hoefsmit, "Isfahan" existed as a composition before the 1963 state tour. Strayhorn scholar Walter van de Leur's research indicates that Strayhorn wrote the song on his own, though it is co-credited to Ellington.

There has been speculation that the Central Intelligence Agency planted an agent amidst the Ellington state tour entourage, particularly for the purpose of observing or influencing the November 1963 Iraqi coup, but no hard evidence of this could be found at the time of this writing by myself or Ellington scholar Arne Neegaard. Neegaard's cache of secret and confidential State Department cables and documents about the 1963 Iraqi tour stop added historical depth to my understanding of the situation. A movie based on these events, coproduced and starring Morgan Freeman as Ellington, is set for release in 2009.

47. Ellington Orchestra 6 September 6–28 November 1963: Synopsis, BECAHC/SCD/UAL; uncited author, "Educational and Cultural Exchange: Annual Report on the Educational Exchange Program for FY 1964," MC-468, box 319, folder 1, BECAHC/SCD/UAL.

48. This account of the events on the tour that occurred after the Kennedy assassination is based on the following sources: Ellington Orchestra 6 September 6–28 November 1963: Synopsis, BECAHC/SCD/UAL; Lucius D. Battle, Assistant Secretary of State, Telegram, 25 November 1963, MC-468, box 61, folder 6, BECAHC/SCD/UAL; Sally Hammond, "Duke Ellington's Wish: To Play in Honor of JFK," *New York Post* (6 December 1963); Drew Pearson, Washington Merry-Go-Round column, *Aberdeen (SD) American News* (12 January 1964); "Jazz Seemed Off Key, Ellington Tour Ended," *New York Herald-Tribune* (29 November 1963);

"Ellington Band Not Swinging on Tour for State Dept. during U.S. Mourning," *Daily Variety* (2 December 1963). Clipping and press release from DES 6:32, NMAH/SI. The reference cables mentioned by Battle were not found in the archives consulted.

49. Logan interview, 1964; Helen McNamara, "The Duke, Quick on Wit, Is Master of Talents," *Toronto Telegraph* (25 March 1964); Stratemann, *Duke Ellington*, 474. Clipping from Duke Ellington clipping file, IJS/RU.

50. Leonard Feather, "Kennedy Tragedy Affects Jazzmen," Life with Feather column, *North Valley Times* (7 December 1963); Atra Baer, Scene and Heard column, *New York Journal-American* (22 December 1963). Clippings from DES 6:32, NMAH/SI.

Chapter Thirteen

1. James Lincoln Collier, *Duke Ellington* (New York, 1987), 278–87, 290–96; Herb Jeffries interview, conducted by Patricia Willard, 22 and 23 September 1989, SIEOHP, tapes 3 and 5, AC/NMAH/SI.

2. Janna Tull Steed, *Duke Ellington: A Spiritual Biography* (New York, 1999), 19; Collier, *Duke Ellington*, 278–87, 290–96.

3. Carl L. Baldwin, "Don't Call It Jazz," *Impact* (December 1968); Stanley Dance interview, conducted by Dr. Marcia M. Greenlee, 28 August 1990, SIEOHP, tape 6, AC/NMAH/SI; Mercer Ellington interview, conducted by Dr. Marcia M. Greenlee, 18 September 1990, 5 and 7 May 1991, SIEOHP, tape 2, AC/NMAH/SI; Donald Hatwell, "He's the Only Duke of Jazz," *Bristol Evening Post* (6 October 1958); Henry Kane, manuscript of Ellington interview feature for his book *How to Write a Song* (published 1962; interview conducted in 1959), collection 301, series 10, AC/NMAH/SI; Simon Kavanaugh, "This Week's Profile: Jazz Is His Life and He Is Jazz," *Coventry Evening Telegraph* (31 October 1958); Msgr. John Saunders interview, conducted by Patricia Willard, 15 September 1989, tape 3, AC/NMAH/SI; Steed, *Duke Ellington*, 21–22. Clippings from DES 4, 11:21, 57, NMAH/SI.

4. This examination of the spiritual influences in Ellington's work before 1965 is based on the following sources: Bob Brier, "The Father and the Duke: Piano-Playing Paulist Priest Sees Mood in Melody as in Prayer," uncited source (4 April 1963), collection 301, series 8, vol. 29, AC/NMAH/SI; Harry T. Cook II, "Jazzman Blends the Sacred, Secular: Duke Ellington Gets Religion into His Music," *Detroit News* (5 July 1969); Helen Oakley Dance interview, conducted by Patricia Willard, 26 and 27 September 1989, SIEOHP, tape 1, AC/NMAH/SI; Stanley Dance, liner notes, *The Ellington Suites* (Pablo, 1976); Duke Ellington interview, CHIC 1956 #1, tape 1, AC/NMAH/SI; Herb Jeffries interview, 22 and 23 September 1989; Mark Tucker, "Retrospection: Ellington, Washington and the Music of Memory" (paper presented at the Ellington '99 International Conference, Washington, D.C., 29 April 1999); "Grace Cathedral Presents a Concert of Sacred Music by Duke Ellington" program, 16 September 1965, San Francisco, collection 301, series 2C, box 15, folder 5, AC/NMAH/SI. Clipping from DES 10:50, NMAH/SI.

For more detail on Ellington's inspirations within the natural world for *The Queens' Suite,* see chapter 10. Many more pre-1965 Ellington compositions than were referenced here can be seen as spiritually influenced; only a sample is presented in this volume.

5. George Avakian interview, conducted by the author, 16 April 2001; Duke Ellington, "My Path of Prayer," *Guideposts* (February 1971), collection 301, series 2C, box 17, folder 2, AC/NMAH/SI; Leonard Feather, "Duke Ellington: New Projects," *International Musician* (April 1967). Clipping from DES 9:47, NMAH/SI.

6. E. Franklin Frazier, *The Black Church in America* (New York, 1964; reprint 1975), 24, 47–50; Nathan O. Hatch, *The Democratization of American Christianity* (New Haven, 1989), 152–

61; LeRoi Jones (Amiri Baraka), *Blues People: Negro Music in White America* (New York, 1963), 38–49; C. Eric Lincoln and Lawrence H. Mamiya, *The Black Church in the African-American Experience* (Durham, 1990), 6–10, 214; Russell Sanjek, *American Popular Music and Its Business,* vol. 1, *From the Beginning to 1790* (New York, 1988), 257–63, Russell Sanjek, *American Popular Music and Its Business,* vol. 2, *From 1790 to 1909* (New York, 1988), 222; Eileen Southern, *The Music of Black Americans: A History* (New York, 1971), 215–17.

7. Frazier, *Black Church in America,* 15–16; Sylvia Frey, *Water from the Rock: Black Resistance in a Revolutionary Age* (Princeton, 1991), 243–65; Hatch, *Democratization of American Christianity,* 102–13; Rhys Isaac, "Evangelical Revolt: The Nature of the Baptist Challenge to the Traditional Order in Virginia, 1765–1775," in *Colonial America,* ed. Stanley Katz, John Murrin, and Douglas Greenberg (New York, 1993), 649–56; Philip D. Morgan, "Slave Life in Piedmont, Virginia, 1720–1800," in *Colonial Chesapeake Society,* ed. Lois Carr, Philip D. Morgan, and Jean Russo (Chapel Hill, 1988), 474–80; Mechal Sobel, *The World They Made Together: Black and White Values in 18th-Century Virginia* (Princeton, 1987), 180–93.

8. Ira Berlin, *Many Thousands Gone: The First Two Centuries of Slavery in North America* (Cambridge, MA, 1998), 151, 252, 272–73, 288–89; Frey, *Water from the Rock*; Hatch, *Democratization of American Christianity*; Allan Kulikoff, "The Origins of Afro-American Society in Tidewater Maryland and Virginia, 1700–1790," in Katz, Murrin, and Greenberg, *Colonial America,* 479–83; Lawrence W. Levine, *Black Culture and Black Consciousness: Afro-American Folk Thought from Slavery to Freedom* (Oxford, 1977), chap. 1; Lincoln and Mamiya, *Black Church in the African-American Experience,* 47; Morgan, "Slave Life in Piedmont."

9. Berlin, *Many Thousands Gone*; Eric Foner, *The Story of American Freedom* (New York, 1998), 44; Frey, *Water from the Rock,* 291–99, 320–22; Lincoln and Mamiya, *Black Church in the African-American Experience,* 52–58, 203; Gayraud S. Wilmore, *Black Religion and Black Radicalism* (Garden City, NJ, 1972), 62–64, 104–24.

10. Frazier, *Black Church in America,* chap. 3; Lincoln and Mamiya, *Black Church in the African-American Experience,* 76; Leon Litwack, *Trouble in Mind: Black Southerners in the Age of Jim Crow* (New York, 1998), 378–403; Wilmore, *Black Religion and Black Radicalism,* 194–200.

11. Levine, *Black Culture and Black Consciousness,* 35–36, 43–47; Litwack, *Trouble in Mind,* 400–401; Wilmore, *Black Religion and Black Radicalism,* 221–35.

Examples of anti-Christian themes in Harlem Renaissance writers: Countee Cullen, "She of the Dancing Feet Sings," in *The New Negro: An Interpretation,* ed. Alain Locke (New York, 1925), 131; Rudolph Fisher, "Shepherd! Lead Us," in *Vestiges: Harlem Sketches,* in Locke, *New Negro,* 75–80; Langston Hughes, "Thursday Afternoon," in *The Portable Harlem Renaissance Reader,* ed. David Levering Lewis (New York, 1994), 595; Claude McKay, *Home to Harlem* (New York, 1928), 52, 176; Claude McKay, "The Negro's Friend," in Lewis, *Portable Harlem Renaissance Reader,* 291; Wallace Thurman, *Infants of the Spring* (Carbondale, IL, 1932; reprint 1979), 102.

12. James B. Gilbert, *Perfect Cities: Chicago's Utopias of 1893* (Chicago, 1991), 38, 170; Lincoln and Mamiya, *Black Church in the African-American Experience,* 359–67; William McLoughlin, *Revivals, Awakenings and Reform: An Essay on Religion and Social Change in America* (Chicago, 1978), 145–60; Alan Rich, "Swinging in Church," *New York Herald Tribune* (16 January 1966); Sanjek, *American Popular Music and Its Business,* 2:210, chap. 8; Brian Ward, *Just My Soul Responding: Rhythm and Blues, Black Consciousness, and Race Relations* (Berkeley, 1998), 192–99. A similar article to Rich's in the religious press, which views the Sacred Concert in the context of centuries of tension between sacred and secular music: Donald P. Hustad, "Music—Jazz in the Church," *Eternity* Looks at the Arts column, *Eternity* (April 1966). Clippings from DES 8:41, 42, NMAH/SI.

13. Taylor Branch, *Parting the Waters: America in the King Years, 1954–1963* (New York, 1988), 228, 335–39, 388–89; Taylor Branch, *Pillar of Fire: America in the King Years, 1963–1965* (New

York, 1998), 24, 46–49, 105; Frazier, *Black Church in America,* 73–79; C. Eric Lincoln, *The Black Church since Frazier* (New York, 1974), 104–9, 135–43; Ward, *Just My Soul Responding*; Cornel West, *Prophetic Fragments* (Grand Rapids, MI, 1988), 161–63. .

14. Branch, *Pillar of Fire,* 302–3; Frazier, *Black Church in America*; Ward, *Just My Soul Responding,* 182–83.

15. Branch, *Pillar of Fire,* chaps. 1 and 18; H. Robert Udkoff interview, conducted by the author, 28 September 1995; Lincoln, *Black Church since Frazier,* chap. 4; Malcolm X, as told to Alex Haley, *The Autobiography of Malcolm X* (New York, 1964), 49, 218–21, 241–43, 247; Wilmore, *Black Religion and Black Radicalism,* 235–37.

16. Grace Cali Burgess, "Jazz Goes to Church," *Sunday San Juan Star* (22 January 1967); Mark S. Harvey, "New World A-Comin': The Sacred Concerts and Duke Ellington's Religious Vision" (paper presented at the Ellington '99 International Conference, Washington, D.C., 30 April 1999); Norman O'Connor, C.S.P, "New Songs unto the Lord," *Saturday Review* (10 April 1965); Steed, *Duke Ellington,* 115–17. Clippings from DES 7, 9:37, 46, respectively, NMAH/SI. In the cited interview, Gensel expressed a view of the relationship between popular music and religion very similar to that expressed by O'Connor in the previous paragraph and footnote.

17. Edward Kennedy Ellington, *Music Is My Mistress* (New York, 1973), 282–85; Rev. John Gensel interview, conducted by the Duke Ellington Society, October 1965, SC Audio C-479, SCBC; Ben Gross, "He Ministers to the Jazzmen," *Sunday Daily News* (12 April 1970); Harvey, "New World A-Comin'"; Joseph Kaye, "Harmonious Blend in Jazz and Religion," *Kansas City Star* (13 January 1963); Lewis K. McMillan, Jr., Swingin' With column, *New York Column* (9 September 1971); Gene Santoro, *Myself When I Am Real: The Life and Music of Charles Mingus* (New York, 2000), 152. Clippings from DES, rolls 5, 13 and 14, vols. 27, 65, and 71, NMAH/SI.

18. Lincoln and Mamiya, *Black Church in the African-American Experience,* 377–80; Daniel Lyman Rideout, "New Church Controversy: Should Jazz Be Played in the Church?" *Baltimore Afro-American* (9 January 1960).

19. This summary of religious music utilizing the jazz, popular, and folk genres before the premiere of Ellington's Sacred Concerts is based on the following sources: Philip E. Elwood, "Regaining the Lost 'Soul': Works of Top Jazz Artists Now Finding a Place in Church," *San Francisco Examiner* (day obscured, September 1965); Leonard Feather, "A Saintly Man Comes Marchin' In," *Los Angeles Times* (17 July 1966); Nat Hentoff, "The Murderous Modes of Jazz: The New Wave Is Telling the Establishment That Modern Jazz Is Out-of-Date," *Esquire* (September 1960); Nat Hentoff, "The 1963 *Playboy* All-Stars: A Look at the Current Jazz Scene and the Winners of the Seventh Annual *Playboy* Poll," *Playboy* (February 1963); Dan Morgenstern, "Newport '66," *Down Beat* (11 August 1966); Thomasina Norford, "Rousing Jazz Revival at Newport," *Amsterdam News* (14 July 1962); O'Connor, "New Songs unto the Lord"; Arnold Rampersad, *The Life of Langston Hughes,* vol. 2, *1941–1967, I Dream a World* (New York, 1988), 381–82, 392–95; Art Seidenbaum, "The Duke in a Different Kingdom," *Los Angeles Times* (8 November 1966); Church of the Redeemer concert program, 26 May 1963, Washington, D.C., collection 301, series 2C, box 15, folder 2, AC/NMAH/SI; "Jazz Goes to Church," *Ebony* (April 1966). Clippings from DES, rolls 3, 5, 8 and 9, vols. 19, 26, 27, 39, and 42–45, NMAH/SI.

20. Reid Badger, *A Life in Ragtime: A Biography of James Reese Europe* (New York, 1995), 54–64; Ted Gioia, *The History of Jazz* (New York, 1997), 31–32; Annie Kuebler, "Spiritual Works of Duke Ellington and Mary Lou Williams: Singing His Praises or Seeking Redemption" (paper presented at the Ellington '99 International Conference, Washington, D.C., 1 May 1999); Mark Tucker, *Ellington: The Early Years* (Urbana, IL, 1991), 6–14, 19–22; Mark Tucker, "Retrospection: Ellington, Washington, and the Music of Memory" (paper presented at the Ellington '99 International Conference, Washington, D.C., 29 April 1999.

21. Reverend C. Julian Bartlett to Duke Ellington, 4 January 1963, collection 301, series 2C, box 15, folder 1, AC/NMAH/SI; interview with the Reverend C. Julian Bartlett, in Steed, *Duke Ellington,* 119; Ellington, "My Path of Prayer"; Sister Mary Felice, W.S., "An Interview with the Duke," *Africa* (Summer 1966), collection 301, series 10, box 4, folder 2, AC/NMAH/SI; Reverend Canon John S. Yaryan to Duke Ellington, 12 February and 1 April 1964, collection 301, series 2C, box 15, folder 1, AC/NMAH/SI.

22. Poppy Cannon White, "God's Gentleman," Poppy's Notes column, *Amsterdam News* (8 January 1966); "In SF Cathedral: Jazz Great Duke Ellington Will Produce Sacred Music Concert," *Sacramento Bee* (27 August 1965). These clippings, and dozens more like them from all over the country, from DES 8:39–41, NMAH/SI.

23. Louis Bellson interview, conducted by the Duke Ellington Society, 1965, SC Audio C-481, SCBC; "The Duke—American Gospel," Upward and Onward column, *Whitehouse Station (NJ) Hunterdon Review* (date obscured—c. January 1966). Clipping from DES 8:41, NMAH/SI.

24. The number of Sacred Concerts from 1966 to 1969 is taken from a list that appears to have been compiled by Duke Ellington, Inc.: uncited author, "Duke Ellington's Sacred Concerts, 1965, 1966, 1967, and 1968 [and 1969]," collection 301, series 2C, box 15, folder 10, AC/NMAH/SI.

For more on the historical background of "Come Sunday" and the spiritual section of *Black, Brown and Beige,* consult chapter 7.

The description of the First Sacred Concert is based on the version of the concert recorded at its second performance in New York City later in 1965, which was released as an album the next year. This was the final version of the program that Ellington toured with for the next three years. In the first performance of the Sacred Concert at Grace Cathedral, two non-Ellington pieces were performed that were dropped from all subsequent performances of the program: a medley of older spiritual songs by the Herman McCoy choir and a piece by Richard I. Purvis called "Purvis a la Jazz Hot": "Grace Cathedral Presents" program, AC/NMAH/SI.

25. Duke Ellington interview, CHIC 1964 #3, tape 1, AC/NMAH/SI; The Smithsonian Institution Ellington Oral History Project: Joya Sherrill interview, conducted by Dr. Marcia M. Greenlee, 15 August 1989, SIEOHP, tape 3, AC/NMAH/SI; Steed, *Duke Ellington,* 120.

26. Louis Cassells, "'Modern' Teachings Result in Friction: Why a Liberal Bishop Faces Heresy Charges," *Boston Traveler* (27 August 1965), from collection 301, series 8, vol. 29, AC/NMAH/SI; Joan Didion, *The White Album* (New York, 1979), 51–52; Gensel interview, October 1965; Ben Williams, "Cathedral and Jazz: Duke's Sacred Concert," *San Francisco Examiner* (27 August 1965). Clipping from DES 8:39, NMAH/SI.

27. This summary of the reaction to the initial Sacred Concert is based on the following sources: Olivia Bartlett, "Duke Ellington at the Cathedral," *Faith at Work* (December 1965), collection 301, series 2C, box 15, folder 5, AC/NMAH/SI; Bunny Briggs interview, conducted by the Duke Ellington Society, 1967, SC Audio C-490, SCBC; Frank Chesley, "The Durable Duke," *The Stars and Stripes* (11 May 1966); Felice, "An Interview with the Duke"; "Cathedral Echoes to Jazzman's Hymns," *San Antonio Evening News* (17 September 1965); Don Mullen, "Duke Swings Prayers in Cathedral Concert: Religious Program in San Francisco Entrances Standing-Room Audience," *Pittsburgh Press* (17 September 1965); "Glimpses: Ellington to New Peak," *Kansas City Times* (18 September 1965). Clipping from DES 8:39, 40, NMAH/SI. Dozens of stories about the Grace Cathedral concert are in these scrapbooks; most of them are dispatches from AP, UPI, or Herald-Tribune news wires—one example of each is provided in the footnote. The Chesley article is from DES 3:15.

28. George Dugan, "Numbers Are Greeted by Loud Applause of Crowded House," *New York Times* (27 December 1965); Reverend John G. Gensel, Dr. Bryant M. Kirkland (two separate press releases), 19 November 1965, collection 301, series 2C, box 15, folder 1, AC/NMAH/SI;

Marnie Mellblom, "On Hearing Jazz in Church," *Lutheran* (2 March 1966); White, "Poppy's Notes"; "Duke Ellington: Concert of Sacred Music," *Fifth Avenue Voice* (newsletter of the Fifth Avenue Presbyterian Church) (December 1965), collection 301, series 2C, box 15, folder 9, AC/NMAH/SI. Clipping from DES 8:40–42, NMAH/SI.

29. Dr. Bryant M. Kirkland, "Jazz and the Ministry of Fifth Avenue Presbyterian Church" draft for program essay (c. December 1965), collection 301, series 2C, box 15, folder 8, AC/NMAH/SI; "Duke Jazz Concert Set for Gotham Church," *Cincinnati Enquirer* (19 December 1965); "Ellington's Church Music: His Personal Statement," *Pittsburgh Courier* (20 January 1966). Clipping from DES 8:40–41, NMAH/SI.

30. Alan Rich, "Ellington's Music as Prayer," *New York Herald-Tribune* (28 December 1965); Peter J. Shaw, "2,000 People Hear Jazz Music Leader: Duke Ellington Gave a Concert in Gotham Church," *Hartford City (IN) News-Times* (27 December 1965); "Ellington's Jazz Fills Historic Church," *New York Journal-American* (27 December 1965); "Praise Him with Sound of Trumpet," *Haddonfield (NJ) Town Crier & Herald* (6 January 1966); "Jazz Goes to Church" *Ebony* (April 1966); Clipping from DES 8:40–41, NMAH/SI.

31. Joe Brieg, "Can Tap Dancing Glorify God?" *Ave Maria* (19 March 1966); Hustad, Music—Jazz in the Church"; Mellblom, "On Hearing Jazz in Church." Clipping from DES 8:40–41, NMAH/SI.

32. Reverend Wm. Vanden Berg, "Life and Character: A Weekly Series of Inspirational Comment," *Boyden (IA) Reporter* (24 February 1966); Rev. Gene Garrison, "Strange Things Are Happening," Ministerially Speaking column, *Altus (OK) Times-Democrat* (6 May 1966); Mrs. Chester M. Hanks, "Repudiates Jazz as Worship Form" letter to the editor, *Baltimore News-American* (17 January 1966); Eleanor Taylor, "Ellington's 'Sacred Jazz Concert'" letter to the editor, *Des Moines Register* (30 January 1966); "Ellington Concert Idea Lauded Here," *Tulsa Tribune* (27 December 1965); "Guest Editorial: Is This Church Worship?" *Norman (OK) Transcript* (10 January 1966); "Jazz in Church Brings Protest from Wyrtzen," *Paterson (NJ) Morning News* (15 January 1966); "Jazz, Tap Dancing—Out of Step in Church," *Tampa Sentinel Bulletin* (22 January 1966). Clipping from DES 8:40–43, NMAH/SI.

For more on the cultural clashes of the 1960s in the United States, consult: Terry H. Anderson, *The Movement and the Sixties: Protest in America from Greensboro to Wounded Knee* (New York, 1995); Tom Engelhardt, *The End of Victory Culture: Cold War United States and the Disillusioning of a Generation* (New York, 1995); Todd Gitlin, *The Sixties: Years of Hope, Days of Rage* (Toronto, 1987).

33. Michael Zwerin, "Kliegs," Jazz Journal column, *Village Voice* (13 January 1966).

34. Aubrey Chalmers, "God Gave Us Talents . . . We Offer Them Back, Says Ellington: Why the Duke Played Jazz in a Cathedral," *Daily Sketch* (22 February 1966). Clipping from DES 8:41, NMAH/SI.

35. Frazier, *Black Church in America*, 21–22; Gioia, *History of Jazz*; Lincoln and Mamiya, *Black Church in the African-American Experience*, 5, 380; Albert Murray, *Stomping the Blues* (New York, 1976), 1–38, 144; "Jazz Goes to Church" *Ebony* (April 1966).

36. Dr. Bryant M. Kirkland to Duke Ellington, 21 January 1966, collection 301, series 2C, box 15, folder 1, AC/NMAH/SI; Jack Smith, "Ella's Not Content and Doesn't Believe She's 'The Greatest,'" *Washington Post* (27 December 1966); *Jet,* "Duke Flooded with Requests for Church Concerts" (10 February 1966). Clippings from DES 8, 9:41, 45, NMAH/SI.

37. The October 1965 booking contracts, along with the 16 September 1965 contract with Grace Cathedral that documents Ellington and the orchestra working for scale that night ($592.38), are located in collection 301, series 3A, boxes 5 and 6, AC/NMAH/SI. The 1966 booking contracts are located in collection 301, series 3A, box 6, AC/NMAH/SI—the Sacred Concerts noted occurred on the following 1966 dates: 25 April: 22 July: 14 August: 17 Septem-

ber: 6 and 20 October: 10 and 20 November: 4, 5, 7, 8 December. At least two 1966 Sacred Concerts were not found in the booking contracts: 18 October at Albion College, and 15 November at Temple Emmanuel in Beverly Hills, CA. It is likely that Ellington elected to receive no compensation for these performances.

The 1968 and 1969 booking contracts are located in collection 301, series 3A, boxes 7 and 8, AC/NMAH/SI. The higher asking price for the band, in both sacred and nonsacred shows, probably also had to do with the return of Cress Courtney to the Ellington fold as a personal manager in late 1967 or early 1968. Courtney, according to many sources, pushed Ellington's booking agency, Joe Glaser's Associated Booking Corporation, to demand higher guarantees. The fact that this policy succeeded in increasing the band's asking price at far beyond the rate of inflation, as seen in comparisons between October 1965 and October 1968, shows that there was credence in the charges leveled by Ellington and George Wein, detailed in chapters 9 and 10, that Glaser habitually undercharged for the Ellington orchestra's bookings.

Cress Courtney interview, conducted by the Duke Ellington Society, 1970, SC Audio-499, SCBC.

Courtney's policy of demanding higher guarantees is spoken about in the following sources: Oscar Cohen interview, conducted by Dr. Marcia M. Greenlee, 17 June 1992, SIEOHP, tape 1, AC/NMAH/SI; Shirley Courtney interview, conducted by Dr. Marcia M. Greenlee, 3 February 1992, SIEOHP, tape 2, AC/NMAH/SI; S. Dance interview, 28 August 1990, tape 5; George Wein interview, conducted by Dr. Marcia M. Greenlee, 9 May 1991, SIEOHP, tape 1, AC/NMAH/SI.

38. ASCAP memos: Weighting Formula (New Section H), 30 September 1960, and ASCAP memo #7854, 2 March 1962, both found in collection 301, series 3, box 102, folder 4, AC/NMAH/SI.

Rev. Robert M. Herhold, "The Duke: Sound for the Sanctuaries," *National Catholic Reporter* (23 November 1966), found in DES 9:45, NMAH/SI...

39. George Armstrong, "Duke Ellington . . . : Music Innovations in Church Urged," *Charleston Mail* (4 October 1966); Ed Bridges, "Jazz Music in Church?" *Hudson (MA) Sun* (20 March 1967); Lester Kinsolving, "The Jazz Mass Movement," News in Religion column, *San Francisco Chronicle* (26 March 1966); Dennis McKeown, "The Sublime Beat—Jazz in Temple," *Daily News* (13 February 1966); "Jazz Trend 'Recognizes an Illness,'" *Lincoln (NE) Journal and Star* (20 February 1966). Clippings from DES, rolls 8 and 9, vols. 41, 42, 44 and 46, NMAH/SI.

40. First AME Zion Church program: "Duke Ellington in a Concert of Sacred Music," 10 March 1966, Brooklyn, NY, collection 301, series 2C, box 15, folder 13, AC/NMAH/SI; "Ellington Concert to Aid AME Zion," *Newburgh News* (2 September 1966). Clipping from DES 9:44, NMAH/SI.

41. John Cogley, "Duke Ellington, at 67, Is Starting a New Chapter: His Religious Jazz Is Now in Demand in Secular Spots; It Started Last Year with a Concert in a Cathedral," *New York Times* (13 August 1966); "At College of Idaho: 'Sell-Out' Audience Hears Duke Ellington," *Boise (ID) Statesman* (10 October 1965). Clippings from DES 8, 9:40, 44, NMAH/SI.

42. Herhold, "The Duke"; Rev. Robert M. Herhold, "Ellington's Way," *Episcopalian* (January 1967); Serge Huff, "Composer Duke Ellington in Top Form: Sacred Jazz Concert Is Effective," *Phoenix Gazette* (11 November 1966). Clippings from DES 9:45, NMAH/SI.

43. Temple Emanuel program, "Temple Emanuel Presents a Concert of Sacred Music by Duke Ellington," 15 November 1966, Beverly Hills, CA, collection 301, series 2C, box 15, folder 21, AC/NMAH/SI; Feather, "Duke Ellington: New Projects"; Leonard Feather, "Duke's Concert Features Spirit of Reverence, Respect," *Los Angeles Times* (17 November 1966); Seidenbaum, "Duke in a Different Kingdom"; *Hep,* gossip column (February 1967). Clippings from DES 9:45, NMAH/SI.

For more on the rifts that developed between American blacks and Jews in the 1960s, consult: Jonathan Kaufman, *Broken Alliance: The Turbulent Times between Blacks and Jews in America* (New York, 1988); Robert G. Weisbord and Arthur Stein, *Bittersweet Encounter: The Afro-American and the American Jew* (Westport, CT, 1970).

44. This account of the December 1966 Sacred Concert in Washington, D.C., is based on the following sources: Eric Blanchard, "Won't Debate Clergymen: The Duke Says His Music Is Sincere and Sacred," *Washington Post* (6 December 1966); John Carmody, "Baptist Ministers Refuse to Endorse the 'Worldly' Music of Duke Ellington," *Washington Post* (1 December 1966); Phil Casey, "The Duke Will Play Despite Rebuff," *Washington Post* (3 December 1966); Kenneth Dole, "Pastor Explains Opposition to Jazz Music in Liturgy," Washington Churchmen column, *Washington Post* (7 January 1967); Duke Ellington, "Duke Ellington Explains His Views on Communications and the Artist," *Washington Post* (3 December 1966); Jean T. Faught and Kenneth C. Turner, "Ellington Shock" letters to the editor, *Washington Post* (5 December 1966); Roy Meachum, "Ellington and the Ministers," WTOP-AM news editorial, 2 December 1966; Larry A. Still, "Ellington's Sacred Music Concert Divides Clergy," *Washington Evening Star* (1 December 1966); "Duke, Pastors Fail to Harmonize," *Cleveland News* (2 December 1966); "Duke Ellington's Sacred Music under Attack," Names and Faces column, *Evansville (IN) Press* (2 December 1966); "Ellington 'Just a Messenger,'" *Athens (GA) News* (3 December 1966); "Duke Responds to Criticism," *Northern Wyoming News* (6 December 1966); "We Ain't Ready Club," *Washington D.C. Capitol Spotlight* (15 December 1966). Clippings and radio editorial from DES 9:45, NMAH/SI.

For more on the history of black Washington, D.C, society from 1880 to 1920, consult chapter 1. For more on the 1951 "we ain't ready" controversy, consult chapter 8.

45. George M. Collins, "Duke's Sacred Concert Swings to Cambridge," *Boston Globe* (18 March 1967); Issachar Miron, "Rocking the Cradle of the Lord," *New York Times* (9 February 1969); John S. Wilson, "Jazz and Church: Oil-Water Mix?" *New York Times* (15 January 1967); "Christmas 1966: Changes in the Churches Reflected in Celebration of the Holiday Season; Jazz, Folk Services Planned; In Chicago Garage, Christ Child Sleeps in Inner Tube; In Harlem, the Pain of Wanting," *Wall Street Journal* (22 December 1966); "Jazz and Religion—End of a Love Affair?" *Down Beat* (23 February 1967); The Week in Religion column, *Erie Morning News* (9 March 1968); "Dave Brubeck Unveils Oratorio on Jesus," *Christianity Today* (29 March 1968). Clippings from DES, rolls 9 and 11, vols. 45, 46, 48, and 58, NMAH/SI.

46. Herhold, "The Duke"; "A Duke (Musical) and a Bishop (Episcopal) Jam: Ellington and Donegan Play, and Discuss Sacred Work, at St. John the Divine," *New York Times* (16 January 1968). Clippings from DES 10:51, NMAH/SI.

47. Marty Bennett, "Ellington's 'Sacred Concert' Fills N.Y. Church with 5,000 Faithful at $15 Top," *Variety* (24 January 1968); Mary Campbell, "6,000 in Church Praise Ellington's 2nd Concert," *Standard Times* (20 January 1968); Joseph Feurey, "The Duke's 'Sermon' Rocks a Cathedral," *New York Post* (20 January 1968); William Maki, "Ellington at Cathedral," *Episcopal New Yorker* (February 1968); Peter McLaughlin, "A Big Turnout—Like Christmas or Easter," *New York Daily News* (20 January 1968); Douglas Watt, "Duke Plays Sacred Concert and 7,500 Jam Cathedral," *New York Daily News* (20 January 1968); John S. Wilson, "Ellington's 'Sacred Concert' Is Given Premiere: 7,500 Throng St. John the Divine for a Sample of the Duke's Artistry," *New York Times* (20 January 1968); "Sacred Concert Presented by Duke Ellington," *Mahanoy City (PA) Record-American* (20 January 1968). Clippings from DES 10:51, NMAH/SI.

48. Whitney Balliett, "Which Ellington Are You?" Jazz Concerts column, *New Yorker* (3 February 1968); Collier, *Duke Ellington*.

49. The sources for this discussion on the theme of freedom in the Second Sacred Concert are: Jerry Carroll, "A Jazzman with Visions of God," *San Francisco Chronicle* (13 April 1968);

Helen Dance, "God Has Those Angels," Mid-Month Recordings column, *Saturday Review* (13 April 1968); Duke Ellington, program notes, *Second Sacred Concert* (Prestige, 1974); Foner, *Story of American Freedom,* introduction, 223, 236–44, 260, 276–79; Hollie I. West, "Ellington Explains His Music," *Washington Post* (12 March 1970). Clippings from DES, rolls 9 and 12, vols. 48, 49, and 63, NMAH/SI.

Chapter Fourteen

1. This performance is from *A Duke Named Ellington* (Council for Positive Images, Inc., 1988), LOC/MPD. Other examples of live Ellington footage from the 1960s and 1970s, all available at the Library of Congress Motion Picture Division, most from the Jerry Valburn Collection: *Concert of Sacred Music* (KQED, San Francisco, 1965), *The Duke* (Canadian Broadcasting Corporation, 1965), *Duke Ellington at the Cote D'Azur* (Norman Granz/Alexander Arens, 1966), *Duke Ellington and Friends* (WHA Radio Madison/WMVS-TV Milwaukee, 1972), *Duke Ellington: Love You Madly* (KQED San Francisco, 1967), *Duke Ellington: Reminiscing In Tempo* (Robert Levi Films, 1992), *Indigo—Musikaliska Intermezzon Med Duke Ellington Orkester* (Danish TV, Arne Arnbom, 1963), *On the Road with Duke Ellington* (NBC, 1967), *Praise God and Dance: The Second Scared Music Concert* (Swedish TV, Arne Arnbom, 1969), *The Twentieth Century: Duke Ellington Swings Through Japan* (CBS News, 1964), *Unidentified Ellington/Valburn #1* (Paris, ORTF, 1970).

2. Dr. Arthur Logan interview, conducted by the Duke Ellington Society, 1964, SC Audio C-452, side 2, SCBC.

3. Leonard Feather, "Jazz—Beginning or Dead End?" *Variety* (25 March 1964); Leonard Feather, "Jazz Hindsight 1969," *International Musician* (February 1970); Nat Hentoff, "Jazz and Pop '68," *Playboy* (February 1968); Nat Hentoff, "Jazz and Pop '69," *Playboy* (February 1969); Nat Hentoff, "Jazz and Pop '70," *Playboy* (February 1970); Bob Micklin, "Jazz on the Upbeat Again?" *Newsday* (14 December 1972); Dan Morgenstern interview, conducted by the Duke Ellington Society, 1966, SC Audio C-485, Schomburg Center for Black Culture; Bill Morrison, "Horrors! *Down Beat* Mixes Jazz and Rock," *Raleigh (NC) News and Observer* (22 June 1967); "'67 Readers Poll," *Down Beat* (28 December 1967). Clippings from DES, rolls 7, 10, 11, 12, and 16, vols. 34, 49, 51, 52, 58, 63, and 76, NMAH/SI.

For more on the artists and organizations mentioned at the start of this paragraph, please consult chapter 9.

4. Talk of the Town column, *New Yorker* (24 June 1967); Leonard Feather, "Teen Music Is Maturing: But Standard Tunes Still Thrive," *Canton Repository* (23 July 1967); Nat Hentoff, Soundings column, *Jazz & Pop* (October 1968); Alan Rich, "Jazz and Classical Styles Converging," *New York World Journal Tribune* (23 April 1967). Clippings from DES, rolls 9, 10, and 11, vols. 47, 49, and 57, NMAH/SI.

For examples of critics viewing Ellington as a serious composer and artist during the 1930s and hassling him about his extended works, consult chapter 4.

5. Burns Bennett, "Rotary Promises Danceable Music," *Montgomery Advertiser and Alabama Journal* (9 February 1969); Henry Butler, "Fiedler, Ellington Show U.S.' Musical Progress," *Indianapolis News* (7 August 1967); Gil Rowland, "What's Doing: Jazz Fans Like Duke," *Greenville (SC) Piedmont* (30 June 1969); Charles H. Roper, "4,800 Enjoy Brilliance of Ellington, His Orchestra," *Memphis Press Scimitar* (31 January 1969). Clippings from DES, rolls 10, 11, and 12, vols. 49, 58, and 61, NMAH/SI.

6. Del Carnes, "He's Not Afraid of the Hippies," Backstage column, *Denver Post* (24 August 1967); Amy Lee, "Duke Ellington Plays to Suburban Swingers," *Christian Science Monitor* (23 October 1967); John S. Wilson, "Ellington Swings at Rock Emporium," *New York Times* (6 December 1968). Clippings from DES, rolls 10 and 11, vols. 49, 50, and 57, NMAH/SI.

7. This discussion of the 1965 Pulitzer Prize controversy, except as indicated, is based on the following sources: "Ellington's Snub Still Draws Raps," *Philadelphia Afro-American* (29 May 1965); "Very Too Bad," *Newsweek* (17 May 1965); "He's Still the Duke," *Boston Record American* (7 May 1965); "Is the Board Deaf?" *Minneapolis Tribune* (30 May 1965) (also in the 1 June 1965 issue of *National Review*); Ralph J. Gleason, "A Prize Insult to Duke Ellington," On the Town column, *San Francisco Chronicle* (12 May 1965); Nat Hentoff, "This Cat Needs No Pulitzer Prize," *New York Times Magazine* (12 September 1965); Irving Kolodin, "No Duke for 'Duke'–BBC, BRdCG," Music to My Ears column, *Saturday Review* (29 May 1965); Laurence P. Neal, "The Genius and the Prize," *Liberator* (October 1965); William F. Woo, "Another Pulitzer Prize Hassle: Furor over Duke Ellington Citation Latest in Series of Controversies," *St. Louis Post-Dispatch* (23 May 1965). Clippings from DES 7:37, 38, NMAH/SI. There are dozens more clippings in these files about the Pulitzer controversy than have been listed here.

8. Robert Bendiner, "The Truth about the Pulitzer Prize Awards," *McCalls* (May 1966). Clipping from DES 8:43, NMAH/SI.

9. Mary Blume, "The Duke Rides Upswing with Lead in Movie," *Los Angeles Times* (12 February 1967); Hentoff, "This Cat"; Roger Kahle, "Special Interview with Duke Ellington," *This Day* (July 1968); A. H. Lawrence, *Duke Ellington and His World* (New York, 2001), 364. Clippings from DES 9, 11:46, 54, NMAH/SI.

For a discussion of the Ellington orchestra's 1945 memorial radio program for Franklin Roosevelt, see chapter 8.

10. Duke Ellington, *Music Is My Mistress* (New York, 1973), 476–78.

11. "Duke Ellington (67) Services to Be Engaged November 16," *Pacific Beach (CA) Sentinel* (10 November 1966); "The 1967 Playboy All-Stars' All-Stars," *Playboy* (February 1967); Digby Diehl, "Panel Discusses Role of Jazz in America," *Los Angeles Times* (22 November 1966); Ron Ellik, "Ellington's Music Epitome of Jazz," *Santa Ana (CA) Register* (20 November 1966); Phillip Elwood, "UC to Honor Ellington," *San Francisco Examiner* (3 July 1969); T. E. Forman, "The Duke: Sound of Music Makes It Good," *Riverside (CA) Press* (19 November 1966); David Otis, "In S. B. Concert: 'The Duke' Speaks: Jazz Sophisticated," *San Bernardino (CA) Sun-Telegram* (19 November 1966); Dale Stevens, "Ellington's 1st Lecture Draws Standing Ovation," *Cincinnati Post* (14 April 1966). Clippings from DES, rolls 8 and 9, vols. 42, 45, and 46, NMAH/SI. The 1969 clipping is from DES 12:61.

12. "1967 Playboy All-Stars' All-Stars," *Playboy;* "Jazz Series Scheduled at Stanford," *Los Angeles Times* (1 June 1965). Clipping from DES 7:38, NMAH/SI.

13. "Jazz on the Upswing at the White House," *Down Beat* (16 July 1964); Willis Conover interview, conducted by the Duke Ellington Society, 1967, SC Audio C-489, Schomburg Center for Black Culture; Dorothy McCardle, "Johnson Wants Art at the Grass Roots to Start Growing," *Washington Post* (14 December 1966); George T. Simon, "Acclaim in Russia, Neglect in U.S.," The Jazz Beat column, *New York Herald-Tribune* (28 May 1961). Clippings from DES 7, 9:35, 45, NMAH/SI. The Simon clipping is from collection 301, series 9, box 7, folder 24, AC/NMAH/SI. .

14. "Name-Dropping: First Kennedy in White House," *Boston Globe* (20 June 1965); Milton Esterow, "White House Art Festival to Be Extensive," *Lakeland (FL) Ledger* (30 May 1965); Bonnie Angelo, "Culture Orgy at the White House," *Long Island Press* (15 June 1965); Eric F. Goldman, "The White House and the Intellectuals," *Harpers* (January 1969); Wauhillau La Hey, "It's White Tie for the Duke," *Cincinnati Post* (10 March 1969); Saul Maloff, "Art and Vietnam: The White House Festival," *Commonweal* (9 July 1965); Nan Robertson, "Arts Hold Sway at White House: Mrs. Johnson Greets 400 at Cultural Festival," *New York Times* (15 June 1965); Howard Taubman, "White House Salutes Culture in America: Dissent of Artists on Foreign

Policy Stirs 400 at All-Day Fete," *New York Times* (15 June 1965). Clippings from DES 7:38, NMAH/SI. The articles from 1969 are from DES 11:58.

Willis Conover says that he, along with George Avakian, recommended Duke Ellington to the White House for the festival to be "the climax of the whole thing . . . you'd have a fair panorama of what American music really is": Conover interview, 1967.

For more on J. E. Ellington's work as a butler in the White House, see chapter 1.

15. "Jazz on the Upswing," *Down Beat;* "LBJ Pledges to End Color Bar in Jobs," *Rocky Mountain News* (5 August 1967); "White House Jam Session: All the Way without LBJ," *Chicago Daily News* (22 November 1968); "First Lady Begins Last Official Trip: Speaks to New Citizens—Visits New Orleans Slum," *New York Times* (23 November 1968); uncited author, press release, "Duke Ellington Is Honored at White House and Joins Mrs. Johnson on New Orleans Trip" (18 November 1968), collection 301, series 11, box 2, folder 6, AC/NMAH/SI; Alice Hughes, "Yale University Awards Honor to Duke Ellington," A Woman's New York column, *Laconia (NH) Citizen* (11 August 1967). Clippings from DES 10, 11:49, 57, NMAH/SI.

16. This section on the 1966 Dakar festival, except as indicated, is based on the following sources: "Negro Arts Festival Receives Wild Sendoff," *Waterbury (CT) Republican* (2 April 1966); Ellington, *Music Is My Mistress,* 337–39; Barry Farrell, "Within the Show's Excitement, the Deeper Issue of Negritude," *Life* (22 April 1966); Sister Mary Felice, W.S., "An Interview with the Duke," *Africa* (Summer 1966); Hoyt W. Fuller, "Assessment and Questions: Festival Postscripts," *Negro Digest* (June 1966); Hoyt W. Fuller, "World Festival of Negro Arts: Senegal Fete Illustrates Philosophy of 'Negritude,'" *Ebony* (July 1966); Lloyd Garrison, "'The Duke, and Those Fabulous Dancers,'" *New York Times* (24 April 1966); Lloyd Garrison, "Debate on 'Negritude' Splits Festival in Dakar," *New York Times* (25 April 1966); Arthur Griffiths, "Little Sermon by the 'Duke,'" *Rochester Times-Union* (14 March 1966); Mary Rodlee Henry, "'The Boom-Boom Never Flagged'—Senegal's First World Festival of Negro Arts," *Vogue* (September 1966); Donald H. Louchheim, "U.S. Artists Impressive at Dakar, but Organizational Effort Is Rapped," *Washington Post* (8 April 1966); Charles Sanders, "Africans Disappointed in U.S.," *Jet* (5 May 1966); Richard F. Shepard, "105 U.S. Negro Artists Prepare for Senegal Arts Fete in April," *New York Times* (11 February 1966); Richard F. Shepard, "10 Painters Quit Negro Festival in Dispute with U.S. Committee," *New York Times* (10 March 1966); Penny Von Eschen, *Satchmo Blows Up the World: Jazz Ambassadors Play the Cold War* (Cambridge, MA, 2004), 150; Edward Wakin, "An African for All Seasons," *Sign* (October 1966). Clippings from DES 8, 9:41–44, NMAH/SI.

The article in *Africa* is from collection 301, series 10, box 4, folder 2, AC/NMAH/SI.

Reports of 75, 105, and 130 American participants are cited in three different articles listed above.

17. Two State Department documents from three years later showed that government officials feared the unpredictability of younger jazz artists like Miles Davis, Dizzy Gillespie, and Thelonius Monk, and strongly discouraged including them in State Department–sponsored tours. Gillespie is described as "anathema," while one official states confidently that Davis would not be approved for state tours. A quote from the second-listed document: "Dept's jazz panel advises no repeat no official involvement Monk or Davis. Both excellent artists but . . . not recommended by Dept's jazz panel because of their eccentricity." Thomas D. Huff, "Meeting on the Duke Ellington Tour," 3 June 1969, MC-468, box 61, folder 10; Richards, State Department telegram, 10 October 1969, MC-468, box 61, folder 19. Both documents from BECAHC/SCD/UAL.

18. The sources for this paragraph are: "African Festival," *Dayton Daily News* (23 April 1966); Fran Allred, "Dr. Garrett Reports: Russian Snow Job Seen at Negro Arts Festival," *Charleston (WV) Gazette* (6 May 1966); Betty Flynn, "Report from Senegal: A Meeting of Artists in Af-

rica," *Chicago Daily News* (14 May 1966); Lloyd Garrison, "A Gentle Cold War Wind Wafts through Senegal's Festival of Negro Arts," *New York Times* (19 April 1966); Garrison, "'The Duke.'" Clippings from DES 8:42, 43, NMAH/SI.

19. Information about the Ellington/Senghor meeting and attendance estimates are from the following State Department documents: Duke Ellington Africa Recapitulation, 31 March–9 April 1966, and Mercer Cook, Senghor Receives American Specialists, 12 April 1966, both MC-468, box 61, folder 7, BECAHC/SCD/UAL.

According to the first document, the Ellington orchestra was paid $37,184 during the ten days of festival and travel, almost exactly split between transportation and compensation.

20. Duke Ellington, *Black, Brown and Beige,* undated and unpublished narrative sketch (c. late 1942 or early 1943), collection 415, series 6, folder 7, AC/NMAH/SI. © 2004 Estate of Mercer K. Ellington, cannot be reproduced without permission from the estate.

21. "Society: The Inaugural Balls," *Jet* (6 February 1969); "Nixon Reviews First 100 Days for Record of 'Good History,'" *Salt Lake Tribune* (28 April 1969); Charlotte Curtis, "Thousands of Jubilant Republicans Celebrate at Six Inaugural Balls: Glittering Assemblages Cheer the Nixon Family," *New York Times* (21 January 1969). Clippings from DES 11, 12:58, 59, NMAH/SI.

22. This section on Ellington's 29 April 1969 appearance at the White House, except as indicated, is based on the following sources: "The 'Duke's' Birthday to Be Held at White House," *Springfield (OH) Sun* (25 April 1969); "White House: Soul Night," *Time* (9 May 1969); "The Duke's Party," *New Yorker* (10 May 1969); "Jazz Night at the White House—Honoring the Duke," *U.S. News and World Report* (12 May 1969); "If You Love Me, Feed My Sheep," *Oklahoma City Black Dispatch* (20 March 1969); Stanley Dance, "Ellington at the White House," *Saturday Review* (31 May 1969); Ellington, *Music Is My Mistress,* 424–28; John Edward Hasse, *Beyond Category: The Life and Genius of Duke Ellington* (New York, 1993), 373–74; Robert E. Johnson, "History-Making Honor for Black American Draws Plaudits," *Jet* (15 May 1969); Irv Kupcinet, "Swinger Nixon Hosts Jazz Greats at White House Bash," *Ashtabula (OH) Star-Beacon* (1 May 1969); Myra MacPherson, "A History-Making Party," *Washington Post* (1 May 1969); Nan Robertson, "Duke Ellington, 70, Honored at White House," *New York Times* (30 April 1969). Clippings from DES 11, 12:58–60, NMAH/SI. For a listing of Billy Strayhorn's "four freedoms," consult chapter 13.

23. Sources for this paragraph: Craig A. Boike, "Duke Ellington—His Music and Moods: 'Duke's' Music Something You Feel," *Saginaw News* (10 May 1969); Amy Lee, "Mood Ellington: Duke's Day," *Christian Science Monitor* (25 April 1969); Sabra Tate, About Town column, *McAlester (OK) News-Capital* (3 May 1969). Clippings from DES 11, 12:58, 59, NMAH/SI.

24. George A. Hoffman to Steven A. Burn, 29 April 1969, series 3E, box 103, folder 38; Steven A. Burn to George A. Hoffman, 2 May 1969, series 3G, box 115, folder 9. Both letters from collection 301, AC/NMAH/SI.

25. "Don't Be Fooled by the Icing on Top the Cake," *Washington D.C. Afro-American* (3 May 1969); "Of Things to Come?" *Louisville Defender* (29 May 1969); Diggs Dietrich, National Hotline column, *Pittsburgh Courier* (24 May 1969); Ethel L. Payne, "Story behind Duke Ellington's Fete," *Chicago Daily Defender* (5 May 1969); Robertson, "Duke Ellington, 70, Honored"; Carl T. Rowan, "Some Domestic Failures: High Score for Nixon," *(New Bedford, MA) Standard Times* (1 May 1969). Clippings from DES 11, 12:58–60, NMAH/SI.

26. Kenneth O'Reilly, *Nixon's Piano: Presidents and Racial Politics from Washington to Clinton* (New York, 1995), 321–22; Anthony Summers, *The Arrogance of Power: The Secret World of Richard Nixon* (New York, 2000), 354–56. Nixon's private anti-Semitic comments are also a matter of public record.

27. Richard Halloran, "'Silent Majority,' U.S.I.A. Film, Fails to Stir Foreigners," *New York Times* (30 January 1970). Clipping from DES 12:63, NMAH/SI.

The film *Duke Ellington at the White House* was not shown domestically, since "a couple" of the band members that night refused to sign waivers to let their performances be released "because they didn't want to be associated with Nixon": Bill Berry interview, conducted by Yale American Studies course, 2 December 1977, #510A, pg. 19, OHAM/YUSC.

28. Betty Beale, "Nixon's Fete Duke Ellington," *New York Daily Column and Knickerbocker* (27 April 1969); Earl Wilson, "The Duke's Got a Secret," It Happened Last Night column, *New York Post* (29 July 1969). Clippings from DES 12:59, 61, NMAH/SI.

29. This discussion of Ellington's conservatism in his later years is based on the following sources: Stanley Dance interview, conducted by Dr. Marcia Greenlee, 28 August 1990, SIEOHP, tape 5, AC/NMAH/SI; Mercer Ellington with Stanley Dance, *Duke Ellington in Person: An Intimate Memoir* (Boston, 1978), 157–58; Mercer Ellington interview, conducted by Dick Buckley, March 1980, OHAM/YUSC, #521B, pg. 4–5; Robert and Evelyn Udkoff interview, conducted by Dr. Marcia Greenlee, 11 March 1991, SIEOHP, tape 3, AC/NMAH/SI; H. Robert Udkoff interview, conducted by the author, 28 September 1995; Walt Whitaker, "Duke Speaks Out on Prayer," *Kansas City Times* (26 September 1969). Clipping from DES 12:62, NMAH/SI.

Ellington's honorary chairmanship of the Portland chapter of the Right to Life Committee: photograph and caption, *Portland (OR) Catholic Sentinel* (3 March 1972). From DES 15:73.

For Mercer Ellington's later comments on his father and homosexuals, see David Hajdu, *Lush Life: A Biography of Billy Strayhorn* (New York, 1996), 79–80

For more on Ellington's view of questioners during his 1963 state-sponsored tour, see chapter 13.

For more on the Ellington/Strayhorn friendship, see chapters 6, 8, 9, and 10.

30. *Time,* "Jazz: Keeping up with the Duke" (14 April 1967); Wally Trabing, "A Chat with Duke Ellington," Mostly about People column, *Santa Cruz (CA) Sentinel* (c. September 1964). Clippings from DES 7, 9:36, 46, NMAH/SI.

"Duke Ellington and His World-Famous Orchestra," 1965 publicity manual, Duke Ellington clipping file, IJS/RU.

31. Leonard Feather, "Duke Ellington: New Projects, New Peaks," *International Musician* (April 1967); Sege, "Concert Reviews: Duke Ellington, Philharmonic Hall, N.Y.," *Variety* (28 April 1971); Kip Shaw, "The Sound of Music: Ellington: Still Great with Old and New," *New Hope (PA) Gazette* (14 July 1966). Clippings from DES, rolls 8, 9, and 14, vols. 43, 47, and 69, NMAH/SI.

32. BBC interview with Duke Ellington, conducted by Charles Melville, October 1958, JVC/LOC, RWC 9212.

33. Wayne Grundish, "Believe It or Not, Duke Ellington Likes Beatles," *Atlantic City Press* (26 July 1964); Nell Lawson, "Melody Fair: Ageless Duke Still Playing Jazz with Vigor of Youth," *Buffalo Evening News* (1 August 1966). Clippings from DES 7, 9:35, 44, NMAH/SI.

For a list of particularly vital film performances, see note 1 of this chapter.

34. Art Buchwald, "A Chat with the Duke" (no date or citation, probably early 1961); Hugh Mitchell, "Drowsy Duke Comes to Life on Stage," *New Bedford (MA) Standard-Times* (26 February 1962); Frank Rasky, "14 People Who've Seen It All," *(Montreal) Gazette* (14 February 1970). Clippings from DES, rolls 4, 5, 9, 11, and 12, vols. 23, 25, 45, 57, and 63, NMAH/SI.

Interview of Duke Ellington by Thomas R. Rees, collection 301, series 4, box 1, folder 5, AC/NMAH/SI.

35. Mercedes Ellington interview, conducted by Valerie Archer, 30 June 1980, #547A, B, pg. 35–36, OHAM/YUSC; Phoebe Jacobs interview, conducted by the author, 27 January 1996; Joya Sherrill interview, conducted by Valerie Archer, 21 November 1979, #534, pg. 52, OHAM/YUSC.

36. Derek Jewell, "The Duke—born 1956," *(London) Times* (23 February 1964); A. Logan in-

terview, 1964; Marion Logan interview, conducted by Sonia Rosario, 27 February 1978, #524, pg. 19, OHAM/YUSC; Msgr. John Saunders interview, conducted by Patricia Willard, 15 September 1989, tape 4, AC/NMAH/SI; Irving Townsend, "Ellington in Private," *Atlantic* (May 1975). Jewell clipping from DES 7:34, NMAH/SI.

37. Rev. O. C. Edwards, "That Unconditional Word, LOVE: The Holy Jazz of Duke Ellington," *Living Church* (8 December 1968); T. E. Foreman, "The Duke: Sound of Music Makes It Good," *Riverside (CA) Press* (19 November 1966). Clippings from DES 9, 11:45, 57, NMAH/SI.

38. Gwen Dobson, "Luncheon with Duke," *Washington (DC) Evening Star* (23 April 1971); Sandra Jobson, "Duke Ellington Looks Us Over: Another Night, Another City," *Sydney Morning Herald* (7 February 1970); Jock Veitch, "The Duke and His Secret Concert," *Sun Herald* (8 February 1970). Clippings from DES 13, 14:64, 69, NMAH/SI.

39. Dan Bied, "Ellington Still at Top of Heap," *(Burlington, IA) Hawk-Eye* (12 April 1964); Ed Bridges, "Ellington and Peace," *Marlboro (MA) Enterprise* (11 January 1963); James Greenwood, "The Duke Who's Been Chasing a Melody for 40 Years," *Daily Mail* (13 February 1965); Nat Hentoff, "The Durable Duke," *Reporter* (7 May 1964); Allen Hughes, "Dr. Ellington Sounds Like Same Old Duke," *New York Times* (3 August 1967); Humphrey Lyttelton, "Tin Pan Alley Can Do Its Worst!" *Melody Maker* (2 February 1963); Larry McCarten, "Don't Talk Retirement, The Duke's in Town," *Seattle Post-Intelligencer* (2 December 1967). Clippings from DES, rolls 5, 7, and 10, vols. 27, 28, 34, 37, 49, and 51, NMAH/SI.

40. "A Conversation with the Duke," hosted by Stanley Dance, BBC Radio 1 broadcast, 1972 (probably recorded 1971), RYJ 3702, JVC/LOC; "The Duke: What Is Music?" *San Diego Union* (31 October 1965); Hentoff, "Durable Duke." Clipping from DES 8:40, NMAH/SI.

41. Leonard Feather, "Jazzing It Up: Duke Ellington Keeps on Bettering His Music," *Washington Post* (29 May 1966); Leonard Feather, "Duke Ellington: New Projects, New Peaks," *International Musician* (April 1967); Klaus Stratemann, *Duke Ellington: Day by Day and Film by Film* (Copenhagen, 1992), 536–37. First clipping from collection 301, series 9, box 16, folder 20, AC/NMAH/SI. Second clipping from DES 9:47, NMAH/SI.

Such wide geographical jumps with consecutive shows were not unusual for the band during this period. A couple more examples from Stratemann: from San Rafael, CA, to Tucson, AZ, 28–29 August 1966; from San Francisco to Amarillo, TX, 2–3 October 1966.

42. Maxine, Big City Beat column, *Houston Chronicle* (15 January 1971); Helen McNamara, "16 Nations in 30 Days: Travel with Duke Just 'Too Exhausting,'" *Toronto Telegram* (25 August 1970). Clippings from DES 13, 14:67, 68, NMAH/SI.

McNamara claims the band visited sixteen countries on their 1970 Europe trip, Stone reports thirteen, but Stratemann's itinerary of the tour lists twelve (pg. 601).

43. Alvin Ailey interview, conducted by Harriet Milnes, 7 September 1983, #577, pg. 13–14, OHAM/YUSC.

44. Ellington, *Music Is My Mistress,* 159–61; Mercer Ellington interview, from the film *Duke Ellington: Reminiscing In Tempo;* Hajdu, *Lush Life,* 253–60.

45. Gregory Morris interview, conducted by Harriet Milnes, 23 August 1984, #590A-C, pg. 21–24, OHAM/YUSC.

46. Hajdu, *Lush Life;* Morris interview, 23 August 1984.

Robert Conaway interview, conducted by Harriet Milnes, 24 August 1984, #590A, pg. 14–15; Helen and Carol Strayhorn interview, conducted by Harriet Milnes, 30 May 1984. Both interviews from OHAM/YUSC.

It was Conaway who claimed that Strayhorn was a multimillionaire upon his death, although Hajdu (258) lists the estate at "under $50,000 in cash, property, and royalties (as they were estimated at the time)." Hajdu does not comment on whether this was the figure after

Morris paid Strayhorn's considerable back taxes and penalties or if this is what Strayhorn had on hand when he passed away. .

47. Benjamin Starr to Ruth Ellington, 28 December 1968, folder 22; Steven Burn to Benjamin Starr, 2 January 1969, folder 23; Benjamin Starr to Carl Bornmann, 3 January 1969. All three of these letters are from collection 301, series 3E, box 103, AC/NMAH/SI.

Stock purchase agreement, Tempo Music, 19 June 1969, collection 301, series 3G, box 115, folder 9, AC/NMAH/SI.

48. The 2 July 1970 French television performance can be found on *Unidentified Valburn/ Ellington #1.*

At the time of the 1970 broadcast, Aaron Bridgers was sometimes known as Aaron Bridges, and "Bridges" is the word Ellington says on the broadcast; this might have been a stage name. For more background on the Strayhorn/Bridgers relationship, see Hajdu, *Lush Life,* 65–74.

49. Mercer Ellington interview, conducted by Dr. Marcia Greenlee, 5 May 1991, SIEOHP, tape 5, AC/NMAH/SI; Clark Terry interview, conducted by Dr. Marcia Greenlee, 10 October 1990, tape 3, AC/NMAH/SI.

50. Duke Ellington, "Orientations: Adventures in the Far East," *Music Journal* (March 1964). Clipping from DES 7:34, NMAH/SI.

51. Stanley Dance, eulogy at the funeral of Duke Ellington, 27 May 1974, WRVR-FM radio broadcast, RWC 9445, JVC/LOC; Stanley Dance interview, conducted by Yale American Studies 430 class, 22 November 1977, #527B, pg. 31, OHAM/YUSC; Paul Gonsalves interview, conducted by the Duke Ellington Society, 1968, SC Audio C-497, side 1, SCBC; Gary Keys interview, conducted by the Duke Ellington Society, 1969, SC Audio C-501, side 1, SCBC.

52. Ellington's monologue on the track "Chinoiserie" from *The Afro-Eurasian Eclipse* album (Fantasy, 1971); Ellington, *Music Is My Mistress,* 203. .

53. The sources for this discussion of audience and repertoire are: Duke Ellington interview, October 1958; Duke Ellington interview, CHIC 1964 #8, tape 1, AC/NMAH/SI; Mercer Ellington interview, 5 May 1991, tape 4; Hentoff, "Durable Duke"; Alan Holbert, "Big Band Is Big Kick for Ellington," *Minneapolis Tribune* (4 September 1966); Michael James interview, conducted by the author, 11 November 1999; Dave Jampel, "Backstage with Duke: Financially an Impossibility to Maintain Band: Ellington," *Mainichi (Japan) Daily News* (11 July 1964); Bill Lorentz, "Ellington Pleases All Fans with Varied Jazz Pieces," *Waukesha (WI) Freeman* (29 May 1965); H. Udkoff interview, 28 September 1995; Clippings found in DES, rolls 6, 7, and 9, vols. 32, 38, and 44, NMAH/SI.

Jazz Casual (NET-TV, 11 July 1960/1961), with Duke Ellington and Billy Strayhorn, RWC 9238, JVC/LOC. The tape box claims a 1961 date, but Klaus Stratemann lists it as 1960.

Cat Anderson interview, 1964, SC Audio C-473, side 2; Aaron Bell interview, 1963, SC Audio C-468, side 2; Louis Bellson interview, 1965, SC Audio C-481, side 1; John Lamb interview, 1968, SC Audio C-492, side 2; John Sanders interview, 1962, SC Audio C-465, side 1; Clark Terry interview, 1960, SC Audio C-459, side 1, All interviews conducted by the Duke Ellington Society, SCBC.

54. *Do You Really Dig The Duke???* Mills Music publication (c. 1965), collection 301 series 11, box 2, folder 52, AC/NMAH/SI.

55. Ralph J. Gleason, "Better Jazz Programming Needed," The Rhythm Section column, *New York Post* (26 September 1968); Ben Gross, "Jazz Popular Globally, Is Neglected in U.S.A.," What's On? column, *(NY) Daily News* (24 August 1964); Ben Gross, "George Wein Denounces the U.S. Neglect of Jazz," What's On? column, *(NY) Daily News* (28 June 1971); Chester Higgins, "Fight Bias in Radio against Famous Blacks," *Jet* (24 June 1971). Clippings from 11, 14:56, 70, NMAH/SI.

56. This discussion of Ellington and jazz on television in the 1960s and 1970s is based on

the following sources: "The Playboy Panel: Jazz—Today and Tomorrow," *Playboy* (February 1964); "Dean Martin Host to Duke," *Newark (NJ) Afro-American* (1 October 1966); Al Legro, "Jazz and Things," *Long Island (NY) Entertainer* (7 February 1964); Willie Ruff, *A Call to Assembly: The Autobiography of a Musical Storyteller* (New York, 1991), 375. Clippings from DES 7:32, 34, NMAH/SI.

For a list of Ellington's TV appearances in the 1960s and 1970s, see Stratemann, *Duke Ellington,* 679–84. For a list of the European and Canadian broadcasts referenced, see note 1 of this chapter.

A Contemporary Memorial (CBS-TV, 8 June 1968; viewed at the Museum of Television and Radio, New York City).

57. "Race Relations—Good and Bad," *Rochester (NY) Democrat and Chronicle* (3 August 1968); "'All-Time Great' Duke Ellington," photo montage, *Sanford (FL) Herald* (7 February 1969); Michael H. Drew, "Duke's Old Magic Spellbinds 22,000," *Washington Post* (1 July 1966); Betty Grainger Reid, "Chic Social Set Pays Tribute to the Duke of Ellington: Sunday Was a 'Swinger'—Both Socially and Musically," *New York Courier* (20 November 1965); Gary Tischler, "Music Review: 'Jazz on Mountain': Unusual Experience," *(San Rafael, CA) Independent-Journal* (29 August 1966). Clippings from DES, rolls 8, 9, and 11, vols. 40, 43, 44, 54, and 58, NMAH/SI.

58. Lamar Crosby, "Duke, Now 62, Likes His Music," *Pocatello (Idaho) State Journal* (4 October 1961); Lee, "Mood Ellington: Duke's Day."

59. "Duke Ellington, Band to Appear Here Aug. 10," *Wisconsin Rapids Tribune* (1 August 1961); "Everyone Likes Ellington Music," *Columbus (OH) Dispatch* (11 January 1962); "Duke Ellington (The Garry Moore Show), CBS, Weekly," *Show* (May 1962); Crosby, "Duke, Now 62, Likes His Music." Clippings from DES 4, 5:24–26, NMAH/SI.

60. "Balanced Show at Steel Pier," *Newark (NJ) Italian Tribune* (17 July 1964); "All Ages and Types: Ellington's Fans Diversified," *Corvallis (OR) State Barometer* (9 October 1964); "They 'Dig' the Duke!: A Favorite with Any Age,"photo montage, *Erie (PA) Morning News* (27 July 1964); Paul Ackerman, "Duke Has No Peers; Is Still a Great U.S. Musical Force," *Billboard* (12 August 1967); Marjorie Jones, "Ageless Duke Ellington Has Faith in Younger Generation," *Seattle Daily Times* (3 December 1967); McCarten, "Don't Talk Retirement"; Jackie Peterson, "3 Generations Impressed: SRO for Ellington Concert," *Sacramento Union* (8 March 1972); Greg Schmidt, "Everyone at Concert Agrees That 'Duke Is Still the King,'" *Minneapolis Tribune* (24 June 1972). Clippings from DES, rolls 7, 10, 15, and 16, vols. 35, 36, 49, 51, 73, and 75, NMAH/SI.

Press release, Melvin L. Goldblatt, 15 February 1972, Tiburon, CA, collection 301, series 11, box 2, folder 28, AC/NMAH/SI.

61. Ollie Stewart, "Ellington Shows on France-Italy Border," Report from Europe column, *Washington D.C. Afro-American* (21 July 1970). Clippings from DES 13:67, NMAH/SI.

Stewart lists the border show occurring on 30 July, but Stratemann lists it as 31 July.

Chapter Fifteen

1. The quotes, in order of reference: Rabenold, American Embassy San José, Educational and Cultural Exchange: Cultural Presentations: Duke Ellington acclaimed in San José Concert, 17 December 1971; Belcher, American Embassy Lima, Duke Ellington Concert in Lima, 16 December 1971; McClintock, American Embassy Caracas, Educational and Cultural Exchange: Cultural Presentations: Duke Ellington and Orchestra, 5 January 1972; Shelton, American Embassy Managua, Duke Ellington Orchestra Concert, 16 December 1971. All documents in this paragraph are from: MC-468, box 61, folder 12, BECAHC/SCD/UAL.

2. This section on Ellington's 1970 and 1972 state-sponsored Burmese tours and the 1970 Laos dates is based on the following sources: schedule for Burma visit of Duke Ellington and his orchestra, 31 January–1 February 1970; Jack Foisle, "Burma Easing Its Isolation," *Washington Post* (13 August 1972). All documents in this paragraph from DES 13:64, 75, NMAH/SI.

Memorandum, John Richardson, Jr., to Secretary of State William P. Rogers, 6 February 1970, Duke Ellington Tour File, Historical Collection, Office of International Information, State Department.

Telegram, Hummel, American Rangoon Embassy to Secretary of State, 23 December 1969, folder 8; "The Duke Ellington Orchestra," *Guardian* (2 February 1970), folder 9; Hummel, American Rangoon Embassy to Department of State, Final Report on Duke Ellington and Orchestra's Performances in Rangoon, 10 February 1970, folder 9; Secretary of State William P. Rogers to President Richard Nixon, Memorandum for the President: Success of Duke Ellington in Burma [undated—c. February 1970], folder 10; Godley, American Embassy Vientiane, Educational and Cultural Exchange: Visit of Duke Ellington and his Orchestra, 16 February 1970, folder 8; Martin, American Embassy Rangoon, Final Report on Duke Ellington Concerts, 26 February 1972, folder 20. All documents in this paragraph from: MC-468, box 61, folder 12, BECAHC/SCD/UAL.

Ellington offered to perform in Vietnam: Penny M. Van Eschen, *Satchmo Blows Up the World: Jazz Ambassadors Play the Cold War* (Cambridge, MA, 2004), 221.

3. This section on the 1970 Yugoslavian tour is based on the following sources: enclosures of press articles, radio interview transcripts and photographs, 10, 16, 17, 24 July 1970; Leonhart, American Embassy Belgrade to Department of State, Educational and Cultural Exchange: Visit and Performances of Duke Ellington Orchestra in Yugoslavia, 24 July 1970; Leonhart, American Embassy Belgrade to Department of State, 20 August 1970. All documents in this footnote from Duke Ellington Tour File, Historical Collection, Office of International Information Programs, State Department.

4. Reinhold Wagnleitner, *Coca-Colonization and the Cold War: The Cultural Mission of the United States in Austria after the Second World War* (Chapel Hill, 1994), 210–12.

5. "Duke Takes Jazz to Reds in September," *Boston Herald Traveler* (8 May 1971); "Duke in the USSR," *Fresno (CA) Bee* (11 May 1971); Anthony Astrachan, "Soviets Invite Ellington's Orchestra," *Washington Post* (8 May 1971); Bernard Lairet, "The Communists Love Our American Duke," *Cleveland News* (10 September 1971); George Sherman, "Harmony Russian-Style," *Washington D.C. Star* (9 May 1971); Hedrick Smith, "Ellington Hailed by Moscow Buffs: He Opens 5-Week Jazz Tour in Leningrad Tonight," *New York Times* (13 September 1971); James Yuenger, "Hope Duke Will Ease Russ Chill," *Chicago Tribune* (7 September 1971). Clippings from DES 14:69, 71, NMAH/SI.

For more on the Soviet refusal of Duke Ellington for a 1962 Soviet tour in favor of Benny Goodman, see chapter 13.

6. Frances Church to Irene Carstones, 12 January 1970; memo, unknown State Department employee to Mark B. Lewis, 18 January 1971; Department of State, memorandum of conversation, "US/USSR Cultural Presentations," 10 February 70. All documents in this paragraph from: MC-468, box 61, folder 14, BECAHC/SCD/UAL.

For more on the tensions between Joe Glaser/ABC and Ellington during the 1963 state tour, see chapter 13.

7. "Contract," folder 14; Cultural Presentations List of Attractions Touring Fiscal Year: Duke Ellington Orchestra, USSR (two different undated copies of this document exist in this folder—most of the information in this paragraph is from the second, seemingly later version), folder 15; John B. Mann to Duke Ellington, Inc., 5 October 1971, folder 14; Joseph A. Presel,

"Duke Ellington in the USSR: Trip Report" (c. late 1971), folder 15. All documents in this paragraph from: MC-468, box 61, BECAHC/SCD/UAL.

Grant Agreement between the Government of the United States of America and Duke Ellington, Inc., 15 June 1971, collection 301, series 3A, box 15, folder 23, AC/NMAH/SI.

According to Stratemann's reckoning, the band played twenty-seven shows in thirty-one days: Klaus Stratemann, *Duke Ellington: Day by Day and Film by Film* (Copenhagen, 1992), 632.

8. Dan Lewis, "Soviets Look Duke Over," *Hackensack (NJ) Record* (4 August 1971). Clipping from DES 14:70, NMAH/SI.

Mark B. Lewis to Cress Courtney, 3 September 1971, MC-468, box 61, folder 14, BECAHC/SCD/UAL.

9. Marlin W. Remick to Irene Carstones, 21 June 1971; Marlin W. Remick to Irene Carstones, 4 August 1971; "Duke Ellington and His Orchestra: Staging and Other Requirements" (undated). The first two documents from: MC-468, box 61, folder 16, BECAHC/SCD/UAL. The last document is from folder 14.

In the last document, it is noted that Mercer Ellington injected his father with vitamin B12 every day, another energy-enhancing regimen.

10. Robert L. Jones interview, conducted by Dr. Marcia Greenlee, 31 January 1992, SIEOHP, tape 3, AC/NMAH/SI; memo, Irene Carstones, "Duke Ellington and His Orchestra: Staging and Other Requirements" (undated—c. summer 1971), MC-468, box 61, folder 14, BECAHC/SCD/UAL.

11. Rudolph Chelminski, "The A-Train Pulls into Russia," *Life* (19 November 1971); Presel, "Duke Ellington in the USSR," 2, 4–5.

12. Chelminski, "A-Train"; Robert G. Kaiser, "Greeting the Great Man," *Washington Post* (13 October 1971); H. Smith, "Ellington Hailed." Clippings from DES 14:71, NMAH/SI.

Duke Ellington, *Music Is My Mistress* (New York, 1973), 364–74.

13. "Enthusiasm of Russian Fans Thrills Ellington," *Toronto Telegram* (15 September 1971); Stephen Broening, "Jazz Heats 'Em Up: Ellington Wow Soviets," *Chicago Sun-Times* (14 September 1971); Ellington, *Music Is My Mistress*; Hedrick Smith, "Leningrad Goes Wild over the Duke" (14 September 1971). Clippings from DES 14:71, NMAH/SI.

Telegram, American Embassy Moscow to USIA Washington, D.C., 19 September 1971; B. H. Klosson, American Embassy Moscow to Department of State, "Duke Ellington in the USSR," 10 December 1971; memo, Mark B. Lewis to Alan A. Reich, "Duke Ellington Phones from Leningrad," 17 September 1971. MC-468, box 61, folders 14, 15 and 16, respectively, BECAHC/SCD/UAL.

Kaiser, "Greeting the Great Man"; Presel, "Duke Ellington in the USSR," 3–4.

14. This section on jam sessions between the Soviets and the Ellington orchestra is based on the following sources: telegram, B. H. Klosson, American Embassy Moscow to Secretary of State, 20 September 1971; telegram, Jacob Beam, American Embassy Moscow to Secretary of State, 9 October 1971. Both documents: MC-468, box 61, folders 13 and 15, respectively, BECAHC/SCD/UAL. Presel, "Duke Ellington in the USSR," 9, 12.

Story of Vladimir Khavkin: Von Eschen, 211.

A photo of Ellington on balalaika at the Moscow jam session is included in Ellington, *Music Is My Mistress*.

15. Klosson "Duke Ellington in the USSR," 1, 5–9; Von Eschen, *Satchmo*, 191.

16. Presel, "Duke Ellington in the USSR"; Von Eschen, *Satchmo*, 198–99.

17. Klosson, "Duke Ellington in the USSR," 6; Presel, "Duke Ellington in the USSR," 4.

18. Telegram, Jacob Beam, American Embassy to Secretary of State, 13 October 1971,

MC-468, box 61, folder 13, BECAHC/SCD/UAL. When the U.S. ambassador writes the telegram himself, one can assume the importance of the message.

Klosson, "Duke Ellington in the USSR," 7; Presel, "Duke Ellington in the USSR," 4.

The State Department gave Ellington a full translation of the *Pravda* article, and he quoted parts of it within the "Russian Journal" in his autobiography, praising its "perceptive comments." No notice was made of *Pravda*'s comments on *Harlem*: Ellington, *Music Is My Mistress*, 368.

19. "Curtain-Raiser," *Brantford (Ontario) Canada Expositor* (15 September 1971); "'Da' for the Duke," *Hartford (CT) Times* (16 September 1971); "Duke Power," *Schnectady (NY) Gazette* (16 September 1971); "Ellington Has the Reds Jumping," *Topeka (KS) State Journal* (18 September 1971). Clippings from DES 14:71, NMAH/SI.

20. This section on the steak controversy is based on the following sources: "12 Steaks Catch Up with Duke in Minsk," *Chicago Sun-Times* (21 September 1971); "Steak and Potatoes: Duke to Eat Royally in Soviet-U.S. Style," *Philadelphia Inquirer* (21 September 1971); Joe Alex Morris, Jr., "Duke Can't Cut It on Russian Steaks," *Los Angeles Times* (20 September 1971). Clippings from DES 14:71, NMAH/SI.

Mark B. Lewis to Alan A. Reich, 17 September 1971; telegram, Secretary of State to American Embassy Moscow, 20 September 1971; telex to Joseph A. Presel (sender unknown, probably State Department, Washington, D.C.), 21 September 1971; B. H. Klosson, American Embassy Moscow to Secretary of State, 22 September 1971; telegram, Secretary of State to American Embassy Moscow, 23 September 1971. All documents in this paragraph from: MC-468, box 61, folder 16, BECAHC/SCD/UAL.

Klosson, "Duke Ellington in the USSR," 9; Presel, "Duke Ellington in the USSR," 5–6.

Ellington in his autobiography and Robert G. Kaiser in his previously referenced *Washington Post* article claimed that Ellington actually gained ten pounds on the tour: Ellington, *Music Is My Mistress*, 373.

The steaks actually came from Gristede's, the New York supplier of the steaks for Reuben's restaurant.

21. Ellington felt he was being bugged by the Soviets: Aaron Bridgers interview, conducted by Patricia Willard, 27 September 1989, SIEOHP, tape 2, AC/NMAH/SI; Robert and Evelyn Udkoff interview, conducted by Dr. Marcia Greenlee, 11 March 1991, SIEOHP, tape 2, AC/NMAH/SI. For more on Ellington's beliefs in communist conspiracies, see chapter 14.

22. Joseph A. Presel to Mark B. Lewis, handwritten letter, 5 October 1971, MC-468, box 61, folder 15, BECAHC/SCD/UAL.

Presel, "Duke Ellington in the USSR," 6–8, 12; Kaiser, "Greeting the Great Man."

23. Kaiser, "Greeting the Great Man"; Presel, "Duke Ellington in the USSR," 5–6; R. and E. Udkoff interview, 11 March 1991.

24. This section on ticket problems and extra shows in Moscow is based on the following sources: Ellington, *Music Is My Mistress*, 368–70; Klosson, "Duke Ellington in the USSR," 2–3; Presel, "Duke Ellington in the USSR," 2, 11.

25. President Richard Nixon to Duke Ellington, 2 November 1971; Senator Hubert Humphrey to Duke Ellington, 14 October 1971. Both letters from collection 301, series 2A, box 6, folder 17, AC/NMAH/SI.

Duke Ellington interview on Radio Moscow, 10 October 1971, RGA 1181, JVC/LOC.

Cultural Presentations List of Attractions Touring Fiscal Year: Duke Ellington Orchestra, USSR, MC-468, box 61, folder 15, BECAHC/SCD/UAL.

Mark Beltaire, The Town Crier column, *Detroit Free Press* (3 April 1972); Christine Salkowski, "Soviets Swing to Jones-Lewis Jazz," *Christian Science Monitor* (11 May 1972). Clippings from DES 15:74, NMAH/SI.

26. John S. Wilson, "Ellington to Take Jazz to the Far East," *New York Times* (3 January 1972). Clipping from DES 15:72, NMAH/SI. Actually, it was probably twenty-two or twenty-three audiences that Ellington faced in the Soviet Union, not twenty-four—it's unclear whether the State Department counted the Spaso House Sacred Concert as one of their officially credited twenty-two Ellington performances in the Soviet Union. .

27. Memo, Martin C. Carroll, Jr., to L. Dayton Coe II, Educational and Cultural Exchange: Cultural Presentations: ARA Tour by Duke Ellington and Orchestra, 8 April 1971; Grant Agreement No. SCC-41279; Mark B. Lewis to George Wein, 20 May 1971; Mark B. Lewis to Alejandro Szterenfeld, 25 August 1971. All documents in this paragraph are from: MC-468, box 61, folder 19, BECAHC/SCD/UAL.

Change in State Department CP policy and Mercer Ellington quote: Von Eschen, *Satchmo*, 188, 217–18.

28. U.S. Embassy reports of Ellington's 1971 Latin American tour stops in Brazil, Buenos Aires, Caracas, Lima, Managua, Montevideo, Quito, and San José can be found in: MC-468, box 61, folders 11 and 12, BECAHC/SCD/UAL.

Nixon, the CIA, and Allende: Anthony Summers, *The Arrogance of Power: The Secret World of Richard Nixon* (New York, 2000), 335–37.

29. However, in an interesting corollary, Blood, Sweat and Tears, the first rock and roll group to go on State Department–sponsored tours, did encounter similar homegrown American resistance during their 1970 tour to what the jazz musicians experienced in decades past: Von Eschen, *Satchmo*, 195.

Chapter Sixteen

1. Sources for this discussion of the 1972 Ellington Festival at the University of Wisconsin: *Duke Ellington and Friends* (WHA Radio Madison/ WMVS-TV Milwaukee, 1972), LOC/ MPD; Duke Ellington Festival press release, 5 April 1972, collection 301, series 11, box 2, folder 31, AC/NMAH/SI; Patricia Willard, "Love and Learn: The Ellingtonians at UW," *Downbeat* (12 October 1972).

2. Ruth Ellington interview, conducted by the Duke Ellington Society, 1960, SC Audio C-451, side 1, SCBC; Derek Jewell interview, conducted by Valerie Archer, 24 March 1981, #559A and B, pg. 11, OHAM/YUSC; Barry Ulanov interview, conducted by the Duke Ellington Society, 1966, SC Audio C-484, SCBC.

3. Marion Logan interview in *Duke Ellington: Reminiscing In Tempo* (Robert Levi Films, 1992); Bernice Wiggins and Juanita Middleton interview, conducted by Martha Oneppo, 20 October 1980, #551A, B, OHAM/YUSC.

4. This section on *Music Is My Mistress* is based on the following sources: Duke Ellington, *Music Is My Mistress* (New York, 1973); John Edward Hasse, *Beyond Category: The Life and Genius of Duke Ellington* (New York, 1993), 383–84.

Helen Oakley Dance interview, conducted by Patricia Willard, 26–27 September 1989, tape 4; Stanley Dance interview, conducted by Dr. Marcia Greenlee, 28 August 1990, tape 1; Mercer Ellington interview, conducted by Dr. Marcia Greenlee, 18 September 1990, tape 1; Brad McCuen interview, conducted by Patricia Willard, 2–3 August 1989, tape 3. All interviews in this paragraph: SIEOHP, AC/NMAH/SI.

Stanley Dance interview, conducted by Yale American Studies class, 22 November 1977, #527 A, B, C, pg. 35–37; Betty McGettigan interview, conducted by Vivian Perlis, 15 July 1980, #546, pg. 35–55; Louise Michelle interview, conducted by Harriet Milnes, 15 July 1983, #574, pg. 6–12; Irving Mills interview, conducted by Irene Kahn Atkins, 23 April 1981, #567 A-E, pg. 9–10. All interviews in this paragraph: OHAM/YUSC.

5. This section on the Conservatory without Walls event at Yale is based on the following sources: Willie Ruff, *A Call to Assembly: The Autobiography of a Musical Storyteller* (New York, 1991), 368–77.

"Yale Establishes Ellington Afro-American Fellowship," *Amsterdam News* (26 August 1972); John Karrel, "Ellington Leads Music at Yale," *Hartford Courant* (9 October 1972); Kathryn Kolkhurst, "Yale Honors 'Conservatory without Walls,'" *New Haven Register* (27 August 1972); Kathryn Kolkhurst, "Some Sour Notes," *New Haven Register* (15 August 1972); John S. Wilson, "Jazz: Duke Opens Yale Fund Drive," *New York Times* (8 October 1972); John S. Wilson, "30 Black Musicians Get Ellington Medal at Yale," *New York Times* (9 October 1972). Clippings from DES 16:75, 76, NMAH/SI.

6. Tom Buckley, "Duke: His Creative Impulse—All That Jazz—Throbs On," *New York Times* (3 July 1972). Clipping from DES 15:74, NMAH/SI. Mercer Ellington interview, 18 September 1990, tape 2.

7. Mercer Ellington with Stanley Dance, *Duke Ellington in Person: An Intimate Memoir* (Boston, 1978), 155; Buckley, "Duke: His Creative Impulse."

Marsha Beff, "Duke Ellington during Interview at State University at Binghamton: Charisma's There While the Music Plays, but Not for Hamburg, Fish," *(Binghamton, NY) Evening Press* (10 February 1973); Sophie Smith, "Performs at Tega Cay: Work 'Regenerating' to 73-year-old 'Duke,'" *Rock Hill (SC) Herald* (13 October 1972). Clippings from DES 16:76, 77, NMAH.

Roy Shields, "Ellington Exuberant over Russia Trip," *Edmonton (Canada) Journal* (24 March 1972). From Duke Ellington clipping file, Yale Music Library. Although Ellington seemed to have increasingly less time for the press, this article suggests he was still chatting up the ladies during this period. As the Beff and Shields articles show, Ellington's shortness with reporters did not result in positive portrayals of him, but he probably could not have cared less at this point.

8. United States tax court petition, *Estate of Edward Kennedy Ellington (Deceased) vs. Commissioner of Internal Revenue,* 20 June 1974, box 114, folder 1; Barry N. Cooper/Internal Revenue Service to Leon Hariton, 15 December 1975, box 112, folder 7; Jerome Kurtz/Internal Revenue Service to Duke Ellington, Inc., 26 May 1977, box 126, folder 1. From collection 301, series 3, AC/NMAH/SI. The last document in this series is the one in which the IRS questions the money Ellington paid his family members from 1969 to 1973.

United States tax court petition, *Estate of Edward Kennedy Ellington (Deceased) vs. Commissioner of Internal Revenue,* 16 September 1974, folder 21; E. Lisk Wyckoff, Jr., to Mercer K. Ellington, 4 February 1975, folder 23 (including all tax documentation with this letter). From collection 704, series 3B, box 2, AC/NMAH/SI.

Waiver of Restrictions on Assessment and Collection of Deficiency in Tax and Acceptance of Overstatement, 12 May 1976, collection 301, series 3I, box 134, folder 16, AC/NMAH/SI.

In a 1998 interview with Stuart Nicholson, H. Robert Udkoff claimed that President Nixon had an interest in helping Ellington with his IRS problems. "It was in process of being taken care of," Udkoff said, but Nixon's Watergate problems supposedly kept him from fully following through: Stuart Nicholson, *Reminiscing In Tempo: A Portrait of Duke Ellington* (Boston, 1999), 388.

In 1981, the Ellington estate was still challenging the IRS's tax assessments for the years 1964–73: Status of Tax Court Cases Involving Estate of Duke Ellington, 4 June 1981, collection 301, series 3G, box 125, folder 29, AC/NMAH/SI.

To settle these huge tax debts, Mercer Ellington eventually sold the songs in Tempo Music to Famous Music during the 1980s: Mercer Ellington interview, 18 September 1990, tape 8.

9. Mercer Ellington interview, 18 September 1990, tape 8; Ruth Ellington interview, con-

ducted by the author, 26 January 1996. For more on Ellington's lifelong financial priorities, see chapter 11.

Ellington's ASCAP royalties for 1973 were $96,017.32: E. Lisk Wyckoff, Jr., to Stanley Roth, CPA, 23 August 1974, collection 301, series 3B, folder 20, AC/NMAH/SI. This figure does not include his recording and publishing royalties, which were probably more than $100,000 and are not listed in the Smithsonian files.

10. Mercer Ellington interview, 18 September 1990; McGettigan interview, 15 July 1980.

E. Lisk Wyckoff, Jr., memo: Estate of Edward K. Ellington, 1 July 1974; E. Lisk Wyckoff, Jr., to Ruth Ellington, 20 August 1974; E. Lisk Wyckoff, Jr., to Stanley Roth, CPA, 23 August 1974. All documents in this paragraph: collection 704, series 3B, folders 19 and 20, AC/NMAH/SI.

11. This section on the Third Sacred Concert is based on the following sources: Edward Anderson interview, conducted by Valerie Archer, 15 October 1980, #550A, pg. 51, OHAM/YUSC; Hasse, *Beyond Category*; Albert Murray interview, conducted by the author, 18 April 2001; Klaus Stratemann, *Duke Ellington: Day by Day and Film by Film* (Copenhagen, 1992), 661, 663; George Wein with Nate Chinen, *Myself Among Others* (Cambridge, MA, 2003), 176. Seating chart for the postshow dinner at 10 Downing Street: collection 301, series 2, box 9, folder 6, AC/NMAH/SI.

12. This section on Ellington's state-sponsored shows in Ethiopia and Zambia are based on the following sources: Duke Ellington and B.B. King to Tour Africa for Department of State press release, 26 October 1973, folder 1; telegram, Secretary of State Henry Kissinger to American Embassy Addis Ababa, 23 November 1973, folder 2; telegram, Wilkowski/American Embassy Lusaka to Secretary of State Henry Kissinger, 25 July 1973, folder 3; Adair/American Embassy Addis Ababa to Department of State, Washington, CU/CP: Duke Ellington and Orchestra Visit to Ethiopia, 20–23 November 1973, 14 December 1973, folder 4; Wilkowski/American Embassy Lusaka to Department of State, 18 December 1973, folder 4; Unsigned Note, American Embassy Addis Ababa to USIA, 23 November 1973, folder 4; Emperor Confers Order of Ethiopia on Duke Ellington press release, 21 November 1973, folder 4. All documents in this paragraph are from: MC-468, box 62, BECAHC/SCD/UAL.

Derek Jewell, *Duke: A Portrait of Duke Ellington* (London, 1977), 169.

13. Mercer Ellington interview, 18 September 1990; Mercer Ellington and Dance, *In Person*, 197–200; Jewell, *Duke: A Portrait*, 168–72; Marion Logan interview, conducted by Sonia Rosario, 27 February 1978, #524, pg. 5–6, 13, OHAM/YUSC; Nicholson, *Reminiscing In Tempo*, 404–5.

14. This section on Ellington's activities during 1974 is based on the following sources: Edward Ellington interview, conducted by Sonia Rosario, 3 March 1978, #523A,B, pg. 15–16, OHAM/YUSC; Mercedes Ellington interview, conducted by Valerie Archer, 30 June 1980, #547A, B, pg. 38–39, OHAM/YUSC; Mercer Ellington interview, conducted by Dick Buckley on WBEZ, Chicago, March 1980, #521B, C (no transcript), OHAM/YUSC; Mercer Ellington and Dance, *In Person*, 199–202; John Gensel interview, conducted by Jeremy Orgel, 14 December 1979, #540A, B, pg. 4, OHAM/YUSC; Jewell, *Duke: A Portrait*, 173; McGettigan interview, 15 July 1980; Irving Mills interview, 23 April 1981, pg. 18; Stuart Nicholson, *Ella Fitzgerald: A Biography of the First Lady of Jazz* (New York, 1993), 209; Stratemann, *Duke Ellington*, 662–63; Patricia Willard, "Love You Madly" and "Diamonds for Duke," *Downbeat* (25 April 1974).

15. This section on Ellington's funeral is based on the following sources: John Joyce interview, conducted by Harriet Milnes, 21 September 1983, #579, OHAM/YUSC; Duke Ellington funeral broadcast, WRVR-FM, 27 May 1974, RWC 9445, JVC/LOC. For the lyrics to "My Mother, My Father (Heritage)," see chapter 12.

INDEX

INDEX OF
DUKE ELLINGTON
MUSIC